ACCA

Paper F6

Taxation

Complete Text

Finance Act 2008
for 2009 examination sittings

British library cataloguing-in-publication data

A catalogue record for this book is available from the British Library.

Published by:
Kaplan Publishing UK
Unit 2 The Business Centre
Molly Millars Lane
Wokingham
Berkshire
RG41 2QZ

ISBN 978-1-84710-519-6

Printed in the UK by CPI William Clowes Beccles NR34 7TL

Acknowledgements

We are grateful to the Association of Chartered Certified Accountants and the Chartered Institute of Management Accountants for permisssion to reproduce past examination questions. The answers have been prepared by Kaplan Publishing.

Contents

Paper Introduction

How to Use the Materials

Paper background

The aim of ACCA Paper F6, **Taxation**, is to develop knowledge and skills relating to the tax system as applicable to individuals, single companies and groups of companies.

Objectives of the syllabus

- Explain the operation and scope of the tax system.
- Explain and compute the income tax liabilities of individuals.
- Explain and compute the corporation tax liabilities of individual companies and groups of companies.
- Explain and compute the chargeable gains arising on companies and individuals.
- Explain and compute the effect of national insurance contributions on employees, employers and the self employed.
- Explain and compute the effects of value added tax on incorporated and unincorporated businesses.
- Identify and explain the obligations of tax payers and/or their agents and the implications of non-compliance.

Core areas of the syllabus

- The UK tax system.
- Income tax liabilities.
- Corporation tax liabilities.
- Capital gains.
- National insurance contributions.
- Value added tax.
- The obligations of tax payers and/or their agents.

Syllabus objectives

We have reproduced the ACCA's syllabus below, showing where the objectives are explored within this book. Within the chapters, we have broken down the extensive information found in the syllabus into easily digestible and relevant sections, called Content Objectives. These correspond to the objectives at the beginning of each chapter.

Syllabus learning objective	Chapter reference
A **THE UK TAX SYSTEM**	
1 The overall function and purpose of taxation in a modern economy	
(a) Describe the purpose (economic, social, etc) of taxation in a modern economy.[2]	
2 Different types of taxes	
(a) Identify the different types of capital and revenue tax.[1]	1
(b) Explain the difference between direct and indirect taxation. [2]	1
3 Principal sources of revenue law and practice	
(a) Describe the overall structure of the UK tax system. [1]	1
(b) State the different sources of revenue law.[1]	1
(c) Appreciate the interaction of the UK tax system with that of other tax jurisdictions.[2]	1
4 Tax avoidance and tax evasion	
(a) Explain the difference between tax avoidance and tax evasion.[1]	1
(b) Explain the need for an ethical and professional approach. [2]	1

Excluded topics:

Anti-avoidance legislation.

B	**INCOME TAX LIABILITIES**	
1	The scope of income tax	
	(a) Explain how the residence of an individual is determined.[1]	2
	Excluded topics: The treatment of a person who comes to the UK to work or a person who leaves the UK to take up employment overseas. Foreign income, non-residents and double taxation relief. Income from trusts and settlements.	
2	Income from employment	
	(a) Recognise the factors that determine whether an engagement is treated as employment or self-employment.[2]	4
	(b) Recognise the basis of assessment for employment income.[2]	4
	(c) Compute the income assessable.[2]	4
	(d) Recognise the allowable deductions, including travelling expenses.[2]	4
	(e) Discuss the use of the statutory approved mileage allowances.[2]	4
	(f) Explain the PAYE system.[2]	13
	(g) Identify P11D employees.[2]	4
	(h) Compute the amount of benefits assessable.[2]	4
	(i) Explain the purpose of a dispensation from HM Revenue & Customs.[2]	4
	(j) Explain how charitable giving can be made through a payroll deduction scheme.[2]	4
	Excluded topics: The calculation of a car benefit where emission figures are not available. Share and share option incentive schemes for employees. Payments of the termination of employment, and other lump sums received by employees.	
3	Income from self employment	
	(a) Recognise the basis of assessment for self employment income.[2]	5
	(b) Describe and apply the badges of trade.[2]	5

(c)	Recognise the expenditure that is allowable in calculating the tax-adjusted trading profit.[2]	5
(d)	Recognise the relief that can be obtained for pre-trading expenditure.[2]	5
(e)	Compute the assessable profits on commencement and on cessation.[2]	8
(f)	Change of accounting date	
	(i) Recognise the factors that will influence the choice of accounting date.[2]	8
	(ii) State the conditions that must be met for a change of accounting date to be valid.[2]	8
	(iii) Compute the assessable profits on a change of accounting date.[2]	8
(g)	Capital allowances	
	(i) Define plant and machinery for capital allowances purposes.[2]	6
	(ii) Compute writing down allowances, first year allowances and annual investment allowances.[2]	6
	(iii) Compute capital allowances for motor cars.[2]	6
	(iv) Compute balancing allowances and balancing charges.[2]	6
	(v) Recognise the treatment of short-life assets.[2]	6
	(vi) Explain the treatment of special rate pool items.[2]	6
	(vii) Define an industrial building for industrial buildings allowance purposes.[1]	7
	(viii) Compute industrial buildings allowance for new buildings.[2]	7
(h)	Relief for trading losses	
	(i) Understand how trading losses can be carried forward.[2]	10
	(ii) Explain how trading losses can be carried forward following the incorporation of a business.[2]	10
	(iii) Understand how trading losses can be claimed against total income and capital gains. [2]	10
	(iv) Explain and compute the relief for trading losses in the early years of a trade.[1]	10
	(v) Explain and compute terminal loss relief.[1]	10
(i)	Partnerships and limited liability partnerships	
	(i) Explain how a partnership is assessed to tax.[2]	9

	(ii) Compute the assessable profits for each partner following a change in the profit-sharing ratio. [2]	9
	(iii) Compute the assessable profits for each partner following a change in the membership of the partnership.[2]	9
	(iv) Describe the alternative loss relief claims that are available to partners.[2]	10
	(v) Explain the loss relief restriction that applies to the partners of a limited liability partnership.[2]	10

Excluded topics:

Rules for capital allowances pre 1 April 2008 for companies and 6 April 2008 for unincorporated businesses
The 100% first-year allowance for information and communication technology equipment.
The 100% first-year allowance for expenditure on renovating business premises in disadvantaged areas.
The 100% first-year allowance for flats above shops.
The 100% first-year allowance for water technologies.
Capital allowances for agricultural buildings, patents, scientific research and know-how.
Enterprise zones.
Capital allowances on second hand industrial buildings.
Non industrial use of an industrial building.
Investment income and charges of a partnership.
The allocation of notional profits and losses for a partnership.
Farmers averaging of profits.
The averaging of profits for authors and creative artists.
Loss relief for shares in unquoted trading companies.

4	Property and investment income	
	(a) Compute property business profits.[2]	3
	(b) Explain the treatment of furnished holiday lettings.[1]	3
	(c) Describe rent-a-room relief. [1]	3
	(d) Compute the amount assessable when a premium is received for the grant of a short lease.[1]	3
	(e) Understand how relief for a property business loss is given. [2]	3
	(f) Compute the tax payable on savings income.[2]	2 & 3
	(g) Compute the tax payable on dividend income.[2]	2 & 3
	(h) Explain the treatment of individual savings accounts (ISAs) and other tax exempt investments.[1]	3

5 The comprehensive computation of taxable income and income tax liability

(a) Prepare a basic income tax computation involving different types of income.[2] 2

(b) Calculate the amount of personal allowance available to people aged 65 and above. [2] 2

(c) Compute the amount of income tax payable.[2] 2

(d) Explain the treatment of reliefs against total income.[2] 2

(e) Explain the treatment of gift aid donations.[1] 2

(f) Explain the treatment of property owned jointly by a married couple, or by a couple in a civil partnership.[1] 2

Excluded topics:

The blind person's allowance and the married couple's allowance.

Tax credits.

Maintenance payments.

The income of minor children.

6 The use of exemptions and reliefs in deferring and minimising income tax liabilities

(a) Explain and compute the relief given for contributions to personal pension schemes.[2] 11

(b) Describe the relief given for contributions to occupational pension schemes.[1] 11

(c) Explain how a married couple or couple in a civil partnership can minimise their tax liabilities.[2] 3

Excluded topics:

The conditions that must be met in order for a pension scheme to obtain approval from HM Revenue & Customs.

The pension rules that applied up to 5 April 2006.

The enterprise investment scheme.

Venture capital trusts.

C CORPORATION TAX LIABILITIES

1 The scope of corporation tax

(a) Define the terms 'period of account', 'accounting period', and 'financial year'.[1] 18

(b) Recognise when an accounting period starts and when an accounting period finishes.[1] 18

	(c) Explain how the residence of a company is determined.[2]	18

Excluded topics:

Investment companies.
Close companies.
Companies in receivership or liquidation.
Reorganisations.
The purchase by a company of its own shares.
Personal service companies.

2	Profits chargeable to corporation tax	
	(a) Recognise the expenditure that is allowable in calculating the tax-adjusted trading profit.[2]	19
	(b) Explain how relief can be obtained for pre-trading expenditure.[1]	19
	(c) Compute capital allowances (as for income tax).[2]	19
	(d) Compute property business profits.[2]	19
	(e) Explain the treatment of interest paid and received under the loan relationship rules.[1]	19
	(f) Explain the treatment of gift aid donations.[2]	19
	(g) Understand how trading losses can be carried forward.[2]	21
	(h) Understand how trading losses can be claimed against income of the current or previous accounting periods.[2]	21
	(i) Recognise the factors that will influence the choice of loss relief claim.[2]	21
	(j) Explain how relief for a property business loss is given.[1]	21
	(k) Compute profits chargeable to corporation tax.[2]	18 & 19

Excluded topics:

Research and development expenditure.
Non-trading deficits on loan relationships.
Relief for intangible assets.

3	The comprehensive computation of corporation tax liability	
	(a) Compute the corporation tax liability and apply marginal relief.[2]	18
	(b) Explain the implications of receiving franked investment income.[2]	18

	(c) Explain how exemptions and reliefs can defer or minimise corporation tax liabilities.[2]	20-23

Excluded topics:

The corporate venturing scheme.

4	The effect of a group corporate structure for corporation tax purposes	
	(a) Define an associated company and recognise the effect of being an associated company for corporation tax purposes.[2]	22
	(b) Define a 75% group, and recognise the reliefs that are available to members of such a group.[2]	22
	(c) Define a 75% capital gains group, and recognise the reliefs that are available to members of such a group. [2]	22
	(d) Calculate double taxation relief for withholding tax and underlying tax.[2]	23
	(e) Explain the basic principles of the transfer pricing rules.[2]	23

Excluded topics:

Relief for trading losses incurred by an overseas subsidiary.
Consortia.
Pre-entry gains and losses.
The anti-avoidance provisions where arrangements exist for a company to leave a group.
The tax charge that applies where a company leaves a group within six years of receiving an asset by way of a no gain/no loss transfer.
Controlled foreign companies.
Foreign companies trading in the UK.
Expense relief in respect of overseas tax.
The restriction of double taxation relief for underlying tax to the full rate of corporation tax.
The carry back and carry forward of unrelieved foreign tax, or any aspect of the on-shore pooling rules.
Transfer pricing transactions not involving an overseas company.

5 The use of exemptions and reliefs in deferring and minimising corporation tax liabilities. (The use of such exemptions and reliefs is implicit within all of the above sections 1 to 4 of part C of the syllabus, concerning corporation tax.)

D CAPITAL GAINS

1 The scope of the taxation of capital gains

(a)	Describe the scope of capital gains tax.[2]	14
(b)	Explain how the residence and ordinary residence of an individual is determined.[2]	14
(c)	List those assets which are exempt.[1]	14

Excluded topics:

Assets situated overseas and double taxation relief.

Partnership capital gains.

2 The basic principles of computing gains and losses.

(a)	Compute capital gains for both individuals and companies.[2]	14 & 20
(b)	Calculate the indexation allowance available to companies.[2]	14 & 20
(c)	Explain the treatment of capital losses for both individuals and companies.[1]	14 & 20
(d)	Explain the treatment of transfers between a husband and wife or between a couple in a civil partnership.[2]	15
(e)	Compute the amount of allowable expenditure for a part disposal.[2]	15
(f)	Explain the treatment where an asset is damaged, lost or destroyed, and the implications of receiving insurance proceeds and reinvesting such proceeds.[2]	15

Excluded topics:

Rules pre 6 April 2008

Assets held at 31 March 1982.

Small part disposals of land.

Losses in the year of death.

Relief for losses incurred on loans made to traders.

Negligible value claims.

3 Gains and losses on the disposal of movable and immovable property

(a) Identify when chattels and wasting assets are exempt. [1]	15
(b) Compute the capital gain when a chattel is disposed of. [2]	15
(c) Calculate the capital gain when a wasting asset is disposed of.[2]	15
(d) Compute the exemption when a principal private residence is disposed of.[2]	17
(e) Calculate the chargeable gain when a principal private residence has been used for business purposes.[2]	17
(f) Identify the amount of letting relief available when a principal private residence has been let out.[2]	17

Excluded topics:

The disposal of leases and the creation of sub-leases.

4 Gains and losses on the disposal of shares and securities

(a) Calculate the value of quoted shares where they are disposed of by way of a gift.[2]	16
(b) Explain and apply the identification rules as they apply to individuals and to companies, including the same day, nine day,and thirty day matching rules.[2]	16 & 20
(c) Explain the pooling provisions.[2]	16 & 20
(d) Explain the treatment of bonus issues, rights issues, takeovers and reorganisations.[2]	16 & 20
(e) Explain the exemption available for gilt-edged securities and qualifying corporate bonds [2]	16

Excluded topics:

The small part disposal rules applicable to rights issues.

Substantial shareholdings.

Gilt-edged securities and qualifying corporate bonds other than the fact that they are exempt.

5 The computation of the capital gains tax payable by individuals

(a) Compute the amount of capital gains tax payable.[2]	14

6 The use of exemptions and reliefs in deferring and minimising tax liabilities arising on the disposal of capital assets

(a)	Explain and apply entrepreneurs' relief for individuals	17
(b)	Explain and apply rollover relief as it applies to individuals and companies.[2]	17 & 20
(c)	Explain and apply holdover relief for the gift of business assets.[2]	17
(d)	Explain and apply the incorporation relief that is available upon the transfer of a business to a company.[2]	17

Excluded topics:
Reinvestment relief.

E NATIONAL INSURANCE CONTRIBUTIONS

1 The scope of national insurance

(a)	Describe the scope of national insurance.[1]	12

2 Class 1 and Class 1A contributions for employed persons

(a)	Compute Class 1 NIC.[2]	12
(b)	Compute Class 1A NIC.[2]	12

Excluded topics:
The calculation of directors' national insurance on a month-by-month basis.
Contracted out contributions.

3 Class 2 and Class 4 contributions for self-employed persons

(a)	Compute Class 2 NIC.[2]	12
(b)	Compute Class 4 NIC.[2]	12

Excluded topics:
The offset of trading losses against non-trading income.

F **VALUE ADDED TAX**

1 The scope of value added tax (VAT)

(a) Describe the scope of VAT.[2] 25

(b) List the principal zero-rated and exempt supplies.[2] 25

2 The VAT registration requirements

(a) Recognise the circumstances in which a person must register for VAT.[2] 25

(b) Explain the advantages of voluntary VAT registration.[2] 25

(c) Explain the circumstances in which pre-registration input VAT can be recovered.[2] 25

(d) Explain how and when a person can deregister for VAT.[1]

Excluded topics:

Group registration.

3 The computation of VAT liabilities

(a) Explain how VAT is accounted for and administered.[2] 26

(b) Recognise the tax point when goods or services are supplied. [2] 25

(c) List the information that must be given on a VAT invoice. [1] 26

(d) Explain and apply the principles regarding the valuation of supplies.[2] 25

(e) Recognise the circumstances in which input VAT is non-deductible.[2] 25

(f) Compute the relief that is available for impairment losses on trade debts.[2] 25

(g) Explain the circumstances in which the default surcharge, serious misdeclaration penalty, and default interest will be applied.[1] 26

Excluded topics:

Imports, exports and trading within the European Community.

Partial exemption.

In respect of property and land: leases, do-it-yourself builders, and a landlord's option to tax.

Penalties apart from those listed here (repeated misdeclarations are excluded).

4 The effect of special schemes

(a)	Describe the cash accounting scheme, and recognise when it will be advantageous to use the scheme.[2]	26
(b)	Describe the annual accounting scheme, and recognise when it will be advantageous to use the scheme.[2]	26
(c)	Describe the flat rate scheme, and recognise when it will be advantageous to use the scheme.[2]	26

Excluded topics:

The second-hand goods scheme.

The capital goods scheme.

The special schemes for retailers.

G THE OBLIGATIONS OF TAX PAYERS AND/OR THEIR AGENTS

1 The systems for self-assessment and the making of returns

(a)	Explain and apply the features of the self-assessment system as it applies to individuals.[2]	13
(b)	Explain and apply the features of the self-assessment system as it applies to companies.[2]	24

2 The time limits for the submission of information, claims and payment of tax, including payments on account

(a)	Recognise the time limits that apply to the filing of returns and the making of claims.[2]	13 & 24
(b)	Recognise the due dates for the payment of tax under the self-assessment system.[2]	13
(c)	Compute payments on account and balancing payments/repayments for individuals.[2]	13
(d)	Explain how large companies are required to account for corporation tax on a quarterly basis.[2]	24
(e)	List the information and records that taxpayers need to retain for tax purposes.[2]	13 & 24

Excluded topics:

The payment of CGT by annual instalments.

3 The procedures relating to enquiries, appeals and disputes

(a) Explain the circumstances in which HM Revenue & Customs can enquire into a self-assessment tax return.[2] — 13 & 24

(b) Explain the procedures for dealing with appeals and disputes.[1] — 13 & 24

4 Penalties for non-compliance

(a) Calculate interest on overdue tax. [2] — 13 & 24

(b) State the penalties that can be charged.[2] — 13 & 24

The superscript numbers in square brackets indicate the intellectual depth at which the subject area could be assessed within the examination.

Level 1 (knowledge and comprehension) broadly equates with the Knowledge module, Level 2 (application and analysis) with the Skills module and Level 3 (synthesis and evaluation) to the Professional level. However, lower level skills can continue to be assessed as you progress through each module and level.

Examination format

The paper will be mainly computational and will have five questions, all of which will be compulsory.

- Questions 1 and 2 will be for a total of 55 marks with one of the questions being for 30 marks and the other for 25 marks.

  Question 1 will focus on income tax and question 2 will focus on corporation tax.

- Question 3 will be for 20 marks, and will focus on capital gains (either personal or corporate).
- Questions 4 and 5 will be on any area of the syllabus and will be for 15 marks and 10 marks respectively.

There will always be at a minimum of 10 marks on value added tax on any paper. These marks will normally be included within question 1 or 2 although there might be a separate question on value added tax.

National insurance contributions will not be examined as a separate question, but may be examined in any question involving income tax or corporation tax.

Groups and overseas aspects of corporation tax will only be examined in Question 2, and will account for no more than 8 marks in total on any one examination paper.

Capital gains can be examined in questions other than Question 3, for example as part of a corporation tax or business income tax scenario.

Any of the five questions might include the consideration of issues relating to the minimisation or deferral of tax liabilities.

Total marks: 100

Total time allowed: 3 hours plus 15 minutes reading and planning time.

How to use these materials

These Kaplan Publishing learning materials have been carefully designed to make your learning experience as easy as possible and to give you the best chances of success in your examinations.

The product range contains a number of features to help you in the study process. They include:

(1) Detailed study guide and syllabus objectives

(2) Description of the examination

(3) Study skills and revision guidance

(4) Complete text or essential text

(5) Question practice

The sections on the study guide, the syllabus objectives, the examination and study skills should all be read before you commence your studies. They are designed to familiarise you with the nature and content of the examination and give you tips on how to best to approach your learning.

The **complete text or essential text** comprises the main learning materials and gives guidance as to the importance of topics and where other related resources can be found. Each chapter includes:

- The **learning objectives** contained in each chapter, which have been carefully mapped to the examining body's own syllabus learning objectives or outcomes. You should use these to check you have a clear understanding of all the topics on which you might be assessed in the examination.
- The **chapter diagram** provides a visual reference for the content in the chapter, giving an overview of the topics and how they link together.
- The **content** for each topic area commences with a brief explanation or definition to put the topic into context before covering the topic in detail. You should follow your studying of the content with a review of the example. These are worked examples which will help you to understand better how to apply the content for the topic.
- **Test your understanding** sections provide an opportunity to assess your understanding of the key topics by applying what you have learned to short questions. Answers can be found at the back of each chapter.
- **Summary diagrams** complete each chapter to show the important links between topics and the overall content of the paper. These diagrams should be used to check that you have covered and understood the core topics before moving on.
- **Question practice** is provided at the back of each text.

Icon Explanations

Definition – these sections explain important areas of Knowledge which must be understood and reproduced in an exam environment.

Key Point – identifies topics which are key to success and are often examined.

Expandable Text – within the online version of the work book is a more detailed explanation of key terms, these sections will help to provide a deeper understanding of core areas. Reference to this text is vital when self studying.

Test Your Understanding – following key points and definitions are exercises which give the opportunity to assess the understanding of these core areas. Within the work book the answers to these sections are left blank, explanations to the questions can be found within the online version which can be hidden or shown on screen to enable repetition of activities.

Example – to help develop an understanding of topics and the test your understanding exercises the illustrative examples can be used.

Exclamation Mark – this symbol signifies a topic which can be more difficult to understand, when reviewing these areas care should be taken.

On-line subscribers

Our on-line resources are designed to increase the flexibility of your learning materials and provide you with immediate feedback on how your studies are progressing.

If you are subscribed to our on-line resources you will find:

(1) On-line referenceware: reproduces your Complete or Essential Text on-line, giving you anytime, anywhere access.

(2) On-line testing: provides you with additional on-line objective testing so you can practice what you have learned further.

(3) On-line performance management: immediate access to your on-line testing results. Review your performance by key topics and chart your achievement through the course relative to your peer group.

Ask your local customer services staff if you are not already a subscriber and wish to join.

Paper-based examination tips

Spend the reading time of the examination reading the paper carefully.

Divide the time you spend on questions in proportion to the marks on offer. One suggestion **for this examination** is to allocate 1.8 minutes to each mark available, so a 10-mark question should be completed in approximately 18 minutes.

Unless you know exactly how to answer the question, spend some time planning your answer. Stick to the question and tailor your answer to what you are asked. Pay particular attention to the verbs in the question.

Spend the last five minutes reading through your answers and making any additions or corrections.

If you **get completely stuck** with a question, leave space in your answer book and return to it later.

If you do not understand what a question is asking, state your assumptions. Even if you do not answer in precisely the way the examiner hoped, you should be given some credit, if your assumptions are reasonable.

You should do everything you can to make things easy for the marker. The marker will find it easier to identify the points you have made if your answers are legible.

Reports, memos and other documents: some questions ask you to present your answer in the form of a report or a memo or other document. So use the correct format – there are easy marks to gain here.

Study skills and revision guidance

This section aims to give guidance on how to study for your ACCA exams and to give ideas on how to improve your existing study techniques.

Preparing to study

Set your objectives

Before starting to study decide what you want to achieve – the type of pass you wish to obtain. This will decide the level of commitment and time you need to dedicate to your studies.

Devise a study plan

Determine which times of the week you will study.

Split these times into sessions of at least one hour for study of new material. Any shorter periods could be used for revision or practice.

Put the times you plan to study onto a study plan for the weeks from now until the exam and set yourself targets for each period of study - in your sessions make sure you cover the course, course assignments and revision.

If you are studying for more than one paper at a time, try to vary your subjects as this can help you to keep interested and see subjects as part of wider knowledge.

When working through your course, compare your progress with your plan and, if necessary, re-plan your work (perhaps including extra sessions) or, if you are ahead, do some extra revision/practice questions.

Effective studying

Active reading

You are not expected to learn the text by rote, rather, you must understand what you are reading and be able to use it to pass the exam and develop good practice. A good technique to use is SQ3Rs – Survey, Question, Read, Recall, Review:

(1) **Survey the chapter** – look at the headings and read the introduction, summary and objectives, so as to get an overview of what the chapter deals with.

(2) **Question** – whilst undertaking the survey, ask yourself the questions that you hope the chapter will answer for you.

(3) **Read** through the chapter thoroughly, answering the questions and making sure you can meet the objectives. Attempt the exercises and activities in the text, and work through all the examples.

(4) **Recall** – at the end of each section and at the end of the chapter, try to recall the main ideas of the section/chapter without referring to the text. This is best done after a short break of a couple of minutes after the reading stage.

(5) **Review** – check that your recall notes are correct.

You may also find it helpful to re-read the chapter to try to see the topic(s) it deals with as a whole.

Note-taking

Taking notes is a useful way of learning, but do not simply copy out the text. The notes must:

- be in your own words
- be concise
- cover the key points
- be well-organised
- be modified as you study further chapters in this text or in related ones.

Trying to summarise a chapter without referring to the text can be a useful way of determining which areas you know and which you don't.

Three ways of taking notes:

(1) **Summarise the key points of a chapter.**

(2) **Make linear notes** – a list of headings, divided up with subheadings listing the key points. If you use linear notes, you can use different colours to highlight key points and keep topic areas together. Use plenty of space to make your notes easy to use.

(3) **Try a diagrammatic form** – the most common of which is a mind-map. To make a mind-map, put the main heading in the centre of the paper and put a circle around it. Then draw short lines radiating from this to the main sub-headings, which again have circles around them. Then continue the process from the sub-headings to sub-sub-headings, advantages, disadvantages, etc.

Highlighting and underlining

You may find it useful to underline or highlight key points in your study text - but do be selective. You may also wish to make notes in the margins.

Revision

The best approach to revision is to revise the course as you work through it. Also try to leave four to six weeks before the exam for final revision. Make sure you cover the whole syllabus and pay special attention to those areas where your knowledge is weak. Here are some recommendations:

Read through the text and your notes again and condense your notes into key phrases. It may help to put key revision points onto index cards to look at when you have a few minutes to spare.

Review any assignments you have completed and look at where you lost marks – put more work into those areas where you were weak.

Practise exam standard questions under timed conditions. If you are short of time, list the points that you would cover in your answer and then read the model answer, but do try to complete at least a few questions under exam conditions.

Also practise producing answer plans and comparing them to the model answer.

If you are stuck on a topic find somebody (a tutor) to explain it to you.

Read good newspapers and professional journals, especially ACCA's Student Accountant – this can give you an advantage in the exam.

Ensure you **know the structure of the exam** – how many questions and of what type you will be expected to answer. During your revision attempt all the different styles of questions you may be asked.

Further reading

You can find further reading and technical articles under the student section of ACCA's website.

RATES AND ALLOWANCES

INCOME TAX		%
Basic rate	£1 – £34,800	20
Higher rate	£34,801 and above	40

Personal allowance	£6,035
Personal allowance aged 65 to 74	£9,030
Personal allowance aged 75 and over	£9,180
Income limit for age related allowances	£21,800

Car Benefit Percentage

The base level of CO_2 emissions is 135 grams per kilometre.

Car Fuel Benefit

The base figure for calculating the car fuel benefit is £16,900.

Pension Scheme Limits

Annual allowance	£235,000

The maximum contribution that can be made without evidence of earnings is £3,600.

Capital allowances

Plant and machinery:	%
Writing down allowance	20
Special rate expenditure:	
Writing down allowance	10
First year allowance	
Low emission motor cars (CO_2 emissions of less than 110 grams per kilometre)	100
Annual investment allowance	£50,000
Industrial buildings:	
Writing down allowance	3

CORPORATION TAX

Financial year	2006	2007	2008
Small companies rate	19%	20%	21%
Full rate	30%	30%	28%
Lower limit	£300,000	£300,000	£300,000
Upper limit	£1,500,000	£1,500,000	£1,500,000
Marginal relief fraction	11/400	1/40	7/400

Marginal Relief

(M – P) × I/P × Marginal relief fraction

VALUE ADDED TAX

	£
Registration limit	67,000
Deregistration limit	65,000

RATES OF INTEREST

Official rate of interest:	6.25%
Rate of interest on underpaid tax:	7.5%
Rate of interest on overpaid tax:	3.0%

CAPITAL GAINS TAX

Annual Exemption

Individuals	£9,600
Rate of CGT	18%
Entrepreneur's relief	£1,000,000

NATIONAL INSURANCE CONTRIBUTIONS

(Not contracted out rates)		%
Class 1 Employee	£1 – £5,435 per year	Nil
	£5,436 – £40,040 per year	11.0
	£40,041– and above per year	1.0
Class 1 Employer	£1 – £5,435 per year	Nil
	£5,436 and above per year	12.8
Class 1A		12.8
Class 2	£2.30 per week	
Class 4	£1 – £5,435 per year	Nil
	£5,436 – £40,040 per year	8.0
	£40,041 and above per year	1.0

TIME LIMITS FOR ELECTIONS AND CLAIMS

Income tax

Election / claim	Time limit	For 2008/09
s83 ITA 2007 – Agree the amount of trading losses to carry forward	5 years from 31 January following the end of the tax year in which the loss arose	31 January 2015
s64 ITA 2007 – Current and prior year set-off of trading losses against total income	12 months from 31 January following the end of the tax year in which the loss arose	31 January 2011
s260 CGTA 1992 – Current and prior year set-off of trading losses against capital gains	12 months from 31 January following the end of the tax year in which the loss arose	31 January 2011
s72 ITA 2007 – Three year carry back of trading losses in the opening years	12 months from 31 January following the end of the tax year in which the loss arose	31 January 2011
s89 ITA 2007 – Three year carry back of terminal trading losses in the closing years	5 years from 31 January following the end of the last tax year of trading	31 January 2015

National Insurance Contributions

Election / claim	Time limit	For 2008/09
Class 1 primary and secondary – pay days	14 days after the end of each tax month under PAYE system	19th of each month
Class 1 A NIC – pay day	19 July following end of tax year	19 July 2009
Class 2 NICs – pay days	Monthly by direct debit or quarterly invoicing	
Class 4 NICs – pay days	Paid under self assessment with income tax	

Capital gains tax

Election / claim	Time limit	For 2008/09
Replacement of business asset relief for individuals (Rollover relief)	5 years from 31 January following the end of the tax year in which the disposal occurred	31 January 2015
Holdover relief of gain on the gift of a business asset (Gift relief)	5 years from 31 January following the end of the tax year in which the disposal occurred	31 January 2015
Disapplication of incorporation relief	2 years from the 31 January following the end of the tax year in which the business is transferred	31 January 2011
Entrepreneurs' relief	12 months from 31 January following the end of the tax year in which the disposal occurred	31 January 2011
Determination of principal private residence	2 years from the acquisition of the second property	

Self assessment – individuals

Election / claim	Time limit	For 2008/09
Self assessment – Pay days for income tax and Class 4 NIC	1st instalment: 31 January in the tax year	31 January 2009
	2nd instalment: 31 July following the end of the tax year	31 July 2009
	Balancing payment: 31 January following the end of the tax year	31 January 2010

Election / claim	Time limit	For 2008/09
Self assessment – Pay day for capital gains tax	31 January following the end of the tax year	31 January 2010
Self assessment – Filing dates: If return issued by 31 October in the tax year	Paper return: 31 October following end of tax year	31 October 2009
	Electronic return: 31 January following end of tax year	31 January 2010
– Filing dates: If return issued after 31 October in the tax year	3 months from the date of issue of the return	
Retention of records – Business records	5 years from 31 January following the end of the tax year	31 January 2015
– Personal records	12 months from 31 January following the end of the tax year	31 January 2011
HMRC right of repair (i.e. to correct mistakes)	9 months from the date the return was filed	
Taxpayers right to amend a return	12 months from 31 January following the end of the tax year	31 January 2011
Taxpayers error or mistake claim	5 years from 31 January following the end of the tax year	31 January 2015
HMRC can open an enquiry	12 months from the actual submission of the return	

Election / claim	Time limit	For 2008/09
HMRC can raise a discovery assessment		
– If suspect incomplete disclosure without negligence/fraud:	5 years from 31 January following the end of the tax year	31 January 2015
– If suspect negligence/fraud:	20 years from 31 January following the end of the tax year	31 January 2030
Taxpayers right of appeal against an assessment	30 days from the assessment – appeal in writing	

Corporation tax

Election / claim	Time limit
Replacement of business asset relief for companies (Rollover relief)	6 years from the end of the chargeable accounting period in which the disposal occurred
s393(1) ICTA 1988 – Agree the amount of trading losses to carry forward	6 years from the end of the chargeable accounting period in which the loss arose
s393(A) ICTA 1988 – Current year set-off of trading losses against total profits (income and gains) and – 12 month carry back of trading losses against total profits (income and gains)	2 years from the end of the chargeable accounting period in which the loss arose
Surrender of current period trading losses to other group companies (Group relief)	2 years after the claimant company's chargeable accounting period
Election for deemed transfer of capital asset to another company at nil gain nil loss prior to a disposal outside the group	2 years from the end of the chargeable accounting period in which the disposal occurred by the company actually making the disposal

Self assessment – companies

Election / claim	Time limit
Self assessment – pay day for small and medium companies	9 months and one day after the end of the chargeable accounting period
Self assessment – pay day for large companies	Instalments due on 14th day of: – Seventh – Tenth – Thirteenth, and – Sixteenth month after the start of the chargeable accounting period
Self assessment – Filing dates	Later of: – 12 months from the end of the chargeable accounting period – 3 months form the issue of a notice to deliver a corporation tax return
HMRC right of repair (i.e. to correct mistakes)	9 months from the date the return was filed
Companies right to amend a return	12 months from the filing date
Companies error or mistake claim	6 years from the end of the chargeable accounting period
HMRC can open an enquiry	12 months from the actual submission of the return
Retention of records	6 years from the end of the chargeable accounting period

Value added tax

Election / claim	**Time limit**
Compulsory registration	
– Historic test	Notify HMRC – 30 days from end of the month in which the threshold was exceeded Charge VAT – Beginning of the month following the month in which the threshold was exceeded
– Future test	Notify HMRC – 30 days from the date it is anticipated that the threshold will be exceeded Charge VAT – the date it is anticipated that the threshold will be exceeded (i.e. the beginning of the 30 day period)
Compulsory deregistration	30 days from cessation
Filing of VAT return and payment of VAT	End of month following the return period

chapter

1

The UK tax system

Chapter learning objectives

Upon completion of this chapter you will be able to:

- describe the purpose (economic, social etc.) of taxation in a modern economy
- identify the different types of capital and revenue tax
- explain the difference between direct and indirect taxation
- describe the overall structure of the UK tax system
- explain the different sources of tax law
- appreciate the interaction of the UK tax system with overseas tax systems
- define the terms tax avoidance and tax evasion and recognise the difference between them
- recognise the purpose of the professional and ethical framework in which the accountant operates.

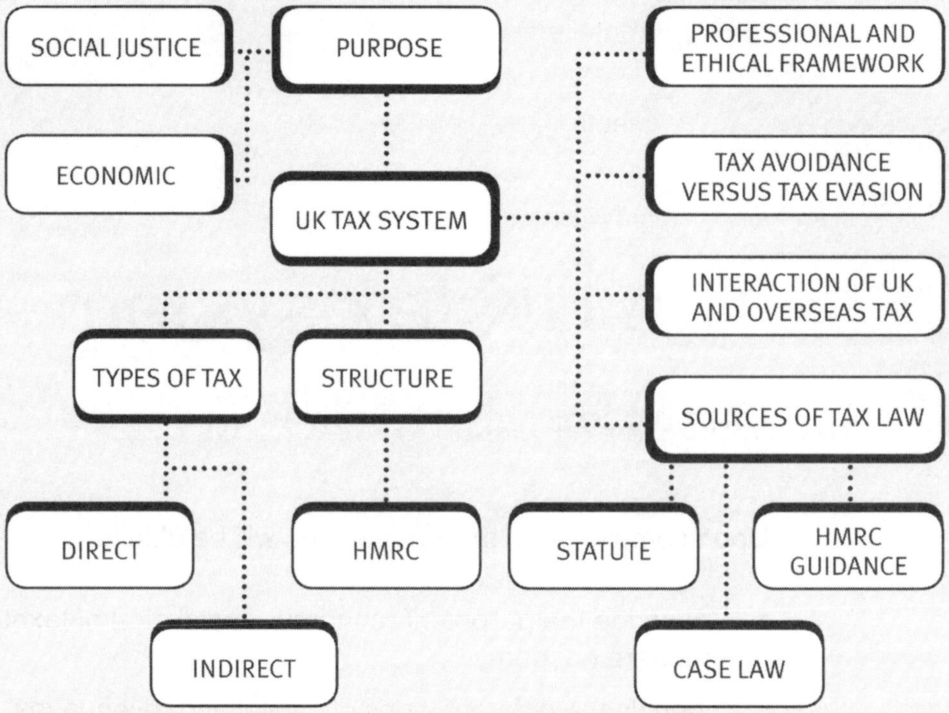

Expandable Text - Purpose of taxation

Economic

- The system of taxation and spending by government impacts on the economy of a country as a whole.
- Taxation polices have been used to influence many economic factors such as inflation, employment levels, imports/exports.
- It is also used to direct the economic behaviour of business and individuals.
  - The current UK tax system encourages:

    (1) individual saving habits by offering tax incentives on savings accounts such as Individual Savings Accounts (ISAs)

    (2) charitable donations by offering tax relief through the Gift Aid scheme

    (3) entrepreneurs and investors by offering tax relief for investments in specified schemes.

  - The current UK tax system discourages:

    (1) motoring by imposing fuel duties

    (2) smoking and alcoholic drinks by imposing significant taxes on these items

(3) environmental pollution by imposing a variety of taxes such as landfill tax, climate change levy and linking CO_2 emissions to the taxation of company cars.

- As government objectives change, taxation policies are altered accordingly.

Social justice

The type of taxation structure imposed has a direct impact on the accumulation and redistribution of wealth within a country.

The main taxation principles are listed below. The arguments for and against each of these are often the matter of significant political debate.

Progressive taxation

- As income rises the proportion of taxation raised also rises.

  For example: 10% on £10,000 of income and 30% on £30,000 of income. Income tax is an example of a progressive tax.

Regressive taxation

- As income rises the proportion of taxation paid falls.

  For example, the tax on a litre of petrol is the same regardless of the level of income of the purchaser.

  This is a regressive tax as it represents a greater proportion of income for a lower income earner than a high income earner.

Proportional taxation

- As income rises the proportion of tax remains constant.

  For example, 10% of all earnings regardless of the level.

Ad Valorem principle

- A tax calculated as a percentage of the value of the item.

  For example, 17.5% VAT on most goods sold in the UK.

1 Types of tax

The UK tax system, administered by HM Revenue and Customs (HMRC), comprises a number of different taxes.

The following taxes are examinable.

Income tax

- Payable by individuals on their earnings and investment income.
- This covers earnings from self-employment and employment.

National insurance contributions (NICs)

- Payable by individuals who are either employed or self-employed.
- Also payable by businesses (e.g. sole trader, company) in relation to their employees.

Capital gains tax

- Payable by individuals on the disposal of capital assets.
- Capital assets include land, buildings and shares, but could include smaller items, such as antiques.

Corporation tax

- Payable by companies on all their income and gains.

Value added tax (VAT)

- Payable on the supply of most goods and services by the final consumer, i.e. us!

2 Direct versus indirect taxation

Direct taxation

- The taxpayer pays direct taxes directly to the Government.
- They are based on income/profits and the more that is earned/received, the more tax is paid.
- Examples of direct taxes include income tax, corporation tax, capital gains tax.

Indirect taxation

- An indirect tax is collected from the taxpayer via an intermediary such as a retail shop.
- The intermediary then pays over the tax collected to the Government.
- An example of indirect taxation is VAT. The consumer pays VAT to the supplier, who then pays it to the Government.

3 Structure of the UK tax system

HM Revenue and Customs

- HM Revenue and Customs is a single body that controls and administers all areas of UK tax law.

Commissioners

- Heading up HMRC are the Commissioners whose main duties are:
  - to implement statute law
  - to oversee the process of UK tax administration.
- To enable the effective running of HMRC across the country, the main body is divided into:
  - District offices
  - Accounting and payments offices.

District offices

- The Commissioners appoint Officers of HM Revenue and Customs to implement the day-to-day work of HMRC.
- There are several hundred district offices covering all areas of the UK.

Accounts and payments offices

- Accounts and payments offices concentrate on the collection and payment of tax liabilities.

4 Sources of tax law

The basic rules of the UK tax system have been established from the following main sources:

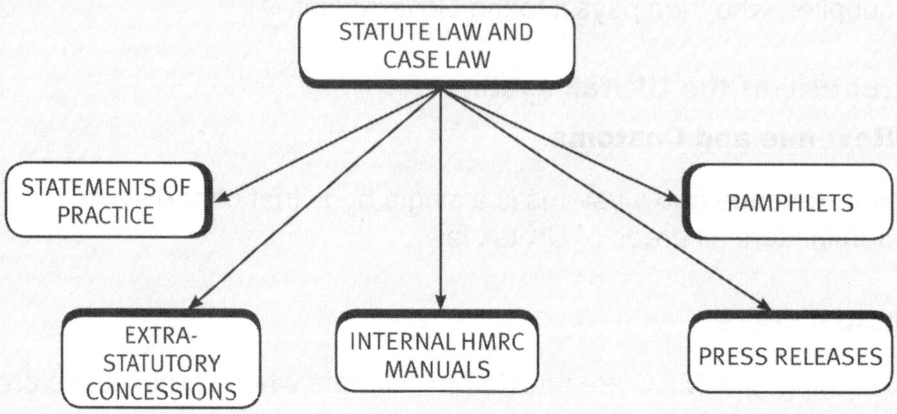

Expandable Text - Sources of tax law

Tax legislation/statutes

- Tax legislation/statutes are law and therefore adherence is mandatory.
- Tax legislation is updated each year by the annual Finance Act that follows from the proposals made by the Chancellor of the Exchequer in his annual Budget statement.
- Statutory instruments are issued where detailed notes are required on an area of tax legislation.

Case law

- Case law refers to the decisions made in tax cases brought before the courts.
- Often the case challenges current tax legislation or argues a certain interpretation of the tax law should be applied.
- These rulings are binding and therefore provide guidance on the interpretation of tax legislation.

HMRC guidance

- As the tax legislation can be complex to understand and open to misinterpretation, further guidance is issued by HMRC in order to:
  - explain how to implement the law
  - give their interpretation of the law.
- The main types of guidance are discussed in the following paragraphs.

Statements of Practice

- Provides HMRC's interpretation of tax law and often provides clarification or detail of how it should be applied.

Extra-statutory concessions

- Extra-statutory concessions allow a relaxation of the strict letter of the law in certain circumstances. A concession is often given where undue hardship or anomalies would otherwise occur.

Internal guidance manuals

- HMRC's own manuals, produced for their staff, are also available to the general public.

Press releases

- Usually provide details of a specific tax issue that has arisen in the year (most commonly used to communicate the Chancellor's annual Budget).

Pamphlets

- Aimed at the general public and provide explanations of various tax issues in non-technical language.

Expandable Text - Interaction of UK and overseas tax systems

Due to the differing tax systems in overseas countries, it is possible that an individual or company could be taxed under two different systems on the same income.

Double taxation relief

Agreements between most countries have been established to decide how a particular individual/company should be taxed.

- These are known as bilateral double taxation treaties.
- Such treaties take precedence over domestic UK tax law and either:
  - exempt certain overseas income from tax in the UK, or
  - provide relief where tax is suffered in two countries on the same income.
- Where no such treaty exists, the UK system still allows for relief to be given where double tax is paid.

Further detail of the operation of the double taxation relief system for companies is found in Chapter 23. Double taxation relief for individuals is not examinable.

Influence of the European Union (EU)

- One of the aims of the EU is to remove barriers and distortions due to different economic and political policies imposed in different member states.
- Although EU members do not have to align their tax systems, members can agree to jointly enact specific laws, known as Directives.
- To date the most important of these has been agreements regarding VAT. EU members have aligned their VAT **policies** according to European legislation. They have not however aligned their **rates** of VAT.
- Many cases have been brought before the European Court of Justice regarding the discrimination of non-tax residents by the UK tax system, some of which have resulted in changes to UK tax law.

5 Tax avoidance versus tax evasion

The difference between tax avoidance and evasion is important due to the legal implications.

Tax evasion

- The term tax evasion summarises any action taken to evade taxes by illegal means.
- The main forms of tax evasion are:
  - suppressing information, e.g. failing to declare taxable income to HMRC
  - submitting false information, e.g. claiming expenses that have not been incurred.
- Tax evasion is an illegal activity and carries a risk of criminal prosecution (fines and/or imprisonment).

Tax avoidance

- Tax avoidance is using the taxation regime to one's own advantage by arranging your affairs to minimise your tax liability.
- It is legal and does not entail misleading HMRC, e.g. making tax savings by investing in ISAs.
- The term is also used to describe tax schemes that utilise loopholes in the tax legislation.
- HMRC have now introduced disclosure obligations regarding tax schemes that involve declaring the details of such schemes to HMRC.

Test your understanding 1

State which of the following is tax evasion:

- Selling a capital asset in May 2008 instead of March 2008 to ensure that the gain is taxed in a later tax year.
- Altering a bill of £700 to read £7,000 on your tax return.
- Moving taxable interest into a tax free ISA account.

6 Professional and ethical guidance

The ACCA 'Professional Code of Ethics and Conduct' has already been covered in your earlier studies. A reminder of the key points is given in expandable text.

Expandable text - Fundamental principles

The ACCA expects its members to:

- adopt an ethical approach to work, employers and clients
- acknowledge your professional duty to society as a whole
- maintain an objective outlook, and
- provide professional, high standards of service, conduct and performance at all times.

To meet these expectations the ACCA 'Code of Ethics and Conduct' sets out five fundamental principles, which members should abide by:

- Integrity
- Objectivity
- Professional competence and due care
- Confidentiality
- Professional behaviour.

Integrity

- Members should act in a straightforward and honest manner in all professional and business judgements.

Objectivity

- Members should not allow bias, conflicts of interest or the influence of others to override objectivity.

Professional competence and due care

- Members have an ongoing duty to maintain professional knowledge and skills to ensure that a client/employer receives competent, professional service based on current developments.
- Members should be diligent and act in accordance with applicable technical and professional standards when providing professional services.

Confidentiality

- Members should respect the confidentiality of information acquired as a result of professional and business relationships and should not disclose any such information to third parties unless:
  - they have proper and specific authority, or
  - there is a legal or professional right or duty to disclose, e.g. Money laundering.
- Confidential information acquired as a result of professional and business relationships, should not be used for the personal advantage of members or third parties.

Professional behaviour

- Members should refrain from any conduct that might bring discredit to the profession.

Advise on taxation issues

A person advising either a company or an individual on taxation issues has duties and responsibilities towards both:

- his client, and
- HM Revenue and Customs.

7 Chapter summary

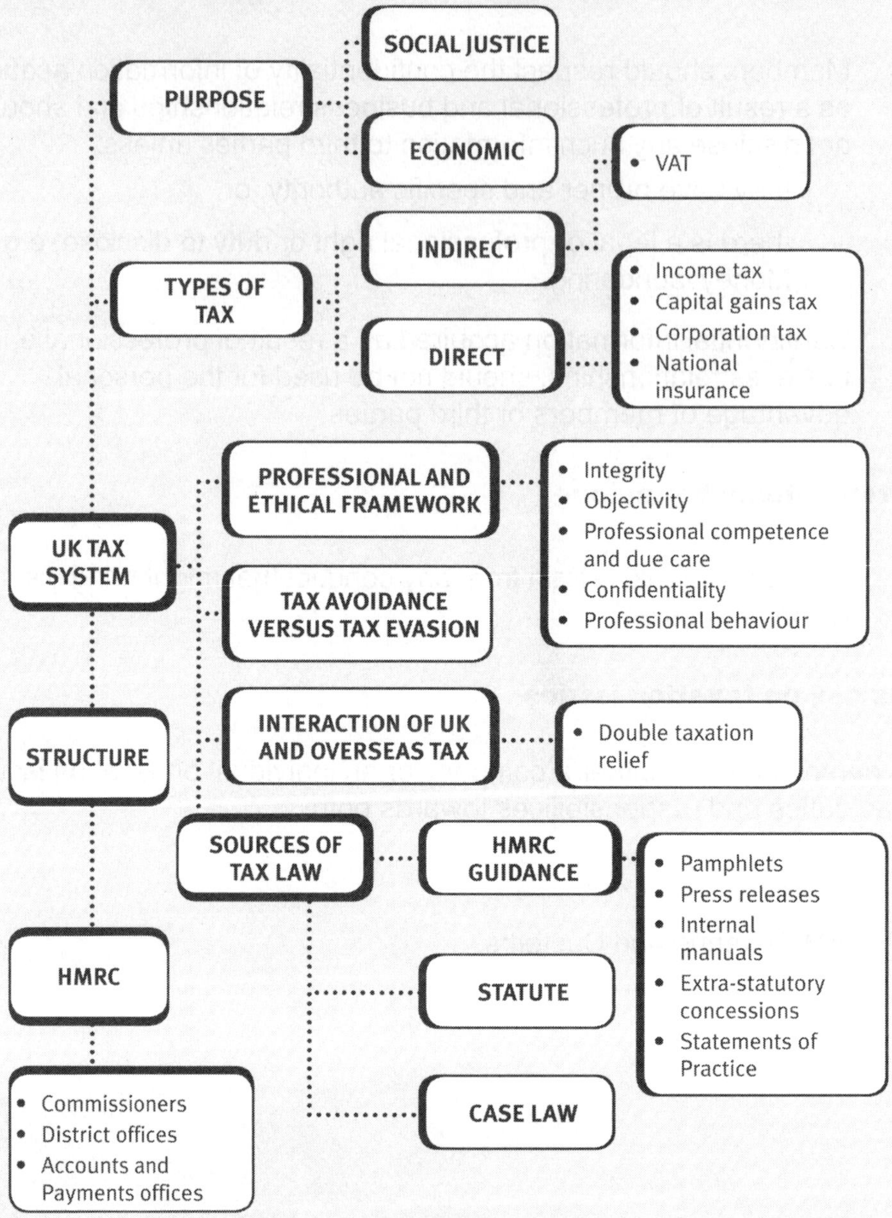

Test your understanding answers

Test your understanding 1

- Changing the timing of the sale of an item so as to delay the tax charge is tax avoidance. Individuals may also do this to take advantage of capital gains tax allowances that are given each year.
- Altering paperwork is tax evasion – submitting false information.
- Moving taxable interest into a tax-free ISA account is tax avoidance – minimising your tax liability within the law.

chapter

2

Basic income tax computation

Chapter learning objectives

Upon completion of this chapter you will be able to:

- identify the scope of income tax and those assessable
- explain how the residence of an individual is determined
- recognise the different types of taxable income for an individual
- calculate the income tax liability arising on different types of income
- distinguish between income tax liability and income tax payable
- recognise qualifying reliefs deductible from total income and explain the tax treatment
- explain the tax treatment of charitable donations
- select and calculate personal age allowances in a variety of situations.

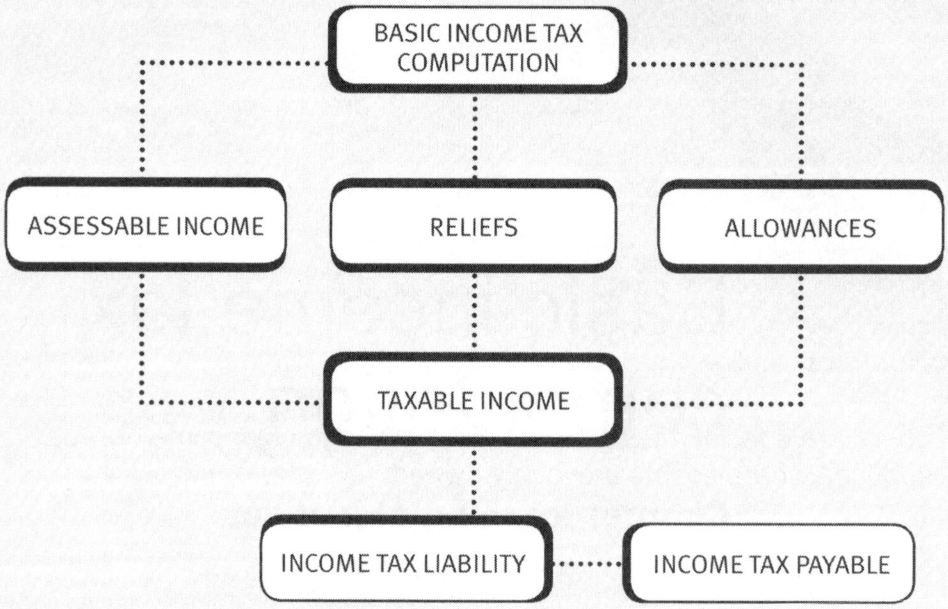

1 The principles of income tax

Introduction

Individuals are assessed to income tax on their income arising in a tax year.

This and the following eight chapters deal in detail with the way in which individuals, whether they are employed, self-employed or simply in receipt of investment income, are assessed to income tax.

Income tax is an important topic as it will be the focus of question one in the examination which will be for either 25 marks or 30 marks.

This first introductory chapter sets out the basis upon which individuals are assessed to income tax and explains how an individual's income tax liability is calculated.

Basis of assessment

Income tax is payable by a UK resident individual on their income for a tax year. This is the year ended on 5 April and is labelled by the calendar years it straddles. Thus the year from 6 April 2008 to 5 April 2009, is referred to as the tax year 2008/09.

Personal allowances

Every taxpayer is entitled to a basic personal allowance (PA). The PA is an amount of tax-free income that every taxpayer is entitled to each tax year. The basic PA in 2008/09 is £6,035. Personal allowances are dealt with in more detail in section 7.

Assessable persons

Each individual is required to pay income tax on his or her taxable income for each tax year. The implications of this are:

- all individuals, including children, are chargeable to income tax
- both spouses within a married couple are treated as separate individuals for the purposes of income tax.

Husband and wife

There are special rules governing the allocation of income between spouses where assets are jointly owned:

- Generally, income generated from assets jointly owned will be split 50:50 between spouses regardless of the actual percentage ownership.
- Where jointly owned assets are held other than in a 50:50 ratio, an election can be made to HM Revenue & Customs (HMRC) for the income to be taxed on the individual spouses according to their actual percentage ownership.
- Civil partnerships are treated in the same way as married couples

Expandable text - Civil partnership

Civil partners are same-sex couples who are registered as a civil partnership under the Civil Partnership Act 2004.

Children

Although a child under the age of 18 is a taxable person, their income typically falls short of their personal allowance in any tax year and therefore no tax liability actually arises on their income.

Residence

- All persons resident in the UK are assessed to UK tax on their worldwide income.
- Broadly, a person is deemed resident in the UK for a tax year if they are present in the UK for a period of six months or more.

Expandable text - Residence

An individual is UK resident if:

- he or she is physically present in the UK for a period (or periods) of six months or more in any tax year, or
- he or she has paid frequent and substantial visits to the UK.

Visits of (in aggregate) three months a year, on average, for four consecutive years are regarded as 'frequent and substantial'. This test is needed to catch the person who deliberately visits the UK on a regular basis over a number of years, but in any one tax year does not satisfy the six months rule.

2 Taxable income

Basic pro forma

- The first stage of the income tax computation is to have a short statement summarising all taxable income.
- All income is included gross in the computation.
- Any exempt income identified can be excluded.

Income tax computation – 2008/09

	£
Earned income	
Trading income	X
Employment income	X
Property income	X
Investment income	
Building society interest (× 100/80)	X
Bank interest (× 100/80)	X
UK dividends (× 100/90)	X
	—
Total income	X
Less: Reliefs	(X)
	—
Net income	X
Less: Personal allowance (PA)	(X)
	—
Taxable income	X
	—

Classification of income

There are a number of different sources of income. For example:

- Income earned from employment and self-employment.
- Income arising from the ownership of property.
- Investment income.
- Income exempt from income tax.

It is important to classify each source of income correctly as the tax rules are different for each source.

All taxable income is included in the income tax computation gross. Some income, such as employment income and bank interest will have had some tax deducted at source. In these instances, the income must be grossed up before being included in the income tax computation.

Earned income

Earned income can be generated in the following ways:

- The profit of a trade, profession or vocation of a self-employed individual is assessed as trading income.
- Earnings derived from an office or employment are assessed as employment income.

Property and investment income

Sources of property and investment income include:

- Property income – typically rental income, but also includes other items such as the income element of a premium on granting a short lease.
- Savings income – usually bank and building society interest. This can be received either net (of 20% income tax) or gross. In both cases it is the gross amount that is included in the tax computation. Credit is given for the tax paid at source in the calculation of income tax payable.
- Dividend income is received net of a 10% tax credit. The grossed up amount (amount received × 100/90) is included in the income tax computation.

Exempt income

Examples of exempt income include:

- Income from certain National Savings products.

- Gaming, lottery and premium bonds winnings.
- Income received from an Individual Savings Account (ISA).
- Some social-security benefits.

Reliefs

Reliefs are deductible from an individual's total income. They include certain payments that an individual makes and certain losses that may be incurred by an individual.

Reliefs are considered in more detail in section 5.

3 Income tax liability

Pro forma – income tax liability

- The second stage of the income tax computation is to compute the income tax liability on the income.
- Different rates of tax apply dependent upon the type of income.

Other income	£		£
On the first £34,800	34,800	@ 20%	X
On excess over £34,800	X	@ 40%	X
Other income	X		
On savings income	X	@ 20/40%	X
On dividend income	X	@10/32.5%	X
Income tax liability			X

Rates of income tax

The rates of income tax for 2008/09 are as follows:

- a basic rate of 20% applies to the first £34,800 of taxable income
- a higher rate of 40% applies where taxable income exceeds £34,800.

These rates are supplied to you in the examination.

These rates apply to all income except dividend income. For example, employment income, trading income, property income and savings income.

Special rates of tax apply to dividend income.

The income tax rates for all sources of income for 2008/09 are summarised below.

Level of income	Other income	Savings income	Dividend income
Basic rate band (first £34,800)	20%	20% (see note below)	10%
Higher rate (excess over £34,800)	40%	40%	32.5%

The income tax liability is calculated firstly on all income except savings income and dividend income (i.e. Other income). This income uses up the basic rate band first.

The income tax liability is then calculated on savings income and finally on dividend income.

In summary the order in which income tax is applied to the different sources of income is as follows:

(1) Other income

(2) Savings income

(3) Dividend income

Note: Special rates may apply to savings income if it falls within the first £2,320 of taxable income.

The special rates for savings and dividend income are considered in more detail in Chapter 3.

Example 1 - Income tax liability

Tony has assessable trading income of £19,535 and employment income of £3,000 for 2008/09. He does not have any savings income or dividend income.

Calculate Tony's income tax liability for 2008/09.

Answer to example 1

Income tax computation – 2008/09

	£
Trading income	19,535
Employment income	3,000
Total income	22,535
Less: Personal allowance	(6,035)
Taxable income	16,500
Income tax liability (£16,500 x 20%)	3,300

Example 2 - Income tax liability

Teresa has assessable trading income of £40,765 and employment income of £4,000 for 2008/09. She does not have any savings income or dividend income.

Calculate Teresa's income tax liability for 2008/09.

Answer to example 2

Income tax computation – 2008/09

	£
Trading income	40,765
Employment income	4,000
Total income	44,765
Less: Personal allowance	(6,035)
Taxable income	38,730

Income tax	£		
Basic rate	34,800	x 20%	6,960
Higher rate	3,930	x 40%	1,572
	38,730		
Income tax liability			8,532

Test your understanding 1

(1) Andrew has income from self-employment of £15,000 and employment income of £2,500.

(2) Alice has income from self-employment of £36,000 and employment income of £21,000.

You should assume that neither taxpayer has any other source of income in 2008/09.

Calculate the income tax liabilities of Andrew and Alice for 2008/09.

4 Income tax payable

Income tax payable

Thus far, calculations have highlighted the income tax liability that arises on the taxable income of the taxpayer.

Certain forms of income, such as:

- savings
- dividends
- most employment income

are received after income tax has been deducted at source.

In determining taxable income all income has been included in the income tax computation gross. To avoid the double payment of income tax, credit is given as the final element of the income tax computation, in order to arrive at the tax payable figure.

The final stage of the income tax computation is to calculate the tax payable, as follows:

	£
Income tax liability	X
Less: Tax credits on dividends	(X)
Tax deducted from savings income	(X)
PAYE on employment income	(X)
Income tax payable	X

The income tax payable is the amount due by the taxpayer. It will be collected via the self-assessment system (see Chapter 13).

In the event that the amount of tax paid during the year is greater than the amount actually due, a refund will be given via the self-assessment system.

In summary:

- **Income tax liability:**
  - The total income tax due on the taxpayer's total gross income, after deducting reliefs and personal allowances.
- **Income tax payable:**
  - The final tax bill to be paid via self-assessment after deducting credits for any tax already suffered/paid at source.

Example 3 - Income tax payable

Akram has assessable trading income of £41,535 and employment income of £9,000 (gross), for 2008/09. He does not have any savings income or dividend income. He suffered tax at source on his employment income (PAYE) of £590.

Calculate Akram's income tax payable for 2008/09.

Answer to example 3

Income tax computation – 2008/09

		£
Trading income		41,535
Employment income		9,000
Total income		50,535
Less: Personal allowance		(6,035)
Taxable income		44,500
Income tax	£	
Basic rate	34,800 x 20%	6,960
Higher rate	9,700 x 40%	3,880
	44,500	
Income tax liability		10,840
Less: PAYE		(590)
Income tax payable		10,250

Test your understanding 2

Waqar provides you with the following information for 2008/09:

Salary	£28,000
Trading income	£20,000

He has no other sources of income for the year, although he does notify you that he suffered £4,390 PAYE, during 2008/09.

Calculate Waqar's income tax payable for 2008/09.

5 Reliefs against total income

Introduction

Tax relief is given for certain losses incurred e.g. trading losses and certain payments made by an individual. Relief is given by deducting the losses/payments from total income.

Losses are covered in detail in Chapter 10.

The only payments deductible from total income which are examinable are certain qualifying interest payments.

In order to maximise the use of reliefs qualifying interest payments should be deducted from total income in priority to losses incurred.

Interest payments

Relief is given for interest paid on loans incurred to finance expenditure for a qualifying purpose.

There are a number of qualifying purposes to which the loan must be applied. The only ones relevant to your examination are as follows:

- **Employees:** The purchase of plant or machinery by an employed person for use in his employment.
- **Partners:** The purchase of a share in a partnership, or the contribution to a partnership of capital or a loan. The borrower must be a partner in the partnership. A loan taken out by a partner for the purchase of plant or machinery for use in the partnership, also qualifies.

Relief is given by deducting the amount of interest **paid** in a tax year from total income.

Example 4 - Reliefs against total income

Gregory has employment income of £34,615, for 2008/09. He paid interest of £2,500 during the year, on a loan taken out to purchase a share in a partnership.

Calculate Gregory's income tax liability for 2008/09.

Answer to example 4

Income tax computation – 2008/09

	£
Employment income	34,615
Reliefs: Interest paid	(2,500)
Net income	32,115
Less: Personal allowance	(6,035)
Taxable income	26,080
Income tax liability (£26,080 x 20%)	5,216

Example 5 - Reliefs against total income

A and B each have total income of £50,000 none of which is savings or dividend income. They made the following payments during 2008/09.

- A made interest payments across the year totalling £2,000 on his mortgage for his principal private residence.
- B made interest payments of £2,000 on a loan to invest in a partnership in which he is a partner.

Calculate the income tax liability for A and B for 2008/09.

Answer to example 5

Income tax computations – 2008/09

	A	**B**
	£	£
Total income	50,000	50,000
Less Reliefs: Qualifying interest paid		(2,000)
Net income	50,000	48,000
Less: Personal allowance	(6,035)	(6,035)
Taxable income	43,965	41,965

Income tax	£	£			
Basic rate	34,800	34,800	x 20%	6,960	6,960
Higher rate	9,165	7,165	x 40%	3,666	2,866
	43,965	41,965			
Income tax liability				10,626	9,826

Note: Mortgage interest paid for a principal private residence is not qualifying interest and therefore not deductible as a relief.

Test your understanding 3

Emmanuel provides the following information in respect of 2008/09

	£
Employment income	27,000
Trading income	19,000
Qualifying interest payment	4,000

He notifies you that PAYE suffered was £4,190, for 2008/09.

Calculate Emmanuel's income tax payable for 2008/09.

6 Charitable giving

Introduction

Tax relief is available for charitable giving in one of two ways:

- Donations under the Gift Aid scheme.
- Payroll giving.

Donations under the Gift Aid scheme are covered below and the payroll giving scheme is covered in Chapter 4.

Donations under the Gift Aid scheme

For those who wish to make gifts of money to charity, the Gift Aid scheme is available.

The key points are as follows:

- Donations made under the scheme attract relief at the donor's highest rate of tax.
- There are no minimum or maximum contribution limits, and gifts can either be one-off or a series of donations.
- The payments must be made with basic rate tax deducted at source. Effectively providing basic rate tax relief at the time the payment is made.
- The basic rate tax is claimed by the charity from HMRC. In addition HMRC will give the charity an additional 2% supplement for donations made in 2008/09 to 2010/11.

Basic rate taxpayers – obtain the tax relief he or she is entitled to at the time of payment, by only paying 80% of the amount due.

Higher rate taxpayers – relief comes in two parts:

- 20% tax relief is granted at the time the payment is made, as above.
- To access the additional higher rate relief, the gross amount of the donation, is added to the basic rate band in the income tax liability calculation. The effect is that income equivalent to the value of the gross donation is taxed at 20%, rather than 40%, giving the additional 20% tax relief that the higher rate taxpayer is entitled to.

Test your understanding 4

Both Paul and Peter earn £44,795 a year. Peter makes donations of £2,000 (net), declaring them to be under the Gift Aid scheme.

Calculate the income tax payable for both for 2008/09.

7 Personal allowances

Every taxpayer (including children) is entitled to a personal allowance (PA).

- The amount for 2008/09 is £6,035.
- The PA is deducted from the taxpayer's net income. It is deducted from the different sources of income in the following order:
  (1) Other income
  (2) Savings income
  (3) Dividend income
- Surplus personal allowances cannot be set against capital gains nor can they be transferred to any other taxpayer.
- There is no restriction to the PA where the individual is only alive for part of the year (i.e. full allowance available in year of birth or death).

Age allowance

Taxpayers aged 65 and over at any time in the year of assessment, are entitled to a higher rate of personal allowance.

- Those aged 65 – 74 are entitled to an increased personal allowance, £9,030 in 2008/09.
- Those aged 75 and over get the highest rate personal allowance, £9,180 in 2008/09.
- The allowance is given for the year of assessment in which the 65th or 75th birthday falls, even if the taxpayer dies before the birthday.
- The allowance is given to attempt to provide some protection for those on lower incomes. An income restriction operates to reduce the level of the allowances, where the taxpayer's net income reaches a certain level. This is set at £21,800 for 2008/09.
- The reduction is calculated as:
  - 50% × (Net income – £21,800)
  - This creates a progressive reduction in the personal age allowance. However, it can never fall below the basic personal allowance of £6,035 for 2008/09.

Example 6 - Personal allowances

Calculate the age allowance in the following situations:

- Dennis will be 71 at the end of 2008/09 and has net income of £23,750
- Nora will be 90 by the end of 2008/09 and has net income of £25,400
- Peter will be 80 at the end of 2008/09 and has net income of £30,900

Answer to example 6

Personal age allowances

	Dennis	Nora	Peter
Age at the end of the tax year:	71	90	80
	£	£	£
Personal age allowance	9,030	9,180	9,180
Less: Restriction			
50% × (23,750 – 21,800)	(975)		
50% × (25,400 – 21,800)		(1,800)	
50% × (30,900 – 21,800) = £4,550 restricted			(3,145)
Personal age allowance	8,055	7,380	6,035

Test your understanding 5

Identify the personal allowances available in 2008/09, to the following:

Taxpayer	Date of birth	Net income
Vera	4 June 1935	£15,900
Agatha	15 March 1932	£22,900
Henry	20 August 1922	£23,900
Leon	7 September 1940	£27,900

8 Chapter summary

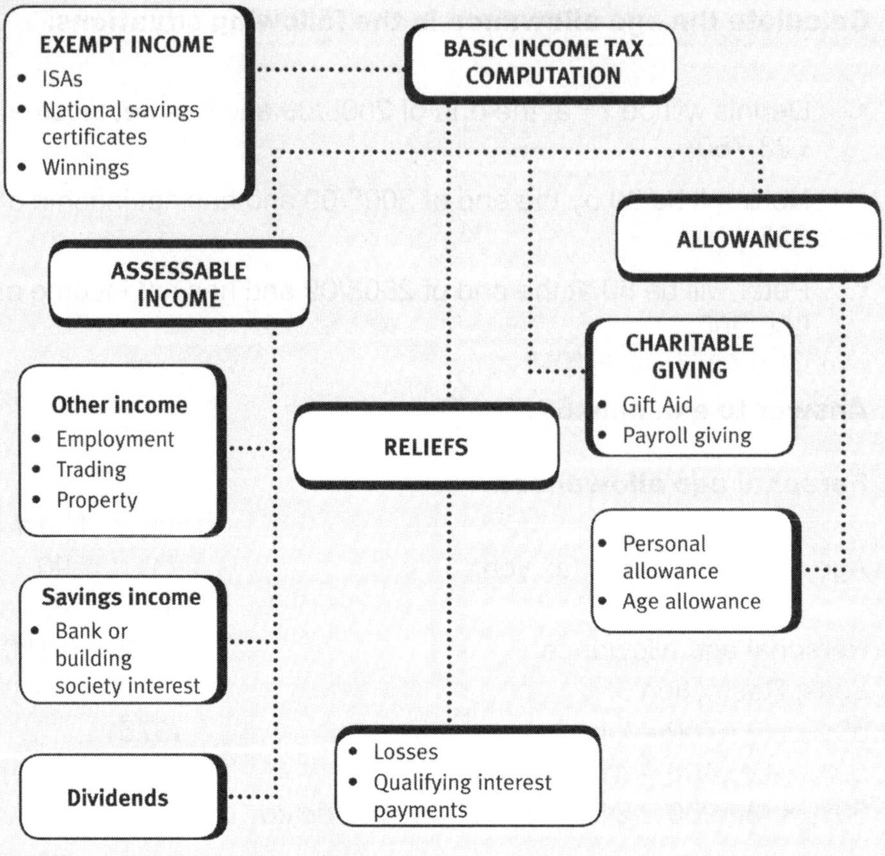

Test your understanding answers

Test your understanding 1

Andrew

Income tax computation – 2008/09			£
Trading income			15,000
Employment income			2,500
Total income			17,500
Less: Personal allowance			(6,035)
Taxable income			11,465
Income tax liability (£11,465 x 20%)			2,293

Alice

Income tax computation – 2008/09			£
Trading income			36,000
Employment income			21,000
Total income			57,000
Less: Personal allowance			(6,035)
Taxable income			50,965
Income tax	£		
Basic rate	34,800	x 20%	6,960
Higher rate	16,165	x 40%	6,466
	50,965		
Income tax liability			13,426

Test your understanding 2

Waqar

Income tax computation – 2008/09			£
Trading income			28,000
Employment income			20,000
Total income			48,000
Less: Personal allowance			(6,035)
Taxable income			41,965
Income tax	£		
Basic rate	34,800	x 20%	6,960
Higher rate	7,165	x 40%	2,866
	41,965		
Income tax liability			9,826
Less: PAYE			(4,390)
Income tax payable			5,436

Test your understanding 3

Emmanuel

Income tax computation – 2008/09			£
Employment income			27,000
Trading income			19,000
Total income			46,000
Less Reliefs: Qualifying interest			(4,000)
Net income			42,000
Less: Personal allowance			(6,035)
Taxable income			35,965
Income tax	£		
Basic rate	34,800	x 20%	6,960
Higher rate	1,165	x 40%	466
	35,965		
Income tax liability			7,426
Less: PAYE			(4,190)
Income tax payable			3,236

Test your understanding 4

Peter and Paul

Income tax computations – 2008/09

					Paul	Peter
					£	£
Income					44,795	44,795
Less: Personal allowance					(6,035)	(6,035)
Taxable income					38,760	38,760
Income tax	£	£				
	34,800	37,300	(W)	x 20%	6,960	7,460
	3,960	1,460		x 40%	1,584	584
	38,760	38,760				
Income tax liability					8,544	8,044

Despite having the same income, Peter's income tax liability is £500 lower than Paul's.

This represents the additional 20% tax saving on the gross payment of £2,500 (£2,000 x 100/80) to the charity.

Working: Peter's basic rate band is extended:

£34,800 + (2,000 × 100/80) = £37,300

Test your understanding 5

Personal age allowances

	Vera	Agatha	Henry	Leon
Age at the end of the tax year:	73	77	86	68
	£	£	£	£
Personal age allowance	9,030	9,180	9,180	9,030
Less: Restriction				
No restriction required	Nil			
50% × (22,900 – 21,800)		(550)		
50% × (23,900 – 21,800)			(1,050)	
50% × (27,900 – 21,800)				(2,995)
= £3,050 restricted				
Personal age allowance	9,030	8,630	8,130	6,035

chapter

3

Property and investment income

Chapter learning objectives

Upon completion of this chapter you will be able to:

- identify savings income
- calculate tax on savings income
- compute the tax payable on dividend income
- recognise the basis for computing property business profits
- explain the rules for allowing expenses and identify the key deductions from property business profits
- demonstrate the reliefs available for a property business loss
- compute the amount assessable when a premium is received for the grant of a short lease
- define when a letting qualifies as furnished holiday lettings
- explain the differences between furnished holiday lettings and normal furnished lettings
- explain when rent a room relief applies
- recognise investments which produce tax free income
- explain the key features of an Individual Savings Account
- explain how a married couple or a couple in a civil partnership can minimise their tax liabilities.

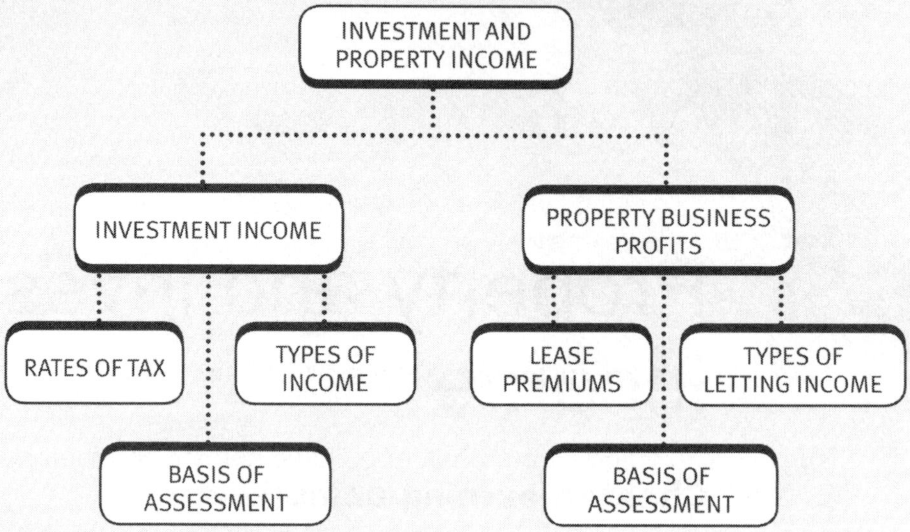

1 Introduction

The primary source of income for most taxpayers is derived from earnings, either from employment or self-employment. These are covered in detail in Chapters 4 to 10. This chapter covers the taxation of income from investments.

The main sources of investment income are:

- Savings income.
- Dividend income.
- Property income.

Certain investments are exempt from income tax. The following tax efficient investments are covered in this chapter:

- Individual Savings Accounts (ISAs).
- National savings products.
- Premium bonds.

2 Savings income

The main types of savings income are bank and building society interest.

Banks and building societies pay interest to individuals net of 20% tax.

Basis of assessment

An individual is taxed on the grossed up amount of the actual savings income **received in a tax year**.

- The amount received will have suffered tax at the lower rate of 20% prior to the taxpayer receiving it.
- The gross amount of interest is calculated as:

interest received × 100/80

- This tax is retained by the bank or building society and then paid direct to HMRC on behalf of the individual taxpayer.

Where the tax credit on bank and building society interest exceeds the individual's tax liability, it is repaid via the self-assessment process (see Chapter 13).

Rates of tax on savings

Savings income is normally taxed in the same way as 'other income' at the basic and higher rates of tax (20% and 40%).

However, with effect from 2008/09, a new starting rate of tax of 10% will apply to the first £2,320 of savings income in certain limited circumstances.

In determining at what rate to tax the savings income, the income is treated as the next slice of a taxpayer's income after his 'other income' (i.e. employment income, trading income and property income) has been taxed.

The new 10% starting rate will only apply where savings income falls into the first £2,320 of taxable income.

Therefore, a taxpayer with taxable savings income will be taxed according to the level of their 'other income' as follows:

'Other income'		Savings income taxed at
None	First £2,320 of taxable savings income	10%
	Next £32,480	20%
	Balance above £34,800	40%
Below £2,320	Taxable savings income falling into the first £2,320	10%
	Next £32,480	20%
	Balance above £34,800	40%
In excess of £2,320	The 10% rate is not applicable	
	Taxable savings income falling into the first £34,800	20%
	Balance above £34,800	40%

The taxpayer has 20% deducted at source, therefore:

- if the recipient is a basic rate taxpayer, there is no additional tax liability to pay on this income. Whilst the income will be recorded gross in the tax computation, the tax paid at source will fully meet the liability
- if the account holder only pays tax at the starting rate (10%) he or she will be entitled to a refund
- for higher rate taxpayers, an additional liability falls due.

Income tax computation

Where an individual has different sources of income, set up the following pro forma using different columns for the different types of income. This will ensure that you:

- calculate the income tax liability on the different sources of income in the correct order, and
- apply the correct rates of income tax.

Taxpayer name

Income tax computation – 2008/09

	Total	Other income	Savings income	Dividends
	£	£	£	£
Employment income	X	X		
Trading profits	X	X		
Property income	X	X		
Interest (× 100/80)	X		X	
Dividends (×100/90)	X			X
Total income	X	X	X	X
Less Reliefs	(X)	(X)		
Net income	X	X	X	X
Personal allowance	(6,035)	(6,035)		
Taxable income	X	X	X	X

- As you practice the examples it is possible that you will become confident enough to identify the different income streams from within the computation and can then revert to the single column approach used to date.

Test your understanding 1

Jamie received bank interest of £1,600 during 2008/09.

Calculate his income tax payable if his income from employment during 2008/09 was:

(a) £25,000

(b) £45,000

(c) £6,900

Set off of reliefs and personal allowances

Personal allowances (PAs) and reliefs are deducted from income in the following order:

(1) Other income.

(2) Savings income.

(3) Dividend income.

This is because the basic rate of tax on other income and savings income (20%) is higher than the corresponding lower rate of tax on dividends (10%). Thus deducting PAs and reliefs in this order produces the highest tax saving.

Example 1 - Set off of reliefs and personal allowances

Simon earned employment income off of £6,500 and received building society interest of £6,000 (net) in 2008/09. He paid qualifying interest of £100 during the year. PAYE of £93 was deducted from his employment income.

Calculate the income tax repayable to Simon.

Answer to example 1

Income tax computation – 2008/09

	Total	Other income	Savings income
	£	£	£
Employment income	6,500	6,500	–
Savings income (£6,000 × 100/80)	7,500	–	7,500
Total income	14,000	6,500	7,500
Less: Interest paid	(100)	(100)	
Net income	13,900	6,400	7,500
Less: Personal allowance	(6,035)	(6,035)	–
Taxable income	7,865	365	7,500

Income tax	£		£
On Other income – basic rate	365	x 20%	73
On Savings income – starting rate	1,955	x 10%	195
	2,320		
On rest of savings income – basic rate	5,545	x 20%	1,109
	7,865		
Income tax liability			1,377
Less: PAYE			(93)
Tax credit on savings income (£7,500 at 20%)			(1,500)
Income tax repayable			(216)

The savings income is partly taxed at the starting rate of 10%, with the balance taxed at the basic rate of 20%.

Here, tax is repayable because tax credits exceeds the tax liability.

Example 2 - Income tax payable or repayable

Patrick has total income in 2008/09 of:

(a) £3,000
(b) £33,000
(c) £42,000

This includes £1,600 (net) of savings income. Patrick has no dividend income.

Calculate Patrick's income tax payable or repayable for the year.

Answer to example 2

(a) Total income £3,000

Income tax computation – 2008/09

	Total	Other income	Savings income
	£	£	£
Other income	1,000	1,000	
Savings income (£1,600 × 100/80)	2,000		2,000
Total income	3,000	1,000	2,000
Personal allowance	(3,000)	(1,000)	(2,000)
Taxable income	Nil	Nil	Nil

Income tax

Income tax liability	Nil
Less: Tax credit on savings income (£2,000 × 20%)	(400)
Income tax repayable	(400)

(b) Total income £33,000

Income tax computation – 2008/09

	Total	Other income	Savings income
	£	£	£
Other income	31,000	31,000	
Savings income (£1,600 × 100/80)	2,000		2,000
Total income	33,000	31,000	2,000
Personal allowance	(6,035)	(6,035)	–
Taxable income	26,965	24,965	2,000

Income tax	£		£
On Other income – basic rate	24,965	x 20%	4,993
On Savings income – basic rate	2,000	x 20%	400
	26,965		
Income tax liability			5,393
Less: Tax credit on savings income (£2,000 × 20%)			(400)
Income tax payable			4,993

(c) Total income £42,000

Income tax computation – 2008/09

	Total	**Other income**	**Savings income**
	£	£	£
Other income	40,000	40,000	
Savings income (£1,600 × 100/80)	2,000		2,000
Total income	42,000	40,000	2,000
Personal allowance	(6,035)	(6,035)	–
Taxable income	35,965	33,965	2,000

Income tax	£		£
On other income – basic rate	33,965	x 20%	6,793
On savings income – basic rate	835	x 20%	167
	34,800		
On rest of savings income – higher rate	1,165	x 40%	466
	35,965		
Income tax liability			7,426
Less: Tax credit on savings income (£2,000 × 20%)			(400)
Income tax payable			7,026

3 Dividend income

Dividends received from a company are charged to income tax in the tax year in which they are received. The receipt date is taken as the date on the dividend voucher.

Tax treatment of dividends

As with savings income, dividends are received net. However for dividends, the process differs slightly:

- Dividends are deemed to be received net of a notional tax credit of 10%. Therefore, any dividends received must be grossed up by 100/90 prior to inclusion within the income tax computation as follows:

Dividend received × 100/90

- As with savings income, the tax credit is available to be set against the taxpayer's tax liability.
- However, as the tax credit is notional (the paying company does not actually make any payment to HMRC on the shareholder's behalf), it can only be used to reduce the taxpayer's income tax liability.

- It is not possible to reclaim this tax credit should it exceed the tax liability for the year.
- Tax credits on dividends are set off, against a taxpayer's income tax liability, in priority to all other tax credits, including PAYE.

Rates of tax on dividends

Level of income	Dividend income
Basic rate band (first £34,800)	10%
Higher rate (over £34,800)	32.5%

There are special rules applicable to the taxation of dividends:

- If the recipient is a basic rate taxpayer, there is no additional liability to pay or refund to claim on any dividend income received.
- For higher rate taxpayers, an additional liability falls due. There is a special higher rate for dividends of 32.5%.

In calculating the income tax liability, dividends are treated as the top slice of income (above 'other income' and savings income). If dividends fall above the higher rate threshold, then they are taxed at the special higher rate of 32.5%.

Example 3 - Dividend income

Jeremy earned employment income of £14,000 and received dividends of £6,750 in 2008/09. PAYE of £1,593 was deducted in respect of the employment income.

Calculate the income tax payable for 2008/09.

Answer to example 3

The dividends are treated as the highest part of Jeremy's income.

As he is only a basic rate taxpayer, all the dividends will be taxed at 10%.

Income tax computation – 2008/09

	Total	Other income	Dividend income
	£	£	£
Employment income	14,000	14,000	
Dividends (£6,750 × 100/90) **Note 1**	7,500		7,500
Total income	21,500	14,000	7,500
Less: PA **Note 2**	(6,035)	(6,035)	–
Taxable income	15,465	7,965	7,500

Income tax

On Other income – basic rate	7,965	x 20%	1,593
On Dividend income **Note 3** – basic rate	7,500	x 10%	750
	15,465		
Income tax liability			2,343
Less: Tax credit on dividend **Note 4**			(750)
PAYE on employment income			(1,593)
Income tax payable			Nil

Note 1: Remember that dividends are always deemed to have been received net of a 10% tax credit and must be grossed up by 100/90, before including in the tax computation.

Note 2: Note that the PA is deducted from 'other income' as this results in the highest tax saving.

Note 3: The 10% rate is charged on dividend income to the extent that it falls within the basic rate band.

Note 4: The dividend credit can never create a refund; at best it can reduce the income tax liability to £nil. It is set off in priority to other tax credits and PAYE.

Example 4 - Dividend income

Jacob earned employment income of £25,300 and received dividends of £15,750 in 2008/09. PAYE of £3,855 was paid in respect of the employment income.

Calculate the income tax payable.

Answer to example 4

Income tax computation – 2008/09

	Total		**Other income**	**Dividend income**
	£		£	£
Employment income	25,300		25,300	
Dividends (£15,750 × 100/90) **Note**	17,500			17,500
Total income	42,800		25,300	17,500
Less: Personal allowance	(6,035)		(6,035)	–
Taxable income	36,765		19,265	17,500
Income tax				
On Other income – basic rate	19,265	x 20%		3,853
On Dividend income **Note** – basic rate	15,535	x 10%		1,553
	34,800			
On Dividend income – higher rate	1,965	x 32.5%		639
	36,765			
Income tax liability				6,045
Less: Tax credit on dividend				(1,750)
PAYE on employment income				(3,855)
Income tax payable				440

Note: The dividends are treated as the highest part of Jacob's income. The first £15,535 of the gross dividend falls into the basic rate band, and is taxed at the lower rate of 10%, the remaining £1,965 (£17,500 – £15,535) falls into the higher rate band, and is taxed at the higher rate of 32.5%.

Example 5 - Dividend income

Simone received dividends of £5,679 in 2008/09. She received no other income during the year.

Calculate the income tax payable/repayable.

Answer to example 5

Income tax computation – 2008/09

	£
Dividends (£5,679 × 100/90)	6,310
Less: Personal allowance	(6,035)
Taxable income	275
Income tax liability (£275 at 10%)	27
Less: Tax credit on dividends (£275 at 10%) **Note**	(27)
Income tax payable	Nil

Note: The tax credit on the dividends in excess of the tax liability (£6,035 × 10%) is not repayable and therefore lost.

Test your understanding 2

Emily has taxable income in 2008/09 as follows:

	£
Employment income	37,000
Bank interest received	1,600
Dividends received	2,700

PAYE deducted in the year is £6,690

Calculate Emily's income tax payable for the year.

Example 6 - Comprehensive scenarios

Gordon Lamont, a single man, received dividend income of £1,350 and bank interest of £300 (net), in 2008/09.

Assume his trading income in 2008/09 is as follows:

Situation:	£
A	2,970
B	7,990
C	22,935
D	39,355
E	43,745

(a) **Calculate the total income tax payable for each situation.**

(b) **If Gordon was married and his wife was a basic rate taxpayer, advise where savings could be made and calculate the tax saved, using situation E only.**

Answer to example 6

Part a – Situation A

Income tax computation – 2008/09

	Total	**Other income**	**Savings income**	**Dividend income**
	£	£	£	£
Trading income	2,970	2,970		
Bank interest				
(£300 × 100/80)	375		375	
Dividends				
(£1,350 × 100/90)	1,500			1,500
Total income	4,845	2,970	375	1,500
Less: Personal allowance (restricted)	(6,035)	(2,970)	(375)	(1,500)
Taxable income	Nil	Nil	Nil	Nil

	£
Income tax	Nil
Less: Tax credit on Dividend income **Note**	Nil
Tax credit on Savings income	(75)
Income tax repayable	(75)

Note: The tax credit on the dividend income is only available to reduce a liability; it cannot create a refund.

Part a – Situation B

Income tax computation – 2008/09

	Total	**Other income**	**Savings income**	**Dividend income**
	£	£	£	£
Trading income	7,990	7,990		
Savings (£300 × 100/80)	375		375	
Dividends (£1,350 × 100/90)	1,500			1,500
Total income	9,865	7,990	375	1,500
Less: PA	(6,035)	(6,035)		
Taxable income	3,830	1,955	375	1,500

Income tax	£		£
On Other income – basic rate	1,955	x 20%	391
On Savings income – starting rate	365	x 10%	36
	2,320		
On rest of savings income – basic rate	10	x 20%	2
On Dividend income – basic rate	1,500	x 10%	150
	3,830		
Income tax liability			579
Less: Tax credit on dividend			(150)
Tax credit on savings			(75)
Income tax payable			354

Part a – Situation C

Income tax computation – 2008/09

	Total	Other income	Savings income	Dividend income
	£	£	£	£
Trading income	22,935	22,935		
Savings (£300 × 100/80)	375		375	
Dividends (£1,350 × 100/90)	1,500			1,500
Total income	24,810	22,935	375	1,500
Less: PA	(6,035)	(6,035)		
Taxable income	18,775	16,900	375	1,500

Income tax	£		£
On Other income – basic rate	16,900	x 20%	3,380
On Savings income – basic rate	375	x 20%	75
On Dividend income – basic rate	1,500	x 10%	150
	18,775		
Income tax liability			3,605
Less: Tax credit on dividend			(150)
Tax credit on savings			(75)
Income tax payable			3,380

Part a – Situation D

Income tax computation – 2008/09

	Total	Other income	Savings income	Dividend income
	£	£	£	£
Trading income	39,355	39,355		
Savings (£300 × 100/80)	375		375	
Dividends (£1,350 × 100/90)	1,500			1,500
Total income	41,230	39,355	375	1,500
Less: Personal allowance	(6,035)	(6,035)		
Taxable income	35,195	33,320	375	1,500

Income tax	£		£
On Other income – basic rate	33,320	x 20%	6,664
On Savings income – basic rate	375	x 20%	75
On Dividend income – basic rate	1,105	x 10%	110
	34,800		
Higher rate	395	x 32.5%	128
	35,195		
Income tax liability			6,977
Less: Tax credit on dividend			(150)
Tax credits on savings			(75)
Income tax payable			6,752

Part a – Situation E

Income tax computation – 2008/09

	Total	Other income	Savings income	Dividend income
	£	£	£	£
Trading income	43,745	43,745		
Savings (£300 × 100/80)	375		375	
Dividends (£1,350 × 100/90)	1,500			1,500
Total income	45,620	43,745	375	1,500
Less: Personal allowance	(6,035)	(6,035)		
Taxable income	39,585	37,710	375	1,500

Income tax	£		£
On Other income – basic rate	34,800	x 20%	6,960
On Other income – higher rate	2,910	x 40%	1,164
On Savings income – higher rate	375	x 40%	150
On Dividend income – higher rate	1,500	x 32.5%	488
	39,585		
Income tax liability			8,762
Less: Tax credit on dividend			(150)
Tax credit on savings			(75)
Income tax payable			8,537

Part b – Tax savings

In Situation E, Gordon is a higher rate taxpayer, paying 40% tax on his savings income and 32.5% on his dividend income.

Gordon could transfer his investments into his wife's name, saving 20% tax (40% - 20%) on his savings income and 22.5% (32.5% – 10%) on the dividend income.

Tax paid by Gordon on investments is £638 = (£150 + £488)

Tax paid by wife:

	£
Savings income (£375 × 20%)	75
Dividend income (£1,500 × 10%)	150
	225
Tax saving: (£638 – £225)	413

Test your understanding 3

Susan has the following income and outgoings for 2008/09:

	£
Trading income	11,615
Employment income (gross)	10,000
Savings income (amount received)	2,800
Dividend income (amount received)	1,800
Qualifying interest (amount paid)	1,000

PAYE of £790 was deducted from the employment income.

Calculate Susan's income tax payable Susan's for 2008/09.

4 Property income

Introduction

For the purposes of the examination, you are required to be able to deal with the following:

- Property business profits arising from the rental/lease of property.
- The premium received on the grant of a short lease.
- Profits arising from the commercial letting of furnished holiday accommodation.
- Rental income received from the rent a room scheme.

Property business profit – basis of assessment

The key assessment rules for property business profits are as follows:

- The assessable income from land and buildings for each tax year is computed as:

	£
Rental income	X
Less: related expenses	(X)
	—
Assessable income	X
	—

- If the landlord lets more than one property, the assessable amount for each year is the aggregate of the profits and losses from each separate property.
- The rental income and related expenses are assessable/deductible on an accruals basis. Accordingly, the due dates for payment of rent and actual payment dates are irrelevant.
- All calculations in the examination are made to the nearest month.

Example 7 - Property income

Hembery owns a property that was let for the first time on 1 July 2008.

The rent of £5,000 pa is paid alternatively:

(a) quarterly in advance

(b) quarterly in arrears.

Hembery paid allowable expenses of £200 in December 2008 (related to redecoration following a burst pipe), and of £400 in May 2009, (related to repair work which was completed in March 2009).

Calculate his property business profit for 2008/09.

Answer to example 7

Property business profit – 2008/09

	£	£
Rent accrued (9/12 × £5,000) **(Note 1)**		3,750
Expenses		
Redecoration	200	
Repairs **(Note 2)**	400	
		(600)
Property business profit for 2008/09		3,150

Note 1: The rent under each alternative is the same – the accruals basis of assessment means the rents accrued between 6 April 2008 to 5 April 2009. The actual payment terms or payment dates are irrelevant.

Note 2: As the work was completed in March 2009 under the accruals basis the expenditure is deductible in 2008/09, the period in which the work was undertaken, and not when the expenditure is paid.

Property business profit – allowable deductions

The expenses allowable against the rental income are computed under the normal rules for the assessment of trading income. These are discussed more fully in Chapter 5.

The main rules are as follows:

- To be allowable, the expenses must have been incurred **wholly** and **exclusively** for the **purposes of the property business.** This covers items such as:
  - insurance
  - agents fees
  - other management expenses
  - repairs
  - interest on a loan to acquire or improve the property.
- Irrecoverable debts are allowable. If a tenant leaves without paying the outstanding rent, the amount owed can be deducted as an expense.

- Relief is available for any expenditure incurred before letting commenced, under the normal pre-trading expenditure rules (see Chapter 5).
- Capital expenditure is not normally an allowable deduction. The main distinction between capital and revenue expenditure is between improvements and repairs.
  - Repairs expenditure would normally be allowable.
  - Improvements expenditure is not allowable.

Expandable text - Distinction between repairs and capital

Caution is required where an item is in need of repair. For example, the replacement of kitchen units with similar standard units would be regarded as a repair. However, had the new units been state of the art new kitchen units, the expenditure would probably have been regarded as an improvement.

- Depreciation may be charged in accounts as a means of writing off the cost of capital expenditure over the life of an asset. Depreciation is not an allowable deduction.
- Normal capital allowances (see Chapter 6) cannot be claimed for expenditure on plant and machinery for use in a dwelling house. However a form of capital allowances known as the 'renewals basis' can be claimed for furnished accommodation.

Renewals basis

- The renewals basis allows relief for the expense of renewing furniture etc. to the same standard.
- The original cost and any improvement element in a replacement is disallowed.
- The record keeping requirements of this method of relief discourage its use in practice.

Wear and tear allowance

The renewals basis of giving relief for capital expenditure is normally replaced by a 'wear and tear' allowance, which is calculated as 10% of the rent received.

If the landlord pays the council tax or water rates on the property, the wear and tear allowance is calculated as 10% of the rent received, net of these expenses.

Wear and tear allowance

= 10% × (rents received — council tax — water rates)

Example 8 - Property income

Giles owns a cottage that he lets out furnished at an annual rent of £3,600, payable monthly in advance. During 2008/09, he incurs the following expenditure:

May 2008	Replacement of one broken kitchen unit with a new unit	£2,000
June 2008	Insurance for year from 5 July (previous year £420)	£480
November 2008	Drain clearance	£380
May 2009	Redecoration (work completed in March 2009)	£750

The tenant had vacated the property during June 2008, without having paid the rent due for June. Giles was unable to trace the defaulting tenant, but managed to let the property to new tenants from 1 July 2008.

Calculate the property business profit for 2008/09, assuming Giles claims the 10% wear and tear allowance.

Answer to example 8

Property business profit – 2008/09

	£	£
Rent accrued		3,600
Expenses		
Irrecoverable debt – June 2008 rent (1/12 × £3,600)	300	
Insurance (3/12 × £420 + 9/12 × £480)	465	
Drain clearance	380	
Redecoration	750	
Wear and tear = 10% × rent received		
10% × (£3,600 – £300)	330	
		(2,225)
Property business profit for 2008/09		1,375

Test your understanding 4

Eastleigh acquired two properties on 1 June 2008, that were first let on 1 July 2008.

Property A is let unfurnished for an annual rent of £4,000, payable quarterly in advance. He incurred the following expenditure in respect of this property.

		£
20.6.08	Repairs to roof following a violent storm on 15 June	1,600
29.6.08	Insurance for year ended 31.5.09	420
1.2.09	Repainting exterior	810

Property B is let furnished for an annual rent of £5,000, payable quarterly in arrears. The tenants were late in paying the amount due on 31 March 2009 – this was not received until 15 April 2009.

Eastleigh incurred the following expenditure in respect of this property in 2008/09.

		£
4.6.08	Letting expenses paid to agent	40
29.6.08	Insurance for year ended 31.5.08	585

Calculate Eastleigh's property business profit for 2008/09.

Property business losses

If rental income for a particular year is less than the allowable expenditure, a loss arises. This is dealt with as follows:

- If the landlord owns more than one property, the profits and losses on all the properties are aggregated to calculate the assessable income for the year. This effectively provides instant loss relief.
- If there is an overall loss on all properties, the property income assessment for the year will be £nil.
- Any unrelieved loss is carried forward indefinitely and offset against the first available future property business profits.

Example 9 - Property losses

Sheila owns three properties that were rented out. Her assessable income and allowable expenses for the two years to 5 April 2009 were:

Property	**1**	**2**	**3**
	£	£	£
Income			
2007/08	1,200	450	3,150
2008/09	800	1,750	2,550
Expenses			
2007/08	1,850	600	2,800
2008/09	900	950	2,700

Calculate Sheila's property business profit/(loss) for 2007/08 and 2008/09.

Answer to example 9

Property	**1**	**2**	**3**	**Total**
	£	£	£	£
2007/08				
Income	1,200	450	3,150	4,800
Less: Expenses	(1,850)	(600)	(2,800)	(5,250)
Profit/(loss)	(650)	(150)	350	(450)
Property business profit 2007/08				Nil
Loss carried forward				450
2008/09				
Income	800	1,750	2,550	5,100
Less: Expenses	(900)	(950)	(2,700)	(4,550)
Profit/(loss)	(100)	800	(150)	550
Less: Loss brought forward				(450)
Property business profit 2008/09				100

Example 10 - Property income and losses

For many years Tom Jones has owned six houses in Upland Avenue that are available for letting unfurnished.

The following details have been provided by the client:

	Property number					
	21	23	25	38	40	67
	£	£	£	£	£	£
Rent due for y/e 5.4.09	2,080	1,820	2,340	1,300	1,300	2,080
Insurance due for y/e 5.4.09	280	220	340	150	150	140

Tom employs a gardener to look after all the properties, and pays him £1,200 a year. There are also accountancy charges of £480 a year; both of these costs are allocated equally to each property.

Numbers 23 and 40, had new tenancies in the year. The cost of advertising for tenants was £50, in respect of number 23 and £100 for number 40. The new tenant at number 23 took over immediately the old tenant moved out. Unfortunately, the old tenant at Number 40 defaulted on rent of £350, due before the new tenant moved in.

During the year Tom had to replace the boiler in number 40, at a cost of £800. During the year he also had to replace the water tank at number 21, at a cost of £100 and a replacement roof for number 25, cost him £5,000.

Tom has loans outstanding on each of the six properties and pays interest of £500 per year on each loan.

(a) **Explain how relief for a property business loss can be obtained.**

(b) **Calculate Tom's property business loss for 2008/09 and state how it will be relieved.**

Answer to example 10

(a) **Relief for property business losses**

Where a taxpayer owns numerous properties, accounts will be prepared for each property for each tax year, resulting in either a profit or loss in each case. These are automatically offset against each other for the tax year to ascertain the property business profit or loss for the year.

Where the aggregated total is a loss, this is carried forward indefinitely, to be offset against the first available future aggregate property business profits.

As it is not necessary to consider profits and losses on each property individually, the accounts could be drawn up to show the total rents, expenses etc. for all the properties, instead of property by property.

(b) **Property business loss – 2008/09**

Upland Avenue no	21	23	25	38	40	67
	£	£	£	£	£	£
Rents accrued	2,080	1,820	2,340	1,300	1,300	2,080
Expenses payable						
Insurance	280	220	340	150	150	140
Gardener	200	200	200	200	200	200
Accountancy	80	80	80	80	80	80
Advertising		50			100	
Repairs	100		5,000		800	
Irrecoverable debt					350	
Interest	500	500	500	500	500	500
	1,160	1,050	6,120	930	2,180	920
Profit/(loss)	920	770	(3,780)	370	(880)	1,160

Summary

	£
No 21	920
No 23	770
No 25	(3,780)
No 38	370
No 40	(880)
No 67	1,160
Loss carried forward (Note)	(1,440)
Assessable property business income for 2008/09	Nil

Note: Losses carried forward are set against future property business profits

5 Premiums received on the grant of a short lease

Premiums

A premium is a lump sum payment made by the tenant to the landlord in consideration for the granting of a lease.

Short lease

A short lease is a lease for a period of less than or equal to 50 years.

- Part of the premium received in respect of a short lease is assessed on the landlord as property business income in the year the lease is granted.
- The amount assessable as property business income is:
  - (a) the amount of the premium **less**
  - (b) 2% of the premium for each complete year of the lease (other than the first).

	£
Premium	X
Less: Premium × 2% × (duration of lease – 1)	(X)
Property business income	X

The duration of the lease = number of complete years (ignore parts of a year).

Example 11 - Premiums received on the grant of a short lease

Rodney granted a 21-year lease to Charles on 1 July 2008, for a premium of £10,500.

Calculate the amount assessable on Rodney as property business income in 2008/09.

Answer to example 11

The amount assessable on Rodney for 2008/09 will be:

	£
Premium	10,500
Less: £10,500 × 2% × (21 – 1)	(4,200)
Property business income	6,300

Test your understanding 5

Albert grants an 18-year lease to Derek for £26,000, on 6 September 2008.

Calculate the amount assessable on Albert as property business income for 2008/09.

Grant of a sub-lease

Where a tenant is granted a short lease on a property and then grants a sub-lease to a subtenant, any premium charged to the subtenant is charged on the tenant as property business income under the normal rules for granting leases.

However, if the tenant originally paid a premium to the landlord on its own lease (known as the head lease) relief is given as follows:

$$\text{Taxable premium for head lease} \times \frac{\text{Duration of sub -lease}}{\text{Duration of head lease}}$$

Example 12 - Grant of a sub-lease

On 1 August 2001 Victor granted a lease to Alex for a period of 20 years. Alex paid a premium of £20,000.

On 1 August 2008 Alex granted a sublease to Max for a period of 5 years. Max paid a premium of £24,000.

Calculate the property business income assessable on Alex in 2008/09.

Answer to example 12

Property business income – 2008/09

	£
Premium received re sub-lease	24,000
Less: £24,000 × 2% × (5 – 1)	(1,920)
	22,080
Less: Relief for premium paid re head lease (W)	
£12,400 × 5/20	(3,100)
Property business income – 2008/09	18,980

Working: Premium paid on head lease

The premium assessed on the landlord in respect of the head lease is:

	£
Premium received	20,000
Less: £20,000 × 2% × (20 – 1)	(7,600)
	12,400

Test your understanding 6

Sasha granted a lease to Irina for a period of 25 years on 1 June 2004. Irina paid a premium of £32,000.

On 1 May 2008 Irina granted a sublease to Anna for a period of 7 years. Anna paid a premium of £21,000.

Calculate the property business income assessable on Irina in 2008/09.

6 Furnished holiday lettings

Introduction

Profits arising from the commercial letting of furnished holiday accommodation is still assessable as property business income but it is treated as though the profits arose from a single and separate trade. There are specific rules and reliefs that apply to such property.

Qualifying conditions

The letting will only be treated as furnished holiday accommodation if it meets the following conditions:

- The property is situated in the UK.
- It is let furnished.
- The letting is on a commercial basis with a view to the realisation of profits.
- It is available for commercial letting, to the public generally, as holiday accommodation for not less than 140 days a year.
- The accommodation is actually let for at least 70 days a year (excluding periods of 'long-term occupation' – see below).

- Where a taxpayer owns more than one property, the 70 days test is satisfied if the average number of days for which the properties are let in the year is at least 70.
- The property must not be let for periods of 'long-term occupation' in excess of 155 days in a year.

Long-term occupation is defined as a period of more than 31 consecutive days when the property is let to the same person.

It is possible for the property to be let to the same person for more than 31 days, however, when aggregating all such periods of longer term occupation (which could be a few periods of letting to different persons), the total must not exceed 155 days.

Tax treatment of furnished holiday lettings

Any profits from commercially let furnished holiday accommodation remain assessable as property income.

However, the profits are treated as arising from a separate trade carried on by the landlord, and are not pooled with other rental property.

The following advantages and reliefs thereby become available:

- Relief may be claimed for any losses sustained as if they were trading losses and not property business losses. The losses can therefore be offset against other income and not just other property income (see Chapter 10).
- The profits are treated as relevant earnings for the purposes of relief for personal pension scheme contributions (see Chapter 11).
- Capital gains tax roll-over relief and entrepreneurs' relief is available (see Chapter 17).
- Normal capital allowances will be available in respect of plant and machinery. This will usually be more beneficial than the wear and tear allowance or the renewals basis.

7 Rent a room relief

Introduction

If an individual lets furnished accommodation in his or her main residence, and the income is liable to tax as property income or trading income, a special exemption applies.

Gross annual rental receipts are equal to or less than £4,250

If the gross annual rental receipts are £4,250 or below, they will be exempt from tax.

- The individual's limit of £4,250 is reduced by half to £2,125 if, during a particular tax year, any other person(s) also received income from letting accommodation in the property while the property was the first person's main residence.
- This rule allows a married couple taking in lodgers to either have all the rent paid to one spouse (who will then have the full limit of £4,250), or to have the rent divided between the spouses (and each spouse will then have a limit of £2,125).
- An individual may elect to ignore the exemption for a particular year, for example, if a loss is incurred when taking account of expenses.

Gross annual rental receipts are more than £4,250

- If the gross annual rental receipts are more than £4,250, an individual may choose between:
  - paying tax on the excess of his gross rent over £4,250
  - being taxed in the ordinary way on the profit from letting (rent less expenses).

Summary: Assess lower of:

Method 1 – Normal assessment		**Method 2 – Rent a room relief**	
	£		£
Rental income	X	Rental income	X
Less Expenses	(X)	Less Rent a room relief	(4,250)
Less Wear and tear allowance	(X)		
	—		—
Profit	X	Profit	X
	—		—

8 Tax-free investments

Introduction

The following investment income is tax-free:

- Income from an Individual Savings Account (ISA).
- Proceeds of National Savings Certificates.
- Premium bond, national lottery, betting winnings.

The objective of these products is to enable the taxpayer to invest and create tax efficient income streams.

Expandable text - Individual savings accounts

Individual savings accounts (ISAs) are the most common form of tax efficient investment. They can be opened by any individual aged 16 or over who is resident and ordinarily resident in the UK.

An ISA offers the following tax reliefs:

- Income (interest and dividends) is received free of income tax.
- Disposals of investments within an ISA are free of capital gains tax.

There is no minimum holding period, so withdrawals can be made from the account at any time.

There are two types of ISAs:

- **Cash ISAs**

  This includes bank and building society accounts, as well as those National Savings products where the income is not exempt from tax.

- **Stocks and shares ISAs**

  Investment is allowed in shares and securities listed on a stock exchange anywhere in the world.

The following stocks and shares qualify:

- Ordinary shares.
- Fixed interest preference shares and convertible preference shares.
- Fixed interest corporate bonds and convertible bonds with at least five years to run until maturity.
- Gilts with at least five years to run until maturity.

In addition, investments in unit trusts, investment trusts and open-ended investment companies also qualify.

Unlisted shares and shares traded on the alternative investment market do not qualify.

It is not possible to transfer newly issued shares (e.g. privatisation issues) into an ISA.

ISA subscription limits

The annual subscription limit is £7,200, of which £3,600 may go into a cash ISA.

Therefore, with effect from 2008/09, an individual can invest in either a cash ISA (limit £3,600 per tax year), a stocks and shares ISA (limit £7,200 per tax year), or both (overall limit £7,200 per tax year).

Husbands and wives each have their own limits.

ISA account providers

Savers have a choice of account providers and account formats. The options are:

- Take separate accounts for cash ISA and stocks and shares ISA with the same provider.
- Take separate accounts for cash ISA and stocks and shares ISA with different providers.

National savings

National savings offer a variety of products, some of which are tax-free.

Tax-free products include:

- National Savings Certificates.
- Children's Bonus Bonds.

National savings also offer products that produce taxable income such as NSB Easy access and Investment accounts. Such income will be:

- taxed as savings income
- usually paid gross.

Historically, investment has been made in National Savings products because of their risk-free nature.

9 Husband and wife planning

Individual spouses have their own personal allowances and income tax rate bands.

Where one spouse is not fully utilising their allowances or basic rate tax band a married couple can transfer income generating assets between them, at no tax cost, to minimise their joint tax liability.

This also applies to partners within a Civil Partnership.

Example 13 - Husband and wife planning

Margaret is married to Alfred. She is aged 45 and has employment income of £50,000 pa. She has various bank accounts from which she receives interest of £4,500 each year.

Alfred, aged 52, earns £20,000 trading profits from self-employment each year. He has no other income.

Calculate the couple's income tax liability for 2008/09 and advise how they could have saved tax by better organising their investments.

Answer to example 13

Margaret – Income tax computation – 2008/09

	Total	Other income	Savings income
	£	£	£
Employment income	50,000	50,000	
Bank interest (£4,500 × 100/80)	5,625		5,625
Total income	55,625	50,000	5,625
Less: Personal allowance	(6,035)	(6,035)	
Taxable income	49,590	43,965	5,625

Income tax:

	£		£
Other income – basic rate	34,800	x 20%	6,960
Other income – higher rate	9,165	x 40%	3,666
	43,965		
Savings income – higher rate	5,625	x 40%	2,250
	49,590		
Income tax liability			12,876

Alfred – Income tax computation – 2008/09

	£
Trading income	20,000
Less Personal allowance	(6,035)
Taxable income	13,965
Income tax liability (£13,965 x 20%)	2,793

Tax saving advice

Margaret is a higher rate taxpayer and has paid tax on her investment income at the rate of 40% in 2008/09. Alfred, however, is a basic rate taxpayer.

If the bank accounts had been in Alfred's name he would have paid tax on the interest at 20% thus saving the couple tax of £1,125 (£5,625 × 20%).

10 Chapter summary

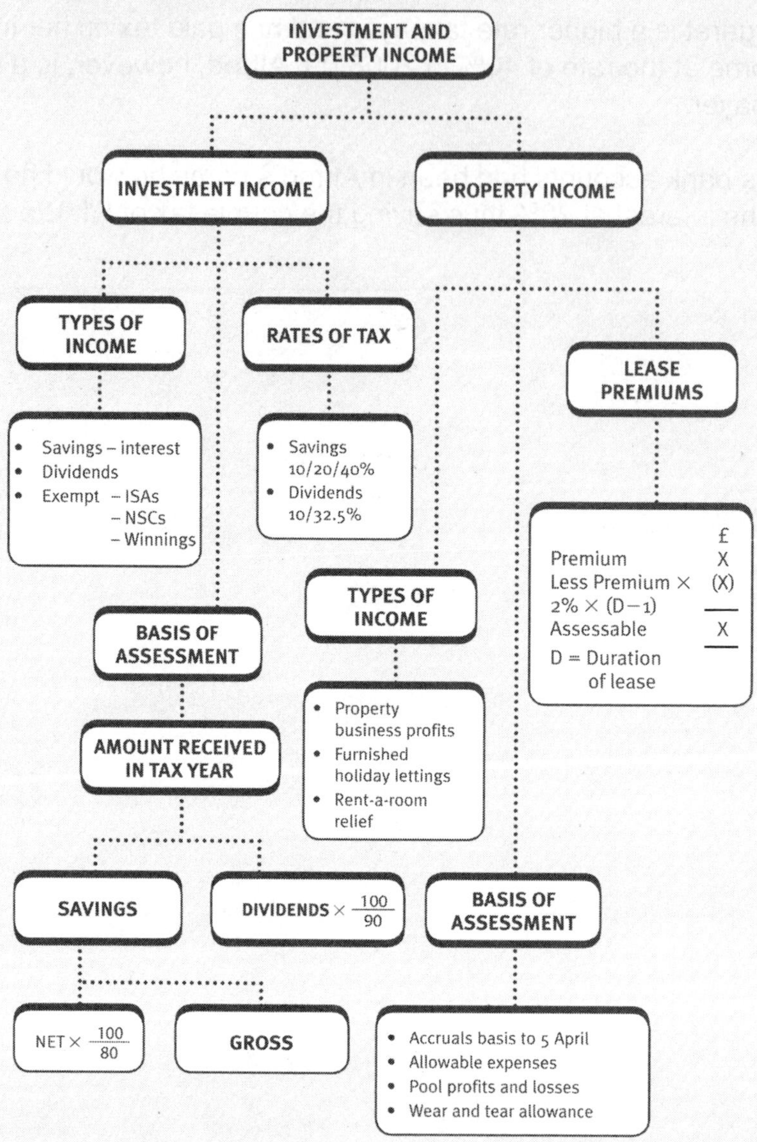

Test your understanding answers

Test your understanding 1

Jamie

(a) **Employment income – £25,000**

Income tax computation – 2008/09

	Total	Other income	Savings income
	£	£	£
Employment income	25,000	25,000	
Savings income (£1,600 × 100/80) **Note 1**	2,000		2,000
Total income	27,000	25,000	2,000
Personal allowance	(6,035)	(6,035)	
Taxable income	20,965	18,965	2,000

Income tax			
On Other income – basic rate	18,965	x 20%	3,793
On Savings income – basic rate	2,000	x 20%	400
	20,965		
Income tax liability			4,193
Less: Tax credit on savings income (£2,000 × 20%)			(400)
Income tax payable			3,793

Note 1: The amount received, must always be grossed up prior to inclusion within the tax computation.

Note 2: The starting rate for savings income is not applicable as 'other income' exceeds the £2,320 band limit. Savings income, to the extent it falls in the basic rate band, is assessed at 20%

(b) **Employment income – £45,000**

	Total	Other income	Savings income
	£	£	£
Employment income	45,000	45,000	
Savings income (£1,600 × 100/80)	2,000		2,000
Total income	47,000	45,000	2,000
Personal allowance	(6,035)	(6,035)	–
Taxable income	40,965	38,965	2,000

Income tax

On other income – basic rate	34,800	x 20%	6,960
On other income – higher rate	4,165	x 40%	1,666
	38,965		
On savings income – higher rate	2,000	x 40%	800
	40,965		
Income tax liability			9,426
Less: Tax credit on savings income (£2,000 × 20%)			(400)
Income tax payable			9,026

Note: In this situation, the starting rate for savings income is not applicable and the savings income falls in the higher rate band. It is therefore assessed at 40%. The deduction for the amount already paid is given, and the additional liability of £400 is settled via the self-assessment process.

(c) **Employment income – £6,900**

Income tax computation – 2008/09

	Total		Other income	Savings income
	£		£	£
Employment income	6,900		6,900	
Savings income (£1,600 × 100/80)	2,000			2,000
Total income	8,900		6,900	2,000
Personal allowance	(6,035)		(6,035)	–
Taxable income	2,865		865	2,000
Income tax				
On other income – basic rate	865	x 20%		173
On savings income – starting rate	1,455	x 10%		145
	2,320			
On rest of savings income – basic rate	545	x 20%		109
	2,865			
Income tax liability				427
Less: Tax credit on savings income (£2,000 × 20%)				(400)
Income tax payable				27

Note: The starting rate band for savings income is firstly reduced by other income before being applied to savings income.

Test your understanding 2

Emily

Income tax computation – 2008/09

	Total	Other income	Savings income	Dividend income
	£	£	£	£
Employment income	37,000	37,000		
Savings (£1,600 × 100/80)	2,000		2,000	
Dividends (£2,700 × 100/90)	3,000			3,000
Total income	42,000	37,000	2,000	3,000
Less: PA	(6,035)	(6,035)		
Taxable income	35,965	30,965	2,000	3,000

Income tax	£		£
On Other income – basic rate	30,965	x 20%	6,193
On Savings income – basic rate	2,000	x 20%	400
On Dividend income – basic rate	1,835	x 10%	183
	34,800		
On Dividend income – higher rate	1,165	x 32.5%	379
	35,965		
Income tax liability			7,155
Less: Tax credit on dividend (see **Note**)			(300)
PAYE on employment income			(6,690)
Tax credit on interest			(400)
Income tax repayable			(235)

Note: Although the tax credit on dividends is not capable of being repaid, it can be set off in priority to other credits, such as PAYE, ensuring maximum relief and enabling Emily to claim a full refund.

Test your understanding 3

Susan

Income tax computation – 2008/09

	Total	Other income	Savings income	Dividend income
	£	£	£	£
Trading income	11,615	11,615		
Employment income	10,000	10,000		
Savings (£2,800 × 100/80)	3,500		3,500	
Dividends (£1,800 × 100/90)	2,000			2,000
Total income	27,115	21,615	3,500	2,000
Less Reliefs: Interest paid	(1,000)	(1,000)		
Net income	26,115	20,615	3,500	2,000
Less: PA	(6,035)	(6,035)		–
Taxable income	20,080	14,580	3,500	2,000

Income tax	£		£
On Other income – basic rate	14,580	x 20%	2,916
On Savings income – basic rate	3,500	x 20%	700
On Dividend income – basic rate	2,000	x 10%	200
	20,080		
Income tax liability			3,816
Less: Tax credit on dividend			(200)
PAYE on employment income			(790)
Tax credit on interest			(700)
Income tax payable			2,126

Whilst the presentation above is the one that you have become used to, the columnar approach takes longer, time that may be valuable in the exam. It is possible to complete the computation with a single column and then separate the income, in the liability calculation at the foot of the computation.

Only use this approach however if you are totally comfortable that you will be able to correctly identify the different sources of income and apply the correct tax rates.

Susan

Income tax computation – 2008/09

	£
Trading income	11,615
Employment income	10,000
Other income	21,615
Savings income (£2,800 × 100/80)	3,500
Dividend income (£1,800 × 100/90)	2,000
Total income	27,115
Less: Reliefs: Interest paid	(1,000)
Net income	26,115
Less: Personal allowance	(6,035)
Taxable income	20,080
Analysis of income:	£
Ohter income (£20,080 – £3,500 – £2,000)	14,580
Savings	3,500
Dividends	2,000

Income tax computation = as before

Test your understanding 4

Eastleigh

Property business profit – 2008/09

Property A	£	£
Rent (9/12 × £4,000)		3,000
Less: Insurance (10/12 × £420)	350	
Repainting exterior	810	
Roof repairs (pre-trading expenditure)	1,600	
		(2,760)
Profit		240
Property B		
Rent (9/12 × £5,000)		3,750
Less: Insurance (10/12 × £585)	488	
Letting expenses	40	(528)
		3,222
Wear and tear allowance (10% × £3,750)		(375)
Profit		2,847
Property business profit for 2008/09 (£240 + £2,847)		3,087

Test your understanding 5

Albert

Albert's assessable property income:

	£
Premium	26,000
Less: £26,000 × 2% × (18 - 1)	(8,840)
Property business income	17,160

Test your understanding 6

Irina

Irina is assessed on the following property business income in 2008/09:

	£
Premium received re sub-lease	21,000
Less: £21,000 × 2% × (7 – 1)	(2,520)
	18,480
Less: Relief for premium paid re head lease (W)	
£16,640 × 7/25	(4,659)
Property business income – 2008/09	13,821

Working: Premium paid on head lease

The premium assessed on the landlord (Sasha) in respect of the head lease is:

	£
Premium received	32,000
Less: £32,000 × 2% × (25 – 1)	(15,360)
Premium assessed on Sasha	16,640

chapter

4

Employment income

Chapter learning objectives

Upon completion of this chapter you will be able to:

- recognise the factors that determine whether an engagement is treated as employment or self-employment
- state the basis of assessment for income from employment
- list the statutory allowable employment income deductions, including explaining how charitable giving can be made through a payroll deduction scheme
- determine when travel expenses are allowable
- explain the basis for other allowable employment income expenses
- determine when the statutory approved mileage allowance is due and calculate it
- explain the purpose of a dispensation from HM Revenue and Customs
- recognise the general principles in calculating benefits
- recognise the exempt benefits
- calculate the benefits assessable on all employees
- explain the basis of determining whether an individual is a P11D employee and state the effect
- calculate the benefits arising on an employer-provided vehicle
- identify the circumstances when the provision of a loan will result in an employee benefit and calculate the loan interest benefit

- calculate the employee benefit where an asset is provided for private use
- calculate the benefit when an asset is transferred to an employee
- calculate the benefit(s) when accommodation is provided to an employee
- given details of a remuneration package calculate the employment income assessable.

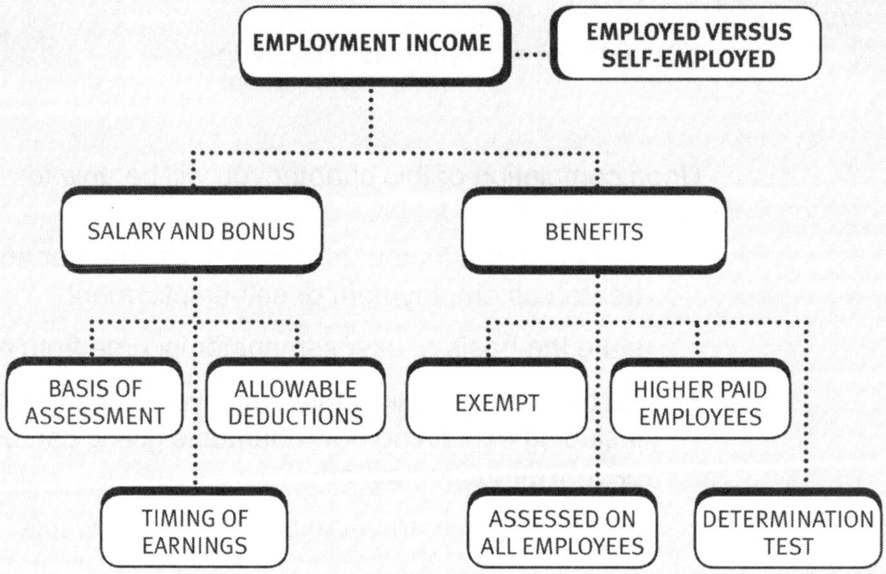

1 The scope of employment income

Employment or self-employment?

The distinction between employment and self-employment is fundamental:

- an employee is taxable under the employment income provisions
- a self-employed person is assessed on the profits derived from his trade, profession or vocation, under the trading income provisions.

The following principles, laid down by statute and case law decisions, are important matters to be taken into account in deciding whether a person is employed or self-employed.

The primary test of an employment is the nature of the contract that exists:

Nature of contract	Status
'of service'	employment
'for services'	self-employment

However, even in the absence of a written contract of service any of the following matters would corroborate the existence of such a contract, and, therefore, employment:

- an obligation by the employer to offer work and an obligation by the employee to undertake the work offered. An employee would not normally be in a position to decline work when offered
- the employer controls the manner and method of the work
- the individual is entitled to benefits normally provided to employees such as sick pay and holiday pay
- the individual is committed to work a specified number of hours at certain fixed times, and is paid by the hour, week or month
- the engagement is for a long period of time
- the individual does not provide his own equipment
- the individual is obliged to work personally and exclusively for the employer, and cannot hire his own helpers
- the work performed by the individual is an integral part of the business of the employer, and not merely an accessory to it
- the economic reality of self-employment is missing – namely the financial risk arising from not being paid an agreed, regular, remuneration
- the individual cannot profit from sound management.

A recent case concerned a vision mixer who was engaged under a series of short-term contracts in the film industry.

Like many persons engaged in a profession or specialised vocation he did not have all the trappings of a business, and did not supply his own equipment. However, it is necessary to look at the overall picture by examining a number of criteria. In his case the number of separate engagements was held to be a deciding factor in the decision to treat him as self-employed.

2 Basis of assessment

Assessable earnings

- All directors and employees are assessed on the amount of earnings received in the year of assessment (the **receipts basis**).
- The term 'earnings' includes not only cash wages or salary, but also bonuses, commission, round sum allowances and benefits made available by the employer.

The date earnings are received

As stated above, employment income assessments are on a receipts basis. Hence, the date that the earnings are received is of critical importance.

The date of receipt is the **earlier** of the following:

- Actual payment of, or on account of, earnings.
- Becoming entitled to such a payment.

In the case of directors, who are in a position to manipulate the timing of payments, there are extra rules. They are deemed to receive earnings on the **earlier** of the two general rules set out above, and:

- when sums on account of earnings are credited in the accounts
- the end of a period of account, where earnings are determined before the end of that period
- when the amount of earnings for a period are determined, if that is after the end of that period.

3 Deductibility of expenses from employment income

General rule

Expenditure will only be deductible if it is incurred **wholly**, **exclusively** and **necessarily** in the **performance of duties**.

Expandable text - General rule for employment income expenses

Expenses must be incurred **wholly**, **exclusively** and **necessarily** in the **performance of the duties** of employment to be allowable deductions against employment income.

- In the performance of the duties.

This aspect of the test means that there is no deduction for expenditure incurred beforehand, to gain the requisite knowledge or experience to do the work. So, for example, the cost of attending evening classes by a schoolteacher has been disallowed.

- Necessarily.

For expenditure to comply with this test, it must be an inherent requirement of the job, not something imposed by the employee's circumstances. Thus an employee with poor eyesight was unable to deduct the cost of spectacles. In other words, to be necessary expenditure, each and every person undertaking the duties would have to incur it.

- Wholly and exclusively.

To be deemed wholly and exclusively incurred, such expenditure must be made with the sole objective of performing the duties of the employment. It does not matter that some personal benefit is acquired from the expenditure, as long as it is incidental.

Two examples show this distinction:

  - If an employee is required to wear clothes of a high standard for his employment and so purchases them, the expenditure is not deductible. The employee's clothes satisfy both professional and personal needs.
  - Expenditure on a home telephone can be partly deductible. Business calls are made 'wholly and exclusively' and so are deductible. But, on the same reasoning as applied to the clothes, no part of the line rental for a home phone may be deducted.

Expenditure allowed by statute

A deduction for certain types of expenditure is specifically permitted by statute as follows:

- contributions to registered pension schemes (within certain limits) (see Chapter 11)
- fees and subscriptions to professional bodies and learned societies, provided that the recipient is approved for the purpose by HMRC, and its activities are relevant to the individual's employment

- payments to charity made under a payroll deduction scheme, operated by an employer
- expenditure on travel and other expenditure, is deductible to the extent that it complies with very stringent rules.
- capital allowances are available for plant and machinery necessarily provided by an employee for use in his or her duties.

Expandable text - Capital allowances

Capital allowances are available for plant and machinery necessarily provided by an employee for use in his or her duties. For example, capital allowances will be available where an employee uses his own computer for business use. Allowances will be restricted to the proportion of business use (see Chapter 6).

Payroll deduction scheme

- Under the payroll deduction scheme an employee authorises his employer to make deductions from his salary and pay the amounts over to specified charities.
- There is no limit on the amount of donations that an employee can make under the scheme.
- The donations are deducted from the employee's gross pay before tax (PAYE) is applied to his taxable pay.

Travel expenditure

Travel expenses may be deducted only where they:

- are incurred necessarily in the performance of the duties of the employment; or
- are attributable to the necessary attendance at any place by the employee in the performance of their duties.

Relief is not given for the cost of journeys that are ordinary commuting or for the cost of private travel.

- Ordinary commuting is the journey made each day between home and a permanent workplace.
- Private travel is a journey between home and any other place that an employee does not have to be, for the purposes of work.

Expandable text - Travel expenditure

- Relief is available for travelling expenditure where an employee travels to visit a client. Where such travel is integral to the performance of the duties, it is allowable. This will include travel undertaken by commercial travellers and service engineers who move from place to place during the day.
- No relief is given for travelling between two separate employments. However, if an employee has more than one place where duties have to be performed for the same employer, then travelling expenses between them are allowable.

In addition, the following rules apply for travel to a temporary workplace:

- Relief is given where an employee travels directly from home to a temporary place of work. A temporary workplace is defined as one where an employee goes to perform a task of limited duration, or for a temporary purpose.
- A place of work will not be classed as a temporary workplace, where an employee works there continuously for a period which lasts, or is expected to last, more than 24 months.
- Where an employee passes their normal permanent workplace on the way to a temporary workplace, relief will still be available provided the employee does not stop at the normal workplace, or any stop is incidental, e.g. to pick up some papers.
- An employee may travel to a temporary workplace without that journey being significantly different from his or her normal commuting. This may be the case where the temporary workplace is situated near the permanent workplace, and in these circumstances relief is denied.

4 Approved mileage allowance (AMA)

Allowable rates

Employees who use their own motor cars for business purposes are normally paid a mileage allowance by their employer. HMRC publish approved mileage rates which apply in these circumstances as follows.

- Provided the mileage allowance paid by the employer is within the statutory approved mileage allowances then no benefit arises.

- Where payments made to the employee are greater than the AMAs, the excess will be assessed on the employee as a benefit.
- Where the payment to the employee is less than the AMA, the individual can make a claim to deduct the difference from their employment income.
- Details of the approved mileage rates will be given if they are needed in an examination question.

The approved rates per mile are as follows:

First 10,000 miles pa	40p
Over 10,000 miles pa	25p

Example 1 - Approved mileage allowance

An employee uses her own 1,800 cc motor car for business travel. During 2008/09, she drove 13,000 miles on business. Her employer paid her 30p per mile.

Calculate the expense claim for 2008/09 that can be made against taxable employment income.

Answer to example 1

The mileage allowance of £3,900 (13,000 at 30p) will be received tax free, but in addition, the employee can make an expense claim of £850 as follows:

	£
10,000 miles at 40p	4,000
3,000 miles at 25p	750
Allowable amount	4,750
Mileage allowance received	(3,900)
Expense claim	850

The £850 can be deducted in arriving at the individual's assessable employment income for 2008/09.

Test your understanding 1

John has travelled 12,000 business miles in 2008/09, in his own car. His employer pays him 38p per mile for each business mile.

(a) **Calculate how much of the mileage allowance is taxable.**

(b) **Explain how your answer would differ, if John's employer paid 35p per mile.**

Test your understanding 2

Underwood is employed as an insurance salesman at a monthly salary of £950. In addition to his basic salary, he receives a bonus that is paid in May each year, and which is related to the sales achieved by Underwood in the year to the previous 31 October. His bonuses are as follows:

Bonus for year to:	Paid during:	£
31 October 2006	May 2007	1,920
31 October 2007	May 2008	1,260
31 October 2008	May 2009	2,700

Underwood made the following payments in respect of his employment in 2008/09.

	£
Contribution to occupational pension scheme	342
Subscription to Chartered Insurance Institute	100
Payroll deduction scheme (in favour of Oxfam)	200

Compute Underwood's assessable income from employment for 2008/09.

Expandable text - P11D Dispensations

Where an employee is reimbursed with business related expenses, (e.g. for rail fares for business trips), the employer should report the expenses to HMRC on the employee's P11D. The reimbursed expenses are treated as taxable employment income and the employee must then make a claim for a deduction against his employment income for the business related expenses in his tax return.

An employer can reduce the administrative burden associated with reporting and recording business related expenses paid to employees, by getting approval in advance that specified expenses do not need to be reported to HMRC. This process is referred to as obtaining a dispensation from HMRC.

The impact of obtaining a dispensation is that it permits:

- The employer to omit information from forms such as the P11D, which would otherwise require reporting.
- It saves employees claiming a deduction in their tax returns for expenses that they have received in reimbursement for expenses incurred wholly, exclusively and necessarily, in the performance of their duties.

The employer is required to apply in advance for permission to make such payments and, upon receiving approval from HMRC, can continue to apply the dispensation until further notice.

5 Employment benefits

Introduction

In addition to salary, the term 'earnings' within the scope of income tax also covers benefits received by the employee.

The general rule for valuing benefits provided to employees has been established by case law (Tennant v Smith, 1892). Employees are taxed on the **cash equivalent of the benefit**.

Exceptions to the general rule

There are, however, a number of exceptions to the general rule outlined above:

- Certain benefits are exempt from tax.
- Some specific benefits that are assessable on all employees, are subject to specific statutory valuation rules e.g. living accommodation.
- Benefits received by employees earning at a rate of £8,500 pa or more, and directors, are assessed under a different general principle imposed by statute. They are assessed on the **actual cost to the employer** of providing the benefit.
- Some specific benefits that are assessable only in the hands of employees earning at a rate of £8,500 pa or more, and directors, are subject to specific statutory valuation rules e.g. car benefits.

6 Exempt benefits

There are a significant number of benefits that the employer can provide to the employee, that do not attract a tax charge. Of these the most commonly examined include:

- An employer's contribution to a registered pension scheme.
- The use of subsidised on-site restaurant or canteen facilities, provided they are available for all employees.
- Luncheon vouchers up to a value of 15p per working day.
- The provision of a car parking space provided at or near the place of work, including the reimbursement of the cost of such a parking place.
- The provision of one mobile telephone by the employer to an employee.
- Certain benefits aimed at encouraging employees to travel to work other than by private car. This exemption includes work buses, subsidies to public bus services, and the provision of bicycles and cycling safety equipment.
- Christmas parties, annual dinner dances, etc. for staff generally, provided they are of modest cost (up to £150 pa per head).
- Workplace nurseries for child care.
- A payment of up to £55 per week to an approved child carer. However, the provision of cash allowances or vouchers to meet child care expenses with non-approved carers are taxable.
- Home worker's additional household expenses of up to £3 per week (£156 per tax year) can be paid tax-free without the need for any supporting evidence.

Expandable Text - Further exempt benefits

Further exempt benefits include:

- Home worker's additionall household expenses:
  For higher amounts than £156 per tax year to be exempt, it is necessary to have supporting evidence that the payments are wholly in respect of additional household expenses incurred by the employee, in carrying out his duties at home.
- Relocation and removal expenses up to £8,000.
- Entertainment provided for an employee, by reason of his or her employment, by a genuine third party, e.g. a ticket or seat at a sporting or cultural event provided by a business contact or client, to generate goodwill.
- Gifts received, by reason of his or her employment, from genuine third parties, provided the cost from any one source does not exceed £250 in a tax year.
- Long service awards in kind (e.g. gold watches) are exempt up to a cost of £50 for each year of service of 20 years or more.
- Provision of travel, accommodation and subsistence during public transport disruption caused by industrial action.
- Employer funded training. Where the expenses of training are paid for by the employer, no taxable benefit arises on the employee.
- Medical insurance for treatment and medical services where the need for treatment arises while abroad in the performance of employment duties.
- Security assets and services. Where a security asset or security service is provided by reason of employment, or where reimbursement is made for the cost of such measures.
- Recreational or sporting facilities. No benefit arises on the provision of such facilities by a person's employer (directly or indirectly).
- Welfare counselling for employees provided the service is available to employees generally.
- Pension's advice for employees. The advice must cost no more than £150 per employee per year and must be available to all employees.

- Expenses incurred by employees whilst away overnight on company business. This includes:
  - Where employers pay personal expenses, such as telephone calls home, laundry etc. for employees who stay away from home on business.
  - No benefit arises on these expenses provided that they fall below the de minimis limit of £5 per night in the UK and £10 per night overseas.

  If an amount above the limit is paid, the whole amount is taxable.

- Employee liability insurance. Liability insurance is aimed at protecting an employee from a work-related liability.
- Provision by employers of eye care tests and/or corrective glasses for VDU use by their employees, provided they are made available to all employees.

This is an extremely comprehensive list and in reality, the examiner is likely to refer to one or two within a question that you will be expected to identify as exempt.

Further details on two of the exempt benefits:

Workplace nurseries

The employer must be responsible for the finance and management of the nursery for it to qualify.

The nursery must either be at the workplace or at other non-domestic premises.

Facilities that are run jointly with other employers or local authorities and similar facilities for older children after school or during school holidays, also qualify.

Relocation and removal expenses

- No assessable benefit arises on payment or reimbursement of removal expenses and benefits, provided that the following criteria are met:

  - the expenses are incurred in connection with either a totally new employment, or a new role with the existing employer; or

- a change in the location at which the employee's duties are carried out. In either case it must be necessary for the employee to acquire a new principal private residence, as a commute to the new place of work would not be viable.

- The costs met or reimbursed must be qualifying expenses. These include costs of disposing of the first house, travel and subsistence when looking for a new house, removal expenses and interest on a bridging loan whilst the employee owns both the old and new homes.
- The expenditure must be incurred by the end of the tax year following the one in which the employment change occurred.

7 Benefits assessable on all employees

The general rule of valuing the benefit by its cash equivalent value on disposal to a third party is used, unless there are specific rules for valuing a benefit.

Specific rules have been established for a number of benefits that are assessable on all employees as follows:

Vouchers and credit tokens

Vouchers are broadly documents with which an individual can obtain goods and services.

- Cash vouchers are subject to tax (PAYE) when handed over to an employee, and thus, no further benefit arises on them since tax has already been paid.
- Non-cash vouchers are assessable on the employee at the cost of providing them. An exception is where vouchers are used to provide benefits which would normally be exempt, e.g. luncheon vouchers up to 15 per day, the excess is still assessable using this rule.
- The use of a credit token (such as a company credit card) is assessed on the value of goods and services bought for private use, with the credit token.

No assessable benefit arises where the employee can show that the use of vouchers or credit tokens was wholly, exclusively and necessarily in the performance of the duties of his or her employment, for example, where a voucher for travel for business purposes is provided.

Living accommodation

Where an employee is provided with living accommodation as a result of his employment, the benefit is assessed as follows:

	Benefit arising
All properties: Basic charge	The employee is assessed on the higher of: • the accommodation's **annual value**, and • the rent actually paid by the employer.
'Expensive' living accommodation	(Cost of providing the accommodation – £75,000) × the appropriate percentage This is charged in addition to the basic charge.

Annual value

The annual value is assumed to be the rateable value of the property. This figure will always be given to you in the examination.

Expensive living accommodation

An additional benefit arises where the 'cost of the accommodation' provided exceeds £75,000.

- The ' cost of providing the accommodation' is the purchase price of the property, plus expenditure on improvements incurred prior to the start of the tax year.

	£
Original cost (or market value)	X
Add: Capital improvements prior to the start of the current tax year	X
Cost of providing accommodation	X

- The appropriate percentage is the official rate of interest (ORI) in force at the start of the tax year. For 2008/09, the ORI is 6.25% and will be provided in the examination.
- Where the employer acquired the accommodation more than **six years** before first providing it to the employee, the calculation of the additional benefit uses the property's **market value when first provided** to the employee, rather than the original cost.
- It is important to note that regardless of the market value, an additional benefit is only imposed if the 'cost of providing the accommodation' exceeds £75,000.

The assessable benefits can be reduced by:

- any amount paid by the employee towards meeting the employer's cost of providing the benefit
- the extent that the accommodation is used wholly, exclusively and necessarily for business purposes
- any periods during the tax year that the property is not available to the employee.

Pro forma calculation:

	£
Basic annual value charge	X
Additional expensive accommodation charge	X
	X
Less: Amounts paid by employee for accommodation	(X)
Assessable benefit	X

Job-related accommodation

There is no assessable benefit if the accommodation is job-related.

To be defined as job related, the property must be provided for one of the following reasons:

- Where it is necessary for the proper performance of the employee's duties (e.g. a caretaker).
- Where it will enable the better performance of the employee's duties and (for that type of employment) it is customary (e.g. hotel-worker).
- Where there is a special threat to the employee's security and he resides in the accommodation as part of special security arrangements.

Expandable text - Exception for directors

A director can only claim one of the first two exemptions if he is a full-time working director and has no material interest in the company (broadly, material means more than 5% of the company's ordinary share capital).

Example 2 - Benefits assessable on all employees

Jack was provided with a house to live in by his employer. It cost them £200,000 in June 2004 and has an annual value of £3,000 pa. Assume the official rate of interest is 6.25%.

Calculate the assessable benefit assuming the accommodation is not job-related.

Answer to example 2

Assessable benefit for accommodation

	£	£
Basic charge:		
Higher of		
(i) annual value	3,000	
(ii) rent paid by employer	Nil	
		3,000
Expensive living accommodation charge		
(£200,000 – £75,000) × 6.25%		7,812
Taxable benefit		10,812

Example 3 - Benefits assessable on all employees

The house cost £90,000, when acquired in June 2003; it has an annual value of £1,700.

Since this time the following improvements have taken place:

Date of expenditure	**Type of expenditure**	**£**
February 2004	Conservatory	15,000
August 2006	Redecoration	2,000
May 2008	Garage extension	10,000

Its market value was as follows:

April 2008	200,000
June 2008	165,000

The accommodation is not job-related and Sachin pays a rent of £100 per month to his employer.

(a) **Calculate the amount assessable for 2008/09 in the following situations:**

(i) **Sachin moved in during June 2008.**

(ii) **Sachin moved in during June 2008, but the property was actually acquired by his employer in June 2000.**

(b) **For each of the scenarios above and assuming Sachin remains in the property, with no further improvements than the ones referred to above, what will be the cost of providing the accommodation for calculating the expensive accommodation charge for 2009/10?**

Assume an official rate of interest of 6.25%.

Answer to example 3

(a) Assessable benefits for accommodation – 2008/09

(i) Property acquired June 2003

	£	£
Basic charge		
Higher of (i) annual value	1,700	
(ii) rent paid by employer	Nil	
		1,700
Expensive living accommodation charge **(W1)**		
(£105,000 – £75,000) × 6.25%		1,875
		3,575

		£
Restriction for part-year occupation		
(June 2008 – March 2009) (10/12 × £3,575)		2,979
Less: Contributions paid by employee (10 months)		(1,000)
Taxable benefit		1,979
(ii) Property acquired June 2000		
Basic charge	£	£
Higher of		
(i) annual value	1,700	
(ii) rent paid by employer	Nil	
		1,700
Expensive living accommodation charge **(W2)**		
(£165,000 – £75,000) × 6.25%		5,625
		7,325
Restriction for part-year occupation (10/12 × £7,325)		6,104
Less: Contributions paid by employee (10 months)		(1,000)
Taxable benefit		5,104

(b) Cost of providing accommodation

	Scenario (a)(i)	Scenario (a)(ii)
	£	£
Original cost + improvements **(W1)**	105,000	
Market value **(W2)**		165,000
Garage extension (May 2008)	10,000	10,000
	115,000	175,000

Workings

(W1) Cost of providing accommodation – 2008/09

	£
Cost (June 2003)	90,000
Improvements:	
Conservatory (Feb 2004)	15,000
Redecoration (Aug 2006) **Note 1**	Nil
Extension (May 2008) **Note 2**	Nil
Cost of providing accommodation	105,000

(W2) Market value

As Sachin has moved in more than 6 years after the employer acquired the property, the cost is the market value at the date the property was made available to Sachin, i.e. £165,000. The cost of the conservatory is already accounted for in the market value as at June 2008.

As in scenario (a)(i) the improvements that take place in 2008/09 do not come into the calculation until the following year.

Note 1: The redecoration does not represent capital expenditure and therefore is not included in the calculation.

Note 2: Only those improvements up to the start of the tax year are included, as this expenditure does not take place until May 2008, it will not be included in the calculation until 2009/10.

Test your understanding 3

Paolo lives in a furnished company flat that cost his employers £105,000 in June 2003. The annual value (i.e. gross rateable value) of the flat is £2,500 and he pays his employers rent of £100 a month. The accommodation is not job-related.

Calculate Paolo's taxable benefit for 2008/09.

Assume the official rate of interest is 6.25%.

8 Benefits assessable on directors and employees earning at a rate of £8,500 or more

Principles of assessment

Special provisions apply to:

- employees earning at a rate of £8,500 p.a. or more
- directors.

These are sometimes referred to as 'P11D employees'.

General rule

The general rule is that the assessable amount of the benefit is the **cost of providing** the benefit.

Under case law this has been held to mean the **additional or marginal cost** incurred by the employer – not a proportion of the total cost. This is particularly relevant where employer's provide in-house benefits, such as free tickets for employees of a bus company.

In addition there are specific rules which specify how certain benefits are to be taxed.

An employee is deemed to be provided with a benefit, not only when it is provided to him directly, but also when it is provided to a member of his family or household.

To be taxed under these principles, a benefit must be provided to the employee by reason of his employment.

The key aspects in this chapter are:

- the basis for determining whether or not an employee is classified as a P11D employee.
- the specific rules to use in calculating certain specified benefits.

The threshold income level

In broad terms, the calculation to ascertain whether a person reaches the threshold income level of £8,500 p.a. assumes that he does so, as follows:

	£
Salary	X
Benefits assessable on all employees	X
Benefits assessable only on £8,500 (or more) earners	X
	—
Total earnings (for test purposes)	X
	—

Note that

- There is no reduction in this calculation for any expenses incurred, apart from contributions to registered pension funds and charitable donations, under an approved payroll deduction scheme.
- In reality, it is likely that the vast majority of employees receiving benefits, would fall within the category of being a P11D employee. However, the examiner retains the right to test this area of the law to determine whether they are or not.

P11D employees

The benefits provided to employees earning at a rate of £8,500 pa or more, are reported to HMRC on form P11D. The term 'P11D employee' is therefore sometimes used to denote an employee earning at a rate of £8,500 pa. The term 'higher-paid' employee can also be used.

Directors are automatically subject to the benefits regime for those earning at a rate of over £8,500 pa, unless he or she:

- earns less than £8,500 pa,
- has no material interest in the company (5% of ordinary share capital), **and**
- is a full-time working director of the company.

Motor cars

The company car is one of the benefits most widely provided for employees.

Where a company car is available to the employee for private use a taxable benefit arises.

The benefit is calculated as follows:

	£
(List price when new) × appropriate %	X
Less: Employee contributions for the private use of the car	(X)
Assessable benefit	X

List price

The list price of a car is calculated as follows:

- Price (including taxes) appropriate for the car on the assumption that it is sold in the UK, as an individual sale in the retail market, on the day before the car's first registration. Consequently employees of large companies cannot benefit from bulk discounts their employer might negotiate.
- Plus the value of all accessories and extras fitted at the time of issue, plus the cost of any added subsequently.
- Less any capital contributions up to £5,000, made by the employee towards the capital cost of the car.
- Subject to a maximum price (after deducting any employee capital contribution) of £80,000.

Appropriate percentage

The car benefit charge is a fixed percentage of the car's list price. The percentage to be applied is determined by the CO_2 emissions of the car.

CO_2 emissions per km	**Petrol car %**	**Diesel car %**
120 grams or less	10	13
121 – 135 grams	15	18
Each complete additional 5 grams emission above 135 grams	An additional 1% is added to the 15% or 18% up to a maximum % of 35%	

Note that:

- With effect from 2008/09, a lower % rate of 10% (petrol) and 13% (diesel) has been introduced for "qualifying low emission cars". Low emission cars for this purpose are defined as those emitting 120 grams or less per km.
- The maximum % that can be applied to any car is 35%.

Employee contributions

A reduction is made where the employee makes a financial contribution towards the running costs, as a condition of the car being available for his private use.

This should not be confused with a capital contribution made towards the purchase cost of the car, which is deducted from the price on which the percentage car benefit is based.

Additional points to note:

- The benefit is reduced proportionately where the car is unavailable for part of the tax year because it was first provided or ceased to be provided part-way through a tax year. This is also relevant where an employee changes their car during the year when a separate calculation needs to be performed in respect of each car.
- Where the car is unavailable for a period during the tax year (but was available both before and after, e.g. if it was under repair after a crash), the benefit charge is again proportionately reduced. This condition applies only if the car was unavailable for a continuous period of at least 30 days.
- The charge for cars available for private use takes into account all of the running expenses of the vehicle, so there is no additional taxable benefit when the employer pays for insurance, road fund licence, maintenance etc. If a chauffeur is provided with the car however, it constitutes an additional benefit.
- A separate benefit charge is made for car fuel (see below).
- When more than one car is made available simultaneously to an employee, the benefit in respect of the second car is computed in exactly the same way as set out above.

Example 4 - Benefits assessable on directors and employees

Boris is provided with a company car which has CO_2 emissions of 205 g/km.

Identify the % to be used in calculating the assessable benefit arising on the provision of the company car.

Comment on the impact on the benefit, if the car provided to Boris had a diesel engine.

Answer to example 4

The percentage is calculated as follows:

	%
Basic % for petrol car	15
Plus (205 – 135) × 1/5	14
	29

If Boris's car had a diesel engine, the charge will be increased by 3% to 32%.

Note that if the CO_2 emissions of the car were 209 g/km the starting point of the calculation would still be 205 g/km as you always round down to the nearest full number divisible by 5.

Test your understanding 4

Louis is provided with a company car by his employer. It has a carbon dioxide emission rate of:

(1) 167 g/km.

(2) 128 g/km.

(3) 232 g/km.

(4) 119 g/km.

Calculate the appropriate percentage assuming the car runs on petrol or diesel.

Expandable text - Pool cars

No individual using a pool car is assessed on a car benefit.

To qualify as a pool car, all of the following conditions must be met during the tax year in question:

- The car must be used by more than one employee (and not usually by one employee to the exclusion of the others).
- It must not normally be kept overnight at or near the residence of any of the employees making use of it.
- Any private use by an employee must be merely incidental to his or her business use of it.

Example 5 - Benefits assessable on directors and employees

During 2008/09 Fashionable plc provided the following employees with company motor cars:

(1) Amanda was provided with a new diesel powered company car on 6 August 2008. The motor car has a list price of £13,500 and an official CO_2 emission rate of 127 g/km.

(2) Betty was provided with a new petrol powered car throughout 2008/09. The motor car has a list price of £16,400 and an official CO_2 emission rate of 193 g/km.

(3) Charles was provided with a new petrol powered car throughout 2008/09. Fashionable plc purchased the car for £21,000 and Charles was required to contribute £3,000 towards the purchase cost. The motor car has a list price of £22,600 and an official CO_2 emission rate of 254 g/km. Charles paid the company £1,200 during 2008/09 for the private use of the motor car.

Calculate the car benefit assessable on each of the above employees of Fashionable plc in 2008/09.

Answer to example 5

Assessable car benefits

Amanda	£
Benefit: (£13,500 × 18%) **(W1)**	2,430
Less: Reduction for non-availability **(W2)**	(810)
Assessable benefit	1,620
Betty	
Benefit: £16,400 × 26% **(W3)**	4,264
Charles	
Benefit: £19,600 × 35% **(W4)**	6,860
Less: Payment for use of car **(W5)**	(1,200)
Assessable benefit	5,660

Workings

(W1) The CO_2 emissions are below the base level figure of 135 g/km, so the relevant percentage is 18% (15% plus a 3% charge for a diesel car).

(W2) Reduction for non-availability

The motor car was not available for four months of 2008/09, so the benefit is reduced by £810 (£2,430 × 4/12).

Alternatively, the benefit can be time apportioned and calculated for the 8 months the car was available as follows:

(£13,500 x 18% x 8/12) = £1,620

(W3) Appropriate percentage	%
Basic % for petrol car	15
Plus (190 – 135) × 1/5	11
	26

The CO_2 emissions figure of 193 is rounded down to 190 so that it is divisible by 5. The minimum percentage of 15% is increased in 1% steps for each 5 g/km above the base level.

(W4) The car benefit is based on the list price of the car. The price paid for the car by the company is not relevant.

Charles has contributed £3,000 towards the purchase price of the car. As this is less than £5,000, the capital contribution of £3,000 is deducted from the list price of the car upon which the benefit is calculated. The price on which the car benefit is calculated is £19,600 (£22,600 – £3,000).

The CO_2 emissions are above the base level of 135 g/km.

	%
Basic % for petrol car	15
Plus (230 – 135) × 1/5	23
	38
Restricted to	35

(W5) The contributions by Charles for the private use of the car reduce the assessable benefit.

Test your understanding 5

Sue is provided with a 2,000cc petrol driven car by her employer. The emission rate shown on the registration document is 201 g of carbon dioxide per kilometre and the list price of the car when new was £16,000. During 2008/09, Sue drove 3,000 business miles and paid her employer £2,000 in respect of her private use of the car.

Paul is provided with a 2,300cc diesel powered car by his employer. The list price of the car when new was £36,000. During 2008/09, Paul drove 28,000 business miles. The emission rating of the car is 237g/km.

Calculate the benefit taxable on Sue and Paul for 2008/09.

Private fuel

In addition to the provision of the motor car, some employees also have all (or part) of their private mileage paid for by their employer.

This is an entirely separate benefit from the provision of the car, the rules are as follows:

- The benefit where car fuel is provided for private motoring in a car provided by reason of a person's employment is also based on the CO_2 emissions of the car.
- The fuel benefit is calculated as a percentage of a base figure, which is set each year. The base figure for 2008/09 is £16,900. The base figure of £16,900 will be given in the tax rates and allowances section of the examination paper.

- The CO_2 percentage used in the calculation of the car benefit is also used to calculate the fuel benefit charge. The percentage will therefore range from 15% to 35% (10% or 13% for low emission cars).
- The fuel benefit is proportionately reduced where the fuel itself is only provided for part of the tax year.

Expandable Text - Fuel provided for part of the tax year

However, it is not possible to opt in and out. If, for example, fuel is provided from 6 April to 30 September 2008, then the fuel benefit for 2008/09 will only be charged for six months as the provision of fuel has permanently ceased.

If fuel is provided from 6 April to 30 September 2008, and then again from 1 January to 5 April 2009, the fuel benefit will not be reduced since the cessation was only temporary.

- No reduction is made to the fuel benefit for payments made by the employee unless he or she pays for all fuel used for private motoring. In that case there would be no fuel benefit.
- The fuel benefit only applies to vehicles for which there is a car benefit charge. It does not therefore apply to pool cars.

Example 6 - Benefits assessable on directors and employees

Continuing with the situations set out in Example 5 Fashionable plc.

Amanda was provided with fuel for private use between 6 August 2008 and 5 April 2009.

Betty was provided with fuel for private use between 6 April and 31 December 2008.

Charles was provided with fuel for private use between 6 April 2008 and 5 April 2009. He paid Fashionable plc £600 during 2008/09, towards the cost of private fuel, although the actual cost of this fuel was £1,000.

Calculate the car fuel benefit assessable on each of the above employees of Fashionable plc in 2008/09.

Answer to example 6

Assessable fuel benefit

	£	£
Amanda		
Benefit: £16,900 × 18% **(W1)**		3,042
Less: Reduction for non-availability **(W2)**		(1,014)
Assessable benefit		2,028
Betty		
Benefit: £16,900 × 26% **(W1)**		4,394
Less: Reduction for non-availability **(W3)**		(1,099)
Assessable benefit		3,295
Charles		
Benefit: £16,900 × 35% **(W4)**		5,915

Workings

(W1) The CO_2 percentage used in the calculation of the car benefit is also used to calculate the fuel benefit charge. The percentage is applied to a base figure, which is £16,900 for 2008/09.

(W2) Reduction for non-availability:

The motor car was not available for four months of 2008/09, so the benefit is reduced by £1,014 (£3,042 × 4/12).

Alternatively the benefit can be time apportioned and calculated for the 8 months fuel was provided:

£16,900 x 18% x 8/12 = £2,028

(W3) Reduction for non-availability:

Fuel was not available for three months of 2008/09, so the benefit is reduced by £1,099 (£4,394 × 3/12).

Alternatively the benefit is calculated as: (£16,900 x 26% x 9/12) = £3,295

(W4) There is no reduction for the contribution paid by Charles towards the cost of private fuel, since he did not reimburse the full cost of the private fuel.

Test your understanding 6

Charles took up employment with Weavers Ltd on 1 July 2008. His remuneration package included a 5-year-old 2,500cc petrol-driven car with a list price of £24,000. He took delivery of the car on 1 August 2008. The car has CO_2 emissions of 220 g/km. As a condition of the car being made available to him for private motoring, Charles paid £100 per month for the car and £50 per month for petrol.

Weavers Ltd incurred the following expenses in connection with Charles's car:

	£
Servicing	450
Insurance	780
Fuel (of which £1,150 was for business purposes)	2,500
Maintenance	240

Calculate Charles's assessable benefits for 2008/09 in connection with his private use of the car.

Test your understanding 7

Joan was employed as sales manager of Wilt Ltd from 1 August 2008 at a salary of £60,000 pa. From 1 November 2008, the company provided her with a 1,800cc car, the list price of which was £15,000 and the emission rate was 164 g/km. Up to 5 April 2009, she drove 6,000 miles of which 4,500 were for private purposes. The company paid for all running expenses.

Between 1 November 2008 and 31 January 2009, the company paid for all petrol usage including private use. Joan made a contribution to her employer of £15 per month towards the provision of the petrol for her private use. From 1 February 2009 her employer only paid for business use petrol.

Calculate Joan's taxable earnings for 2008/09.

Vans

The benefit rules for vans are different from those for the motor car. They are as follows:

- The benefit for the private use of a van for 2008/09 is a flat rate scale charge of **£3,000 p.a.**
- No benefit arises where the private use of a van is insignificant. When determining the level of private use, journeys between home and work are ignored. This is not the case for cars.
- Proportionate reductions in the scale charge are made where a van is unavailable (using the same definition as for cars) for part of the tax year.
- A reduction in the benefit is made for payments by the employee for the private use of the van.
- Where employees share the private use of the van, the scale charge is divided equally between the employees who made any private use of the van during the tax year, regardless of the amount of private use.
- In addition a benefit of **£500 p.a.** arises where fuel is provided for private mileage.

9 Beneficial loans

Introduction

Beneficial loans are those made to an employee below the **official rate** of interest. The examiner will assume that 6.25% applies throughout 2008/09.

Employees are liable to a benefit charge on:

	£
Interest that would be payable on the loan (had interest been charged at the official rate)	X
Less: Interest actually paid in respect of the tax year	(X)
	—
Assessable benefit	X
	—

- An exemption for small loans applies where all an employee's cheap or interest free loans (excluding loans which qualify for tax relief) total no more than £5,000.
- There are two methods of calculating the benefit:
  - **The simple (or average) method** – this uses the average balance of the loan outstanding during the year.

    (Balance outstanding at beginning of tax year + Balance outstanding at end of tax year) x 1/2

    If the loan was taken out or redeemed during the tax year, that date is used instead of the beginning or end of the tax year.
  - **The accurate (or precise) method** – this calculates the benefit day by day on the balance actually outstanding.

  Either the taxpayer or HMRC can decide that the precise method should be used.

- If an interest free or cheap loan is used for a purpose that fully qualifies for tax relief (e.g. loan to buy plant used wholly for employment), then there is no benefit.
- If all or part of a loan to an employee (whether or not made on low-interest or interest-free terms) is written off, the amount written off is treated as a benefit and charged to income tax.

Example 7 - Beneficial loans

Daniel was granted a loan of £35,000 by his employer on 31 March 2008, to help finance the purchase of a yacht. Interest is payable on the loan at 3% pa. On 1 June 2008, Daniel repaid £5,000 and on 1 December 2008, he repaid a further £15,000. The remaining £15,000 was still outstanding on 5 April 2009. Daniel earns £30,000 pa.

Calculate the assessable benefit for 2008/09 using:

(a) **the average method**

(b) **the precise method.**

You should assume that the official rate of interest is 6.25% pa.

Answer to example 7

Assessable benefit for beneficial loans

(a) Average method

	£	£
(£35,000 + £15, 000) x 1/2 × 6.25%		1,562
Less: Interest paid		
6.4.08 – 31.5.08: £35,000 × 3% × 2/12	175	
1.6.08 – 30.11.08: £30,000 × 3% × 6/12	450	
1.12.08 – 5.4.09: £15,000 × 3% × 4/12	150	
		(775)
Benefit		787

(b) Precise method

	£
6.4.08 – 31.5.08: £35,000 × 6.25% × 2/12	365
1.6.08 – 30.11.08: £30,000 × 6.25% × 6/12	937
1.12.08 – 5.4.09: £15,000 × 6.25% × 4/12	312
	1,614
Less: Interest paid (as above)	(775)
Benefit	839

In this situation HMRC could opt to switch to the precise method, although it is likely that they would accept £787 as the difference is not significant.

Test your understanding 8

Bob is loaned £10,000, interest free, by his employer on 6 August 2007. He repaid £2,000 on 6 September 2008.

Calculate the amount taxable on Bob in 2008/09. Assume an official rate of interest of 6.25%.

Expandable text - Exemption for commercial loans

There is an exemption for loans made to employees on commercial terms by employers who lend to the general public e.g. banks. The exemption will apply where:

- the loans are made by an employer whose business includes the lending of money
- loans are made to employees on the same terms and conditions as are available to members of the public
- a substantial number of loans on these terms are made to public customers.

10 Assets provided to employees

Private use of an asset provided by the employer

As seen with the rules on the motor car, it is possible for an asset to be provided for an employee's use, while legal ownership remains with the employer. The car is the most common example, but there is a general rule that applies to other assets.

The general rule is that an employee is taxed on an annual benefit of:

20% of an asset's market value at the time it is first provided.

- Where the employer rents the asset made available to the employee instead of buying it, the employee is taxed on the rental paid by the employer, rather than 20% of market value if the rental is the higher figure.
- Payments made by the employee for the use of the asset reduce (or eliminate) the taxable benefit.
- The provision of one mobile phone to an employee is an exempt benefit. The above rules however, will apply to any additional mobile phones provided.
- These rules do not apply to cars, vans and living accommodation. As we have already seen special rules apply to the provision of these assets.

Example 8 - Use of assets

An employee is provided with a computer by his employer, which cost £800.

Compute the benefit arising on the employee. How does your answer vary if the employer rents the computer for £200 pa?

Answer to example 8

The benefit taxed as employment income is £160 (£800 × 20%). The benefit is assessed for **each** tax year in which it is provided (not just the one in which it was first made available).

In the event that the company rents the computer for £200 p.a. rather than owns it as the rent is higher than the general rule calculation, it will be the rent paid that is assessed on the employee.

Gifts of assets

If an employer purchases a new asset and gives it to an employee immediately, the employee is taxed on the cost to the employer.

Private use followed by gift of the asset

Where an asset is given to an employee that he has previously had the use of, different rules apply.

The employee is taxed on the higher of:

	£	£
Asset market value when gifted		X
		—
Asset market value at the time it was **first made available** to the employee	X	
Less: The benefits assessed on the employee during the time he or she had the use of it, but did not own it	(X)	
	—	
		X
		—

Any amount paid for the asset by the employee is deducted from either figure in the above calculation.

The purpose of the special rule for gifts of used assets is to prevent employees gaining from gifts of assets that depreciate in value rapidly once they are used.

Where the asset being given to an employee is a used car or van, the above rules do not apply. Instead, the benefit is the market value at the date of transfer.

Example 9 - Use of assets

Brian's employer, X Ltd, purchased a dishwasher for his use on 1 June 2007, costing £600. On 6 April 2008, X Ltd gave the dishwasher to Brian (its market value then being £150).

Calculate the benefit assessable on Brian on the basis of:

(a) the circumstances as set out above

(b) if Brian paid X Ltd £100 for the dishwasher.

Answer to example 9

Assessable benefits for use of assets

(a) Sale for nil proceeds	£
Market value when first made available to Brian	600
Less: Benefit already assessed 2007/08:	
£600 × 20% × 10/12	(100)
Taxable benefit on gift: 2008/09	500

The benefit is £500 since this is greater than the dishwasher's market value when given to Brian (£150).

(b) Sale of dishwasher to Brian for £100

	£
Benefit as calculated in (a) above	500
Less: Price paid	(100)
Taxable benefit on gift: 2008/09	400

Brian would also have been taxed on the benefits of using the dishwasher in 2007/08.

Note: Where the benefit is provided for only part of a tax year the benefit is reduced proportionately.

Test your understanding 9

A suit costing £300 was purchased for Bill's use by his employer on 6 April 2007. On 6 August 2008, the suit is purchased by Bill for £20, when the market value was £30. Bill earns £30,000 pa.

Calculate the amounts taxable on Bill for each of the tax years affected by the information above.

11 Expenses connected with living accommodation

In addition to the provisions outlined in section 7, which apply to all employees, expenses connected with living accommodation, such as lighting and heating, are taxable on higher paid employees where the cost is met by his employer.

Job-related accommodation

Such costs can total a considerable sum and so there is a limit on the amount taxable as a benefit where the employee's accommodation is job-related.

The limit applies to the following types of expense:

- Heating, lighting and cleaning.
- Repairing, maintaining or decorating the premises.
- Furniture and other goods normal for domestic occupation.

The taxable element of the expenses is limited to 10% of net earnings (i.e. employment income excluding this benefit for living accommodation).

Example 10 - Expenses connected with living accommodation

Amy is a hotel manager and is provided with accommodation on the site of the hotel (job-related). Her salary is £25,000. She has other employment benefits of £500 and makes payments into her employer's registered occupational pension scheme of £2,000 pa.

The accommodation has an annual value of £1,500 and cost her employer £90,000 four years ago. The accommodation contains furniture which cost the employer £10,000 four years ago (when she first occupied the accommodation). The employer pays all of her household bills totalling £1,000.

Calculate the taxable benefit for 2008/09. How does this differ if the accommodation is not job-related?

Assume the official rate of interest is 6.25%.

Answer to example 10

Job-related accommodation

	£
Basic charge (exempt)	Nil
Expensive accommodation charge (exempt)	Nil
Provision of services – furniture (20% × £10,000)	2,000
– household bills	1,000
Total benefit	3,000
Restricted to (10% × net earnings) **(W)**	
10% × £23,500	2,350

Note: Be careful when calculating the accommodation benefit. Before starting to calculate consider all the factors that can impact the calculation (e.g. is it job related, does it cost more than £75,000, is it owned or rented by the employer?)

Workings: Net earnings

	£
Salary	25,000
Other benefits	500
Less: Allowable expenses	(2,000)
Net earnings	23,500

Not job-related accommodation

	£
Basic charge – Annual value	1,500
Expensive accommodation charge	
(£90,000 – £75,000) × 6.25%	937
Provision of services – furniture (20% × £10,000)	2,000
– household bills	1,000
Total benefit	5,437

There is no restriction in the expenses benefit as the accommodation is not job-related. In addition, the property elements of the benefit are chargeable as well.

12 Comprehensive examples

Example 11 - Employment benefits

Mr Darcy, managing director of the Pemberley Trading Co Ltd, is paid an annual salary of £36,000 and also bonuses based on the company's performance. Pemberley Trading Co Ltd's accounting year ends on 31 December each year and the bonuses are normally determined and paid on 31 May thereafter. In recent years bonuses have been:

	£
Year to 31 December 2006	4,000
Year to 31 December 2007	8,000
Year to 31 December 2008	4,000

Mr Darcy uses a company car (3,500cc) purchased in 2002, at its list price of £20,000. Running expenses, including diesel paid by the company, were £2,600 in the year. The car has CO_2 emissions of 225 g/km.

Compute Mr Darcy's income tax liability for 2008/09. Briefly give reasons for your treatment of items included or excluded, in arriving at his taxable income.

Answer to example 11

Mr Darcy – Income tax computation – 2008/09

	£
Salary	36,000
Bonus **(Note 1)**	8,000
	44,000
Car benefit (£20,000 × 35% **(W)**	7,000
Car fuel benefit (£16,900 × 35% **(Note 2)**	5,915
Total income	56,915
Less: Personal allowance (PA)	(6,035)
Taxable income	50,880

	£	£
Basic rate	34,800 x 20%	6,960
Higher rate	16,080 x 40%	6,432
	50,880	
Income tax liability		13,392

Explanation of treatment

Note 1: Under the receipts basis for directors the bonus is treated as received, and therefore taxed, when it is determined. Thus the bonus determined in May 2008, is taxable in 2008/09.

Note 2: A fuel benefit will arise if Mr Darcy is provided with fuel for private motoring. It has been assumed that this is the case.

Working: Car benefit

The car benefit percentage has been calculated as follows:

	%
Basic % for diesel car	18
Plus (225 – 135) x 1/5	18
	36

The maximum percentage of 35% therefore applies.

Test your understanding 10

Mr Drake is employed as the sales director of Drakemain Ltd at a salary of £20,000 pa. Details of expenses and benefits paid by his employer for the year ended 5 April 2009, are as follows:

	£
Entertainment expenses reimbursed	683
Travelling and subsistence expenses	
(including £385 rail fares home to office)	826
Motor car benefit	4,800
Gross annual value of company house	650
Medical subscription	409
Home telephone (calls)	160
Private fuel – taxable benefit	4,200
	11,728

You are given the following further information.

(1) £10 per month is deducted from Mr Drake's net salary to cover his private use of the motor car and £40 per month as rent for the house.

(2) Mr Drake paid the council tax on the company house in the year 2008/09. This amounted to £325.

(3) The telephone installed in the company house is used only 40% for business.

(4) Unless otherwise indicated, all expenses reimbursed to Mr Drake were incurred for business purposes.

(5) The company purchased a TV on 6 April 2007 and allowed Mr Drake the use of it for the whole of the years ended 5 April 2008 and 2009. The set was then given to him on 5 April 2009. The set cost £500 and was worth £150 in April 2009.

Calculate Mr Drake's taxable employment income for 2008/09.

Test your understanding 11

Mrs Cornell is a senior executive with Berkeley plc. Her salary is £20,000 pa. In the tax year 2008/09 her employers will make the following benefits available to her:

(1) A Ford Granada 2,300cc motor car from 6 October 2008. Its list price will be £18,000 in October 2008 and its CO_2 emissions will be 189 g/km. The company will pay all running expenses including private diesel.

(2) She will continue to have the use of a stereo system owned by the company which cost £2,000 two years ago and which is kept at her home.

(3) Berkeley plc has provided Mrs Cornell with a television for her personal use since 6 April 2006 when it cost £1,200. On 6 April 2008 the television was sold to Mrs Cornell for £225 when its market value was £375.

(4) Berkeley plc provided Mrs Cornell with an interest-free loan of £30,000 on 1 January 2008. She will repay £10,000 of the loan on 30 June 2008. The loan is not used for a qualifying purpose.

In addition she has been offered the choice of luncheon vouchers of £2 per day (for 200 working days) or free meals worth £3 per day in the company's canteen (for 200 working days). Meals are available free of charge to all other employees.

After making the most tax efficient choice in respect of the lunch facilities, calculate the total value for taxation purposes of the benefits Mrs Cornell will receive for the tax year 2008/09.

Test your understanding 12

Basil Ransom is managing director of Boston plc. He is also a substantial shareholder in the company.

The company's accounts show the following information:

Years ended 30 April:	**2007**	**2008**	**2009**
	£	£	£
Salary, as managing director	13,620	43,560	44,100
Performance bonus	10,000	15,000	18,000

The performance bonus is determined and paid in the July following the accounting year end.

Mr Ransom has the use of a 2,800cc Porsche motor car with a list price of £34,000. The CO_2 emissions were 242g/km. All petrol and expenses were paid by the company. Mr Ransom drove a total of 18,000 miles in 2008/09, of which 10,000 were for private purposes.

He reimbursed the company £50 in respect of private petrol.

Mr Ransom also has had the use of a company house since 6 April 2008, whose annual value is £1,200 and which is provided rent free. The house had cost £90,000 in 2001 and its market value in April 2008 was £135,000.

The company pays private medical insurance for all its employees. Mr Ransom's share of the group premium was £320 for 2008/09. In June 2008 he needed to have treatment following a motor accident and the cost to the insurance company was £1,720.

In 2008/09 Mr Ransom was reimbursed £1,500 in respect of business travelling in the UK.

Calculate the assessable earnings of Mr Ransom for 2008/09 after his claim for a deduction from employment income.

13 Chapter summary

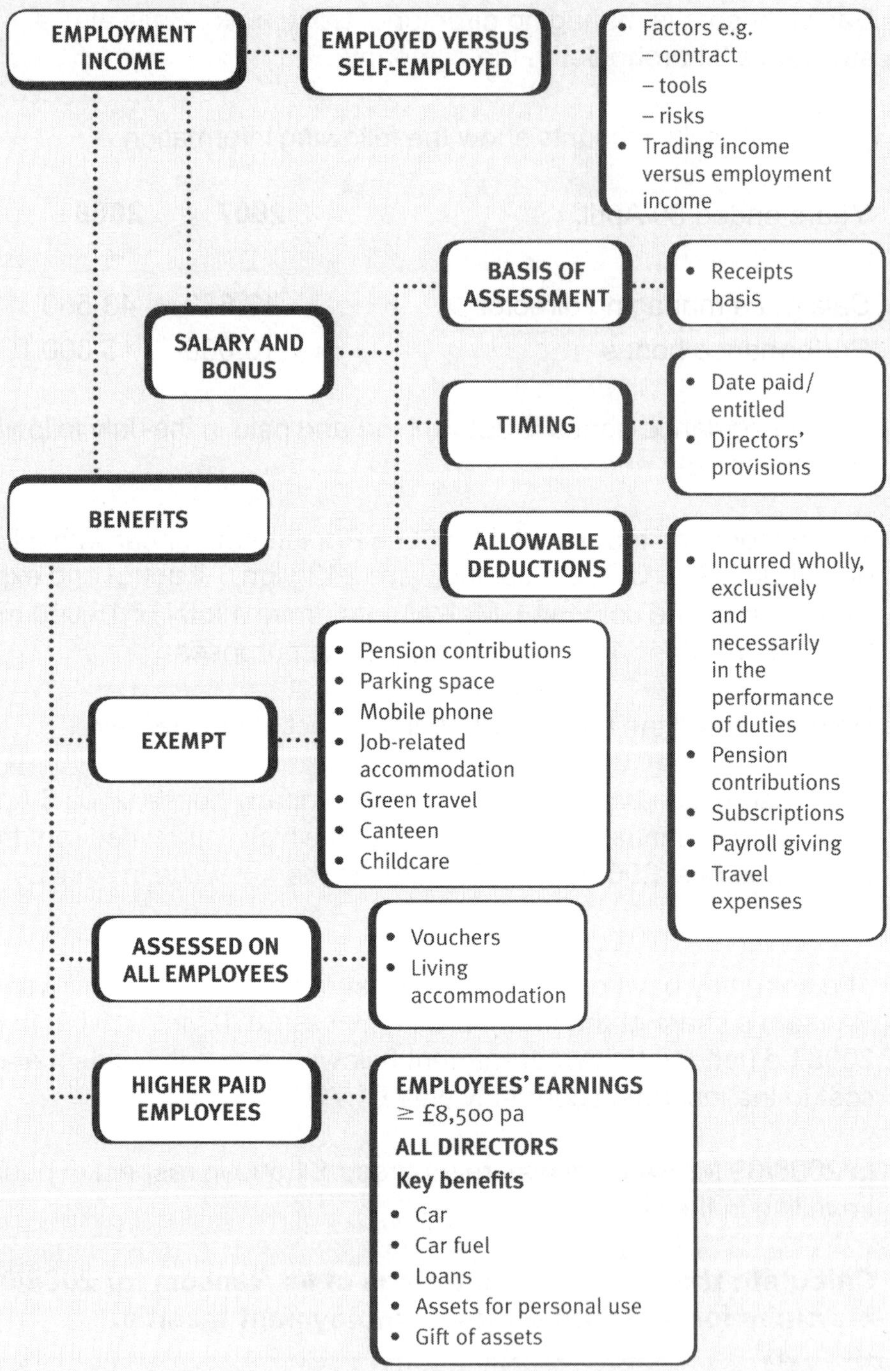

Test your understanding answers

Test your understanding 1

John

(a) **Taxable amount**

	£	£
Income (12,000 × 38p)		4,560
Less: Allowable expenses		
10,000 × 40p	4,000	
2,000 × 25p	500	
		(4,500)
Taxable amount		60

(b) **If employer paid 35p**

If John's employer paid 35p per mile, the total paid would be 12,000 × 35p = £4,200.

John could deduct the shortfall of £300 (£4,500 – £4,200) from his employment income, as an allowable expense.

Test your understanding 2

Underwood

Underwood's taxable earnings for 2008/09 are as follows:

	£	£
Basic salary (£950 × 12)		11,400
Bonus paid in May 2008 (receipts basis)		1,260
		12,660
Less: Allowable expenses		
Subscription	100	
Pension contribution	342	
Payroll deduction scheme	200	
		(642)
Taxable employment income		12,018

Test your understanding 3

Paolo

Assessable benefit for accommodation – 2008/09

	£
Basic charge – annual value (no rent paid by employer)	2,500
Expensive living accommodation charge £105,000 – £75,000) = £30,000 × 6.25%	1,875
	4,375
Less: Contribution by employee (£100 × 12)	(1,200)
Taxable benefit	3,175

Test your understanding 4

Louis

CO_2 emissions		**Petrol %**	**Diesel %**
167 g/km	Basic %	15	18
	Plus (165 – 135) x 1/5	6	6
		21	24
128 g/km	Basic %	15	18
232 g/km	Basic %	15	18
	Plus (230 – 135) x 1/5	19	19
		34	37
	Restricted to maximum		35%
119 g/km	Basic % – low emission car	10	13

Test your understanding 5

Assessable car benefits

Sue

	£
£16,000 × 28% (W)	4,480
Less: Contribution	(2,000)
Benefit	2,480

Working: Appropriate %	%
Basic % for petrol car	15
Plus (200 – 135) x 1/5	13
	28

Paul

Benefit = £36,000 × 35% (W) = £12,600

Working: Appropriate %	%
Basic % for diesel car	18
Plus (235 – 135) x 1/5	20
	38
Restricted to	35

Note that the business mileage driven is of no relevance to the calculation.

Test your understanding 6

Charles

	£
Car benefit: (£24,000 × 32% **(W1)** x 8/12) **(W2)**)	5,120
Less: Payment for use **(W3)**	(800)
	4,320
Fuel: (£16,900 × 32% **(W4)** x 8/12 **(W2)**	3,605
Total assessable benefits	7,925

Workings

		%
(W1)	Appropriate %	
	Basic % for petrol car	15
	Plus (220 – 135) x 1/5	17
		32

(W2) Reduction for non-availability – car

Car first made available on 1 August 2008, therefore not available for 4 months of 2008/09. It has been available for 8 months.

(W3) Payment for use

Payment made for 8 months @ £100/month = £800.

(W4) Car fuel

The fuel benefit is calculated using the same percentage as the car benefit of a fixed amount, which is £16,900 for 2008/09. Same proportionate reduction for non-availability applies as for car benefit charge.

Note: Charles cannot deduct the £50 per month paid for petrol and does not qualify for a reduction of the fuel scale charge, because he does not pay for all fuel used for private motoring.

Test your understanding 7

Joan

Taxable earnings

	£
Salary (£60,000 × 8/12)	40,000
Car benefit (£15,000 × 20% **(W1)** x 5/12)	1,250
Fuel benefit (£16,900 × 20% × 3/12) **(W2)**	845
Taxable earnings	42,095

Workings

(W1) Appropriate %

	%
Basic % for petrol	15
Plus (160 – 135) x 1/5	5
	20

The car has only been available for 5 months.

(W2) The petrol was only provided for 3 months in 2008/09. The contribution towards the cost of private petrol does not reduce the fuel benefit, as the cost of the private petrol was not reimbursed in full.

Test your understanding 8

Bob

The assessable benefit is computed as follows:

(a) Average method

	£
6.25% × ½ × (£10,000 + £8,000)	562
Interest paid by employee	–
Taxable benefit	562

(b) Precise method

	£
6.4.08 – 5.9.08: (£10,000 × 6.25% × 5/12)	260
6.9.08 – 5.4.09: (£8,000 × 6.25% × 7/12)	292
	552

In this situation, whilst Bob can opt for the precise method it is likely he will accept an assessment of £562.

Test your understanding 9

Bill

The assessable benefits are computed as follows:

	£	£
2007/08		
Annual value (20% × £300)		60
2007/08		
Annual value (20% × £300) × 4/12		20
Assessment upon gift, greater of:		
Suit's current market value	30	
Less: Price paid by employee	(20)	
	10	
Suit's original market value	300	
Less: Taxed in respect of use to date:		
2007/08	(60)	
2008/09	(20)	
	220	
Less: Price paid by employer	(20)	
	200	200
Amount assessable in 2008/09		220

Note: Essentially, Bill has received a £300 suit for £20 and been assessed on taxable income of £280 (£60 + £220).

Test your understanding 10

Mr Drake

Employment income

	£	£
Salary		20,000
Expenses and benefits		11,728
		31,728
Less: Entertaining (disallowed in the employer's tax computation)	683	
Travelling, etc. (other than home to office)	441	
Telephone (£160 less private 60%)	64	
Payments for accommodation (£40 per month)	480	
Payments for use of company car	120	(1,788)
		29,940
Benefit for use of TV (20% of £500)		100
Benefit for gift of TV (£500 – £100 – £100)		300
Employment income assessment		30,340

Note: Council tax is the personal liability of Mr Drake. If his employer were to meet this cost, it would be taxed on Mr Drake as a benefit.

Test your understanding 11

Mrs Cornell

Taxable benefits – 2008/09

	£
Car **(W1)**	2,520
Fuel **(W2)**	2,366
Stereo system (20% × £2,000)	400
Television **(W3)**	495
Beneficial loan **(W4)**	1,406
Lunch facility **(W5)**	Nil
Assessable benefits	7,187

Workings:

(W1) Car

The CO_2 emissions figure of 189 is rounded down to 185 g/km, so that it is divisible by five:

	%
Base % for diesel car	18
(185 - 135) = (50 ÷ 5)	10
	28

Benefit = (28% × £18,000) = £5,040.

Time apportion benefit as the car was only available from 6 October 2008:
(£5,040 × 6/12) = £2,520.

(W2) Fuel

(28% × £16,900) = £4,732.

Time apportion as only available from 6 October 2008
(£4,732 × 6/12) = £2,366.

(W3) Television

Greater of:	£
(1) Original cost less benefits assessed	
£1,200 – (£240 + £240)	720
(2) Current market value	375
Original cost less benefits assessed	720
Less: Amount paid to employer	(225)
Assessable benefit	495

(W4) Beneficial Loan

Average method	£
(£30,000 + £20,000) × ½ × 6.25% =	1,562

Precise method	£
£30,000 × 3/12 (April/May/June) × 6.25%	469
£20,000 × 9/12 (July to March) × 6.25%	937
	1,406

Therefore Mrs Cornell should elect for the precise method.

(W5) Lunch facilities

Luncheon vouchers	
200 days × (£2 - 15p)	£370
Canteen: 200 days × £3/day	Exempt

Test your understanding 12

Basil Ransom

Assessable earnings – 2008/09

	£
Salary (1/12 × £43,560 + 11/12 × £44,100)	44,055
Performance bonus (received in July 2008)	15,000
Benefits:	
Car benefit (35% × £34,000) **(W1)**	11,900
Fuel benefit (35% × £16,900) **(W1)**	5,915
Living accommodation:	
Annual value	1,200
Expensive accommodation charge	
(£135,000 - £75,000) @ 6.25% **(W2)**	3,750
Private medical insurance	320
Reimbursed expenses	1,500
	83,640
Less: Deduction from employment income claim	(1,500)
Assessable earnings	82,140

Workings:

(W1) Car and fuel

The CO_2 emissions are above 135 g/km.

The CO_2 emissions figure of 242 g/km is rounded down to 240 g/km so that it is divisible by five.

	%
Basic % for petrol car	15
(240 – 135) = (105 ÷ 5)	21
	36

Restricted to 35%.

There is no deduction for the reimbursement of part of the cost of the private petrol provided.

(W2) Accommodation

The house was acquired by the employer more than six years before it was made available to the employee, therefore the market value at the date it was provided to Mr Ransom is used instead of the cost.

chapter

5

Income from self-employment

Chapter learning objectives

Upon completion of this chapter you will be able to:

- state the basis of assessment for income from self-employment
- describe and apply the badges of trade
- prepare the tax adjusted trading profit/loss
- recognise the relief that can be obtained for pre-trading expenditure.

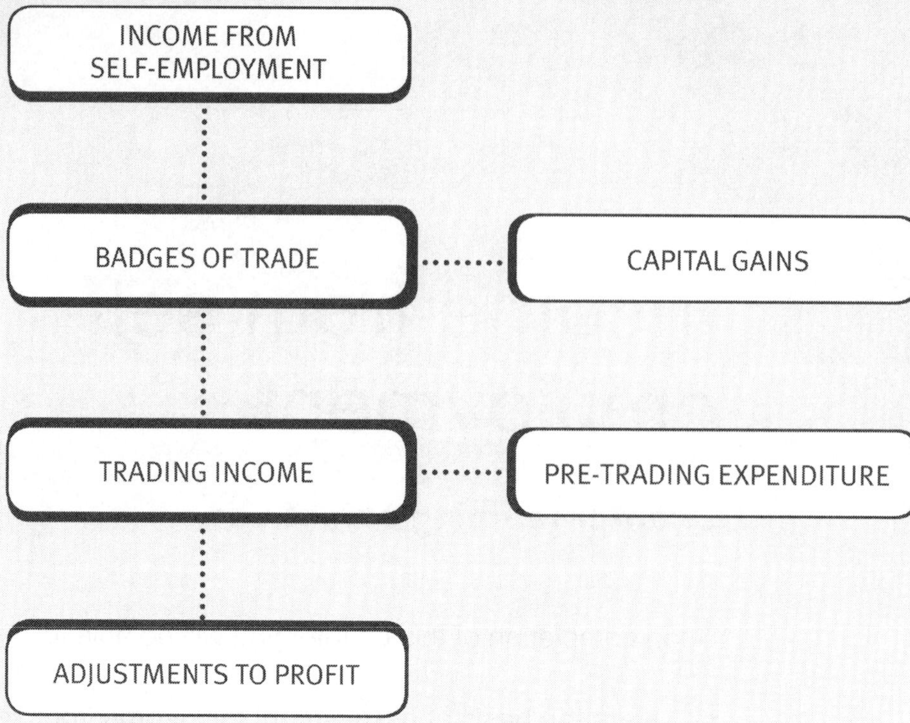

1 Introduction

Trading income

The profits of an unincorporated trader arising from a trade, profession or vocation are assessed as trading income. Typically these individuals are referred to as self-employed or sole traders.

Basis of assessment

The profits are assessed on a current year basis. This means the profits assessed in a tax year are those of the twelve month accounting period ending in that tax year.

Test your understanding 1

A sole trader prepares his accounts to December each year.

In which tax year will the profits be assessed?

Basis of assessment is covered in more detail in Chapter 8.

2 Badges of trade

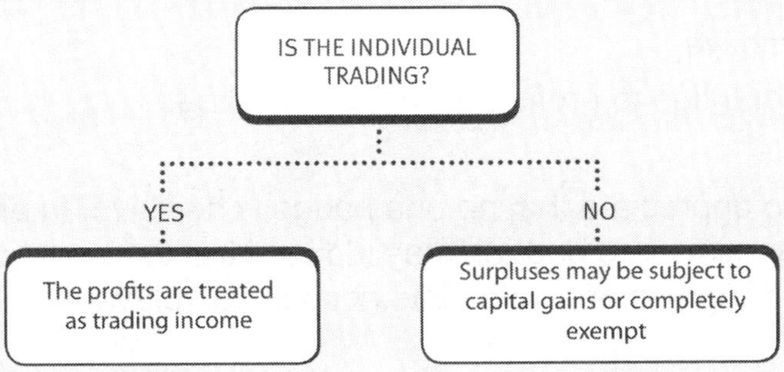

To determine whether an individual is trading, a number of tests, known as the 'badges of trade', have been developed.

Expandable text - Nature of trade

'Trade includes every trade, manufacture, adventure or concern in the nature of trade.'

Although the above is the statutory definition of a trade, in practice it is not a very helpful one. What constitutes a trade has been reviewed numerous times by the Courts and the criteria that emerged were set out by a Royal Commission. These criteria are known as the 'badges of trade'.

The badges of trade which are used to determine if an activity is in the nature of a trade are as follows:

- The subject matter of the transaction:
  - are the goods of a type normally used for trading?
- The length of the period of ownership.
  - short period of ownership is more likely to indicate trading.
- The frequency or number of similar transactions by the same person.
  - frequent transactions indicate trading.
- Supplementary work and marketing.
  - work performed on goods to make them more marketable indicates trading.

- The circumstances responsible for the sale.
  - forced sale indicates not trading.
- The motive.
  - intention to profit may indicate trading.

It is vital to appreciate that no one badge is decisive. In any set of circumstances some badges may indicate trading whilst others may not. It is the overall impression, taking into account all relevant factors, that is important.

Expandable text - Badges of trade

Subject matter of the transaction

The type of goods involved in a transaction is relevant in deciding the nature of the transaction. An asset is said to have been acquired for one of three reasons:

- an investment – in which case it is capital in nature and not subject to income tax
- goods for the private use of the individual (or family) – therefore not subject to tax
- stock in trade – therefore a trading transaction and subject to income tax.

Normally, to be considered as an investment, the goods must either be income producing (such as land or shares), or liable to be held for aesthetic reasons (such as works of art).

So, when an individual acquired 1,000,000 rolls of toilet paper and resold them at a profit, he was held not to have acquired and resold an investment and consequently was judged to have made a trading profit.

The length of the period of ownership

As a general rule, the longer the period between the date of acquisition and the date of disposal of an asset, the greater the likelihood that the transaction will not be treated as trading in nature.

Care must be taken in applying this principle and in particular the nature of the asset has to be taken into account.

For instance, it would be necessary to hold land for far longer than quoted shares to obtain the benefit of this rule, since normally the market in land operates much more slowly than that in shares.

The frequency or number of similar transactions by the same person

As was seen in the toilet rolls case above, a single transaction may be enough for a person to be regarded as trading. However, the usual situation is that the more often similar transactions are entered into, the more likely they will be regarded as trading activities.

Again the nature of the assets involved is important:

- A taxpayer was held to be trading on the evidence of over 200 Stock Exchange sales and purchases over a period of three years.
- A director of a spinning company was engaged in buying the shares of mill-owning companies and then selling the assets of the companies (asset stripping). One transaction of this kind might have been regarded as capital in nature, but when he had done the same thing four times over, he was held to be trading.

Supplementary work and marketing

Supplementary work done on an asset to make it more marketable before it is sold is an indication of trading.

For example, the purchase of brandy in bulk and subsequent blending and re-casking before resale was held to be a trade.

The circumstances responsible for the sale

A forced sale to raise cash for an emergency is an indication that the transaction was not of a trading nature.

Similarly, an individual who deliberately purchases goods is more likely to be regarded as trading than one who acquires them accidentally, for example, by inheritance or by gift.

The motive

The more obvious an individual's intention to profit from a transaction the more likely it is that it will be viewed as trading.

For example, an individual purchased a large quantity of silver bullion as a hedge against the devaluation of sterling. The profit resulting from its resale was regarded as a trading profit, on the basis that the motive for the transaction was to make a profit in sterling terms.

It is important to appreciate, however, that the absence of a profit motive does not of itself preclude the transaction from being treated as trade.

3 Adjusting the accounting profit

The net profit per the financial accounts and the taxable trading profit figure are rarely the same figure. A number of adjustments need to be made to the accounting profit for tax purposes in order to calculate the taxable trading profit (tax-adjusted trading profit).

It is necessary to compute the tax-adjusted trading profit before going on to calculate the tax liability.

Adjustments

There are four types of adjustment that need to be made to move from accounting profit to the tax-adjusted trading profit. These are as follows:

Reason for adjusting profits	Adjustment required to arrive at tax-adjusted trading profit
Expenditure which tax law prevents from being an allowable deduction may have been charged in the profit and loss account.	**Add back** to the accounting profit.
Taxable trading income may not be included in the profit and loss account.	**Add back** to the accounting profit.
Expenditure that is deductible for tax purposes may not be charged in the profit and loss account.	**Deduct** from accounting profit.
Income may be included in the profit and loss account that is not taxable as trading income.	**Deduct** from accounting profit.

Pro forma – Tax adjusted trading profit

	£	£
Net profit per accounts		X
Add: Expenditure not allowable for taxation purposes	X	
Taxable trading income not credited in the accounts	X	
	—	
		X
		—
		X
Less: Expenditure not charged in the accounts but allowable for the purposes of taxation	X	
Income included in the accounts that is not taxable as trading income	X	
Capital allowances (see Chapters 6 & 7)	X	
	—	
		(X)
		—
Tax-adjusted trading profit		X
		—

Before considering the adjustments in detail, two important points need to be emphasised:

- It is only the trading profit that is being calculated. The fact that an item of income (such as rental income) is excluded in calculating the tax-adjusted trading profit, does not mean that it is not taxable, only that it is not taxable as trading income. As we saw in Chapter 3, rental income is taxable as property business income.
- The starting point in deciding whether or not an adjustment is necessary, is that the principles of normal commercial accountancy apply unless overridden by tax law.

4 Non-deductible expenditure

Non-deductible/disallowable expenditure is the most common form of adjustment. The following are the main examples that you can expect to come across in the examination.

Expenditure not incurred wholly and exclusively for trading purposes

The general rule to follow in deciding whether expenditure is an allowable deduction from trading profits is that only expenditure incurred wholly and exclusively for the purposes of the trade is allowable.

Expenditure may be disallowed because:

- it is too remote from the purposes of the trade – the remoteness test
- it has more than one purpose and one of them is not trading – the duality principle.

More detail on these two types of expenditure not incurred wholly and exclusively for the purposes of the trade is given in expandable text.

Expandable text - Remoteness test and duality principle

Remoteness test

Expenditure is regarded as being too remote from the trade, when it is incurred in some other capacity than that of trading. For example, normal accountancy and taxation fees are allowable, but the cost of any personal tax work is not.

Duality principle

- The duality principle is best illustrated by decided cases:
  - A self-employed trader was unable to eat lunch at home and claimed the extra cost of eating out as a tax deduction. It was held that the expenditure was not allowable. The duality of purpose lay in the fact that the taxpayer needed to eat to live, not just to work.
  - A self-employed barrister was refused a tax deduction for her expenditure on the black clothing necessary for court appearances. It was held that the expenditure had been for her personal as well as professional needs.
- Where expenditure has been incurred for both trading and non-trading purposes, a deduction can be claimed for the business use proportion, provided it can be separately identified. This is particularly relevant to expenditure on motor cars, where business and private mileage can be identified.

Appropriations

Appropriations are the withdrawal of funds from a business i.e. profit extraction rather than expenses incurred in earning them and, as such, are disallowed expenses. The most common examples are:

- A business owner's salary.
- Interest paid to the owner on capital invested in the business.

- Drawings made by a sole trader or partner.
- Any private element of expenditure relating to the owner's motor car, telephone etc.

Example 1 - Non-deductible expenditure

Jim is a self-employed solicitor. During the year ended 31 December 2008, Jim drove a total of 20,000 miles and his motor expenses amounted to £10,800.

Each working day Jim drives from his home to his office, which is ten miles away. He works five days a week and 50 weeks a year.

Jim drove 1,500 miles on a holiday in August 2008, but for the rest of the year his wife's car was used for private journeys. Jim's wife owns her own car, and is not involved in Jim's business.

Calculate the amount of Jim's motor expenses that are allowable.

Answer to example 1

Jim's motor expenses will be apportioned according to his proportion of business mileage to total mileage for the year.

Travel from home to work and back is classed as private mileage, so Jim's total private mileage is 6,500 miles (10 × 5 × 50 × 2 + 1,500). His business mileage is therefore 13,500 miles (20,000 - 6,500).

Of the motor expenses, £7,290 (£10,800 × 13,500/20,000) is allowable and £3,510 (£10,800 × 6,500/20,000) is disallowed.

Excessive salary paid to a sole trader's family

- Business owners (especially sole traders) often employ their spouses or members of their families in their business.
- Any salary paid to the family of the owner of an unincorporated business must not be excessive. In other words it must be at the commercial rate for the work performed. Any excessive salary payments are disallowed.

Test your understanding 2

Sheila is in business running her own advertising agency. Her husband Richard has given up work to look after their daughter who was born three years ago.

Until 2008 Sheila employed a part-time typist, who was paid £4,500 pa, but the typist then left and Sheila could not find a suitable replacement. Richard therefore agreed to do Sheila's typing at home. During the year ended 5 April 2009, Sheila paid Richard a salary of £10,000.

Explain the probable adjustment in calculating the tax-adjusted trading income for the year ended 5 April 2009?

Interest payable

- Interest on borrowings such as business account overdrafts, credit cards or hire purchase contracts, is an allowable trading expense calculated on an accruals basis.
- For unincorporated businesses, interest paid on overdue tax is never allowable and likewise interest received on overpaid tax is not taxable.

Capital expenditure

- Expenditure on capital assets is not an allowable trading expense. Any expense in the form of depreciation, loss on sale of fixed assets or the amortisation of a lease is also disallowed for tax purposes.
- The distinction between revenue expenditure (allowable) and capital expenditure (disallowable) is not always clear-cut. This is especially the case when deciding if expenditure is in respect of a repair to an asset (revenue expenditure) or is an improvement (capital expenditure).

Expandable text - Repair v Improvement

Whilst you are not required to know the legal cases from which the following decisions were reached, it is important to understand the legal principles behind case decisions regarding capital expenditure as this will help with exam questions:

- The cost of initial repairs in order to make an asset usable is not deductible.

  For example, a taxpayer failed to obtain a deduction for repair work on a newly bought ship, in order to make the ship seaworthy prior to using it.

- The cost of initial repairs is deductible if the asset can be put into use before any repairs are carried out.

  For example, a taxpayer obtained a deduction for the cost of renovating newly acquired cinemas. The work was to make good normal wear and tear and the purchase price was not reduced to take account of the necessary repair work.

- The treatment of restoration costs is another disputed area. To be allowable, it needs to be proven that the restoration renews a subsidiary part of an asset.

  For example, the replacement of a factory chimney, was held to be a repair to the factory.

  Where it is deemed as the renewal of a separate asset it is treated as non-allowable capital expenditure.

  For example, the replacement of an old stand with a new one at a football club, was held to be expenditure on a new asset and thus capital expenditure.

- Expenditure on plant and machinery and industrial buildings attracts capital allowances. They are effectively a form of tax depreciation. Capital allowances are covered in Chapters 6 and 7.

Car leasing

- Rental charges payable for an 'expensive' leased motor car are restricted where the motor car would have cost more than £12,000 when new.
- The **allowable** portion of the rental charge is the amount given in the following formula:

$$\text{Annual rental charge} \times \frac{£12{,}000 + 1/2\ (\text{Cost of car when new} - £12{,}000)}{\text{Cost of car when new}}$$

Example 2 - Expensive car leasing

Roger enters into a leasing contract for a motor car with an original cost of £30,000, paying £8,000 pa in rental charges.

Calculate the amount of the rental charge that is disallowed.

Answer to example 2

Disallowable rental charge

The annual allowable amount would be:

£8,000 × £12,000 + 1/2 (£30,000 - £12,000)/£30,000 = £5,600

£5,600 is the amount of the expenditure already charged in the accounts that is allowable in arriving at the tax-adjusted trading profit.

Hence, Roger must disallow £2,400 (£8,000 - £5,600) of the rental charges. He must therefore add £2,400 on to his profits per the accounts.

Test your understanding 3

Ray decides to sell his car that he uses in his business in January 2008. Instead of buying a new car, he decided to lease the replacement car. He leased a used car, worth approximately £17,000. When new it had an original cost of £27,500. The lease payments are £700 per month.

Calculate the amount of the lease payments that will be an allowable deduction from his trading income.

Subscriptions and donations

- Trade or professional association subscriptions are normally deductible since they will be made wholly and exclusively for the purposes of the trade.
- In the case of charitable donations they must meet three tests to be allowable:
  - First, they must be wholly and exclusively for trading purposes (for example, promoting the business name).
  - Second, it must be local and reasonable in size in relation to the business making the donation.
  - Third, it must be made to an educational, religious, cultural, recreational or benevolent organisation.
- If the donation is disallowed but the payment was made to a charity, the taxpayer can instead claim relief under the Gift Aid provisions.
- Subscriptions and donations to political parties are not deductible.
- Non-charitable gifts are not allowable, except as set out below.

Entertaining and gifts

- Entertainment expenditure is disallowed.
- The only exception is for expenditure relating to employees, provided it is not incidental to the entertainment of others.

Gifts to employees

- Gifts to employees are normally treated as allowable trading expenditure.
- Care must be taken, however, as the gift may fall within the benefit rules and be assessed on the employee as employment income.

Gifts to customers

- Gifts to customers are only allowable if:
  - they cost less than £50 per recipient per year; and
  - the gift is not of food, drink, tobacco or vouchers exchangeable for goods; and
  - the gift carries a conspicuous advertisement of the business making the gift.
- The cost of a gift that does not meet these conditions is disallowed.
- If the total of gifts in the tax year exceeds £50, it is the full cost of the item that is disallowable, not just the excess.

Legal and professional charges

In order to determine whether legal and professional charges are allowable, it is important to review the reasons for the business incurring the costs.

As a general principle, where expenditure is incurred for the purposes of the trade, the expenditure is allowable. Examples include:

- legal fees chasing trading debts
- charges incurred in defending the title to fixed assets.

Where expenditure is of a capital nature, it is disallowable. For example:

- Fees associated with acquiring new fixed assets
- There are the following exceptions:
  - Fees and other costs of obtaining long-term debt finance are allowable for a sole trader.
  - The cost of registering patents is allowable.
  - The expense of renewing a short lease (i.e. less than 50 years) is allowable, although the legal expenses incurred on the initial granting of the lease are not.

Impaired debts and allowances for debtors

The following are allowable items:

- The write-off of a trade debt (therefore, the recovery of a trade debt previously written-off is taxable).
- An allowance for trade debtors to reflect the potential irrecoverability or impairment of debtors, provided it is calculated in accordance with UK generally accepted accounting practice (UK GAAP). Again, the reduction in an allowance for trade debtors is taxable income.

The following items are disallowable:

- The write-off of a non-trade debt, e.g. a loan to a customer or an employee.

Example 3 - Impaired debtor and allowance for debtor

The profit and loss account of Mary for the year ended 30 June 2008, includes a figure for impaired debts of £200. This is made up as follows:

	£	£
Trade debts written-off		500
Staff loan written-off		200
Allowance for impaired debtors		
As at 1 July 2007	900	
As at 30 June 2008	700	
		(200)
Trade debts recovered		(400)
Loan to supplier written-off		250
Loan to a customer recovered		(150)
		200

The loan to supplier written-off relates to a loan to a supplier with cash flow problems. The loan to the customer recovered is in respect of a loan written-off two years ago.

Calculate the adjustment required in preparing Mary's tax adjusted trading profit.

Answer to example 3

	£
Staff loan written-off	200
Loan to supplier written-off	250
	450
Less: Loan to customer recovered	(150)
Amount to add back to profit	300

To be allowed, debt write-offs must be in respect of normal trade debts. The recovery of such debts already written-off is taxable.

The write-off of other debts is not allowable when computing trading profit and their recovery, after being written-off, is not taxable and will therefore not be included in the tax adjusted trading profit.

Amounts charged or credited to the profit and loss account in respect of allowances for trade debts are allowable deductions against trading profits.

Other items

Set out below is a list of some other items you may encounter and a brief description of how to treat each.

Type of expenditure	**Treatment in computation**	**Notes**
Provisions for future costs (e.g. provision for future warranty costs)	Allow	Provided they are calculated in accordance with UK GAAP and their estimation is sufficiently accurate
Compensation for loss of office paid to an employee	Allow	Only if for benefit of trade
Counselling services for redundant employees	Allow	
Damages paid	Allow	Only if paid in connection with trade matter
Defalcations (e.g. theft/ fraud)	Allow	Only if by employee, not the business owner/director
Educational courses	Allow	Only if for trade purposes
Fines	Disallow	Unless parking fines incurred on business by employee, but not business owner/director
Payment that constitutes a criminal offence	Disallow	
Pension contributions to registered pension scheme	Allow	Provided paid (not accrued) by the year end

Premiums for insurance against an employee's death or illness	Allow	
Redundancy pay in excess of the statutory amount	Allow	On the cessation of trading the limit is 3 × the statutory amount
Removal expenses	Allow	Provided not an expansionary move
Salaries accrued at year end	Allow	Provided paid not more than 9 months after year end

Test your understanding 4

For each item of income or expenditure state whether you need to adjust for the item for tax purposes by adding or deducting an amount from the accounting profit.

Item of expenditure/income	**Add back/deduct**
Drawings of the proprietor	
£45,000 salary paid to the proprietor's spouse. Typical market rate is estimated at £15,000	
Subscription to golf club where sole trader might meet/entertain clients	
Legal fees to acquire a short lease (7 years)	
Trade related NVQ training course for apprentice employee	

5 Other adjustments

Taxable trading income not included in the profit and loss account

This adjustment is normally only needed when a trader removes goods from the business for his or her own use.

- The trader is treated as making a sale to himself based on the selling price of the goods concerned.
- Note that this rule does not apply to the supply of services.

Example 4 - Goods for own use

A car dealer removes a vehicle from stock for his own personal use. It had originally cost the business £10,000 and has a market value of £12,500. No entries have been made in the accounts to reflect this transaction, other than the original purchase.

Explain the adjustment, if any, that should be made to the car dealer's accounts, for tax purposes, to reflect the above transaction.

Answer to example 4

Goods taken for own use

The tax-adjusted trading profit must reflect the transaction as if the owner has sold the vehicle to himself based on the selling price of the goods concerned.

In determining the adjustment required, it is important to identify the entries made in the accounts to date. In this example, only the original cost has been recorded, therefore the adjustment is to add the market value £12,500 to the accounting profit to arrive at the tax-adjusted trading profit.

Deductible expenditure not charged in the profit and loss account

- The most important item of deductible expenditure not charged in the profit and loss account is the figure for capital allowances. These are deductible as if they were a trading expense. Capital allowances are covered in detail in Chapters 6 and 7.
- In addition to this, other examples include:
  - Allowable trading element of lease premiums paid on short leases.
  - Where a business owner uses their private residence partly for business purposes for example, uses a room in their private house as an office, the business portion of running expenses is allowable.
  - Business calls from the private telephone of the sole trader.
  - Expenses that are wholly and exclusively for the trade that have been met from the private funds of the owner.

Short lease premiums

- When a landlord receives a premium for the grant of a short lease a proportion of the lease premium is charged to income tax as a property income business (see Chapter 3).
- Where a business pays a premium for a short lease, for premises which he uses in his business, he is entitled to deduct a proportion of the amount assessable on the landlord in calculating his taxable trading profit. This will not be reflected in the accounts, however, the cost of the lease will be reflected in an annual amortisation charge.

The adjustments required for the lease are therefore as follows:

- Add back: the amortisation charged in the accounts (disallowable as capital).
- Deduct: proportion of the lease premium.

The allowable deduction for the trader is the property business income element of the premium (see Chapter 3) spread evenly over the period of the lease.

The property business income assessable on the landlord is calculated as:

P – (P × 2% × (D – 1))

Where:

P = total premium
D = duration of lease in years.

Example 5 - Lease premium

Lawrie prepares accounts to 31 March. On 1 April 2008 he paid a premium of £25,200 for the grant of a 21-year lease on business premises.

Calculate the deduction Lawrie can claim in his tax-adjusted trading profit.

Answer to example 5

Lease premium adjustment

The amount of the lease premium paid that will be assessed on the landlord as property business income is:

	£
Premium	25,200
Less (£25,200 × 2% × 20)	(10,080)
	15,120

The trading deduction for Lawrie is therefore £720 (£15,120 × 1/21) each year. This would have been time apportioned for the year ended 31 March 2009, if the premium had not been paid at the start of the accounting period.

Example 6 - Use of home for business

Sam is in business as a central heating engineer. She uses one room of her five-room house as an office, and no adjustment has been made in her accounts for the year ended 5 April 2009, in respect of this.

Sam has listed her household expenses relating to the year ended 5 April 2009, as follows:

	£
Electricity	400
Gas	250
Rates	450
Television repairs	50
Groceries	600
Video rental	200
Mortgage interest on £20,000 mortgage	900

Calculate the amount Sam can claim as a trading expense for her use of an office at home.

Answer to example 6

Use of home for business

Sam uses one room out of five as an office and therefore it is appropriate to allow one fifth of her expenses that relate to running the home.

Sam's television repairs, groceries and video rental are all of a private nature.

The total of the remaining items is £2,000 (£400 + £250 + £450 + £900). One fifth of this is £400, and this will be Sam's deductible trading expense for the use of the office.

Income included in the profit and loss account that is not taxable trading income

There are three categories of income which need to be adjusted for as follows:

- Capital receipts (which may be treated as chargeable gains – see Chapter 14). In addition, any profit on the sale of a capital asset should also be deducted in calculating the tax adjusted trading profit.
- Other forms of income (such as savings income or dividends) must be deducted in arriving at the taxable trading profit. However, they may be subject to income tax by being included elsewhere in an individual's income tax computation.
- Income that is exempt from tax (such as interest received on overpaid income tax).

6 Relief for pre-trading expenditure

Any revenue expenditure, incurred in the **seven years** before a business commences to trade, is treated as an expense on the day that the business starts trading.

Example 7 - Relief for pre-trading expenditure

Able commenced trading on 1 April 2008. He had spent £6,000 in the previous six months advertising the fact that he was about to start trading.

Explain how the expenditure of £6,000 on advertising treated for tax purposes.

Answer to example 7

Pre-trading expenditure

The £6,000 advertising expenditure is treated as a trading expense as if it had been incurred on 1 April 2008.

7 Comprehensive example

Test your understanding 5

On 1 June 2008 William Wise, aged 38, commenced in self-employment running a retail clothing shop. William's profit and loss account for the year ended 31 May 2009 is as follows:

	£	£
Gross profit		139,880
Expenses:		
Depreciation	4,760	
Light and heat **(Note 1)**	1,525	
Motor expenses **(Note 2)**	4,720	
Professional fees **(Note 3)**	2,300	
Rent and rates **(Note 1)**	3,900	
Repairs and renewals **(Note 4)**	5,660	
Sundry expenses **(Note 5)**	2,990	
Wages and salaries **(Note 6)**	83,825	
		(109,680)
Net profit		30,200

Notes

1: Private accommodation

William and his wife live in a flat that is situated above the clothing shop. Of the expenditure included in the profit and loss account for light, heat, rent and rates, 40% relates to the flat.

2: Motor expenses

During the year ended 31 May 2009, William drove a total of 12,000 miles, of which 9,000 were for private journeys.

3: Professional fees

Professional fees are as follows:

	£
Accountancy	700
Legal fees in connection with the purchase of the clothing shop	1,200
Debt collection	400
	2,300

Included in the figure for accountancy is £250 in respect of personal tax work.

4: Repairs and renewals

The figure of £5,660 for repairs and renewals includes £2,200 for decorating the clothing shop during May 2008, and £1,050 for decorating the private flat during June 2008. The building was in a usable state when it was purchased.

5: Sundry expenses

The figure of £2,990 for sundry expenses, includes £640 for gifts to customers of food hampers costing £40 each, £320 for gifts to customers of pens carrying an advertisement for the clothing shop costing £1.60 each, £100 for a donation to a national charity, and £40 for a donation to a local charity's fête. The fête's programme carried a free advertisement for the clothing shop.

6: Wages and salaries

The figure of £83,825 for wages and salaries includes the annual salary of £15,500 paid to William's wife. She works in the clothing shop as a sales assistant. The other sales assistants doing the same job are paid an annual salary of £11,000.

7: Goods for own use

During the year ended 31 May 2009, William took clothes out of the shop for his personal use without paying for them. The cost of these clothes was £460, and they had a selling price of £650.

8: Plant and machinery

The capital allowances available for the year ended 31 May 2009 are £13,060. (In the actual examination you will be required to do a capital allowances computation and work out this figure.)

Calculate William's tax adjusted trading profit for the year ended 31 May 2009.

8 Chapter summary

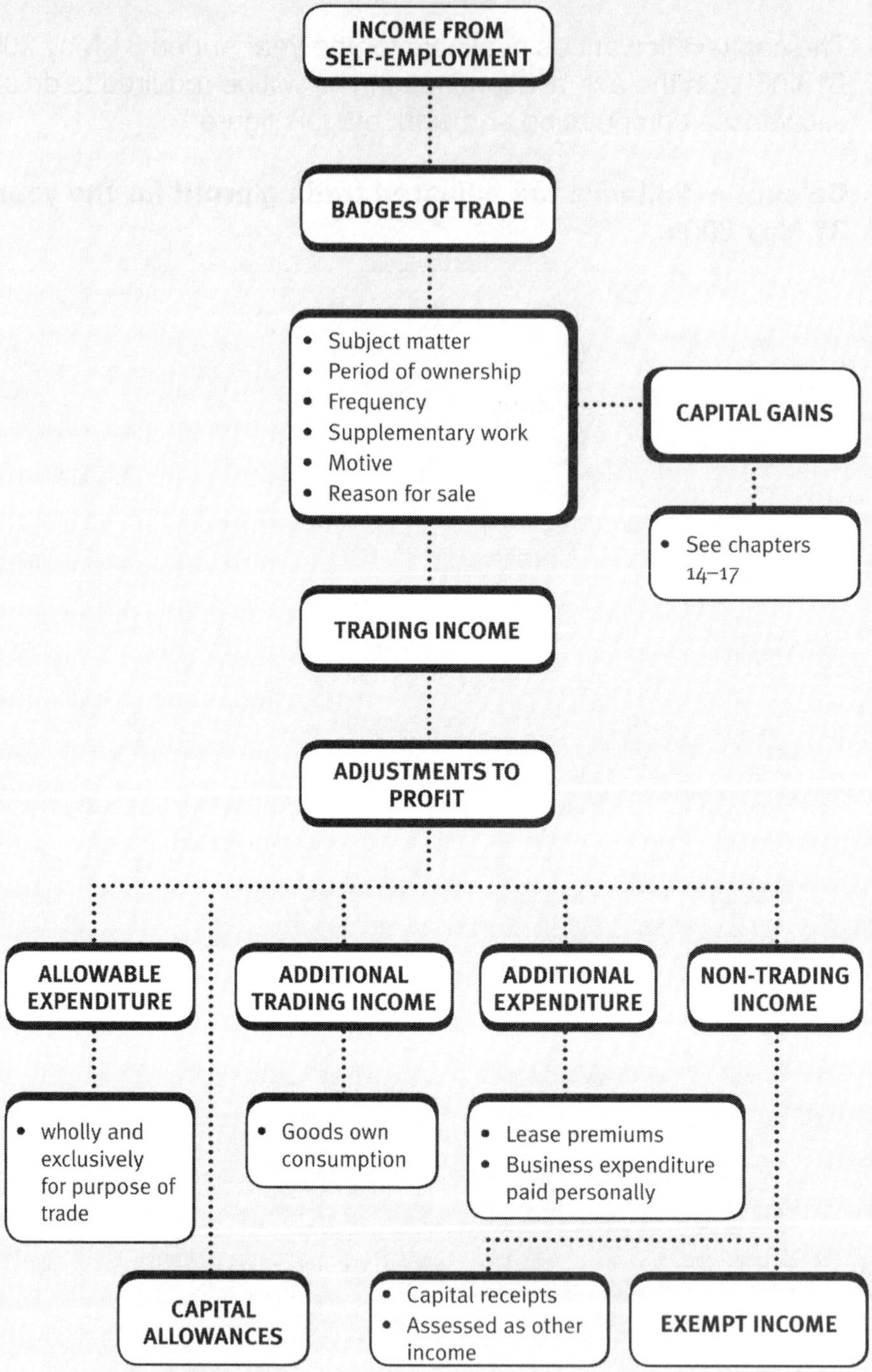

Test your understanding answers

Test your understanding 1

Sole trader

For the tax year 2008/09 the profits assessed will be for year ended 31 December 2008.

Test your understanding 2

Sheila

Excessive salary adjustment

Richard's salary of £10,000 appears to be excessive, and a disallowance of £5,500 (£10,000 - £4,500) is probably appropriate.

In real life the exact adjustment would depend on such matters as the nature of Richard's duties, and the hours that he works, as compared to the part-time typist.

Test your understanding 3

Ray

Allowable lease payments

Annual rental payments = (£700 × 12) = £8,400

The annual allowable amount would be:

$$\pounds 8,400 \times \frac{\pounds 12,000 + 1/2 \times (\pounds 27,500 - \pounds 12,000)}{\pounds 27,500} = \pounds 6,033$$

Assuming that Ray has charged the full lease payments each month through his accounts, then he needs to add back £2,367 (£8,400 - £6,033) in arriving at the tax-adjusted trading profit.

Test your understanding 4

Item of expenditure/income	Add back/deduct	Reason
Drawings of the proprietor	Add back	Appropriation of profit and therefore disallowed
£45,000 salary paid to the proprietor's spouse. Typical market rate is estimated at £15,000	Add back £30,000	HMRC will only allow that amount which represents a market rate
Subscription to golf club where sole trader might meet/entertain clients	Add back	Not wholly and exclusively for the purposes of the trade
Legal fees to acquire a short lease (7 years)	Add back	Legal fees incurred on the RENEWAL of a short lease only are allowed
Trade related NVQ training course for apprentice employee	No adjustment	Provided the course is for the purpose of the trade it will be allowable

Test your understanding 5

William Wise

Tax adjusted trading profit for the year ended 31 May 2009

	£	£
Net profit as per accounts		30,200
Add: Items debited in P&L a/c not allowed for tax purposes		
Depreciation	4,760	
Light and heat (40% × £1,525)	610	
Motor expenses (9,000/12,000 × £4,720)	3,540	
Personal tax work	250	
Purchase of new shop	1,200	
Rent and rates (40% × £3,900)	1,560	
Decorating private flat	1,050	
Gift of food hampers	640	
Donation to national charity	100	
Excessive remuneration to William's wife (£15,500 – £11,000)	4,500	
Goods own consumption	650	
		18,860
Adjusted trading profit		49,060
Less: Capital allowances (given)		(13,060)
Tax adjusted trading profit		36,000

chapter

6

Capital allowances: plant and machinery

Chapter learning objectives

Upon completion of this chapter you will be able to:

- define plant and machinery for capital allowance purposes
- calculate writing down allowances for an accounting period
- determine the correct treatment of disposals
- recognise that First Year allowances (FYAs) are available for certain types of business and expenditure
- calculate the correct FYA for a period
- recognise that the Annual Investment Allowance (AIA) is available for certain types of expenditure
- calculate and allocate the correct AIA for the period
- identify the treatment of motor cars for capital allowance purposes
- recognise the impact of private use of an asset on capital allowances
- define a short-life asset
- identify and calculate the allowances available for a short-life asset
- identify when the special rate pool treatment will apply and calculate the allowances available
- compute the capital allowances for a sole trader, over more than one period of account, dealing with additions and disposals.

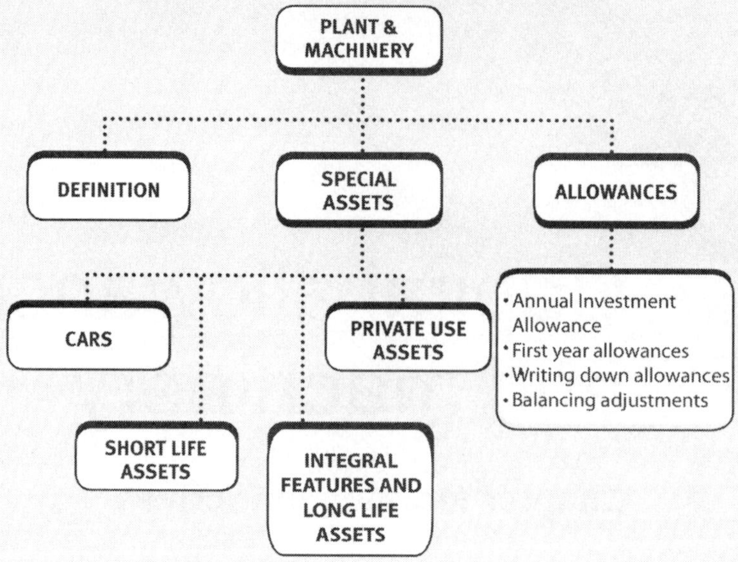

1 Eligibility

Purpose

Capital allowances are provided to give a business tax relief for capital expenditure on qualifying assets over the life of those assets. Remember that depreciation charged in the accounts is not an allowable deduction in computing taxable trading profits.

Qualifying assets

Capital allowances are given on expenditure on certain qualifying assets.

The allowances are given on the original cost of the asset and all subsequent qualifying expenditure of a capital nature, such as improvements.

The capital allowances covered in the syllabus are for expenditure on:

- plant and machinery
- industrial buildings and qualifying hotels (see Chapter 7).

Capital allowances are also given for expenditure on various other types of asset, but these are not examinable.

Who may claim capital allowances?

Capital allowances are available to persons who buy qualifying assets for use in a trade or profession.

Relief for capital allowances

Capital allowances are deducted as a trading expense in calculating the tax-adjusted trading income. Capital allowances are calculated for a trader's period of account (i.e. the period for which they draw up accounts).

2 Meaning of plant and machinery

Definition

'Machinery' has a commonly understood meaning. It includes all machines, computers, office equipment, etc.

The term 'plant' however, is not clearly defined in the tax legislation. HMRC has however codified some rules based on decided cases and specifically deemed certain types of expenditure to be plant and machinery.

Key principles

The key principles to apply in deciding the appropriate treatment is to consider the function that the asset performs for the business:

In carrying out the business, does the asset perform:	This means that the asset is:	Plant and machinery?
An active function	Apparatus with which the business is carried on	Yes
A passive function	The setting in which the business is carried on	No

Assets deemed to be plant

In addition there are certain types of expenditure that would not be thought of as plant using the above principles but are treated as plant by specific legislation.

These include:

- capital expenditure incurred on complying with fire regulations
- the cost of alterations to buildings needed for the installation of plant
- expenditure on acquiring computer software.

Land and buildings

Statute also makes it clear that land, buildings and structures cannot be plant.

Summary

Determining what is and what is not plant can be difficult in practice. In the exam the most common examples of plant and machinery that you will come across are:

- computers and software
- machinery
- cars and lorries
- office furniture
- moveable partitions
- air-conditioning
- alterations of buildings needed to install plant and machinery.

Expandable text - Definition of plant and machinery

The origins of plant and machinery are extremely detailed having been forged initially more than 100 years ago. Although there is no comprehensive statutory definition of plant, the Courts have produced considerable comment upon the topic.

The original interpretation was provided in the case of Yarmouth v France (1887). Plant was said to include:

'Whatever apparatus is used by a businessman for carrying on his business – not his stock-in-trade that he buys or makes for sale – but all goods and chattels, fixed or moveable, live or dead, which he keeps for permanent employment in his business.'

This is obviously a very far-reaching definition. It includes not only the obvious items of plant and machinery, but also such items as moveable partitions, office furniture and carpets, heating systems, motor vehicles, computers, lifts and any expenditure incurred to enable the proper functioning of the item, such as reinforced floors or air conditioning systems for computers.

The Courts' interpretation of 'plant'

The original definition of plant in Yarmouth v France provides a good starting point but has been subsequently refined by the Courts.

In particular, the test that has been applied is a functional one. It asks whether the item is simply part of the setting or premises in which the trade is carried on or is it something with which the trade is carried on? If it is part of the setting or premises it is not plant, and thus no capital allowances are available, but if it fulfils a function it is plant.

The dividing line between an asset that is functional and one that is merely part of the setting in which the trade is carried on, is not always clear. Examples below show how the Courts have reacted to claims for capital allowances in these circumstances:

- A canopy covering petrol pumps at a petrol station was held to be part of the setting and not plant and machinery (it did not assist in serving petrol to customers).
- False ceilings in a restaurant were held not to be plant (all they did was hide unsightly pipes).
- Swimming pools at a caravan park were held to be plant and machinery (the caravan park as a whole was the setting but the pool and its associated pumping and filtering equipment had an active role of providing leisure apparatus).

Plant and buildings

There are statutory provisions that state that land, buildings and structures cannot be plant.

The provisions give detailed lists of items associated with buildings that are part of the building and not plant. The term 'buildings' includes:

- walls, floors, ceilings, doors, windows and stairs
- mains services, and systems, of water, electricity and gas.

The following however may fall within the definition of a building but will nevertheless normally qualify as plant:

- electrical, cold water and gas systems provided mainly to meet the particular requirements of the trade, or to serve particular machinery used for the purposes of the trade
- space or water heating systems, systems of ventilation and air cooling, and any ceiling or floor comprised in such systems

- manufacturing or processing equipment, storage equipment, display equipment, counters, check outs and similar equipment
- cookers, washing machines, dishwashers, refrigerators and similar equipment
- wash basins, sinks, baths, showers, sanitary ware and similar equipment
- furniture and furnishings
- lifts, escalators and moving walkways
- sprinkler equipment and fire alarm systems
- movable partition walls
- decorative assets provided for the enjoyment of the public in a hotel, restaurant or similar trade
- advertising hoardings, signs and similar displays.

3 Calculating the allowances

The general pool (or main pool)

Generally expenditure on plant and machinery becomes part of a pool of expenditure upon which capital allowances are claimed. Normally capital allowances are not calculated on individual assets.

- Most items of plant and machinery purchased are included within the general pool (also known as the main pool).
- When an addition is made, the purchase price increases the value of the pool.
- When an asset is disposed of, the pool value is reduced by the sale proceeds.

Exceptionally, certain items are not included in the general pool. For unincorporated businesses, these are:

- motor cars costing more than £12,000 (i.e. 'expensive' cars)
- assets that are used partly for private purposes by the owner of the business
- expenditure incurred on short-life assets where an election to de-pool is made
- expenditure incurred on items that form part of the 'special rate pool'.

These exceptional treatments are dealt with later in this chapter.

The Annual Investment Allowance (AIA)

The Annual Investment Allowance (AIA) is a 100% allowance for the first £50,000 of expenditure incurred by a business on plant and machinery.

The key rules for the allowance are as follows:

- available to **all** businesses regardless of size;
- available on acquisitions of general plant and machinery and acquisitions of 'special rate pool' items (see later);
- **not** available on cars;
- limited to a maximum of £50,000 expenditure incurred in each accounting period of 12 months in length;
- for long and short accounting periods the £50,000 allowance is pro-rated;
- not available in the accounting period in which the trade ceases.

Where a business spends more than £50,000 in a 12 month accounting period on assets qualifying for the AIA:

- the expenditure above the £50,000 limit will immediately qualify for writing down allowances (WDA) (see below).

Note also that:

- the taxpayer does not have to claim all / any of the AIA if he does not want to
- any unused AIA can not be carried forward or carried back, the benefit of the allowance is just lost.

Example 1 - AIA

Matthew commenced trading on 1 May 2008. In his first year of trading he made the following purchases:

• plant and machinery for the factory he rented	£120,000
• office furniture and equipment	£35,000
• a car for his office manager	£11,000

(a) **Calculate Matthew's annual investment allowance for the year ended 30 April 2009 and state how much is eligible for writing down allowances.**

(b) **What if Matthew did not purchase the plant and machinery?**

Answer to example 1

(a) Year ended 30 April 2009

	£	General pool £
Additions:		
Not qualifying for AIA:		
Car		11,000
Qualifying for AIA:		
Plant and machinery	120,000	
Office furniture	35,000	
	155,000	
Less AIA (Maximum)	(50,000)	
		105,000
Eligible for WDA		116,000

(b) If Matthew did not purchase the plant and machinery

	£	General pool £
Additions:		
Not qualifying for AIA:		
Car		11,000
Qualifying for AIA:		
Office furniture	35,000	
Less AIA (Note)	(35,000)	
		Nil
Eligible for WDA		11,000

Note: The unused AIA of £15,000 (£50,000 – £35,000) is lost.

Writing down allowances (WDA)

- An annual WDA of 20% is given on a reducing balance basis
- It is given on:
  - the unrelieved expenditure in the pool brought forward at the beginning of the period of account (i.e. tax written down value) (TWDV).
  - any additions eligible for WDAs
  - any additions on which the AIA is not claimed
  - after taking account of disposals
- The TWDV brought forward includes all prior expenditure, less allowances already claimed.

Example 2 - Writing down allowances

Grace commenced trading on 1 August 2008. Her trading profits, adjusted for tax purposes but before capital allowances, are as follows:

	£
Year ended 31 July 2009	25,500
Year ended 31 July 2010	30,000

On 9 November 2008, she bought plant and machinery for £20,000 and a motor car for £6,000.

Calculate Grace's tax-adjusted trading profit for both years.

Answer to example 2

Grace – Capital allowances calculation

		General pool	Total allowances
	£	£	£
Year ended 31 July 2009			
Additions:			
Not qualifying for AIA:			
Car		6,000	
Qualifying for AIA:			
Plant and machinery	20,000		
Less: AIA	(20,000)	Nil	20,000
		6,000	
WDA (20% x £6,000)		(1,200)	1,200
TWDV c/f		4,800	
Total allowances			21,200
Year end 31 July 2010			
WDA (20% x £4,800)		(960)	960
TWDV c/f		3,840	
Total allowances			960

Taxable trading income

Year ended	Adjusted trading profit	Capital allowances	Tax-adjusted trading profit
	£	£	£
31 July 2009	25,500	(21,200)	4,300
31 July 2010	30,000	(960)	29,040

Test your understanding 1

Gayle commenced trading on 1 May 2008. Her trading profits, adjusted for tax purposes but before capital allowances, are as follows:

	£
Year ended 30 April 2009	60,500
Year ended 30 April 2010	54,000

On 1 May 2008, Gayle acquired plant and machinery for £52,000 and a new motor car £10,000.

Calculate Gayle's tax-adjusted trading profit for both years.

Short or long periods of account

- The AIA and WDAs are given for periods of account, i.e. the period for which a trader draws up accounts. The £50,000 AIA and the percentage of 20% is based on a period of account of 12 months.
- Shorter or longer periods of account result in the allowances being pro-rated.
- If the period of account exceeds 18 months it must be split into a 12-month period and a second period of account to deal with the remaining months.
- The most common occasion for a business having a non 12-month period of account is at the start of trading.

Example 3 - WDA: long period of account

Giles commenced trading on 1 August 2008. His trading profits, adjusted for tax purposes but before capital allowances, are as follows:

	£
14-month period ended 30 September 2009	128,000
Year ended 30 September 2010	135,000

On 1 November 2008, he bought plant and machinery for £56,000 and a motor car for £9,000.

Calculate his tax-adjusted trading profit for each of the periods of trading.

Answer to example 3

Giles – Capital allowances calculation

		General pool	Total allowances
	£	£	£
Period ended 30 September 2009			
Additions:			
Not qualifying for AIA:			
Car		9,000	
Qualifying for AIA:			
Plant and machinery	56,000		
Less AIA (Note)	(56,000)		56,000
		Nil	
		9,000	
WDA (20% x £9,000 x 14/12)		(2,100)	2,100
TWDV c/f		6,900	
Total allowances			58,100
Year ended 30 September 2010			
WDA (20% x £6,900)		(1,380)	1,380
TWDV c/f		5,520	
Total allowances			1,380

Note: The AIA is pro-rated to £58,333 (£50,000 x 14/12) and therefore all of the £56,000 expenditure is eligible for the allowance in the 14 months ended 30 September 2009. The unused allowance is lost.

Both the AIA and the WDA are pro-rated to reflect the 14 month-period.

Period ended	**Adjusted trading profit**	**Capital allowances**	**Tax adjusted trading profit**
	£	£	£
30 September 2009	128,000	(58,100)	69,900
30 September 2010	135,000	(1,380)	133,620

Test your understanding 2

Graham commenced trading on 1 May 2008. His trading profits, adjusted for tax purposes but before capital allowances, are as follows:

	£
4-month period ended 31 August 2008	32,000
Year ended 31 August 2009	45,000

On 1 May 2008, he bought plant and machinery for £18,000 and a motor car for £11,500.

Calculate the tax-adjusted trading profit for each of the periods of trading.

Length of ownership in the period of account

It is important to distinguish between the length of the period of account and the date of acquisition of the asset during the period:

- The WDA is never restricted by reference to the length of ownership of an asset in the period of account.
- If a business prepares accounts for the year ended 31 March 2009, the same WDA is given whether an asset is purchased on 1 April 2008 or on 31 March 2009.

  This is because it is ownership of an asset on the last day of the period of account that determines whether the allowance is available, not the length of ownership.

4 Sale of plant and machinery

At the point an asset is sold or scrapped the following steps are taken:

- The disposal value (sale proceeds) is deducted from the total of the: (TWDV brought forward on the pool plus additions).
- The WDA for the year is then calculated on the remaining figure.

- If sale proceeds exceed the original cost of the asset, the sale proceeds deducted from the pool are restricted to the original cost of the asset. An excess of sale proceeds over original cost may then be charged as a capital gain.

- Therefore on a disposal always deduct from the pool the lower of the sale proceeds and the original cost.

Example 4 - Sale of plant and machinery

Glyn prepares accounts to 31 March. In the year to 31 March 2009, the following transactions took place:

5 June 2008	Plant sold (originally purchased for £8,000) for £1,200
3 September 2008	Plant purchased for £40,000

Compute the capital allowances for the year ended 31 March 2009, assuming that the TWDV on 1 April 2008, was £10,000.

Answer to example 4

Glyn – Capital allowances computation

		General pool	Total allowances
	£	£	£
Year ended 31 March 2009			
TWDV b/f		10,000	
Additions:			
Qualifying for AIA:			
Plant and machinery	40,000		
Less AIA	(40,000)		40,000
		Nil	
		10,000	
Disposals			
(lower of cost or sale proceeds)		(1,200)	
		8,800	
WDA (20% x £8,800)		(1,760)	1,760
TWDV c/f		7,040	
Total allowances			41,760

Balancing charges

If, on disposal of an asset in the pool, disposal proceeds exceed the pool balance brought forward, the excess allowances previously given will be recovered and charged to tax by means of a balancing charge.

A balancing charge is added to the taxable trading profit.

Balancing allowances

The following rules apply:

- The basic idea underlying capital allowances is that the business will over time obtain relief for the actual cost of an asset to the business i.e. cost less sale proceeds (if any).

- When the business is permanently discontinued, and there is still a balance of unrelieved expenditure in the pool, a business can claim relief for the unrelieved balance by way of a balancing allowance.
- The only time a balancing allowance will arise in the pool is when the trade is permanently discontinued.
- A balancing allowance is computed by reference to the excess of the pool balance at the end of the final period of account over the sale proceeds received on the ultimate disposal of plant and machinery.
- No AIA or WDAs are available in the final period of account.

Example 5 - Cessation or trade

Gene has previously prepared accounts to 31 March. He decided to cease to trade on 31 December 2009, after a period of ill health.

The following transactions have recently taken place:

21 February 2009	Plant sold (originally purchased for £2,000) for £320
10 June 2009	Plant purchased for £4,000

On the completion of the sale of his business, Gene received £5,400 for his plant and machinery. No item was sold for more than its original cost.

The WDV on 1 April 2008, was £9,000.

Compute the capital allowances for the year ended 31 March 2009, and the period ended 31 December 2009.

Answer to example 5

Gene

Capital allowances computation

		General pool	Total allowances
	£	£	£
Year ended 31 March 2009			
TWDV b/f		9,000	
Disposals			
(lower of cost or sale proceeds)		(320)	
		8,680	
WDA (20% x £8,680)		(1,736)	1,736
TWDV c/f		6,944	
Total allowances			1,736
Period ended 31 December 2009			
Additions:			
Qualifying for AIA:			
Plant and machinery	4,000		
Less AIA (Note)	Nil		
		4,000	
		10,944	
Disposals			
(lower of cost or sale proceeds)		(5,400)	
		5,544	
Balancing allowance		(5,544)	5,544
Total allowances			5,544

Note: There is no AIA or WDA available in the final period of account.

Test your understanding 3

Gloria has owned and run her own business for many years. She prepares accounts to 30 June each year. During the year ended 30 June 2009, the following transactions took place:

21 February 2009	Purchased a motor car for £11,000.
14 March 2009	Sold a piece of plant for £3,000, she had paid £15,000 for this when she acquired it many years ago.
31 May 2009	Purchased plant for £19,500.

The TWDV at 1 July 2008, was £21,000.

Compute the capital allowances for the year ended 30 June 2009.

5 Motor cars

Motor cars costing £12,000 or less

Motor cars are included in the general pool unless:

- the cost of the motor car is more than £12,000
- the motor car is used by the owner of the business partly for private purposes
- the car is a low emission car.

Note that the AIA is not available against expenditure on cars, whether or not they are included in the general pool.

Motor cars costing more than £12,000 (expensive cars)

Where cars cost more than £12,000:

- The cost of a motor car must not be brought into the general pool. The capital allowances on each 'expensive' car must be separately computed.
- Each expensive car will have its own separate column in the capital allowances computation.
- The AIA is not available.
- The WDA is restricted to a maximum (for a 12-month period of account) of £3,000.

- Once the motor car has a written down value of below £15,000, the WDA will be computed in the normal way (i.e. 20% of TWDV) but the motor car remains in its separate column of the computation. It must not be brought into the general pool.
- When each 'expensive' motor car is sold, a balancing allowance or charge must be computed on the difference between the TWDV and the sale proceeds.

Example 6 - Motor cars

Glenda prepares accounts to 31 March. At 1 April 2008, the TWDVs are as follows:

	£
Pool	21,200
Expensive motor car	13,600

The following transations took place during the year ended 31 March 2009:

25.08.08	Purchased a motor car for £10,600
15.12.08	Sold the expensive motor car for £9,400
16.03.09	Purchased a motor car for £18,000

Calculate the capital allowances for the year to 31 March 2009.

Answer to example 6

Glenda

Capital allowances computation

	General pool	Exp Car 1	Exp Car 2	Total allowances
Y/e 31 March 2009	£	£	£	£
TWDV b/f	21,200	13,600		
Additions:				
Not qualifying for AIA:				
Cars	10,600		18,000	
Disposals				
(lower of cost or sale proceeds)		(9,400)		
	31,800	4,200	18,000	
Balancing allowance		(4,200)		4,200
WDA (20% x £31,800)	(6,360)			6,360
WDA (restricted to max £3,000)			(3,000)	3,000
TWDV c/f	25,440		15,000	
Total allowances				13,560

Test your understanding 4

Glen prepares accounts to 31 March. At 1 April 2008, the TWDVs are as follows:

	£
General pool	43,500
Expensive motor car 1	14,500
Expensive motor car 2	15,600

The following transactions took place during the year ended 31 March 2009:

10.5.08	Purchased plant for £53,300
25.6.08	Purchased a motor car for £10,600
15.2.09	Sold expensive motor car 1 for £9,400
16.2.09	Purchased a motor car for £18,000

Calculate the capital allowances for the year to 31 March 2009.

Low emission motor cars

- The AIA is not available on any type of car.
- However, expenditure on low emission cars by all businesses (regardless of size) is eligible for a 100% first year allowance.
- A low emission car is one which emits 110 or less grams per kilometre of carbon dioxide.
- In the exam you will be told if a car qualifies as a low emission car. You do not need to learn the definition.

The relief for FYA is calculated as follows:

- In the period of acquisition, a 100% FYA is given instead of the WDA.
- Unlike the WDA, the FYA is not pro-rated for periods of greater or less than 12 months.
- FYAs are not given in the final period of trading.

Test your understanding 5

Gwen runs a business preparing accounts to 31 March. The TWDV on the general pool on 1 April 2008 was £11,000.

During the year ended 31 March 2009 the following transactions took place:

25 May 2008	Purchased plant for £29,000
31 August 2008	Purchased two cars for £13,000 each, one of which is a low emission car
30 March 2009	Sold plant for £4,600 (originally purchased for £9,500)

Calculate the capital allowances for the year ended 31 March 2009.

6 Assets with private use by the owner of the business

- Where an asset is used by the owner of the business, partly for business and partly for private purposes, only the business proportion of the available capital allowances are available as a tax deduction.
- The following rules must be followed when computing capital allowances:

  – The cost of the privately used asset is not brought into the general pool, but must be the subject of a separate computation (in the same way as a motor car costing over £12,000).

  – The AIA, WDA or FYA on the asset is based on its full cost but only the business proportion of any allowance is actually deductible in computing the taxable trading profit.

  – Note that if applicable, the business can choose the expenditure against which the AIA is matched.

  – It will therefore be most beneficial for the AIA to be allocated against the general pool expenditure rather than any private use asset as only the business proportion of any AIA available can be claimed.

  – However note that in examinations the assets most commonly used for private purposes are cars, which are not eligible for the AIA.

- On disposal of the asset, a balancing adjustment is computed by comparing sale proceeds with the TWDV. There is a balancing charge if there is a profit, and a balancing allowance if there is a loss.
- Having computed the balancing adjustment, the amount assessed or allowed is then reduced to the business proportion.
- Where the asset concerned is an expensive motor car, WDAs are first restricted to the £3,000 limit and then the business proportion of £3,000 is actually given as an allowance.
- Private use by an employee of an asset owned by the business has no effect on the business's entitlement to capital allowances.

Example 7 - Assets with private use by the owner of the business

George runs a small business and prepares his accounts to 31 March. As at 1 April 2008, the tax written down values are as follows:

	£
General pool	11,700
Expensive motor car (used 60% for private purposes by George)	11,600

The following transactions took place during the year ended 31 March 2009:

- Purchased plant for £8,800
- Purchased a motor car for £9,400
- Sold the expensive motor car for £5,500
- Purchased a motor car for £16,000 (used 45% for private purposes by George)

Calculate the capital allowances for the year to 31 March 2009.

Answer to example 7

George – Capital allowances computation

		General pool	Exp Car 1 (B.U. 40%)	Exp Car 2 (B.U. 55%)		Total CAs
	£	£	£	£	B.U.%	£
Y/e 31 March 2009						
TWDV b/f		11,700	11,600			
Additions:						
No AIA:						
Cars		9,400		16,000		
Qualifying for AIA:						
Plant	8,800					
Less AIA	(8,800)					8,800
	———	Nil				
Disposals proceeds			(5,500)			
		21,100	6,100	16,000		
Balancing allowance			(6,100)		x 40%	2,440
WDA (20% x £21,100)		(4,220)				4,220
WDA (max £3,000)				(3,000)	x 55%	1,650
TWDV c/f		16,880		13,000		
Total allowances						17,110

Test your understanding 6

Georgina runs a small business and prepares accounts to 5 April. At 6 April 2008, the TWDVs are as follows:

	£
Pool	21,200
Expensive motor car (used 30% for private purposes by Georgina)	13,600

The following transactions took place during the year ended 5 April 2009:

10.5.08	Purchased plant for £6,600
25.6.08	Purchased a motor car for £10,600
15.2.09	Sold the expensive motor car for £9,400
16.2.09	Purchased a motor car for £16,000 (used 30% for private purposes by Georgina)

Calculate the capital allowances for the year to 5 April 2009.

7 Short-life assets

Purpose

The short-life asset election exists to enable businesses to accelerate capital allowances on certain qualifying expenditure.

Qualifying expenditure

For the purposes of the exam, all plant and machinery, with the exception of motor cars, constitute eligible expenditure, where it is the intention to sell or scrap the item within four years of the end of the period of account in which the asset is acquired.

Process for computation

The following steps must be taken:

- The treatment of short-life assets corresponds in most respects to that applied to motor cars costing over £12,000.
- Each short-life asset is the subject of a separate column within the capital allowances computation.
- On disposal within four years of the end of the period of account in which the asset was acquired, a separate balancing allowance or balancing charge is calculated.
- An election (written application to HMRC) must be made to enable assets to be treated separately in the capital allowances computation as short-life assets. This is known as de-pooling.
- This election must be made by the first anniversary of 31 January following the end of the tax year in which the trading period of expenditure ends.

- If no disposal has taken place within four years of the end of the period of account in which the acquisition took place, the unrelieved balance is transferred to the general pool. The transfer takes place in the first period of account following the four-year anniversary.
- However, note that the AIA is available against short life assets and the business can choose the expenditure against which the AIA is matched.
- If eligible for the AIA, there will be no expenditure left to "de-pool" and the short life asset election will not be made.
- If there is expenditure in excess of the maximum £50,000 on expenditure eligible for the AIA, it may be advantageous for the AIA to be allocated against the general pool expenditure rather than a short life asset and for the short life asset election to be made.
- It will be advantageous if it is anticipated that a balancing allowance will arise within the following four accounting periods.

Example 8 - Short-life assets

Gina has traded for many years preparing accounts to 31 March each year. The TWDV on the general pool was £15,000 on 1 April 2008.

In May 2008, she acquired a new machine costing £10,000. She anticipated that the machine would last two years and she eventually sold it on 30 June 2010, for £1,750.

In August 2008, she acquired general plant and machinery for £52,000.

Calculate the allowances available for each year, illustrating whether or not an election to treat the new machine as a short life asset would be beneficial.

Answer to example 8

Gina – Capital allowances computation – without making a short life asset election

		General pool	Total allowances
	£	£	£
Year ended 31 March 2009			
TWDV b/f		15,000	
Additions:			
Qualifying for AIA:			
Plant and machinery	62,000		
Less AIA (Max)	(50,000)		50,000
	———	12,000	
		27,000	
WDA (20% x £27,000)		(5,400)	5,400
TWDV c/f		21,600	
Total allowances			55,400
Year ended 31 March 2010			
WDA (20% x £21,600)		(4,320)	4,320
TWDV c/f		17,280	
Total allowances			4,320
Year ended 31 March 2011			
Disposal proceeds		(1,750)	
		15,530	
WDA (20% x £15,530)		(3,106)	3,106
TWDV c/f		12,424	
Total allowances			3,106

Gina – Capital allowances computation – with a short life asset election

		General pool	Short life asset	Total CAs
Year ended 31 March 2009	£	£	£	£
TWDV b/f		15,000		
Additions:				
Qualifying for AIA:				
Plant and machinery	62,000			
Less AIA (Max)	(50,000)			50,000
	———	2,000	10,000	
		———	———	
		17,000	10,000	
WDA (20% x £17,000/£10,000)		(3,400)	(2,000)	5,400
		———	———	
TWDV c/f		13,600	8,000	
				———
Total allowances				55,400
				———
Year ended 31 March 2010				
WDA (20% x £13,600)		(2,720)		2,720
WDA (20% x £8,000)			(1,600)	1,600
		———	———	
TWDV c/f		10,880	6,400	
				———
Total allowances				4,320
				———
Year ended 31 March 2011				
Disposal proceeds			(1,750)	
		———	———	
		10,880	4,650	
Balancing allowance			(4,650)	4,650
			———	
WDA (20% x £10,800)		(2,176)		2,176
		———		
TWDV c/f		8,704		
		———		———
Total allowances				6,826
				———

The total allowances claimed without making the election are £62,826 (£55,400 + £4,320 + £3,106). In the event Gina makes the election, the allowances available for the three years are £66,546 (£55,400 + £4,320 + £6,826).

Note that the election just accelerates allowances available and only changes the timing of the allowances. However, if not covered by the AIA it is recommended that the short life treatment is taken if it is expected that a balancing allowance can be accelerated.

8 Special rate pool

The 'special rate pool' is a pool of expenditure eligible for a reduced rate of WDA.

The pool operates in the same way as the general pool except that:

- the WDA is 10% for a 12 month period, calculated on a reducing balance basis.

Note that:

- the AIA is available against this expenditure, and
- the business can choose the expenditure against which the AIA is matched.

It will therefore be most beneficial for the AIA to be allocated against expenditure in the following order:

(1) the 'special rate pool'.

This is because assets in the 'special rate pool' are eligible for 10% WDA whereas general plant and machinery is eligible for 20% WDA.

(2) the general pool

(3) short life assets

(4) private use assets.

Qualifying expenditure

The 'special rate pool' groups together expenditure incurred on the following type of assets:

- long-life assets
- 'integral features' of a building or structure (with effect from 6 April 2008)
- thermal insulation of a building (with effect from 6 April 2008).

Long-life assets

Long-life assets are defined as:

- Plant and machinery with an expected working life of 25 years or more.
  - Examples of long-life assets might include aircraft used by an airline and agricultural equipment used by a farm.
  - The 25 year working life is from the time that the asset is first brought into use, to the time that it ceases to be capable of being used. It is not sufficient to just look at the expected life in the hands of the current owner.

Where the business spends less than £100,000 pa on long-life assets, they are treated as normal additions in the general pool.

The following can never be classed as long-life assets:

- Motor cars.
- Plant and machinery situated in a building that is used as a retail shop, showroom, hotel or office.

Long-life assets have been treated as a separate pool of expenditure for a number of years.

With effect from 6 April 2008, the special rate pool now includes:

- expenditure on long-life assets incurred on/after 6 April 2008, and
- any existing long-life asset pool TWDV b/f from previous years.

Integral features of a building or structure and thermal insulation

'Integral features of a building or structure' include expenditure incurred with effect from 6 April 2008 on the following:

- electrical (including lighting) systems;
- cold water systems;
- space or water heating systems;
- powered systems of ventilation, air cooling or air purification;
- lifts and escalators.

Thermal insulation in all business buildings (except residential buildings in a property business) is also included in the special rate pool.

Example 9 - Long-life assets

Apple runs a manufacturing business and prepares her accounts to 31 March each year. As at 1 April 2008 the tax written down values are as follows:

	£
General pool	103,000
Expensive motor car	16,200
Long life asset pool	40,000

During the year ended 31 March 2009 Apple incurred the following expenditure:

- Spent £120,000 on a new air-conditioning system for the factory which is expected to last 30 years.
- Purchased a new computer and related software for £25,000 and £5,000 respectively.
- Spent £15,000 on a new packing machine. Apple also incurred £4,000 on alterations to the factory in order to accommodate the new machine.

In addition she sold old machinery for £10,000 (original cost £60,000).

Calculate the capital allowances available to Apple for the year ended 31 March 2009.

Answer to example 9

Apple – Capital allowances computation

		General pool	Special rate pool	Expensive car	Total CAs
	£	£	£	£	£
Y/e 31 March 2009					
TWDV b/f		103,000		16,200	
Long-life asset pool b/f			40,000		
Additions:					
Qualifying for AIA:					
Long-life asset (Note 1)	120,000				
Less AIA (max) (Note 2)	(50,000)				50,000
			70,000		
Qualifying for AIA:					
Computer and software	30,000				
Machine (Note 3)	19,000				
	49,000				
Less AIA (Note 2)	(Nil)				
		49,000			
Disposal proceeds		(10,000)			
		142,000	110,000	16,200	
WDA (20% x £142,000)		(28,400)			28,400
WDA (10% x £110,000)			(11,000)		11,000
WDA (max £3,000)				(3,000)	3,000
TWDV c/f		113,600	99,000	13,200	
Total allowances					92,400

Notes:

(1) The air-conditioning unit has an expected life of more than 25 years and is therefore a long-life asset. As Apple has incurred more than £100,000 on such assets in the year the air-conditioning unit is included in the 'special rate pool' and WDAs are restricted to 10%.

(2) The AIA is allocated to the additions in the 'special rate pool' in priority to the additions in the general pool. The maximum £50,000 is therefore all allocated to the special rate pool and there is no AIA available against the general pool expenditure.

(3) Software and the cost of altering buildings to accommodate plant are specifically deemed by statute to be items of general plant and machinery.

9 The small pool WDA

The WDA of 20% or 10% is claimed each accounting period and if there are no additions in an accounting period in excess of the £50,000 AIA, the WDA will be claimed on an ever decreasing amount for many years.

To prevent the inconvenience of continually claiming small amounts of WDA and keeping records of small balances of expenditure, a 'small pool WDA' has been introduced with effect from 6 April 2008.

The annual WDA available:

- applies only to the general pool and 'special rate pool'
- is any amount up to £1,000, and
- is pro rated for long or short accounting periods.

Therefore, an allowance of up to £1,000 can be claimed on either or both of the pools where the unrelieved expenditure on the pool (after dealing with additions qualifying for WDAs and disposals in the period) is £1,000 or less.

The claim therefore allows the balance on a 'small pool' to be written off at once.

The claim is optional. However, it is likely that the taxpayer will want to claim as much as possible and reduce the remaining balance on the pool to £Nil.

Test your understanding 7

Angelina is in business as a sole trader and prepares accounts to 31 March each year.

During the year ending 31 March 2009 she incurred the following expenditure:

15 May 2008	Purchased new office furniture for £23,800.
2 June 2008	Purchased a new car (not a low emission car) for £10,000 which Angela will use 20% of the time for private purposes.
10 June 2008	Installed a new water heating system in her business premises at a cost of £15,000 and a new lighting system at a cost of £20,000.

In addition on 1 July 2008 she sold office equipment for £10,000 (original cost £18,000).

As at 1 April 2008 the tax written down value on her general pool was £2,000.

Calculate Angelina's capital allowances for the year ended 31 March 2009.

10 Summary of computational technique

- Capital allowances are an important element of the syllabus and are certain to appear in the exam, within at least one of the questions.
- To be successful answering these questions, it is vital to use a methodical approach to work through the information in the question.
- Always follow the approach to computational questions outlined below and always ensure that you answer the question using the following pro-forma, amended to reflect the particular circumstances of the question.

Approach to computational questions

For plant and machinery capital allowances, adopt the following step-by-step approach:

(1) Read the information in the question and decide how many columns / pools you will require.

(2) Draft the layout and insert the TWDV b/f (does not apply in a new trade).

Remember that if applicable, the TWDV on a long-life asset pool is entered into the special rate pool.

(3) Insert additions not eligible for the AIA or FYAs into the appropriate column.

(4) Insert additions eligible for the AIA in the first column, then allocate the AIA to the additions. Allocate the AIA to 'special rate pool' additions in priority to additions of plant and machinery in the general or special asset pools.

(5) Deal with any disposal by deducting the lower of cost or sale proceeds.

(6) Work out any balancing charge / balancing allowance for assets in individual pools.

Remember to adjust for any private use if an unincorporated business.

(7) Consider whether the 'small pool' WDA applies to the general pool and / or the 'special rate pool'.

(8) Calculate the WDA on each of the pools at the appropriate rate (20% or 10%).

Remember to:

- restrict the WDA on expensive cars to a maximum of £3,000 p.a.
- time apportion if the accounting period is not 12 months
- adjust for any private use if an unincorporated business.

(9) Calculate the TWDV to carry forward to the next accounting period and add the 'total allowances' column.

(10) Deduct the total allowances from the tax adjusted trading profits.

	Notes		General pool	Special rate pool	Expensive car 1	Expensive car 2	Short life asset	Private use asset (Note 4)	x Business Use %	Allowances
		£	£	£	£	£	£	£		£
TWDV b/f			X	–	X		X	X		
Long-life assets b/f	1			X						
Additions:										
Not qualifying for AIA or FYA:										
- Cars (not low-emission cars)			X			X				
Qualifying for AIA:										
- Integral features		X								
- Long-life assets		X								
- Thermal insulation		X								
		X								
Less AIA (Max £50,000 in total)	2	(X)								X
Transfer balance to special rate pool				X						
Qualifying for AIA:										
- plant and machinery		X								
Less AIA (Max £50,000 in total)	2	(x)								X
Transfer balance to general pool			X							
Disposals (lower of original cost or sale proceeds)			(X)		(X)					
			X	X	X / (X)	X	X	X		
BA / (BC)					(X) / X					X / (X)
Small pools WDA	3									
WDA at 20%			(X)				(X)	(X)	x B.U.%	X
WDA at 20% (maximum £3,000 p.a.)						(X)				X
WDA at 10%				(X)						X
Additions qualifying for FYAs:										
Low emission cars		X								
Less FYA at 100%		(X)								X
			Nil							
TWDV c/f			X	X		X	X	X		
Total allowances										X

Notes to the proforma capital allowances computation

(1) The opening balance on the long-life asset pool is transferred to the 'special rate pool' at the beginning of the accounting period.

(2) Allocate the AIA to the 'special rate pool' expenditure in priority to plant and machinery assets on which WDA at 20% is available.

(3) 'Small pool' WDA: can claim up to a maximum WDA of £1,000 but on the general pool and/or 'special rate pool' only.

(4) The taxpayer does not have to claim all or any of the AIA or WDA.

11 Comprehensive examples

Example 10 - Comprehensive example

Ashley runs a manufacturing business and prepares accounts to 31 March each year.

During the year ending 31 March 2009 Ashley incurred the following expenditure:

1 May 2008	Spent £120,000 on a new air-conditioning system for the factory which is expected to last 30 years.
1 June 2008	Purchased new machinery for £40,000.
3 June 2008	Purchased a new low-emission car for £17,000.
15 July 2008	Purchased a new car for £18,000.

In addition on 1 July 2008 Ashley sold an old machine for £10,000 (original cost £15,000) and a car for £7,000, which had originally cost £15,000.

As at 1 April 2008 the tax written down values were as follows:

General pool	£64,000
Expensive car	£9,000
Long-life asset pool	£90,000

Calculate Ashley's capital allowances for the year ended 31 March 2009.

Answer to example 10

Ashley – Capital allowances computation

		General pool	Special rate pool	Exp car 1	Exp car 2	Total CAs
	£	£	£	£	£	£
Y/e 31 March 2009						
TWDV b/f		64,000		9,000		
Long-life assets b/f			90,000			
Additions:						
No AIA:						
Cars					18,000	
Qualifying for AIA:						
Air conditioning	120,000					
Less AIA (Note)	(50,000)					50,000
	———		70,000			
Qualifying for AIA:						
Machine	40,000					
Less AIA (Max)	(Nil)					
	———	40,000				
Disposals proceeds		(10,000)		(7,000)		
		94,000	160,000	2,000	18,000	
Balancing allowance				(2,000)		2,000
WDA (20% x £94,000)		(18,800)				18,800
WDA (10% x £160,000)			(16,000)			16,000
WDA (max)					(3,000)	3,000
Additions:						
Qualifying for FYA						
Low emission car	17,000					
Less FYA (100%)	(17,000)					17,000
	———	Nil				
TWDV c/f		75,200	144,000		15,000	
Total allowances						106,800

Note: The AIA is allocated to the additions in the 'special rate pool' (WDA 10%) in priority to the additions in the general pool (WDA 20%).

Test your understanding 8

On 1 January 2009, Gordon commenced in self-employment running a music-recording studio. He prepared his first set of accounts for the 3 months to 31 March 2009. The following information relates to the 3 months of trading to 31 March 2009:

(1) The tax adjusted trading profit for the period is £22,590. This figure is before taking account of capital allowances.

(2) Gordon purchased the following assets:

		£
1 January 2009	Recording equipment	21,625
15 January 2009	Motor car (used by Gordon – 60% business use)	15,800
20 February 2009	Motor car (used privately by employee – 20% private use)	10,400
4 March 2009	Recording equipment (expected to be scrapped in 2 years)	3,250

Calculate Gordon's taxable trading income for the period ended 31 March 2009.

12 Chapter summary

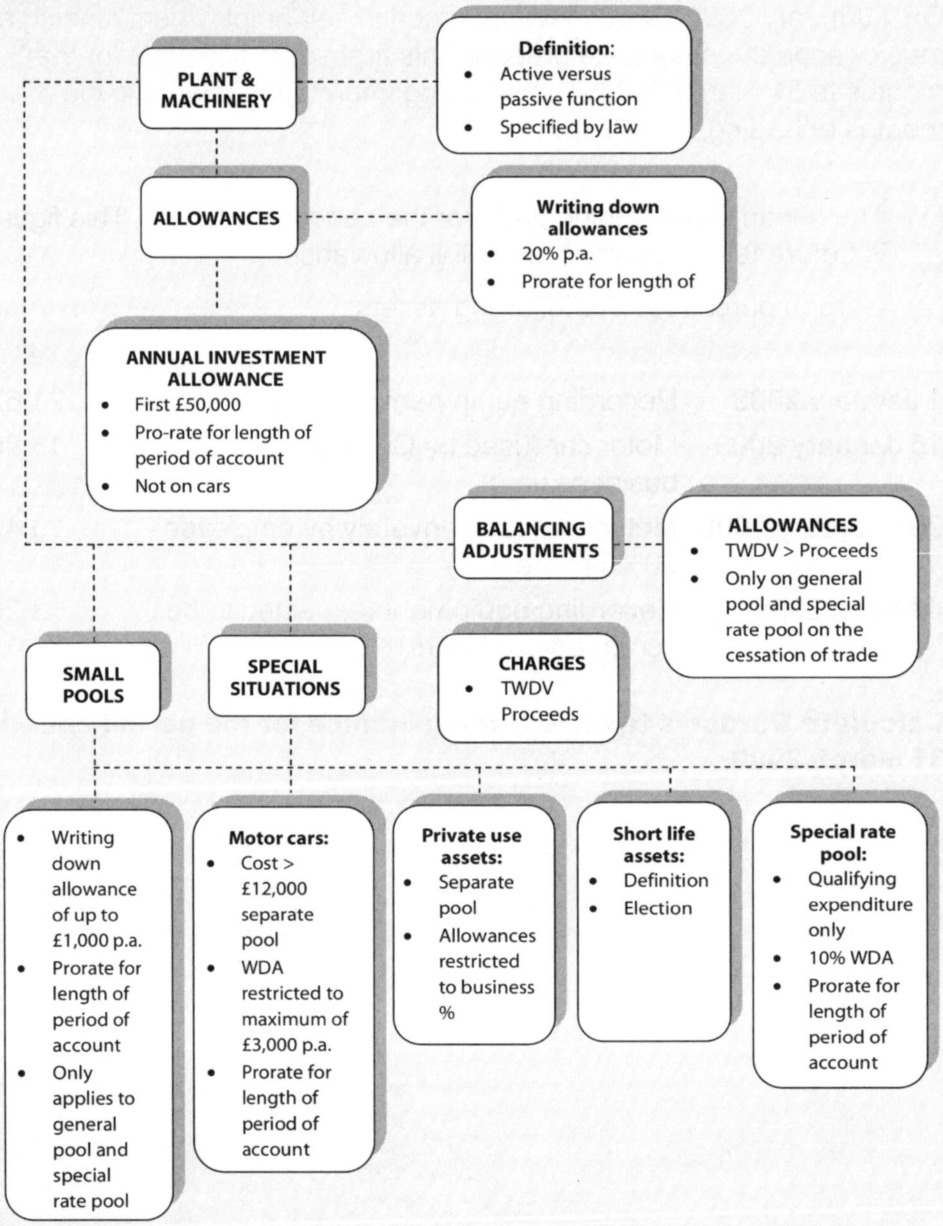

Test your understanding answers

Test your understanding 1

Gayle

Capital allowances computation

		General pool	Total allowances
	£	£	£
Year ended 30 April 2009			
Additions:			
Not qualifying for AIA			
Car		10,000	
Qualifying for AIA:			
Plant and machinery	52,000		
Less: AIA (maximum)	(50,000)		50,000
		2,000	
		12,000	
WDA (20% x £12,000)		(2,400)	2,400
TWDV c/f		9,600	
Total allowances			52,400
Year end 30 April 2010			
WDA (20% x £9,600)		(1,920)	1,920
TWDV c/f		7,680	
Total allowances			1,920

Taxable trading income

Year ended	Adjusted profit	Capital allowances	Tax-adjusted trading profit
	£	£	£
30 April 2009	60,500	(52,400)	8,100
30 April 2010	54,000	(1,920)	52,080

Test your understanding 2

Graham

Capital allowances computation

	£	General pool £	Total allowances £
Period ended 31 August 2008			
Additions:			
Not qualifying for AIA:			
Car		11,500	
Qualifying for AIA:			
Plant and machinery	18,000		
Less AIA (Note)	(16,667)		16,667
		1,333	
		12,833	
WDA (20% x £12,833 x 4/12)		(856)	856
TWDV c/f		11,977	
Total allowances			17,523
Year ended 31 August 2009			
WDA (20% x £11,977)		(2,395)	2,395
TWDV c/f		9,582	
Total allowances			2,395

Note: The maximum AIA is pro-rated to £16,667 (£50,000 x 4/12). Both the AIA and the WDA are pro-rated to reflect the 4 month-period.

Trading income assessments

	Adjusted trading profit £	Capital allowances £	Tax-adjusted trading profit £
Period ended 31 August 2008	32,000	(17,523)	14,477
Year ended 31 August 2009	45,000	(2,395)	42,605

Test your understanding 3

Gloria

Capital allowances computation

	£	General pool £	Total allowances £
Year ended 30 June 2009			
TWDV b/f		21,000	
Additions:			
Not qualifying for AIA:			
Car		11,000	
Qualifying for AIA:			
Plant and machinery	19,500		
Less AIA (Note)	(19,500)		19,500
		Nil	
		32,000	
Disposals			
(lower of cost or sale proceeds)		(3,000)	
		29,000	
WDA (20% x £29,000)		(5,800)	5,800
TWDV c/f		23,200	
Total allowances			25,300

Test your understanding 4

Glen

Capital allowances computation

		General pool	Exp Car 1	Exp Car 2	Exp Car 3	Total CAs
	£	£	£	£		£
Y/e 31 March 2009						
TWDV b/f		43,500	14,500	15,600		
Additions:						
No AIA:						
Cars		10,600			18,000	
Qualifying for AIA:						
Plant	53,300					
Less AIA (Max)	(50,000)					50,000
		3,300				
Disposals proceeds			(9,400)			
		57,400	5,100	15,600	18,000	
Balancing allowance			(5,100)			5,100
WDA (20% x £57,400)		(11,480)				11,480
WDA (max £3,000)				(3,000)	(3,000)	6,000
TWDV c/f		45,920		12,600	15,000	
Total allowances						72,580

Test your understanding 5

Gwen

Capital allowances computation

		General pool	Expensive car	Total allowances
Y/e 31 March 2009	£	£	£	£
TWDV b/f		11,000		
Additions:				
Not qualifying for AIA or FYA:				
Car (Note 1)			13,000	
Qualifying for AIA:				
Plant	29,000			
Less AIA	(29,000)			29,000
	———	Nil		
Disposal proceeds		(4,600)		
		———	———	
		6,400	13,000	
WDA (20% x £6,400) (Note 2)		(1,280)		1,280
WDA (20% x £13,000) (Note 1)			(2,600)	2,600
		———	———	
		5,120	10,400	
Additions:				
Qualifying for FYA:				
Low emission car (Note 3)	13,000			
Less FYA (100%)	(13,000)			
	———	Nil		13,000
		———	———	
TWDV c/f		5,120	10,400	
		———	———	———
Total allowances				45,880
				———

Notes:

(1) The cars cost more than £12,000 each and are therefore expensive cars. However, one is a low emission car and is therefore dealt with separately.

The other car must be put into a separate pool of its own. It is not put into the general pool. The WDA on this expensive car is calculated in the normal way at 20% which is below the maximum of £3,000 as the cost of the car is below £15,000.

(2) There is no balancing allowance in the general pool except in the period when trade is permanently discontinued. A WDA is claimed on the unrelieved expenditure after recording the disposal.

(3) The low emission car is dealt with at the end of the computation as it is not eligible for either the AIA or a WDA. It is eligible for 100% FYA.

Test your understanding 6

Georgina

Capital allowances computation

		General pool	Exp Car 1 (B.U. 70%)	Exp Car 2 (B.U. 70%)		Total CAs
	£	£	£	£	B.U.%	£
Y/e 5 April 2009						
TWDV b/f		21,200	13,600			
Additions:						
No AIA:						
Cars		10,600		16,000		
Qualifying for AIA:						
Plant	6,600					
Less AIA	(6,600)					6,600
		Nil				
Disposals proceeds			(9,400)			
		31,800	4,200	16,000		
Balancing allowance			(4,200)		x 70%	2,940
WDA (20% x £31,800)		(6,360)				6,360
WDA (max £3,000)				(3,000)	x 70%	2,100
TWDV c/f		25,440		13,000		
Total allowances						18,000

Test your understanding 7

Angelina

Capital allowances computation

		General pool	Special rate pool	Private use car (B.U. 80%)		Total CAs
	£	£	£	£	B.U.%	£
Y/e 31 March 2009						
TWDV b/f		2,000				
Additions:						
No AIA:						
Cars				10,000		
Qualifying for AIA:						
Water system and lighting system	35,000					
Less AIA (Note)	(35,000)					35,000
	———	Nil				
Qualifying for AIA:						
Furniture	23,800					
Less AIA (Max)	(15,000)					15,000
	———	8,800				
Disposals proceeds		(10,000)				
		800	Nil	10,000		
Small pool WDA		(800)				800
WDA (20% x £10,000)				(2,000)	x 80%	1,600
TWDV c/f		Nil	Nil	8,000		
Total allowances						52,400

Note: The AIA is allocated to the additions in the 'special rate pool' (WDA 10%) in priority to the additions in the general pool (WDA 20%).

Test your understanding 8

Gordon

Capital allowances computation

		General pool	Short life asset	Exp Car (B.U. 60%)		Total CAs
	£	£	£	£	B.U.%	£
3 m/e 31 March 2009						
Additions:						
No AIA or FYA:						
Cars (Note 1)		10,400		15,800		
Qualifying for AIA:						
Equipment	21,625					
Less AIA (Note 2)	(12,500)					12,500
	———	9,125				
Equipment	3,250					
Less AIA (Note 2)	Nil		3,250			
	———	———	———	———		
		19,525	3,250	15,800		
WDA (20% x £19,525 x 3/12)		(976)				976
WDA (20% x £3,250 x 3/12)			(163)			163
WDA (max £3,000 x 3/12)				(750)	x 60%	450
		———	———	———		
TWDV c/f		18,549	3,087	15,050		
		———	———	———		———
Total allowances						14,089
						———

Notes:

(1) Private use by an employee is not relevant. A separate private use asset column is only required where there is private use by the owner of the business.

(2) The AIA is pro-rated for the three month period. The maximum allowance is therefore £12,500 (£50,000 x 3/12). The AIA is allocated to the general plant and machinery in priority to the short life asset.

Taxable trading profit – 3 months ended 31 March 2009

(£22,590 – £14,089) = £8,501

chapter

7

Capital allowances: industrial buildings allowances

Chapter learning objectives

Upon completion of this chapter you will be able to:

- recognise qualifying and non-qualifying expenditure for industrial buildings allowance purposes
- compute the industrial buildings allowances for a new building used solely for industrial purposes

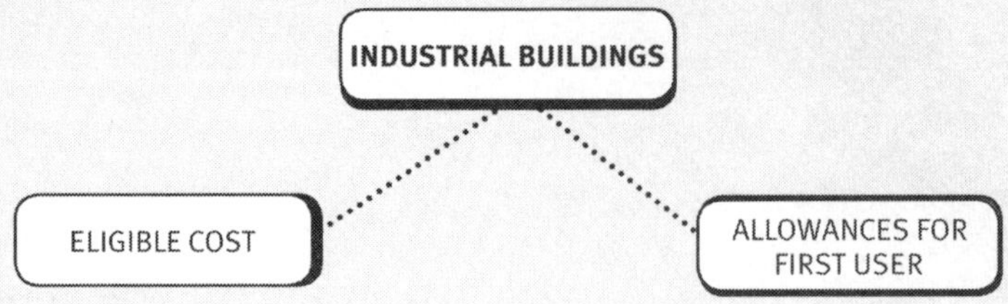

1 Introduction

Purpose

The purpose of industrial buildings allowances is to provide the business with tax relief for the acquisition of qualifying industrial buildings.

Qualifying assets

- Those buildings acquired by a business for use within a qualifying trade.

Relief for capital allowances

- Industrial building allowances (IBAs) are deducted as a trading expense in calculating the tax-adjusted trading profit.
- IBAs are calculated for a trader's period of account (i.e. the period for which they draw up accounts).

2 Definition of an industrial building

Industrial buildings are those used for the purposes of a qualifying trade. The more important of these qualifying trades are:

- a trade carried on in a mill, factory or similar premises
- a trade in the manufacture of goods or materials or the subjection of goods or materials to any process
- a trade in the storage of:
  - goods or materials used for manufacturing purposes, or which are to be subjected to any process
  - finished goods or materials that have been manufactured or subjected to any process.

In addition, the following structures are also industrial buildings:

- Any building or structure provided by the company carrying on one of the above trades for the welfare of its employees, for example, a canteen or workplace nursery.
- A drawing office used for the preparation of plans for manufacturing or processing operations.

Expandable text - Definition of an industrial building

The definition of an industrial building has been developed further by case law.

- Where an IBA claim is made for a building on the grounds that it is used to subject goods to a process the nature of the 'goods' is important:
  - The screening and packing of coal into paper bags was held to be subjecting goods to a process and therefore a qualifying building.
  - On the other hand, a building used for the cremation of human bodies does not qualify (human bodies are not goods). Neither does a building used for packing wages into envelopes (notes and coins are not goods).
- A building for maintaining and repairing hired-out plant does not qualify because the plant is not being subjected to a process.
- A building used for storage of manufactured goods before delivery to a customer qualifies. Where a retailer or wholesaler stores goods, the building does not qualify, as the retailer or wholesaler is the customer to whom the manufacturer has delivered the goods.

Hotels

Provided that a hotel meets all the following four conditions, it is treated as an industrial building:

- The building must be a hotel.
- The hotel must be open for at least four months (120 days) in the season (1 April to 31 October each year).
- When open in the season, the hotel must have at least ten bedrooms that are available for short-term letting to the public (not more than 30 days per letting).
- When open in the season, the services provided for guests must normally include breakfast, evening meal, room cleaning and the making of beds.

Excluded buildings

Buildings specifically excluded from being industrial buildings are:

- dwelling houses
- retail or wholesale premises
- showrooms
- offices.

3 Qualifying cost of construction

- The qualifying cost of an industrial building includes only that expenditure actually incurred in its construction.
- The cost of the land (and the incidental expenses associated with acquiring the land) does not qualify for IBAs.
- As well as the actual cost of constructing the building the following are also qualifying elements of the construction cost:
  - costs in connection with the land that are preliminary to construction do qualify, including:
    (1) the preparation of the site in order to lay foundations
    (2) cutting, tunnelling and levelling the land in connection with the construction.
  - professional fees, notably those of architects, incurred as part of the construction project.
  - capital expenditure on alterations to an existing industrial building.
- Where part of a building is not used for a qualifying purpose and the expenditure on that non-industrial part does not exceed 25% of the total qualifying cost of the whole building, then IBAs will be given on the cost of the whole building.
- If the non-industrial part represents more than 25%, IBAs will only be given on the industrial cost element.
- The total cost of constructing a qualifying building is eligible for IBAs (subject to the rule on non-qualifying parts of a building) if built by or for the trader.
- If the building was acquired after construction (but before use) the eligible cost depends on the type of vendor:
  - When purchased from a builder the eligible expenditure is the purchase price (including the builder's profit margin).
  - For any other vendor the eligible cost is always the lower of the purchase price and the construction expenditure incurred.

Example 1 - Qualifying cost of construction

Harry erected a factory for use in his manufacturing business. The total construction cost of £370,000, was apportioned as follows:

	£
Freehold land	60,000
Cutting and levelling of site	2,000
Construction of building comprising	
Employees' canteen	12,000
General offices	29,000
Factory	267,000
	370,000

Calculate the expenditure qualifying for IBAs.

Answer to example 1

The expenditure qualifying for IBAs is as follows:

	£
Total cost	370,000
Less: Land	(60,000)
Cost of construction of whole building	310,000

The cost of the non-qualifying part of the building (i.e. the offices) of £29,000 does not exceed 25% of the cost of the whole building of £310,000. Therefore, IBAs are available on the cost of the whole building.

If the offices had actually cost say £100,000, then as a proportion of the qualifying cost (£100,000/£310,000) is 32.258% > 25% and hence would be disallowed.

In this situation, the eligible cost would be £210,000.

Test your understanding 1

Harriet acquired a new factory at a cost of £409,300, on 1 January 2006. It was brought into industrial use on the same day. The total cost was made up as follows:

	£
Land	90,000
Levelling the land	10,000
Architects' fees	25,000
Air-conditioning system	19,300
Strengthened concrete floor to support machinery	10,200
General offices	62,500
Factory	192,300
	409,300

(a) **Compute the expenditure qualifying for IBAs.**

(b) **Compute the qualifying expenditure if the offices had cost £82,500 and the total spend remains as above at £409,300.**

4 Calculating industrial buildings allowances for a new building

Writing down allowance (WDA)

The following rules apply:

- WDAs for industrial buildings are given on a straight-line basis on the eligible cost of the qualifying building.
- The rate of WDA for 2008/09 and year ended 31 March 2009 is 3%.
- Prior to 31 March 2008, the WDA was 4% p.a.
- The WDA is proportionately reduced where the period of account is less than 12 months.
- A WDA is given provided the building is in use as an industrial building at the end of the period of account.
- A period of temporary disuse of an industrial building does not affect the allowances given.

Sale of buildings

Where a building is disposed of on or after 21 March 2007 there are no capital allowance implications for the vendor, other than he will cease to claim IBAs in the period of account in which the building is disposed of.

Contrast this with plant and machinery where a balancing charge or allowance may arise on a disposal (see Chapter 6).

The position of buildings disposed of prior to 21 March 2007 is not examinable.

Example 2 - Calculating industrial buildings allowances for a new

Assume the expenditure on industrial buildings was as in the previous illustration, Harry. The factory was completed and paid for on 1 June 2005 and taken into use on 1 August 2005. Harry prepares accounts to 31 March.

On 1 August 2009, the factory was sold for £500,000 (including £100,000 for the land), to Henry.

Compute the IBAs available to Harry for each of the years concerned.

Answer to example 2

Qualifying expenditure incurred (June 2005) = £310,000

	Allowances
Year ended 31 March 2006	£
WDA (4%) on cost (in use 31.3.06)	12,400
Years ended 31 March 2007 and 2008	
WDA (4%) x 2 years	24,800
Year ended 31 March 2009	
WDA (3%) on cost	9,300
Total allowances	46,500

Year ended 31 March 2010

The building was not in use on 31 March 2010 (sold 1 August 2009) and therefore no allowances are available in the year to 31 March 2010.

Test your understanding 2

Henrietta incurred £300,000 on the purchase of a new industrial building on 1 January 2007. It was taken into industrial use on 1 February 2007. Henrietta prepares accounts to 31 March each year.

On 15 August 2009 the building was sold for £424,000 including £109,000 for the land.

Calculate the IBAs available to Henrietta for each of the years concerned.

5 Comprehensive example

Example 3 - Comprehensive example

Chris commenced to trade on 1 January 1992 and prepares his accounts regularly to 31 March each year.

He acquired a new industrial building on 1 September 2003 and brought it into use immediately. The total cost of £112,500, was made up as follows:

	£
Land	12,500
Site clearance	2,500
Foundation	7,500
General office	5,000
Drawing (design) office	2,500
Canteen	3,750
Accounts office	4,500
Other allowable costs	74,250
Total expenditure	112,500

On 1 July 2009 Chris sold the building to Freddy for £130,000.

Compute the IBAs available to Chris for all relevant years to 31 March 2010.

Answer to example 3

Chris

Qualifying expenditure incurred (W1) = £100,000

	Allowances
	£
y/e 31 March 2004 – 31 March 2008	
Building is in industrial use at the end of each of these POA	
WDA (4% x £100,000 x 5 years)	20,000
y/e 31 March 2009	
WDA (3% x £100,000)	3,000
y/e 31 March 2010	
No allowances – building sold 1.7.09	Nil
Total allowances	23,000

Workings: Qualifying cost

		£
Total cost		112,500
Less: Land		(12,500)
Potential qualifying cost		100,000 × 25% = £25,000
General office	£5,000	
Accounts office	£4,500	
Total	£9,500	↓
= Less than £25,000 and therefore allowed		
Qualifying cost		100,000

6 Chapter summary

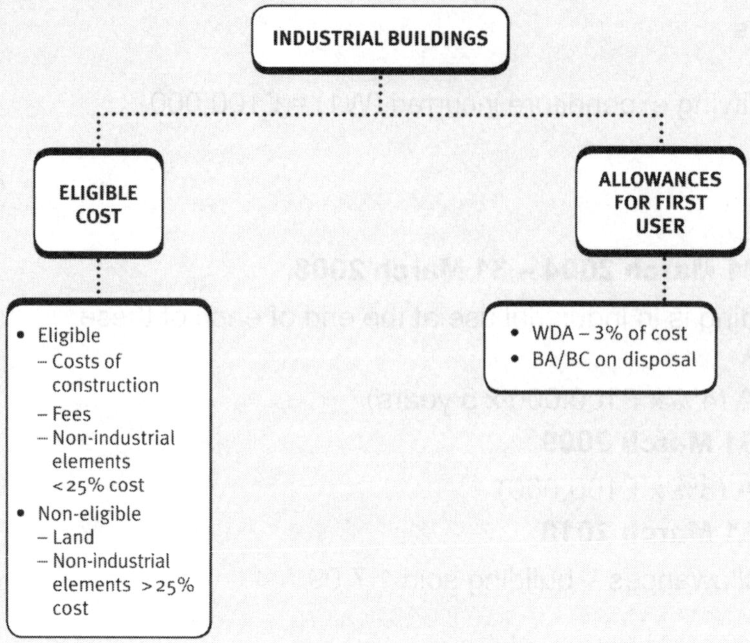

Test your understanding answers

Test your understanding 1

Harriet

(a) Qualifying expenditure

	£
Total cost	409,300
Less: Land	(90,000)
Air-conditioning system	(19,300)
Potential qualifying cost	300,000
£300,000 × 25% = £75,000	
General office £62,500 = less than £75,000	
Therefore qualifying cost	300,000

(b) If offices cost £82,500

General office £82,500 = more than £75,000 therefore not allowed	
Therefore qualifying cost (£300,000 – £82,500)	217,500

Test your understanding 2

Henrietta

Qualifying expenditure incurred (Jan 2007) = £300,000

	Allowances
Year ended 31 March 2007	£
WDA (4%) on cost (in use 31.3.07)	12,000
Year ended 31 March 2008	
WDA (4%) on cost	12,000
Year ended 31 March 2009	
WDA (3%) on cost	9,000
Total allowances	33,000

Year ended 31 March 2010

The building was not in use on 31 March 2010 (sold 15 August 2009) and therefore no allowances are available in the year ended 31 March 2010.

chapter

8

Sole traders: Basis of assessment

Chapter learning objectives

Upon completion of this chapter you will be able to:

- Recognise the basis of assessment for income from self-employment
- Compute the assessable trading profits for a new business
- Compute the assessable trading profits on cessation of a business
- Recognise the factors that will influence the choice of accounting date for a new business
- State the conditions that must be met for a change of accounting date to be valid
- Compute the assessable profits on a change of accounting date

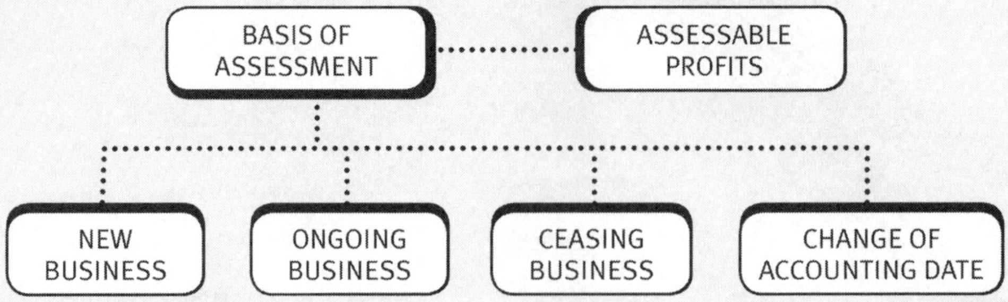

1 Introduction

Once the tax-adjusted trading profit has been calculated for a period of account, it is important to identify in which tax year it will be assessed.

- Income tax is charged for a tax year or year of assessment which runs from 6 April to the following 5 April.
- Since traders do not necessarily prepare their profit and loss accounts to coincide with the tax year, there needs to be a system for attributing profits earned in a period of account to a particular tax year.

The profit-earning (or loss-making) period of account that is attributed to a particular tax year is known as the 'basis period' for that tax year.

- In the examination, where the apportionment of trading profits into different tax years is required, the apportionment should be performed on a monthly basis as shown in all the illustrations below.

2 Ongoing year rules

Basic principles

The basic rule is:

- The profits for a year of assessment are the tax-adjusted trading profits for the 12 months period of account ending in that year.
- This is sometimes referred to as the current year basis of assessment (or CYB for short).

Test your understanding 1

A sole trader prepares his accounts to 31 December each year. He has been operating for several years.

State which profits will be assessed in 2008/09?

Test your understanding 2

Jerry prepares accounts to 30 September annually. His recent taxable trading profits have been as follows:

	£
Year to 30 September 2007	20,000
Year to 30 September 2008	22,000

State in which tax years will these profits be assessed.

3 Opening year rules

Assuming a business starts to trade on 1 January 2008 and prepares accounts for calendar years, the first tax year it is trading is in 2007/08.

However, the first accounting period will not end until 31 December 2008 and using the basic principle above this period will not be taxed until 2008/09.

In order to ensure that there is an assessment for each tax year that a business is trading, the following special provisions apply:

Year 1 The actual profits from commencement of trading to the following 5 April are assessed to tax in that year (known as the **actual basis** of assessment).

Year 2 If there is a 12 month period of account ending in the second tax year, then this is the basis period (CYB). Otherwise apply the following rules:

Period of account	**Basis of assessment**
The period of account ending in the second tax year is: – **LESS than 12 months** after the commencement of trading. – **MORE than 12 months** after the commencement of trading.	First 12 months of trading. Twelve months ended on the new permanent accounting date.
There is **no period of account** ending in the second tax year.	Tax the actual profits arising between 6 April and 5 April (continuing the actual basis applied in first tax year).

Year 3 Assess the 12 months ending with the accounting date in that year.

Example 1 - Opening year rules

Jenny commenced trading on 1 January 2008 and prepared her first set of accounts to 31 December that year.

Her tax-adjusted trading profits were £12,000.

Explain which profits will be assessed in Jenny's first two tax years.

Answer to example 1

Basis of assessment – opening years

First tax year

Using the current year basis approach above, there is not a 12 months accounting period ending in 2007/08, but Jenny has traded in this tax year.

In this situation the profits assessed for 2007/08 will be the actual profits falling in the period on a pro rata basis.

Tax year	Basis period	Calculation	Assessable profits
2007/08	01.01.08 - 05.04.08	(3/12 × £12,000)	£3,000

Second tax year

In the second tax year there is a 12 month period of account ending in the tax year. The current year basis can therefore be applied.

Tax year	Basis period	Assessable profits
2008/09	CYB (y/e 31 December 2008)	£12,000

You will notice that in the two years above, the profits for the period 1 January to 5 April (£3,000) have been assessed twice.

These are referred to as **overlap profits**.

Overlap profits

- Profits that are assessed in more than one tax year are known as the overlap profits.
- Overlap profits arise in every scenario at commencement of trade other than when the trader opts to take a 31 March year-end.
- The overlap profits are carried forward and are normally deducted from the assessment for the period in which the business ceases.
- Whilst this does mean that the trader will get relief for overlap profits, relief may not be obtained for many years if the business continues for a long while.
- Overlap profits may also be relieved when a business changes its accounting date (see section 7).

Test your understanding 3

Rob started to trade on 1 September 2007 and prepared his first accounts for the year ended 31 August 2008. His tax-adjusted trading profits were £18,000.

Calculate his assessable profits for 2007/08 and 2008/09.

Identify the months that have been taxed more than once and the overlap profits arising.

Summary of opening year rules

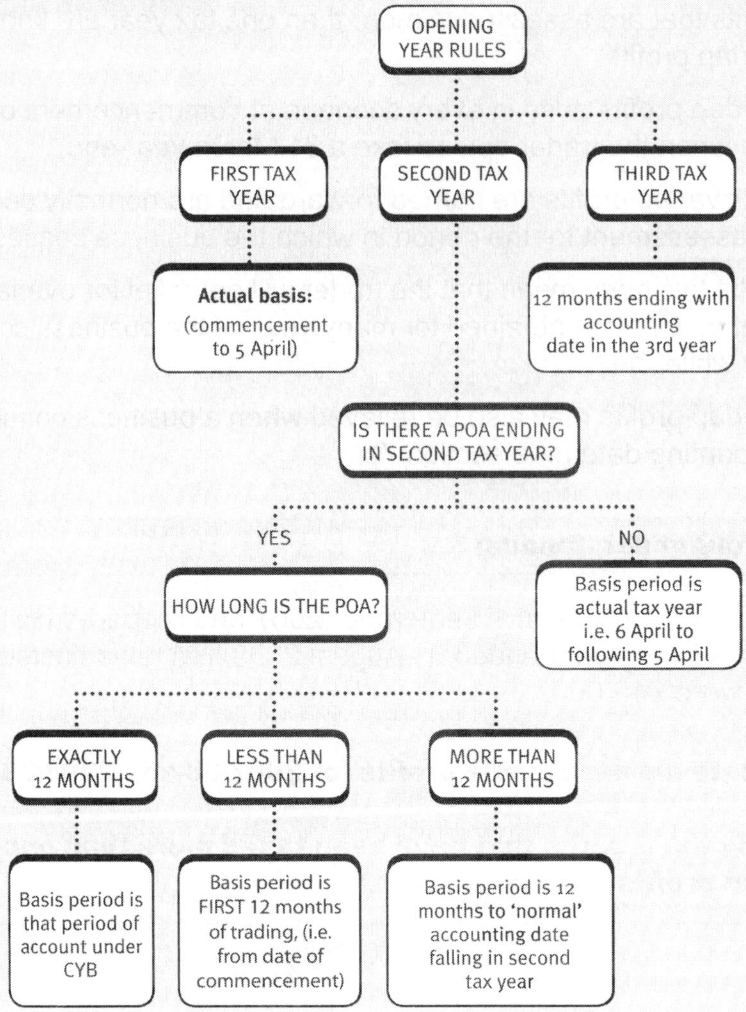

Example 2 - Opening year rules

Arthur commenced trading on 1 May 2006. He prepares accounts to 30 June each year. His tax-adjusted trading profits were as follows:

	£
Period ended 30.6.07	28,000
Year ended 30.6.08	30,000

Calculate Arthur's trading income assessments for his first three tax years and his overlap profits.

Answer to example 2

Tax year	Basis period	Calculation	Assessable profits
			£
2006/07	1.5.06 - 5.4.07:	11/14 x £28,000 (actual basis)	22,000
2007/08	Year to 30.6.07 (Note)	12/14 x £28,000	24,000
2008/09	Y/e 30.6.08 – CYB		30,000

Note: As the period of account ending in 2007/08 is 14 months long, the basis period is the 12 months to the normal accounting date (i.e. 30 June).

The overlap profits are for the period 1 July 2006 to 5 April 2007 (i.e. £28,000 × 9/14 = £18,000).

Test your understanding 4

George commenced trade on 1 October 2005 and decided to prepare accounts to 31 December each year.

His tax-adjusted trading profits are:

	£
Period to 31 December 2006	30,000
Year ended 31 December 2007	36,000
Year ended 31 December 2008	40,000

Calculate the trading profits assessed on George for all relevant years. State the overlap profits arising.

Example 3 - Opening year rules

Pattie commenced trading on 1 September 2006. She prepared accounts to 30 June 2007 and annually thereafter.

Her tax-adjusted trading profits for the first two periods were as follows:

	£
Period ended 30 June 2007	30,000
Year ended 30 June 2008	48,000

Calculate Pattie's trading income assessments for her first three tax years and her overlap profits.

Answer to example 3

Tax year	Basis period	Calculation	Assessable profits
			£
2006/07	1.9.06 - 5.4.07	(£30,000 × 7/10) (actual)	21,000
2007/08	1.9.06 - 31.8.07	(£30,000 + (2/12 × £48,000) (Note)	38,000
2008/09	y/e 30.6.08 – CYB		48,000

Note: Because the accounting date ending in the second year of assessment is less than 12 months after the commencement of trading, the basis of assessment is the first 12 months of trading.

Overlap profits = £29,000: £21,000 (1.9.06 to 5.4.07) and £8,000 (1.7.07 to 31.8.07: 2/12 × £48,000).

Test your understanding 5

Fred commenced a new trade on 1 June 2005 and decided that his normal accounting date would be 30 April each year.

Given below are the tax-adjusted trading profits since commencement:

	£
Period to 30 April 2006	11,000
Year ended 30 April 2007	18,000
Year ended 30 April 2008	22,000

Calculate the trading profits assessable on Fred for all relevant years.

Example 4 - Opening year rules

Cordelia commenced trading on 1 July 2006. She prepared accounts to 30 April 2008 and annually thereafter.

Her tax-adjusted trading profits for the first two periods were as follows:

	£
Period ended 30.04.08	55,000
Year ended 30.04.09	32,000

Calculate Cordelia's trading income assessments for her first three tax years and her overlap profits.

Answer to example 4

Tax year	**Basis period**	**Calculation**	**Assessable profits**
			£
2006/07	(01.07.06 – 05.04.07)	£55,000 × 9/22 (actual)	22,500
2007/08	(06.04.07 – 05.04.08)	£55,000 × 12/22 (Note 1)	30,000
2008/09	(Year to 30.04.08)	£55,000 × 12/22 (Note 2)	30,000
2009/10	Year to 30.04.09	CYB	32,000

Note 1: Because there is no accounting date in the second year of assessment, the basis of assessment is the actual basis for the period from 6.4.07 to 5.4.08.

Note 2: In year three, the basis period is the profits of the 12-months ending with the accounting date in that year.

Overlap profits: £27,500 (01.05.07 to 05.04.08 = 11/22 × £55,000)

Test your understanding 6

Maria commenced business on 1 January 2005 and prepared her first accounts for the period to 30 June 2006, and thereafter to 30 June in each year.

Her tax-adjusted trading profits have been:

	£
Period to 30 June 2006	27,000
Year ended 30 June 2007	30,000
Year ended 30 June 2008	40,000

Calculate the trading profits assessed on Maria for all relevant years. State the overlap profits.

4 Closing year rules

- The objective in the final year of assessment is to ensure that any profits not previously assessed are assessed here.
- Any overlap profits from commencement are deducted from the assessment for the final year.
- The easiest approach to identify the basis period of assessment for the final tax year is:
  - Identify the tax year in which the trade ceases. This is the last year that profits must be assessed.
  - For the immediately preceding tax year, identify the assessment under normal CYB rules.
  - All profits after this period of account will not have been assessed and so fall into the assessment for the final tax year of trade.
  - Remember to deduct overlap profits in this final assessment.

Example 5 - Closing year rules

Michael ceased trading on 31 March 2009. His tax-adjusted trading profits for the final three periods of trading are as follows:

	£
Year ended 30.4.07	40,000
Year ended 30.4.08	42,000
Period ended 31.3.09	38,000

He has unrelieved overlap profits of £27,000.

Calculate Michael's final two trading income assessments.

Answer to example 5

The final year of assessment is 2008/09, the year in which trade ceases.

		£
2007/08	CYB (Year to 30.4.07)	40,000
2008/09	(23 months from 1.5.07 to 31.3.09)	
	(£42,000 + £38,000)	80,000
	Less overlap profits	(27,000)
	Final assessable amount	53,000

Test your understanding 7

Major, who has been trading for many years, decides to cease trading on 31 December 2008. Major regularly prepared accounts to 30 June in each year.

The recent tax-adjusted trading profits have been:

	£
Period to 31 December 2008	6,000
Year ended 30 June 2008	12,000
Year ended 30 June 2007	15,000
Year ended 30 June 2006	20,000
Year ended 30 June 2005	18,000

The overlap profits on commencement were £7,500.

Calculate the trading profits that will be assessed on Major for all tax years affected by the above accounts.

Test your understanding 8

Benny commenced to trade on 1 July 2003 and prepared his first accounts to 31 August 2004 and thereafter to 31 August annually. Benny ceased to trade on 31 December 2008.

Given below are the tax adjusted trading profits for all the relevant periods:

	£
Period ended 31 August 2004	10,500
Year ended 31 August 2005	18,000
Year ended 31 August 2006	22,500
Year ended 31 August 2007	31,500
Year ended 31 August 2008	27,000
Period ended 31 December 2008	8,400
	117,900

Compute the trading profits that will have been assessed on Benny for each tax year.

5 Choice of accounting date

Options available

There are various factors to consider in identifying the accounting date that a business adopts:

- An accounting date of just after, rather than just before, 5 April (such as 30 April) will ensure the maximum interval between earning profits and having to pay the related tax liability.
- However, an accounting date just after 5 April will result in increased overlap profits upon the commencement of trading. Although there is relief for overlap profits, there may be a long delay before relief is obtained.
- Alternatively an accounting date of just before 5 April, such as 31 March, will give the shortest interval between earning profits and having to pay the related tax liability. However, there will be no overlap profits.

6 Change of accounting date – conditions

Provided certain conditions are met, an unincorporated business is allowed to change its accounting date. There may be tax advantages in doing so, or the change may be made for commercial reasons. For example, it may be easier to take stock at certain times of the year.

The detailed conditions and consequences of failing to meet the conditions are covered in expandable text.

Expandable text - Conditions to be met for a valid change

A change in accounting date will only be valid if the following conditions are met:

- The change of accounting date must be notified to HMRC on or before 31 January following the tax year in which the change is to be made.
- The first accounts to the new accounting date must not exceed 18 months in length.
- If the period between the old accounting date and the proposed new accounting date is longer than 18 months, then two sets of accounts will have to be prepared.
- There must not have been another change of accounting date during the previous five tax years. This condition may be ignored if HMRC accept that the present change is made for genuine commercial reasons.

Failure to meet the conditions

If the conditions are not met, the old accounting date will continue to apply. If accounts are prepared to the new accounting date, then the figures will have to be apportioned accordingly.

7 Change of accounting date – calculations

Calculation of assessable profits

If the conditions are met, then the period of account for the tax year in which the change of accounting date is made, will either be less than or more than 12 months in length.

Change of accounting date – calculations

A trader has previously prepared accounts to 30 June. If he changes his accounting date to 30 September, the next set of accounts are going to be for either 3 or 15 months.

However, all basis of assessments other than for the first and final tax years must be of 12 months in duration.

As the latest period of account will not be, the assessment will either be made up to 12 months, by creating further overlap profits, or reduced back to 12 months by relieving earlier overlap profits.

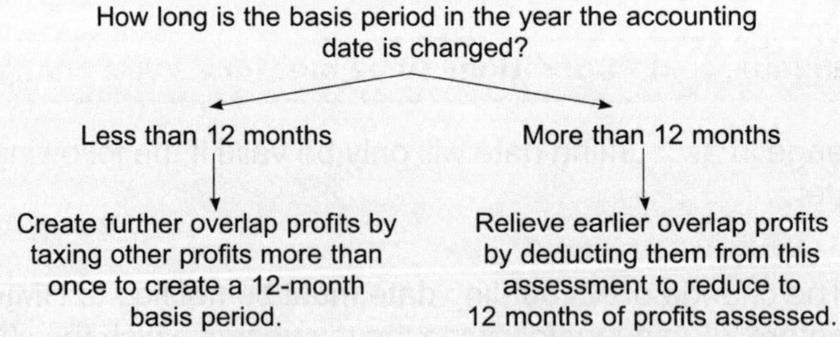

Expandable Text - New date is earlier in the tax year

Where the new accounting date is earlier in the tax year than the old one, the basis period for the tax year of change will be the **12 month period ending with the new accounting date**.

This will result in some profits being assessed more than once. Overlap profits will therefore arise, which are treated in exactly the same way as overlap profits arising on the commencement of trade.

Example 6 - New date earlier - short period

Andrea, a sole trader, has always prepared her accounts to 31 March. She decides to change her accounting date to 30 June by preparing accounts for the three-month period to 30 June 2008.

Andrea's tax-adjusted trading profits are as follows:

	£
Year ended 31 March 2008	60,000
Three months to 30 June 2008	20,000
Year ended 30 June 2009	85,000

Calculate Andrea's trading income assessments for 2007/08 to 2009/10.

Answer to example 6

Note that the new accounting date (June) is earlier in the tax year than the previous accounting date (March).

The tax year of change is the year in which accounts to the new accounting date are prepared. The basis period for the tax year of change is the 12 months to the new accounting date.

The trading profits assessable will be as follows:

Tax year	**Basis period**	**Assessable profits**
		£
2007/08	Year to 31.3.08 – Normal CYB	60,000
2008/09	12-month period to new accounting date of 30.6.08	
	Year to 31.3.08: (£60,000 × 9/12)	45,000
	Period to 30.6.08	20,000
		65,000
2009/10	Year to 30.6.09 (CYB)	85,000

Note: The change in accounting date has created further overlap profits of £45,000, as the 9 months to March 2008 are assessed in both 2007/08 and 2008/09. The overlap profits will be offset in the final year of assessment.

As well as moving to an earlier date in the tax year with a short accounting period, it is possible to do this with a long accounting period.

Example 7 - New date earlier - long period

If Andrea had instead prepared accounts for the 15-month period to 30 June 2009, then the result would have been virtually the same. Assume the tax adjusted profit for the 15-month period ended 30 June 2009 is £105,000.

Calculate Andrea's trading income assessments for 2007/08 to 2009/10.

Answer to example 7

The tax year in which the change takes place is still 2008/09 as Andrea does not adopt her normal 31 March year-end here.

Because all the criteria are met, she is allowed to adopt the new accounting date in this year, preparing accounts for the 12 months to the new accounting date – 30 June.

Tax year	**Basis period**	**Assessable profits**
		£
2007/08	Year to 31.3.08	60,000
2008/09	12-month period to new accounting date of 30.6.08	
	Year to 31.3.08: (£60,000 × 9/12)	45,000
	Period to 30.6.09: (£105,000 × 3/15)	21,000
		66,000
2009/10	Year to 30.6.09: (£105,000 × 12/15)	84,000

Overlap profits still arise in respect of the nine months to 31 March 2008, as before = £45,000.

Expandable Text - New date is later in the tax year

Where the new accounting date is later in the tax year than the old one the basis period for the tax year of change will be the period ending with the new accounting date.

As the resulting basis period may be more than 12 months, a corresponding proportion of any overlap profits that arose upon the commencement of trading are offset against the assessable profits.

Again, it is possible to have either a short accounting period creating the new date, or a long period.

Example 8 - New date later - long period

Peter, a sole trader, commenced trading on 1 July 2005, and has always prepared his accounts to 30 June. He has now decided to change his accounting date to 30 September by preparing accounts for the 15-month period to 30 September 2008.

Peter's tax-adjusted trading profits are as follows:

	£
Year ended 30 June 2006	18,000
Year ended 30 June 2007	24,000
Period ended 30 September 2008	30,000
Year ended 30 September 2009	36,000

Calculate Peter's trading income assessments for 2005/06 to 2009/10.

Answer to example 8

The tax year of change is the tax year in which accounts are prepared to the new accounting date (i.e. 2008/09). As the new accounting date is later in the tax year, the basis period is the period ending with the new accounting date.

The trading income assessments will be as follows:

Tax year	Basis period	Assessable profits
		£
2005/06	1.7.05 to 5.4.06: Actual (£18,000 × 9/12)	13,500
2006/07	Year to 30.6.06: CYB	18,000
2007/08	Year to 30.6.07: CYB	24,000
2008/09	15 months period to 30.9.08	30,000
	Less: Overlap profits (£13,500 × 3/9)	(4,500)
		25,500
2009/10	Year to 30.9.09: CYB	36,000

The overlap profits on commencement of trade are £13,500, representing the 9 months (1.7.05 to 5.4.06) that have been taxed twice.

In 2008/09 the period of account is 15 months. No assessment can be for more than 12 months and in this case, Peter is allowed to offset three months' worth of his overlap profits.

The remaining 6 months of overlap profits are carried forward as normal and available for relief, either on a further change in accounting date, or on the cessation of trade.

8 Chapter summary

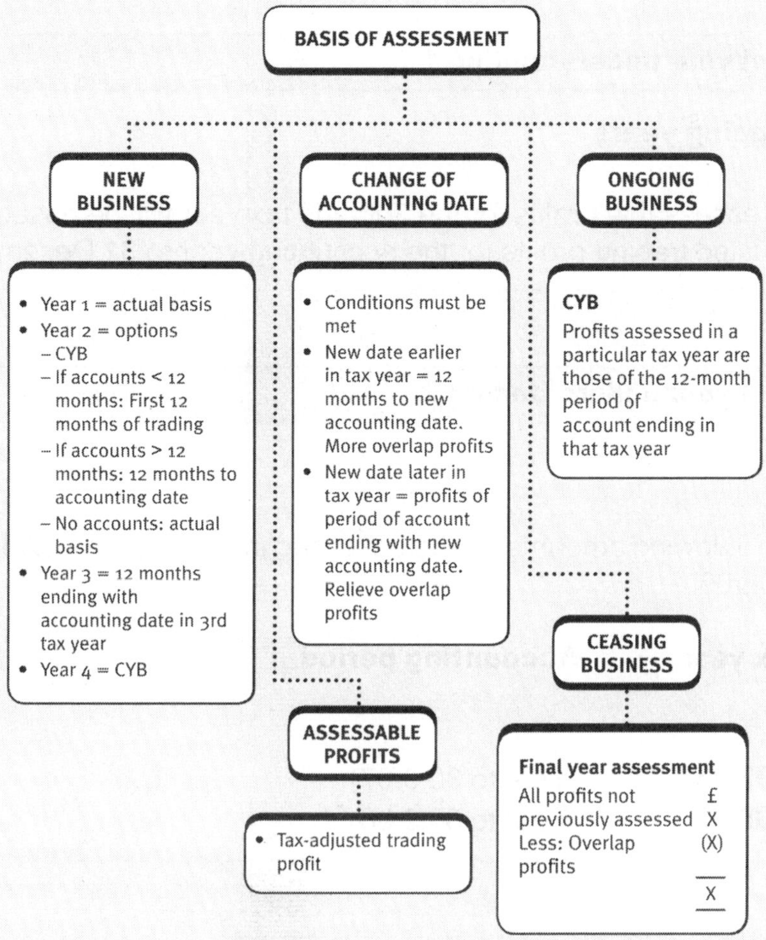

Test your understanding answers

Test your understanding 1

Ongoing years

His assessable profits for the 2008/09 tax year will be based on the tax-adjusted trading profits for the accounting year to 31 December 2008.

Test your understanding 2

Jerry

The following amounts will be assessed in the tax years 2007/08 and 2008/09:

Tax year	Accounting period	Assessable profits
		£
2007/08	(Year to 30.9.07)	20,000
2008/09	(Year to 30.9.08)	22,000

Test your understanding 3

Rob

Tax year	Basis period	Calculation	Assessable profits
			£
2007/08	01.09.07 – 05.04.08	(7/12 × 18,000)	10,500
2008/09	CYB (y/e 31 August 2008)		18,000

The profits between 1 September 2007 and 5 April 2008 (7 months) are taxed in both tax years.

Overlap profits are therefore £10,500 (7/12 × £18,000).

Test your understanding 4

George

Tax year	Basis period	Assessable profits £
2005/06 (actual basis)	01/10/05 to 05/04/06 6/15 × £30,000	12,000
2006/07 (12 months ending on the accounting date)	01/01/06 to 31/12/06 12/15 × £30,000	24,000
2007/08 (CYB)	y/e 31/12/07	36,000
2008/09 (CYB)	y/e 31/12/08	40,000

Overlap profits: £6,000, i.e. 1/1/06 to 5/4/06 (3/15 × £30,000)

Test your understanding 5

Fred

Tax year	Basis period	Assessable profits £
2005/06 (Actual basis)	01/06/05 to 05/04/06 10/11 × £11,000	10,000
2006/07 (First 12 months)	01/06/05 to 31/05/06 £11,000 + (1/12 × £18,000)	12,500
2007/08 (CYB)	y/e 30/04/07	18,000
2008/09 (CYB)	y/e 30/04/08	22,000

As the period of account ending in the second year is less than 12 months long, the basis period is the first 12 months of trading.

Overlap profits = £11,500, i.e. 01/06/05 to 05/04/06 (£10,000) and 01/05/06 to 31/05/06 (1/12 × £18,000).

Test your understanding 6

Maria

Tax year	**Basis period**	**Assessable profits** £
2004/05 (Actual basis)	01/01/05 to 05/04/05	
	3/18 × £27,000	4,500
2005/06 (Actual basis)	06/04/05 to 05/04/06	
	12/18 × £27,000 **(Note)**	18,000
2006/07 12m to the	01/07/05 to 30/06/06	
accounting date	12/18 × £27,000	18,000
2007/08 (CYB)	y/e 30/06/07	30,000
2008/09 (CYB)	y/e 30/06/08	40,000

Note: There is no period of account ending in the second year. The profits are therefore assessed on the actual basis.

Test your understanding 7

Major

Tax year	**Basis period**	**Assessable profits** £
2005/06 (CYB)	y/e 30/06/05	18,000
2006/07 (CYB)	y/e 30/06/06	20,000
2007/08 (CYB)	y/e 30/06/07	15,000
2008/09	01/07/07 to 31/12/08	
	(£12,000 + £6,000 – £7,500)	10,500

The final year of assessment is 2008/09, the year in which trade ceases.

Test your understanding 8

Benny

Tax year	**Basis period**	**Assessable profits**
		£
2003/04 (Actual basis)	01/07/03 to 05/04/04	
	(9/14 × £10,500)	6,750
2004/05 (12 months to	01/09/03 to 31/08/04	
accounting date)	(12/14 × £10,500)	9,000
2005/06 (CYB)	y/e 31/08/05	18,000
2006/07 (CYB)	y/e 31/08/06	22,500
2007/08 (CYB)	y/e 31/08/07	31,500
2008/09	01/09/07 to 31/12/08	
	(£27,000 + £8,400 – £5,250)	30,150
		117,900

Overlap profits: 01/09/03 to 05/04/04 = 7/14 × £10,500 = £5,250

Note that over the life of the business the total profits of £117,900 have been assessed to tax.

chapter

9

Partnerships

Chapter learning objectives

Upon completion of this chapter you will be able to:

- explain how a partnership is assessed to tax
- show the allocation of profits/losses between partners for the period of account
- show the allocation of profits/losses between partners for the period of account following a change in the profit-sharing ratio
- calculate the assessable profit for ongoing/new and ceasing partners.

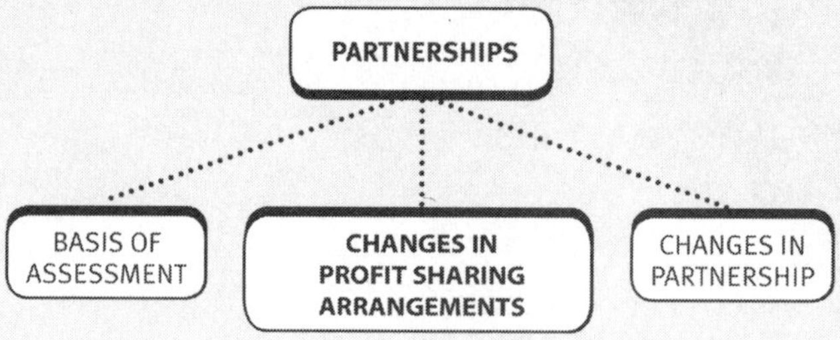

1 Introduction

Definition

- A partnership is a body of persons carrying on business together with a view to profit (Partnership Act 1890).

Basis of assessment

- Each partner is taxed individually, despite the partnership being a single trading entity.
- Each partner is assessed on his share of the partnership profits as if he were a sole trader.
- To determine a partner's assessable profits:
  - firstly, the trading profits per the partnership accounts are adjusted for tax purposes as for a sole trader (see Chapter 5).
  - secondly, the tax-adjusted trading profits of the partnership are allocated to the individual partners.
  - finally, apply the basis of assessment rules to determine the partner's assessable profits in a tax year (see Chapter 8).

2 The allocation of profits and losses

The computation of partnership profits and losses

- The principles of computation of a partnership's total tax-adjusted trading profits for a period of account are the same as those for a sole trader.
- Partners' salaries and interest on capital are not deductible expenses, since these are an allocation of profit.

The allocation of the profit or loss

- The tax-adjusted trading profit or loss is allocated (divided) between the partners according to their profit-sharing arrangements for that period of account.
- Partners may be entitled to salaries (a fixed allocation of profit) and interest on capital. The balance of profits will be allocated in the profit-sharing ratio (PSR).
- Whether it is described as salary, interest on capital or profit share, the total allocated to a partner is assessable as trading income.

Example 1 - The allocation of profits and losses

Dan and Phil have been in partnership for a number of years. The partnership agreement provides that each should take a salary of £25,000, 5% interest on capital balances at the start of the accounting period and then split the profit remaining 60:40 in Phil's favour.

Calculate the trading income assessable for each partner for 2008/09, if the tax-adjusted trading profits for the year ended 30 September 2008, were £74,000.

Their respective capital balances at 1 October 2007, were

Phil	£75,000
Dan	£60,000

Answer to example 1

Allocation of partnership profits

Year ended 30 September 2008	**Total**	**Phil**	**Dan**
	£	£	£
Salary	50,000	25,000	25,000
Interest on capital (£75/60k × 5%)	6,750	3,750	3,000
	56,750	28,750	28,000
Balance (£74,000 – £56,750) (60:40)	17,250	10,350	6,900
Total allocation	74,000	39,100	34,900

Trading income assessment – 2008/09
(CYB = Year ended 30 September 2008)

Phil	£39,100
Dan	£34,900

Test your understanding 1

Paul and Art have been in partnership for many years preparing accounts to 31 December each year.

The partnership agreement provides Paul with a salary of £3,000 and Art is entitled to 15% interest on his capital balance at the start of the period. His capital balance was £27,000 on 1 January 2008. Paul and Art agreed to split any remaining profits equally.

Calculate Paul and Art's share of profits, if in the year ended 31 December 2008, the trading profits as adjusted for tax were £30,000.

Expandable text - Partnership capital allowances

Capital allowances are calculated in the same way as for a sole trader:

- Capital allowances are deducted as an expense in calculating the tax-adjusted trading profit or loss of the partnership. The profit allocated between the partners is therefore after deducting capital allowances.
- Individual partners cannot claim capital allowances on their own behalf.
- If assets are owned privately (such as motor cars), then the business proportion of such assets must be included in the partnership's capital allowances computation. The total capital allowances are then deducted as an expense.

3 Changes in profit-sharing ratio

The profit-sharing ratio may change for a number of reasons:

- The existing partners decide to allocate profits in a different way. This may be as a result of a change in duties, seniority or simply by agreement of the parties concerned.
- The membership of a partnership may change as the result of the admission, death or retirement of a partner.
- Provided that there is at least one partner common to the business before and after the change, the partnership will automatically continue.
- Where there is a change in membership, the commencement or cessation basis of assessment rules will apply to the individual partner who is joining or leaving the partnership only.

4 The effect of a change in the profit-sharing ratio

- If a partnership changes its basis of profit-sharing during a period of account, then the accounting period is split, with a different allocation of profits in the different parts.

Example 2 - The effect of a change in the profit-sharing ratio

David and Peter are in partnership. Their tax-adjusted trading profit for the year ended 30 September 2008, was £16,500.

Up to 30 June 2008, profits were shared between David and Peter 3:2, after paying annual salaries of £3,000 and £2,000 respectively.

From 1 July 2008, profits are shared 2:1 after paying annual salaries of £6,000 and £4,000.

Show the trading income assessments for David and Peter for 2008/09.

Answer to example 2

The partnership profits for year ended 30 September 2008 will be allocated as follows:

	Total	David	Peter
	£	£	£
1.10.07 to 30.6.08			
(Profits £16,500 × 9/12 = £12,375)			
Salaries (9/12)	3,750	2,250	1,500
Balance (3:2)	8,625	5,175	3,450
	12,375	7,425	4,950
1.7.08 to 30.9.08			
(Profits £16,500 × 3/12 = £4,125)			
Salaries (3/12)	2,500	1,500	1,000
Balance (2:1)	1,625	1,083	542
	4,125	2,583	1,542
Total allocation	16,500	10,008	6,492

Trading income assessments – 2008/09
(CYB = Year ended 30 September 2008):

David	£10,008
Peter	£6,492

Test your understanding 2

John and Major have been in partnership for many years preparing accounts to 31 December.

Their profit-sharing arrangement provides for salaries of £4,500 and £3,000 pa and the balance in the ratio of 3:2 respectively.

From 1 July 2008, John will receive a salary of £9,000 pa and Major a salary of £6,000 pa, with the balance in the ratio 2:1 in John's favour. Their recent tax-adjusted trading profits for the accounting year ended 31 December 2008, are £24,800.

Show the division of profits for the relevant period of account and the trading income assessment to be raised on each partner for 2008/09.

5 Commencement and cessation

Changes in membership

The normal opening year and closing year basis of assessment rules apply upon commencement and cessation of a partnership.

- A change in the membership of the partnership will normally affect only the partner joining or leaving.

Commencement

The normal commencement rules apply for the partner being admitted to the partnership.

The steps taken are:

- Identify the start date of the new partner.
- Allocate the profits between the old and new partner(s):
  - If the new start date is part way through the period of account, the allocation of profits will need to be split between the two periods concerned.
  - If the new partner joins at the start of a new period of account, profits in the period will be allocated throughout using the new PSR.
- Determine the assessable trading profits for the tax year.
  - For those partners common to the old and new partnerships, there will be no change in the method of calculating their assessable trading income and the normal CYB approach applies.
  - For the partner joining, they must apply the opening year rules, as for the sole trader in Chapter 8. A partner will be treated as commencing when he or she joins the partnership.
  - Each partner has his or her own overlap profits, available for overlap relief.

Example 3 - Commencement and cessation

Alex, Arsene and Jose have been in partnership for a number of years. Their recent results have been as follows:

	£
Year ended 30 September 2007	103,500
Year ended 30 September 2008	128,000

The relationship is often fractious and there have been a number of disputes over the years. In an attempt to improve the dynamics, on 1 January 2008, Rafa was admitted to the partnership.

Profits had been shared equally, after allocating salaries and interest on capital, prior to the admission of Rafa.

Partner	**Salary**	**Capital balance**	**Rate of interest on capital**
	£	£	
Alex	15,000	100,000	5%
Arsene	12,000	80,000	5%
Jose	10,000	40,000	5%

Rafa's admission changed the profit-sharing arrangements as follows:

Partner	**Salary**	**Capital balance**	**Rate of interest on capital**	**Profit share**
	£	£		
Alex	20,000	100,000	5%	35%
Arsene	18,000	80,000	5%	30%
Jose	15,000	40,000	5%	25%
Rafa	10,000	Nil	n/a	10%

The projected result for year ended 30 September 2009, is a profit of £140,000.

Calculate the assessable trading income for each of the partners from 2007/08 to 2009/10.

Answer to example 3

Alex, Arsene, Jose and Rafa

Step 1: Allocate the tax-adjusted trading profits for each accounting period between the partners

Profits will be allocated between the partners as follows:

	Total	**Alex**	**Arsene**	**Jose**	**Rafa**
	£	£	£	£	£
Y/e 30.9.07					
Salary	37,000	15,000	12,000	10,000	
Interest at 5% on capital	11,000	5,000	4,000	2,000	
PSR	55,500	18,500	18,500	18,500	
Total	103,500	38,500	34,500	30,500	
Y/e 30.9.08					
1.10.07–31.12.07					
£128,000 × 3/12 = £32,000					
Salary (3/12)	9,250	3,750	3,000	2,500	
Interest at 5% (× 3/12)	2,750	1,250	1,000	500	
PSR	20,000	6,667	6,667	6,666	
	32,000	11,667	10,667	9,666	
1.1.08–30.9.08					
£128,000 × 9/12 = £96,000					
Salary (9/12)	47,250	15,000	13,500	11,250	7,500
Interest at 5% (× 9/12)	8,250	3,750	3,000	1,500	Nil
PSR (35:30:25:10)	40,500	14,175	12,150	10,125	4,050
	96,000	32,925	28,650	22,875	11,550
Total	128,000	44,592	39,317	32,541	11,550

	Total	Alex	Arsene	Jose	Rafa
	£	£	£	£	£
Y/e 30.9.09					
Salary	63,000	20,000	18,000	15,000	10,000
Interest at 5% on capital	11,000	5,000	4,000	2,000	Nil
PSR (35:30:25:10)	66,000	23,100	19,800	16,500	6,600
Total	140,000	48,100	41,800	33,500	16,600

Step 2: Compute each partner's assessable trading profits, as though they were a sole trader.

Each of Alex, Arsene and Jose will be assessed on a current year basis for each tax year.

	Alex	Arsene	Jose
	£	£	£
2007/08	38,500	34,500	30,500
2008/09	44,592	39,317	32,541
2009/10	48,100	41,800	33,500

Rafa will be treated as commencing on 1 January 2008, and will be assessed on his share of the partnership profits as follows:

Tax year	Basis period	Assessable profits
		£
2007/08	1 January 2008 to 5 April 2008 (£11,550 × 3/9)	3,850
2008/09	First 12 months (£11,550 + ((£16,600 × 3/12))	15,700
2009/10	Year ended 30 September 2009	16,600

He will carry forward overlap profits of £8,000 (£3,850 + 4,150).

Note: This question tests knowledge of a wide range of issues in relation to partnerships. It is unlikely that such a wide range of issues would be tested in a single question in the examination.

Test your understanding 3

Able and Bertie have been in partnership since 1 July 2006 preparing their accounts to 30 June each year. On 1 July 2008, Carol joins the partnership.

The partnership's tax-adjusted trading profits are as follows:

	£
Year ended 30 June 2007	10,000
Year ended 30 June 2008	13,500
Year ended 30 June 2009	18,000

Profits are shared equally.

Show the amounts assessed on the individual partners for 2006/07 to 2009/10.

Cessation

As for commencement, the normal rules for a sole trader are applied to a partner leaving a partnership.

The steps taken are:

- Identify the partner ceasing to be a member.
- Allocate the profits, remembering that if this is part-way through the period of account it will affect the profit-sharing ratio for that period of account and this will need to be calculated in two parts.
- For the partners continuing, use the normal CYB method of assessment.
- For the partner ceasing, use the closing year rules and deduct any overlap profits they have available.

Example 4 - Commencement and cessation

Ball, Sphere, Globe and Bauble have been in partnership for a number of years, drawing up accounts to 30 September each year. The profit sharing arrangements have been as follows:

Partner	Annual salary	Capital balance	Rate of interest on capital	Profitshare
	£	£		
Ball	20,000	100,000	5%	35%
Sphere	18,000	80,000	5%	30%
Globe	15,000	40,000	5%	25%
Bauble	10,000	Nil	n.a.	10%

Ball has decided to resign as a partner at the end of March 2010.

The existing salary and interest arrangements will remain in place, but the balance of the profit will then be split equally between the three remaining partners.

Profits for the year end 30 September 2009 and 2010 are expected to be £180,000 and £210,000 respectively.

Calculate the assessable trading profits of each partner for 2009/10 and 2010/11. Ball informs you he had £15,000 of overlap profits from commencement.

Answer to example 4

Ball, Sphere, Globe and Bauble

Profits for year end 30 September 2009 and 2010, are expected to be £180,000 and £210,000 respectively.

	Total	Ball	Sphere	Globe	Bauble
	£	£	£	£	£
Y/e 30.9.09					
Salary	63,000	20,000	18,000	15,000	10,000
Interest at 5% on capital	11,000	5,000	4,000	2,000	Nil
PSR (35:30:25:10)	106,000	37,100	31,800	26,500	10,600
Total	180,000	62,100	53,800	43,500	20,600

	Total	Ball	Sphere	Globe	Bauble
	£	£	£	£	£
Y/e 30.9.10					
1.10.09 – 31.3.10					
£210,000 × 6/12 = £105,000					
Salary (6/12)	31,500	10,000	9,000	7,500	5,000
Interest at 5% (× 6/12)	5,500	2,500	2,000	1,000	Nil
PSR (35:30:25:10)	68,000	23,800	20,400	17,000	6,800
	105,000	36,300	31,400	25,500	11,800
1.4.10 – 30.9.10					
£210,000 × 6/12 = £105,000					
Salary (6/12)	21,500	Nil	9,000	7,500	5,000
Interest at 5% (6/12)	3,000	Nil	2,000	1,000	Nil
PSR (1:1:1)	80,500	Nil	26,834	26,833	26,833
	105,000	Nil	37,834	35,333	31,833
Total	210,000	36,300	69,234	60,833	43,633

Sphere, Globe and Bauble will continue to be assessed on the current year basis:

	Sphere	Globe	Bauble
	£	£	£
2009/10	53,800	43,500	20,600
2010/11	69,234	60,833	43,633

Ball will be treated as ceasing to trade on 31 March 2010, his share of the partnership profits will be as follows:

Tax year	Basis period	Assessable profits
		£
2009/10	Year ended 30 September 2009	62,100
	Period ended 31 March 2010	36,300
		98,400
	Less: Overlap relief	(15,000)
	Assessable trading income	83,400

Test your understanding 4

Continuing the TYU3 above with Able, Bertie and Carol.

After suffering a period of ill health, Bertie plans to retire on 31 December 2009.

Profits for year ended 30 June 2010, are expected to be £24,000.

The profit-sharing ratio will remain unchanged until Bertie retires. Thereafter it will be split 65:35 in Able's favour.

Calculate Bertie's assessable trading income for 2009/10 and Able and Carol's assessable trading income for 2010/11.

6 Chapter summary

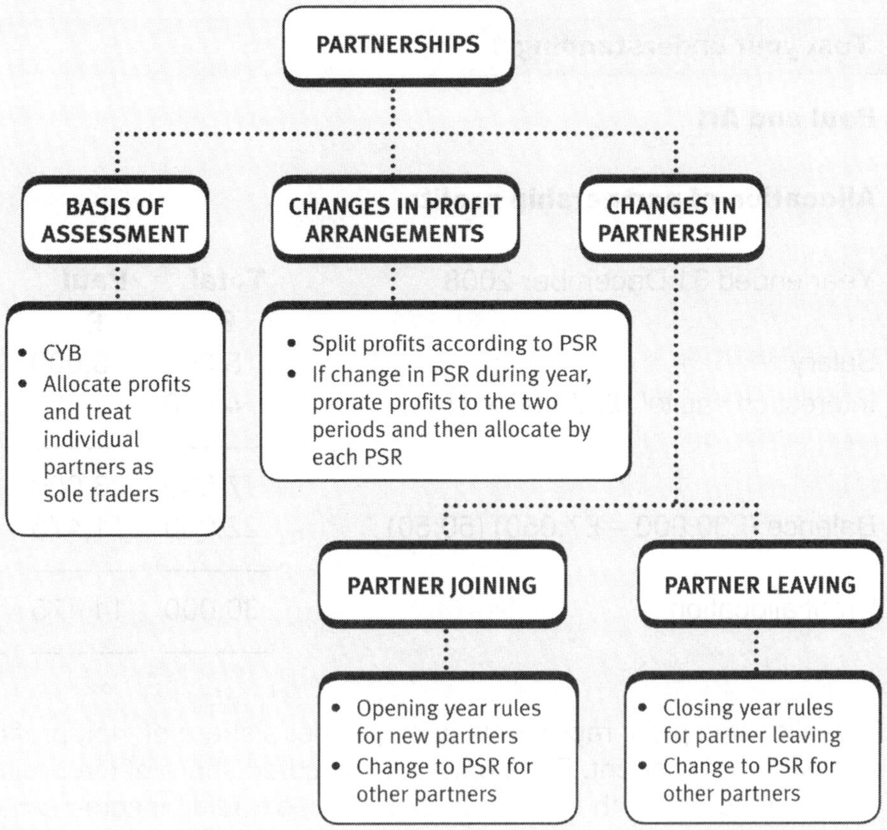

Test your understanding answers

Test your understanding 1

Paul and Art

Allocation of partnership profits

Year ended 31 December 2008	**Total**	**Paul**	**Art**
	£	£	£
Salary	3,000	3,000	
Interest on capital (£27,000 × 15%)	4,050		4,050
	7,050	3,000	4,050
Balance (£30,000 – £7,050) (50:50)	22,950	11,475	11,475
Profit allocation	30,000	14,475	15,525

The allocated profit represents each partner's share of their profits for this period of account. Each partner's allocated share of the profit is then assessed to tax on the individual partners as trading income using the basis of assessment rules for a sole trader.

Trading income assessment for 2008/09
(CYB, Year ended 31 December 2008)

Paul	£14,475
Art	£15,525

Test your understanding 2

John and Major

Allocation of partnership profits

The partnership profits for year ended 31 December 2008, will be allocated as follows:

	Total	John	Major
	£	£	£
1.1.08 to 30.6.08			
(Profits £24,800 × 6/12 = £12,400)			
Salaries (6/12)	3,750	2,250	1,500
Balance (3:2)	8,650	5,190	3,460
	12,400	7,440	4,960
1.7.08 to 31.12.08			
(Profits £24,800 × 6/12 = £12,400)			
Salaries (6/12)	7,500	4,500	3,000
Balance (2:1)	4,900	3,267	1,633
	12,400	7,767	4,633
Total allocation	24,800	15,207	9,593

Trading income assessments for 2008/09 (CYB Year ended 31 December 2008):

John	£15,207
Major	£9,593

Test your understanding 3

Able and Bert

Step 1: Allocate the tax-adjusted trading profits for accounting periods between the partners.

Profits will be allocated between the partners as follows:

	Total	Able	Bertie	Carol
	£	£	£	£
Y/e 30.6.07	10,000	5,000	5,000	
Y/e 30.6.08	13,500	6,750	6,750	
Y/e 30.6.09	18,000	6,000	6,000	6,000

Step 2: Compute each partner's assessable trading profits, as though they were a sole trader.

Able and Bertie will both be assessed as follows, based upon a commencement on 1 July 2006:

Tax year	Basis period		Assessable profits
			£
2006/07	1 July 2006 to 5 April 2007	(£5,000 × 9/12)	3,750
2007/08	Year ended 30 June 2007		5,000
2008/09	Year ended 30 June 2008		6,750
2009/10	Year ended 30 June 2009		6,000

They will each carry forward overlap profits of £3,750 in respect of the period 1 July 2006 to 5 April 2007.

Carol will be treated as commencing on 1 July 2008, and will be assessed on her share of the partnership profits as follows:

Tax year	Basis period		Assessable profits
			£
2008/09	1 July 2008 to 5 April 2009	(£6,000 × 9/12)	4,500
2009/10	Year ended 30 June 2009		6,000

She will carry forward overlap profits of £4,500 in respect of the period 1 July 2008 to 5 April 2009.

Test your understanding 4

Able, Bertie and Carol

Profits will be allocated between the partners as follows:

	Total	Able	Bertie	Carol
Y/e 30 June 2010	£	£	£	£
1.7.09 – 31.12.09				
£24,000 × 6/12 (1/3:1/3:1/3)	12,000	4,000	4,000	4,000
1.1.10 – 30.6.10				
£24,000 × 6/12 (65:35)	12,000	7,800	–	4,200
Total	24,000	11,800	4,000	8,200

Able and Carol will both be assessed on the current year basis:

Tax year	Basis period	Able	Carol
		£	£
2010/11	Year ended 30 June 2010	11,800	8,200

Bertie will be treated as ceasing to trade on 31 December 2009. His final tax year of trade is 2009/10.

Tax year	Basis period	Assessable profits
		£
2009/10	Year ended 30 June 2009	6,000
	Period ended 31 December 2009	4,000
		10,000
	Less: Overlap relief	(3,750)
	Assessable trading income	6,250

chapter

10

Trading losses for individuals

Chapter learning objectives

Upon completion of this chapter you will be able to:

- understand how to calculate a trading loss for a tax year
- explain how trading losses can be carried forward for an ongoing business
- demonstrate when a trading loss can be used against total income and capital gains
- explain how a trading loss can be relieved in the early years of a trade
- calculate a terminal loss
- explain how a terminal loss can be relieved
- demonstrate the optimum use of trading loss reliefs
- describe the alternative loss relief claims that are available to partners
- explain the loss relief restriction to the partners of a limited liability partnership
- identify the circumstances when trading losses can be carried forward and used on the incorporation of a business.

1 Introduction

Identifying a trading loss

- A trading loss arises when:
  - the accounting profit or loss as adjusted for tax purposes is negative
  - the result for a period of account is a loss and therefore the assessable profit for that period will be £nil.
- In the tax year in which a loss arises the figure entered in the income tax computation for trading income is £nil. The losses are available for relief in a number of ways as set out below.

Although you are not required to learn the section numbers of the legislation for your examination, loss reliefs are often referred to by their section number.

- The section numbers are from the Income Tax Act (ITA) 2007.

Key reliefs

The main reliefs available for a trading loss, as explained in the following sections, are as follows:

s83 ITA 2007 – carry forward against future trading profits.

s64 ITA 2007 – relief against total income.

s72 ITA 2007 – opening year loss relief against total income.

s89 ITA 2007 – terminal loss relief against previous trading profits.

2 Carry forward of trading losses (s83 ITA 2007)

Principles of the relief

This is the simplest form of loss relief available to the taxpayer. The key rules are as follows:

- It is possible to choose to carry forward a trading loss.
- The carried forward loss must be set against the **first available** profit arising from the **same trade**.
- If carried forward, it is mandatory to set off as much as possible of the loss, no claim can be made on a partial basis.
- If the subsequent profits are not high enough to use all the loss, the loss is firstly used to reduce the trading profits to nil, with the remainder carried forward against future trading profits and set off in the same way until the loss is fully extinguished.
- This carrying forward of the loss is automatic. However, a claim must be made to establish the amount of the loss to be carried forward within 5 years of 31 January following the end of the tax year in which the loss arose. For 2008/09 loss, the claim must be made by 31 January 2015.

When dealing with loss questions it is useful to adopt a columnar layout, presenting each year in a separate column. In addition keep a separate working to show when, and how much of, the loss has been used up.

Example 1 - Carry forward of trading losses (s83 ITA 2007)

Edward has had the following recent tax-adjusted trading results:

		£
Year to 31 December 2006	Loss	(5,000)
Year to 31 December 2007	Profit	3,000
Year to 31 December 2008	Profit	10,000

Assuming that Edward wishes to carry the loss forward under s83 ITA 2007, calculate his assessable trading profits for 2006/07 to 2008/09 inclusive.

Answer to example 1

	2006/07	2007/08	2008/09
	£	£	£
Trading income	Nil	3,000	10,000
Less: s83 relief **(Working)**	Nil	(3,000)	(2,000)
Assessable trading income	Nil	Nil	8,000

Working – Loss memorandum

	£
Trading loss – year to 31 December 2006	5,000
Less: s83 relief in 2007/08	(3,000)
	2,000
Less: s83 relief in 2008/09	(2,000)
Loss carried forward to 2009/10	Nil

Test your understanding 1

Michael has been trading for many years as a retailer. His recent tax-adjusted trading results are as follows:

		£
Year to 31 August 2006	Loss	(9,000)
Year to 31 August 2007	Profit	6,000
Year to 31 August 2008	Profit	19,000

Michael has had no other sources of income and therefore carried forward the loss arising in the year to 31 August 2006.

Calculate Michael's assessable trading income for the years affected by the above assuming he carries the loss forward under s83 ITA 2007.

3 Loss relief against total income (s64 ITA 2007)

Introduction

Carry forward loss relief is useful as the taxpayer gets the potential of an unrestricted period over which to utilise the available loss, providing that he continues to trade and makes subsequent future profits.

However, there are a number of disadvantages to carrying losses forward:

- In a prolonged difficult period for a business, relief may take a long time to materialise.
- Obtaining relief in a later period is less advantageous from the perspective of cash flow and time value of money.
- There is no certainty about the levels of future trading income and whether it will be possible to utilise the loss.

Consequently taxpayers are likely to consider the alternative loss relief which allows losses to be offset against the taxpayer's other income (s64 ITA 2007). This permits the taxpayer to relieve trading losses against:

- the total income of the tax year of the loss, **and/or**
- the total income of the previous tax year.

Tax year of loss

- Losses are identified with tax years in the same way as tax-adjusted trading profits.
- A loss for the year ended 31 December 2008 arises in the tax year 2008/09. Under s64 ITA 2007 it can be relieved against total income of 2008/09 and/or 2007/08.

Example 2 - Loss relief against total income (s64 ITA 2007)

Graham prepares his accounts to 31 December annually. His recent tax-adjusted results are as follows:

		£
Year to 31 December 2007	Profit	10,000
Year to 31 December 2008	Loss	(6,000)
Year to 31 December 2009	Profit	12,000

Explain how Graham can utilise the loss in respect of the year to 31 December 2008 assuming he claims to offset it against his total income under s64 ITA 2007.

Answer to example 2

The loss of £6,000 arises in the tax year 2008/09. This is available for relief against total income of 2008/09 and/or 2007/08 under s64 ITA 2007.

Obtaining relief for the loss

- The options available to the taxpayer, enable him to relieve the loss against total income of:
  - the year of the loss, followed by a claim against total income of the previous year; or
  - the previous year, followed by a claim against total income of the current year; or
  - either year in isolation.
- In each case, any unrelieved loss can be carried forward under s83 ITA 2007.

The key point to note is that the taxpayer cannot decide to set only part of his loss against total income; it must be set off to the maximum possible extent for a given year.

Other points to note:

- Qualifying interest payments (see Chapter 2) are also deducted from total income. In order not to waste the relief for interest payments, these should be deducted from total income in priority to losses.
- Personal allowances are deducted from net income (i.e. total income after deducting reliefs). Therefore, a claim under s64 ITA 2007 may involve wasting personal allowances.
- The two years available for potential claims are treated separately and thus a claim is required for each year.
- A written claim must be made within one year of 31 January following the end of the tax year of loss. For a 2008/09 loss the claim must be made by 31 January 2011.
- A taxpayer may have losses for two consecutive tax years and wish to relieve both under s64 ITA 2007. In these circumstances the total income of a year is relieved by the loss of that year, in priority to the loss carried back from the following year.

Example 3 - Loss relief against total income (s64 ITA 2007)

Adrian prepares accounts to 31 December each year. His recent results have been:

		£
Year ended 31 December 2007	Profit	34,000
Year ended 31 December 2008	Loss	(48,000)
Year ended 31 December 2009	Profit	60,000

In 2007/08, Adrian has other income of £5,000. In 2008/09, he had other income of £6,000 and he paid qualifying interest of £2,500.

(a) **Show how relief for the loss would be given against total income under s64 ITA 2007, assuming that Adrian makes all claims to the extent that they are beneficial.**

(b) **What loss, if any, is available for, carry forward against trading profits after all s64 ITA 2007 claims have been made?**

Answer to example 3

(a) **Relief under s64**

	2007/08	**2008/09**
	£	£
Trading income	34,000	Nil
Other income	5,000	6,000
Total income	39,000	6,000
Less Reliefs: Interest paid	Nil	(2,500)
	39,000	3,500
Less: Loss relief s64 **(W)**	(39,000)	–
Net income	Nil	3,500
Less: PA **(Note)**	–	(3,500)
Taxable income	Nil	Nil

(b) **Loss carried forward**

Losses of £9,000 (see Working) remain unrelieved after a claim for 2007/08 has been made under s64 and they are thus available for carry forward under s83.

Working – Loss memorandum

	£
2008/09 – loss of y/e 31.12.08	48,000
Less: s64 relief in 2007/08	(39,000)
Loss carried forward against future trading profits	9,000

Note

By only making a claim for 2007/08 under s64 ITA 2007, Adrian obtained relief for his loss as rapidly as possible. This approach also avoided needlessly wasting his personal allowance for 2008/09.

This approach maximised the amount of loss to carry forward to use against future trading profits.

The best course of action would depend on the personal circumstances of each case but as a general principle there is clearly no point in claiming s64 ITA 2007 where personal allowances already cover all or most of the total income.

Test your understanding 2

Derek has been trading for some time preparing accounts to 31 July.

His recent tax-adjusted trading results are as follows:

		£
Year ended 31 July 2006	Profit	18,000
Year ended 31 July 2007	Loss	(43,200)
Year ended 31 July 2008	Profit	13,000
Year ended 31 July 2009	Profit	15,000

Derek's other income each year is £12,000 (gross).

Show Derek's net income for all tax years affected by the above results assuming:

(a) **No claim is to be made against total income for a relevant year under s64 ITA 2007 for the trading loss.**

(b) **Full s64 ITA 2007 claims are to be made to obtain relief as early as possible.**

Expandable text - Relief under s64 ITA 2007 in opening years

- It is vital to remember that a loss may only be relieved once.
- When basis period rules are followed in the opening years to ascertain which profits are assessed in each tax year, overlap profits occur unless the trader prepares their accounts to 5 April.
- If, in the opening years, a loss has been taken into account in one tax year, it is treated as nil when calculating the assessment for the next tax year.

Example 4 - Loss relief against total income (s64 ITA 2007)

Geraldine starts trading on 1 August 2007. Her results, as adjusted for tax purposes, are:

		£
10 months to 31 May 2008	Loss	(20,000)
Year ended 31 May 2009	Profit	48,000

Calculate Geraldine's assessable trading income for 2007/08 and 2008/09.

Answer to example 4

	Trading income assessments	Loss available
2007/08 (Actual basis)	£	£
1.8.07 – 5.4.08 (8/10 × 20,000) = (£16,000)	Nil	16,000
2008/09 (First 12 months)		
1.8.07 – 31.7.08		
Loss	(20,000)	Nil
Less: Taken into account in 2007/08	16,000	
	(4,000)	
Profits (2/12 × £48,000)	8,000	
	4,000	

Test your understanding 3

Georgina started trading on 1 May 2005. The results of her initial periods of trading were as follows:

		£
Year ended 30 April 2006	Loss	(36,000)
Year ended 30 April 2007	Profit	30,000
Year ended 30 April 2008	Profit	35,000

Calculate Georgina's assessable trading income and available loss for each year affected by the above results.

Relief of trading losses against capital gains (s261B TCGA 1992)

- A trader is permitted to set trading losses off against capital gains, provided the following conditions are satisfied:
  - total income of the year in question has been reduced to zero by the trading loss under a normal s64 ITA 2007 claim
  - unrelieved losses remain.
- There is no need to make a s64 ITA 2007 claim for the previous year (or any other claim for loss relief), but relief against capital gains is only granted if total income has been reduced to nil in the same tax year.

The loss relief available is offset as follows:

	£
Gains in year	X
Less: Capital losses in year	(X)
	—
	X
Less: s261B TCGA 1992 trading losses	(X)
Capital losses b/f	(X)
	—
Net capital gains before annual exemption	X
	—

In summary:

- The unrelieved trading loss, is treated as a current year capital loss.
- It takes precedence over both the CGT annual exemption and any capital losses brought forward.

Test your understanding 4

Charles prepares accounts annually to 31 December. He made a trading profit of £3,000 and a loss of £14,000 in his periods of account ended 31 December 2008 and 2009 respectively.

He has other income of £4,500 (gross) in 2008/09 and also realised capital gains of £16,000 and capital losses of £5,000 in that tax year.

Calculate the amounts that remain in charge to tax for 2008/09, assuming that Charles claims loss relief against both total income and gains for that year and no other year.

4 Relief for trading losses incurred in the early years of a trade (s72 ITA 2007)

Introduction

- To help new businesses survive the initial years of trading, a special loss relief is available in the first four tax years of a trade.
- s72 ITA 2007 relief is available, in addition to s83 and s64 ITA 2007 relief described earlier in this chapter.

Relief under s72 ITA 2007

- s72 ITA 2007 permits the taxpayer to relieve a loss in any of the **first four tax years of trade** against total income of the **three tax years preceding the tax year of the loss**.
- There is no need for the trade to have been carried on in the earlier years.
- Unlike s64 ITA 2007 relief, where separate claims are required for relief in the current year and the previous year, relief under s72 ITA 2007 operates automatically for all three years.
- It is applied on a FIFO basis (i.e. beginning with the earliest and ending with the latest tax year).
- The loss available for s72 ITA 2007 relief must be computed in the same way as described for s64 ITA 2007 relief, i.e. in the same way as profits.
- The additional relief against capital gains is not available.

Example 5 - Relief for trading losses incurred in the early years of

Caroline started her business on 1 July 2007. Her trading results, as adjusted for tax purposes, for the first two years are as follows:

		£
Year ended 30 June 2008	Loss	(12,000)
Year ended 30 June 2009	Profit	2,500

Before becoming self-employed, Caroline had been employed as a dressmaker. Her remuneration from this employment, which ceased on 30 September 2006, for recent years, was:

	£
2006/07	6,678
2005/06	11,860
2004/05	11,330

Caroline has other income of £4,500 (gross) pa.

Calculate taxable income for all years:

(a) **after claiming relief under s72 ITA 2007, and**

(b) **after claiming relief under s64 ITA 2007, instead of claiming under s72 ITA 2007.**

Assume the allowances for 2008/09 apply throughout.

Answer to example 5

(a) **Taxable income computations – s72 ITA 2007 relief**

	2004/05	**2005/06**	**2006/07**	**2007/08**
	£	£	£	£
Employment income	11,330	11,860	6,678	–
Other income	4,500	4,500	4,500	4,500
Total income	15,830	16,360	11,178	4,500
Less: s72 relief **(W2)**	(9,000)	(3,000)	–	–
Net income	6,830	13,360	11,178	4,500
Less: PA	(6,035)	(6,035)	(6,035)	(6,035)
Taxable income	795	7,325	5,143	Nil

	2008/09	**2009/10**
	£	£
Trading income **(W1)**	Nil	2,500
Other income	4,500	4,500
Total income	4,500	7,000
Less: Personal Allowance	(6,035)	(6,035)
Taxable income	Nil	965

Notes

(1) Under s72 ITA 2007 the loss of 2007/08 is set initially against total income of 2004/05. Any loss remaining would then be set automatically against total income of 2005/06 and finally against total income of 2006/07.

(2) The loss of 2008/09 is set initially against total income of 2005/06 before relieving 2006/07 and 2007/08 (had any loss remained).

Workings

(W1) New business – assessments

Tax year	Basis period	Assessable profits
		£
2007/08	1.7.07 – 5.4.08 **(W2)**	Nil
2008/09	(y/e 30.6.08) **(W2)**	Nil
2009/10	(y/e 30.6.09)	2,500

(W2) Loss arising

Tax year	Basis period	Assessable profits
		£
2007/08	(1.7.07 – 5.4.08): (9/12 × £12,000)	(9,000)
2008/09	(y/e 30.6.08): (£12,000 – £9,000)	(3,000)

(b) Taxable income computations – s64 ITA 2007 relief

	2004/05	2005/06	2006/07	2007/08
	£	£	£	£
Employment income	11,330	11,860	6,678	–
Other income	4,500	4,500	4,500	4,500
Total income	15,830	16,360	11,178	4,500
s64 loss relief	–	–	(9,000)	(3,000)
Net income	15,830	16,360	2,178	1,500
Less: PA	(6,035)	(6,035)	(6,035)	(6,035)
Taxable income	9,795	10,325	Nil	Nil

	2008/09	2009/10
	£	£
Trading income **(W1)**	Nil	2,500
Other income	4,500	4,500
Net income	4,500	7,000
Less: Personal allowance	(6,035)	(6,035)
Taxable income	Nil	965

Notes

(1) The personal allowance is assumed throughout to be £6,035.

(2) Under s64 ITA 2007:

- the loss for 2007/08 (£9,000) is set against total income of 2007/08 and/or 2006/07
- the loss for 2008/09 (£3,000) is set against total income of 2008/09 and/or 2007/08.

In the example, relief is taken in the earliest year possible.

There is no requirement that the trade be carried on in the earlier year for which a s72 claim is made.

Test your understanding 5

Knight started a business on 1 May 2006. His taxable trade profits are as follows:

		£
Year ended 30 April 2007	Profit	6,120
Year ended 30 April 2008	Loss	(28,480)
Year ended 30 April 2009	Profit	7,630

Prior to commencing in business Knight had been in salaried employment.

His employment earnings for 2004/05 and 2005/06 were £9,400 and £13,660 respectively. In addition he enjoys savings income amounting to £1,700 (gross) each year.

Show how Knight will obtain relief for the loss if he makes a claim under s72 ITA 2007.

Test your understanding 6

Norman commenced trading on 6 April 2006. He had had no taxable income prior to 2006/07.

His trading results, adjusted for income tax and capital allowances were:

		£
Period ended 30 September 2006	Loss	(22,000)
Year ended 30 September 2007	Loss	(12,000)
Year ended 30 September 2008	Profit	11,000

He received gross bank interest as follows:

	£
2006/07	4,025
2007/08	3,400
2008/09	2,150

In 2006/07 he had also realised a capital gain, before the annual exemption, of £15,300.

(a) **State in what ways the trading losses may be relieved.**

(b) **Show how the trading losses can be utilised most effectively by Norman, giving your reasoning.**

Note: Assume that the allowances for 2008/09 apply throughout the question.

5 Terminal loss relief (s89 ITA 2007)

Introduction

- The only relief for trading losses incurred in the final year of trade would be a current year (and/or previous year) claim under s64 ITA 2007.
- No claim will be possible under s83 ITA 2007 as there will be no trade to generate future profits.
- A special terminal loss relief is provided under s89 ITA 2007.

It permits the trading loss of the final 12 months of trade that remain unrelieved to be set against:

- the trading profits for the year of cessation; and
- then carried back and set against the trading profits for the three preceding tax years (LIFO basis).

Calculating the terminal loss

The terminal loss is made up by totalling the following elements:

(1) Trading loss incurred in the final tax year (i.e. from 6 April to date of cessation).

(2) Trading loss incurred from 12 months before cessation to the start of the final tax year.

In calculating these amounts bear the following in mind:

- Any overlap relief created when the trade commenced is deductible in the final year of assessment thereby increasing any trading loss (or, perhaps, turning a trading profit into a loss) appearing in (1) above.
- If the calculation of trading losses in either (1) or (2) above in fact shows a profit, treat it as £nil.
- If any of the losses that might appear in the terminal loss calculation have been relieved by some other means (e.g. s64 ITA 2007), they must be excluded.

Test your understanding 7

Yves ceased trading on 30 June 2009. His final period of trade was the nine months to 30 June 2009 and beforehand he made up accounts annually to 30 September. His tax-adjusted trading results are as follows:

		£
Nine months to 30.6.09	Loss	(7,200)
Year to 30.9.08	Profit	100
Year to 30.9.07	Profit	7,300
Year to 30.9.06	Profit	7,500

There was overlap relief of £1,800 brought forward.

Yves had no other sources of income.

Calculate the terminal loss available to Yves and show how relief may be obtained for it.

6 Choice of loss reliefs

Utilising loss relief

The aims in utilising loss relief claims will be to:

- obtain relief as rapidly as possible
- ensure that the taxpayer's personal allowances are not wasted
- obtain relief at the highest marginal rate of tax.

The specific circumstances faced by the taxpayer will help to determine which of these is most important.

Factors to consider

In understanding the position of the taxpayer, it is important to understand the comparative features of the various reliefs.

Loss relief	Income relieved	Timing of relief	Flexibility
s64 ITA 2007	Total income (possibly also capital gains)	Current and/or previous tax year	Either, neither or both tax years (in either order). All or nothing
s72 ITA 2007	Total income	Preceding three tax years on a FIFO basis	Only in opening years. All or nothing. Can be used with s64 claim
s83 ITA 2007	Future trading income	As soon as possible in future	None

Expandable text - Choice of loss relief

Although the reliefs against total income, s64 and s72 ITA 2007, obtain relief more quickly than relief by carry forward under s83 ITA 2007, they frequently involve loss of personal allowances.

However, there is no point in choosing s83 for a large loss that will eliminate several years' modest trading profits if there is no non-trading income in those future years to obtain relief for personal allowances. All that will have happened is that future personal allowances rather than current ones will be wasted.

The taxpayer can choose when to claim relief first under s64, that is, against total income of the tax year of the loss; or against total income of the preceding year, as the legislation does not dictate that either takes priority.

If neither a current nor a previous year claim under s64 appears appropriate (on the grounds of wasting personal allowances), look further afield.

Where the taxpayer has made a large capital gain, a claim under s261B TCGA 1992 may be appropriate. Since the claim can only be made once total income for the year is reduced to zero, it will undoubtedly involve wasting at least one year's personal allowance.

7 Partnership losses

The allocation of trading losses

Trading losses are allocated between partners in exactly the same way as trading profits.

Loss relief claims available

Claims available to partners are the same as those for sole traders.

- A partner joining a partnership may be entitled to claim relief under s72 ITA 2007, where a loss is incurred in the first four tax years of his membership of the partnership.

This relief would not be available to the existing partners.

- A partner leaving the partnership may be entitled to claim for a terminal loss under s89 ITA 2007.

Again, this relief would not be available to the partners remaining in the partnership.

Test your understanding 8

Diane, Lynne and John are in partnership preparing their accounts to 5 April. During 2008/09, John left the partnership and Rose joined in his place.

For the year ended 5 April 2009, the partnership made a tax-adjusted loss of £40,000.

State the loss relief claims that will be available to the partners.

Example 6 - Partnership loss

Jake and Milo have been in partnership together since 1998, but ceased trading on 30 September 2008.

The tax-adjusted trading profits and losses for the final four years before allocation between the partners are as follows:

	Profit/ (Loss)
	£
2005/06	15,000
2006/07	14,000
2007/08	11,200
2008/09	(33,500)

Profits and losses have always been shared 40% to Jake and 60% to Milo.

Jake is single and had no other income or outgoings.

Milo is single and also has no other income or outgoings apart from bank interest of £4,350 (gross) received on 1 December 2008 from investing a recent inheritance. He has a capital gain of £23,400 for 2008/09 in respect of the disposal of an asset on 18 July 2008.

Assume that the 2008/09 rates and allowances apply to all years. Ignore overlap relief.

(a) **Advise the partners of the possible ways of relieving the partnership loss for 2008/09.**

(b) **Advise the partners as to which loss relief claims would be the most beneficial.**

(c) **After taking into account the advice in (b), calculate the partners' taxable income for 2005/06 to 2008/09.**

Answer to example 6

(a) **Options for relieving loss**

There are two possible ways that the partnership loss can be relieved:

(1) A claim can be made under s64 ITA 2007 against total income for 2008/09 and/or 2007/08. Subject to this claim being made, it would then be possible to extend the claim under s261B TCGA 1992 against capital gains of the same year.

(2) Terminal loss relief can be claimed under s89 ITA 2007.

The tax-adjusted trading profits will be split between the partners as follows:

	Jake 40%	**Milo 60%**
	£	£
2005/06	6,000	9,000
2006/07	5,600	8,400
2007/08	4,480	6,720
2008/09	(13,400)	(20,100)

(b) **Most beneficial relief**

The most beneficial loss relief claim available to Jake would appear to be a terminal loss claim under s89 ITA 2007.

Milo could also make a terminal loss claim, but this would waste his personal allowances for several years. He would be advised to make a claim under s64 ITA 2007 against his total income of £4,350 for 2008/09, and then claim under s261B TCGA 1992 against his capital gains of £23,400 for 2008/09.

(c) **Jake – Taxable income**

	2005/06	2006/07	2007/08	2008/09
	£	£	£	£
Trading income	6,000	5,600	4,480	–
Terminal loss	(3,320)	(5,600)	(4,480)	–
Net income	2,680	–	–	–
PA (restricted)	(2,680)	–	–	–
Taxable income	–	–	–	–

Milo – Taxable income

	2005/06	2006/07	2007/08	2008/09
	£	£	£	£
Trading income	9,000	8,400	6,720	–
Bank interest	–	–	–	4,350
Total income	9,000	8,400	6,720	4,350
s64 ITA 2007 loss claim	–	–	–	(4,350)
Net income	9,000	8,400	6,720	–
PA	(6,035)	(6,035)	(6,035)	–
Taxable income	2,965	2,365	685	–

Limited liability partnerships (LLP)

- An LLP is a special type of partnership where the amount that each partner contributes towards the partnership losses, debts and liabilities is limited by agreement.
- It is generally taxed in the same way as other partnerships.
- The normal loss reliefs are available.
- The losses that may be set against income not deriving from the partnership is, however, limited to the amount of capital that the partner has contributed to the partnership.

Test your understanding 9

Rob and Linda are partners in a limited liability partnership (LLP) to which they contributed capital of £45,000 and £15,000 respectively.

The LLP prepares its accounts to 31 March each year and Rob and Linda share profits and losses 2:1. For the year to 31 March 2009, the LLP made a trading loss of £60,000.

State the amount of the loss available to Rob and Linda to off set against total income in 2008/09.

8 Businesses transferred to companies (s86 ITA 2007)

Overview of the relief

- When a business ceases to trade, any accumulated trading losses are normally lost.
- If, however, the business is sold to a company controlled by the former proprietor(s) then:
  - the losses may be carried forward, and
  - set against the first available income (of the former proprietor(s)) from the company,
  - but not the company profits.
- The relief applies to trading losses at the date of cessation.
- For the relief to apply, the consideration for the business given by the company must be wholly or mainly (at least 80%) shares in the company.
- The losses may be carried forward indefinitely (awaiting sufficient income from the company) provided that:
  - the former proprietor retains his or her shares in the company; and
  - the company continues to carry on the former business' trade.
- The losses brought forward can be set off against all income from the company such as salaries, directors' fees, interest and dividends.
- The loss must be set off as soon as possible against the first available income, but there is no prescribed order of set off.
- The most beneficial order of set off will be against employment income first, then savings, then dividends.

9 Chapter summary

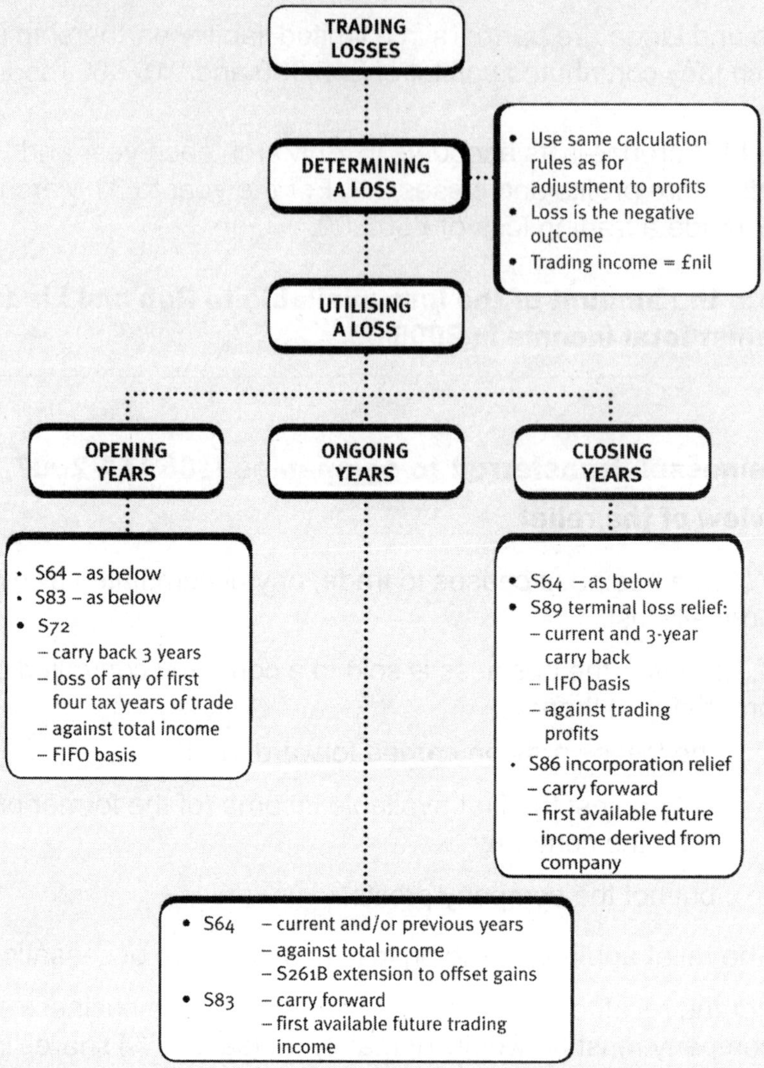

Test your understanding answers

Test your understanding 1

Michael	2006/07	2007/08	2008/09
	£	£	£
Trading income	Nil	6,000	19,000
Less: s83 relief **(working)**	Nil	(6,000)	(3,000)
Net trading income	Nil	Nil	16,000

Working – Loss memorandum

	£
Trading loss – year to 31 August 2006	9,000
Less: s83 relief in 2007/08	(6,000)
	3,000
Less: s83 relief in 2008/09	(3,000)
Loss carried forward to 2009/10	Nil

Test your understanding 2

Derek

(a) **No s64 relief claim**

If no claim is made under s64 then the trading loss of 2006/07 is carried forward against future trading profits under s83.

	2006/07	2007/08	2008/09	2009/10
	£	£	£	£
Trading profits	18,000	Nil	13,000	15,000
Less s83 relief	–	–	(13,000)	(15,000)
	18,000	Nil	Nil	Nil
Other income	12,000	12,000	12,000	12,000
Net income	30,000	12,000	12,000	12,000

Working – Loss memorandum

		£
Year ended –	31 July 2007	43,200
s83 relief –	2008/09	(13,000)
	2009/10	(15,000)
Carry forward to –	2010/11	15,200

(b) **Full s64 relief claims**

s64 claims can only be made for 2006/07 and/or 2007/08 and any balance is carried forward for relief against future trading profits.

	2006/07	2007/08	2008/09	2009/10
	£	£	£	£
Trading profits	18,000	Nil	13,000	15,000
s83 relief			(1,200)	–
			11,800	15,000
Other income	12,000	12,000	12,000	12,000
Total income	30,000	12,000	23,800	27,000
s64 relief	(30,000)	(12,000)	–	–
Net income	Nil	Nil	23,800	27,000

Working – Loss memorandum

		£
Year ended –	31 July 2007	43,200
s64 relief –	2006/07	(30,000)
	2007/08	(12,000)
		1,200
s83 carry forward –	2008/09	(1,200)
		Nil

Test your understanding 3

Georgina

		Trading income assessments	Loss available
2005/06 (Actual basis)		£	£
1.5.05 – 5.4.06 11/12 × £36,000 = £33,000		Nil	(33,000)
2006/07 (CYB)	£		
Year ended 30 April 2006	36,000		
Less: Used in 05/06	(33,000)		
	(3,000)	Nil	(3,000)
2007/08 (CYB)			
Year ended 30 April 2007		30,000	Nil
2008/09 (CYB)			
Year ended 30 April 2008		35,000	Nil

Test your understanding 4

Charles

Income tax computation – 2008/09

	£
Trading income (y/e 31.12.08)	3,000
Other income	4,500
Total income	7,500
Less: s64 relief against total income	(7,500)
Taxable income	Nil

Capital gains computation – 2008/09

Capital gains	16,000
Less: Capital losses – current year	(5,000)
Net capital gains	11,000
Less: s261B TCGA 1992 relief against capital gains (£14,000 – £7,500)	(6,500)
Net capital gains before annual exemption	4,500

Test your understanding 5

Knight

	Loss available	Taxable trade profits
	£	£
2006/07		
(1 May 2006 – 5 April 2007)		
£6,120 × 11/12		5,610
2007/08		
(Year ended 30 April 2007)		6,120
2008/09		
(Year ended 30 April 2008)	28,480	–
2009/10		
(Year ended 30 April 2009)		7,630

Note: 2008/09 is the year of the loss.

The loss of £28,480 sustained in 2008/09 will be set off under s72 as follows:

	2005/06	2006/07	2007/08
	£	£	£
Employment income	13,660	–	–
Trading profits	–	5,610	6,120
Savings income	1,700	1,700	1,700
Total income	15,360	7,310	7,820
Less: s72 loss relief	(15,360)	(7,310)	(5,810)
Net income	Nil	Nil	2,010

Working – Loss memorandum

	£
Trading loss	28,480
Less: s72 claim 2005/06	(15,360)
	13,120
Less: s72 claim 2006/07	(7,310)
	5,810
Less: s72 claim 2007/08	(5,810)
	Nil

Test your understanding 6

Norman

(a) **Loss relief options**

The trading losses sustained may be relieved as follows:

- s83 ITA 2007 – carry forward the loss to be set against the first available future tax-adjusted trading profit of the same trade.
- s64 ITA 2007 – set off the loss against the total income in the tax year of the loss and/or the previous year.
- s 261B TCGA 1992 – set off the balance of the loss after s64 relief against capital gains.

Tutorial note

It was not possible to claim any relief under s72 ITA 2007. Although the loss arises within the first four years of a new trade, the question states that there was no taxable income prior to 2006/07.

(b) **Tax efficient utilisation of trading losses**

	2006/07	**2007/08**	**2008/09**
	£	£	£
Trading income	Nil	Nil	11,000
s83 relief (£8,675 + £2,325) **(W2)**			(11,000)
			Nil
Bank interest	4,025	3,400	2,150
Total income	4,025	3,400	2,150
s64 relief **(W2)**	(4,025)		
	Nil	3,400	2,150
Less: PA (Wasted/restricted to)	–	(3,400)	(2,150)
Taxable income	Nil	Nil	Nil
Net gain	15,300		
s261B TCGA 1992 relief **(W2)**	(15,300)		
	Nil		

Tutorial notes

- In 2006/07 Norman had to make a claim under s64 because he wanted to make a claim under s261B TCGA 1992 – without the s64 claim, he cannot make a s72 claim. Therefore although it leads to wasting the PA, it also avoids any capital gains tax as the remaining gain is now nil.
- In 2007/08 he does not need to make a s261B claim as there are no gains – therefore there is no need to make a s64 claim as the total income is less than the personal allowance.

(W1) Allocation of loss to respective tax years

Tax year	Basis period	Loss allocated	s64 relief is possible in
		£	
2006/07	6/4/06 to 5/4/07	28,000	2006/07 and/or
	£22,000 + 6/12 × £12,000		2005/06 **(Note 1)**
2007/08	y/e 30/9/07 (CYB)	6,000	2007/08 and/or
	£12,000 – £6,000 **(Note 2)**		2006/07

Note 1: No income for 2005/06 – therefore loss relief starts from 2006/07.

Note 2: £6,000 of the loss for the year to 30/9/07 has already been allocated to 2006/07.

Note that as losses arise in 2006/07 and 2007/08, the trading income assessments are £Nil.

(W2) Loss available and its utilisation

	£
Loss of 2006/07 **(W1)**	28,000
Utilisation: s64 relief – 2006/07	(4,025)
	23,975
s261B TCGA 1992 relief	(15,300)
Excess carried forward	8,675
s83 – first available future trading profit (2008/09)	(8,675)
	Nil

	£
Loss of 2007/08 **(W1)**	6,000
Utilisation:	
None in 2006/07 as no income remaining	–
s64 claim not made in 2007/08 as it would lead to a wastage of personal allowance	–
Therefore carry forward under s83	
– against first available future trading profit – 2008/09	6,000
(£11,000 – £8,675)	(2,325)
Carry forward to 2009/10	3,675

Test your understanding 7

Yves

	2006/07	2007/08	2008/09	2009/10
	£	£	£	£
Trading income	7,500	7,300	100	Nil
TLR (W2)	(iii) (1,575)	(ii) (7,300)	(i) (100)	Nil
Net income	5,925	Nil	Nil	Nil

Workings

(W1) Calculation of terminal loss

	£
6.4.09 to 30.6.09: Actual loss (3/9 × £7,200)	2,400
1.7.08 to 5.4.09: Actual loss	
(6/9 × £7,200) – (3/12 × £100)	4,775
Overlap relief	1,800
Terminal loss	8,975

(W2) Terminal loss relief (TLR)

The terminal loss is then relieved on a LIFO basis in the final year of assessment and the previous three years, against the trading profits.

Test your understanding 8

Diane, Lynne and John

All the partners will be entitled to relief against total income under s64 ITA 2007.

All the partners except John will be entitled to carry forward loss relief under s83 ITA 2007.

John will be entitled to terminal loss relief under s89 ITA 2007 since he has ceased trading.

Rose will be entitled to claim opening years relief under s72 ITA 2007 since she has commenced trading.

Diane and Lynne will not be entitled to s89 or s72 relief.

Test your understanding 9

Rob and Linda

Rob will be entitled to £40,000 (£60,000 × 2/3) of the loss arising in the year ended 31 March 2009. This figure is less than the capital that he has contributed of £45,000 and the full amount of the loss (£40,000) is therefore available to be offset against Rob's non-partnership income for 2008/09 under s64 ITA 2007.

Linda will be entitled to £20,000 (£60,000 × 1/3) of the loss arising in the year ended 31 March 2009.

The amount of the loss, which may be set against income not deriving from the partnership in 2008/09, is however limited to £15,000, being the amount of capital that she has contributed to the LLP.

The balance of the loss, £5,000 (£20,000 – £15,000), can only be claimed against partnership income, for example under s83 ITA 2007.

chapter

11

Pensions

Chapter learning objectives

Upon completion of this chapter you will be able to:

- explain the basis for calculating the maximum annual contributions to a registered pension scheme for an individual
- calculate the tax relief available and explain how relief for pension contributions is given
- explain the concept of the lifetime allowance and the implications of the allowance being exceeded.

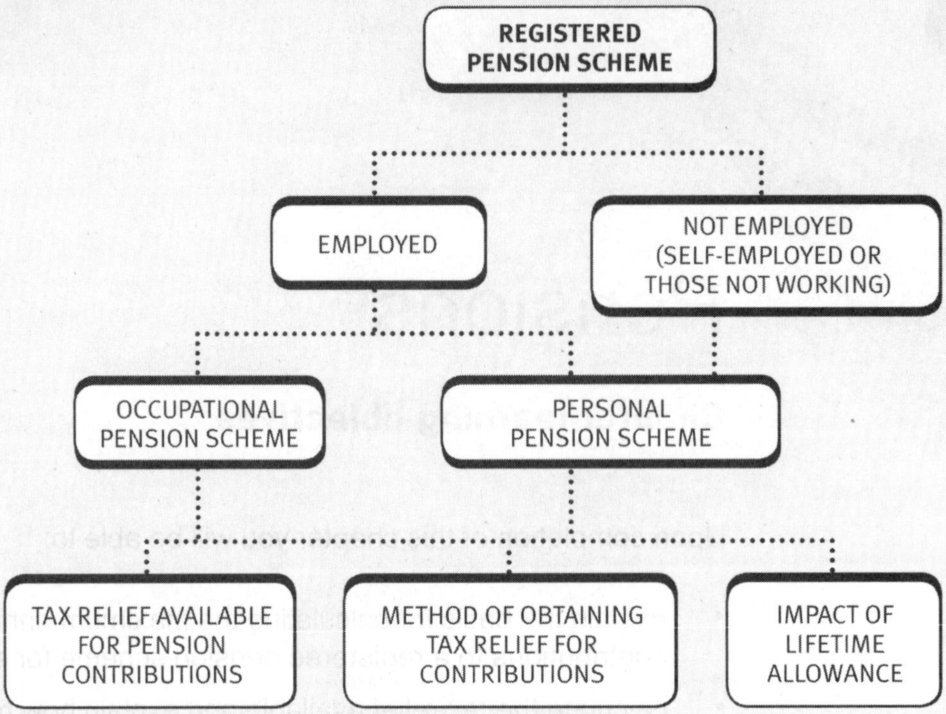

1 Types of registered pension schemes

Introduction

An individual can set up an investment of funds to provide an income during his retirement in a tax-efficient way by making payments into a registered pension scheme.

A pension scheme is a savings plan for retirement that enjoys special tax privileges, but only if the scheme is registered with HM Revenue and Customs (HMRC).

Investing in a registered pension scheme is a long-term investment and is very tax efficient for the following reasons:

- The individual obtains tax relief on the contributions made into the scheme.
- Where an employer contributes into the scheme, tax relief for the employer contributions is available without there being a taxable benefit for the employee.
- Registered pension scheme funds can grow tax-free as the scheme is exempt from income tax and capital gains tax.
- On retirement, part of the funds can be withdrawn as a tax-free lump sum.

The two main types of registered pension schemes available are:

- Occupational pension schemes
- Personal pension schemes.

If self-employed or unemployed, the individual can only set up a personal pension scheme.

If employed, the individual may:

- join an occupational pension scheme if one is provided by his employer, or
- choose not to join the employer's scheme and set up a personal pension scheme, or
- contribute into both his employer's occupational scheme and set up a personal pension scheme.

Occupational pension schemes

An occupational pension scheme is a scheme set up by an employer for the benefit of his employees.

Employers may use an insurance company to provide a pension scheme for its employees, or it may set up its own self-administered pension fund.

Contributions into occupational schemes may be made by the employer, and the employee.

Expandable text - Occupational pension schemes

Registered occupational pension schemes may be 'defined benefit' or 'money purchase' schemes.

Under a **defined benefit scheme** :

- the benefits obtained on retirement are linked to the level of earnings of the employee.

Under a **money purchase scheme** (also known as a 'defined contribution' scheme):

- the benefits obtained depend upon the performance of the investments held by the pension fund.

Personal pension schemes

Personal pension schemes can be established by **any** individual:

- the employed
- the self-employed
- those not working (including children).

Contributions into personal pension schemes may be made by:

- the individual, and
- any third party on behalf of the individual (for example the employer, a spouse, parent or grandparent).

Personal pension schemes are usually 'money purchase' schemes administered by financial institutions on behalf of the individual.

Overview of the tax relief rules for registered pension schemes

- The **amount** of tax relief available for pension contributions is the same regardless of whether the scheme is an occupational or personal pension scheme.
- The **method** of obtaining tax relief for the contributions is different depending on whether the scheme is an occupational or a personal pension scheme.
- Once the funds are invested in the scheme, all registered pension schemes are governed by the same rules.

2 Tax relief for pension contributions

The relief for contributions made by individuals

Tax relief is available for pension contributions if both:

- the pension scheme is a registered scheme
- the individual is resident in the UK and aged under 75.

Regardless of the level of earnings, an individual may make pension contributions of **any amount** into either:

- a pension scheme, or
- a number of different pension schemes.

However, **tax relief** is only available for a **maximum annual amount** each tax year.

The total maximum annual gross contribution for which an individual can obtain tax relief is calculated as follows.

The higher of:

- £3,600, and
- 100% of the individual's 'relevant earnings', chargeable to income tax in the tax year.

Relevant earnings includes taxable trading profits, employment income and furnished holiday lettings but not investment income.

- The above maximum limit applies to the total gross contributions made into all schemes where:
  - an employee contributes to both an occupational and a personal pension scheme, or
  - an individual contributes into more than one personal pension scheme.
- An individual with no relevant earnings can still obtain tax relief on gross contributions of up to £3,600 pa. This figure will be provided in the examination.

Example 1 - Maximum tax relief for individuals

The following individuals made gross pension contributions into a personal pension scheme in 2008/09:

	Pension contributions (gross)	**Relevant earnings**
	£	£
Amy	2,500	Nil
Brenda	6,000	Nil
Caroline	36,000	75,000
Deborah	96,000	75,000

Explain the maximum amount of pension contribution for which tax relief is available for each individual in 2008/09.

Answer to example 1

	Tax relief available £	Explanation
Amy	2,500	Relief = contributions made as they are below the maximum annual amount of £3,600 (higher of £3,600 and £nil).
Brenda	3,600	Contributions (£6,000) exceed the maximum annual amount (higher of £3,600 and £nil). Relief = restricted to maximum annual amount of £3,600.
Caroline	36,000	Relief = contributions made (£36,000) as they are below the maximum annual amount of £75,000 (higher of £3,600 and £75,000).
Deborah	75,000	Contributions (£96,000) exceed the maximum annual amount (higher of £3,600 and £75,000). Relief = restricted to the annual maximum amount of £75,000.

The tax charge on contributions in excess of the annual allowance

As we have seen tax relief for pension contributions is restricted to the **maximum annual amount**.

In addition however, a tax charge is levied on the individual if the total of all contributions on which tax relief has been obtained exceed an **annual allowance** of £235,000 for 2008/09.

This limit will be provided in the examination.

Tax charge

The tax charge is a **40% income tax charge**, which is:

- added to the individual's income tax liability in his income tax computation, and
- paid through the self-assessment system.

Relevant contributions

There is no income tax charge where excess contributions have **not** qualified for tax relief.

Therefore, the combined total of all contributions paid into an individual's registered pension scheme(s) **for which tax relief is obtained** is compared with the £235,000 limit.

Expandable text - Combined contributions

The total contributions paid into the scheme which are considered are therefore as follows:

- Contributions made by the individual within the maximum annual amount (see above).
- Contributions made by other individuals (for example: spouse, parents, grandparents) that have obtained tax relief.
- All contributions made by an employer.

In Example 1 above:

- The £75,000 would be the contributions taken into account to calculate whether or not there is an annual allowance charge for Deborah (not the gross contributions of £96,000 she paid into the scheme).
- The £75,000 would be added to any contributions made by her employer or other third parties to decide whether the annual allowance charge should be levied.

Summary

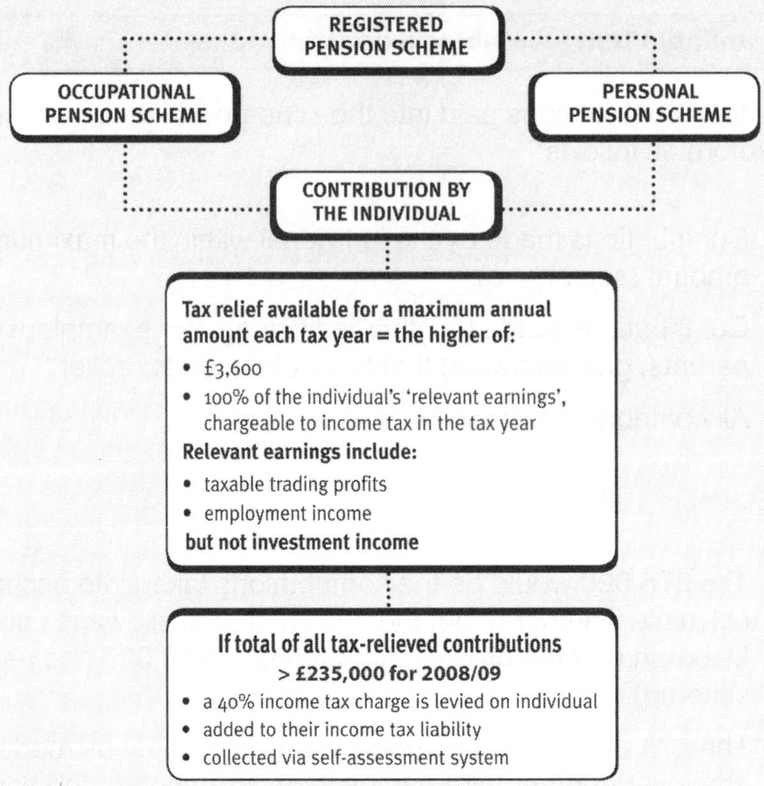

3 The method of obtaining relief for pension contributions

Personal pension schemes

The method of obtaining tax relief for contributions into a personal pension scheme is the same whether they are made by an employee, a self-employed individual or an individual who is not working.

Relief is given as follows:

Basic rate tax relief

- Basic rate tax relief is automatically given by deduction at source when contributions are paid, as an individual makes contributions net of the basic rate of income tax (20%).
- Contributions into a personal pension scheme benefit from basic rate tax relief, even if the taxpayer is paying tax at the starting rate, higher rate or not paying tax at all.

Higher rate tax relief

- For higher rate taxpayers, basic rate relief of 20% is given at source (as above) and higher rate relief is given by extending the basic rate tax band by the gross amount of pension payments paid in the tax year.
- This means that an amount of income equal to the gross pension contributions is removed from the charge to higher rate tax and is taxed at the basic rate instead.
- For example, if an individual pays a contribution of £8,000 (net), this is equivalent to a gross contribution of £10,000 (£8,000 × 100/80).
- The individual's higher rate threshold is therefore extended to £44,800 (£34,800 + £10,000).

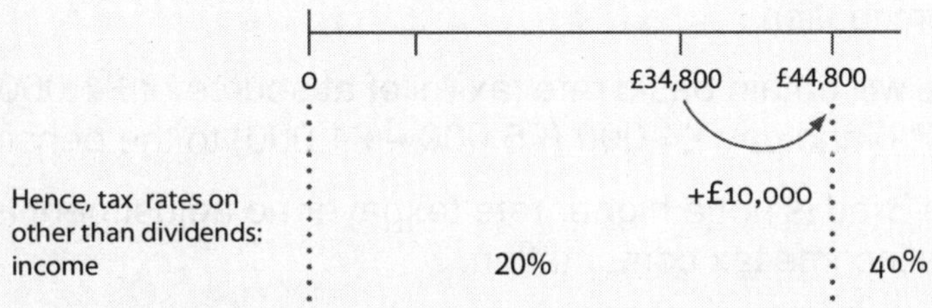

Example 2 - The method of obtaining relief for pension

The following individuals made gross pension contributions into a personal pension scheme in 2008/09 and had the following trading profits:

	Pension contributions (gross)	**Trading profits**
	£	£
Andy	5,000	Nil
Brad	5,000	20,000
Cindy	25,000	20,000
Don	40,000	85,000
Ed	100,000	85,000

Explain how tax relief for the pension contributions will be given in 2008/09 for each individual and calculate the income tax liability of Don and Ed for 2008/09.

Answer to example 2

Andy

- As Andy has no earnings he will obtain tax relief on a maximum gross amount of £3,600.
- He will obtain basic rate tax relief at source of £720 (£3,600 × 20%) and pay £4,280 (£5,000 – £720) to the pension scheme.

Brad

- Brad's pension contributions are less than his earnings for the year and he will therefore receive tax relief on the full amount of the contribution.
- He will obtain basic rate tax relief at source of £1,000 (£5,000 × 20%) and pay £4,000 (£5,000 – £1,000) to the pension scheme.
- As Brad is not a higher rate taxpayer no adjustment is required in his income tax computation.

Cindy

- The tax relief available on Cindy's pension contributions is restricted to 100% of her earnings, i.e. £20,000.
- She will obtain basic rate tax relief at source of £4,000 (£20,000 × 20%) and pay £21,000 (£25,000 – £4,000) to the pension scheme.
- As Cindy is not a higher rate taxpayer no adjustment is required in her income tax computation.

Don

- Don's pension contributions are less than his earnings for the year and he will therefore receive tax relief on the full amount of the contribution.
- He will obtain basic rate tax relief at source of £8,000 (£40,000 × 20%) and pay £32,000 (£40,000 – £8,000) to the pension scheme.
- Higher rate tax relief will be given by extending the basic rate band by £40,000 from £34,800 to £74,800.

Don's income tax computation for 2008/09 will be:

		£
Trading income		85,000
Less: Personal allowance		(6,035)
Taxable income		78,965
	£	
Basic rate	74,800 @ 20%	14,960
Higher rate	4,165 @ 40%	1,666
	78,965	
Income tax liability		16,626

Ed

- The tax relief available on Ed's pension contributions is restricted to 100% of his earnings, i.e. £85,000.
- He will obtain basic rate tax relief at source of £17,000 (£85,000 × 20%) and pay £83,000 (£100,000 – £17,000) to the pension scheme.
- Higher rate tax relief will be given by extending the basic rate band by £85,000 from £34,800 to £119,800.

Ed's income tax computation for 2008/09 will be:

			£
Trading income			85,000
Less: Personal allowance			(6,035)
Taxable income			78,965
	£		
Basic rate	78,965	@ 20%	15,793

Example 3 - Contributions in excess of the annual allowance

Julie has been a self-employed interior designer for a number of years. In the year to 31 March 2009 she made taxable trading profits of £286,000. Julie made a gross contribution of £240,000 into her personal pension scheme in 2008/09.

Explain how tax relief will be obtained for the pension contribution made by Julie and calculate her income tax liability for 2008/09.

Answer to example 3

Julie can obtain tax relief for a pension contribution up a maximum of 100% of her earnings, i.e. £286,000 in 2008/09. She will therefore obtain relief on the gross contribution of £240,000.

Julie will have paid the pension contribution net of basic rate tax of £48,000 (£240,000 × 20%) and paid £192,000 (£240,000 – £48,000) into the pension scheme.

As a higher rate taxpayer, higher rate relief is obtained by extending the basic rate band by £240,000 from £34,800 to £274,800.

However Julie's gross contributions of £240,000 have exceeded the annual allowance of £235,000. She will therefore have an additional income tax liability in 2008/09 of £2,000 (£240,000 – £235,000 = £5,000 × 40%).

Julie's income tax computation for 2008/09 will be:

	£
Trading income	286,000
Less: Personal allowance	(6,035)
Taxable income	279,965

Income tax liability	£		
Basic rate	274,800	@ 20%	54,960
Higher rate	5,165	@ 40%	2,066
	279,965		
			57,026
Annual allowance charge	5,000	@ 40%	2,000
Income tax liability			59,026

Occupational pension schemes

Where employees make pension contributions into an occupational pension scheme, payments are made gross and tax relief is given at source by the employer through the PAYE system.

Tax relief is given at basic and higher rates of tax depending on the individual's level of income as follows:

- The employer will deduct the pension contribution from the individual's earned income, before calculating income tax under the PAYE system.
- Tax relief is therefore automatically given at both the basic and higher rate at source.

Test your understanding 1

Henry is employed by Lloyd Ltd on an annual salary of £80,000 pa. He is a member of the company's occupational pension scheme.

Henry pays 3% and Lloyd Ltd pays 5% of his salary into the scheme each year. He has no other income.

Calculate Henry's income tax liability for 2008/09, showing how tax relief is obtained for his pension contributions.

Contributions made by employers into registered pension schemes

Contributions paid by an employer into a registered pension scheme are:

- tax deductible in calculating the employer's taxable trading profits, provided the contributions are paid for the purposes of the trade
- an exempt employment benefit for the employee
- added to the pension contributions paid by the employee on which tax relief is given to determine whether the annual allowance has been exceeded and an income tax charge levied.

Expandable text - Employer contributions as a trading deduction

The deduction against the employer's trading profits is given in the accounting period in which the contribution is **paid**; the accounting treatment is not followed.

Therefore, in the adjustment to profit computation:

- any amount charged in the profit and loss account is added back, and
- the amount paid in the accounting period is tax deductible.

Test your understanding 2

Hugh is a self-employed builder, who prepares accounts to September each year. His recent tax-adjusted trading profits have been:

	£
Year ended 30 September 2007	140,000
Year ended 30 September 2008	150,000

Hugh's wife, Holly, has employment income from a part-time job of £3,500 pa.

They also have a joint bank account on which they earned interest of £5,000 (gross) in 2008/09.

During the year to 5 April 2009, Hugh paid £79,400 into his registered personal pension scheme. Holly paid £2,600 into her employer's registered occupational pension scheme and Holly's employer contributed a further £4,500.

Calculate how much of the pension contributions made by Hugh, Holly and Holly's employer in 2008/09 will obtain tax relief and explain how the tax relief will be obtained.

Test your understanding 3

Marcus has been employed for many years.

In 2008/09 Marcus earned £292,500 and made a gross contribution of £250,000 into his personal pension scheme.

Calculate Marcus' income tax liability for 2008/09.

Summary

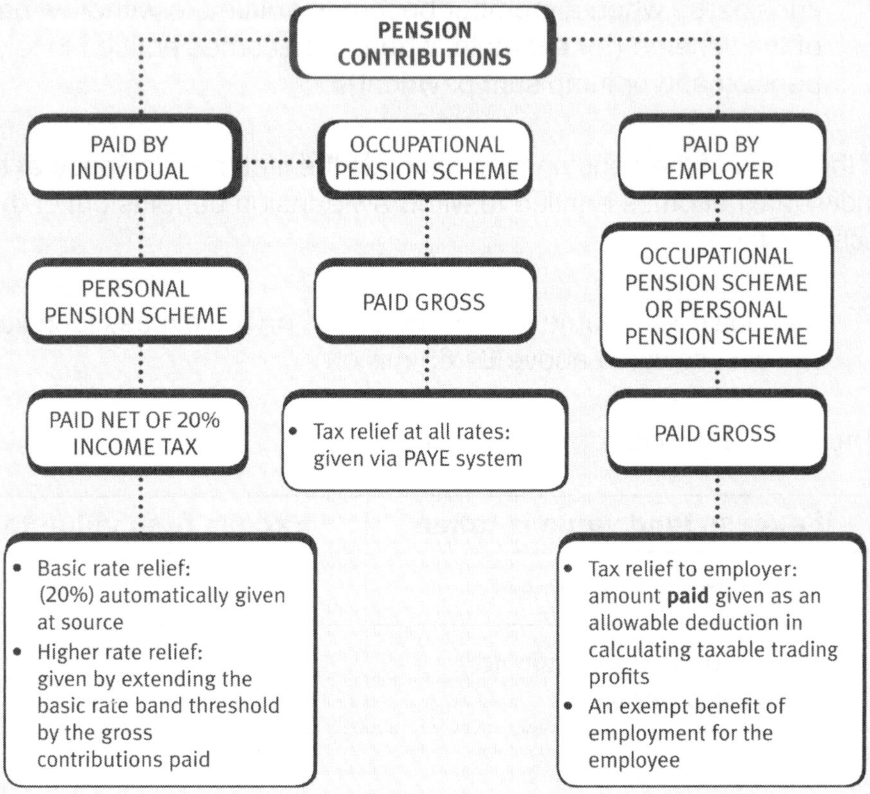

4 The lifetime allowance

There is no restriction on the **total** contribution that an individual may make into a registered pension scheme. There is only a limit upon the annual contributions upon which **tax relief** will be available.

Funds invested in a registered pension scheme each year will be accumulated and can grow in value, tax free, as the scheme is:

- exempt from income tax in respect of any income earned from the assets invested
- exempt from capital gains tax in respect of any capital disposals made by the trustees over the life of the scheme.

As funds in a registered pension scheme can grow tax free there is a maximum limit to the amount that an individual can accumulate in a pension scheme to obtain the benefit of tax-free growth, known as the 'lifetime allowance'.

Lifetime allowance

The lifetime allowance is:

- £1.65 million for 2008/09
- considered when a member becomes entitled to withdraw benefits out of the scheme (for example, when he becomes entitled to take a pension and/or lump sum payment).

If the value of the pension fund exceeds the lifetime allowance at the time the individual becomes entitled to withdraw pension benefits out of the pension scheme then:

- an additional income tax charge arises on the excess fund value (i.e. the excess value above £1.65 million).

The income tax charge is as follows:

If excess fund value is taken	Excess fund value taxed at
• as a lump sum payment	55%
• to purchase an annuity to provide a pension	25%

This income tax charge is normally taken out of the pension scheme assets.

5 Chapter summary

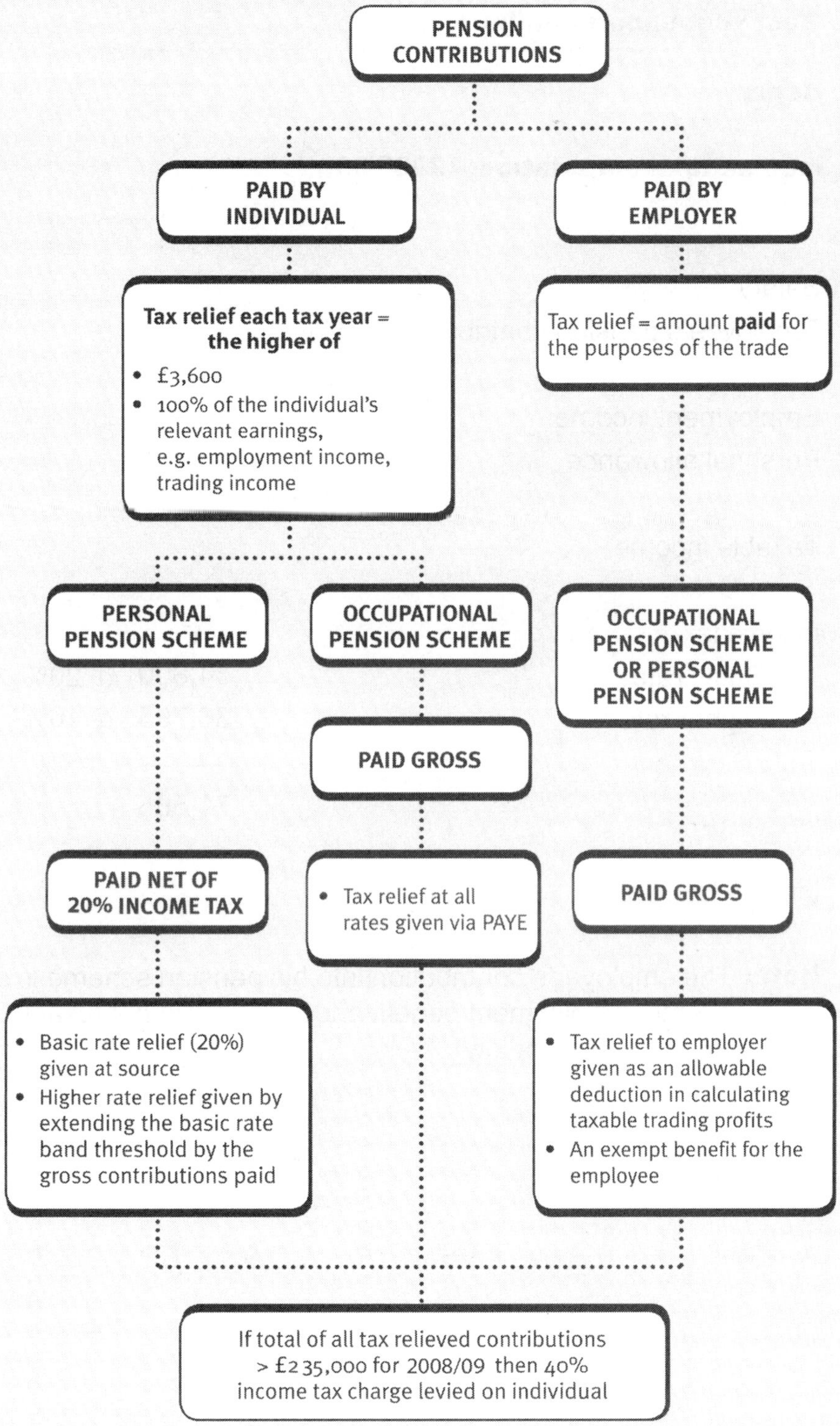

Test your understanding answers

Test your understanding 1

Henry

Income tax computation – 2008/09

			£
Salary			80,000
Employee's pension contributions (3%)			(2,400)
Employment income			77,600
Personal allowance			(6,035)
Taxable income			71,565
Income tax	£		
Basic rate	34,800	@ 20%	6,960
Higher rate	36,765	@ 40%	14,706
	71,565		
Income tax liability			21,666

Note: The employer's contribution into his pension scheme is an exempt employment benefit and is therefore not taxable income for Henry (see below).

Test your understanding 2

Hugh

- Hugh can obtain tax relief for a pension contribution of up to a maximum of 100% of his earnings in 2008/09.
- His earnings are his assessable trading profits for 2008/09, i.e. £150,000 (year ended 30 September 2008).
- Unearned income such as bank interest is not included.
- Hugh will have paid the pension contribution net of basic rate tax of £19,850 (£79,400 × 20/80).
- The gross pension contribution is £99,250 (£79,400 × 100/80).
- As a higher rate taxpayer, higher rate tax relief is obtained by extending the basic rate band threshold by £99,250 from £34,800 to £134,050.

Holly

- Holly can obtain tax relief for a gross pension contribution of up to a maximum of the higher of £3,600 or 100% of her employment earnings in 2008/09 (i.e. £3,500).
- Her gross pension contribution of £2,600 is less than £3,600, therefore she can obtain tax relief for all £2,600 contributions paid.
- Holly's employer will deduct the gross contribution of £2,600 from her employment income before calculating her income tax liability under PAYE.

Holly's employer

- Holly's employer will obtain tax relief for all of the £4,500 contribution made into the occupational pension scheme.
- Relief is given as an allowable deduction in the calculation of the employer's taxable trading profits.

Test your understanding 3

Marcus

- Marcus can obtain tax relief for a gross pension contribution of up to a maximum of 100% of his earnings, i.e. £292,500 in 2008/09.
- However, he only made a gross contribution of £250,000. Tax relief is therefore available on the full contribution of £250,000.
- Marcus will have paid the pension contribution net of basic rate tax of £50,000 (£250,000 × 20%) and paid £200,000 (£250,000 × 80%) into the pension scheme.
- As a higher rate taxpayer, higher rate relief is obtained by extending the basic rate band threshold by £250,000 from £34,800 to £284,800.
- However the gross contributions paid into the scheme on which tax relief has been given in 2008/09 of £250,000 exceeds the annual allowance of £235,000.
- Marcus will therefore have an additional income tax liability in 2008/09 of £6,000 (£250,000 – £235,000 = £15,000 × 40%).

Marcus' income tax computation for 2008/09 will be:

			£
Employment income			292,500
Less: Personal allowance			(6,035)
Taxable income			286,465
Income tax	£		
Basic rate	284,800	@ 20%	56,960
Higher rate	1,665	@ 40%	666
	286,465		
			57,626
Annual allowance charge (£15,000 × 40%)			6,000
Income tax liability			63,626

chapter

12

National insurance

Chapter learning objectives

Upon completion of this chapter you will be able to:

- identify the different types of National Insurance Contributions (NICs) and the persons who are liable
- define earnings for the purposes of Class 1 NICs
- calculate the Class 1 NIC primary and secondary liabilities on earnings
- state how and when Class 1 NICs are collected
- explain the basis of the Class 1A NIC charge and calculate the amount of Class 1A NICs payable
- state how and when Class 1A NICs are payable
- calculate Class 2 NICs for relevant self-employed persons
- explain how Class 2 NICs are collected
- identify the relevant earnings for Class 4 NICs and calculate the liability
- demonstrate the mechanism for the payment of Class 4 NICs
- calculate the total NIC liability for a self-employed person.

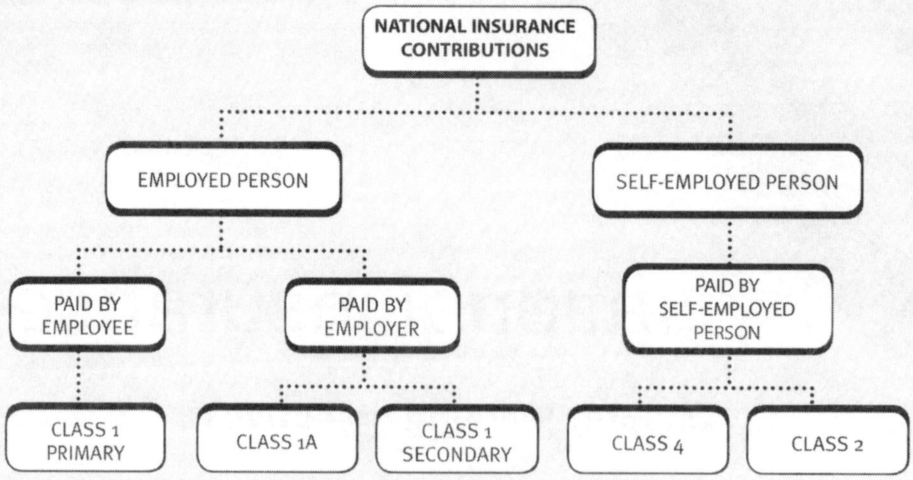

1 Classes of national insurance contributions

The amount of National Insurance Contribution (NIC) a person pays and the statutory rules governing the payment of contributions depend on the class of contribution.

The main classes and persons who are liable are summarised in the table below.

Class of contribution	**Basis of assessment**	**Person liable**
Class 1 primary	A percentage-based contribution levied on employee earnings in excess of £5,435 for 2008/09	Employee
Class 1 secondary		Employer
Class 1A	A percentage-based contribution levied on assessable benefits provided to employees	Employer
Class 2	A flat rate weekly contribution	Self-employed person
Class 4	A percentage-based contribution levied on taxable trading profits in excess of £5,435 for 2008/09	Self-employed person

Example 1 - Classes of NICs

Nicholas has been self-employed for many years. He employs a full-time salesman and six part-time employees. Nicholas' taxable trading profits for 2008/09 are £86,000.

The salesman earns a salary of £14,000 pa and is provided with a Company car. The remaining members of staff earn £3,000 pa.

Explain which classes of NICs are payable by Nicholas in respect of 2008/09.

Answer to example 1

Nicholas will pay:

(1) Flat rate Class 2 contributions in respect of his self employed business.

(2) Class 4 contributions in respect of his self-employed business based on his taxable trading profits as they are in excess of £5,435.

(3) Class 1 secondary contributions as Nicholas is an employer. The contributions will be based on the salesman's salary of £14,000 as his earnings are in excess of £5,435.

(4) Class 1A contributions based on the assessable employment benefit arising from the provision of a company car to the salesman

Notes

(1) No NICs are payable in respect of the remaining six part-time staff members as they each earn less than £5,435 pa.

(2) The salesman is liable to pay Class 1 primary contributions based on his salary of £14,000.

Example 2 - Classes of NICs

Stephen works for Camberley Cars Ltd on a part-time basis earning a salary of £19,000 pa. He is provided with a company car; petrol for both business and private mileage; and a place is provided for his daughter at the company's workplace nursery while he is working for them.

Stephen also runs a small bed and breakfast business from his home. In the year to 31 March 2009 his taxable trading profit from the business is £10,300.

Explain which classes of NICs are payable by Stephen and Camberley Cars Ltd in respect of 2008/09.

Answer to example 2

Stephen

Stephen will pay:

(1) Class 1 primary contributions based on his salary from Camberley Cars Ltd of £19,000 as his earnings are in excess of £5,435.

(2) Flat rate Class 2 contributions in respect of his bed and breakfast business.

(3) Class 4 contributions in respect of his bed and breakfast business based on his taxable trading profits as they are in excess of £5,435.

Camberley Cars Ltd

Camberley Cars Ltd will pay:

(1) Class 1 secondary contributions based on Stephen's salary of £19,000 as his earnings are in excess of £5,435.

(2) Class 1A contributions based on the assessable employment benefit arising from the provision of a company car and private petrol to Stephen.

Note: Class 1A contributions are not required in respect of the provision of a nursery place as it is an exempt benefit.

2 NICs payable in respect of employees

The following NICs are payable in respect of employees:

- Class 1 primary contributions
- Class 1 secondary contributions
- Class 1A contributions.

Class 1 primary and secondary NICs

Both the primary Class 1 contribution paid by the employee and the secondary contribution paid by the employer are a percentage-based contribution levied on the 'gross earnings' of the employee in excess of £5,435 for 2008/09.

The definition of earnings for Class 1 NIC purposes

'Earnings' for the purpose of Class 1 NICs consists of **any** remuneration derived from the employment and paid in **cash** or assets which are readily convertible into cash.

The calculation of Class 1 NICs is based on **gross earnings** with **no allowable deductions** (i.e. earnings before deductions that are allowable for income tax purposes, such as employee occupational pension scheme contributions and subscriptions to professional bodies).

Gross earnings **includes**:

- wages, salary, overtime pay, commission or bonus
- sick pay, including statutory sick pay
- tips and gratuities paid or allocated by the employer
- payment of the cost of travel between home and work
- vouchers (exchangeable for cash or non-cash items, such as goods).

'Gross earnings' **does not include**:

- exempt employment benefits
- most taxable **non-cash benefits** except remuneration received in the form of financial instruments, readily convertible assets and non-cash vouchers (see above)
- tips received from customers

- mileage allowance received from the employer provided it does not exceed the authorised HMRC approved allowance mileage rate of 40p per mile
- business expenses paid for or reimbursed by the employer, including reasonable travel and subsistence expenses.

Note that dividends are not subject to NICs, even if they are drawn by a director/shareholder in place of a monthly salary.

Expandable text - Exempt employment benefits

'Gross earnings' excludes items paid for, or provided by, the employer to the extent that these items are exempt from income tax (Chapter 4).

For example, items such as:

- employer contributions into a pension scheme
- relocation expenses
- provision of a workplace nursery
- a mobile phone
- work buses

Example 3 - Definition of Class 1 earnings

Janet and John are employed by Garden Gnomes Ltd. Their remuneration for 2008/09 is as follows:

	Janet	**John**
	£	£
Salary	30,000	55,000
Bonus	Nil	4,000
Car benefit	Nil	3,950
Childcare vouchers	£75 per week for 35 weeks	Nil
Employer's occupational pension scheme contribution	2,300	4,575
Employee's occupational pension scheme contribution	1,650	3,800

Calculate Janet and John's 'gross earnings' for Class 1 NIC purposes.

Answer to example 3

	Janet	John
	£	£
Salary	30,000	55,000
Bonuses	Nil	4,000
Childcare vouchers in excess of £55 per week		
(£75 – £55) × 35 weeks	700	Nil
Gross earnings for Class 1 NICs	30,700	59,000

Notes

(1) The employer's pension contributions are excluded as they are an exempt benefit.

(2) The employee's pension contributions are ignored as these are not deductible in calculating earnings for NIC purposes.

(3) The car benefit is excluded as it is a non-cash benefit which will be assessed to Class 1A NICs, not Class 1.

Eligible employees

Class 1 contributions are payable where the individual:

- is employed in the UK, and
- is aged 16 or over, and
- has earnings in excess of the lower earnings threshold of £5,435 for 2008/09.

Class 1 primary contributions

Class 1 primary contributions are payable by employees:

- aged 16 or over until
- attaining pensionable age (65 for a man, 60 for a woman).

The employer is responsible for calculating the amount of Class 1 primary NICs due and deducting the contributions from the employee's wages or salary.

Note that Class 1 primary contributions:

- are not an allowable deduction for the purposes of calculating the individual employee's personal income tax liability
- do not represent a cost to the business of the employer, as they are ultimately paid by the employee. Therefore, they are not a deductible expense when calculating the employer's taxable trading profits.

Calculating Class 1 primary contributions

Primary contributions are normally calculated by reference to an employee's earnings period:

- if paid weekly, the contributions are calculated on a weekly basis
- if paid monthly, the contributions are calculated on a monthly basis.

In the examination, the Class 1 NIC limits are usually shown on an annual basis and Class 1 NIC calculations should therefore be performed on an annual basis unless you are clearly told otherwise.

The primary contributions payable are calculated as:

- 11% on gross earnings between £5,435 and £40,040
- 1% on gross earnings in excess of £40,040

Expandable text - Earnings period

The annual earnings thresholds can be used to calculate the rate of Class 1 NICs payable where the employee's wages or salary does not fluctuate during the year.

However, where an employee's salary fluctuates during the year:

- the calculations must be performed on an earnings period basis
- the annual limits are divided into weekly or monthly thresholds.

The apportioned lower limit is £105 per week (£5,435/52) or £453 per month (£5,435/12); and the upper limit is £770 a week (£40,040/52) or £3,337 a month (£40,040/12).

Class 1 secondary contributions

Class 1 secondary contributions are payable by employers in respect of employees:

- aged 16 or over until
- the employee ceases employment.

There is no upper age limit for employer contributions, the employer is liable in full even if the employee is above pensionable age.

Secondary contributions are an additional cost of employment and are a deductible expense when calculating the employer's taxable trading profits.

Calculating Class 1 secondary contributions

Secondary contributions are calculated by reference to an employee's earnings period.

In the examination, the Class 1 NIC limits are usually shown on an annual basis and Class 1 NIC calculations should therefore be performed on an annual basis unless you are clearly told otherwise.

Secondary contributions are calculated as:

- 12.8% on all gross earnings above £5,435.

Note that there is:

- no upper earnings limit
- no change in rate of NIC payable for employer contributions.

Example 4 - Class 1 NICs

Millie is employed by Blue Forge Ltd and is paid an annual salary of £43,000. Millie is also provided with the following taxable benefits:

	£
Company car	5,000
Vouchers for the local gym	2,000

Calculate the employee's and the employer's Class 1 NIC liability due for 2008/09.

Answer to example 4

Millie

Class 1 NICs are due on annual earning of £45,000 (salary £43,000 and vouchers £2,000). The company car is a non-cash benefit and is therefore not subject to Class 1 NICs.

	£
Employee's Class 1 NICs	
(£40,040 – £5,435) @ 11%	3,806
(£45,000 – £40,040) @ 1%	50
	3,856
Employer's Class 1 NICs	
(£45,000 – £5,435) × 12.8%	5,064

Test your understanding 1

Alex is paid £7,950 per year and Betty is paid £41,440 per year.

Calculate the employee's and the employer's Class 1 NIC liability due for 2008/09.

Company directors

Special rules apply to company directors to prevent the avoidance of NICs by paying low weekly or monthly salaries, and then taking a large bonus in a single week or month.

Therefore, when an employee is a company director, his Class 1 NICs are calculated as if he had an annual earnings period.

Payment of Class 1 contributions

The administration and payment of Class 1 NICs is carried out by the employer as follows:

- The employer is responsible for calculating the amount of Class 1 primary and secondary contributions at each weekly or monthly pay date.
- Primary contributions are deducted from the employee's wages or salary by the employer and paid to HMRC on the employee's behalf.
- The total primary and secondary contributions are payable by the employer to HMRC, along with income tax deducted from the employees under PAYE.
- The payment is normally due on the 19th of each month (i.e. due not later than 14 days after the end of each PAYE month).
- The specific payment rules for very small employers and those paying electronically are covered in detail in Chapter 13.

Class 1A NICs

Employers are required to pay Class 1A contributions on 'taxable benefits' provided to employees earning at a rate of £8,500 pa and directors (i.e. higher paid employees).

No Class 1A contributions are payable in respect of:

- exempt benefits
- benefits provided to employees earning at a rate of less than £8,500 pa (i.e. lower paid employees)
- benefits already treated as earnings and assessed to Class 1 NICs, such as remuneration received in the form of non-cash vouchers (see above).

The contributions are calculated as:

- 12.8% on the value of the taxable benefits.

Class 1A contributions are an additional cost of employment and are a deductible expense when calculating the employer's taxable trading profits.

Example 5 - Class 1A NICs

Simon is employed by Dutton Ltd at an annual salary of £52,000.

He was provided with a company car throughout 2008/09 that had a list price of £15,000. The car has CO_2 emissions of 193 g/km. Petrol for both business and private mileage is provided by his employer.

Calculate the employee's and the employer's Class 1 and Class 1A NIC liabilities due for 2008/09.

Answer to example 5

(a) Class 1 NICs

Employee's Class 1 NICs	£
(£40,040 – £5,435) x 11% (maximum)	3,806
(£52,000 – £40,040) x 1%	120
	3,926
Employer's Class 1 NICs	
(£52,000 – £5,435) x 12.8%	5,960

(b) Class 1A NICs

Simon's taxable benefits for Class 1A purposes are as follows:

Company motor car	£
15% + ((190 – 135) / 5) = 26% × £15,000	3,900
Private fuel provided by company (26% × £16,900)	4,394
Taxable benefits for Class 1A	8,294
Employer's Class 1A NICs (£8,294 at 12.8%)	1,062

Test your understanding 2

Sally is paid £25,000 per year and has the following taxable benefits for 2008/09:

	£
Company motor car	5,250
Private fuel provided by company	4,200
Beneficial loan	2,600
Vouchers to be used at the local department store	250

The company also provided Sally with a mobile phone, which cost £135, and the following contributions were made into her personal pension scheme:

	£
Employer's contribution	2,540
Employee's contribution	1,380

Calculate the employee's and the employer's Class 1 and Class 1A NIC liabilities due for 2008/09.

Payment of Class 1A contributions

Class 1A contributions are payable to HMRC by 19 July following the end of the tax year (i.e. by 19 July 2009 for 2008/09).

Summary

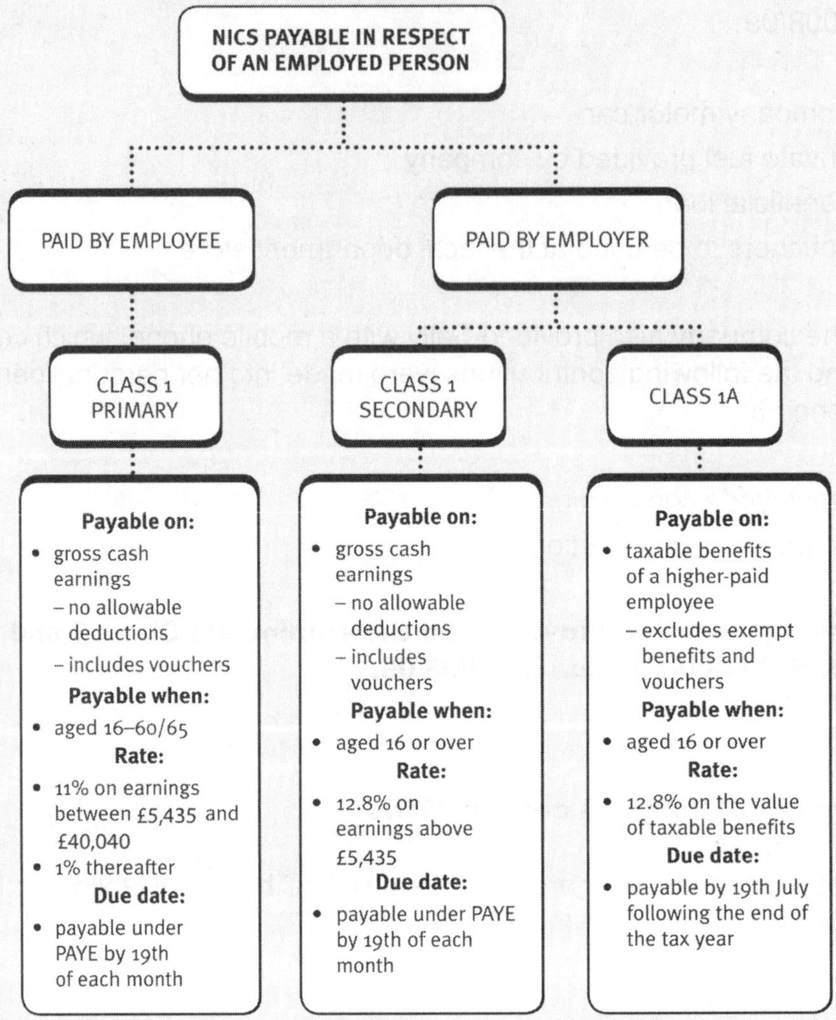

3 NICs payable in respect of self-employed individuals

The following NICs are payable by self-employed individuals:

- Class 2 contributions
- Class 4 contributions.

Class 2 contributions

Class 2 contributions are payable by individuals:

- aged 16 or over until
- attaining pensionable age (65 for a man, 60 for a woman).

Amount payable

Class 2 contributions are a flat rate payment of £2.30 per week.

The maximum total Class 2 NICs payable for 2008/09 is therefore £120 (£2.30 × 52 weeks).

Note that Class 2 contributions:

- are not an allowable deduction for the purposes of calculating the individual's income tax liability
- are not a deductible expense when calculating the business' taxable trading profits.

Payment of Class 2 contributions

Class 2 contributions are collected by HMRC on a monthly basis by direct debit, or by quarterly billing in arrears.

Class 4 contributions

In addition to Class 2 NICs, a self-employed individual may also be liable to Class 4 NICs.

Class 4 contributions are payable by self-employed individuals who:

- at the start of the tax year, are aged 16 or over.

They continue to pay **until**:

- the end of the tax year in which they attain pensionable age (65 for a man, 60 for a woman).

Class 4 NICs are a percentage-based contribution levied on the 'profits' of the individual in excess of £5,435 for 2008/09.

Note that Class 4 contributions:

- are not an allowable deduction for the purposes of calculating the individual's income tax liability
- are not a deductible expense when calculating the business' taxable trading profits.

The definition of Class 4 profits

'Profits' for the purposes of Class 4 NICs consists of:

- the taxable trading profits of the individual that are assessed for income tax after deducting trading losses (if any).

Note that 'profits' for Class 4 NICs are **before** deducting the individual's personal allowance that is available for income tax purposes.

If the individual has more than one business, the aggregate of all profits from all self-employed occupations are used to calculate the Class 4 NIC liability.

Calculating Class 4 NICs

The contributions payable are calculated as:

- 8% on profits between £5,435 and £40,040
- 1% on profits in excess of £40,040.

Example 6 - Class 4 NICs

James has been trading as a self-employed painter and decorator since 1998. His taxable trading profits for 2008/09 are £56,000 and he has trading losses brought forward of £10,000.

His wife, Poppy, is a part-time mobile hairdresser. Her taxable trading profits for 2008/09 are £6,560.

Calculate the Class 4 NICs payable by James and Poppy for 2008/09.

Answer to example 6

James

	£
Taxable trading profits for 2008/09	56,000
Less trading losses brought forward	(10,000)
Profits for Class 4 purposes	46,000

Class 4 NICs	£
(£40,040 – £5,435) × 8% (maximum)	2,768
(£46,000 – £40,040) × 1%	60
	2,828
Poppy	
Class 4 NICs	
(£6,560 – £5,435) × 8%	90

Test your understanding 3

Jack is a self-employed builder who has been in business for many years and prepares accounts to 31 March each year.

His taxable trading profit for the year ended 31 March 2009 is £43,850.

Calculate Jack's Class 2 and Class 4 NICs liability for 2008/09.

Payment of Class 4 contributions

Class 4 contributions are paid to HMRC at the same time as the individual's income tax due under self assessment, as follows:

Payment	**Due date**	**Amount**
Payments on account	• 31 January in the tax year (i.e. 31.1.2009 for 2008/09) • 31 July following the end of the tax year (i.e. 31.7.09 for 2008/09)	Two equal instalments of: • 50% of the amount paid by self assessment in the preceding year
Balancing payment	• 31 January following the end of the tax year (i.e. 31.1.10 for 2008/09)	Under or overpayment for the year

The detailed administration and payment rules are covered in Chapter 13.

Summary

NICs PAYABLE IN RESPECT OF A SELF-EMPLOYED INDIVIDUAL

CLASS 2

Payable when:

- aged 16–60/65

Rate:

- fixed rate £2.30 per week

Due date:

- collected monthly by direct debit or quarterly billing

CLASS 4

Payable on:

- taxable trading profits after trading losses

Payable when:

- aged 16–60/65 at the start of the tax year

Rate:

- 8% on profits between £5,435 and £40,040
- 1% thereafter

Due date:

- payable with income tax due under self assessment

4 Total NICs payable by a self-employed individual

A self-employed individual pays both Class 2 and Class 4 NICs in respect of his trading profits.

If the self-employed individual employs staff, he will be required to account for:

- Class 2 and Class 4 NICs in respect of his trading profits
- Class 1 primary, Class 1 secondary and Class 1A NICs in respect of earnings and benefits provided to employees.

Test your understanding 4

Diane has been a self-employed computer consultant for many years. Her taxable trading profits for 2008/09 are £50,000.

Diane employs a full-time personal assistant at a salary of £14,000 pa. She also provides the assistant with a diesel-engined company car, which has a list price of £13,500 and CO_2 emissions of 161 g/km. Diane pays for the assistant's private and business fuel.

Calculate the total NICs that Diane must account for to HMRC in respect of 2008/09.

5 Chapter summary

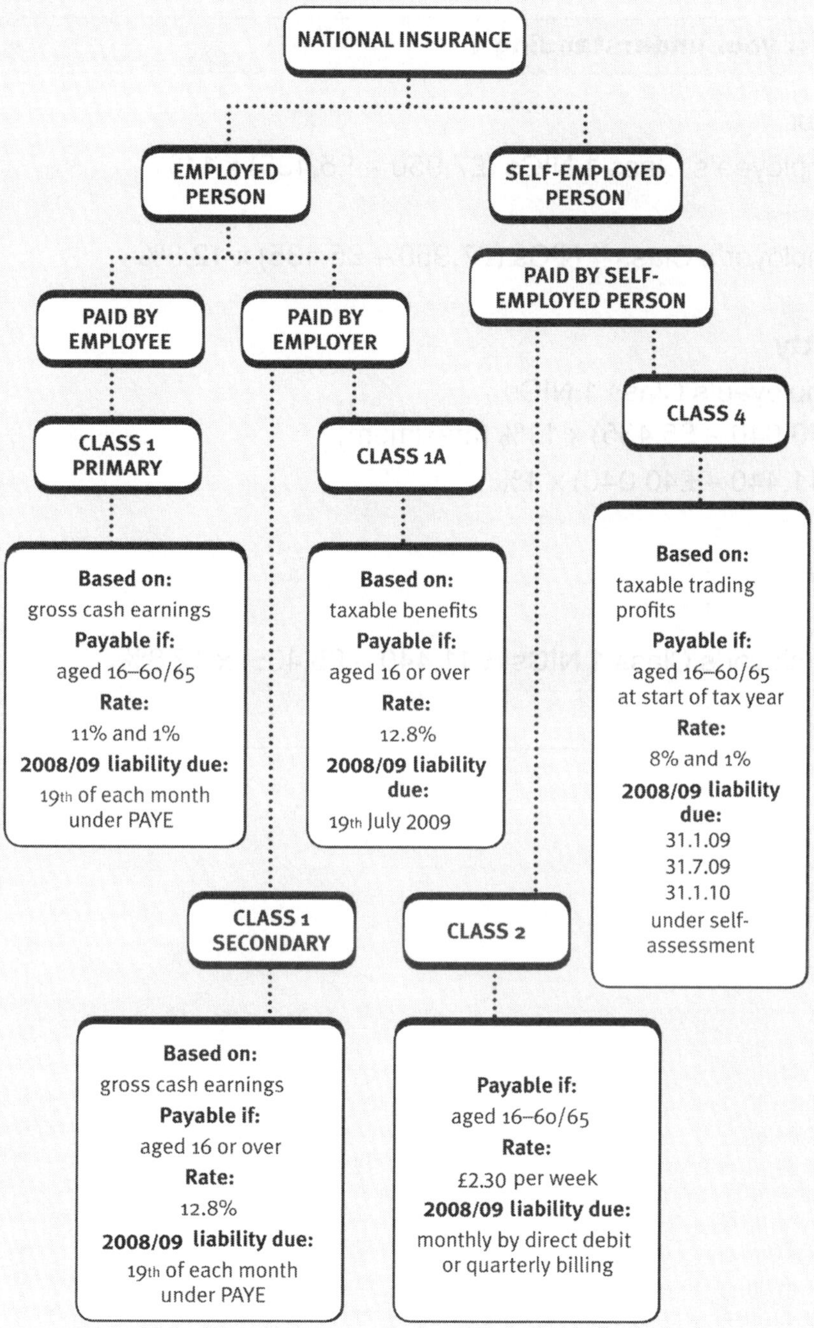

Test your understanding answers

Test your understanding 1

Alex	£
Employee's Class 1 NICs (£7,950 —£5,435) x 11%	277
	———
Employer's Class 1 NICs (£7,950 – £5,435) x 12.8%	322
	———
Betty	£
Employee's Class 1 NICs	
(£40,040 – £5,435) x 11% (maximum)	3,806
(£41,440 – £40,040) x 1%	14
	———
	3,820
	———
Employer's Class 1 NICs (£41,440 – £5,435) x 12.8%	4,609
	———

Test your understanding 2

Sally

Class 1 NICs

Sally's earnings for Class 1 purposes are as follows:

	£
Salary	25,000
Vouchers	250
Cash earnings for Class 1 NICs	25,250
Employee's Class 1 NICs (£25,250 – £5,435) x 11%	2,180
Employer's Class 1 NICs (£25,250 – £5,435) x 12.8%	2,536

Notes

(1) The provision of one mobile phone per employee, and employer pension contributions, are excluded as they are exempt benefits.

(2) The employee pension contributions are not allowable deductions in calculating earnings for NIC purposes.

(3) The car, fuel and beneficial loan benefits are excluded as they are non-cash benefits which are assessed to Class 1A NICs, not Class 1.

Class 1A NICs

Sally's taxable benefits for Class 1A purposes are as follows:

	£
Company motor car	5,250
Private fuel provided by company	4,200
Beneficial loan	2,600
Taxable benefits for Class 1A	12,050
Employer's Class 1A NICs (£12,050 at 12.8%)	1,542

Test your understanding 3

Jack	£
Class 2 NICs (£2.30 × 52 weeks)	120
Class 4 NICs	
(£40,040 – £5,435) × 8% (maximum)	2,768
(£43,850 – £40,040) × 1%	38
	2,806

Test your understanding 4

Diane

Diane will pay

(1) Flat rate Class 2 contributions in respect of her self-employed business.

Class 2 NICs	
(£2.30 × 52 weeks)	£120

(2) Class 4 contributions in respect of her self-employed business based on her taxable trading profits as they are in excess of £5,435.

Class 4 NICs	£
(£40,040 – £5,435) × 8% (maximum)	2,768
(£50,000 – £40,040) × 1%	100
	2,868

(3) Class 1 secondary contributions as she is an employer. The contributions will be based on her personal assistant's salary of £14,000.

Employer's Class 1 NICs	
(£14,000 – £5,435) x 12.8%	£1,096

(4) Class 1A contributions based on the assessable employment benefit arising from the provision of a company car to the personal assistant.

Taxable company car benefits for Class 1A purposes:

Company motor car	£
18% + ((160 – 135) / 5) = 23% × £13,500	3,105
Private fuel provided (23% × £16,900)	3,887
Taxable benefits for Class 1A	6,992
Employer's Class 1A NICs	
(£6,992 at 12.8%)	895

(5) Class 1 primary contributions are levied on the personal assistant. However, it is Diane's responsibility to deduct the NICs from the assistant's salary and pay them to HMRC along with the Class 1 secondary contributions on the 19th of each month.

Employee's Class 1 NICs	
(£14,000 – £5,435) x 11%	£942

Summary	£
Class 2	120
Class 4	2,868
Class 1 secondary	1,096
Class 1A	895
Diane's total liability	4,979
Class 1 primary	942
Total amount Diane must account for to HMRC	5,921

chapter

13

Tax administration for individuals

Chapter learning objectives

Upon completion of this chapter you will be able to:

- explain the self-assessment system as it applies to individuals
- state the time limits for notifying a liability and filing a return
- state the penalties for late submission of returns and notifying HMRC of liability
- list the information and records that the taxpayer needs to retain for tax purposes together with the retention period
- state the due dates for payment of tax under self-assessment
- compute payments on account and balancing payments/repayments
- state the effect of making a late payment on account/balancing payment
- calculate interest on overdue tax
- state the penalties that can be charged on a late payment of tax
- determine the time limits for key claims
- explain the circumstances in which HMRC can enquire into a self-assessment tax return
- describe the procedures for dealing with appeals and disputes
- explain the PAYE system
- list the key PAYE forms and explain their purpose.

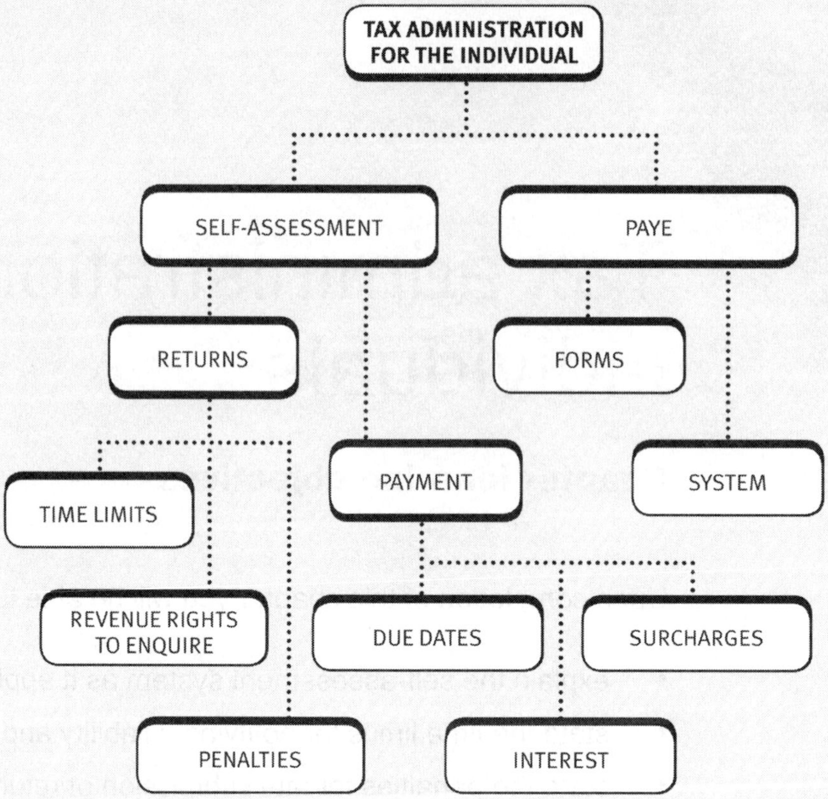

1 The self-assessment system

Introduction

The key aspects of the self-assessment system for the individual are as follows.

- The onus is placed on the taxpayer to calculate his or her own tax liability.
- The taxpayer will be sent a self-assessment tax return annually.
- Different filing deadlines exist for paper and electronic (online) returns.
- The final due date for the payment of the year's income tax, Class 4 NIC and CGT liability is 31 January following the end of the tax year to which it relates.
- Interim payments on account may be required on 31 January in the tax year and 31 July following the tax year for certain taxpayers.

The self-assessment tax return

The filing deadline for the 2008/09 self-assessment tax return depends on how the return is filed.

The filing deadline is the later of:

- 31 October 2009 for a paper return
- 31 January 2010 for an electronic (online) return (known as the filing date)
- three months after the issue of the return.

The different filing deadlines were introduced for 2007/08 onwards to encourage taxpayers to file their returns online. Prior to 2007/08 the filing deadline for all returns was 31 January following the end of the tax year.

The return comes in two parts.

- In the first part, the taxpayer needs to provide all the information required to calculate his tax liability for the year. This will be some or all of:
  - taxable income from all sources
  - any capital gains for the tax year concerned
  - reliefs and allowances.

  Self-employed people: The return includes a section for standardised accounts information.

  Employees: Generally pay their tax liability under PAYE and often a self-assessment tax return will not be required as there is no further tax liability.

  Partnerships: Although partners are dealt with individually, a partnership return will have to be completed to aid self-assessment on the individual partners. This will give details of the partners, and includes a partnership statement detailing the partnership's tax-adjusted income and how this is allocated between the partners.

- In the second part of the return, there is a section for the taxpayer to calculate his or her own tax liability (hence the term 'self-assessment'). This self-assessment is required even if the tax due is £Nil or if a repayment is due.
- Where a return is filed electronically a calculation of the tax liability is automatically provided as part of the online filing process.
- Where a paper return is submitted the taxpayer has the option of requesting HMRC to calculate the tax liability on behalf of the taxpayer provided the return is submitted by the 31 October deadline. The calculation by HMRC is treated as a self-assessment on behalf of the taxpayer.

- Note that in this situation, HMRC makes no judgement of the accuracy of the figures included in the return, but merely calculates the tax liability based on the information submitted.
- HMRC normally communicate with the taxpayer by issuing a statement of account.

  The statement of account sets out:

  – the tax charges
  – any charges of interest or surcharges (see later)
  – any payments already made by the taxpayer.

  The statement is not a notice to pay but merely a reminder of the taxpayer's indebtedness.

Amendments to the return

Either party may amend the return:

- HMRC may correct any obvious errors or mistakes within nine months of the date that the return is filed with them. These would include arithmetical errors or errors of principle. This does not mean that HMRC has necessarily accepted the return as accurate.
- The taxpayer can amend the return within 12 months of 31 January following the end of the tax year. For 2008/09, amendments must therefore be made by 31 January 2011. Note that the deadline is the same regardless of whether the return is filed on paper or electronically.

If an error is discovered at a later date then the taxpayer can make an error or mistake claim (see later) to recover any tax overpaid.

Notification of chargeability

Self-assessment places the onus on the taxpayers, therefore:

- Taxpayers who do not receive a return are required to notify HMRC if they have income or chargeable gains on which tax is due.
- The time limit for notifying HMRC of chargeability is six months from the end of the tax year in which the liability arises.
- Notification is not necessary if there is no actual tax liability. For example, if the income or capital gain is covered by allowances or exemptions.

Penalties for failure to submit a return

The following penalties apply where the taxpayer is late submitting the return:

- The initial penalty for not filing a return by the due date is £100.
- A daily penalty of up to £60 per day can be imposed, provided leave is given by the General or Special Commissioners (see later).
- If a daily penalty has not been imposed within six months of the filing date, and the return is not submitted by this date, then there is a further penalty of £100.
- The fixed penalties of £100 cannot exceed the amount of tax due.
- If the failure to file a return continues for more than 12 months after the filing date, then a tax-geared penalty may be imposed. The tax-geared penalty is in addition to the fixed and daily penalties, although it cannot exceed the tax liability for the tax year in question.

Example 1 - The self-assessment system

A taxpayer submits his return electronically for 2008/09 (which was issued during April 2009) on 10 October 2010. The tax due is £175.

Identify the penalties that will be charged.

Answer to example 1

Two fixed penalties of £100 will be due as the return is submitted more than six months after the filing date of 31 January 2010. The penalties will be reduced to the tax due of £175.

If a daily penalty was imposed, then this would run from the date when the Commissioners imposed it to 10 October 2010. The second fixed penalty of £100 will not be due if the daily penalties commenced before 31 July 2010 (six months after the filing date).

Test your understanding 1

Mandy had previously not submitted a tax return. She notified HMRC of her need to submit a return for 2008/09 and they issued her with one in April 2009. She eventually got around to submitting the form online in April 2010.

Identify the penalties that HMRC will charge. Note, that Mandy's eventual tax liability was in excess of £10,000.

Determination of tax due if no return is filed

Where a self-assessment tax return is not filed by the filing date, HMRC may determine the amount of tax due. The impact of this is:

- The determination is treated as a self-assessment by the taxpayer.
- The determination can only be replaced by the actual self-assessment when it is submitted by the taxpayer.
- There is no appeal against a determination, which therefore encourages the taxpayer to displace it with the actual self-assessment.
- A determination can be made at any time within five years of the filing date.

Records

Taxpayers are required to keep and preserve records necessary to make a correct and complete return.

For a business (including the letting of property), the records that must be kept include:

- all receipts and expenses
- all goods purchased and sold
- all supporting documents relating to the transactions of the business, such as accounts, books, contracts, vouchers and receipts.

These taxpayers (i.e. the self-employed), must keep all their records (not just those relating to the business) until five years after the 31 January filing date. For 2008/09 records must therefore be retained until five years after 31 January 2010, i.e. 31 January 2015.

For other taxpayers, they are likely to have many fewer records, but should keep evidence of income received such as dividend vouchers, P60s, copies of PIIDs and bank statements.

The records for these taxpayers must be retained until the later of:

- 12 months after the 31 January filing date (31 January 2011 for 2008/09)
- the date on which an enquiry into the return is completed
- the date on which it becomes impossible for an enquiry to be started.

A penalty of up to £3,000 may be charged for failure to keep or retain adequate records. The maximum penalty is only likely to be imposed in the most serious cases such as where a taxpayer deliberately destroys his records in order to obstruct an HMRC enquiry.

2 Payment of tax

Introduction

A taxpayer will be required to settle liabilities by 31 January following the end of the tax year for:

- income tax
- national insurance
- capital gains.

For 2008/09 this is 31 January 2010.

Payments on account

For certain taxpayers, payments on account may also be required.

If the taxpayer had an income tax liability in the previous year in excess of any tax deducted at source, a payment on account is normally required for the following year. The exceptions to this are if:

- the relevant amount for the previous year is less than £500 or
- more than 80% of the income tax liability for the previous year was met by deduction of tax at source.

The impact of these provisions is that most employed people will not have to make payments on account, since at least 80% of their tax liability is paid through PAYE.

For those taxpayers who are required to make payments on account, the dates for 2008/09 are:

- first payment on account – 31 January 2009
- second payment on account – 31 July 2009.

Any remaining liability is then settled on the 31 January 2010 due date.

The payments on account are only for:

- income tax
- Class 4 National Insurance Contributions (NICs).

No payments on account are ever required for capital gains tax.

The payments on account are calculated using the previous year's tax liability. Therefore the payments on account for 2008/09 are based on the tax liability for 2007/08.

This is referred to as the relevant amount and is calculated as:

	£
Total tax liability for the year	X
Less: Amounts paid at source, e.g. PAYE, tax on bank and building society interest, dividend tax credits	(X)
Relevant amount	X

Note: No payments on account are required if there is no relevant amount in the previous year. A taxpayer who commences self-employment on 1 May 2008 will not have to make payments on account for 2008/09, since he or she will not have a relevant amount for 2007/08.

Example 2 - Payment of tax

Roderick, who is 47, is required to make payments on account of his 2008/09 tax liability. His income tax payable for 2007/08 was £5,100. Of this, £1,250 was collected via PAYE.

What are Roderick's payments on account in respect of his 2008/09 income tax liability?

Answer to example 2

The amounts payable as 'payments on account' are based on an **equal** division of the relevant amount for the previous year's tax payable, hence £3,850 **(W)** × 1/2 = £1,925.

Roderick is required to make two payments of account of £1,925 on 31 January 2009 and 31 July 2009.

Working: Relevant amount

The relevant amount for the previous year is £3,850 (£5,100 – £1,250).

Test your understanding 2

Ahmed's tax liability for 2007/08 was as follows:

	£
Income tax	9,400
Less: Tax deducted at source	(2,100)
	7,300
Class 4 NIC	700
CGT	3,500
Total tax liability	11,500

Calculate the payments on account for 2008/09.

Claims to reduce payments on account

- At any time before 31 January following the tax year, a taxpayer can claim to reduce the payments on account.
- A taxpayer would claim to reduce the payments on account if he expected the actual income tax and Class 4 NIC liability (net of tax deducted at source) for 2008/09 to be lower than 2007/08.
- The claim must state the grounds for making the claim.

Following a claim to reduce payments on account:

- The payments on account will be reduced.
- Each payment on account will be for half the reduced amount, unless the taxpayer claims that there is no tax liability at all.
- If payments on account are paid before a claim is made, then HMRC will refund the overpayment.

Incorrect claims to reduce payments on account

A taxpayer should only claim to reduce payments on account if the tax liability (net of tax deducted at source) for the current year is expected to be less than the payments on account based on the previous years relevant amount.

In the event that the claim is incorrect and the actual tax liability for the current year turns out to be higher than the original payments on account, then the following consequences arise:

- Interest will be charged on the tax underpaid.
- A penalty will be charged if a taxpayer fraudulently or negligently claims to reduce payments on account. The maximum penalty is the difference between the amounts actually paid on account, and the amounts that should have been paid.
- A penalty will not be sought in cases of innocent error. The aim is to penalise taxpayers who claim large reductions in payments on account without any foundation to the claim.

Balancing payments

The balancing payment is due on 31 January following the tax year. For 2008/09 this will be 31 January 2010.

The balancing payment is calculated as:

	£	£
Total tax liability for the year		X
(Income tax, Class 4 NIC and CGT)		
Less:		
Amounts deducted at source	X	
Payments on account	X	(X)
	—	—
Balancing payment		X
		—

- It is possible that a balancing repayment will be due, in which case HMRC will repay the amount of tax overpaid.
- Where the amount of tax due changes as a result of an amendment to the self-assessment (by either the taxpayer or HMRC), any additional tax due must be paid within 30 days of the notice of amendment if this is later than the normal due date.

Example 3 - Payment of tax

Continuing the example of Roderick from above. You now learn that his final liability for 2008/09 has been agreed as £7,629. Of this amount £1,635 has been collected via the PAYE system.

State the total amount payable by Roderick on 31 January 2010 and what the payments relate to.

Answer to example 3

The payment made on 31 January 2010 will comprise two parts:

- the balancing payment for 2008/09
- first payment on account for 2009/10.

The balancing payment for 2008/09 will be based on the final liability for 2008/09 less amounts collected at source and the payments on account already made.

	£
2008/09 IT liability	7,629
PAYE	(1,635)
Payments on account	(3,850)
Final payment	2,144

The first payment on account for 2009/10 will be 50% of the relevant amount using the 2008/09 position.

	£
2008/09 IT liability	7,629
PAYE	(1,635)
Relevant amount	5,994

The first payment on account is (£5,994 × 1/2) = £2,997

Summary:

	£
Balancing payment 2008/09	2,144
First payment on account 2009/10	2,997
Total payable 31 January 2010	5,141

Test your understanding 3

Peter's tax liability for 2008/09 is as follows:

	£
Income tax	10,800
Less: Tax deducted at source	(2,500)
	8,300
Class 4 NIC	800
CGT	4,600
Total tax liability	13,700

He made payments on account of £8,000 in respect of 2008/09.

Identify the balancing payment to be made for 2008/09, the first payment on account for 2009/10 and state the due date for payment of both.

3 Interest and surcharges

The interest rate will be provided in the Tax Rates and Allowances section of the exam.

For the June 2009 and December 2009 exams, the rate to use is 7.5% pa.

Interest on tax paid late

Interest will automatically be charged if any tax is paid late.

Interest can arise in respect of:

- payments on account
- balancing payments
- any tax payable following an amendment to a self-assessment
- any tax payable following a discovery assessment.

The date from which interest runs depends on the payment made late:

- For payments on account, interest runs from the due date of the relevant payment on account (i.e. 31 January in the tax year or 31 July following it).
- In other instances, interest runs from 31 January following the tax year to the date of payment. This is the case even if the tax was not actually due until a later date (i.e. following the amendment of the self-assessment).

The only exception to this is where the return was issued late, in which case the due date will be three months after the issue of the return if this is later.

Interest is charged on penalties from the date they become due to the date that they are paid. The actual interest charge is calculated for the period from the due date to the day before actual payment takes place.

Example 4 - Interest and surcharges

A taxpayer pays his 2008/09 payments on account on 15 March 2009 and 10 August 2009. The balancing payment is paid on 15 April 2010.

Identify the payments that will attract interest and state the period for which interest will be charged.

Answer to example 4

Interest will be charged as follows:

- first payment on account: from 31 January 2009 to 14 March 2009
- second payment on account: from 31 July 2009 to 9 August 2009
- balancing payment: from 31 January 2010 to 14 April 2010.

Test your understanding 4

Rodney was due to make the following payments of tax for 2008/09.

Due Date	**Payment**	**Actual date of payment**
31 January 2009	£2,100	28 February 2009
31 July 2009	£2,100	31 August 2009
31 January 2010	£1,000	31 March 2010

Identify the periods for which interest will be charged. Calculate the amount of interest payable assuming a 7.5% interest rate.

Interest on incorrect claims to reduce payments on account

- Interest will be charged where an excessive claim is made to reduce payments on account.
- The charge is based on the difference between the amounts actually paid and the amounts that should have been paid. The amount that should have been paid is the lower of:
  - the original payments on account based on the relevant amount for the previous year
  - 50% of the final tax liability (excluding CGT, and net of tax deducted at source) for the current year.

Interest runs from the due dates of 31 January in the tax year and 31 July following the tax year to the date of payment. The date of payment will be 31 January following the tax year when the balancing payment is due, unless the balancing payment is made late.

Example 5 - Interest and surcharges

A taxpayer's relevant amount for 2007/08 is £5,000 (payments on account for 2008/09 are therefore £2,500), but a claim is made to reduce the payments on account to £1,000 each. These payments are made on time.

Subsequently the taxpayer identifies the actual tax liability (net of tax deducted at source) for 2008/09 to be £4,500. The correct balancing payment (i.e. £4,500 – £2,000 = £2,500) is paid on 31 January 2010.

Identify the amounts on which interest is to be charged and state the period(s) for which interest will be charged.

Answer to example 5

Payments on account should have been reduced to £2,250 (£4,500 × 1/2) rather than £1,000. Interest will therefore be charged as follows:

- on £1,250 from 31 January 2009 to 30 January 2010
- on £1,250 from 31 July 2009 to 30 January 2010.

Test your understanding 5

Herbert's payments on account for 2008/09 based on his income tax liability for 2007/08 were £4,500 each. However, Herbert made a claim to reduce these amounts to £3,500. He made his interim payments on account for 2008/09 as follows:

Payment	£	Date
First payment on account	3,500	29 January 2009
Second payment on account	3,500	12 August 2009

When Herbert's eventual liability for 2008/09 was agreed, it was as follows:

	£
Income tax liability	10,000
Capital gains	2,500

Herbert paid the balance of the tax due £5,500 on 19 February 2010.

Identify the amounts on which interest is to be charged and state the period(s) for which interest will be charged.

Interest paid on overpayments of tax

Interest is paid by HMRC on any overpayment of tax.

The interest rate will be provided in the Tax Rates and Allowances section of the exam. For the June 2009 and December 2009 exams the rate to use is 3%.

Interest runs from the later of:

- the due date
- the actual payment date

to the date of repayment.

Interest is only paid on the amount of tax that should have been paid (i.e. deliberate overpayments will not attract interest).

Surcharge on unpaid tax

Interest on tax paid late is not a penalty, since it merely compensates for the advantage of paying late. Therefore, to further encourage compliance, surcharges can also be imposed where income tax, Class 4 NIC or CGT is paid late.

The surcharge does not apply to payments on account.

Surcharges are calculated as follows:

- Where a balancing payment is not paid until more than 28 days after the due date (31 January following the tax year), a surcharge equal to 5% of the tax unpaid is imposed.
- A further 5% surcharge arises if the tax is still unpaid after six months.

Where additional tax becomes due as a result of an amendment to a self-assessment, a surcharge is only imposed if the additional tax is not paid within 28 days of the due date for the amendment (30 days after the amendment).

Note: This last provision differs from interest that runs from the normal due date; 31 January following the tax year.

There is also an interest charge on the surcharge, if the surcharge is not paid within 30 days of the date that it is imposed.

A surcharge may be mitigated by HMRC, for example if there is a reasonable excuse for the non-payment of the tax. Insufficiency of funds is not a reasonable excuse.

Example 6 - Interest and surcharges

A taxpayer's balancing payment due for 2008/09 is £5,000. Only £1,200 of this was paid on 31 January 2010.

Set out the interest and surcharges that will be payable and state the implication of continued non-payment of the liability.

Answer to example 6

Interest

Interest will be charged on £3,800 from 31 January 2010 to the date of payment.

In the event that either of the surcharges are not paid within 30 days of their issue, interest will be assessed on these amounts as well.

Surcharges

A surcharge of £190 (£3,800 at 5%) will be due if the tax of £3,800 is not paid by 28 February 2010.

A further surcharge of £190 will be due if the tax is not paid by 31 July 2010.

Interest will arise on these surcharges, if they remain unpaid for 30 days from the date of issue.

Test your understanding 6

Rowena's final tax payable (after credits but before payments on account) is computed for 2008/09 as follows:

Income tax	£6,000
Capital gains tax	£3,000

Payments on account of £4,000 in total were made on the relevant dates. The balance of the tax due was paid as follows:

Income tax	1 March 2010
Capital gains tax	1 April 2010

Calculate the interest and surcharges due. (Assume the rate of interest on unpaid tax is 7.5%)

4 Claims

Introduction

- A claim for a relief, allowance or repayment must be quantified at the time that the claim is made. For example, if loss relief is claimed, then the amount of the loss must be stated.
- Wherever possible the taxpayer must include claims in his or her self-assessment tax return.

Claims for earlier years

Certain claims will relate to earlier years. The most obvious example of this is the claiming of loss relief for earlier years.

The basic rule is that such a claim is:

- established in the later year
- calculated based on the tax liability of the earlier year.

This means that the tax liability for the earlier year is not adjusted. Instead, the tax reduction resulting from the claim will be set off against the tax liability for the later year. The logic behind this is that it avoids re-opening self-assessments for earlier years.

If the taxpayer does make a claim in the return for the later year, the HMRC will refund the tax due.

As the claim is only quantified by reference to the earlier year, payments on account that are based on the relevant amount for the earlier year, will not change.

Example 7 - Claims

A taxpayer's relevant amount for 2007/08 is £4,400. In 2008/09 the taxpayer makes a trading loss of £1,000, and makes a claim to offset this against his total income of 2007/08.

Explain how the taxpayer will receive the tax refund arising as a result of the relief for the loss arising in 2008/09.

Answer to example 7

The taxpayer's payments on account for 2008/09 are £2,200 (£4,400 × 1/2), and these will not change as a result of the loss relief claim.

The tax refund due will be calculated at the taxpayer's marginal income tax rate(s) for 2007/08. The tax refund due will either be set off against the 2008/09 tax liability, thereby affecting the balancing payment on 31 January 2010, or if there is insufficient tax left owing, HMRC will make a refund.

Error or mistake claims

Where an assessment is excessive due to an error or mistake in a return, the taxpayer can claim relief.

The claim must be made within five years of the 31 January filing date for the tax year concerned. For 2008/09 an error or mistake claim must be made by 31 January 2015.

A claim can be made in respect of errors made, and mistakes arising from not understanding the law.

5 Enquiries into returns

HMRC's right of enquiry

HMRC have the right to enquire into the completeness and accuracy of any self-assessment tax return.

The enquiry may be made as a result of any of the following:

- a suspicion that income is undeclared
- deductions being incorrectly claimed
- other information in HMRC's possession
- being part of a random review process.

Additional points:

- HMRC do not have to state a reason for the enquiry and are unlikely to do so.
- An enquiry can be made even if HMRC calculated a taxpayer's tax liability.
- HMRC must give written notice before commencing an enquiry.
- The written notice must be issued within 12 months of the date the return is filed with HMRC. Once this deadline is passed, the taxpayer can normally consider the self-assessment for that year as final.

Enquiry procedures

HMRC can demand that the taxpayer produces any or all of the following:

- documents
- accounts
- other written particulars
- full answers to specific questions.

The information requested should be limited to that connected with the return.

The taxpayer has 30 days to comply with the request. An appeal can be made against the request.

The enquiry ends when HMRC gives written notice that it has been completed. The notice will state the outcome of the enquiry. If the taxpayer believes that HMRC have no grounds for continuing an enquiry, he is entitled to ask the General or Special Commissioners that a date be set for its completion.

The closure notice must include either:

- confirmation that no amendments are required
- HMRC's amendments to the self-assessment.

The taxpayer has 30 days to appeal against any amendments by HMRC. The appeal must be in writing.

Discovery assessments

Despite the fact that HMRC must normally begin enquiries into a self-assessment return within 12 months of the date the return is filed, a discovery assessment can be raised at a later date to prevent the loss of tax.

The detail procedure for discovery assessments is given in expandable text.

Expandable text - Discovery assessment

The use of a discovery assessment is restricted where a self-assessment has already been made:

- Unless the loss of tax is due to fraud or negligence, a discovery assessment cannot be raised where full disclosure was made in the return, even if this is found to be incorrect.
- HMRC will only accept that full disclosure has been made if any contentious items have been clearly brought to their attention – perhaps in a covering letter or in the 'white space' on the tax return.
- Information lying in the attached accounts will not constitute full disclosure if its significance is not emphasised.
- Only a taxpayer who makes full disclosure in the self-assessment tax return therefore has absolute finality 12 months after the date the return is filed.

The time limit for making a discovery assessment is five years from the 31 January filing date, i.e. 31 January 2015 for 2008/09 returns. This is extended to 20 years from the 31 January filing date in the case of fraud or negligence.

A discovery assessment may be appealed against.

Penalties

In addition to interest on the late payment of tax, HMRC can impose a penalty for submitting incorrect returns (i.e. for omitting information from a return, or where the return includes false information).

For returns commencing on/after 1 April 2008 where the return is due to be filed on / after 1 April 2009, the penalty is determined according to:

- The amount of tax understated
- The reason for the understatement
- The extent of disclosure by the taxpayer.

The level of the penalty is a percentage of the revenue lost as a result of the inaccuracy or under assessment and depends on the behaviour of the taxpayer as follows:

Taxpayer behaviour	**Maximum penalty (% of revenue lost)**
Genuine mistake	No penalty
Failure to take reasonable care	30%
Serious or deliberate understatement	70%
Serious or deliberate understatement with concealment	100%

The penalties may be reduced depending on the type of penalty and whether the taxpayer makes an unprompted disclosure.

Where the return is incorrect through deliberate intention of a third party, the penalty can be charged on the third party.

6 Appeals

Introduction

The taxpayer can appeal against an amendment to the self-assessment following a HMRC enquiry, and against discovery assessments.

Disputes that cannot be settled between HMRC and the taxpayer are usually adjudicated by either:

- General Commissioners or
- Special Commissioners.

Both the General and the Special Commissioners are appointed by the Lord Chancellor.

The Commissioners will hear the appeal at which HMRC and the taxpayer (or his representative, e.g. his accountant) present their cases. The Commissioners then adjudicate on the dispute.

Their findings are conclusive on a point of **fact**, but disputes on points of **law** (i.e. interpretation of the Taxes Acts) may be continued through the High Court – Chancery Division, the Court of Appeal and finally to the House of Lords.

At the Commissioners' stage of appeal, both sides will normally meet their own costs; although the Special Commissioners can award costs against a party that has acted unreasonably in bringing or persisting with the case.

Special Commissioner cases are published where the decision is likely to be of interest to other taxpayers.

The costs of appeal incurred by the taxpayer are not allowable expenses for tax purposes.

Expandable text - The General and Special commissioners

The General Commissioners

The key features of the General Commissioners are that they:

- are lay persons
- are appointed by the Lord Chancellor
- have no special legal or taxation qualifications.

The appointments are honorary and part-time.

All appeals are heard by them automatically, unless an election is made for the appeal to be determined by the Special Commissioners. This election, however, is not available unless the General Commissioners direct that they are satisfied that the case should be heard by the Special Commissioners.

The General Commissioners are able to transfer appeals to the Special Commissioners subject only to obtaining their agreement. They are likely to do this because of either:

- the complexity of the appeal
- the length of time likely to be required for hearing it.

The Special Commissioners

Unlike the General Commissioners, the Special Commissioners are:

- full-time paid officials
- independent of HMRC
- barristers, advocates or solicitors of not less than ten years' standing.

They hear all appeals where an election has been made for them to do so.

Certain appeals on special points must be heard by the Special Commissioners – normally those involved with complex interpretations of the Taxes Acts.

7 The PAYE system

Introduction

Pay as you earn (PAYE) is the system used for collecting income tax and national insurance at source from the earnings paid to employees:

- All payments of earnings assessable as employment income are subject to deduction of tax under the PAYE system.
- In many cases, the PAYE system removes the need to file a formal self-assessment tax return since the correct amount of tax will have been deducted from earnings.
- All employers making payments of earnings are required to deduct the appropriate amount of tax from each payment (or repay over-deductions) by reference to PAYE tax tables.
- The aim of the tax tables is for the tax deducted from payments to date to correspond as closely as possible to the correct proportion to date of the total tax liability (after allowances and reliefs) of the employee for the year.

Coding notice

To enable the employer to match the tax collected with the particular tax affairs of the individual taxpayer, HMRC issues a tax coding.

The system enables different amounts of tax to be collected from different taxpayers according to their personal circumstances. The detail rules for tax coding are given in expandable text.

Expandable text - coding notice

- From the information supplied in his or her tax return, each employee is sent a coding notice that sets out the total reliefs and allowances available to him for the year.
- The last digit is removed to arrive at the code number shown. Thus, allowances of £6,035 become 603.
- The employer is also notified of the code number.
- Using this code number and a set of tax tables, the employer can calculate the correct amount of tax each week or month.
- Most code numbers issued to the employer carry a suffix of which the most usual is L. The letter L denotes that just the ordinary personal allowance of £6,035 has been given.

- These letters are added in order to simplify the revision of codes, e.g. when the personal allowance is increased from one tax year to the next, all code numbers with the suffix L can easily be increased by the employer, so that PAYE can continue to operate effectively.
- Some code numbers carry a K prefix. This indicates that the deductions, such as benefits, to be made from allowances actually exceed the allowances. The code number is effectively 'negative'.
- Where an employee has not been allocated a code number (perhaps because the individual was previously self-employed), the employer must deduct tax under PAYE in accordance with an emergency code that reflects only the personal allowance (i.e. Code 603L). This code is applied until the correct code number is supplied by HMRC.

Tax code calculation

Tax code calculation 2008/09

Allowances	£	**Deductions**	£
Personal allowance	X	Benefits	X
Allowable expenses	X	Adjustment for underpaid tax (must be less that £2,000)	X
Adjustment for overpaid tax	X	Other income	X
	—		—
Total allowances	X	Total deductions	X
	—		—

The tax code is:

(Total allowances less total deductions) × 1/10

The answer is then rounded down to the nearest whole number.

Calculation of deductions

PAYE is calculated on a tax deductions working sheet (P11), using tax tables provided by HMRC.

The tax tables are as follows.

Pay adjustment tables:	Based on an employee's tax code, this set of tables shows the cumulative amount of tax-free pay to which an employee is entitled for each week or month of the year.
Taxable pay tables:	Deducting tax-free pay from pay gives a figure for taxable pay. The taxable pay tables can then be used to calculate the amount of income tax due.

The tax is calculated for any given pay week or month on a cumulative basis, i.e. the tax for, say month five, is the difference between the cumulative total tax due at the end of month five compared with the cumulative total due at the end of month four.

Payments to HMRC

Employers are generally required to make monthly payments of income tax and NIC to HMRC as follows:

- The income tax and NIC that the employer deducts during each tax month is due for payment to HMRC not later than 14 days after the month ends.
- The tax month runs from sixth to fifth of each month.
- Therefore the payment due date is the 19th of each month.
- Employers whose average monthly payments of PAYE and NICs are less than £1,500 in total are allowed to make quarterly, rather than monthly, payments. Payments are due by the 19th of the month following the quarters ending 5 July, 5 October, 5 January and 5 April.
- Employers with 250 or more employees must make their monthly PAYE payments electronically on the 22nd of each month.

8 Key PAYE forms

Introduction

To standardise the correspondence with HMRC, specific forms are issued for use in certain circumstances. This ensures all appropriate information is gathered and simplifies the process.

They key forms that you are required to know are:

Form	Purpose of use	Timing
P45	When employee leaves	Ongoing with staffing changes
P46	When new employee joins without P45	Ongoing with new starters
P35	Year end summary	Annually following end of tax year
P14 – P60	Year end summary	Annually following end of tax year

The procedure to be adopted when an employee leaves or joins a business, and the year end procedures, is given in expandable text.

Expandable text - Procedures on leaving or joining

Procedure to be adopted when an employee leaves

When an employee leaves an employment the PAYE system is interrupted. Forms P45 must be completed for each employee in order that either:

- a new employer can carry on making PAYE deductions using the appropriate code and cumulative totals from the last employment
- the employee can claim a tax repayment.

Procedure to be adopted when an employee joins

The operation of the PAYE system depends upon having a tax code for each employee. The form P45 details his or her tax code, pay to date and tax to date and will allow the new employer to operate PAYE for the employee's pay.

Where form P45 cannot be produced the employee has to complete form P46 to identify the individual's circumstances so that the appropriate amount of tax can be deducted. If:

- it is the employee's first full-time job they are allocated a tax code equivalent to the basic personal allowance (603L for 2008/09) on a full cumulative basis.

- it is the employee's main employment an emergency tax code equivalent to the basic personal allowance (603L for 2008/09), and this will be operated on a non-cumulative basis.
- the employee is in receipt of a pension all his employment earnings then have tax deducted under PAYE at the basic rate (i.e. code BR applies).

If none of the above circumstances apply the employer will have to operate a basic rate code by deducting basic rate tax on the full amount of pay.

End-of-year procedure

The following returns will need to be completed at the end of each tax year.

P35 employer's annual statement, declaration and certificate

This has to be submitted by 19 May, and performs the role of:

- an overall summary of tax and NIC deducted by the employer for the year
- a questionnaire to ensure compliance with PAYE arrangements
- a declaration and certificate to be signed by the employer confirming that all year-end returns have been completed.

P14 – P60 certificate of pay and tax deducted

Not later than 19 May the employer must send the first two copies of the form (P14) to HMRC, showing for each employee:

- Employee's National Insurance number
- Employer's name and address
- Personal details
- Total earnings for the year
- Final PAYE code
- Total income tax deducted for the year
- Total NIC for the year.

The third part of the form (P60) is given to the employee by 31 May in order to complete the employment pages of his self-assessment return.

9 Chapter summary

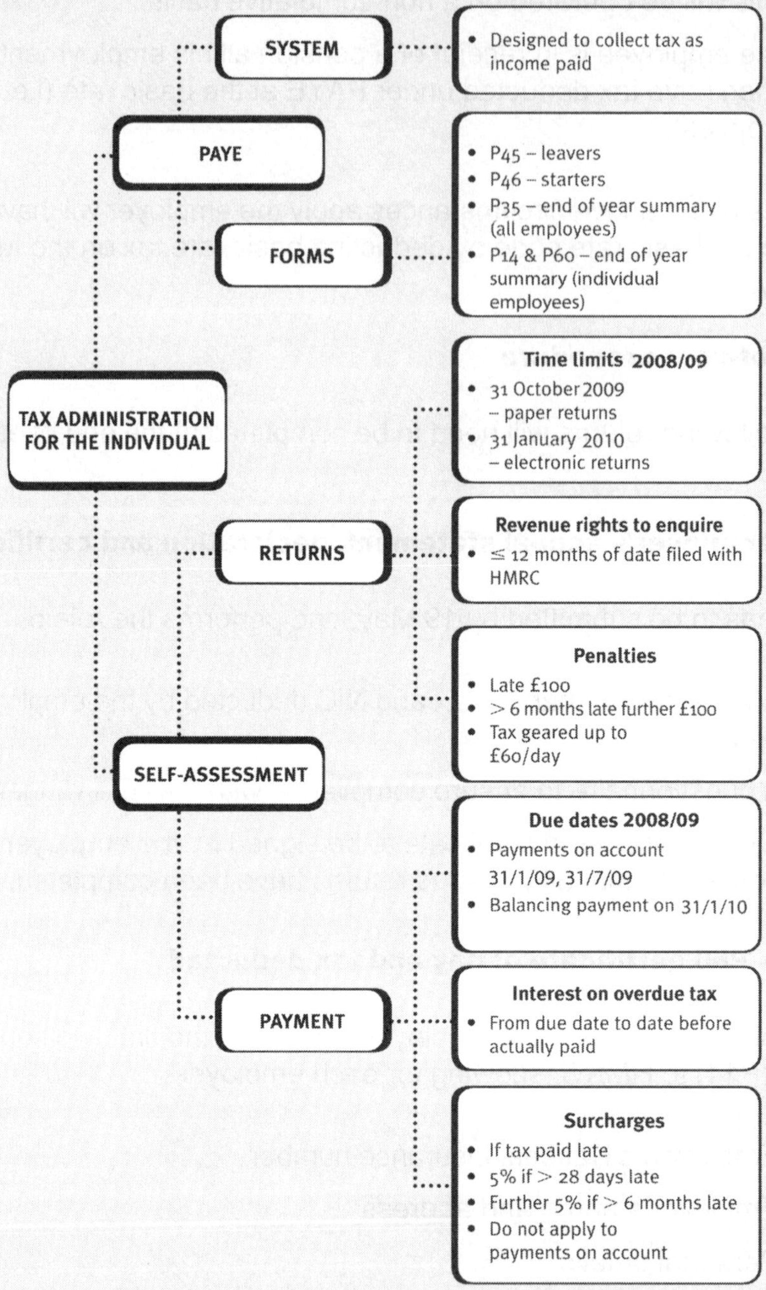

Test your understanding answers

Test your understanding 1

Mandy

Mandy will be charged £100 fixed penalty for failing to submit her tax return by 31 January 2010. There is also likely to be interest and surcharges levied.

Test your understanding 2

Ahmed

The relevant amount for income tax is £7,300.

The relevant amount for Class 4 NIC is £700.

Payments on account will be due for 2008/09 as follows:

	£
31 January 2009 (£7,300 + £700 = £8,000 × 1/2)	4,000
31 July 2009	4,000

No payments on account of capital gains tax are ever required.

Test your understanding 3

Peter

	£
Total tax liability	13,700
Less: Payments on account	(8,000)
Balancing payment due 31 January 2010	5,700

The balancing payment comprises:

	£
Income tax and National Insurance (£8,300 + £800 – £8,000)	1,100
CGT	4,600
Balancing payment	5,700

The first payment on account for 2009/10 will be 50% of the relevant amount using the 2008/09 position.

	£
2008/09 IT liability (after deducting PAYE)	8,300
Class 4 NIC	800
Relevant amount	9,100

The first payment on account is (£9,100 × 1/2) = £4,550

Summary:

	£
Balancing payment 2008/09	5,700
First payment on account 2009/10	4,550
Total payable on 31 January 2010	10,250

Test your understanding 4

Rodney

Periods on which interest is charged:

On first POA	31 January 2009 – 27 February 2009	28 days
On second POA	31 July 2009 – 30 August 2009	31 days
On final payment	31 January 2010 – 30 March 2010	59 days

Interest payable:

On first POA	(£2,100 × 7.5% × 28/365) = £12.08
On second POA	(£2,100 × 7.5% × 31/365) = £13.38
On final payment	(£1,000 × 7.5% × 59/365) = £12.12

Test your understanding 5

Herbert

Payments on account should not have been reduced, therefore the amounts that should have been paid, on each of the due dates was £4,500.

First payment on account:

£3,500 is paid on time.

Interest charge therefore only levied on £1,000 that should also have been paid.

Levied for the period 31 January 2009 to 18 February 2010.

Second payment on account:

£3,500, as well as being the wrong amount, was also paid late.

On £3,500, interest charged 31 July 2009 to 11 August 2009.

On the additional £1,000, interest levied for the period 31 July 2009 to 18 February 2010.

On balancing payment:

Income tax of £9,000 (£4,500 × 2) has been dealt with above, so it is only the remaining £1,000 that will incur an interest charge, from 31 January 2010 to 18 February 2010.

Capital gains tax of £2,500 incurs interest from 31 January 2010 to 18 February 2010.

Test your understanding 6

Rowena

The relevant date for balancing payments is 31 January 2010.

No payments on account are ever required for CGT.

The amounts due were therefore as follows:

		£
31 January 2010	Income tax	2,000
	Capital gains tax	3,000

Interest will run as follows:

Income tax	£2,000 from 31 January 2010 to 28 February 2010, i.e. 1/12 × 7.5% × £2,000 = £12.50
CGT	£3,000 from 31 January 2010 to 31 March 2010, i.e. 2/12 × 7.5% × £3,000 = £37.50

In addition a surcharge is due on the CGT and income tax (as they are more than 28 days late) of 5% of £5,000 = £250.

Total payable £12.50 + £37.50 + £250 = £300.

The surcharge may be reduced if HMRC accept there was a reasonable excuse for late payment.

chapter

14

Computation of gains and tax payable

Chapter learning objectives

Upon completion of this chapter you will be able to:

- identify the persons and the transactions that are liable to UK tax on capital gains
- define 'residence' and 'ordinary residence' for an individual and state its relevance for capital gains tax
- identify which assets are exempt
- understand how to calculate the gain on the disposal of an asset
- calculate the capital gain on the disposal of an asset for an individual
- used for both business and non-business purposes
- demonstrate how capital losses can be relieved against gains for an individual
- calculate the capital gains on assets after losses
- compute the amount of capital gains tax payable.

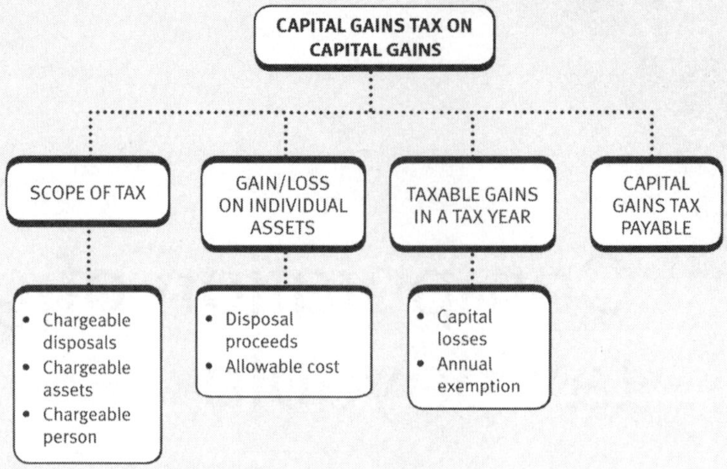

1 Introduction

This and the following three chapters deal with the way in which **individuals** are subject to tax on their capital gains.

Companies also pay tax on their chargeable gains and many of the rules set out in these capital gains tax chapters also apply to companies. There are, however, some differences and these are explained within the chapters on corporation tax.

The taxation of capital gains is an important topic as it will be the focus of question three, for **20 marks**, in the examination. Questions one and two may also contain an element of capital gains.

2 Scope of capital gains tax (CGT)

Capital gains tax (CGT) is charged on gains arising on **chargeable disposals** of **chargeable assets** by **chargeable persons**.

Chargeable disposal

An asset is disposed of for capital gains purposes when its ownership changes. The following are treated as chargeable disposals:

- sale of the whole or part of an asset
- gift of the whole or part of an asset
- exchange of an asset
- receipt of a capital sum derived from an asset, e.g. compensation for damage to an asset
- loss or total destruction of an asset.

Note that a disposal as a result of the death of an individual is an exempt disposal for CGT purposes.

Chargeable assets

All forms of property, wherever situated, are chargeable assets unless specifically exempted. Exempt assets are covered in more detail below.

Chargeable persons

Chargeable persons include:

- individuals
- companies.

Chargeable individuals

In these CGT chapters we are only concerned with disposals by individuals.

- Only individuals who are either:
  - UK resident or
  - UK ordinarily resident

  in the tax year in which the disposal takes place are subject to capital gains tax on their gains.

- Chargeable individuals are subject to CGT on all disposals of assets, regardless of where in the world the assets are situated.
- An individual who is neither UK resident nor UK ordinarily resident does not pay UK CGT even though the assets may be situated in the UK.

Definition of residence

The definition of residence is the same as for income tax purposes, which was covered in Chapter 2. Broadly, an individual will be a UK resident in a tax year if he is physically present in the UK for a period of six months or more.

Expandable text - Residence

An individual is UK resident if either:

- they are physically present in the UK for a period (or periods) of six months or more in any tax year or
- they have paid frequent and substantial visits to the UK.

HM Revenue and Customs (HMRC) regard stays of three months a year, on average, for four consecutive years as, 'frequent and substantial'.

Definition of ordinary residence

Ordinary residence implies residence with some degree of continuity, ignoring incidental or temporary absences.

It is the place where the individual normally resides as opposed to his place of occasional residence.

Expandable text - Ordinary residence

- An individual who has previously been resident and ordinarily resident in the UK may still be regarded as UK ordinarily resident for a year that he spends wholly overseas if it is their intention to return to the UK.
- An individual must be absent from the UK for at least three years before they will be regarded as having lost their ordinarily residence status.

Exempt assets

Exempt assets are outside the scope of CGT. Consequently:

- gains are not taxable
- losses are not allowable.

The main types of exempt assets are:

- motor vehicles (including vintage cars)
- certain types of chattels (see Chapter 15).
- principal private residence
- securities and qualifying corporate bonds
- national savings certificates
- foreign currency acquired for personal use
- prizes and betting winnings
- assets held in Individual Savings Accounts (ISA).

Test your understanding 1

Which of the following disposals may give rise to a capital gain?

- **Sale of shares in an unquoted trading company.**
- **Gift of antique painting.**
- **Sale of 13% Treasury stock 2012.**
- **Exchange, with a friend, of a house for an apartment.**
- **Sale of a motor car to brother at less than market value.**
- **Gift of a London flat by an individual who is neither resident nor ordinarily resident in the UK.**

Complete the table below:

Not chargeable	Chargeable disposals

3 Calculation of capital gain/loss on individual disposals

An individual is subject to CGT on the taxable gains realised on all assets disposed of in a tax year.

The following steps should be carried out to compute the capital gains tax payable by an individual for a tax year:

(1) Calculate the capital gains/allowable loss arising on the disposal of each chargeable asset separately

(2) Calculate the net capital gains arising in the tax year = (capital gains less allowable losses)

(3) Deduct capital losses brought forward = net capital gains

(4) Deduct the annual exemption = taxable gains

(5) Calculate the CGT payable at a flat rate of 18%.

This section deals with Steps 1 and 2, the calculation of the capital gain/allowable loss arising on the disposal of each individual asset, and the calculation of net capital gains in the tax year.

Pro forma – individual

The following basic CGT pro forma should be used for the disposal of all assets by an individual.

	£	£
Disposal proceeds		X
Less: Allowable selling costs		(X)
		—
Net proceeds		X
Less: Allowable expenditure		
Cost of acquisition	X	
Incidental costs of acquisition	X	
Additional (capital) enhancement expenditure	X	(X)
	—	—
Capital gain/(allowable loss)		X/(X)
		—

Disposal proceeds

The disposal proceeds used in the computation is normally the consideration received for the asset. Market value may, however, be used in certain circumstances instead of the actual consideration.

- Market value is substituted for actual proceeds either because:
  - the deal was not made at arm's length, e.g. a gift
  - the law assumes that it was not made at arm's length, e.g. transfers between connected parties.
- An individual is connected with family members, business partners and any company that he controls. For this purpose family members are:
  - ancestors, lineal descendants and their spouses/civil partners
  - brothers, sisters and their spouses/civil partners
  - his or her spouse/civil partner
  - the relatives (as above) of his or her spouse/civil partner.

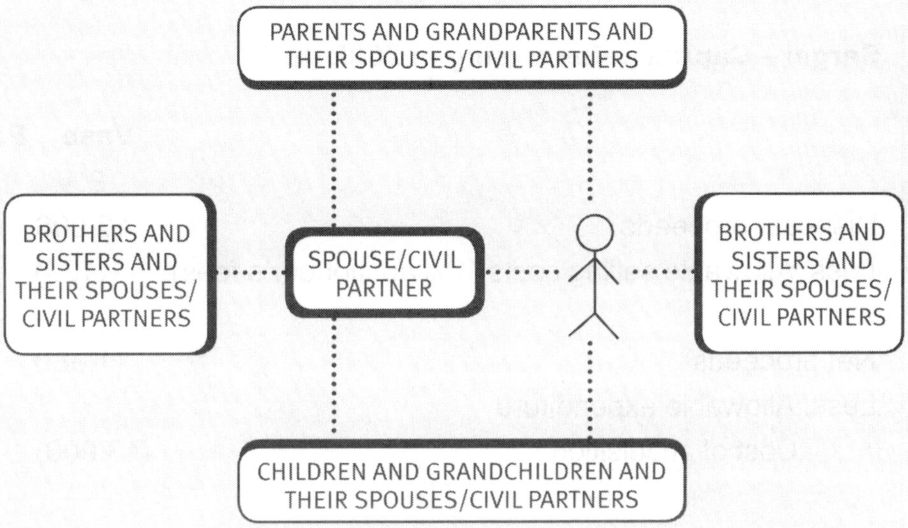

- Incidental costs arising on disposal are deducted from the gross proceeds, e.g. auctioneer's fees, estate agent fees.

Allowable expenditure

The types of expenditure that rank as allowable deductions are:

- cost of acquisition (e.g. purchase cost)
- expenditure on enhancing the value of the asset (improvement expenditure)
- expenditure incurred to establish, preserve or defend the taxpayer's title to the asset
- incidental costs arising on the acquisition of the asset.

Where an individual acquires an asset where the previous owner was required to use the asset's market value in calculating their own gain, e.g. gift of an asset, then that same market value is used by the current owner as their cost of acquisition.

Where an individual inherits an asset on death, the cost of acquisition when they later dispose of the asset is the asset's market value at the date of the death (i.e. probate value).

Example 1 - Calculation of capital gain/loss on individual

On 1 May 2008 Sergei sold an antique vase for £12,000 and a painting for £20,000. He incurred auctioneer's fees of 1% of the proceeds. He acquired both assets on 1 July 1991 for £13,000 and £5,000, respectively.

Calculate the net capital gain arising in 2008/09.

Answer to example 2

Sergei – Capital gains arising in 2008/09

	Vase	Painting
	£	£
Disposal proceeds	12,000	20,000
Less: Allowable selling costs (1% auctioneer's fees)	(120)	(200)
Net proceeds	11,880	19,800
Less: Allowable expenditure		
Cost of acquisition	(13,000)	(5,000)
Capital gain/(allowable loss)	(1,120)	14,800
Net capital gain for 2008/09 (£14,800 – £1,120)	£13,680	

Test your understanding 2

On 1 May 2008, Margaret sold a holiday villa to her sister for £25,000. Its market value at that date was £100,000. Margaret had acquired the villa on 1 June 1997 for £20,000 and had paid legal fees on acquisition of £500. On 1 May 2002, she had added a conservatory at a cost of £10,000.

Calculate the capital gain arising on the sale of the villa.

Test your understanding 3

Amanda sold a holiday cottage for £75,000 on 13 August 2008. It cost £53,500 in May 1999 and was extended in September 2003 at a cost of £16,000. The estate agent and solicitor fees for the purchase totalled £2,300 and for the sale totalled £5,400.

She also sold her grandmother's engagement ring for £12,000. She had inherited the ring on the death of her grandmother in August 2005 when the ring was valued at £9,000.

Calculate the net capital gain arising in 2008/09.

4 Calculation of CGT payable

An individual is subject to capital gains tax on the taxable gains realised on all assets disposed of in a tax year.

This section covers Steps 3 to 5 in the procedure to calculate the CGT payable by an individual, once the net capital gains for the tax year have been calculated.

Proforma capital gains tax payable computation – 2008/09

	£
Net capital gains for the tax year	X
Less: Capital losses brought forward (see later)	(X)
Net capital gains	X
Less: Annual exemption (2008/09)	(9,600)
Taxable gains	X
CGT payable (18% x taxable gains)	X

Annual exemption

Every individual is entitled to an annual exemption for each tax year.

- For 2008/09 the annual exemption is £9,600.
- If an individual's taxable gains for the tax year do not exceed that amount, they are not chargeable to tax. Otherwise, they are chargeable on gains over and above the annual exemption.

- If the annual exemption is not utilised in any particular tax year, then it is wasted. It cannot be carried forwards or backwards against capital gains of another tax year.

For the purpose of examination requirements, the term **taxable gain** means the **net capital gains after deducting the annual exemption**.

Capital losses

Current year capital losses

Capital losses arising on assets in the current tax year are set off:

- against capital gains arising in the same tax year
- to the maximum possible extent, i.e. they cannot be restricted to avoid wasting all or part of the annual exemption.

Any unrelieved/unused capital losses are carried forward to offset against net capital gains in future years.

Brought forward capital losses

The maximum amount of brought forward losses that can be set off against gains in any tax year is restricted to the amount required to reduce the total net capital gains in the tax year to the level of the annual exemption.

Example 2 - Calculation of taxable gains in the tax year

Tom and Jerry made capital gains and allowable losses for the years 2007/08 and 2008/09 as set out below.

	Tom	**Jerry**
2007/08	£	£
Capital gains	12,000	4,000
Allowable losses	8,000	7,000
2008/09		
Capital gains	12,500	10,800
Allowable losses	2,000	1,000

Calculate the taxable gains for Tom and Jerry for both 2007/08 and 2008/09 and the amount of any losses carried forward at the end of 2008/09.

Answer to example 2

Tom

2007/08	£
Capital gains	12,000
Allowable losses – current year	(8,000)
Net capital gains	4,000

Net capital gains are covered by the annual exemption. There are no losses to carry forward to 2008/09.

2008/09	£
Capital gains	12,500
Allowable losses – current year	(2,000)
Net capital gains	10,500
Annual exemption	(9,600)
Taxable gains	900

Tom is taxed on gains of £900 in 2008/09.

Jerry

2007/08	£
Capital gains	4,000
Allowable losses – current year	(4,000)
Net capital gains	Nil

Jerry is unable to use his 2007/08 annual exemption since his gains are all covered by current year losses. He has losses of £3,000 (£7,000 – £4,000) to carry forward to 2008/09.

2008/09	£
Capital gains	10,800
Allowable losses – current year	(1,000)
Net capital gains in the tax year	9,800
Losses brought forward (2007/08)	(200)
Net capital gains	9,600
Annual exemption	(9,600)
Taxable gains	Nil

Jerry used £200 of his losses brought forward, to reduce his capital gains to the level of the annual exemption. He still has losses of £2,800 (£3,000 – £200) to carry forward to 2009/10.

Test your understanding 4

Fred and Barney made capital gains and allowable losses for the years 2007/08 and 2008/09 as set out below.

	Fred	**Barney**
2007/08	£	£
Capital gains	15,000	5,000
Allowable losses	10,000	9,000
2008/09		
Capital gains	20,900	12,800
Allowable losses	11,000	2,500

Calculate the taxable gains for Fred and Barney for both 2007/08 and 2008/09 and the amount of any losses carried forward at the end of 2008/09.

5 Payment of CGT

CGT is due as follows:

- On 31 January following the tax year, i.e. for 2008/09 payment must be made by 31 January 2010.
- No payments on account are ever made.

Test your understanding 5

Jade sold an investment property on 1 May 2008 for £650,000. She had acquired the building for £80,000 in June 1995 and had extended it at a cost of £30,000 in June 1997.

Jade also disposed of a painting on 1 June 2008 for £20,000, incurring auctioneer's fees of 1%. She had acquired the painting for £35,000 in April 1997.

Jade had capital losses brought forward of £16,000. Jade's taxable income in 2008/09 was £31,000.

Calculate Jade's capital gains tax payable for 2008/09 and state the due date for payment.

6 Chapter summary

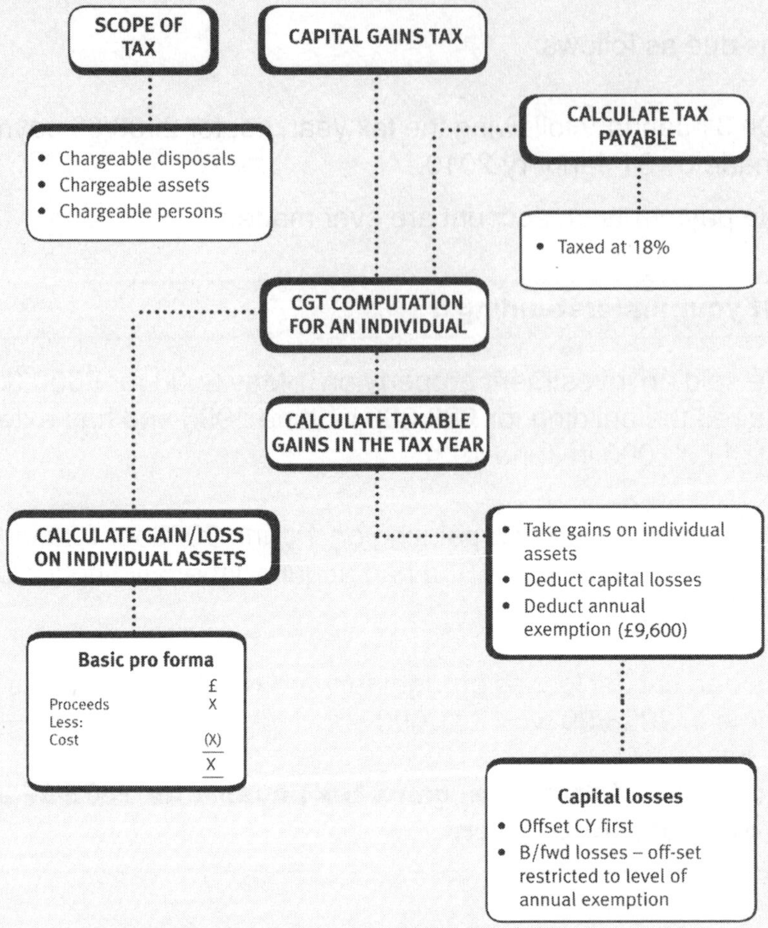

Test your understanding answers

Test your understanding 1

Not chargeable	Chargeable disposals
Sale of 13% Treasury stock 2012 (gilt-edged security – exempt asset)	Sale of shares in an unquoted trading company
Sale of a motor car to brother at less than market value (motor vehicle – exempt asset)	Gift of antique painting
Gift of a London flat by an individual who is neither resident nor ordinarily resident in the UK (not a chargeable individual)	Exchange, with a friend, of a house for an apartment

Test your understanding 2

Margaret

Capital gain arising in 2008/09

	£	£
Disposal proceeds – deemed market value (**Note 1**)		100,000
Less: Allowable expenditure		
Cost of acquisition	20,000	
Incidental costs of acquisition – legal fees	500	
Enhancement expenditure (**Note 2**)	10,000	
		(30,500)
Capital gain		69,500

Notes

1: Market value is substituted for actual proceeds as the sale was to a connected person (Margaret's sister) and is therefore deemed to not be an 'arm's length transaction'.

2: The conservatory is allowable expenditure as it enhanced the value of the villa.

Test your understanding 3

Amanda

Capital gains arising in 2008/09

	Cottage	**Ring**
	£	£
Disposal proceeds	75,000	12,000
Less: Allowable selling costs	(5,400)	(Nil)
Net proceeds	69,600	12,000
Less: Allowable expenditure		
cost of acquisition	(53,500)	
Incidental costs of acquisition	(2,300)	
Extension	(16,000)	
Probate value		(9,000)
Capital gain/(allowable loss)	(2,200)	3,000
Net capital gain for 2008/09 (£3,000 – £2,200)	£800	

Test your understanding 4

Fred

2007/08	£
Capital gains	15,000
Allowable losses – current year	(10,000)
Net capital gains	5,000

Net capital gains are covered by the annual exemption. There are no losses to carry forward to 2008/09.

2008/09	£
Capital gains	20,900
Allowable losses – current year	(11,000)
Net capital gains	9,900
Annual exemption	(9,600)
Taxable gains	300

Fred is taxed on gains of £300 in 2008/09.

Barney

2007/08	£
Capital gains	5,000
Allowable losses – current year	(5,000)
Net capital gains	Nil

Barney is unable to use his 2007/08 annual exemption since his gains are all covered by current year losses. He has losses of £4,000 (£9,000 – £5,000) to carry forward to 2008/09.

2008/09	£
Capital gains	12,800
Allowable losses – current year	(2,500)
Net capital gains for year	10,300
Losses brought forward (2007/08)	(700)
Net capital gains	9,600
Annual exemption	(9,600)
Taxable gains	Nil

Barney used £700 of his losses brought forward, to reduce his capital gains to the level of the annual exemption. He still has losses of £3,300 (£4,000 – £700) to carry forward to 2009/10.

Test your understanding 5

Jade

Capital gains tax computation – 2008/09

	£	£
Investment property		
Disposal proceeds	650,000	
Less: Allowable expenditure		
Cost of acquisition	(80,000)	
Enhancement expenditure	(30,000)	
Capital gain	540,000	540,000
Painting		
Disposal proceeds	20,000	
Less: Allowable selling costs	(200)	
Net proceeds	19,800	
Less: Allowable expenditure		
Cost of acquisition	(35,000)	
Loss	(15,200)	(15,200)
Net capital gains arising in the tax year		524,800
Less: Capital losses brought forward		(16,000)
Net capital gains		508,800
Less: Annual exemption		(9,600)
Taxable gains		499,200
Capital gains tax payable		
(£499,200 x 18%)		89,856

chapter

15

Computation of gains: special rules

Chapter learning objectives

Upon completion of this chapter you will be able to:

- show the tax treatment of a capital asset when the transfer is between spouses or registered civil partners
- calculate the gain when there is a part disposal of an asset
- define a wasting and non-wasting chattel
- identify when chattels and wasting assets are exempt
- compute the capital gain/allowable loss when a chattel is disposed of
- calculate the gain when a chargeable wasting asset is disposed of
- explain why the disposal of plant and machinery does not create a capital loss
- identify the tax treatment where an asset is lost/destroyed
- identify the tax treatment where an asset is damaged.

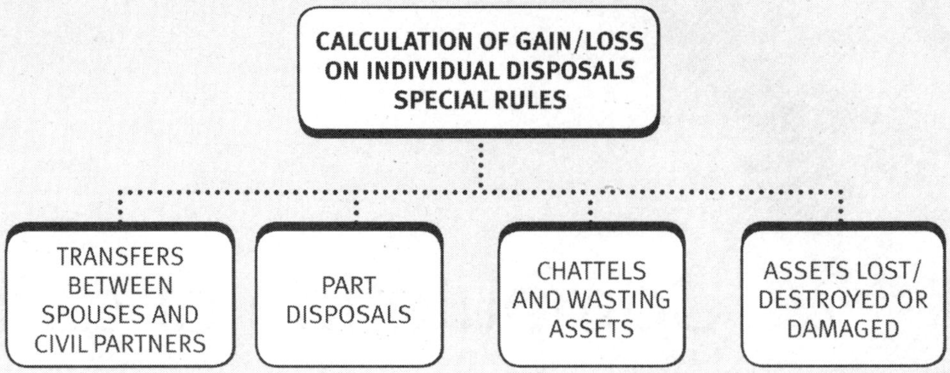

1 Introduction

Building on from the previous chapter, and using the basic pro forma for all disposals of assets, we can now develop this with the following special rules that may need to be considered:

- transfers between spouses and civil partners
- part disposals
- chattels and wasting assets
- assets lost or destroyed
- damaged assets.

2 Transfers between spouses and civil partners

Where an asset is transferred between spouses or civil partners:

- no gain or loss arises on the transfer
- any actual proceeds are ignored
- if the transfer is on/after 6 April 2008, the transferor is deemed to dispose of the asset at its acquisition cost
- if the transfer is before 6 April 2008, the transferor is deemed to dispose of the asset at a 'base cost' which ensured that there was no gain or loss on the transfer under the 'pre 6 April 2008' capital gains tax rules.

  If applicable, the examiner will give you the appropriate 'base cost' to use in the examination question.

- the deemed proceeds of the transferor are treated as the deemed acquisition cost (base cost) of the transferee.

Expandable text - pre-6 April 2008

Pre 6 April 2008, individuals were entitled to an indexation allowance.

The base cost of an inter-spouse transfer was therefore its acquisition cost plus indexation allowance up to the date of the transfer.

However, the examiner has stated that knowledge of the pre-6 April 2008 rules for individuals is not required.

These rules only apply whilst the spouses/civil partners are living together (i.e. not separated).

Example 1 - Transfers between spouses and civil partners

David purchased some jewellery in August 1995 for £50,000. In June 2009 he gave it to his wife Victoria when it was worth £200,000.

Calculate the deemed sale proceeds of David's disposal and state Victoria's deemed acquisition cost.

Answer to example 1

The interspouse transfer occurred after 6 April 2008, therefore David is deemed to have transferred the asset at its acquisition cost of £50,000 so that no gain or loss arises on the transfer.

The deemed proceeds are therefore £50,000 and Victoria's deemed acquisition cost is the same as David's deemed proceeds, i.e. £50,000.

Subsequent disposal by transferee

On a subsequent disposal of the transferred asset by the transferee the following rules apply:

- The deemed acquisition cost (often referred to as the base cost of the asset) is the deemed proceeds on the nil gain, nil loss transfer.

Example 2 - Subsequent disposal

Jack acquired a holiday cottage for £25,000 on 1 September 1987 and transferred it to his wife, Jill, on 31 January 1990. The base cost of the cottage was £29,175. Jill sold the cottage to a third party on 1 August 2008 for £42,000.

Compute the capital gain on Jill's disposal in August 2008.

Answer to example 2

	£
Disposal proceeds	42,000
Less: Deemed acquisition cost (base cost)	(29,175)
Capital gain	12,825

Test your understanding 1

John acquired a warehouse for £100,000 on 1 September 1994. On 1 May 2008 he gave the warehouse to his wife, Tania, when it was worth £300,000. Tania sold the warehouse for £350,000 on 1 July 2008.

Tania had no other capital disposals in 2008/09, but has capital losses brought forward of £11,300.

Calculate Tania's capital gains tax payable in 2008/09.

Planning opportunities

Married couples and civil partners can transfer assets between them at no tax cost (i.e. the assets are transferred at no gain/no loss). This provides opportunities to minimise their total capital gains tax liability.

They can transfer assets between them to maximise the use of:

- each individual's annual exemption
- capital losses.

Example 3 - Planning opportunities

Adam, who is married to Kerry, made three chargeable disposals in the tax year 2008/09, as follows:

Asset 1	Gain	£10,000
Asset 2	Gain	£20,000
Asset 3	Gain	£14,800

(a) **Calculate Adam's CGT payable for 2008/09.**

(b) **Advise how savings could have been made by the couple, and calculate the revised CGT payable by the couple assuming they had taken your advice.**

Answer to example 3

(a) **Adam's CGT payable – 2008/09**

	£
Asset 1	10,000
Asset 2	20,000
Asset 3	14,800
Total net capital gains	44,800
Less: Annual exemption	(9,600)
Taxable gain	35,200
CGT payable (£35,200 × 18%)	6,336

(b) **Advice**

As a married couple, Kerry and Adam can transfer assets between themselves at nil gain/nil loss, (i.e. at no tax cost).

Accordingly, they should consider transferring assets between themselves to ensure that they both use their annual exemptions.

If Adam had transferred Asset 3 to Kerry, then the gain on the asset would be reduced by her annual exemption of £9,600, leaving only £5,200 chargeable to CGT.

Adam's revised CGT payable for the year is as follows:

	£
Asset 1	10,000
Asset 2	20,000
	30,000
Less: Annual exemption	(9,600)
Taxable gain	20,400
CGT payable (£20,400 × 18%)	3,672

Kerry's CGT payable would be:	£
Asset 3	14,800
Annual exemption	(9,600)
Taxable gain	5,200
CGT payable (£5,200 x 18%)	936
Total CGT payable (£3,672 + £936)	4,608
Tax saving (£6,336 – £4,608)	1,728
Alternative calculation:	
Use of Kerry's annual exemption (£9,600 x 18%)	1,728

3 Part disposals

When there is a part disposal of an asset, we need to identify how much of the original cost of the asset relates to the part of the asset disposed of as follows.

- The allowable expenditure of the part of the asset disposed of is calculated using the following formula:

$$\textbf{Cost} \times \frac{\textbf{A}}{\textbf{A + B}}$$

Where:
A = Value of the part disposed of
B = Market value of the remainder at the time of the part disposal.

- The allowable expenditure, calculated using the formula, is then used in the basic capital gains tax computation as normal.

Example 4 - Part disposal

Yayha acquired 20 acres of land in March 1988 for £6,000. On 1 June 2008, he disposed of 8 acres for £8,000. The value of the remaining 12 acres at this date was £15,000.

On 1 September 2008, Yayha sold the reminder of the land for £18,000.

Calculate the capital gains arising on the disposals of land on 1 June 2008 and 1 September 2008.

Answer to example 4

1 June 2008 disposal

	£
Proceeds	8,000
Cost £6,000 × £8,000/(£8,000 + £15,000)	(2,087)
Capital gain	5,913

Note that the number of acres is irrelevant in calculating the cost of the land disposed of.

Always use the (A/A + B) formula, which uses the **value** of the asset disposed of and retained.

1 September 2008 disposal

	£
Sale proceeds	18,000
Cost (£6,000 – £2,087(above))	(3,913)
Capital gain	14,087

Test your understanding 2

Jacob bought 10 acres of land for £8,000 in August 1992. He sold 3 acres of the land for £20,000 in January 2009. At that time the remaining land was worth £60,000.

In March 2009 Jacob sold the remaining acres for £75,000.

Calculate the capital gains tax payable for 2008/09 and state the due date of payment.

Test your understanding 3

Gemma bought an investment property in May 2000 for £50,000. On 1 July 2006 she disposed of part of the land attached to the property for £40,000. The value of the property and the remaining land at this date was £100,000.

On 1 August 2008 Gemma sold the property and remaining land for £200,000.

Calculate the capital gains tax payable for 2008/09.

4 Chattels and wasting assets

It is important to be able to identify a chattel and a wasting asset as there are special rules for calculating the gain or loss arising on them.

Chattels

Chattels are defined as tangible moveable property, e.g. a picture or table.

Note that the asset must be:

- moveable – therefore a building is not a chattel
- tangible – therefore shares are not chattels.

Wasting assets

A wasting asset is an asset with a predictable life not exceeding 50 years.

Chattels may be wasting or non-wasting assets as follows.

	Wasting chattels	Non-wasting chattels
Expected life	Not exceeding 50 years	More than 50 years
Examples	Greyhound Boat Plant and machinery Racehorse	Antiques Jewellery Paintings

Plant and machinery is deemed to have a useful life of less than 50 years and is therefore **always** a wasting asset.

Chattels – exempt disposals

Certain disposals of chattels are exempt from capital gains tax as follows.

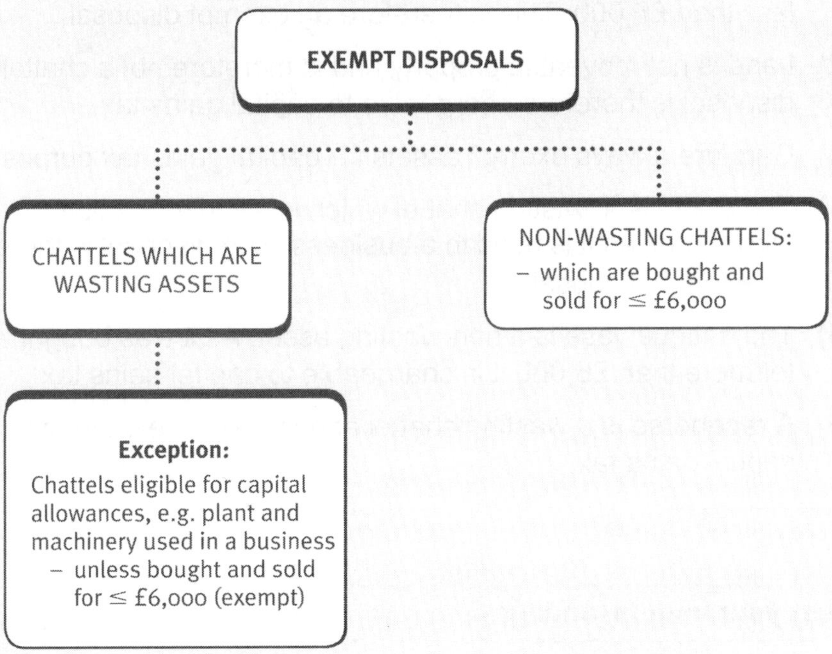

Example 5 - Chattels and wasting assets

Mr Windsor has made the following disposals in 2008/09.

(1) A painting was sold in July 2008 for £5,600. He originally bought it in February 1990 for £3,500.

(2) A piece of land, which he bought in April 2005 for £2,000 (an investment property), was sold in September 2008 for £5,000.

(3) He sold a vintage car for £25,000 in June 2008 that had originally cost him £5,500 in June 1999.

(4) He bought a moveable crane for £20,000 in August 1992, which he used in his haulage business. He sold the crane for £10,000 in January 2009.

(5) An antique vase was sold in August 2008 for £10,000. It originally cost £8,000 in April 2000.

(6) In May 2008 he sold his half share in a racehorse for £5,000, which he had acquired in June 2001 for £4,000.

For each of the above transactions, state whether they are chattels (wasting or non-wasting) and whether they will be subject to capital gains tax.

Answer to example 5

(1) The painting is a non-wasting asset which was bought and sold for less than £6,000. This is therefore an exempt disposal.

(2) Land is not moveable property and is therefore not a chattel. The disposal is therefore chargeable to capital gains tax.

(3) Cars are always exempt assets for capital gains tax purposes.

(4) The crane is a wasting chattel which is eligible for capital allowances as it is used in a business. The disposal is therefore **not** an exempt disposal.

(5) The antique vase is a non-wasting asset. As it was bought and sold for more than £6,000 it is chargeable to capital gains tax.

(6) A racehorse is a wasting chattel and is therefore exempt from capital gains tax.

Test your understanding 4

Which of the following disposals are exempt from, and which are chargeable to, capital gains tax?

(1) Gift of a necklace which was bought for £4,000. Its market value at the date of the gift was £7,000.

(2) Sale of shares in a quoted trading company for £2,000 which were bought for £1,000.

(3) Sale of a motor car, for £5,000, which was used for business purposes. It was acquired for £6,000.

(4) Sale of a boat for £20,000, which was acquired for £15,000.

(5) Sale of a painting for £5,000, which was acquired for £1,000.

(6) Sale of a greyhound for £10,000, which was acquired for £5,000

Complete the box below.

Exempt disposals	Chargeable disposals

Chattels – non-wasting assets

When a non-wasting chattel is disposed of the following rules apply:

(1) asset bought **and** sold for £6,000 or less – exempt

(2) asset bought and sold for more than £6,000 – the capital gain is computed in the normal way

(3) asset either bought or sold for £6,000 or less – then special rules apply as follows.

- **Sold at a gain**
  Calculate the capital gain as normal but the gain is then restricted to a maximum of:
  5/3 × (gross disposal consideration – £6,000).
- **Sold at a loss**
  Sale proceeds are deemed to be£6,000.

The above rules are referred to as **the £6,000 rule**.

	Cost	
	£6,000 or less	**More than £6,000**
Sale proceeds:		
£6,000 or less	Exempt	Allowable loss but proceeds are deemed = £6,000
More than £6,000	Normal calculation. If result is a gain compare with: 5/3 × (gross proceeds – £6,000). Take lower gain	Chargeable in full = normal CGT computation

Example 6 - Non-wasting chattel

Andrew sold a picture on 1 February 2009 for £6,600. He had acquired it on 1 March 2004 for £3,200.

Calculate the capital gain arising on the disposal.

Answer to example 6

As the picture is a non-wasting chattel, that was sold for more than £6,000, the disposal is not an exempt disposal.

	£
Disposal proceeds	6,600
Less: Cost	(3,200)
Gain	3,400

But the gain is limited to: 5/3 × (£6,600 – £6,000) = £1,000

The lower gain of £1,000 is taken.

Example 7 - Non-wasting chattel

Brian bought an antique table for £6,500 in September 2001 and sold it for £5,600 in December 2008. He incurred £250 to advertise it for sale.

Calculate the allowable loss arising, if any.

Answer to example 7

This is a disposal of a non-wasting asset that cost more than £6,000 but which was sold for less than £6,000. The disposal is not an exempt disposal but the allowable loss is restricted as follows.

	£
Deemed sale proceeds	6,000
Less: Expenses of sale	(250)
Cost	(6,500)
Allowable loss	(750)

Test your understanding 5

Marjory bought two antique tables in March 1985 each for £1,000. She sold them both in June 2008 for £6,400 and £13,600 respectively.

Calculate the capital gains arising on the disposal of the two antique tables.

Test your understanding 6

Brian bought a picture in April 1983 for £10,000 plus purchase costs of £500. The market for the artist's work slumped and Brian sold the picture on 10 April 2008 for £500, less disposal costs of £50.

Calculate the allowable loss on disposal of the picture.

Test your understanding 7

During January 2009, Sally sold four paintings, which she had acquired in May 1999. Details were as follows.

Painting	Cost	Proceeds
	£	£
1	2,000	7,000
2	8,000	4,500
3	3,000	5,500
4	7,000	9,500

Calculate Sally's net capital gains for 2008/09.

Chattels – summary

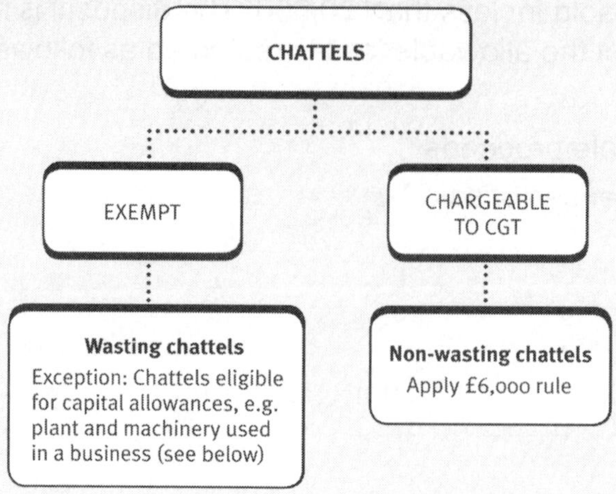

Wasting assets

Wasting assets (i.e. predictable life of less than 50 years) can be split into the following categories:

- Chattels not eligible for capital allowances = exempt from capital gains tax.
- Chattels eligible for capital allowances.
- Other wasting assets.

Expandable Text - Wasting assets

Wasting chattels eligible for capital allowances

For example, plant and machinery that has been used for the purposes of a trade.

Where capital allowances have been claimed on an asset we must take into account the tax relief for the actual cost of the asset, given through the capital allowances system, as follows:

- Where a trader acquires a machine for £10,000 and sells it for £7,000 he will receive capital allowances (net of any balancing adjustments) of £3,000. The net allowances match the actual £3,000 cash loss that he has realised.

- Where a trader acquires a machine for £10,000 and sells it for £14,000, proceeds of £10,000 will be used in calculating the net capital allowances (proceeds in the capital allowance computation are restricted to lower of sales proceeds and original cost). In this case, as the trader has made a gain the capital allowances given will be £nil (net of any balancing adjustments) and the gain will be subject to capital gains tax.

Accordingly the following rules apply:

- Sold at a gain

  Calculate the gain as normal, applying the £6,000 rule if applicable.

- Sold at a loss

  The capital loss is restricted as relief for the loss has already been given through the capital allowances system.

  In the capital loss computation, the net capital allowances given (i.e. net of balancing charges on disposal) are deducted from the asset's allowable expenditure.

Plant and machinery sold at a loss, which is eligible for capital allowances, results in a no gain/no loss situation for capital gains tax purposes.

Example 8 - Wasting assets - Sarah

Sarah bought a machine for use in her trade for £35,000 in May 2006. In October 2008 she decided to replace it and sold the old machine for £40,000.

Calculate the capital gain arising on the disposal in October 2008.

Answer to example 8

The asset was sold at a gain. The capital gain is therefore calculated as normal.

	£
Disposal proceeds	40,000
Less: Cost	(35,000)
Capital gain	5,000

Example 9 - Wasting assets - Fred

Fred bought a machine for use in his trade for £35,000 in April 2002. In October 2008 he decided to replace it and sold the old machine for £26,500.

Calculate the capital gain or allowable loss arising on the disposal in October 2008.

Answer to example 9

Fred has sold the machine for a real loss of £8,500 (£35,000 – £26,500). He is compensated for this loss through the capital allowances system, i.e. he receives net capital allowances of £8,500 during his period of ownership of the machine. The allowable capital loss computation is therefore adjusted to reflect the relief for the loss already given through the capital allowances system as follows:

	£	£
Disposal proceeds		26,500
Less: Cost	35,000	
Less: Net capital allowances	(8,500)	
		(26,500)
Allowable loss		Nil

Example 10 - Wasting assets - Rasheed

Rasheed bought a machine for use in his trade for £12,000 in April 2005. In May 2008 he decided to replace it and sold the old machine for £10,000.

Calculate the capital gain or allowable loss arising on the disposal in May 2008.

Answer to example 10

Rasheed sold the machine for a real loss of £2,000. He is compensated for this loss through the capital allowances system, i.e. he receives net capital allowances of £2,000 (£12,000 – £10,000) during his period of ownership of the machine. The allowable capital loss computation is therefore adjusted to reflect the relief for the loss already given through the capital allowances system as follows:

	£	£
Disposal proceeds		10,000
Less: Cost	12,000	
Less: Net capital allowances	(2,000)	
		(10,000)
Allowable loss		Nil

Expandable Text - Other wasting assets

This category covers wasting assets that are not chattels, e.g. copyright.

The special point about wasting assets that are not chattels is that the allowable expenditure is deemed to waste away over the life of the asset.

Consequently, when a disposal is made:

- the allowable expenditure is restricted to take account of the asset's natural fall in value
- the asset's fall in value is deemed to occur on a straight line basis over its predictable useful life

- the allowable cost is calculated as:

$$C - \left[\frac{P}{L} \times C\right]$$

where

P is the disposer's period of ownership

L is the asset's predictable life

C is the cost of the asset

Example 11 – Other wasting assets - Ian

On 1 February 1999 Ian bought a wasting non-business asset at a cost of £24,000. It had an estimated useful life of 30 years. He sold the asset for £38,000 on 1 February 2009.

Calculate the capital gain or allowable loss arising from the disposal in February 2009.

Answer to example 11

	£
Disposal proceeds	38,000
Less: Allowable element of acquisition cost (W)	(16,000)
Capital gain	22,000

Working: Allowable element of acquisition cost

	£
Cost	24,000
Less: Wasting asset depreciation	
10/30 × £24,000	(8,000)
	16,000

Example 12 – Other wasting assets - Jan

On 1 March 2004 Jan bought a wasting non-business asset at a cost of £19,000. It had an estimated useful life of 40 years. She sold the asset for £30,000 on 1 March 2009.

Calculate the capital gain or allowable loss arising from the disposal in March 2009.

Answer to example 12

	£	£
Disposal proceeds		30,000
Less: Purchase cost	19,000	
Less: Wasting asset depreciation		
5/40 × £19,000	(2,375)	
Allowable element of acquisition cost		(16,625)
Capital gain		13,375

Wasting assets – summary

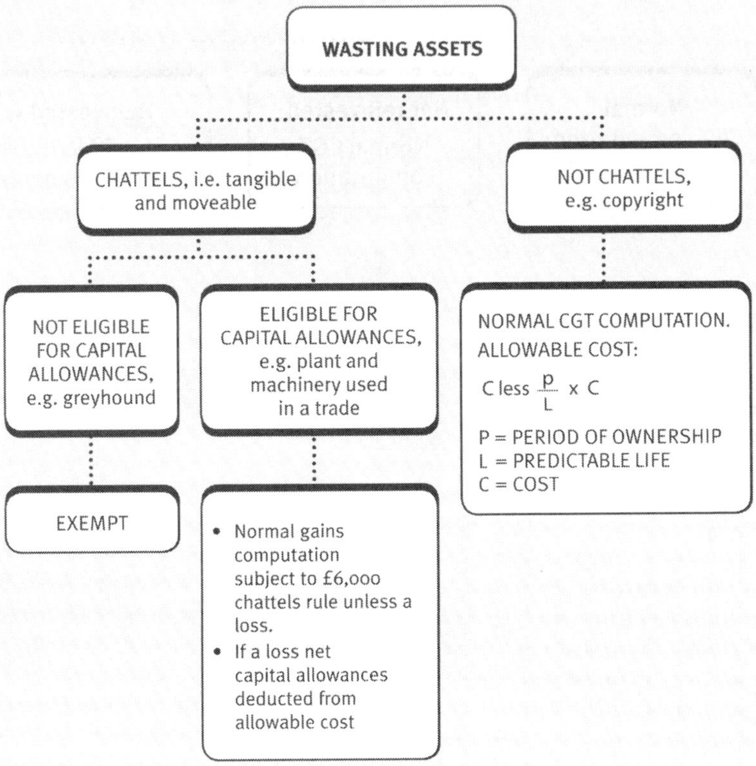

5 Assets lost or destroyed or damaged

Introduction

In most circumstances a capital transaction has two parties, a buyer and a seller.

However, when an asset is damaged, destroyed or lost and the asset's owner receives compensation (either from the perpetrator or an insurance company) the position is different. The owner has received a capital sum without disposing of the asset and the payer has received nothing in return. Consequently, a special set of rules is required.

The rules vary according to whether:

- the asset has been completely lost/destroyed or merely damaged
- the owner has replaced or restored the asset.

Asset lost or destroyed

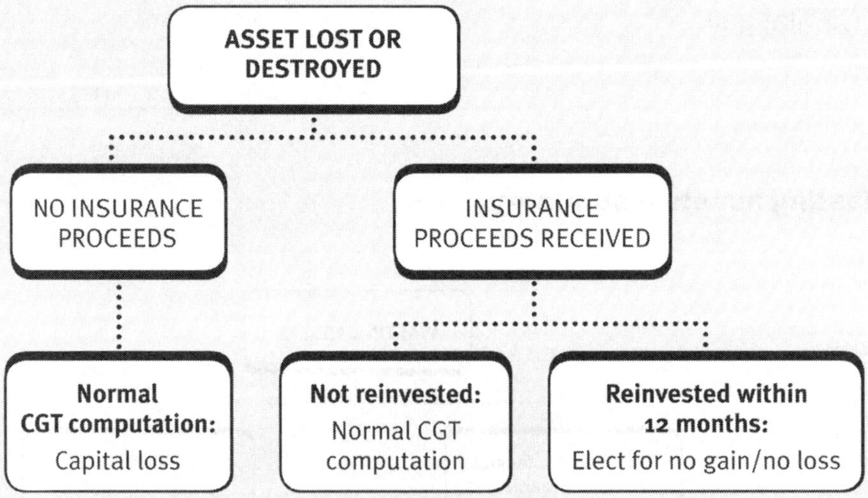

Expandable text - Assets lost or destroyed

Where an asset is lost or destroyed there is a deemed disposal for capital gains tax purposes as follows:

(a) **No insurance proceeds**

Compute a capital loss using the normal capital gains tax computation pro forma:

- Disposal proceeds will be £nil.
- Deduction of the allowable expenditure will create a loss.

(b) **Insurance proceeds received – no replacement of asset**

Where an asset is lost or destroyed and insurance proceeds are not used to replace the asset, a capital gain/loss is computed using the normal capital gains tax computation proforma.

(c) **Insurance proceeds received – asset replaced**

Where an asset is lost or destroyed and the insurance proceeds are used to buy a replacement asset within 12 months the following rules apply:

- The taxpayer can claim that the destruction/loss of the asset is treated as a no gain/no loss disposal (as for husband and wife transfers).
- If the insurance proceeds are greater than the deemed disposal proceeds under the no gain/no loss computation, the excess is deducted from the replacement asset's allowable cost.

The date of disposal is the date that the insurance proceeds are received, not when the destruction or loss of the asset occurred.

Example 13 – Assets lost or destroyed – Nadir

Nadir purchased a business asset for £15,000 on 1 April 1990, which was destroyed by fire on 31 July 2008. The asset was not insured.

Calculate the allowable loss arising from the destruction of the asset.

Answer to example 13

	£
Proceeds	Nil
Cost	(15,000)
Allowable loss	(15,000)

Example 14 – Assets lost or destroyed – Padma

Padma purchased an antique table for £35,000 on 1 May 1992, which was destroyed by fire on 30 June 2008. She received insurance proceeds of £50,000 on 1 September 2008. She did not replace the table.

Calculate the capital gain arising from the destruction of the antique table.

Answer to example 14

	£
Proceeds	50,000
Cost	(35,000)
Capital gain	15,000

Example 15 – Assets lost or destroyed – Silvio

Silvio purchased a painting for £50,000 on 1 June 1993, which was destroyed in a fire on 31 May 2008. He received insurance proceeds of £57,000 on 1 September 2008. He did not replace the painting.

Calculate the capital gain or allowable loss arising from the destruction of the painting.

Answer to example 15

	£
Proceeds	57,000
Cost	(50,000)
Allowable loss	(7,000)

Example 16 – Assets lost or destroyed – Bill

Bill purchased an asset for £25,000 on 1 October 1990, which was destroyed by fire on 30 September 2008. He received compensation of £35,000 from his insurance company on 1 January 2009. He purchased a replacement asset for £40,000 on 1 February 2009.

Assuming that Bill claims the loss by fire to be a no gain/no loss disposal, calculate the allowable expenditure (base cost) of the replacement asset.

Answer to example 16

	£	£
Cost of replacement asset		40,000
Less: Compensation	35,000	
Less: Deemed disposal proceeds of old asset **(W)**	(25,000)	
		(10,000)
Replacement asset base cost		30,000

Working – deemed disposal proceeds

Since the disposal of the old asset is assumed to be on a no gain/no loss basis and the no gain/no loss transfer is on/after 6 April 2008. The disposal proceeds are the allowable cost of the asset.

	£
Allowable cost = Deemed disposal proceeds	25,000

Example 17 – Assets lost or destroyed – Belinda

Belinda purchased an antique necklace for £20,000 on 1 October 1996, which she lost on 30 June 2007. She received compensation of £45,000 from her insurance company on 1 October 2007 and purchased a replacement necklace for £50,000 on 1 November 2007. The base cost of the necklace on 1 October 2007 was £21,140.

She sold the replacement necklace for £65,000 on 1 March 2009.

Assuming that Belinda claims the loss of the necklace to be a no gain/no loss disposal, calculate the capital gain arising on the sale of the replacement necklace on 1 March 2009.

Answer to example 17

	£
Proceeds	65,000
Cost **(W)**	(26,140)
Capital gain	38,860

Working – Replacement asset base cost

	£	£
Cost of replacement necklace		50,000
Less: Insurance proceeds	45,000	
Less: Deemed disposal proceeds of lost necklace = Base cost	(21,140)	
		(23,860)
Replacement asset base cost		26,140

Asset damaged

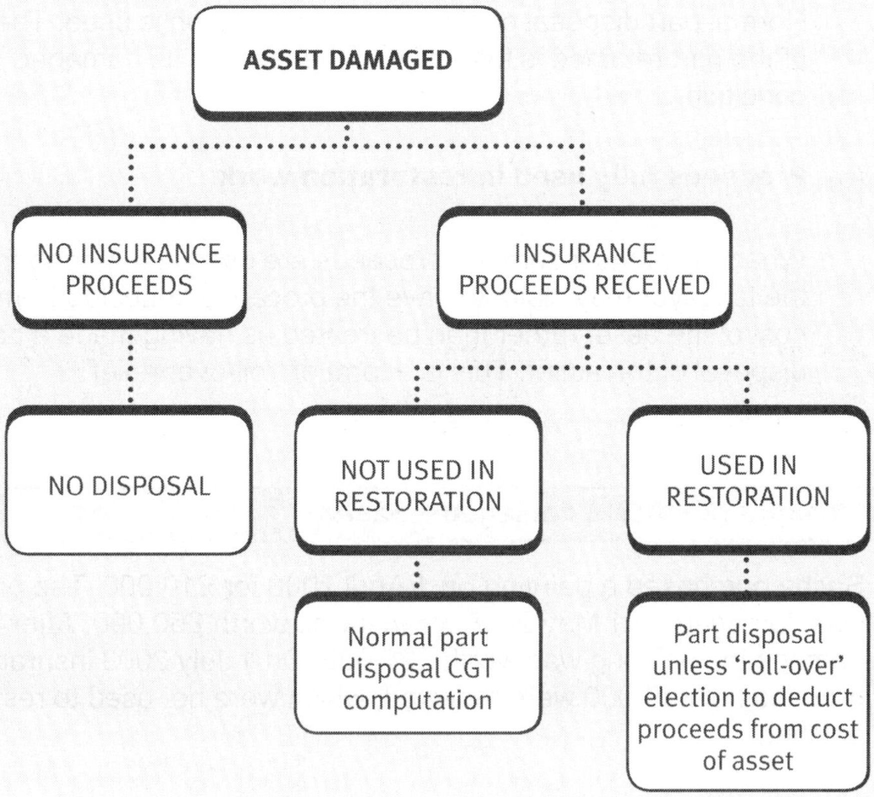

Expandable text - Asset damaged

Where an asset is damaged there are no implications for capital gains tax purposes unless compensation, e.g. insurance proceeds, is received.

Where an asset is damaged and compensation is received there is a part disposal for capital gains tax purposes.

The allowable cost is calculated using the normal part disposal formula:

Cost × A / A + B

Where

A = Compensation received
B = Market value of the remainder at the time of the part disposal.

The computation is varied depending on how the insurance proceeds are applied.

(a) **Proceeds not used in restoration work**

Normal part disposal capital gains computation is used. The value of the part retained is the value of the asset in its damaged condition.

(b) **Proceeds fully used in restoration work**

Where all of the insurance proceeds are used in restoring the asset the taxpayer may claim to have the proceeds deducted from the cost of the asset rather than be treated as having made a part disposal of the asset. This is a form of 'roll-over relief'.

Example 18 – Asset damaged – Sasha

Sasha purchased a painting on 1 April 2000 for £10,000. The painting was damaged on 1 May 2008 when it was worth £50,000. After the damage the painting was worth £25,000. On 1 July 2008 insurance proceeds of £30,000 were received, which were not used to restore the painting.

Calculate the capital gain arising in respect of the painting.

Answer to example 18

	£
Deemed proceeds	30,000
Cost £10,000 × £30,000/(£30,000 + £25,000)	(5,455)
Capital gain	24,545

Example 19 – Asset damaged – Amy

Amy purchased a painting on 1 April 2000 for £10,000. The painting was damaged on 1 May 2008 when it was worth £50,000. After the damage the painting was worth £40,000. On 1 July 2008 insurance proceeds of £8,000 were received. All of the proceeds were used to restore the painting.

Assuming Amy elects for the insurance proceeds to be rolled over against the cost of the painting, calculate the revised base cost for capital gains tax purposes of the painting after it has been restored.

Answer to example 19

As Amy has elected for the proceeds to be rolled over against the cost of the painting there is no part disposal and the revised base cost of the painting is as follows:

	£
Original cost	10,000
Insurance proceeds	(8,000)
Revised base cost	2,000

Example 20 – Asset damaged – Sari

Sari purchased an investment property on 1 May 2002 for £200,000. In June 2008 it was damaged by fire. On 1 August 2008 insurance proceeds of £100,000 were received which were used to restore the property. After the restoration the property was worth £500,000.

Assuming Sari elects for the insurance proceeds to be rolled over against the cost of the property calculate the revised base cost for capital gains tax purposes of the property after it has been restored.

Answer to example 20

As the proceeds are fully used for restoring the property and Sari has made a 'roll over' election there is no part disposal and the revised base cost of the property is as follows:

	£
Original cost	200,000
Insurance proceeds	(100,000)
Revised base cost	100,000

6 Chapter summary

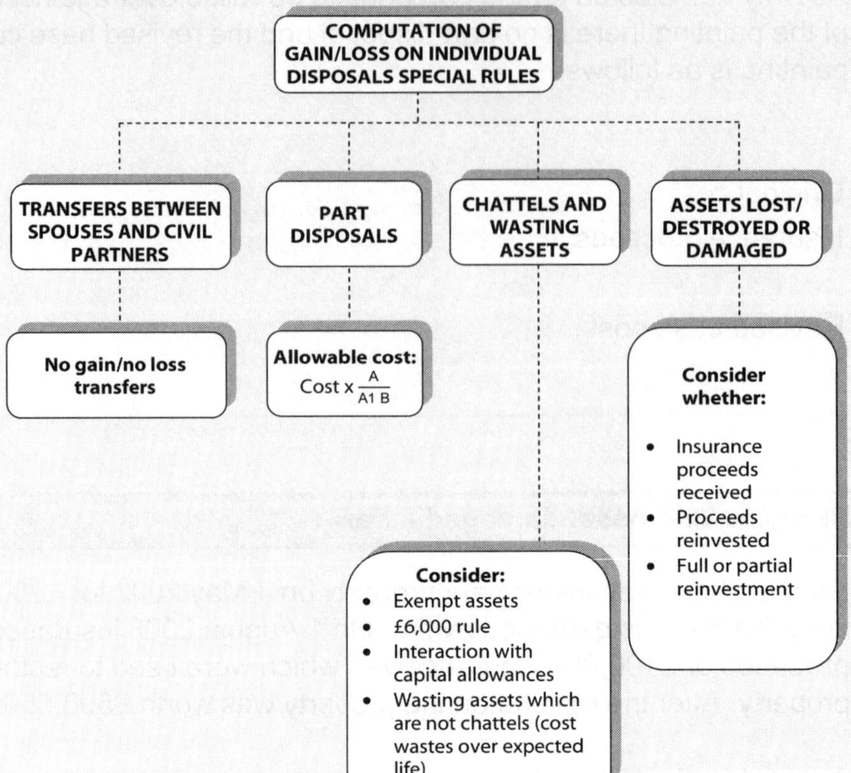

Test your understanding answers

Test your understanding 1

Tania

Capital gains tax computation – 2008/09

	£
Warehouse	
Disposal proceeds	350,000
Less: Deemed acquisition cost	(100,000)
Capital gain	250,000
Less: Capital losses brought forward	(11,300)
Net capital gains	238,700
Less: Annual exemption	(9,600)
Taxable gains	229,100
Capital gains tax payable (£229,100 x 18%)	41,238

Test your understanding 2

Jacob

Disposal in January 2009

	£	£
Sale proceeds	20,000	
Less: Allowable cost		
£8,000 × A/(A + B)		
£8,000 × £20,000/(£20,000 + £60,000)	(2,000)	
Capital gain		18,000
Disposal in March 2009		
Sales proceeds	75,000	
Less: Allowable cost (£8,000 – £2,000)	(6,000)	
		69,000
Net capital gains		87,000
Less: Annual exemption		(9,600)
Taxable gains		77,400
Capital gains tax @ 18%		13,932
Due date		31.1.2010

Test your understanding 3

Gemma

Disposal in 2008/09

	£
Proceeds	200,000
Cost (£50,000 – £14,286) **(W)**	(35,714)
Capital gain	164,286
Less: Annual exemption	(9,600)
Taxable gain	154,686
Capital gains tax @ 18%	27,843

Working – Allowable expenditure

The allowable expenditure in relation to the part disposal of the land on 1 July 2006 was:

$$£50,000 \times \frac{£40,000}{(£40,000 + £100,000)} \quad £14,286$$

Test your understanding 4

Exempt disposals	**Chargeable disposals**
(3) Motor car – exempt asset	(1) Necklace (deemed proceeds £7,000). Non-wasting chattel not sold and bought for ≤ £6,000
(4) Boat – wasting chattel	(2) Shares – not chattels (not tangible property)
(5) Painting – chattel bought and sold for ≤ £6,000	
(6) Greyhound – wasting chattel	

Test your understanding 5

Marjory

Disposals in June 2008

	Table A	Table B
	£	£
Proceeds (June 2008)	6,400	13,600
Less: Cost (March 1985)	(1,000)	(1,000)
Capital gains	5,400	12,600
The gains calculated above are restricted to:		
5/3 × (sale proceeds – £6,000)	667	12,667
Decision = take the lower gain	667	12,600

Test your understanding 6

Brian

	£
Sale proceeds: actually £500 but deemed to be	6,000
Less: Selling costs	(50)
Net proceeds	5,950
Less: Cost (including acquisition expenses)	(10,500)
Allowable loss	(4,550)

Note: It is the **gross** sale proceeds **before** deducting selling costs that are deemed to be £6,000.

Test your understanding 7

Sally

Net capital gains – 2008/09

	Painting		
	1	2	4
	£	£	£
Proceeds	7,000		9,500
Deemed proceeds		6,000	
Cost	(2,000)	(8,000)	(7,000)
Capital gain/(allowable loss)	5,000	(2,000)	2,500
Gain restricted to 5/3 × (£7,000 – £6,000)	1,667		

Net capital gains (£1,667 – £2,000 + £2,500) = £2,167.

Note: Painting 3 is exempt as the cost and proceeds are both less than £6,000.

chapter

16

CGT: Shares and securities for individuals

Chapter learning objectives

Upon completion of this chapter you will be able to:

- identify the exemption for government securities and qualifying corporate bonds
- calculate the value of quoted shares where they are disposed of by way of a gift
- understand why identification rules are required when acquiring and disposing of shares
- apply the correct matching rules on a disposal of shares by an individual
- explain the pooling principle
- calculate a gain on the disposal of shares by an individual
- identify the treatment of a bonus issue
- identify the treatment of a rights issue
- explain the tax treatment on a takeover or reorganisation of a shareholding in exchange for other shares
- explain the treatment on a takeover where there is cash and shares consideration
- calculate the capital gain on the cash element on a takeover.

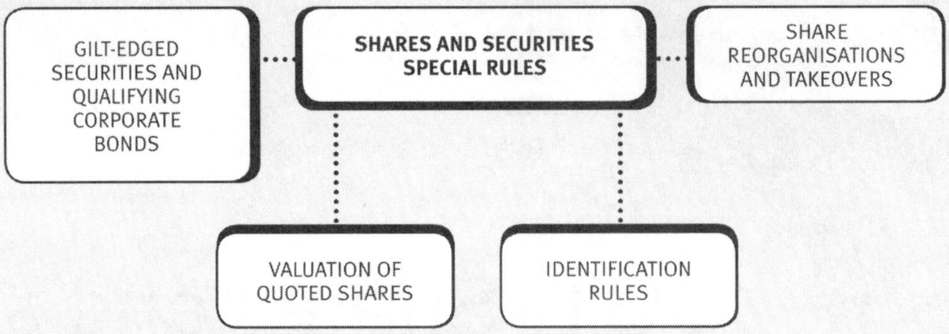

1 Introduction

The basic capital gain computation, as seen in Chapter 15, is used as normal on a disposal of shares or securities but because shares are indistinguishable from each other there are special rules to identify the allowable cost.

This chapter covers the rules as they apply to disposals by an individual. Similar rules apply for the disposal of shares by companies. These are covered in Chapter 20.

2 Government securities and qualifying corporate bonds

All shares and securities disposed of by an individual are subject to capital gains tax except for the following, which are exempt:

- listed government securities (gilt-edged securities or gilts)
- qualifying corporate bonds (broadly company loan notes)
- shares held in an Individual Savings Account (ISA).

Expandable text - Definition of a qualifying corporate bond

A qualifying corporate bond is one that:

(a) represents a normal commercial loan;

(b) is expressed in sterling and has no provision for either conversion into, or redemption in, any other currency; and

(c) was issued after 13 March 1984 or was acquired by the disposer after that date (whenever it was issued).

The term 'corporate bond' is also extended to permanent interest-bearing shares in building societies, provided they meet the condition set out in (b) above.

Test your understanding 1

Which of the following shares and securities are exempt assets for capital gains tax purposes when disposed of by an individual?

(1) £1 ordinary shares in the unquoted property development company, Sealand Ltd.

(2) 10½% Exchequer Stock 2016.

(3) 10% preference shares in the quoted trading company, Ace plc.

(4) 6% loan stock issued by Amble plc in 2007.

(a) (3) and (4) only

(b) (2) and (4) only

(c) (1) and (2) only

(d) (2), (3) and (4) only.

3 Valuation of quoted shares

On a sale of shares between unconnected parties, the actual proceeds are used in the capital gains computation.

However, it is necessary to identify the market value of quoted shares when shares are either:

- gifted
- transferred to a connected party.

Their market value is taken from prices quoted in the Stock Exchange Daily Official List and is the lower of:

- the value using the '¼ up method', i.e. lower quoted price + ¼ (higher price – lower price)
- the average of the highest and lowest recorded bargains.

Example 1 - Valuation of quoted shares

Shares in XYZ plc are quoted in the Stock Exchange Daily Official List at 230p to 270p. On the same day the highest and lowest recorded bargains were 224p and 276p.

If a disposal of XYZ plc shares were made on that day to a connected party, what would their value be for capital gains tax purposes?

Answer to example 1

The value of XYZ plc shares is the lower of:

(a) ¼ up rule: Lower price	230p
Add: (270p – 230p) × ¼	10p
	——
	240p
	——
(b) Average of lowest and highest recorded bargains	
(224p + 276p) × ½	250p
	——

The value is therefore 240p per share.

Test your understanding 2

Shares in Sawyer plc are quoted in the Stock Exchange Daily Official List at 460p to 540p.

On the same day the highest and lowest recorded bargains were 552p, 500p and 448p.

If a gift of Sawyer plc shares were made on that day, what would their value be for capital gains tax purposes?

4 Identification rules

It is necessary to have identification (or matching) rules to determine which shares have been disposed of as:

- Shares and securities that are bought in a particular company of the same class are not distinguishable from one another.
- Each time shares are bought in any quoted company the price paid may be different.
- They enable you to decide which shares have been sold and to work out the allowable cost to use in the capital gains computation.

Identification rules for disposals by individuals

When shares are disposed of they are matched against shares acquired of the same class in the following order:

- Same day as the date of disposal.
- Within **following** 30 days.
- The share pool (shares acquired before the date of disposal are pooled together).

Expandable text - Shares acquired within the following 30 days

It may appear strange that a disposal is matched with acquisitions following the date of sale. The reason for this is that it prevents a practice known as 'bed and breakfasting'.

Typically, shares would have been sold at the close of business one day and then bought back at the opening of business the next day. A gain or loss would have been established without making a genuine disposal of the shares. It might have been useful for an individual to establish a capital loss, e.g. in the same tax year that he or she has chargeable gains, or a capital gain to use his or her annual exemption, if it had not been used already.

The 30-day matching rule makes the practice of bed and breakfasting much more difficult, since the subsequent acquisition cannot take place within 30 days.

Example 2 - Identification rules

Frederic had the following transactions in the shares of DEF plc, a quoted company.

			£
1 June 1986	Bought	4,000 shares for	8,000
30 July 1995	Bought	1,800 shares for	9,750
30 April 1999	Bought	500 shares for	4,000
20 May 2000	Bought	1,000 shares for	8,500
15 March 2009	Sold	3,500 shares for	36,000
28 March 2009	Bought	800 shares for	6,400

Identify with which acquisitions the shares sold on 15 March 2009 will be matched.

Answer to example 2

		Number of shares
Shares sold		3,500
1. Shares acquired on same day		(Nil)
2. Shares acquired in following 30 days		
28 March 2009		(800)
		2,700
3. Share pool		
(Shares pre 15 March 2009))		
1 June 1986	4,000	
30 July 1995	1,800	
30 April 1999	500	
20 May 2000	1,000	
	7,300	
The disposal from the share pool is therefore 2,700 shares out of 7,300 shares		(2,700)
		Nil

The share pool

The share pool may also be referred to as the 's104 pool' or the 'FA 1985 pool'.

For an individual, with effect from 6 April 2008, the share pool contains shares in the same company, of the same class purchased before the date of disposal.

- The share pool simply keeps a record of the number of shares acquired and sold and the cost of those shares.
- When shares are disposed of out of the share pool, the appropriate proportion of the cost which relates to the shares disposed of is calculated. The shares are disposed of at their average cost.

  Thus if there are 4,000 shares in the pool with a cost of £8,000 and 2,000 shares are disposed of:

  – the cost of the shares removed is £4,000 ((2,000/4,000) × £8,000).

5 Calculating the gain/loss on the disposal of shares

Once the identification rules have been used to identify which shares have been disposed of, the cost of those shares is used in the normal capital gains tax computation.

Example 3 - Calculating the gain/loss on the disposal of shares

Frances sold 11,000 ordinary shares in Hastings Co plc, a quoted company, on 18 December 2008 for £50,000. She had bought ordinary shares in the company on the following dates.

	Number of shares	Cost
		£
6 April 1998	8,000	7,450
12 December 1999	4,000	5,500
10 January 2009	2,000	6,000

Calculate the capital gain arising on the disposal of shares on 18 December 2008.

Assume that Hastings Co plc is not Frances' personal trading company.

Answer to example 3

Capital gains computation – 2008/09

Stage 1 Use the identification rules to identify the shares disposed of.

Shares disposed of by individuals are matched with acquisitions as follows:

		Number
Shares sold		11,000
1	Shares acquired on same day	(Nil)
2	Shares acquired in following 30 days 10 January 2009	(2,000)
		9,000
3	Share pool (9,000 out of 12,000 shares)	(9,000)
		Nil

Stage 2 Calculate the capital gain arising on each of the individual parcels of shares disposed of.

(a) Shares acquired on 10 January 2009

	£
Proceeds (2,000/11,000 × £50,000)	9,091
Less: Acquisition cost	(6,000)
Capital gain	3,091

(b) Shares in the share pool

	£
Proceeds (9,000/11,000 × £50,000)	40,409
Less: Acquisition cost **(W)**	(9,712)
Capital gain	31,197
Total capital gains on disposal of 11,000 shares:	34,288

Working: share pool

	Number	Cost
		£
Acquisition – 6 April 1998	8,000	7,450
Acquisition – 12 December 1999	4,000	5,500
	12,000	12,950
Disposal – 18 December 2008 (Note) 9,000/12,000 × £12,950	(9,000)	(9,712)
Balance carried forward	3,000	3,238

Note: The 'average cost' method is used to calculate the cost removed from the share pool on the disposal.

If the individual disposes of shares in his personal trading company and is also an employee of that company, entrepreneurs' relief is available.

This relief is covered in detail in chapter 17.

Test your understanding 3

Zoe purchased 2,000 shares in XYZ Ltd on 16 April 1985 for £10,000.

In addition she acquired 1,500 shares in the company on 30 April 2008 for £18,000, and 500 shares on 31 May 2008 for £7,000. On 10 February 2009, Zoe bought a further 200 shares in XYZ Ltd for £3,600.

Zoe sold 3,500 shares in XYZ Ltd on 31 January 2009 for £70,000.

Calculate Zoe's capital gain on the disposal of shares on 31 January 2009.

Assume that XYZ Ltd is not Zoe's personal trading company.

6 Bonus issues and rights issues

Bonus issues

A bonus issue is the distribution of free shares to shareholders based on their existing shareholding.

For capital gains tax purposes they are treated as follows:

- For the purposes of the share identification rules the bonus shares acquired will be included in the share pool.
- The bonus shares are not treated as a separate holding of shares.
- The number of shares are included in the pool, but at Nil cost.

Example 4 - Bonus issues

Blackburn had the following transactions in the shares of Gray Ltd:

January 2008	Purchased 3,500 shares for £7,350
May 2008	Purchased 500 shares for £1,750
June 2008	Bonus issue of one for five
September 2008	Sold 2,600 shares for £10,400

Calculate the capital gain arising on the disposal in September 2008.

Assume that Gray Ltd is not Blackburn's personal trading company.

Answer to example 4

Gain on shares

	£
Sale proceeds	10,400
Less Cost (Working)	(4,929)
Capital gain	5,471

Working: Share pool

		Number	Cost
			£
Jan 2008	Purchase	3,500	7,350
May 2008	Purchase	500	1,750
		4,000	9,100
June 2008	Bonus issue (1:5)	800	Nil
		4,800	9,100
September 2008	Sale	(2,600)	(4,929)
Balance c/f		2,200	4,171

Test your understanding 4

Kieran had the following transactions in Black plc shares:

January 2005	Purchased 3,000 shares for £6,000
May 2008	Bonus issue of one for three
June 2008	Purchased 500 shares for £1,500
February 2009	Sold 3,000 shares for £12,000

Calculate the capital gain arising on the disposal in February 2009.

Assume that Black plc is not Kieran's personal trading company.

Rights issues

A rights issue is the offer of new shares to existing shareholders in proportion to their existing shareholding, usually at a price below the market price.

Rights issues are similar in concept to bonus issues, however because money is paid for the new shares there are additional factors to consider:

- As for bonus issues, for the purposes of the share identification rules the rights shares acquired will be included in the share pool.

- The rights shares are not treated as a separate holding of shares.
- The number of shares are included in the pool, and the cost, in the same way as a normal purchase.

Example 5 - Rights issue

Carmichael had the following transactions in Rudderham Ltd shares:

January 2007	Purchased 2,700 shares for £5,400
May 2008	Purchased 600 shares for £1,500
June 2008	Took up 1 for 3 rights issue at £2.30 per share
August 2008	Sold 4,000 shares for £14,000

Calculate the capital gain on the disposal in August 2008.

Assume that Rudderham Ltd is not Carmichael's personal trading company.

Answer to example 5

Gain on shares

	£
Sale proceeds	14,000
Less Cost (Working)	(8,573)
Capital gain	5,427

Working: Share pool

		Number	Cost
			£
Jan 2007	Purchase	2,700	5,400
May 2008	Purchase	600	1,500
		3,300	6,900
June 2008	Rights issue (1:3) @ £2.50 per share	1,100	2,530
		4,400	9,430
August 2008	Sale	(4,000)	(8,573)
Balance c/f		400	857

Test your understanding 5

Victor had the following transactions in the ordinary shares of Victorious Vulcanising plc, a quoted company:

April 1999	Purchased 1,000 shares for £11,000
September 1999	Rights issue of 1 for 2 at £6 each
August 2008	Sold 1,200 shares for £46,000

Calculate Victor's capital gains for 2008/09.

Assume that Victorious Vulcanising plc is not Victor's personal trading company.

7 Reorganisations and takeovers

Reorganisations

A reorganisation involves the exchange of existing shares in a company for other shares of another class in the same company.

Takeovers

A takeover occurs when one company acquires the shares in another company either in exchange for shares in itself, cash or a mixture of both.

Consideration: shares for shares

Where the consideration for the reorganisation or takeover only involves the issue of shares in the acquiring company, the tax consequences are:

- No capital gains tax is charged at the time of the reorganisation/takeover.
- The cost of the original shares becomes the cost of the new shares.
- Where the shareholder receives more than one type of share in exchange for the original shares, the cost of the original shares is allocated to the new shares by reference to the market values of the various new shares on the first day of dealing in them.

This treatment is automatic.

However, where the share exchange takes place after 5 April 2008, the shareholder can elect for the event to be treated as a disposal for CGT purposes.

If the election is made, entrepreneurs' relief may be available against the gain. This relief is considered in detail in Chapter 17.

Example 6 - Reorganisations and takeovers

Major purchased 2,000 ordinary shares in Blue plc for £5,000 in June 2002. In July 2008, Blue plc underwent a reorganisation and Major received two 'A' ordinary shares in exchange for each of his ordinary shares.

In December 2008, Major sold all his holding of 'A' ordinary shares for £8,000.

Calculate the capital gain or allowable loss arising on the disposal in December 2008.

Assume that Blue plc is not Major's personal trading company.

Answer to example 6

	£
Disposal proceeds	8,000
Less: Cost **(Note)**	(5,000)
Capital gain	3,000

Note: The cost of the original ordinary shares (£5,000) becomes the cost of the new 'A' ordinary shares.

Example 7 - Reorganisations and takeovers

In July 2008, Craig sold his entire holding of ordinary shares in Corus plc for £75,000. Craig had originally purchased 20,000 £1 ordinary shares in BNB plc at a cost of £20,000 in April 2001.

In July 2004, BNB plc was taken over by Corus plc. Craig received one ordinary 50p share and one 50p 6% preference share in Corus plc for each ordinary share he held in BNB plc.

Immediately after the takeover the values of these new shares were quoted as:

50p ordinary share	£1.80 each
50p preference shares	£0.80 each

Compute the capital gain arising on the disposal by Craig in July 2008.

Assume that Craig has never worked for Corus plc or BNB plc.

Answer to example 7

	£
Proceeds	75,000
Less: Allocated acquisition cost **(W)**	(13,846)
Capital gain	61,154

Working

Following the takeover in July 2004 of BNB plc by Corus plc, Craig now owns the following shares in Corus plc as per the terms of the takeover:

	Total M.V.	**Original cost**
	£	£
20,000 50p ordinary shares @ £1.80	36,000	13,846
20,000 50p preference shares @ £0.80	16,000	6,154
	52,000	20,000

Allocate the original cost incurred in April 2001 to the shares now owned in July 2004, using the normal average cost method.

£36,000/£52,000 × £20,000 = £13,846

£16,000/£52,000 × £20,000 = £6,154

Test your understanding 6

In June 2008, Marie purchased 2,000 ordinary shares in Black Ltd for £5,000. In July 2008 Black Ltd was taken over by Red plc, and Marie received 2 ordinary shares and 1 preference share in Red plc for each ordinary share in Black Ltd.

Immediately after the takeover the ordinary shares in Red plc were valued at £2 and the preference shares in Red plc were valued at £1.

In December 2008, Marie sold all her holding of ordinary shares in Red plc for £8,000.

Calculate the capital gain or allowable loss arising on the disposal in December 2008.

Assume that Marie has never worked for Red plc or Black Ltd.

Takeovers: consideration in cash and shares

If the consideration for the takeover includes a cash element:

- there is a part disposal of the original shares
- a gain arises on the cash element of the consideration on the date the cash is received.

Cash proceeds – part disposal computation

In these circumstances the part of the cost of the original holding apportioned to the cash is calculated as:

$$\frac{\text{Cash received}}{\text{Cash received + M.V. of new shares}} \times \text{cost of original shares}$$

Example 8 - Reorganisations and takeovers

Patrick bought 10,000 shares in Target plc in May 2004 for £20,000. On 3 November 2008, the entire share capital of Target plc was acquired by Bidder plc. Target plc shareholders received 2 Bidder plc shares and £0.50 cash for each share held. Bidder plc shares were quoted at £1.25.

Calculate the capital gain as a result of the takeover in November 2008.

Assume that Patrick has not worked for Target plc or Bidder plc.

Answer to example 8

The total consideration provided by Bidder plc is:

	£
Shares (20,000 @1.25)	25,000
Cash (10,000 × £0.50)	5,000
	30,000

As Patrick has received part of the consideration in cash he has made a part disposal of the original shares.

	£
Disposal proceeds (cash)	5,000
Less: Original cost	
£5,000/£30,000 × £20,000	(3,333)
Capital gain	1,667

Patrick's allowable cost on the future disposal of his shares in Bidder plc will be £16,667 (£20,000 – £3,333).

Test your understanding 7

Paula bought 25,000 shares in Tiny plc in May 2005 for £20,000. On 3 October 2008 the entire share capital of Tiny plc was acquired by Big plc. Tiny plc shareholders received 2 Big plc shares and £1.20 cash for each share held. Big plc shares were quoted at £1.75.

Calculate the capital gain as a result of the take-over in October 2008 and state the allowable cost of Paula's shares in Big plc.

Assume that Paula has not worked for either Tiny plc or Big plc.

8 Chapter summary

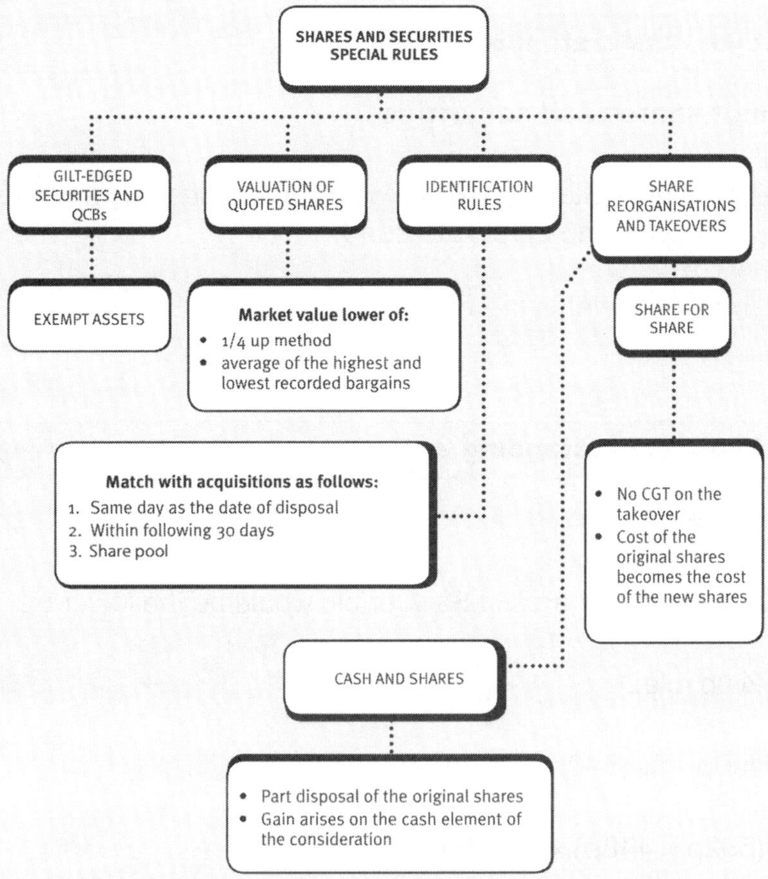

Test your understanding answers

Test your understanding 1

Exempt shares and securities

10½ Exchequer Stock 2016 is a government security and the 6% loan stock is a qualifying corporate bond.

The correct answer is therefore (b).

Test your understanding 2

Sawyer plc

The value of the shares in Sawyer plc would be the lower of:

(1) ¼ up rule:

460p + ¼ (540p – 460p) = 480p

(2) (552p + 448p) x ½ = 500p

The value is therefore 480p or £4.80 per share.

Test your understanding 3

Zoe

(a) Match with acquisitions within following 30 days (10 February 2009) (200 shares)

	£
Disposal proceeds (£70,000 × 200/3,500)	4,000
Less: Purchase price	(3,600)
Capital gain	400

(b) Match with acquisitions in the share pool (balance of 3,300 shares)

	£
Disposal proceeds (£70,000 × 3,300/3,500)	66,000
Less: Purchase price **(W)**	(28,875)
Capital gain	37,125
Total capital gains (£400 + £37,125)	37,525

Working – Share pool

	Number	**Cost**
		£
Acquisitions		
16/4/85	2,000	10,000
30/4/08	1,500	18,000
31/5/08	500	7,000
	4,000	35,000
Sale 31/1/09 £35,000 x 3,300/4,000	(3,300)	(28,875)
Balance carried forward	700	6,125

Test your understanding 4

Kieran

Gain on shares

	£
Sale proceeds	12,000
Less Cost (Working)	(5,000)
Capital gain	7,000

Working: Share pool

		Number	Cost
			£
Jan 2005	Purchase	3,000	6,000
May 2008	Bonus issue (1:3)	1,000	Nil
June 2008	Purchase	500	1,500
		4,500	7,500
February 2009	Sale	(3,000)	(5,000)
Balance c/f		1,500	2,500

Test your understanding 5

Victor

Gain on shares

	£
Sale proceeds	46,000
Less Cost (Working)	(11,200)
Capital gain	34,800

Working: Share pool

		Number	Cost
			£
April 1999	Purchase	1,000	11,000
September 1999	Rights issue (1:2) @ £6 per share	500	3,000
		1,500	14,000
August 2008	Sale	(1,200)	(11,200)
Balance c/f		300	2,800

Test your understanding 6

Marie

Capital gains computation – 2008/09

	£
Disposal proceeds	8,000
Less: Cost **(W)**	(4,000)
Capital gain	4,000

Working – Cost of ordinary shares in Red Plc

Marie received:

4,000 ordinary shares, valued at (4,000 × £2) = £8,000

2,000 preference shares, valued at (2,000 × £1) = £2,000

Cost attributable to the ordinary shares is thus:

£5,000 × £8,000/£10,000 = £4,000

Test your understanding 7

Paula

The total consideration provided by Big plc is:

	£
Shares (50,000 × 1.75)	87,500
Cash (25,000 × £1.20)	30,000
	117,500

Paula has made a part disposal on 3 October 2008 in relation to the cash consideration.

	£
Disposal proceeds (cash)	30,000
Less: Original cost	
£20,000 × £30,000/£117,500	(5,106)
Capital gain	24,894

Paula's allowable cost on the future disposal of her shares in Big plc will be £14,894 (£20,000 – £5,106).

chapter

17

CGT: Reliefs for individuals

Chapter learning objectives

Upon completion of this chapter you will be able to:

- define 'principal private residence'
- calculate the relief on disposal of a principal private residence
- calculate the gain when a principal private residence has been used partly for business purposes
- identify when letting relief is available on a principal private residence and calculate the relief
- explain and calculate entreprenneurs relief
- explain and apply roll-over relief as it applies to individuals
- explain and apply hold-over relief for the gift of business assets
- explain when incorporation relief is available upon the transfer of a business to a company
- apply incorporation relief.

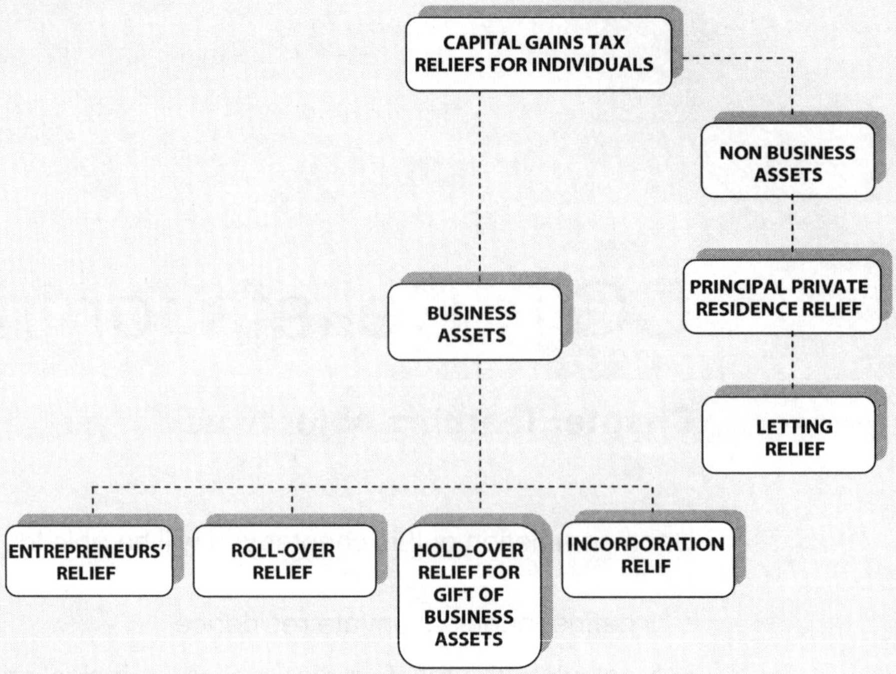

1 Introduction

In certain situations a gain on the disposal of an asset may be reduced or delayed by capital gains tax reliefs.

The reliefs are applied to the capital gain **before** deducting capital losses.

The main reliefs available to individuals are as follows.

	Relief	**On**
Non-business assets	Principal private residence relief	Individual's private residence
Business assets	Entrepreneurs relief	Exemption on the disposal of certain business assets
	Roll-over relief	Reinvestment in new business assets
	Hold-over relief	Gift of business assets
	Incorporation relief	The incorporation of a business

2 Principal private residence relief

Principal private residence (PPR) relief applies when an individual disposes of:

- a dwelling house (including normally up to half an acre of adjoining land)
- which has at some time during his ownership been his only or main private residence.

The relief

The relief applies where the PPR has been occupied for either the whole or part of the period of ownership.

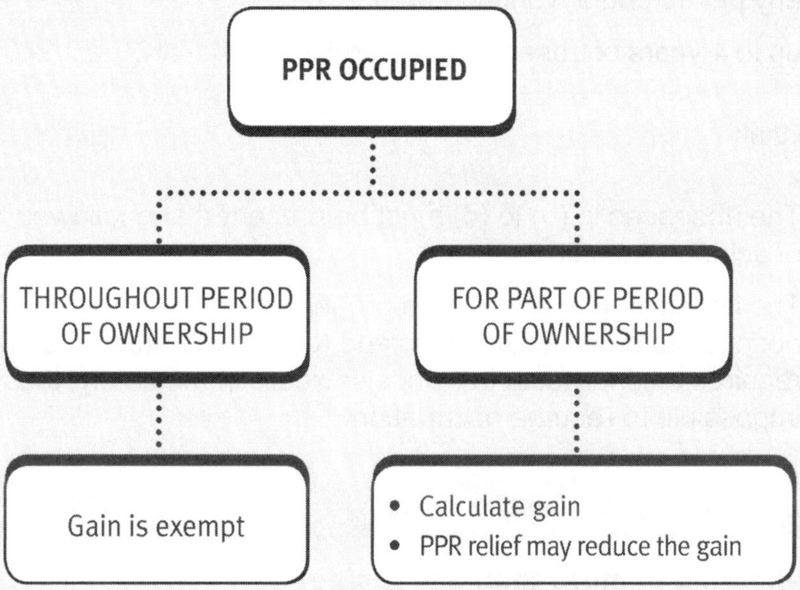

Calculating the relief

Where there has been a period of absence from the PPR the procedure is as follows.

- Calculate the capital gain on the disposal of the property
- Compute the total period of ownership.
- Calculate the periods of occupation (see below).
- Calculate the PPR exemption as follows:

  Gain × (Periods of occupation/Total period of ownership)

Periods of occupation

The period of occupation includes periods of both:

- actual occupation
- deemed occupation.

Deemed occupation

Periods of deemed occupation are:

(a) the last 3 years of ownership

(b) up to 3 years of absence for any reason

(c) any period spent working abroad

(d) up to 4 years of absence while working in the UK.

Note that:

- The absences in (b) to (d) must be preceded and followed by a period of actual occupation.
- The condition to reoccupy the property after the period of absence does not need to be satisfied for (c) and (d) above where an employer requires the individual to work elsewhere immediately, thus making it impossible to resume occupation.

Expandable text - Further points

Ownership of more than one residence

Where an individual has more than one residence he is entitled to nominate which of them is to be treated as his principal residence for capital gains purposes by notifying HM Revenue and Customs in writing.

The election must be made within two years of acquiring an additional residence otherwise it is open to HMRC, as a question of fact, to decide which residence is the main residence.

Married couples/civil partners

Provided that they are not treated as being separated or divorced, a married couple (or civil partnership) is entitled to only one residence between them for the purposes of the principal private residence exemption.

Example 1 - Principal private residence relief

On 1 May 1984 Mr Flint purchased a house in Southampton for £25,000, which he lived in until he moved to a rented flat on 1 July 1985.

He remained in the flat until 1 October 1987, when he accepted a year's secondment to his firm's New York office.

On coming back on 1 October 1988 he moved into a relative's house, where he stayed until he returned to his own home on 31 January 1989.

On 1 July 2000 he changed jobs and rented a flat near his new employer's offices in Newcastle. Here he remained until he sold his Southampton house on 1 February 2009 for £95,000.

Calculate the capital gain after reliefs, if any, arising on the disposal of the house on 1 February 2009.

Answer to example 1

	£
Disposal proceeds	95,000
Less: Cost	(25,000)
Capital gain before reliefs	70,000
Less: Principal private residence (PPR) exemption **(W)**	(54,209)
Chargeable gain after relies	15,791

Working – Chargeable and exempt periods of ownership

	Chargeable months	Exempt months
May 1984 – June 1985 (actual occupation)	–	14
July 1985 – September 1987 (absent – any reason)	–	27
October 1987 – September 1988 (absent – employed abroad)	–	12
October 1988 – January 1989 (absent – any reason)	–	4
Feb 1989 – June 2000 (actual occupation)	–	137
July 2000 – January 2006 (absent – see note)	67	–
February 2006 – January 2009 (final 36 months)	–	36
	67	230

Total period of ownership (67 + 230) = 297 months.

Exempt element of gain is 230/297 × £70,000 = £54,209.

Notes

(1) After Mr Flint left his residence to work in Newcastle he never returned. Consequently the exemption for working away from home in the UK is not available as there is not actual occupation both before and after the period of absence.

(2) The remaining 5 months (3 years – 27 months – 4 months) for 'any reason' is also not available for exemption as Mr Flint never reoccupied the property after leaving for Newcastle.

(3) In contrast, the exemption for the final 36 months of ownership has no such restriction and is therefore still available.

Test your understanding 1

Arthur bought a house on 1 January 1990 and sold it on 30 September 2008 making a capital gain of £189,000.

He occupied the house as follows:

1 January 1990 – 31 December 1991	Lived in house
1 January 1992 – 30 June 1998	Employed overseas
1 July 1998 – 31 December 2002	Travels the world
1 January 2003 – 30 September 2008	Lived in house

Calculate the chargeable gain after reliefs, if any, arising on the disposal of the house on 30 September 2008.

Business use

Where a house, or part of it, is used wholly and exclusively for business purposes, this part loses its PPR exemption and becomes taxable.

It should be noted that:

- The taxpayer cannot benefit from the rules of deemed occupation for any part of the property used for business purposes.
- However where part of the property was used for business purposes but was also at any time used as the taxpayer's main residence, the exemption for the last 36 months applies to the whole property.
- The 36 month exemption does not however apply to any part of the property used for business purposes **throughout** the period of ownership.

Example 2 - Principal private residence relief

On 30 June 2008 Alex sold his house for £125,000, resulting in a capital gain of £70,000. The house had been purchased on 1 July 1996, and one of the five rooms has always been used for business purposes.

Calculate the chargeable gain after reliefs arising on the disposal of the house.

Answer to example 2

Alex owned the house for 144 months and used 1/5th of the house (one of the five rooms) for business purposes. The 36 month exemption does not apply to the part of the property used for business purposes as it has never been used at any time for private purposes.

The capital gain is therefore: (£70,000 × 1/5) = £14,000

Alternative approach:

	£
Capital gain before reliefs	70,000
Less: PPR exemption (£70,000 x 4/5)	(56,000)
Chargeable gain after reliefs	14,000

Test your understanding 2

On 30 April 2008 Todd sold his house for £150,000, resulting in a capital gain of £60,000. The house had been purchased on 1 May 2001, and one of the seven rooms had always been used for business purposes.

Calculate the chargeable gain after reliefs arising on the disposal of the house.

Letting relief

Letting relief is available where an individual's PPR is let out for residential use.

It applies when:

- the owner is absent from the property and lets the house out, or
- the owner lets part of the property whilst still occupying the remainder.

It does not apply to let property which is not the owner's PPR, e.g. buy-to-let properties.

The relief

Letting relief is the lowest of:

- £40,000
- the amount of the gain exempted by the normal PPR rules
- the part of the gain (still in charge) attributable to the letting period.

Example 3 - Letting relief

Mr Hill bought a house on 1 April 1985. He occupied the house as follows:

1 April 1985 – 31 March 1986	Lived in as PPR
1 April 1986 – 30 September 1990	Travelled the world and let the house
1 October 1990 – 31 March 1995	Lived in as PPR
1 April 1995 – 1 May 2008	House empty

He sold the house on 1 May 2008 giving a capital gain of £209,730.

Calculate the chargeable gain after reliefs arising on the sale of the house.

Answer to example 3

(1) Calculate the capital gain using normal rules (given) = £209,730.

(2) Compute the total period of ownership:

1 April 1985 – 1 May 2008 = 23 years 1 month (277 months).

(3) Compute periods of occupation:

		Actual (months)	Deemed (months)	Absent (months)	Total (months)
(1)	1.4.85 – 31.3.86	12	–	–	12
(2)	1.4.86 – 30.9.90 (3 years any reason)	–	36	18	54
(3)	1.10.90 – 31.3.95	54	–	–	54
(4)	1.4.95 – 30.4.05	–	–	121	121
(5)	1.5.05 – 1.5.08 (Last 3 years of ownership)	–	36	–	36
		66	72	139	277

Exempt periods = (66 + 72) = 138

(4) Capital gain before letting relief is calculated is:

	£
Capital gain before reliefs	209,730
Less: PPR relief	
(£209,730 × 138/277)	(104,486)
	105,244

(5) Calculate letting relief

The house was let for the period 1.4.86 – 30.9.90, i.e. four years and six months (54 months) but of the 54 months of letting there are three years of deemed occupation qualifying for PPR relief.

Thus the letting relief is restricted to the gain on 18 months as only this portion of the chargeable gain is attributable to the letting.

Letting relief = lowest of:

1 Maximum £40,000
2 PPR = £104,486
3 Gain on letting = £209,730 × 18/277 £13,629

(6) Calculate chargeable gain after reliefs

	£
Chargeable gain after PPR	105,244
Less: Letting relief	(13,629)
Chargeable gain after reliefs	91,615

Test your understanding 3

On 30 September 2008 Jane Smith made a gift of a house to her grandson Norman. The house had been bought by Jane on 1 September 1999 for £45,000, and was extended at a cost of £10,600 during June 2000. A market value of £140,000 at 30 September 2008 had been agreed by HM Revenue and Customs.

Jane occupied the house as her main residence until 30 September 2001 when she went to live with her sister. The house was rented out from 1 October 2002 to the date of the deemed sale.

Calculate the chargeable gain after reliefs arising on the gift of the house.

Summary

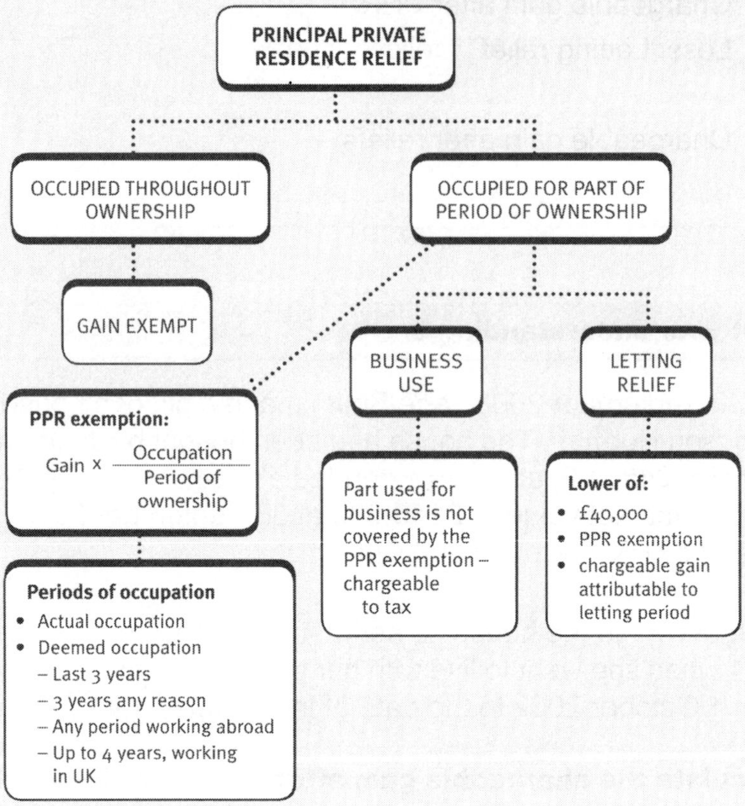

3 Entrepreneurs' relief

Entrepreneurs' relief reduces the capital gains tax payable on certain qualifying business disposals.

The relief operates as follows:

- The first £1 million of gains on 'qualifying business disposals' on or after 6 April 2008 will be reduced by 4/9ths.
- The remaining 5/9ths of the first £1 million of gains are taxed at the new flat rate of 18% resulting in an effective rate of 10% on the first £1 million of gains (18% x 5/9 = 10%).
- Any gains above the £1 million limit are taxed in full at the 18% rate.

The relief is given **before** the deduction of:

- allowable losses (other than any losses on assets that are part of the disposal of the business), and
- the annual exemption.

The relief must be claimed within 12 months of the 31 January following the end of the tax year in which the disposal is made.

For 2008/09 disposals, the relief must be claimed by 31 January 2011.

The £1 million limit is a lifetime limit which is diminished each time a claim for the relief is made.

Qualifying business disposals

The relief applies to the disposal of:

- the whole or part of a business carried on by the individual either alone or in partnership
- assets of the individual's or partnership's trading business that has **now ceased**
- shares **provided**:
  - the shares are in the individual's 'personal trading company', **and**
  - the individual is an employee of the company (part time or full time).

An individual's 'personal trading company' is one in which the individual:

- owns at least 5% of the ordinary shares
- which carry at least 5% of the voting rights.

Note that:

- the disposal of an individual business asset used for the purposes of a continuing trade does not qualify. There must be a disposal of the whole or part of the trading business. The sale of an asset in isolation will not qualify.
- "Part of a business" is likely to be interpreted as meaning a "substantial part" which is "capable of independent operation".
- Where the disposal is a disposal of assets (i.e. not shares), relief is not available on gains arising from the disposal of those assets held for investment purposes.

Qualifying ownership period

The asset(s) being disposed of must have been owned by the individual making the disposal in the 12 months prior to the disposal.

Where the disposal is an asset of the individual's or partnership's trading business that has now ceased the disposal must also take place within three years of the cessation of trade.

Example 4 - Entrepreneurs' relief

In 2008/09, Katie sold her trading business which she set up in 1990 and realised the following gains:

	£
Factory	275,000
Goodwill	330,000
Warehouse	(100,000)
Investment property	200,000

All of the assets have been owned for many years.

Katie also sold her shares in an unquoted trading company and realised a gain of £600,000. She owned 25% of the ordinary shares of the company which she purchased ten years ago. She has worked for the company on a part time basis for the last three years.

Katie has not made any other capital disposals in 2008/09.

Calculate Katie's capital gains tax payable for 2008/09.

Answer to example 4

		£	£
Net gains qualifying for Entrepreneurs' relief			
Sale of trading business			
Factory		275,000	
Goodwill		330,000	
Warehouse		(100,000)	
	£	505,000	
Less: Entrepreneur's relief	505,000	x 4/9 (224,444)	
			280,556
Sale of trading company shares			
Gain on shares		600,000	
Less: Entrepreneur's relief	495,000	x 4/9 (220,000)	
	1,000,000		380,000
			660,556
Net gains not qualifying for Entrepreneurs' relief			
Sale of investment property			200,000
Net chargeable gains			860,556
Less: Annual exemption			(9,600)
Taxable gains			850,956
Capital gains tax payable (£850,956 x 18%)			153,172

Test your understanding 4

In 2008/09 Paul sold shares in Dual Ltd, an unquoted trading company, and realised a gain of £430,000. Paul has worked for Dual Ltd for many years and has owned 10% of the ordinary shares of the company for the last five years.

Paul set up a trading business in 2003 and in 2008/09 he sold a warehouse used in the business, realising a gain of £245,000.

In 2009/10 Paul sold the rest of the business and realised the following gains:

	£
Factory	495,000
Goodwill	130,000

All of the assets in the business have been owned for many years.

He also sold an antique grandfather clock and realised a gain of £5,325.

Calculate Paul's capital gains tax payable for 2008/09 and 2009/10. Assume that the annual exemption for 2008/09 continues in the future.

Interaction with other reliefs

Note that other specific capital gains tax reliefs (e.g. gift relief, roll-over relief and incorporation relief) are given before entrepreneurs' relief.

This means that if entrepreneurs' relief is applicable it is applied to the remaining gain:

- **after** other reliefs have been considered, but
- **before** deducting capital losses and the annual exemption.

More detail on how the interaction work is given later with the detail on the specific reliefs.

Interaction with takeovers

With a share for share exchange, it is possible that:

- the old shares would qualify for entrepreneurs' relief if it were treated as a disposal
- but the new company is not the shareholder's personal trading company and so the later disposal of its shares would not qualify for relief.
- where the share exchange takes place after 5 April 2008, the shareholder can elect for the event to be treated as a disposal for CGT such that entrepreneurs' relief may be available against the gain.

4 Roll-over relief

Roll-over relief allows the gain arising on the disposal of a business asset to be rolled over (i.e. deferred) when the sale proceeds are reinvested in a new business asset.

The relief

The relief operates as follows:

- The gain arising on the disposal of the business asset is deducted from (rolled over against) the acquisition cost of the new asset.
- Provided the proceeds are fully reinvested, no tax is payable at the time of the disposal.
- Roll-over relief effectively increases the gain arising on the disposal of the replacement asset, as its base cost has been reduced by the amount of deferred gain.
- Gains may be 'rolled over' a number of times such that a tax liability will only arise when there is a disposal without replacement.
- The relief is not automatic, it must be claimed.

Example 5 - Roll-over relief

Smith purchased an asset qualifying for roll-over relief in January 1987 for £160,000. In May 2008, he sold the asset for £180,000 and spent £200,000 in August 2008 on a new qualifying asset.

Calculate the chargeable gain arising on the disposal of the asset assuming that roll-over relief is claimed.

Calculate the base cost of the new asset acquired.

Answer to example 5

Gain on disposal of asset	£
Proceeds	180,000
Less cost	(160,000)
Capital gain	20,000
Less Roll-over relief	(20,000)
Chargeable gain	Nil
Base cost of new asset	
Acquisition cost	200,000
Less Gain rolled over on asset disposed of	(20,000)
Revised base cost	180,000

Conditions

Where a **qualifying business asset** is sold at a gain, the taxpayer may roll over the gain provided the proceeds are reinvested in a replacement qualifying business asset within the **qualifying time period**.

Qualifying business assets

The following assets qualify for roll-over relief on a disposal by an individual:

- goodwill
- land and buildings
- fixed plant and machinery, i.e. not moveable.

Both the old and the replacement assets must be qualifying business assets and have been used in a trade.

Qualifying time period

The replacement assets must be acquired within a period beginning **one** year before and ending **three** years after the date of sale of the old asset.

Example 6 - Rollover relief

Jones purchased a warehouse in February 1999 for £170,000. In July 2008, he sold the warehouse for £300,000. He used the warehouse for the purposes of his trade throughout the period of ownership

In December 2010 Jones bought a new warehouse for £360,000 for the purposes of his trade. He plans to sell the warehouse in January 2012 for £550,000.

Calculate the chargeable gains arising on the sale of the two warehouses.

Answer to example 6

First warehouse – July 2008

	£
Sale proceeds	300,000
Less Cost	(170,000)
Capital gain	130,000
Less Roll-over relief (Note)	(130,000)
Net chargeable gain	Nil

Note: The full gain of £130,000 can be rolled over (i.e. deferred) as:

- the asset disposed of is a qualifying business asset
- the replacement asset is a qualifying business asset
- the reinvestment has been made in December 2010 (i.e. within the qualifying period of July 2007 to July 2011)
- the amount reinvested exceeds the sale proceeds received (i.e. purchase price of new warehouse of £360,000 exceeds the sale proceeds of £300,000).

Second warehouse – January 2012

	£	£
Sale proceeds		550,000
Less Base Cost		
Cost	360,000	
Less deferred gain	(130,000)	
		(230,000)
Net chargeable gain		320,000

Note: Entrepreneurs' relief is not available as this is the disposal of an individual asset used for the purposes of a continuing trade. The trade itself is not being disposed of.

Gains deferred before 6 April 2008

If the disposal of a qualifying asset was made prior to 6 April 2008 and a roll-over relief claim is made, the calculation of the deferred gain may have been different to the current rules.

Knowledge of the different rules is not required. Therefore, if applicable, the examiner will either:

- give the amount of the deferred gain, or
- the calculation will be the same as the current rules (i.e. sale proceeds less cost).

Note however that regardless of how the gain is calculated, the deferred gain arising would have been deducted from the base cost of the replacement asset and deferred until the subsequent disposal of the replacement asset in the same way as before.

Expandable Text - Gain deferred pre 6 April 2008

Pre 6 April 2008 an individual was entitled to an indexation allowance on purchases from March 1982 to April 1998. The indexed gain was deferred when a roll-over relief claim was made.

Test your understanding 5

Chris acquired a freehold building in April 1995. In May 1998 he sold the building for £100,000 and realised a gain of £56,360. In August 1999, another freehold building was bought for £140,000 and this was sold in November 2008 for £380,000.

All of the buildings were used for the purposes of a trade by Chris.

Calculate the chargeable gain arising on the disposal of the second building in 2008/09.

Partial reinvestment of proceeds

Full roll-over relief is only available when all of the proceeds from the sale of the old asset are reinvested.

Where there is partial reinvestment of the proceeds, part of the gain is chargeable at the time of the disposal.

The gain which is chargeable (cannot be rolled over) is the lower of:

- the amount of the proceeds not reinvested
- the full indexed gain.

Test your understanding 6

Jarvis bought a factory in September 1987 and in December 2008, wishing to move to a more convenient location, he sold the factory for £750,000. The gain arising on the disposal of the factory was £115,000.

Jarvis moved into a rented factory until March 2009 when he purchased and moved into a new factory.

Calculate the amount of the gain which is chargeable, if any, on the sale of the original factory and calculate the base cost of the new factory assuming the new factory was purchased for (a) £700,000, or (b) £550,000?

Non-business use

Full roll-over relief is only available where the asset being replaced (the old asset) was used entirely for trade purposes throughout the trader's period of ownership.

Where this condition is not met, roll-over relief is still available but it is scaled down in proportion to the non-trade use.

Example 7 - Roll-over relief

Robert acquired a freehold building in April 1995 for £65,500. He only used 60% of the freehold building for the purposes of his trade. The building was sold in November 2008 for £162,000.

A replacement building was acquired in January 2008 for £180,000 and this was used 100% for trade purposes by Robert.

The replacement building was sold for £250,000 in May 2009.

Calculate the gain rolled over and the chargeable gains arising on the disposals in November 2008 and May 2009.

Answer to example 7

First building – November 2008

	£
Sale proceeds	162,000
Less Cost	(65,500)
Capital gain	96,500

Note: The asset disposed of is a qualifying business asset, but as only 60% of the building has been used for trade purposes, the gain eligible for roll-over relief must be restricted by 60%

	Business portion	Non-business portion
	£	£
Split of capital gain	57,900	38,600
Less Rollover relief (Note)	(57,900)	(N/A)
Chargeable gain – 2008/09	Nil	38,600

Note:

- the replacement asset is a qualifying business asset, used 100% for the purposes of the trade
- the reinvestment has been made in January 2008 (i.e. within the qualifying period of November 2007 to November 2011)
- the amount reinvested for the purposes of the trade exceeds the sale proceeds received relating to the trade use of the building (i.e. purchase price of new warehouse of £180,000 exceeds the portion of the sale proceeds on the first building relating to the trade of £97,200 (£162,000 x 60%)).
- therefore roll-over relief is available on all of the business portion of the gain.

Sale of replacement building – May 2009

	£	£
Sale proceeds		250,000
Less Base Cost		
Cost	180,000	
Less deferred gain	(57,900)	
		(122,100)
Capital gain – 2009/10		127,900

Note: Entrepreneurs' relief is not available as this is the disposal of an individual asset used for the purposes of a continuing trade.

Test your understanding 7

Hadley purchased a factory in November 1988 and not needing all the space, he let out 15% of it.

In August 2008 he sold the factory for £560,000 and realised a capital gain of £45,000.

In October 2008 Hadley bought another factory which he used 100% for business purposes for £500,000 claiming roll-over relief.

(a) **Calculate the chargeable gain arising on the disposal in August 2008?**

(b) **Calculate the base cost of the new factory.**

Depreciating assets

Roll-over relief is modified where the new asset purchased is a depreciating asset:

- If the replacement asset acquired is a depreciating asset, the gain cannot be rolled over, instead it is deferred until the earliest of the following three events:
  - Disposal of replacement asset.
  - The depreciating asset ceases to be used for the purposes of the trade.
  - Ten years from the date of acquisition of the replacement asset.
- The deferred gain is not deducted from the acquisition cost of the new asset.
- The deferred gain is just 'frozen' and becomes chargeable on the earliest of the three events above.

A depreciating asset is a wasting asset (i.e. with a predictable life of 50 years or less), or an asset that will become a wasting asset within ten years, (e.g. fixed plant and machinery or leasehold property with ≤ 60 years remaining on the lease).

- If prior to the deferred gain crystallising, a non-depreciating asset is bought, then the original deferred gain can now be rolled over.

Example 8 - Depreciating assets

Cooper purchased a freehold factory in June 1985 for £250,000. In May 2008 he sold it for £420,000 and in June 2008 bought fixed plant and machinery for £450,000. In March 2010, Cooper sold the fixed plant and machinery for £475,000.

Calculate the chargeable gains arising in 2009/10 assuming Cooper claims to roll over the gains where possible.

Answer to example 8

Freehold factory – May 2008

	£
Sale proceeds	420,000
Less Cost	(250,000)
Capital gain	170,000
Less deferred gain (see Note)	(170,000)
Chargeable gain in 2008/09	Nil

Note:

- the asset disposed of is a qualifying business asset
- the replacement asset is a qualifying business asset, but is a depreciating asset (fixed plant and machinery)
- the reinvestment has been made in June 2008 (i.e. within the qualifying period of May 2007 to May 2011)
- the amount reinvested exceeds the sale proceeds received (i.e. purchase price of new plant and machinery of £450,000 exceeds the sale proceeds on the factory of £420,000)
- therefore all of the gain can be deferred, but the deferred gain is not deducted from the base cost of the plant and machinery
- the gain of £170,000 is frozen and becomes chargeable on the earliest of:
  - the sale of the fixed plant and machinery (March 2010)
  - the date the plant and machinery ceases to be used in the trade (presumably March 2010)
  - ten years from the acquisition of the plant and machinery (June 2018)

Sale of plant and machinery – March 2010

	£	£
Sale proceeds	475,000	
Less Cost	(450,000)	
Capital gain on plant and machinery		25,000
Deferred gain becomes chargeable		170,000
Chargeable gains in 2009/10		195,000

Note: Entrepreneurs' relief is not available as this is the disposal of an individual asset used for the purposes of a continuing trade.

Test your understanding 8

Amir purchased a freehold factory in May 1985 and in May 1997 he sold it for £350,000 realising a capital gain of £150,000. In June 1999 Amir bought fixed plant and machinery for £400,000. In March 2010 Amir sold the fixed plant and machinery for £500,000.

Calculate the chargeable gains arising in respect of the sale of the freehold factory and the fixed plant and machinery, assuming Amir claims to roll over the gains where possible.

Clearly identify in which tax year the gains arise.

Summary

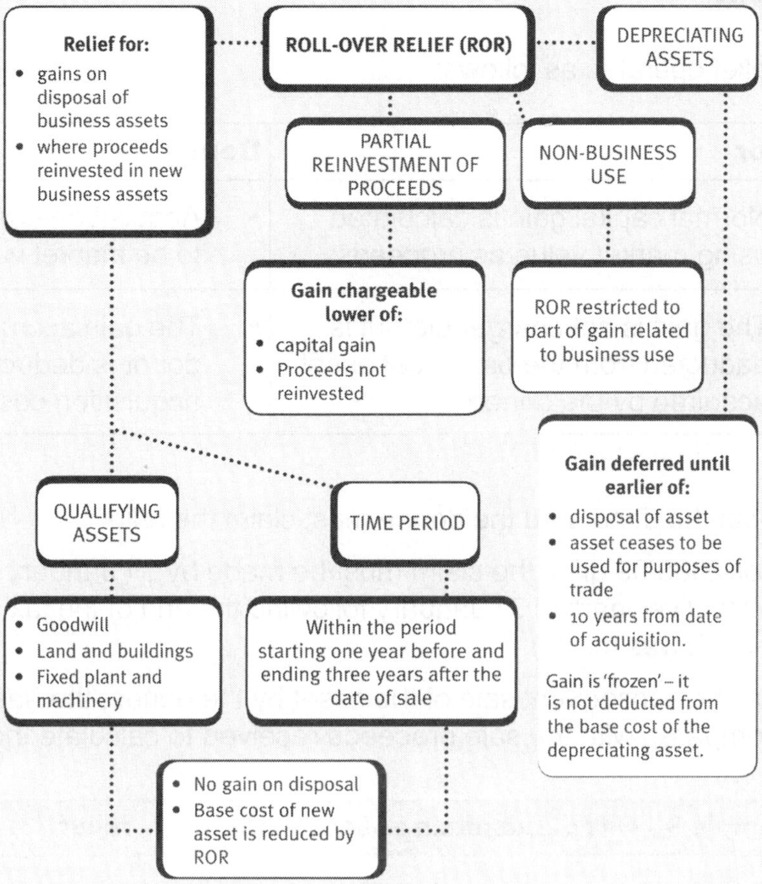

5 Gift of business assets – hold-over relief

The gift of an asset is a chargeable disposal which gives rise to a capital gains tax liability for the donor, however the donor has not received any funds with which to pay the tax.

Gift of business assets relief allows the gain to be held over (i.e. deferred) until the asset is eventually sold by the donee.

The relief however is only available for:

- business assets
- gifts by individuals.

The relief

The relief operates as follows:

Donor	Donee
• Normal capital gain is calculated using market value as proceeds	• Acquisition cost = deemed to be market value
• The gain is not chargeable but is deducted from the base cost asset acquired by the donee	• The gain accruing to the donor is deducted from the acquisition cost

- Both the donor and the donee must claim the relief.
- For 2008/09 gifts, the claim must be made by 31 January 2015 (i.e. within five years of 31 January following the end of the tax year in which the gift was made).
- On the subsequent sale of the asset by the donee, the base cost is compared with the sale proceeds received to calculate the capital gain.

Example 9 - Gift of business assets – hold-over relief

Jones bought a business asset for £25,000 in September 2003. In June 2008 he gifted it to Smith, when its market value was £40,000. Jones and Smith have made an election to hold over any gain arising.

Show Jones's capital gains tax position on the gift to Smith and calculate Smith's base cost in the asset.

Answer to example 9

Gift to Smith – June 2008

	£
Market value of asset	40,000
Less: Cost	(25,000)
Capital gain	15,000
Less: Hold-over relief for business assets	(15,000)
Chargeable gain	Nil

Smith's base cost

Smith has allowable expenditure to set against a future disposal, calculated as follows:

	£
Market value of asset acquired	40,000
Less: Held over capital gain	(15,000)
Base cost	25,000

Qualifying assets

The relief is only available where there is a gift of a qualifying asset.

The following are the main categories of qualifying asset.

- Assets used in the trade of:
  - the donor (i.e. where he is a sole trader)
  - the donor's personal company (this extends the relief to assets owned by the individual but not used by him directly for trading purposes).
- Shares and securities of trading companies provided that one of the following conditions apply:
  - the shares or securities are not quoted on a recognised stock exchange
  - the shares or securities gifted are those of the individual's personal company.

A company qualifies as an individual's personal company if at least 5% of the voting rights are owned by the individual.

Note that gift relief is given **before** entrepreneurs' relief.

This means that if entrepreneurs' relief is applicable:

- the deferred gain is **not** reduced by entrepreneurs' relief
- the donee **may** be able to make his or her own claim to entrepreneurs' relief on a subsequent disposal if the conditions are satisfied
- to donor may **choose not to claim** gift relief in order to crystallise a gain and claim entrepreneurs' relief instead if this is advantageous (i.e. if the donee will not qualify for the relief, for example if they would not satisfy the one-year ownership rule).

Gift before 6 April 2008

If the gift was made prior to 6 April 2008 and a gift relief claim is made, the calculation of the deferred gain may have been different to the current rules.

Knowledge of the different rules is not required. Therefore, if applicable, the examiner will either:

- give the amount of the deferred gain, or
- the calculation will be the same as the current rules (i.e. sale proceeds less cost).

Note however that regardless of how the gain is calculated, the deferred gain arising would have been deducted from the base cost of the donee and deferred until the subsequent disposal of the asset by the donee.

Sales at an undervalue

The relief applies not just to outright gifts but also to sales at an undervalue, where there is an element of gift.

For sales at an undervalue the relief is modified as follows:

- Any proceeds received which exceed the **original cost** of the asset gifted are chargeable to capital gains tax at the date of the gift.
- The gain held over is reduced by the amount chargeable.

Example 10 - Gift of business assets – hold-over relief

Ronald bought a business asset on 4 July 1998 for £20,000. He gave this asset to his son, Regan, on 1 September 2000 when the market value was £52,000. Ronald and Regan made a joint election to hold over any gain arising. Regan sold the asset on 18 December 2008 for £95,000.

(a) **Calculate the gain 'held over' and the chargeable gain arising on the eventual disposal by Regan in 2008/09.**

(b) **Calculate the gain eligible for gift relief and the base cost for Regan, assuming the same facts as above, but Regan pays his father on 1 September 2000:**

(i) **£28,000 or**

(ii) **£18,000.**

Answer to example 10

(a) **Ronald – Capital gains computation – 2000/01**

	£
Deemed disposal proceeds (MV @ date of gift)	52,000
Less: Acquisition cost	(20,000)
Capital gain	32,000

As Ronald and Regan have made a joint election the gain of £32,000 can be 'held over' (i.e. deferred) from Ronald to Regan (under the gift relief for business assets provisions).

Therefore there would be no chargeable gain on Ronald in 2000/01.

Regan – Capital gains computation – 2008/09

	£	£
Sale proceeds		95,000
Less Base cost:		
MV @ date of gift	52,000	
Less: Gain held over from Ronald	(32,000)	(20,000)
Capital gain		75,000

Note: Entrepreneurs' relief is not available as this is the gift of an individual asset, not the disposal of a whole or substantial part of a business.

(b) **Sale at undervaluation**

(i) **Ronald – Capital gains computation – 2000/01**

	£	£
Deemed disposal proceeds (MV @ date of gift)		52,000
Less: Acquisition cost		(20,000)
Potential gain (as before)		32,000
Actual proceeds	28,000	
Less: Original cost	(20,000)	
Excess proceeds over cost chargeable now	8,000	
Less: Gain eligible to be held over		(24,000)
Chargeable gain in 2000/01		8,000

Regan – Base cost (for future disposal)

	£
Deemed acquisition cost (MV at date of gift)	52,000
Less: Gain held over from Ronald	(24,000)
Base cost	28,000

(ii) **Ronald – Capital gains computation – 2000/01**

	£
Deemed disposal proceeds (MV at date of gift)	52,000
Less: Acquisition cost	(20,000)
Potential gain (as before)	32,000
Actual proceeds of £18,000 are less than original cost of £20,000 therefore the entire gain is eligible for gift relief.	
Less: Gain eligible to be held over	(32,000)
Chargeable gain in 2000/01	Nil

Regan – Base cost (for future disposal)

	£
Deemed acquisition cost	52,000
Less Gain held over from Ronald	(32,000)
Base cost	20,000

Test your understanding 9

Alice bought a business asset in May 2006 for £120,000. She gave this asset to her brother, Adam, on 1 June 2008 when the market value was £150,000. Alice and Adam made a joint election to hold over any gain arising. Adam sold the asset on 1 May 2009 for £180,000.

(a) **Calculate the gain 'held over' and the capital gain arising on the eventual disposal by Adam in 2009/10.**

(b) **Calculate the gain eligible for gift of business assets relief and the base cost of Adam if, instead of giving the asset to Adam, Alice had sold it to him for £130,000.**

Assets not used wholly for trade purposes

The relief is restricted where either:

- only part of an asset is used for trading purposes
- an asset is used for trading purposes for only part of the donor's period of ownership.

Assets apart from shares

Only the gain relating to the period that the asset was used in the trade or the part of the asset used for trading purposes is eligible for relief.

The restriction to the relief operates in the same way as roll-over relief where assets have not been wholly used in the trade.

Example 11 - Gift of business assets – hold-over relief

David acquired a freehold building in May 2005 for £160,000. He used 60% of the freehold building in his trade for business purposes. In June 2008 he gifted the building to his son, Ben, when its market value was £250,000. David and Ben signed an election to hold over the gain arising on the gift.

Calculate the gain held over and the chargeable gain arising on the gift of the building in June 2008.

Answer to example 11

David – Capital gains computation – 2008/09

	£
Market value at date of gift	250,000
Less: Acquisition cost	(160,000)
Potential gain	90,000
As only 60% of the building has been used for the purposes of a trade, the gain eligible to be held over must also be restricted by the same %.	
Less: Gain eligible to be held over (60% × £90,000)	(54,000)
Chargeable gain in 2008/09 (40% of £90,000)	36,000

Note: Entrepreneurs' relief is not available as this is the gift of an individual asset, not the disposal of a whole or substantial part of a business.

Shares

Where the assets being gifted are shares the gain eligible to be held over is restricted in the following situation:

- the shares are in the donor's personal company (at least 5% of the voting rights are owned by the donor); and
- the company owns chargeable non-business assets.

In this situation the gain eligible for gift relief is:

$$\text{Total gain} \times \frac{\text{M.V. of chargeable business assets (CBA)}}{\text{M.V. of chargeable assets (CA)}}$$

Note that where the donor holds less than 5% of the voting rights in the company there is no restriction to the relief when shares are gifted.

Chargeable assets

A chargeable asset is one that, if sold, would give rise to a chargeable gain (or an allowable loss). Exempt assets such as motor cars are therefore excluded.

Chargeable business assets

These are defined as assets used for the purposes of a trade other than those assets on the disposal of which no chargeable gain arises (i.e. stocks, debtors, cash, etc) and **excludes** shares, securities or other assets held for investment.

Note that if the individual disposes of shares in a personal trading company:

- gift relief is available:
  - subject to the (CBA / CA) restriction above
  - regardless of whether the individual works for the company
- entrepreneurs' relief is also available provided:
  - the individual works for the company, and
  - it has been the individual's personal trading company
  - for the 12 months prior to the disposal.

Remember that gift relief is given before entrepreneurs' relief.

Example 12 - Gift of business assets – hold-over relief

Jin Ming has been a full-time working director of Porcelain Products Ltd since 1 December 1994 and has owned 10% of the company's ordinary shares since 1 December 1998. He resigned from the company on 1 December 2008 and gifted his 10% shareholding, valued at £950,000, to his daughter Jun Ying. The agreed capital gain on the disposal of the shares was £700,000. Jin and Jun signed an election to hold over the gain on the gift.

The market values of the assets in the balance sheet at 1 December 2008 were as follows.

	£
Land and buildings	550,000
Motor cars	80,000
Cash	45,000
Debtors	35,000
Stock	50,000
Shares held as investments	60,000

Calculate Jin Ming's chargeable gain before the annual exemption in 2008/09; and the base cost of the shares acquired by Jun Ying.

Answer to example 12

Jin Ming – Capital gains computation – 2008/09

	£
Total gain on disposal of shares	700,000
Less: Gift relief	
$\text{£}700{,}000 \times \dfrac{\text{£}550{,}000}{\text{£}550{,}000 + \text{£}60{,}000}$	(631,148)
	68,852
Less: Entrepreneurs' relief (£68,852 x 4/9)	(30,601)
Chargeable gain	38,251

Base cost for Jun Ying

	£
MV @ date of gift	950,000
Less: Gain held over from Jin Ming	(631,148)
Base cost	318,852

Test your understanding 10

Fred owned 100% of the shares in Fred Ltd and has always worked for his company. On 20 February 2009 he made a gift of the shares to his son, and this resulted in a capital gain of £400,000.

At the time of the gift the market value of the assets owned by Fred Ltd were as follows.

	£
Freehold trading premises	400,000
Investments – Shares in UK companies	100,000
Stock and work in progress	130,000
Debtors	100,000
Cash	30,000
	760,000

Calculate the amount of Fred's capital gain that can be held over as a gift of business assets.

Summary

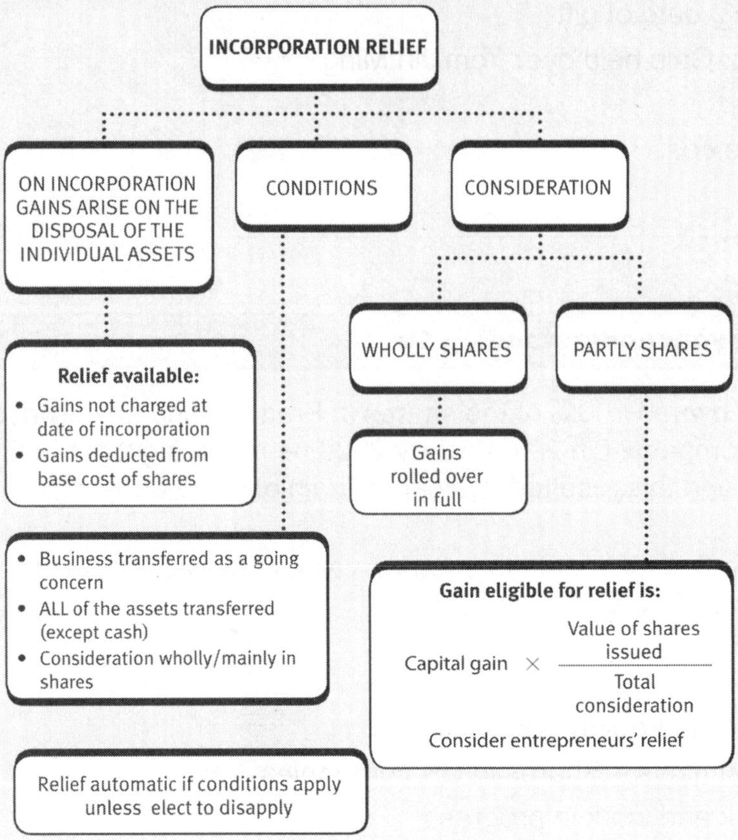

6 Incorporation relief

Where an individual transfers their business to a company, the individual assets of the business are deemed to have been disposed of at market value for capital gains tax purposes.

Incorporation relief is a form of roll-over relief to allow the gains arising on incorporation to be deferred until the shares in the newly formed company are disposed of.

The conditions

Incorporation relief is available where the following conditions apply:

- The unincorporated business is transferred as a going concern.
- All of the assets of the business (other than cash) are transferred.
- The consideration for the transfer of the business must be wholly or mainly shares in the company.

The relief

Incorporation relief operates as follows:

- The gains arising on the deemed disposal of the individual assets are rolled over against the acquisition cost of the shares in the new company.
- The rolled over gain is deducted from the base cost of the shares.
- Where the consideration for the transfer of the business to the company is wholly shares, the full gain is rolled over.
- Where part of the consideration for the transfer of the business is not shares, e.g. cash or debentures, the gain eligible for relief is:

$$\text{Capital gains} \times \frac{\text{Value of shares issued}}{\text{Total consideration}}$$

- The relief is automatic provided certain conditions are met.
- An individual can elect for incorporation relief not to apply (i.e. disapply the relief).

Note that, if applicable, incorporation relief is given before entrepreneurs' relief.

This means that if entrepreneurs' relief is available:

- the deferred gain is not reduced by entrepreneurs' relief
- but where part of the consideration is in the form of cash, the remaining gain can be reduced by entrepreneurs' relief
- the subsequent disposal of the shares should normally qualify for entrepreneurs' relief provided the conditions are satisfied
- however if this in unlikely, the individual may **disapply** incorporation relief in order to crystallise a gain and claim entrepreneurs' relief instead if this is advantageous (i.e. if the individual plans to dispose of the shares within one year and fails the one-year ownership rule).

Example 13 - Incorporation relief

Sarah incorporated her sewing business on 1 June 2008. The assets transferred to the new company, Sarah Ltd, are set out below. In exchange for the transfer of the business she received 100,000 £1 ordinary shares.

Assets transferred	**Market value at 1.6.08**	**Original cost**
	£	£
Freehold premises – acquired May 2000	150,000	70,000
Furniture and fittings	5,000	10,000
Plant and machinery	5,500	15,000
Stock	25,500	25,000
Goodwill	54,000	–
	240,000	120,000

All items of plant and machinery and furniture and fittings were bought and sold for less than £6,000.

Calculate the chargeable gains, if any, arising on the incorporation of Sarah's business and state Sarah's base cost in the shares in Sarah Ltd.

Answer to example 13

Sarah – Capital gains computation – 2008/09

Gains arising on the incorporation of the existing business

	£	£
Freehold premises		
MV on incorporation	150,000	
Less: Acquisition cost	(70,000)	
Potential gain		80,000
Goodwill		
MV on incorporation	54,000	
Less: Acquisition cost	(Nil)	
Potential gain		54,000
Total capital gains		134,000
Less Incorporation relief **(Note)**		(134,000)
Chargeable gain		Nil
Base cost of shares in Sarah Ltd		
Market value of shares		240,000
Less: Capital gains rolled over		(134,000)
Base cost		106,000

Note: As the consideration is wholly in shares the gains arising on incorporation can be rolled over in full.

Test your understanding 11

On 8 March 2009 Chandra incorporated a wholesale business that she had run as a sole trader since 1 May 2006. The market value of the business on 8 March 2009 was £250,000.

All of the business assets were transferred to a new limited company, with the consideration consisting of 200,000 £1 ordinary shares valued at £200,000 and £50,000 in cash.

The only chargeable asset of the business was goodwill and this was valued at £100,000 on 8 March 2009. The goodwill has a nil cost.

Calculate the chargeable gains arising from Chandra's disposals during 2008/09.

Example 14 - Incorporation relief

Sam started a retail business in 1985. On 1 May 2008 he transferred his business to a company, Sam Ltd. The assets transferred are set out below. In exchange he received 4,000 £1 ordinary shares, valued at £80,000 and £20,000 cash.

Assets transferred	**Market value at 1.5.08**	**Gain**
	£	£
Freehold premises	35,000	25,000
Furniture and fittings	8,000	–
Plant and machinery	14,000	–
Stock	25,000	–
Goodwill	18,000	18,000
	100,000	43,000

On 1 February 2009 Sam sold his entire holding in Sam Ltd for £150,000.

Calculate Sam's chargeable gains for 2008/09.

Consider any tax advice you may wish to give Sam.

Answer to example 14

Capital gain on transfer of business – May 2008

		£
Total gains		43,000
Less: Gain rolled over	$\frac{£80,000}{£80,000 + £20,000} \times £43,000$	(34,400)
		8,600
Less: Entrepreneurs' relief (£8,600 x 4/9)		(3,822)
Chargeable gain		4,778

Disposal of shares – February 2009

	£	£
Sale proceeds		150,000
Less Base cost:		
Market value of shares	80,000	
Less: Rolled over gain	(34,400)	
		(45,600)
Capital gain (Note)		104,400

Total chargeable gains in 2008/09 are £109,178 (£4,778 + £104,400).

Note: Entrepreneurs' relief is not available on the disposal of the shares as Sam has owned them for less than 12 months.

Tax advice

In these circumstances it would be advantageous to disapply incorporation relief.

As a result the total chargeable gains in 2008/09 would be £93,889 (W) (£23,889 + £70,000).

Working

	£
Total gains on transfer of business	43,000
Less: Entrepreneurs' relief (£43,000 x 4/9)	(19,111)
Chargeable gain	23,889
Disposal of shares	
Sale proceeds	150,000
Cost	(80,000)
Capital gain	70,000

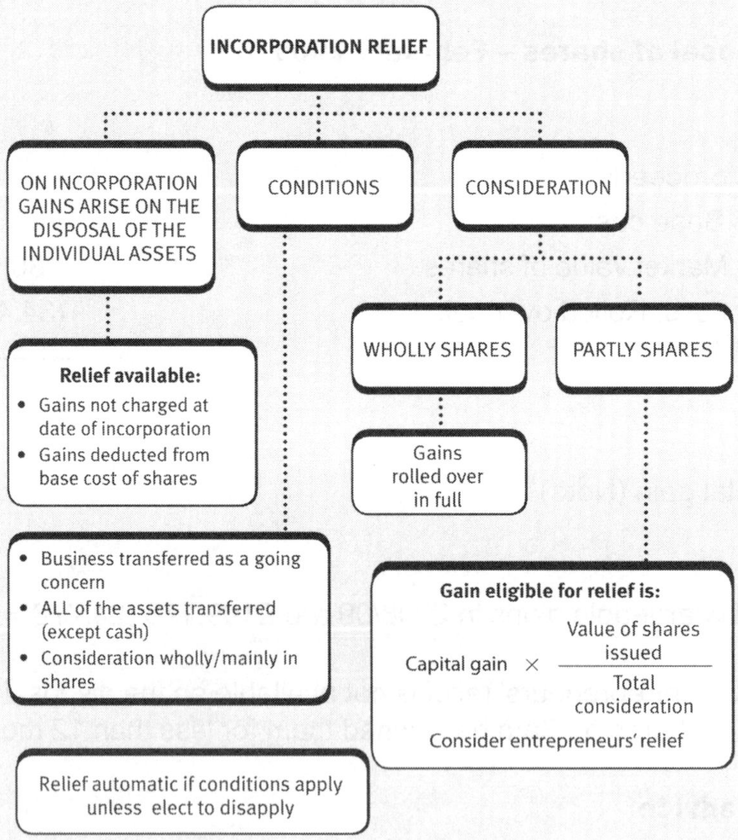

7 Chapter summary

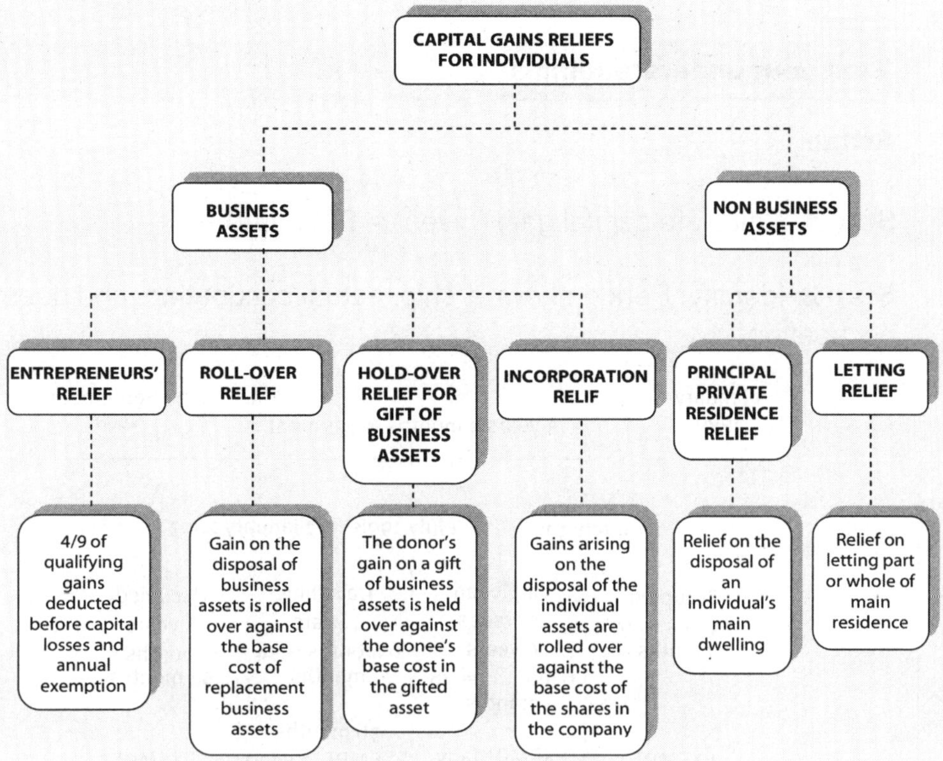

Test your understanding answers

Test your understanding 1

Arthur

Step 1 Calculate capital gain (given) = £189,000.

Step 2 Identify: Period of ownership, actual occupation, and deemed occupation.

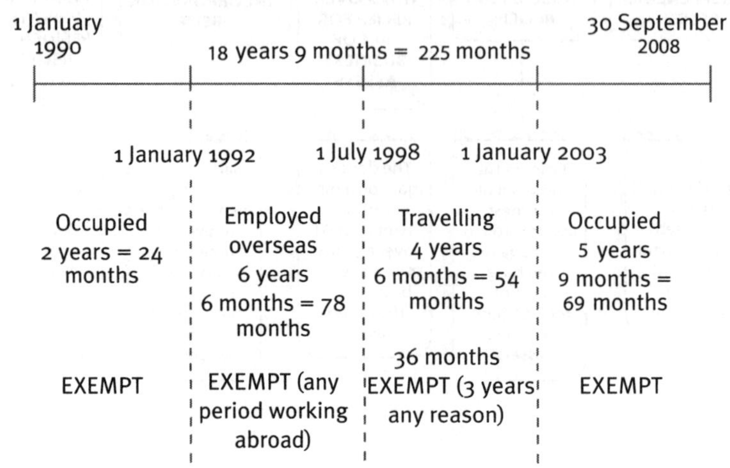

PPR exemption

	Months	
Occupied	24	
Employed overseas	78	
Any reason	36	
Occupied	69	
PPR exemption	207	out of 225

Note

The periods of occupation before and after deemed occupation do **not** need to be **immediately** before and after (for example the employment overseas ended on 30 June 1998 and is followed by actual occupation which did not start until 1 January 2003).

Step 3 Apply PPR exemption.

	£
Capital gain before reliefs	189,000
Less: PPR exemption 207/225 × £189,000	(173,880)
Chargeable gain after reliefs	15,120

Test your understanding 2

Todd

Todd owned the house for six years and used 1/7th of the house (one of the seven rooms) for business purposes.

The last 36 months exemption does not apply to the business element of the gain as this part of the house has never been used for private purposes.

The chargeable gain after reliefs = (£60,000 × 1/7) = £8,571.

Test your understanding 3

Jane Smith

	£
Deemed proceeds (market value)	140,000
Less: Cost	(45,000)
Enhancement expenditure	(10,600)
Capital gain before reliefs	84,400

		Total (months)	Exempt (months)	Chargeable (months)	Property let (months)
1.9.99 to 20.9.01	Actual	25	25		
1.10.01 to 30.9.02	Empty	12		12	
1.10.02 to 30.9.05	Living elsewhere, property let	36			36
1.10.05 to 30.9.08	Last 3 years	36	36		
		109	61	12	36

	£
Capital gain before reliefs (as above)	84,400
Less: PPR relief (£84,400 × 61/109)	(47,233)
	37,167
Less: Letting relief = lowest of:	
(a) £40,000	
(b) £47,233 (the part of the gain exempt as a principal private residence)	
(c) £84,400 × 36/109= £27,875 (the gain attributable to the period of letting)	(27,875)
Chargeable gain after reliefs	9,292

Test your understanding 4

Paul

2008/09

			£	£
Net gains qualifying for Entrepreneurs' relief				
Sale of trading company shares				
Gain on shares			430,000	
Less: Entrepreneurs' relief	£430,000	x 4/9	(191,111)	
				238,889
Net gains not qualifying for Entrepreneurs' relief				
Sale of Warehouse (Note)				245,000
Net chargeable gains				483,889
Less: Annual exemption				(9,600)
Taxable gains				474,289
Capital gains tax payable				
(£474,289 x 18%)				85,372

Note: The disposal of the warehouse in 2008/09 is the disposal of an individual business asset used for the purposes of a continuing trade. To qualify there must be a disposal of the whole or part of the trading business. The sale of an asset in isolation will not qualify.

2009/10

		£	£
Net gains qualifying for Entrepreneurs' relief			
Sale of trading business			
Factory		495,000	
Goodwill		130,000	
		625,000	
Less: Entrepreneurs' relief			
Rest of the lifetime allowance			
(£1,000,000 – £430,000)	£570,000 x 4/9	(253,333)	
			371,667
Net gains not qualifying for Entrepreneurs' relief			
Sale of Grandfather clock			5,325
Net chargeable gains			376,992
Less: Annual exemption			(9,600)
Taxable gains			367,392
Capital gains tax payable			
(£367,392 x 18%)			66,131

Test your understanding 5

Chris

Second building – November 2008

	£	£
Sale proceeds		380,000
Less: Base cost		
Cost	140,000	
Less: deferred gain	(56,360)	
		(83,640)
Chargeable gain		296,360

Note: The full gain of £56,360 can be rolled over (i.e. deferred) as:

- the asset disposed of is a qualifying business asset
- the replacement asset is a qualifying business asset
- the reinvestment has been made in August 1999 (i.e. within the qualifying period of May 1997 to May 2001)
- the amount reinvested exceeds the sale proceeds received (i.e. purchase price of new warehouse of £360,000 exceeds the sale proceeds of £300,000).

Test your understanding 6

Jarvis

	(a)	(b)
New factory purchased for	**£700,000**	**£550,000**
	£	£
Chargeable gain now = Lower of:		
(i) Sale proceeds not reinvested		
(£750,000 – £700,000)	50,000	
(£750,000 – £550,000)		200,000
(ii) Capital gain on the disposal of original factory	115,000	115,000
Therefore, **chargeable in 2008/09** (Note)	**50,000**	**115,000**
Roll-over relief		
(£115,000 – £50,000)	65,000	
(£115,000 – £115,000)		Nil
Base cost of new replacement factory		
Cost	700,000	550,000
Less Roll-over relief	(65,000)	(Nil)
	635,000	550,000

Note: Entrepreneurs' relief is not available as this is the disposal of an individual asset used for the purposes of a continuing trade.

Test your understanding 7

Hadley

Disposal of factory – August 2008

	£
Capital gain	45,000

Note: the asset disposed of is a qualifying business asset, but as only 85% of the building has been used for trade purposes, the gain eligible for roll-over relief must be restricted by 85%.

	Business portion	**Non-business portion**
	£	£
Split of capital gain	38,250	6,750
Less: Rollover relief (Note)	(38,250)	(N/A)
Chargeable gain – 2008/09	Nil	6,750

Note:

- the replacement asset is a qualifying business asset, used 100% for the purposes of the trade
- the reinvestment has been made in October 2008 (i.e. within the qualifying period of August 2007 to August 2011)
- the amount reinvested for the purposes of the trade exceeds the sale proceeds received relating to the trade use of the building (i.e. purchase price of new warehouse of £500,000 exceeds the portion of the sale proceeds on the first building relating to the trade of £493,000 (£560,000 x 85%))
- therefore roll-over relief is available on all of the business portion of the gain.
- Entrepreneurs' relief is not available as this is the disposal of an individual asset used for the purposes of a continuing trade and the gain is arising on an investment asset.

Base cost of replacement factory – October 2008

	£
Cost	500,000
Less: Deferred gain	(38,250)
	461,750

Test your understanding 8

Amir

Freehold factory – May 1997

	£
Capital gain	150,000
Less: Deferred gain (see Note)	(150,000)
Chargeable gain in 1997/98	Nil

Note:

- the asset disposed of is a qualifying business asset
- the replacement asset is a qualifying business asset, but is a depreciating asset (fixed plant and machinery)
- the reinvestment has been made in June 1999 (i.e. within the qualifying period of May 1996 to May 2000)
- the amount reinvested exceeds the sale proceeds received (i.e. purchase price of new plant and machinery of £400,000 exceeds the sale proceeds on the factory of £350,000)
- therefore all of the gain can be deferred, but the deferred gain is not deducted from the base cost of the plant and machinery
- the gain of £150,000 is frozen and becomes chargeable on the earliest of:
  - the sale of the fixed plant and machinery (March 2010)
  - the date the plant and machinery ceases to be used in the trade (presumably March 2010)
  - ten years from the acquisition of the plant and machinery (June 2009)

Chargeable event – June 2009

	£	£
Deferred gain becomes chargeable		150,000

Sale of plant and machinery – March 2010

	£	£
Sale proceeds	500,000	
Less: Cost	(400,000)	
Capital gain on plant and machinery		100,000
Chargeable gains in 2009/10		250,000

Test your understanding 9

Alice

(a) **Alice – Capital gains computation – 2008/09**

	£
MV @ date of gift	150,000
Less: Acquisition cost	(120,000)
Capital gain	30,000

As Alice and Adam made a joint election this gain of £30,000 can be 'held over' from Alice to Adam (under the 'gift relief' provisions). Therefore there would be no chargeable gain on Alice in 2008/09.

Adam – Capital gains computation – 2009/10

	£	£
Sale proceeds		180,000
Less: Base cost		
MV @ date of gift	150,000	
Less: Gain held over from Alice	(30,000)	(120,000)
Capital gain		60,000

Note: Entrepreneurs' relief is not available as this is the gift of an individual asset, not the disposal of a whole or substantial part of a business.

(b) **Alice – Capital gains computation – 2008/09**

	£	£
MV @ date of gift		150,000
Less: Acquisition cost		(120,000)
Potential gain (as above)		30,000
Actual proceeds	130,000	
Less: Original cost	(120,000)	
Excess proceeds over cost	10,000	
Less: Gain eligible to be held over		(20,000)
Chargeable gain in 2008/09		10,000

Adam – Base cost (for future disposal)

	£
Deemed acquisition cost (MV at date of gift)	150,000
Less: Gain held over from Alice	(20,000)
Base cost	130,000

Test your understanding 10

Fred

Fred Ltd's chargeable business assets total £400,000 (premises), whilst the chargeable assets total £500,000 (premises and shares held as investments).

Therefore £320,000 (£400,000 × £400,000/£500,000) of the capital gain can be held over.

Note: Gift relief is given before entrepreneurs' relief. Entrepreneurs' relief is available on the remaining gain.

Test your understanding 11

Chandra

Capital gains computation – 2008/09

Gain arising on the incorporation of the existing business:

	£
Goodwill	
MV on incorporation	100,000
Less: Acquisition cost	(Nil)
Potential capital gain	100,000
Less: Incorporation relief	
£100,000 × £200,000/£250,000 **(Note 1)**	(80,000)
	20,000
Less Entrepreneurs' relief (£20,000 x 4/9)	(8,889)
Chargeable gain	11,111

chapter

18

Introduction to corporation tax

Chapter learning objectives

Upon completion of this chapter you will be able to:

- define the terms 'period of account', 'accounting period', and 'financial year'
- explain the rules for determining when an accounting period starts and ends
- identify the correct accounting period for corporation tax from information supplied
- define the rules of residence for a company and determine a company's residence using those rules
- identify the different taxable profits for a company and the basis of assessment
- explain the implications of receiving franked investment income
- compute the corporation tax liability for a single company.

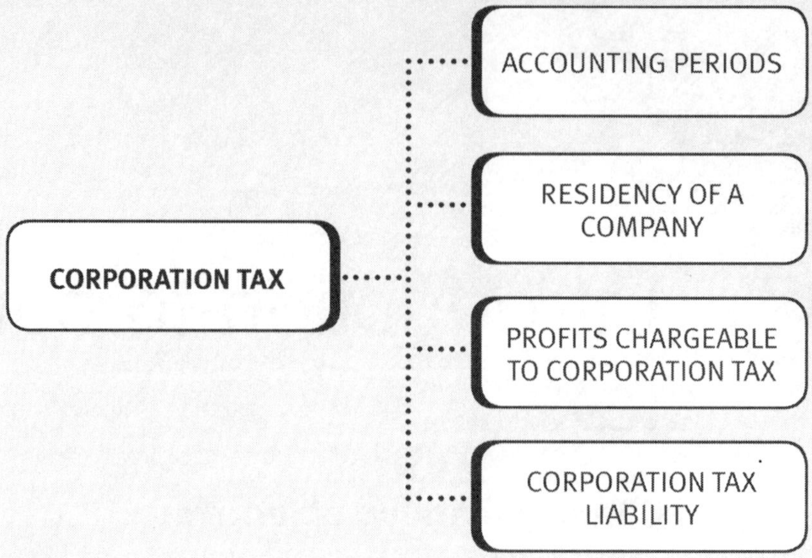

1 Introduction

UK resident companies are assessed to corporation tax on their income and chargeable gains arising in an accounting period.

This and the following five chapters deal with the way in which companies are assessed to corporation tax.

Corporation tax is an important topic as it will be the focus of question two in the examination, which will be either for either **25** or **30 marks**.

This first introductory chapter sets out the basis upon which companies are assessed to corporation tax and explains how a company's corporation tax liability is calculated.

2 Basis of assessment

- Corporation tax is assessed on a company's income and chargeable gains arising in an accounting period.
- The accounting period is not necessarily the same period as the company's set of accounts (period of account).

It is important when dealing with corporation tax to understand the terms 'period of account' and 'accounting period'.

Period of account

A period of account is any period for which a company prepares accounts. It is usually 12 months in length, but may be shorter or longer than this.

Accounting period

An accounting period is the period for which a charge to corporation tax is made. It may never be longer than 12 months.

3 Accounting periods

When does an accounting period start?

An accounting period starts when:

- a company starts to trade (or receives income chargeable to corporation tax)
- the previous accounting period ends.

When does an accounting period end?

An accounting period ends on the earliest of:

- twelve months after the beginning of the accounting period
- the end of the company's period of account
- the date the company begins or ceases to trade.

Expandable text - Defining the accounting period

An accounting period begins when:

- a company starts to trade, or when the profits of a company first become liable to corporation tax, or
- the previous accounting period ends, providing that the company is still liable to corporation tax.

An accounting period ends on the earliest of:

- twelve months after the beginning of the accounting period
- the end of the company's period of account
- the company beginning or ceasing to trade
- the company beginning or ceasing to be resident in the UK
- the company ceasing to be liable to corporation tax

- the company goes into administration or moves out of liquidation into administration
- the company ceases to be in administration, or
- the commencement of the winding up of the company.

Long periods of account

For corporation tax purposes, an accounting period can never exceed 12 months. Therefore, if a company prepares accounts for a period of more than 12 months, there must be two accounting periods for tax purposes.

The long period of account is divided into chargeable accounting periods (CAPs) as follows:

- CAP for the first 12 months.
- a separate CAP for the balance.

A corporation tax computation is prepared for each CAP.

Illustration – Accounting periods

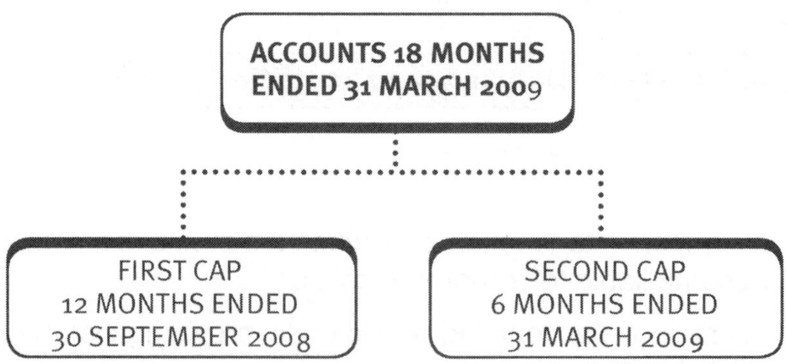

The method of allocating the accounting profits between the two chargeable accounting periods is covered in Chapter 19.

4 The tax residence of a company

Companies **resident** in the UK are chargeable to corporation tax on all profits and chargeable gains **wherever they arise**. It is therefore important to correctly determine where a company is resident.

Determining residence

A company is UK resident as follows:

- a company **incorporated** in the UK is resident in the UK for corporation tax purposes
- if a company is incorporated elsewhere, it is regarded as resident in the UK if it is **centrally managed and controlled** in the UK.

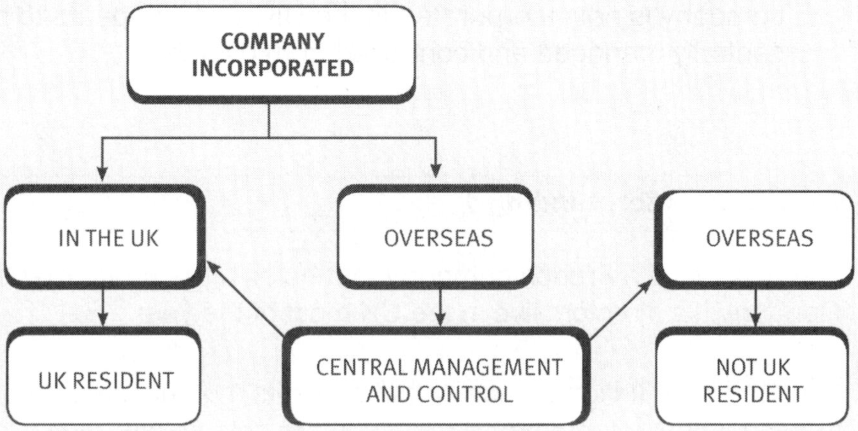

A company that is incorporated in the UK is resident in the UK regardless of where it is centrally managed and controlled.

Example 1 - The tax residence of a company

X Ltd is incorporated in the UK. The directors hold monthly board meetings overseas when major policy decisions are made.

Y Ltd is incorporated overseas. The directors hold frequent board meetings in the UK, which is where the directors are based.

Z Ltd is incorporated overseas. The directors hold weekly meetings overseas, but have quarterly meetings in the UK because this is where the non-executive directors are based.

State which of the above companies will be treated as resident in the UK.

Answer to example 1

- X Ltd is resident in the UK. If a company is incorporated in the UK it is irrelevant where meetings are held and decisions are made.
- Y Ltd would probably be treated as resident in the UK for corporation tax purposes. Although not incorporated in the UK, it would appear that the company is centrally managed and controlled from the UK.
- Z Ltd would probably not be treated as resident in the UK. The company is not incorporated in the UK, and it appears to be centrally managed and controlled from overseas.

Test your understanding 1

Matthew Ltd is a French company that holds all its board meetings in Germany. Its directors live in the UK most of the year.

Mark Ltd is an Italian company that holds its monthly board meetings in London. Other interim board meetings are held in Italy, which is where some of the directors are based. Most of the directors are based in the UK.

Luke Ltd is a UK company. Board meetings are held in France.

State which of the above companies will be treated as resident in the UK for corporation tax purposes.

5 Profits chargeable to corporation tax

Introduction

- A company's corporation tax liability for an accounting period is calculated by computing profits from all sources, and deducting Gift Aid payments.
- Included in the computation of profits are the world-wide income and chargeable gains of a company.
- The resultant figure is known as profits chargeable to corporation tax (or 'PCTCT' for short).

Layout of a corporation tax computation

An example of a corporation tax computation is as follows:

X Ltd – Corporation tax computation for the 12 months ended 31 March 2009

	£
Trading profit	X
Interest income	X
Dividends from non-UK companies	X
Property business profit	X
Chargeable gains	X
	—
Total profits	X
Less: Gift Aid	(X)
	—
Profits chargeable to corporation tax (PCTCT)	X
	—

Trading profit

Covers all trading income and expenditure. More detail is given in Chapter 19.

Interest income

Covers all interest receivable and some interest payable. More detail is given in Chapter 19.

Dividends

Dividends received from UK companies are exempt from corporation tax.

- Although exempt from corporation tax, dividends received have an impact on the rate of corporation tax that is applicable.
- In Chapter 23 you will see how dividends from non-UK companies are subject to corporation tax.

Property business profit

This is the profit (or loss) from letting furnished or unfurnished property and is calculated on the accruals basis. More detail is given in Chapter 19.

Chargeable gains/losses

- Corporation tax is also charged on any chargeable gains that a company makes during an accounting period.

It is essential to understand that companies pay corporation tax on their chargeable gains rather than capital gains tax, which is paid by individuals on their gains.

- Chargeable gains for companies are covered in detail in Chapter 20.

Gift Aid

It is important to realise that the tax treatment of Gift Aid payments made by a company is different from that applied to payments made by an individual.

- For companies, Gift Aid payments are deducted from total profits.
- Further detail of Gift Aid payments made by a company is given in Chapter 19.

Example 2 - Profits chargeable to corporation tax

Westmorland Ltd has the following income and outgoings for the year ending 31 March 2009.

	£
Tax-adjusted trading profit	1,456,500
Property business profit	25,000
Interest receivable	10,000
Chargeable gains	35,000
Dividends from UK companies	14,400
Gift Aid donation	(10,000)

Compute the profits chargeable to corporation tax for the year ending 31 March 2009.

Answer to example 2

Corporation tax computation for the chargeable accounting period of 12 months ended 31 March 2009

	£
Tax-adjusted trading profits	1,456,500
Property business profit	25,000
Interest receivable	10,000
Chargeable gains	35,000
	1,526,500
Less: Gift Aid donation	(10,000)
PCTCT	1,516,500

Note: Dividends from UK companies are ignored when calculating PCTCT.

Test your understanding 2

Cumberland Ltd has the following income and outgoings for the year ended 31 March 2009.

	£
Tax-adjusted trading profit	81,500
Property business profit	1,300
Non-trading loan interest receivable	2,200
Chargeable gains	3,000
Dividends from non-UK companies	3,500
Dividends from UK companies	900
Gift Aid donation	1,000

Compute the profits chargeable to corporation tax for the year ended 31 March 2009.

6 The corporation tax liability

The company's corporation tax liability is calculated by applying the appropriate rate of corporation tax to the company's profits chargeable to corporation tax (PCTCT).

Rate of corporation tax

The rate of corporation tax is determined by:

(1) financial year

(2) 'profits' of the company.

Financial year

- The rate of corporation tax is fixed by reference to financial years.
- A financial year runs from 1 April to the following 31 March and is identified by the calendar year in which it begins.
- The year commencing 1 April 2008 is the financial year 2008 (FY 2008). Financial years should not be confused with the tax years for income tax, which run from 6 April to the following 5 April.
- The following rates apply to the 2008 financial year (FY 2008), i.e. year ended 31 March 2009.

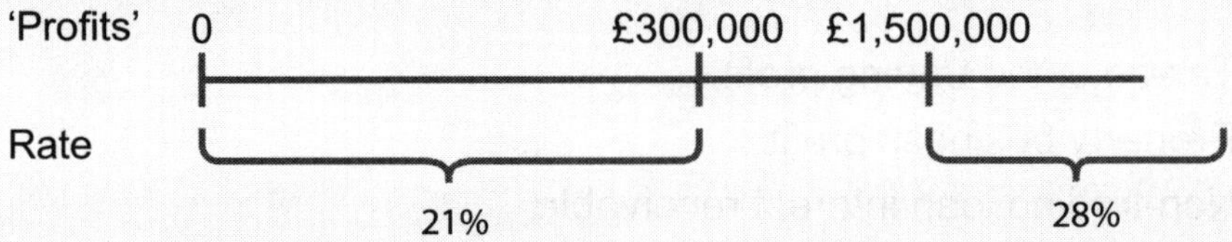

These rates and limits are provided in the Tax Rates and Allowances tables provided in the examination.

- If the 'profits' are below £300,000 (the 'lower limit') then the 'profits chargeable to corporation tax' are charged at the small company's rate of 21%.
- If the 'profits' exceed £1,500,000 (the 'upper limit') then the 'profits chargeable to corporation tax' are charged at the full rate of 28%.
- Where 'profits' are between £300,000 and £1,500,000 a special marginal relief applies.
- These limits for 'profits' are fixed for each financial year.

'Profits'

To determine the rate of corporation tax, a special definition of 'profits' applies as follows:

	£
PCTCT	X
Franked investment income (FII)	X
	—
'Profits'	X
	—

The 'profits' figure is compared to the 'profits' limits for the relevant financial year to determine the rate of corporation tax applicable. The appropriate rate of tax is then applied to the company's PCTCT.

Franked investment income

Although dividends received from UK companies are exempt from corporation tax, they can have an impact on the rate of corporation tax that is applicable.

- Dividends received from UK companies plus the associated 10% tax credit are known as franked investment income (FII).
- To calculate FII, take dividends received and multiply by 100/90.
- FII is added to the PCTCT in order to arrive at the 'profit' figure.

- Although corporation tax is calculated on the PCTCT, it is the 'profit' figure that determines which **rate** of corporation tax is applicable.
- There are two types of dividend that are not included as FII:
  - dividends received from overseas companies (see Chapter 23)
  - dividends received from 51% group companies (see Chapter 22).

Test your understanding 3

Zachary Ltd has profits chargeable to corporation tax of £148,000 in the year ended 31 March 2009, and dividends received from other UK companies of £4,500.

Calculate Zachary Ltd's corporation tax liability for the year ended 31 March 2009.

Test your understanding 4

Argo Ltd has profits chargeable to corporation tax of £1,450,000 in the year ended 31 March 2009, and UK dividends received of £72,000.

Calculate Argo Ltd's corporation tax liability for the year ended 31 March 2009.

Marginal relief

If 'profits' fall between the 'lower and upper limits,' i.e. between £300,000 and £1,500,000, then the company is 'marginal' and its 'profits chargeable to corporation tax' are charged as follows:

	£
PCTCT @ full rate (28%)	X
Less Marginal relief	
7/400 × (M – P) × I/P	(X)
Corporation tax liability	X

where:

M = Relevant 'profits' upper limit for the financial year (FY 2008 = £1,500,000)

P = 'Profits'

I = PCTCT

Example 3 - The corporation tax liability

Small Ltd has the following PCTCT for the year ended 31 March 2009.

	£
Trading profit	260,000
Property business profit	40,000
	300,000
Less: Gift Aid paid	(10,000)
PCTCT	290,000

Calculate the company's corporation tax liability if:

(a) **no dividends are received from UK companies.**

(b) **£9,000 of dividends are received from UK companies.**

(c) **£45,000 of dividends are received from UK companies.**

Answer to example 3

(a) No dividends received

	£
PCTCT	290,000
FII	Nil
'Profits'	290,000

'Profits' are below the lower limit of £300,000 therefore:

Corporation tax liability = £290,000 × 21% = £60,900.

(b) Dividends received = £9,000

	£
PCTCT	290,000
FII (£9,000 × 100/90)	10,000
'Profits'	300,000

'Profits' are equal to the lower limit and therefore the small companies rate applies:

Corporation tax liability = £290,000 × 21% = £60,900, as before.

The 'profits' level has not altered the decision.

(c) Dividends received = £45,000

	£
PCTCT	290,000
FII (£45,000 × 100/90)	50,000
'Profits'	340,000

'Profits' are above £300,000 but below £1,500,000; therefore marginal relief applies:

	£
Corporation tax (£290,000 × 28%)	81,200
Less: Marginal relief 7/400 × (£1,500,000 – £340,000) × £290,000/£340,000	(17,315)
Corporation tax liability	63,885

Test your understanding 5

Sycamore Ltd has the following results for the year ended 31 March 2009:

	£
Tax-adjusted trading profit	320,000
Chargeable gain	10,000
Dividends received from UK companies	18,000

Calculate Sycamore Ltd's corporation tax liability for the year ended 31 March 2009.

Short accounting periods

- The upper and lower 'profits' limits of £1,500,000 and £300,000 apply for accounting periods of 12 months.
- If an accounting period is for less than 12 months, the limits must be reduced proportionately.

Example 4 - The corporation tax liability

Minnow Ltd has the following results for the three-month accounting period ended 31 March 2009:

	£
Tax-adjusted trading profit	250,000
Dividends from UK companies (amounts received)	18,000

Compute the company's corporation tax liability for the accounting period ended 31 March 2009.

Answer to example 4

Corportion tax computation – year ended 31 March 2009

	£
Profits chargeable to corporation tax	250,000
Franked investment income (£18,000 × 100/90)	20,000
'Profits'	270,000

	£
Corporation tax (£250,000 × 28%)	70,000
Marginal relief	
7/400 × (£375,000 – £270,000) × £250,000/£270,000	(1,701)
Corporation tax liability	68,299

Note: As the accounting period is only three months long, the lower limit is reduced to £75,000 (£300,000 × 3/12) and the upper limit is reduced to £375,000 (£1,500,000 × 3/12).

As 'profits' fall between these reduced limits, marginal relief applies.

Note that the reduced upper limit of £375,000 is used in the marginal relief calculation.

Test your understanding 6

Petal Ltd has the following results for the nine months ended 31 March 2009:

	£
Tax-adjusted trading profit	1,100,000
Chargeable gain	60,000
Dividends from UK companies	45,000

Calculate the company's corporation tax liability for the nine months ended 31 March 2009.

Accounting periods straddling 31 March

Where a company's accounting period falls into two financial years then the corporation tax liability must be calculated for each financial year if either:

- the corporation tax rates, or
- the 'profits' limits have changed between the financial years.

The rates of corporation tax and the marginal relief fractions are different for the financial years 2006, 2007 and 2008. Therefore two-part computations are required for accounting periods straddling 31 March 2008 and 31 March 2009.

The following tables will be provided to you in the Tax Rates and Allowances section of the exam:

	2006	2007	2008
Small companies rate	19%	20%	21%
Full rate	30%	30%	28%
Lower limit	£300,000	£300,000	£300,000
Upper limit	£1,500,000	£1,500,000	£1,500,000
Marginal relief fraction	11/400	1/40	7/400

The corporation tax liability must be calculated for each financial year separately applying the appropriate rates of tax for each year.

Example 5 - Accounting periods straddling 31 March

Flute Ltd had profits chargeable to corporation tax of £400,000 and received dividends from UK companies of £45,000 in the year ended 30 September 2008.

Calculate Flute Ltd's corporation tax liability for the year ended 30 September 2008.

Answer to example 5

Corporation tax computation – year ended 30 September 2008

	£
PCTCT	400,000
FII (£45,000 × 100/90)	50,000
'Profits'	450,000

As 'profits' are between the small companies lower limit of £300,000 and the upper limit of £1,500,000 marginal relief applies.

The company's accounting period straddles 31 March 2008. Six months (1 October 2007 to 31 March 2008) fall into financial year 2007 and six months (1 April 2008 to 30 September 2008) fall into financial year 2008.

The corporation tax liability is calculated for each of the financial years as follows:

	£	£
FY2007		
(£400,000 x 30% x 6/12)	60,000	
Less: Marginal relief		
1/40 x (£1,500,000 – £450,000) x £400,000/£450,000 x 6/12	(11,667)	
		48,333
FY2008		
(£400,000 x 28% x 6/12)	56,000	
Less: Marginal relief		
7/400 x (£1,500,000 – £450,000) x £400,000/£450,000 x 6/12	(8,167)	
		47,833
Corporation tax liability		96,166

Test your understanding 7

Oboe Ltd had profits chargeable to corporation tax of £100,000 and franked investment income of £20,000 for the year ended 31 December 2008.

Calculate Oboe Ltd's corporation tax liability for the year ended 31 December 2008.

Test your understanding 8

Bassoon Ltd had profits chargeable to corporation tax of £850,000 and received dividends from UK companies of £16,200 in the year ended 30 June 2008.

Calculate Bassoon Ltd's corporation tax liability for the year ended 30 June 2008.

7 Chapter summary

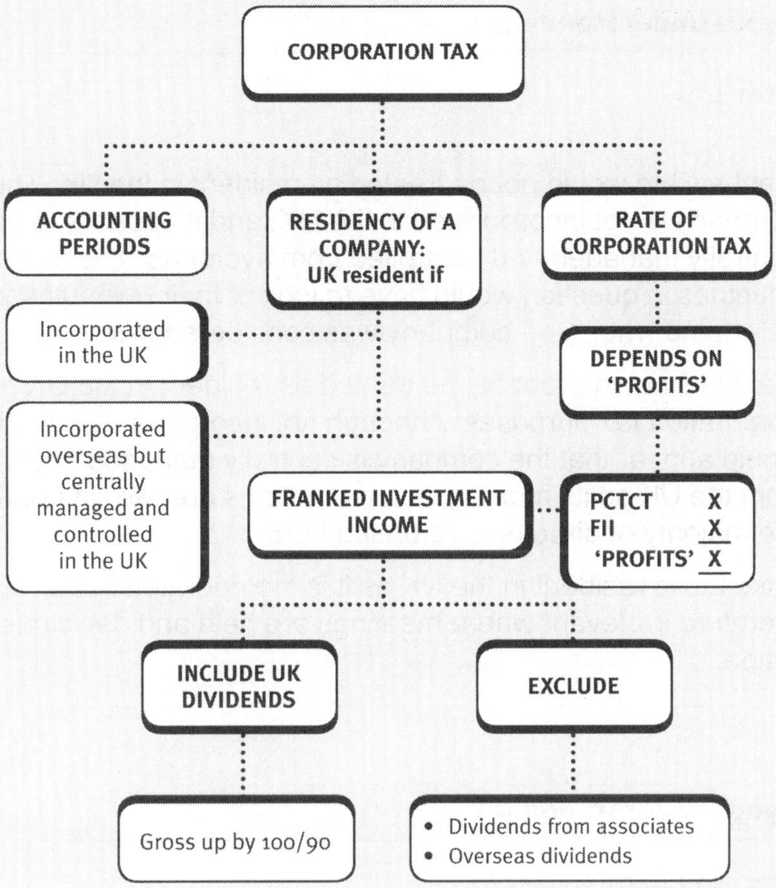

Test your understanding answers

Test your understanding 1

Matthew Ltd

- Matthew Ltd would not be treated as resident in the UK. The company is not incorporated in the UK, and it appears to be centrally managed and controlled from overseas. The overseas countries in question would have to look at their own rules to determine where the company was considered resident.
- Mark Ltd would probably be treated as resident in the UK for corporation tax purposes. Although not incorporated in the UK, it would appear that the company is centrally managed and controlled from the UK as its monthly board meetings are held in London and the majority of directors are based here.
- Luke Ltd is resident in the UK as it is incorporated in the UK. It is therefore irrelevant where meetings are held and decisions are made.

Test your understanding 2

Cumberland Ltd

Corporation tax computation for the chargeable accounting period of 12 months ended 31 March 2009

	£
Tax-adjusted trading profits	81,500
Property business profit	1,300
Interest receivable	2,200
Dividends from non-UK companies	3,500
Chargeable gains	3,000
	91,500
Less: Gift Aid donation	(1,000)
Profits chargeable to corporation tax (PCTCT)	90,500

Test your understanding 3

Zachary Ltd

Step 1: Calculate 'profits':

	£
PCTCT	148,000
FII (£4,500 × 100/90)	5,000
'Profits'	153,000

Step 2: From 'profits' determine the rate of corporation tax:

As 'profits' are less than £300,000, then PCTCT is taxed at 21%.

Step 3: Apply rate to PCTCT:

Corporation tax liability (£148,000 × 21%) = £31,080.

Test your understanding 4

Argo Ltd

	£
PCTCT	1,450,000
FII (£72,000 × 100/90)	80,000
'Profits'	1,530,000

As 'profits' are more than £1,500,000, then PCTCT is taxed at 28%.

Corporation tax liability (£1,450,000 × 28%) = £406,000.

Note: The fact that PCTCT is below the limit of £1,500,000 is irrelevant. 'Profits' determine the tax rate.

Test your understanding 5

Sycamore Ltd

Corporation tax computation – year ended 31 March 2009

	£
Tax-adjusted trading profit	320,000
Chargeable gain	10,000
Profits chargeable to corporation tax (PCTCT)	330,000
Franked investment income (£18,000 × 100/90)	20,000
'Profits'	350,000

The 'profits' are between £300,000 and £1,500,000 andtherefore PCTCT is charged at the full rate with marginal relief.

	£
Corporation tax (£330,000 x 28%)	92,400
Less: Marginal relief	
7/400 × (£1,500,000 – £350,000) × £330,000/£350,000	(18,975)
Corporation tax liability	73,425

Test your understanding 6

Petal Ltd

Corporation tax computation – 9 m/e 31 March 2009

	£
Tax-adjusted trading profit	1,100,000
Chargeable gain	60,000
Profits chargeable to corporation tax	1,160,000
Franked investment income (£45,000 × 100/90)	50,000
'Profits'	1,210,000

	£
Corporation tax liability (£1,160,000 at 28%)	324,800

Note: As the accounting period is only nine months long, the small company rate lower limit is reduced to £225,000 (£300,000 × 9/12) and the upper limit is reduced to £1,125,000 (£1,500,000 × 9/12).

As 'profits' fall above the upper limit of £1,125,000 the tax rate is 28%.

Test your understanding 7

Oboe Ltd

Corporation tax computation – year ended 31 December 2008

	£
PCTCT	100,000
FII	20,000
"Profits"	120,000

As "profits" are below the lower limit of £300,000 the small companies rate applies.

The company's accounting period straddles 31 March 2008. Three months (1 January 2008 to 31 March 2008) fall into financial year 2007 and nine months (1 April 2008 to 31 December 2008) fall into financial year 2008.

The corporation tax liability is calculated for each of the financial years as follows:

	£
FY 2007: (£100,000 × 3/12 × 20%)	5,000
FY 2008: (£100,000 × 9/12 × 21%)	15,750
Corporation tax liability	20,750

Test your understanding 8

Bassoon Ltd

Corporation tax computation – year ended 30 June 2008

	£
PCTCT	850,000
FII (£16,200 × 100/90)	18,000
"Profits"	868,000

As "profits" are between the small companies lower limit of £300,000 and the upper limit of £1,500,000 marginal relief applies.

The company's accounting period straddles 31 March 2008. Nine months (1 July 2007 to 31 March 2008) fall into financial year 2007 and three months (1 April 2008 to 30 June 2008) fall into financial year 2008.

The corporation tax liability is calculated for each of the financial years as follows:

	£	£
FY2007		
(£850,000 x 30% x 9/12)	191,250	
Less: Marginal relief		
1/40 x (£1,500,000 – £868,000)		
x £850,000/£868,000 x 9/12	(11,604)	
		179,646
FY2008		
(£850,000 x 28% x 3/12)	59,500	
Less: Marginal relief		
7/400 x (£1,500,000 – £868,000)		
x £850,000/£868,000 x 3/12	(2,708)	
		56,792
Corporation tax liability		236,438

hapter

19

Profits chargeable to corporation tax

Chapter learning objectives

Upon completion of this chapter you will be able to:

- identify the different taxable profits for a company and the basis of assessment
- calculate the tax-adjusted trading profit or loss for a company
- explain how relief can be obtained for pre-trading expenditure
- compute capital allowances on plant and machinery and industrial buildings for companies
- compute property business profits
- distinguish between trading and non-trading loans and deposits
- identify the tax treatment of trade and non-trade interest and associated costs
- show the treatment of Gift Aid donations made by a company
- prepare a computation of profits chargeable to corporation tax for an accounting period
- calculate profits chargeable to corporation tax for a long period of account.

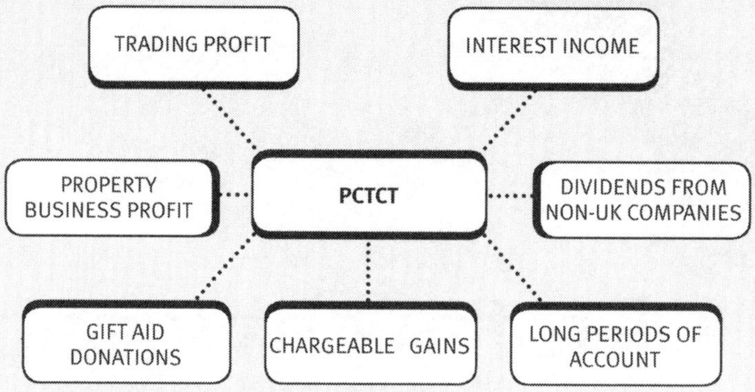

1 Profits chargeable to corporation tax

Companies pay corporation tax on their profits chargeable to corporation tax (PCTCT) for an accounting period.

As illustrated in Chapter 18, PCTCT is calculated as follows:

	£
Trading profit (section 2)	X
Interest income (section 3)	X
Dividends from non-UK companies (Chapter 23)	X
Property business profit (section 4)	X
Chargeable gains (Chapter 20)	X
Total profits	X
Less: Gift Aid (section 5)	(X)
Profits chargeable to corporation tax (PCTCT)	X

Chapter 18 briefly discussed the different elements which make up PCTCT and then showed how the corporation tax liability is calculated on PCTCT.

This and the following chapters show in detail how each item within PCTCT is calculated.

2 Trading profit

In Chapter 5 we studied how to adjust a sole trader's trading profit for tax purposes. The rules for companies are very similar.

For reference, a summary of the main adjustments is given below:

- Disallow expenditure which is not wholly and exclusively for the purposes of the trade.
- Disallow entertaining (except entertaining staff).
- Disallow expenditure on capital items.
- Adjust for expensive leased cars.
- Adjust for gifts to customers.
- Disallow depreciation.
- Adjust for profits/losses on disposal of capital items.
- Adjust for non-trading income.
- Add back Gift Aid donations.

All the above rules apply for companies.

There are, however, a number of key differences which apply when computing the taxable trading profits for a company.

Differences relating to companies

The main differences are in relation to:

- private use adjustments
- interest payable/receivable
- dividends payable
- capital allowances.

Expandable text - Key differences

Private use adjustments

The restrictions studied in Chapter 5 related to private use by a sole trader.

There are no such restrictions for companies:

- Any private use of assets by a director or employee of the company is ignored in the capital allowances calculation. There is no restriction for private usage.
- Any private expenses of a director or employee of a company are fully allowable, when calculating the tax-adjusted trading profit.

  The director or employee may however suffer income tax on the employment benefit received (Chapter 4).

Interest payable/receivable

Companies have special rules which cover interest payments and interest income. These are known as the loan relationship rules.

The detail of the rules is covered in section 3, however, when adjusting trading profits the following rules apply:

- Any interest payable in relation to trading activities is fully allowable as a deduction against trading profits, therefore no adjustment is required.
- Any interest payable in relation to non-trading activities must be added back to trading profit.
- Any interest receivable must be deducted from trading profit.

Dividends payable

Dividends payable by a company are an appropriation of profit and are not allowable as a trading expense.

Example 1 - Trading profit

The accounts of Helen Ltd show the following for the year ended 31 December 2008

	£	£
Gross profit from trading		280,000
Interest receivable	6,320	
Rent income	2,850	
		9,170
		289,170
Less Expenses:		
Rent and rates	10,950	
Depreciation	6,730	
Interest payable **(Note 1)**	3,560	
Entertaining and gifts **(Note 2)**	7,420	
Delivery costs	2,890	
Motor expenses **(Note 3)**	5,480	
Miscellaneous **(Note 4)**	12,000	
		(49,030)
Profit before tax		240,140

Notes

(1) Interest payable was in respect of a loan to acquire the rental property (non-trading interest).

(2) Entertaining and gifts comprise:

	£
Gifts to customers (Christmas champagne: cost £25 per customer)	1,500
Staff Christmas party	3,430
Client Christmas party	2,490

(3) Motor expenses represent costs for the director's car. He uses the car 60% for private use.

(4) Miscellaneous includes a £3,500 gross charitable donation under the Gift Aid scheme.

Calculate the tax-adjusted trading profit for Helen Ltd, for the year ended 31 December 2008.

Answer to example 1

Helen Ltd

Tax-adjusted trading profit for the year ended 31 December 2008

	£	£
Profit before tax		240,140
Add: Disallowable expenditure:		
Depreciation	6,730	
Non-trading interest payable **(Note 1)**	3,560	
Gifts to customers: Drink **(Note 2)**	1,500	
Client entertaining **(Note 2)**	2,490	
Gift Aid donation **(Note 4)**	3,500	
		17,780
		257,920
Less: Income not chargeable as trading income		
Non-trading interest receivable	6,320	
Property business income	2,850	
		(9,170)
Tax-adjusted trading profit		248,750

Notes

(1) No adjustment is required for the private use motor expenses of the director. These are fully deductible when calculating company taxable trading profits. The director will be taxed on the benefit of private use as an employment benefit.

(2) As for a sole trader, Gift Aid is disallowable as trading expenditure but will be deductible when calculating PCTCT.

(3) Gifts to customers are disallowed unless they amount to £50 or less per customer during the year and display a conspicuous advert for the business. Gifts of food or drink or tobacco are disallowed irrespective of their cost.

Test your understanding 1

You are presented with the accounts of Cornelius Ltd, for the year to 31 December 2008 (see below). Cornelius Ltd runs a small printing business and the managing director wishes to know the amount of the company's tax-adjusted trading profit for the year ended 31 December 2008.

Calculate Cornelius Ltd's tax-adjusted trading profit before capital allowances for the year ended 31 December 2008.

	£	£
Gross profit from trading		21,270
Interest receivable		4,350
Profit on sale of business premises **(Note 1)**		1,750
		27,370
Advertising	642	
Impaired debts **(Note 2)**	80	
Depreciation	2,381	
Light and heat	372	
Miscellaneous expenses **(Note 3)**	342	
Motor car expenses **(Note 4)**	555	
Rates	1,057	
Repairs and renewals **(Note 5)**	2,598	
Staff wages **(Note 6)**	12,124	
Telephone	351	
		(20,502)
Profit before tax		6,868

Notes

(1) The profit on the sale of premises relates to the sale of a small freehold industrial unit in which the company stored paper, before building the extension (see **Note 5**).

(2) The charge for impaired debts is made up as follows:

	£
Write-off of loan to customer	55
Write-off of trade debts	32
Increase in specific allowance for debtors	10
Recovery of trade debts previously written off	(17)
Charge to profit and loss account	80

(3) Miscellaneous expenses is made up as follows:

	£
Subscription to Printers' association	40
Contribution to national charity under Gift Aid	45
Gifts to customers:	
– Calendars costing £7.50 each and bearing the company's name	75
– Two food hampers bearing the company's name	95
Other allowable expenses	87
	342

(4) A director uses the motor car 75% for business purposes and 25% for private purposes.

(5) Repairs and renewals comprise the following expenditure:

	£
Redecorating administration offices	951
Building extension to enlarge paper store	1,647
	2,598

(6) Staff wages included an amount of £182 for a staff Christmas lunch.

Capital allowances

Chapters 6 and 7 covered the main principles of calculating capital allowances and industrial building allowances for sole traders.

The same rules apply for companies, but in addition, the following points should be noted when calculating capital allowances for companies:

Short and long accounting periods

- Allowances are given for **accounting periods** by reference to acquisitions and disposals in that accounting period.
- If the accounting period is less than 12 months:
  - the annual investment allowance and the writing down allowance is proportionately reduced.
  - but first year allowances on low emission cars are always given in full. They are never reduced for a short accounting period.
- Where a company has a long period of account:
  - there will be two accounting periods
  - two capital allowances computations will be required; one for each of these accounting periods
  - the balance period will be a short accounting period.

Private use adjustments

- There are no private use adjustments where company assets are used by directors or employees, when calculating capital allowances for companies.

Example 2 - Trading profit

Bill Ltd prepares accounts to 31 March.

The company's tax written down value on the general pool on 1 April 2008, was £23,500.

In the two years ended 31 March 2010, the following transactions took place:

Year ended 31 March 2009

1 November 2008	Purchased plant costing £13,260.
10 November 2008	Sold two lorries (purchased for £8,450 each) for £2,500 each. Purchased two replacement lorries for £5,250 each.
1 December 2008	Purchased a motor car for £16,600, which is used by the managing director for 25% of the time for private purposes.

Year ended 31 March 2010

1 November 2009	Purchased a motor car for £7,500.
1 December 2009	Sold the motor car purchased on 1 December 2008 for £12,000.

Compute the capital allowances available to Bill Ltd for the years ended 31 March 2009 and 31 March 2010.

Answer to example 2

Bill Ltd – Capital allowances computation

		General pool	Expensive car	Total CAs
	£	£	£	£
Year ended 31 March 2009				
TWDV b/f		23,500		
Additions:				
No AIA:				
Cars			16,600	
Qualifying for AIA:				
Plant and machinery	13,260			
Lorries	10,500			
	23,760			
Less AIA	(23,760)			23,760
		Nil		
		23,500	16,600	
Disposal proceeds		(5,000)		
		18,500		
WDA (20% x £18,500)		(3,700)		3,700
WDA (restricted)			(3,000)	3,000
TWDV c/f		14,800	13,600	
Total allowances				30,460

	£	General pool £	Expensive car £	Total CAs £
Year ended 31 March 2010				
TWDV b/f		14,800	13,600	
Additions				
No AIA: Cars		7,500		
		22,300	13,600	
Disposal proceeds			(12,000)	
Balancing allowance			1,600	
			(1,600)	1,600
WDA (20% x £22,300)		(4,460)		4,460
TWDV c/f		17,840		
Total allowances				6,060

Test your understanding 2

Expansion Ltd is a UK resident company that manufactures aeroplane components. The company has always prepared accounts to 31 March in each year and has now decided to change its accounts preparation date to 30 June, after having prepared accounts to 31 March 2008.

The results for the 15 months ended 30 June 2009, included the following.

Expansion Ltd acquired a new factory at a cost of £400,000, on 1 April 2008. It was brought into industrial use on the same day. The total cost was made up as follows:

	£
Land	80,000
Levelling the land	9,200
Architects' fees	24,300
Heating system	12,800
Fire alarm system	7,200
Strengthened concrete floor to support machinery	16,500
General offices	62,500
Factory	187,500
	400,000

On 1 April 2008, the tax written-down values of plant and machinery were as follows:

	£
General pool	149,280
Short-life asset	13,440

In addition to any items of plant and machinery included in the cost of the industrial building, the following assets were purchased and sold during the 15 months period ended 30 June 2009.

		£
5 June 2008	Purchased equipment	100,800
22 September 2008	Purchased a motor car	11,760
11 December 2008	Purchased a motor car	12,200
14 May 2009	Purchased plant	50,000
15 January 2009	Sold a lorry	(14,160)
12 March 2009	Sold the short-life asset	(5,520)

The motor car purchased on 11 December 2008, is a low emission motor car. The lorry sold on 15 January 2009, for £14,160 originally cost £21,600.

Compute the capital allowances for the 15 months ended 30 June 2009.

Assume that the current rate of allowances for FY2008 continue in the future.

Pre-trading expenditure

The rules for pre-trading expenditure are the same for companies and sole traders (see Chapter 5) and are as follows:

- Any revenue expenditure incurred in the **seven years** before a company commences to trade is treated as an expense, on the day that the company starts trading.
- Any capital expenditure is treated as if bought on the first day, when the trade commences. Any capital allowances will be claimed in the first capital allowances computation.

3 Interest income – loan relationship rules

All interest paid or received by a company is dealt with under the loan relationship rules.

The rules apply to:

- Payments in connection with borrowing money, e.g. interest paid on overdrafts, bank loans, corporate debt (company debentures and loan stock) and other costs such as arrangement fees.
- Income received from the lending of money, i.e. interest income. This includes interest from deposits, loans, government stocks and corporate bonds.

- In order to apply the loan relationship rules correctly, all interest paid/received must first be distinguished as either 'trading' or 'non-trading'.

Trade v non-trade purposes

- Generally, all interest receivable by a company is non-trade interest, unless it is the company's trade to lend money, (e.g. a bank).
- Examples would be:
  - interest receivable on investments such as gilts, debentures, loan stock and bonds.
- Examples of trading interest payable would be:
  - Interest on a loan taken out to purchase plant and machinery for the business.
  - Loan or overdraft to fund the daily operations (i.e. working capital).
  - Issue of debentures to fund trading operations.

- Examples of non-trading interest payable would be:
  - interest payable on a loan to purchase a commercially let property (where the rent would be taxable as property business income – section 4).
  - Interest payable on a loan to acquire the shares of another company.

Interest income

- All interest receivable by a company is normally assessable as non-trading interest income.
- Interest receivable should be deducted when calculating trading income and included in the corporation tax computation as interest income.
- Interest received and receivable is usually credited in the company accounts on an 'accruals' basis. As interest receivable is taxed on an accruals basis, the figure included in the accounts is the figure which is taxed as interest income.
- Interest income is received **gross** by companies. No grossing up calculations are therefore required in the corporation tax computation.

Interest paid

- Interest paid and payable on borrowings for a trading purpose is deductible as a trading expense.
- Interest payable on borrowings for a non-trading purpose is:
  - added back to trading profit
  - deducted from interest income.

Assessment in PCTCT

- All interest paid by a company is deductible on the accruals basis.
- As the company accounts are also prepared on the accruals basis, the figure included in the accounts is also the figure used for tax purposes.
- If only cash payments are provided, these would have to be adjusted for opening and closing accruals of interest payable/receivable.
- Where interest income exceeds interest payable,
  - the net profit is assessed as interest income in PCTCT.
  - the situation where interest payable exceeds interest income is not examinable.

Example 3 - Interest income – loan relationship rules

Trinity Ltd, a clothing manufacturer, received bank interest of £2,800, on 14 December 2008 and paid debenture interest of £19,500, on 26 September 2008.

The debentures were issued in January 2008, to raise finance for the purchase of a new packing machine.

The company prepares accounts to 31 December each year. Accrued debenture interest payable at 31 December 2008 was £9,000. There was no interest receivable at either 31 December 2007 or 31 December 2008.

Explain how the bank and debenture interest will be treated in the corporation tax computation for the year to 31 December 2008.

Answer to example 3

Bank interest receivable

The bank interest receivable in the period will be taxable as non-trading interest income. As there was no interest receivable at the beginning or end of the year, the taxable interest income will be the amount received of £2,800.

Debenture interest payable

The debenture interest paid relates to finance issued for the purposes of the trade, i.e. to purchase new machinery. It is therefore allowed as a trading expense. The interest will be recorded in the accounts on the accruals basis, i.e. interest payable of £28,500 (£19,500 paid + £9,000 accrued). No adjustment will therefore be required for tax purposes.

Note: The interest on the debentures is paid gross and the interest income is received gross.

Example 4 - Interest income – loan relationship rules

PQR Ltd prepares its accounts to 31 December.

The company issued £100,000 of 12% debentures on 1 May 2007. The proceeds of the issue were used to purchase a new factory.

Explain how the interest on the debentures is treated for tax purposes for the year ended 31 December 2008.

Answer to example 4

For the year ended 31 December 2008, PQR Ltd will be entitled to a deduction against trading profits of £8,000 (£100,000 at 12% × 8/12).

Provided this amount is included in the accounts, no adjustment will be necessary when calculating the tax-adjusted trading profit.

The amount of debenture interest actually paid is irrelevant as interest payable is deductible on the accruals basis.

Test your understanding 3

The net profit of Simon Ltd per the accounts for the year ended 31 December 2008, is £105,940.

This profit includes the following:

	£
Depreciation	9,750
Debenture interest payable (on loan to purchase machinery)	12,760
Bank interest payable (on loan to purchase an investment property)	6,590
Bank interest receivable	15,860

Notes:

1 Bank interest receivable includes an accrual of £2,340 as at 31 December 2008 and £1,210, as at 31 December 2007. There were no accruals in respect of the debenture or bank interest payable at either the beginning or the end of the year.

2 The company's capital allowances for the year are £11,800.

Calculate Simon Ltd's profits chargeable to corporation tax for the year ended 31 December 2008.

Summary – interest payable/receivable

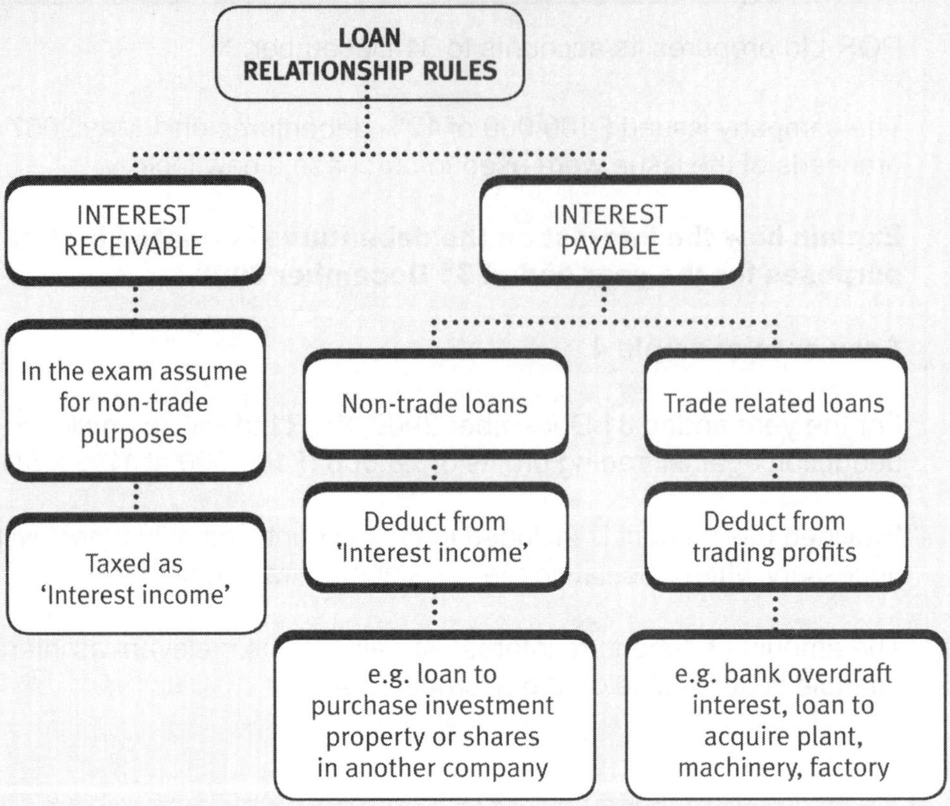

4 Property business profits

A trading company may hold property for investment purposes or have premises which are rented out, as they are surplus to the company's current trading requirements. The income from these properties is assessed as property business income.

Treatment for companies

The rules in connection with property business income were set out in Chapter 3.

The main points, which are still relevant for companies, are as follows:

- Property business profits are taxed on the accruals basis.
- Allowable expenses are those associated with the normal running and upkeep of the property (generally revenue expenses, like property maintenance, repairs, insurance and irrecoverable debts).

There are, however, a few differences in the way that companies are assessed on their property business profits, compared to individuals.

These can be summarised as follows:

- The company is assessed on the property business profit arising in the accounting period (not the tax year as for individuals).
- The treatment of interest payable.
- The treatment of capital losses.

Interest on loan to buy a property

- Interest payable on a loan to acquire or improve an investment property, is not allowed as a deduction from property business income. Instead, it is taxed under the 'Loan Relationship' rules and is therefore deducted from interest income (see section 3).

Property business losses

- Profits and losses on various let properties are 'pooled' together to obtain an overall 'property business profit or loss' for an accounting period.
- A property business loss is:
  - first set-off against total profits (before Gift Aid) of the same accounting period
  - then carried forward to be set against total profits (before Gift Aid) in the future.
- A property business loss is also available for 'group relief' (Chapter 22).

Lease premiums

Where a company receives a premium for the grant of a lease, an element of the premium is taxed as property business income.

The rules on how to find the revenue element of a lease premium were covered in Chapter 3 in relation to unincorporated businesses, and apply in exactly the same way for companies.

Example 5 - Property business profits

Speed Ltd prepares accounts for the year ended 31 March 2009 and during the year received a premium of £12,000 on the grant of a seven-year lease.

The building was rented out from 1 September 2008, for an annual rent of £6,000. It lay empty until this date. Rent is received quarterly in advance.

Calculate the amount of property business income that Speed Ltd will be assessed to corporation tax on in the accounting period ended 31 March 2009.

Answer to example 5

	£
Premium	
£12,000 – (2% × (7 – 1) × £12,000)	10,560
Rent	
(£6,000 × 7/12) = £3,500	3,500
Total property business profit	14,060

Test your understanding 4

Tasman Ltd is a UK resident company that manufactures components for washing machines.

Tasman Ltd lets out two warehouses that are surplus to requirements.

The company's results regarding income from property for the year ended 31 March 2009, are as follows:

- The first warehouse was empty from 1 April to 31 August 2008, but was let from 1 September 2008. On that date the company received a premium of £47,000, for the grant of a seven-year lease, and the annual rent of £10,500, which is payable in advance.

- The second warehouse was let until 31 January 2009, at an annual rent of £11,200. On that date the tenant left owing three months' rent, which the company is not able to recover. The roof of the warehouse was repaired at a cost of £7,200, during March 2009.

Calculate the property business profit to be included in the company's corporation tax computation for the year ended 31 March 2009.

5 Gift Aid for companies

The tax treatment of Gift Aid payments is different for companies and individuals. It is important that you understand and can apply the different treatments.

For **individuals**, Gift Aid payments are treated as follows:

- Gift Aid payments are paid net of basic rate tax.
- Tax relief is given by extending the basic rate band by the gross amount of the Gift Aid paid in the tax year.

For **companies**, Gift Aid payments are treated as follows:

- Gift Aid payments by companies are made gross.
- The amount **paid** in the accounting period is deducted from total profits in calculating a company's profits chargeable to corporation tax.
- If the amount of Gift Aid paid exceeds the total profits of the company, no relief for the excess is given.

6 Comprehensive examples

Test your understanding 5

Superscoff Ltd is a trading company operating a fast food retailing business. The profit and loss account for the 12 months to 31 March 2009, shows the following:

	£		£
Salaries and wages	146,323	Gross profit	1,490,515
Rates, light and heat	11,650	Bank deposit interest	1,200
Travelling expenses	13,200	Dividends from UK companies	6,000
Entertaining **(Note 1)**	6,000		
Advertising **(Note 2)**	18,600	Capital gain **(Note 5)**	798
Depreciation	27,800		
Director's remuneration	40,000		
General expenses **(Note 3)**	3,150		
Debenture interest paid **(Note 4)**	8,800		
Net profit	1,222,990		
	1,498,513		1,498,513

Notes:

(1) The entertaining expenses comprise £4,750 cost of entertaining customers, and £1,250 for the staff Christmas party.

(2) Advertising includes the cost of 500 calendars, bearing the company's name, at a cost of £2 each.

(3) General expenses comprise:

	£
Subscriptions to BHRCA, a trade association	40
Gift Aid payments to Oxfam – paid 1 January 2009	500
Fine for breach of hygiene regulations	250
Allowable expenses	2,360
	3,150

(4) The debenture interest is on £88,000, 10% debentures issued in 1999, to raise funds to purchase new retail premises. The interest is payable half-yearly on 30 September and 31 March.

(5) The gain arises on the sale of 5,000 shares in Finefish Ltd, purchased and sold in May 2008. The investment represented a holding of less than 1% in Finefish Ltd.

(6) The written-down value of the plant and machinery for capital allowances purposes on 1 April 2008, was as follows:

	£
General pool	200
Car costing £18,750 used 60% privately by managing director	6,750

During the year ended 31 March 2009, the following transactions took place:

1 May 2008	Machinery purchased for £3,765.
1 August 2008	Sold the MD's car for £6,350 and purchased a replacement for £18,000. Private use remains at 60%.
1 March 2009	Sold a cold food display cabinet for £1,200 (cost £2,500).

Compute Superscoff Ltd's PCTCT for the 12 months ended 31 March 2009.

Test your understanding 6

Geronimo Ltd is a UK resident company that manufactures motorcycles. The company's summarised profit and loss account for the year ended 31 March 2009 is as follows:

	£	£
Gross profit		921,540
Operating expenses		
Impaired debts (**Note 1**)	22,360	
Depreciation	83,320	
Gifts and donations (**Note 2**)	2,850	
Professional fees (**Note 3**)	14,900	
Patent royalties (**Note 4**)	7,200	
Repairs and renewals (**Note 5**)	42,310	
Other expenses (all allowable)	136,520	
		(309,460)
		612,080
Other operating income **(Note 6)**		24,700
Operating profit		636,780
Income from investments		
Bank interest (**Note 7**)	2,800	
Loan interest (**Note 8**)	22,000	
Dividends (**Note 9**)	36,000	
		60,800
		697,580
Interest payable **(Note 10)**		(45,000)
Profit before taxation		652,580

Notes:

(1) Impaired debts

Impaired debts are as follows:

	£
Trade debts written off	19,890
Loan to customer written off	600
Increase in allowance for trade debtors	1,870
	22,360

(2) Gifts and donations

Gifts and donations are as follows:

	£
Donation to national charity (made under the Gift Aid scheme)	1,800
Donation to national charity (not made under the Gift Aid scheme)	100
Donation to local charity (Geronimo Ltd received free advertising in the charity's magazine)	50
Gifts to customers (food hampers costing £30 each)	900
	2,850

(3) Professional fees

Professional fees are as follows:	£
Accountancy and audit fee	4,100
Legal fees in connection with the renewal of a 20-year property lease	2,400
Legal fees in connection with the issue of a debenture loan (see **Note 10**)	8,400
	14,900

(4) Patent royalties

The patent royalties were trade related. The figure for patent royalties payable is calculated as follows:

	£
Accrued at 1 April 2008	Nil
Paid 31 July 2008	3,500
Paid 31 January 2009	2,300
Accrued at 31 March 2009	1,400
	7,200

(5) Repairs and renewals

The figure of £42,310 for repairs includes £6,200 for replacing part of a wall that was knocked down by a lorry, and £12,200 for initial repairs to an office building that was acquired during the year ended 31 March 2009.

The office building was not usable until the repairs were carried out, and this fact was represented by a reduced purchase price.

(6) Other operating income

Other operating income consists of patent royalties derived from patents which the company registered in 2001 to protect a manufacturing technique it has developed.

Royalties of £8,900 and £15,800 were received on 30 September 2008 and 31 March 2009 respectively. The amounts received are the amounts accrued in the six months to that date.

(7) Bank interest received

The bank interest was received on 31 March 2009. The bank deposits are held for non-trading purposes.

(8) Loan interest received

The figure for loan interest received is calculated as follows:

	£
Accrued at 1 April 2008	(5,500)
Received 30 June 2008	11,000
Received 31 December 2008	11,000
Accrued at 31 March 2009	5,500
	22,000

The above figures are all gross. The loan was made for non-trading purposes.

(9) Dividends received

The dividends were received from other UK companies. The figure of £36,000 is the actual amount received.

(10) Interest payable

Geronimo Ltd raised a debenture loan on 1 July 2008. The loan was used for trading purposes. Interest of £30,000 was paid on 31 December 2008, and £15,000 was accrued at 31 March 2009.

(11) Plant and machinery

On 1 April 2008 the tax written down value of the general pool of plant and machinery was £66,000. There were no purchases or sales of plant and machinery during the year ended 31 March 2009.

(12) Other information

Geronimo Ltd has no associated companies.

(a) **Calculate Geronimo Ltd's tax-adjusted trading profit for the year ended 31 March 2009.**

(b) **Calculate the corporation tax payable by Geronimo Ltd for the year ended 31 March 2009.**

7 Long periods of account

Where a company has a period of account of more than 12 months, it must be split into two accounting periods as follows:

- First 12 months.
- Remainder of the period of account.

There are rules to determine how to allocate taxable income between these two accounting periods.

Allocation of taxable income

Income	Method of allocation
Trading profits before capital allowances.	Adjust profit for period of account for tax purposes and then apportion on a time basis.
Capital allowances.	Separate calculation for each accounting period. AIA and WDAs will be restricted if accounting period is less than 12 months.
Property business profit.	Apportion on a time basis.
Interest receivable.	Allocated to the period in which receivable.
Chargeable gains.	Taxed within the accounting period in which disposal takes place.
Gift Aid.	Deducted from profits of the accounting period in which donations are paid.
Franked investment income.	Allocate to the accounting period in which it is received.

Having allocated profits and Gift Aid to the two separate accounting periods, two separate corporation tax computations are prepared.

Example 6 - Long periods of account

Oak Ltd prepared accounts for the 15 months period to 30 June 2009, with the following results:

	£
Trading profit (adjusted for tax purposes, but before capital allowances)	383,880
Bank interest (received 31 December 2008)	22,000
Property business profit	10,000
Chargeable gain (asset disposed of 1 June 2009)	16,000
Gift Aid payment (1 February 2009)	24,000
Bank interest (income) accrued was as follows:	
At 1 April 2008	5,200
At 1 April 2009	4,100
At 30 June 2009	9,780

The company bought plant costing £120,000, for use in its trade on 31 August 2008. It had made no previous acquisitions qualifying for capital allowances.

Calculate Oak Ltd's PCTCT for the 15 months period to 30 June 2009.

Answer to example 6

Oak Ltd – Profits chargeable to corporation tax

	Year ended 31 March 2009	**3 months to 30 June 2009**
	£	£
Trading profit (12:3)	307,104	76,776
Less: Capital allowances (W)	(64,000)	(2,800)
Trading income	243,104	73,976
Interest income		
(£22,000 – £5,200 + £4,100)	20,900	
(£9,780 – £4,100)		5,680
Property income (12:3)	8,000	2,000
Chargeable gain	Nil	16,000
	272,004	97,656
Less: Gift Aid payment	(24,000)	
PCTCT	248,004	97,656

Working: Capital allowances computation

	£	General pool £	Total allowances £
Year ended 31 March 2009			
Plant and machinery	120,000		
Less AIA (max)	(50,000)		50,000
		70,000	
WDA (20% x £70,000):		(14,000)	14,000
TWDV c/f		56,000	
Total allowances			64,000
3 m/e ended 30 June 2009			
WDA (20% x £56,000 x 3/12)		(2,800)	2,800
TWDV c/f		53,200	
Total allowances			2,800

Test your understanding 7

Ash Ltd prepared accounts for the 17 month period to 30 September 2009, with results as follows:

	£
Trading profit (adjusted for tax purposes but before capital allowances)	485,390
Bank interest (received 31 December 2008)	11,540
Property business profit	25,500
Chargeable gain (asset disposed of 1 March 2009)	12,995
Gift Aid payment (1 February 2009)	16,500

Bank interest (income) accrued was as follows:

At 1 May 2008	7,400
At 1 May 2009	5,600
At 30 September 2009	10,540

The company bought plant costing £95,000, for use in its trade on 1 January 2009. It had made no previous acquisitions qualifying for capital allowances.

Calculate Ash Ltd's PCTCT for the 17 month period

8 Chapter summary

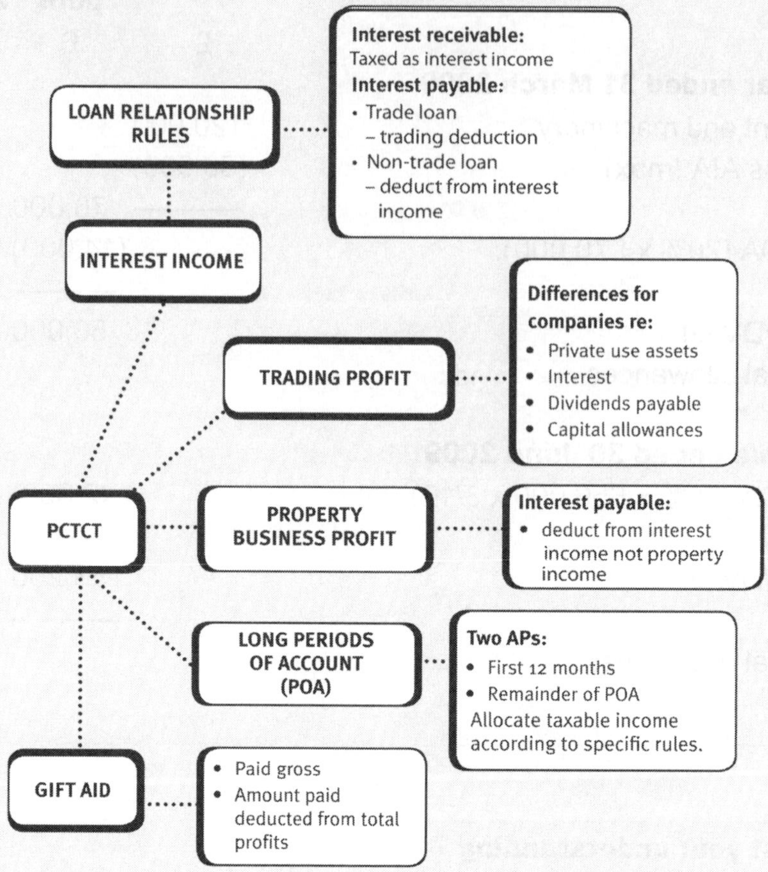

Test your understanding answers

Test your understanding 1

Cornelius Ltd

Tax-adjusted trading profit for the year ended 31 December 2008

	£	£
Profit before tax		6,868
Add: Disallowable expenditure		
Depreciation	2,381	
Impaired debts **(Note 1)**	55	
Gift Aid **(Note 2)**	45	
Gifts to customers (food hampers) **(Note 3)**	95	
Repairs (capital) **(Note 5)**	1,647	4,223
		11,091
Less: Income not chargeable as trading income		
Interest receivable		(4,350)
Profit on sale of premises		(1,750)
Tax-adjusted trading profit		4,991

Notes

(1) The write-off of a non-trade debt (e.g. loan to a customer) is not an allowable trading deduction.

(2) Gift Aid is disallowable as trading expenditure but will be deductible when calculating PCTCT.

(3) Gifts to customers are disallowed, unless they amount to £50 or less per customer during the year and display a conspicuous advert for the business. Gifts of food or drink or tobacco are disallowed irrespective of their cost.

(4) The expenditure on the Christmas lunch is an allowable deduction for the employer.

(5) Motor car expenses are all allowable for the company, although the director will be taxed as an employee on the private use of the car.

Test your understanding 2

Expansion Ltd: Industrial buildings allowance

	£
Total cost	400,000
Less: Land	(80,000)
Heating system **(Note 2)**	(12,800)
Fire alarm system **(Note 2)**	(7,200)
Potential qualifying cost	300,000
£300,000 × 25% = £75,000	
General office £62,500 = less than £75,000	
Therefore qualifying cost	300,000
IBA @ 3%	9,000
Per question: Assume the rate of 3% continues in the future.	
AP to 31.3.09 (first 12 months)	9,000
AP to 30.6.09 (remainder = 3 months)	
3/12 × £9,000	2,250

Notes

1 The cost of the land does not qualify.

2 The costs of the heating and fire alarm systems qualify as plant and machinery.

3 The cost of the strengthened floor, despite being to support machinery, is part of the factory structure (it is not an alteration to an existing building).

Capital allowances computation

		General pool	Expensive car	Special rate pool	Total CAs
	£	£	£	£	£
Year ended 31 March 2009					
TWDV b/f		149,280	13,440		
Additions:					
No AIA:					
Cars		11,760			
Qualifying for AIA:					
Heating system	12,800				
Less AIA	(12,800)				12,800
				Nil	
Equipment	100,800				
Fire alarm system	7,200				
	108,000				
Less AIA (Note)	(37,200)				37,200
		70,800			
		231,840	13,440	Nil	
Disposal proceeds		(14,160)	(5,520)		
		217,680	7,920		
Balancing allowance			(7,920)		7,920
WDA (20% x £217,680)		(45,536)			43,536
Additions:					
Qualifying for FYA:					
Low emission car	12,200				
Less FYA (100%)	(12,200)				12,200
		Nil			
TWDV c/f		174,144		Nil	
Total allowances					113,656

Note: The AIA is allocated to the additions in the 'special rate pool' (WDA 10%) in priority to the addition in the general pool (WDA 20%).

Capital allowances computation

		General pool	Total CAs
	£	£	£
TWDV b/f		174,144	
3 m/e 30 June 2009			
Additions:			
Qualifying for AIA:			
Plant	50,000		
Less AIA (max x 3/12)	(12,500)		12,500
		37,500	
		211,644	
WDA (20% x £211,644 x 3/12)		(10,582)	10,582
TWDV c/f		201,062	
Total allowances			23,082

Test your understanding 3

Simon Ltd

PCTCT computation – year ended 31 December 2008

	£	£
Profit per accounts		105,940
Add: Non-trading interest payable	6,590	
Depreciation	9,750	
		16,340
Less: Non-trading interest receivable	(15,860)	
Capital allowances	(11,800)	
		(27,660)
Tax-adjusted trading profit		94,620
Interest income:		
Non-trading interest receivable	15,860	
Non-trading interest payable	(6,590)	
		9,270
PCTCT		103,890

Test your understanding 4

Tasman Ltd

Property business profit – Year to 31 March 2009

		Warehouse 1	**Warehouse 2**	**Total**
	£	£	£	£
Rent receivable:				
7/12 × £10,500		6,125		6,125
10/12 × £11,200			9,333	9,333
Premium	47,000			
Less:				
2% × (7 – 1) × £47,000	(5,640)	41,360		41,360
		47,485	9,333	56,818
Less: Allowable expenses				
Irrecoverable debt				
(3/12 × £11,200)			(2,800)	(2,800)
Roof repairs			(7,200)	(7,200)
Profit/(loss)		47,485	(667)	46,818

Profit and losses are pooled to obtain an overall property business profit of £46,818, for the year ended 31 March 2009.

Test your understanding 5

Superscoff Ltd

Corporation tax computation: 12 months ended 31 March 2009

	£
Trading profit **(W1)**	1,242,127
Interest income	1,200
Chargeable gain	798
	1,244,125
Less: Gift Aid	(500)
PCTCT	1,243,625

Workings

(W1) Trading profit

	£	£
Net profit per accounts		1,222,990
Add: Entertaining customers		4,750
Gift Aid payment		500
Fine		250
Depreciation		27,800
		1,256,290
Less: Bank deposit interest	1,200	
Dividend received	6,000	
Chargeable gain	798	
		(7,998)
		1,248,292
Less: Capital allowances **(W2)**		(6,165)
Trading profit		1,242,127

(W2) Capital allowances computation

		General pool	Expensive Car 1	Expensive Car 2	Total CAs
	£	£	£	£	£
Y/e 31 March 2009					
TWDV b/f		200	6,750		
Additions:					
No AIA:					
Cars				18,000	
With AIA:					
Machinery	3,765				
Less AIA	(3,765)				3,765
	———	Nil			
Disposal proceeds		(1,200)	(6,350)		
		———	———	———	
		(1,000)	400	18,000	
Balancing charge		1,000			(1,000)
Balancing allowance			(400)		400
WDA (max £3,000)				(3,000)	3,000
		———	———	———	
TWDV c/f		Nil	Nil	15,000	
		———	———	———	———
Total allowances					6,165
					———

Test your understanding 6

Geronimo Ltd

(a) **Tax-adjusted trading profit – year ended 31 March 2009**

	£	£
Operating profit	636,780	
Depreciation	83,320	
Loan to customer	600	
Gift Aid donation	1,800	
Donation to national charity	100	
Gifts to customers	900	
Initial repairs to office building	12,200	
Interest payable		45,000
Capital allowances (£66,000 @ 20%)		13,200
	735,700	58,200
	(58,200)	
Tax-adjusted trading profit	677,500	

Tutorial note

The alternative approach of commencing with the profit before taxation figure of £652,580 is acceptable, and would be awarded equivalent marks.

Notes:

(1) The loan to a customer is for non-trade purposes (money lending is not the company's trade). The write off of the loan is therefore not an allowable deduction in calculating taxable trading profits. The write off is allowable against interest income under the loan relationship rules.

(2) The Gift Aid donation is deducted in the corporation tax computation from total profits and is therefore added back in calculating trading profits.

(3) The costs of renewing a short lease (less than 50 years) are allowable.

(4) The legal fees in connection with the issue of the debenture are incurred in respect of a trading loan relationship and are therefore deductible as a trading expense.

(5) The patent royalties paid are for trading purposes and are allowed as an expense on an accruals basis so no adjustment is required.

(6) The replacement of the wall is allowable since the whole structure is not being replaced. The repairs to the office building are not allowable, being capital in nature, as the building was not in a usable state when purchased and this was reflected in the purchase price.

(7) The patent royalties received are included in the trading profit (on an accruals basis) as they clearly relate to the company's trading activities – no adjustment is therefore needed.

(8) Interest on the debenture loan used for trading purposes is deductible in calculating the taxable trading profit on an accruals basis.

(b) **Geronimo Ltd**

Corporation tax computation – year ended 31 March 2009

		£	£
Trading profit			677,500
Interest income	– Bank interest	2,800	
	– Loan interest	22,000	
	– Customer loan written off	(600)	
			24,200
Total profits			701,700
Gift Aid donation			(1,800)
PCTCT			699,900
Franked investment income (£36,000 × 100/90)			40,000
Profits			739,900
Corporation tax (£699,900 @ 28%)			195,972
Marginal relief			
7/400 × (£1,500,000 – £739,900) × £699,900/£739,900			(12,583)
Corporation tax payable			183,389

Test your understanding 7

Ash Ltd

Profits chargeable to corporation tax

	Year ended 30.4.09	5 months to 30.9.09
	£	£
Trading profit (12:5)	342,628	142,762
Less: Capital allowances (W)	(59,000)	(3,000)
	———	———
Trading income	283,628	139,762
Interest income		
(£11,540 – £7,400 + £5,600)	9,740	
(£10,540 – £5,600)		4,940
Property income (12:5)	18,000	7,500
Chargeable gain	12,995	Nil
	———	———
	324,363	152,202
Less: Gift Aid payment	(16,500)	Nil
	———	———
Profits chargeable to corporation tax	307,863	152,202
	———	———

Working: Capital allowances computation

		General pool	Total allowances
	£	£	£
Year ended 30 April 2009			
Additions:			
Qualifying for AIA:			
Plant and machinery	95,000		
Less AIA (max)	(50,000)		50,000
		45,000	
WDA (20% x £45,000):		(9,000)	9,000
TWDV c/f		36,000	
Total allowances			59,000
3 m/e ended 30 September 2009			
WDA (20% x £36,000 x 5/12)		(3,000)	3,000
TWDV c/f		33,000	
Total allowances			3,000

hapter

20

Chargeable gains for companies

Chapter learning objectives

Upon completion of this chapter you will be able to:

- understand how to calculate the gain on the disposal of an asset by a company
- recognise when indexation is available for a company and calculate the indexation allowance
- calculate the indexed gain on the disposal of an asset for a company
- demonstrate how capital losses can be relieved against gains
- apply the correct matching rules for a company disposal of shares and securities
- calculate the gain on the disposal of shares by a company
- identify the treatment of a bonus issue
- identify the treatment of a rights issue
- demonstrate the effect on a holding where there is both a rights and bonus issue
- explain the tax treatment on a takeover or reorganisation of a shareholding in exchange for other shares
- explain the treatment on a takeover where there is cash and shares consideration
- calculate the chargeable gain on the cash element
- explain and apply roll-over relief as it applies to companies.

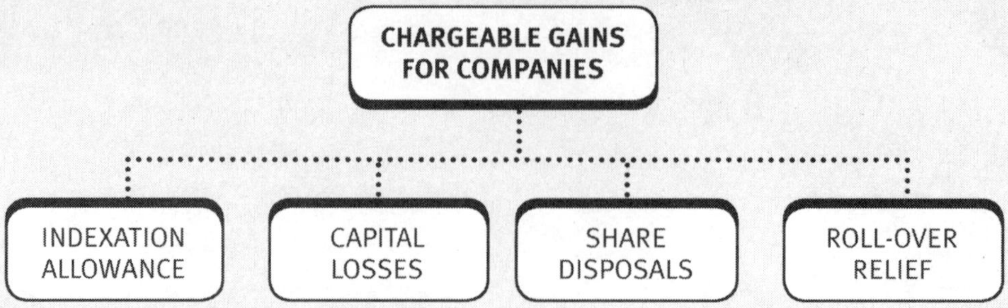

1 Introduction

The main principles of calculating chargeable gains for individuals were set out in chapters 14 – 17. Some of the content is applicable to companies, but there are some notable differences in the calculation of chargeable gains for companies.

Chargeable gains for a company

- Any chargeable gains that a company makes during an **accounting period** are included in the PCTCT computation.
- It is important to note that companies pay corporation tax on their chargeable gains and not capital gains tax.

Calculation of chargeable gains for a company

The following steps should be carried out to compute the chargeable gains to be included in a company's PCTCT computation:

(1) Calculate the capital gains/allowable loss arising on the disposal of each chargeable asset separately

(2) Calculate the total net capital gains arising in the accounting period = (capital gains less allowable losses)

(3) Deduct capital losses brought forward = total net chargeable gains

(4) Include in PCTCT computation.

Note that there is no annual exemption available to companies, the total net chargeable gains is simply included in the company's PCTCT computation.

Proforma – companies

The following basic proforma should be used for the disposal of all assets by a company:

	£
Disposal proceeds	X
Less: Incidental disposal costs	(X)
Net proceeds	X
Less: Allowable expenditure (as for individuals)	(X)
Unindexed gain	X
Less: Indexation allowance (section 2)	(X)
Chargeable gain/(allowable loss)	X

Note that:

- The calculation of capital gains is the same as for individuals except that companies are entitled to an indexation allowance (see section 2).
- There are a few other key differences when dealing with the disposal of assets by companies. These include
  - the treatment of capital losses (section 3)
  - the treatment of shares and securities (section 4), and
  - the availability of reliefs (section 7).
- There is no annual exemption available to companies, the net chargeable gains are included in the PCTCT computation.

2 Indexation allowance

The indexation allowance (IA) gives a company some allowance for the effects of inflation in calculating a gain.

The aim is to ensure that capital gains are subject to tax only to the extent that they represent an increase in real terms of an asset's value on disposal.

The rules for the IA are as follows:

- the IA is based on the cost of the asset and the movement in the retail price index
- it is available:
  - **from** the month of purchase
  - **to** the month of disposal

- the IA is calculated separately for each item of expenditure (e.g. calculate a different IA for the original acquisition cost and any enhancement expenditure because they have different purchase dates).
- the IA cannot create or increase a capital loss.

Calculation of the indexation allowance

The IA is calculated as follows:

IA = indexation factor x allowable cost

The indexation factor is calculated as follows:

$$\frac{\textbf{RPI in month of disposal — RPI in month of expenditure}}{\textbf{RPI in month of expenditure}}$$

- Note that the indexation factor must be rounded to three decimal places.

Example 1 - Indexation allowance

Kane Ltd sold a chargeable asset in June 2008, which it had bought in February 1987.

The RPI for February 1987 is 100.4 and for June 2008 it is 213.4.

Calculate the indexation factor used in the calculation of Kane Ltd's chargeable gain.

Answer to example 1

Indexation factor is

(213.4 – 100.4)/100.4 = 1.125 (rounded to three decimal places).

Example 2 - Indexation allowance

Pye Ltd bought a factory for £250,000, on 1 April 1983. On 15 July 1986, the company spent £70,000 on an extension to the factory. The factory was sold on 30 September 2008, for £800,000.

Assume the relevant RPIs are as follows:

April 1983	84.28
July 1986	97.52
September 2008	214.5

Calculate Pye Ltd's chargeable gain on the disposal of the factory.

Answer to example 2

	£
Sale proceeds	800,000
Cost	(250,000)
Enhancement expenditure	(70,000)
Unindexed gain	480,000
Indexation allowance:	
Cost (£250,000 × 1.545) **(W)**	(386,250)
Enhancement expenditure (£70,000 × 1.200) **(W)**	(84,000)
Chargeable gain	9,750

Working: Indexation factors

The indexation factor from April 1983 to September 2008 is:

(214.5 – 84.28)/84.28 = 1.545 (rounded to three decimal places)

The indexation factor from July 1986 to September 2008 is:

(214.5 – 97.52)/97.52 = 1.200 (rounded to three decimal places)

Test your understanding 1

Hobbit Ltd bought a factory for £175,000 on 1 June 1984. On 15 September 1990, the company spent £62,000 on an extension to the factory. The factory was sold on 31 August 2008, for £650,000.

Assume the relevant RPIs are as follows:

June 1984	89.20
September 1990	129.3
August 2008	214.1

Calculate Hobbit Ltd's chargeable gain on the disposal of the factory.

3 Capital losses

Calculation of a capital loss

- A capital loss arises if the proceeds received for an asset, are lower than the allowable expenditure.
- Remember that indexation cannot create or increase a capital loss.

Test your understanding 2

JNN Ltd is considering selling a field at auction in July 2008. It acquired the field in August 1984, for £10,000 and the sale proceeds are likely to be one of three figures:

(a) £25,000

(b) £12,000

(c) £8,000

Calculate the chargeable gain or loss under each of these alternatives.

Assume the indexation factor from August 1984 to July 2008 is 1.376.

Utilisation of a capital loss

- Where allowable losses arise, they are set off against capital gains arising in the same accounting period.
- Any loss remaining, is carried forward against **chargeable gains** of future accounting periods, as soon as they arise.
- Capital losses can never be set-off against any other income of a company.

Example 3 - Capital losses

Jump Ltd prepares its accounts to 31 March.

For the year ended 31 March 2009, the company has a tax-adjusted trading profit of £65,000, and a chargeable gain of £3,600.

As at 1 April 2008, Jump Ltd had unused capital losses brought forward of £6,000.

Calculate Jump Ltd's corporation tax liability for the year ended 31 March 2009.

Answer to example 3

Jump Ltd
Corporation tax liability – year ended 31 March 2009

	£
Trading profit	65,000
Net chargeable gain (W)	Nil
PCTCT	65,000
Corporation tax at 21%	13,650

Working: Net chargeable gain

	£
Chargeable gain	3,600
Less: Capital loss b/f	(6,000)
Capital loss c/f	(2,400)

Net chargeable gain in the accounting period is therefore £Nil.

Note: Capital losses can never be set against the other income of the company.

Test your understanding 3

High Ltd prepares its accounts to 31 December.

For the year ended 31 December 2008, the company has a tax-adjusted trading profit of £200,000, and a chargeable gain of £17,000.

As at 1 January 2008, High Ltd had unused capital losses brought forward of £23,000.

Calculate High Ltd's corporation tax liability for the year ended 31 December 2008.

4 Shares and securities

The issues regarding the disposal of shares by a company are similar to those set out in chapter 16 for disposals by individuals.

Remember that:

- Shares and securities present a particular problem for capital gains computations, because any two shares in a company (of a particular class) are indistinguishable.
- Matching rules are therefore needed, to solve the problem of being unable to identify acquisitions with disposals. They apply, when there has been more than one purchase of shares or securities, of the same class in the same company.

Matching rules

The matching rules for shares disposed of by companies, are different from those for an individual.

For a company, disposals are matched against acquisitions in the following order:

- Shares acquired on the same day (as the sale).
- Shares acquired during the nine days before the sale.
- Shares in the share pool (also know as the s104 pool or the 1985 pool).

Example 4 - Disposal of shares and securities

Minnie Ltd sold 3,000 shares in Mickey plc for £15,000, on 15 February 2009. The shares in Mickey plc were purchased as follows:

Date	Number	Cost
		£
1 July 1989	1,000	2,000
1 September 1999	1,000	2,500
8 February 2009	500	1,200
15 February 2009	1,500	6,000

Explain which shares Minnie Ltd sold.

Answer to example 4

Using the matching rules, the 3,000 shares sold are as follows:

		Number
(1)	Same day purchases:	
	15 February 2009	1,500
(2)	Previous 9 days purchases:	
	8 February 2009	500
		2,000

(3) Share pool:

All other shares were purchased more than 9 days ago, therefore they must be in the share pool.

1 July 1989	1,000	
1 September 1999	1,000	
Total number of shares in pool	2,000	
Disposal from the pool	(1,000)	
Left in share pool	1,000	
Shares disposed of		3,000

Calculation of gains on same day and previous 9 day purchases

There is no indexation available on either of these calculations, even if the dates of acquisition and disposal straddle a month.

- Hence, the gain is calculated as:

	£
Sale proceeds	X
Less: Allowable cost	(X)
Chargeable gain	X

Example 5 - Disposal of shares and securities

From the above example (Minnie Ltd), calculate the gains on the shares purchased:

(1) **on the same day**

(2) **in the previous 9 days.**

Answer to example 5

Calculate sale proceeds per share:

3,000 shares are sold for £15,000.

Hence: 1 share is sold for £5.00 (£15,000/3,000)

Gain on same day purchases (1,500 shares):

	£
Sale proceeds (£5 × 1,500)	7,500
Less: Allowable cost	(6,000)
Chargeable gain	1,500

Gain on previous 9 days, purchases (500 shares):

	£
Sale proceeds (£5 × 500)	2,500
Less: Allowable cost	(1,200)
Chargeable gain	1,300

The share pool for companies is different to the share pool for individuals as follows:

- it contains shares in the same company, of the same class, purchased **up to 9 days before** the date of disposal.
- The pool keeps a record of the:
  - number of shares acquired and sold
  - cost of the shares, and
  - indexed cost of the shares (i.e. cost plus indexation allowance)
- Each purchase and sale is recorded in the pool, but the indexed cost must be updated **before** recording the "operative event"
- When calculating the IA in the share pool, the indexation factor is not rounded to three decimal places.

  Note that this is the only situation where a non-rounded factor is ever used.

- When shares are disposed of out of the share pool, the appropriate proportion of the cost and indexed cost which relates to the shares disposed of is calculated on an average cost basis (as for individuals).

Pro forma for a company's share pool

The following pro forma, should be used to ensure that additions to and disposals from the share pool, are correctly dealt with.

	Number	Cost	Indexed cost
		£	£
Purchase	X	X →	X
IA to next operative event			X
Purchase	X	X →	X
	X	X	X
IA to next operative event			X
	X	X	X
Disposal	(X)	(X)	(X)
		W1	W2
Pool carried forward	X	X	X

Note:

- (W1) Calculates the average pool cost of shares disposed of
- (W2) Calculates the average indexed cost of shares disposed of

Workings 1 and 2 then feed into a normal chargeable gain computation, as follows:

	£
Sale proceeds	X
Cost (W1)	(X)
Unindexed gain	X
Indexation (W2 – W1)	(X)
Chargeable gain	X

Example 6 - Disposal of shares and securities

Continuing the example of Minnie Ltd (above), calculate the gain on the disposal from the share pool.

Assume the RPIs are as follows:

July 1989	115.5
September 1999	166.2
February 2009	216.5

Answer to example 6

Gain on share pool shares disposed of:

	£
Sale proceeds (£5 × 1,000)	5,000
Less: Allowable cost (W)	(2,250)
	2,750
Less: Indexation allowance (£3,503 – £2,250) (W)	(1,253)
Chargeable gain	1,497

Hence, the total chargeable gain on the 3,000 shares sold is £4,297 (£1,500 + £1,300 + £1,497).

Working: Share pool	Number	Cost	Indexed cost
		£	£
July 1989 purchase	1,000	2,000	2,000
IA to next operative event:			
(July 1989 to September 1999)			
(166.2 – 115.5)/115.5 × £2,000			878
September 1999 purchase	1,000	2,500	2,500
	2,000	4,500	5,378
IA to next operative event			
(September 1999 to February 2009)			
(216.5 – 166.2)/166.2 × £5,378			1,628
	2,000	4,500	7,006
February 2009 sale			
(1,000 out of 2,000) (Note)	(1,000)	(2,250)	(3,503)
Pool carried forward	1,000	2,250	3,503

Note: Multiply each of the sub-totals above by the fraction 1,000/2,000.

Test your understanding 4

Braganza Ltd sold 10,000 ordinary shares in the FRP Co plc, a quoted company, on 20 December 2008, for £70,000.

Braganza Ltd always prepares its financial statements to 31 December each year.

The company had bought the ordinary shares on the following dates:

	Number of shares	Cost	Indexed cost
		£	£
1 April 1998 – Balance b/fwd	8,000	17,450	25,250
22 December 2000	4,000	7,500	

Calculate the chargeable gain arising on the disposal of the shares.

Assume retail price indices are:

April 1998	162.6
December 2000	172.2
December 2008	215.7

5 Bonus and rights issues

The key points to remember are as follows:

- A bonus issue is the distribution of free shares to shareholders, based on existing shareholdings.
- A rights issue involves shareholders paying for new shares, usually at a rate below market price and in proportion to their existing shareholdings.
- In both cases, therefore, the shareholder is making a new acquisition of shares.
- However, for matching purposes, such acquisitions arise out of the original holdings. They are not treated as a separate holding of shares.
- Bonus and rights issues therefore, attach to the original shareholdings, for the purposes of the identification rules.

Bonus issues

As a bonus issue is free shares (i.e. no cost is involved), there is no indexation to be calculated.

A bonus issue is not an operative event in the share pool.

Simply, add the bonus issue shares to the share pool. When the next operative event occurs (e.g. next sale or purchase), index from the operative event before the date of the bonus issue.

Rights issue

- A rights issue is simply a purchase of shares (usually at a price below the market rate).
- Hence, it should be treated as an operative event, in the same way as a purchase in the share pool:
  - Index up to the date of the rights issue; then
  - Add in the number of shares and their cost.

Example 7 - Bonus and rights issues

Alma Ltd acquired shares in S plc, a quoted company, as follows:

2,000 shares acquired in June 1987, for £11,500.

In October 1988, there was a 1 for 2 bonus issue.

Set up the share pool and deal with the events up to and including the bonus issue.

Answer to example 7

Share pool	**Number**	**Cost**	**Indexed cost**
		£	£
Purchase (June 1987)	2,000	11,500	11,500
Bonus issue (October 1988)			
(1 for 2) 1/2 × £2,000	1,000	Nil	Nil
	3,000	11,500	11,500

Note: DO NOT index up to the date of the bonus issue as no cost is involved. The next time there is an operative event, IA will be calculated from June 1987 (the last operative event).

Test your understanding 5

Michael Ltd sold 2,000 ordinary shares out of a holding of 5,000 shares in Ryan Ltd, on 30 September 2008, for £15,400.

Michael Ltd prepares accounts every year to 31 March. The holding of shares in Ryan Ltd had been built up as follows:

Date acquired	**Number of shares**	**Cost £**
May 1995	4,000	7,000
March 1996 – bonus issue 1 for 4	1,000	Nil

Compute the chargeable gain arising on the sale of shares, in the year to 31 March 2009.

Assume the retail price indices are:

May 1995	149.6
March 1996	151.5
September 2008	214.5

Example 8 - Bonus and rights issues

Amber Ltd sold 2,600 shares in Pearl Ltd in December 2008 for £30,000.

Amber Ltd originally acquired 3,000 shares in Pearl Ltd in June 1987 for £11,500. In December 1994 Amber Ltd took up its entitlement to a 1 for 4 rights issue at £3 per share.

Calculate the chargeable gain arising on disposal of the shares, in December 2008.

Assume the following RPIs apply:

June 1987	101.9
December 1994	146.0
December 2008	215.7

Answer to example 8

	£
Sale proceeds	30,000
Cost (W)	(9,533)
Unindexed gain	20,467
Indexation (£19,182 – £9,533) (W)	(9,649)
Chargeable gain	10,818

Working: share pool	Number	Cost	Indexed cost
		£	£
Purchase – June 1987	3,000	11,500	11,500
IA to December 1994			
(146.0 – 101.9)/101.9 × £11,500			4,977
	3,000	11,500	16,477
Rights issue (1 for 4) at £3 – December 1997	750	2,250	2,250
	3,750	13,750	18,727
IA to December 2008			
(215.7 – 146.0)/146.0 × £18,727			8,940
	3,750	13,750	27,667
Disposal – December 2008			
(2,600/3,750) × £13,750/£27,667	(2,600)	(9,533)	(19,182)
Balance to c/f	1,150	4,217	8,485

Note: The indexed cost is updated prior to the rights issue, because there is a purchase which involves additional cost (i.e. it is an operative event).

Following the disposal, there are 1,150 shares in the pool, with a cost of £4,217 and an indexed cost of £8,485.

This will be used as the starting point, when dealing with the next operative event.

6 Takeovers/reorganisations

Consideration: shares for shares

Where the consideration for the reorganisation or takeover, only involves the issue of shares in the acquiring company, the tax consequences are:

- No chargeable gain arises at the time of the reorganisation or takeover.
- The cost of the original shares becomes the cost of the new shares.

- Where the shareholder receives more than one type of share, in exchange for the original shares, the cost of the original shares is allocated to the new shares, by reference to the market values of the various new shares, on the first day of dealing in them.

Mixed consideration

When both cash and shares are received on a takeover:

- There is a part disposal of the original shares. A chargeable gain arises on the cash element of the consideration.

Example 9 - Takeovers/reorganisations

In June 1997, Major Ltd purchased 2,000 ordinary shares in Blue plc, for £5,000.

In July 2008, Blue plc was taken over by Red plc, and Major Ltd received 2 ordinary shares and 1 preference share in Red plc, for each ordinary share in Blue plc.

Immediately after the takeover, the ordinary shares in Red plc, were quoted at £2 and the preference shares in Red plc, were quoted at £1.

In December 2008, Major Ltd sold all of its holding of ordinary shares in Red plc, for £8,000. The indexation factor from June 1997 to December 2008, should be taken as 0.370.

Calculate the chargeable gain arising on the disposal in December 2008.

Answer to example 9

	£
Sale proceeds	8,000
Less: Cost **(W)**	(4,000)
Unindexed gain	4,000
Indexation allowance (£4,000 × 0.370)	(1,480)
Chargeable gain	2,520

Working: Cost of ordinary shares in Red plc

Major Ltd received:

	£
4,000 ordinary shares, valued at £2	8,000
2,000 preference shares, valued at £1	2,000
	10,000

The cost attributable to the ordinary shares is therefore:

£5,000 × (8,000/10,000) = £4,000

Test your understanding 6

In July 2008, Concert Ltd sold its entire holding of ordinary shares in Corus plc, for £75,000. Concert Ltd had originally purchased 20,000 £1 ordinary shares in BNB plc, at a cost of £20,000, in April 1992.

In July 1998, BNB plc was taken over by Corus plc. Concert Ltd received one ordinary 50p share and one 50p 6% preference share in Corus plc, for each ordinary share it held in BNB plc.

Immediately after the takeover, the values of these new shares were quoted as:

50p ordinary share	£1.80 each
50p preference shares	£0.80 each

Compute the chargeable gain arising on the disposal by Concert Ltd, who has always prepared financial statements to 31 December each year.

The relevant indexation factor to be used is:

April 1992 to July 2008	0.540

7 Reliefs available to companies

The **only** relief available to companies is roll-over relief. The other reliefs covered in Chapter 17 are not applicable to companies.

Roll-over relief for companies

The detail of roll-over relief was discussed in Chapter 17. There are generally no differences in the application of roll-over relief for companies. The rules are summarised in expandable text.

Expandable text - Summary of roll-over relief

- Roll-over relief exists, to allow companies to replace assets used in their trade, without incurring a corporation tax liability, on the related chargeable gains.
- The gain arising on the disposal of the business asset, is deducted from (rolled over against), the acquisition cost of the new asset.
- Provided the proceeds are fully reinvested, no tax is payable at the time of the disposal.
- Assets which qualify for roll-over relief:
  - Land and buildings that are both occupied and used for trading purposes.
  - Fixed plant and machinery (in this context 'fixed' means immovable).
- The acquisition of the replacement asset, must occur during a period that begins **one year before** the sale of the old asset and ends **three years after** the sale.
- Where disposal proceeds of the old asset are not fully reinvested, the surplus retained, reduces the amount of chargeable gain that can be rolled over.
- When an asset has not been used entirely for business purposes throughout the company's period of ownership, the roll-over relief is scaled down in proportion to the non-business use.
- If reinvestment is in a depreciating asset, the capital gain is deferred until the earliest of:
  - disposal of the depreciating asset
  - depreciating asset ceases to be used for trading purposes
  - 10 years since the asset was acquired.
- Any asset with a predictable life of not more than 60 years, is a depreciating asset.
- If a new non-depreciating asset is acquired before the deferred gain becomes chargeable, roll-over relief can be reinstated.

The key differences in the rules for companes are as follows:

- **goodwill is not a qualifying asset** for companies
- the gain deferred is the 'indexed gain' (i.e. the gain **after** IA).

Test your understanding 7

Medway Ltd has been offered £160,000 for a freehold factory that it owns, and is considering disposing of the factory in January 2009.

The company acquired the factory on 15 March 1984, for £120,000 (this figure is already indexed to January 2009). The factory has always been used by Medway Ltd for business purposes.

Explain the capital gains implications of each of the following alternative courses of action that Medway Ltd is considering taking:

(a) **Acquiring a larger freehold factory in April 2009, for £170,000.**

(b) **Acquiring a smaller freehold factory in April 2009, for £155,000 and using the remainder of the proceeds as working capital.**

(c) **Using the proceeds to pay a premium of £180,000 in April 2009, for a 40-year lease of a new factory (it is possible that a freehold warehouse will be bought in the next two or three years for an estimated cost of £200,000).**

8 Chapter summary

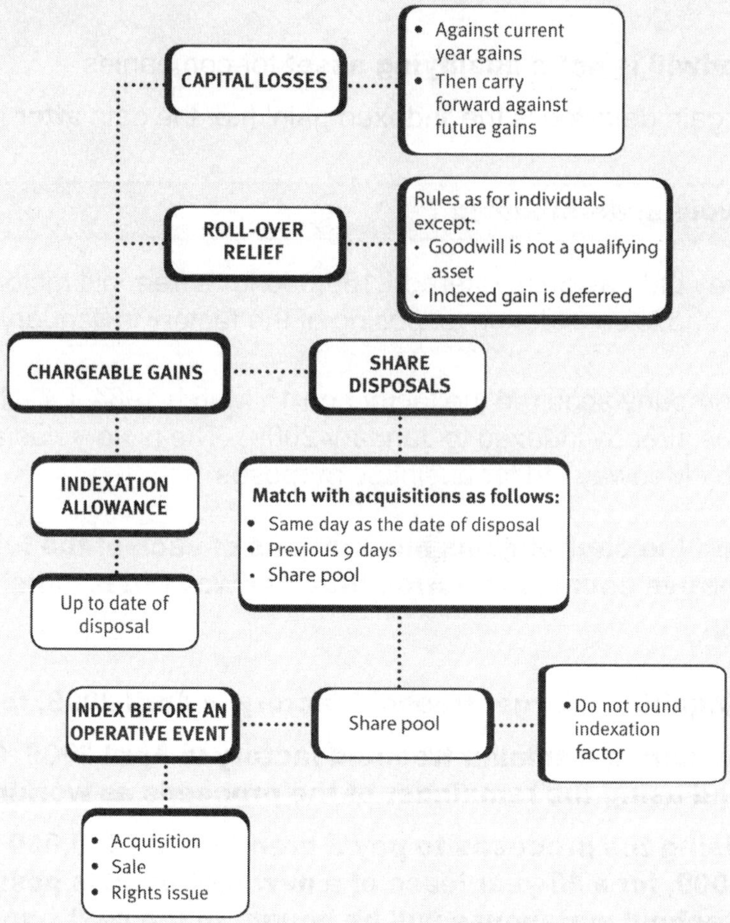

Test your understanding answers

Test your understanding 1

Hobbit Ltd

Chargeable gain computation

	£
Sale proceeds	650,000
Cost	(175,000)
Enhancement expenditure	(62,000)
	–––––––
Unindexed gain	413,000
Indexation allowance:	
Cost (£175,000 × 1.400) **(W)**	(245,000)
Enhancement expenditure (£62,000 × 0.656) **(W)**	(40,672)
	–––––––
Chargeable gain	127,328
	–––––––

Working: indexation factors

The indexation factor from June 1984 to August 2008 is:

(214.1 – 89.20)/89.20 = 1.400 (rounded to three decimal places)

The indexation factor from September 1990 to August 2008 is:

(214.1 – 129.3)/129.3 = 0.656 (rounded to three decimal places)

Test your understanding 2

JNN Ltd

	(a)	(b)	(c)
	£	£	£
Sale proceeds	25,000	12,000	8,000
Cost	(10,000)	(10,000)	(10,000)
Unindexed gain/(loss)	15,000	2,000	(2,000)
Indexation allowance			
£10,000 x 1.376	(13,760)		
Restricted (see note)		(2,000)	Nil
Chargeable gain/(allowable loss)	1,240	Nil	(2,000)

Note: In part (b) the IA is restricted because indexation cannot create a loss.

In part (c) there is no IA because indexation cannot increase a loss.

Test your understanding 3

High Ltd

Corporation tax liability – year ended 31 December 2008

	£
Trading profit	200,000
Net chargeable gain	Nil
PCTCT	200,000
Corporation tax liability	
FY 2007 (3 months) (£200,000 × 20% × 3/12)	10,000
FY 2008 (9 months) (£200,000 × 21% × 9/12)	31,500
	41,500

Working: net chargeable gain

	£
Chargeable gain	17,000
Less: Capital loss b/f	(23,000)
Capital loss c/f	(6,000)

Therefore the net chargeable gain is Nil.

Test your understanding 4

Braganza Ltd

Chargeable gain computation – year to 31 December 2008

	£
Sale proceeds	70,000
Less: Acquisition cost **(W)**	(20,792)
Unindexed gain	49,208
Less: Indexation allowance (£35,742 – £20,792) **(W)**	(14,950)
Chargeable gain	34,258

Working: share pool

	Number	Cost	Indexed cost
		£	£
Balance at 1.4.98	8,000	17,450	25,250
IA to December 2000			
(172.2 – 162.6)/162.6 × £25,250			1,491
December 2000 acquisition	4,000	7,500	7,500
	12,000	24,950	34,241
IA to December 2008			
(215.7 – 172.2)/172.2 × £34,241			8,650
	12,000	24,950	42,891
Disposal – December 2008	(10,000)	(20,792)	(35,742)
Balance c/f	2,000	4,158	7,149

Proportion of cost and indexed cost relating to the disposal:

Cost: (10,000/12,000) × £24,950 = £20,792
Indexed cost: (10,000/12,000) × £42,891 = £35,743

Test your understanding 5

Michael Ltd
Chargeable gain computation – year to 31 March 2009

	£
Sale proceeds	15,400
Less: Acquisition cost (W)	(2,800)
Unindexed gain	12,600
Less: Indexation allowance (£4,015 – £2,800) (W)	(1,215)
Chargeable gain	11,385

Working: share pool	**Number**	**Cost**	**Indexed cost**
		£	£
May 1995	4,000	7,000	7,000
March 1996 – bonus issue	1,000	Nil	Nil
	5,000	7,000	7,000
Index to September 2008 from May 1995			
(214.5 – 149.6)/149.6 × £7,000			3,037
	5,000	7,000	10,037
Disposal **(Note)**	(2,000)	(2,800)	(4,015)
Balance	3,000	4,200	6,022

Note: The proportion of cost and indexed cost relating to the disposal is calculated as: (2,000/5,000) × £7,000 and £10,037 respectively.

Test your understanding 6

Concert Ltd

Chargeable gain computation – year to 31 December 2008

	£
Sales proceeds	75,000
Less: Deemed acquisition cost **(W)**	(13,846)
Unindexed gain	61,154
Less: Indexation allowance (£13,846 × 0.540)	(7,477)
Chargeable gain	53,677

Working: Deemed acquisition cost

Following the takeover in July 1998 of BNB plc by Corus plc, Concert Ltd now owns the following shares in Corus plc as per the terms of the takeover.

	Total market value	Original cost
	£	£
20,000 50p ordinary shares @ £1.80	36,000	13,846
20,000 50p preference shares @ £0.80	16,000	6,154
	52,000	20,000

Allocation of original cost incurred in April 1992, to the shares now owned in July 1998, using the average cost method.

To ordinary shares: (£36,000/£52,000) × £20,000 = £13,846

To preference shares (£16,000/£52,000) × £20,000 = £6,154

Test your understanding 7

Medway Ltd

The chargeable gain on the disposal of the freehold factory is £40,000 (£160,000 – £120,000).

(a) **Larger freehold factory**

The gain will be rolled over against the base cost of the new factory as all the proceeds are reinvested:

	£
Cost of factory	170,000
Gain rolled over	(40,000)
Base cost of new factory	130,000

(b) **Smaller freehold factory**

As only part of the proceeds are reinvested, the capital gain element that cannot be rolled over will be £5,000 (£160,000 – £155,000).

This will be immediately chargeable to corporation tax. The balance of the gain will be rolled over as above.

	£
Cost of factory	155,000
Gain rolled over (£40,000 – £5,000)	(35,000)
Base cost of new factory	120,000

(c) **Lease**

All of the proceeds are being used to acquire a depreciating asset (one with an expected life of less than 60 years). The capital gain is therefore not rolled over, but is instead 'frozen'.

It will become chargeable to corporation tax on the earlier of:

- the date that the lease is sold
- the date the lease ceases to be used in the trade
- the expiry of ten years from April 2009.

Therefore, the base cost of the lease remains at £180,000.

If, before the 'frozen' gain becomes chargeable, a non-depreciating asset is acquired, the gain can be rolled over in the usual way.

In this question, if the freehold warehouse is acquired in the next 2 – 3 years, all the proceeds will be reinvested and so the roll-over claim would switch to the freehold warehouse cost of £200,000.

hapter

21

Losses for companies

Chapter learning objectives

Upon completion of this chapter you will be able to:

- determine a trading loss and explain the various ways of giving relief in a single company
- demonstrate the application of the trading loss reliefs in a corporation tax computation
- show how a trading loss is relieved on cessation of a trade
- identify the factors that influence the choice of a loss relief claim
- explain how relief for a property business loss is given
- demonstrate how capital losses can be relieved against gains.

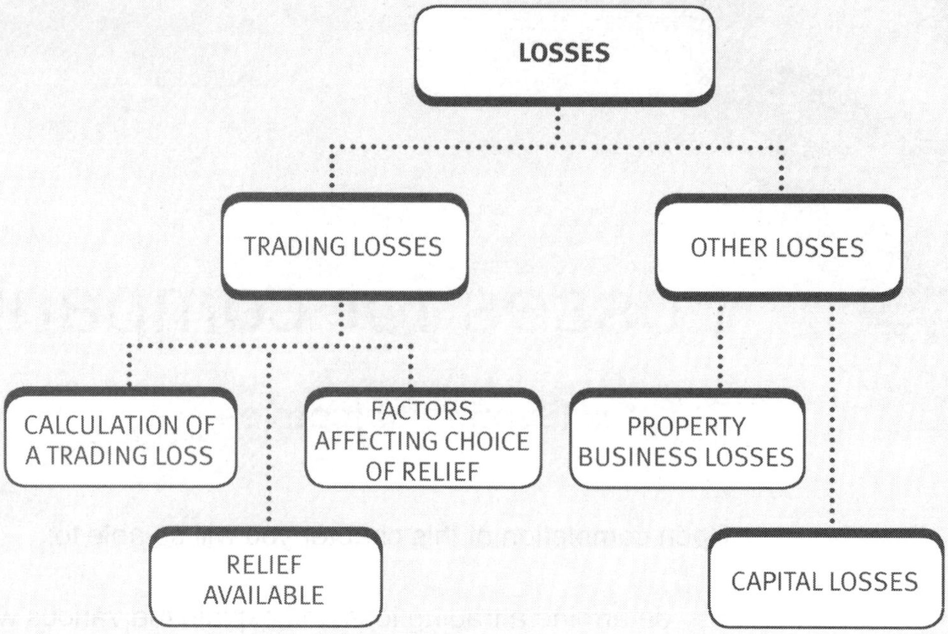

1 Introduction

This chapter deals with the different losses that a company can incur and the ways in which relief for those losses can be obtained.

The following losses are dealt with:

- Trading losses (section 2).
- Property business losses (section 5).
- Capital losses (section 6).

2 Trading losses

Calculation of a trading loss

- Trading losses are computed in the same way as tax-adjusted trading profits:

	£
Tax-adjusted net profit/(loss)	X/(X)
Less: Plant and machinery capital allowances	(X)
Less: Industrial buildings allowances	(X)
Adjusted trading loss	(X)

- The above adjustments would also apply if the net figure per the accounts was a loss.

- When a company has made an adjusted trading loss, then nil is entered in the corporation tax PCTCT computation for trading income for that period.

Example 1 - Trading losses

Carlos Ltd has had the following results for its year ended 31 March 2009:

	£	£
Gross profit		30,000
Less: Expenditure		
Depreciation	5,000	
Allowable costs	12,000	(17,000)
Net profit per accounts		13,000

The capital allowances for the year amount to £21,000.

(a) **Calculate the tax-adjusted trading profit/(loss) for the year ended 31 March 2009.**

(b) **Calculate the tax-adjusted trading loss for the year ended 31 March 2009 assuming the facts are the same except that the company made a net loss per the accounts of £10,000.**

Answer to example 1

(a) **Tax-adjusted trading profit/(loss) – year ended 31 March 2009**

	£
Net profit per accounts	13,000
Add: Depreciation	5,000
	18,000
Less: Capital allowances	(21,000)
Tax-adjusted trading loss	(3,000)
Trading income assessment	Nil

The trading income to be entered in the corporation tax PCTCT computation is nil.

(b) **Tax-adjusted trading loss**

	£
Net loss per accounts	(10,000)
Add: Depreciation	5,000
	(5,000)
Less: Capital allowances	(21,000)
Tax-adjusted trading loss	(26,000)

The trading income entered in the corporation tax PCTCT computation is nil.

Relief for trading losses

There are three ways in which a company can offset trading losses:

(1) Carry forward and off-set against first available **future trading profits** only.

(2) Off-set against **current period total profits**, before Gift Aid payments.

(3) Off-set first against **total profits** (before Gift Aid) of the **current period** and then relieve against **total profits** (before Gift Aid) of the **previous 12 months**.

A company which ceases to trade, may also utilise trading losses through a terminal loss claim (section 3).

Carry forward relief – s393(1) ICTA 1988

The key features of this relief are:

- The loss is carried forward for offset in future accounting periods.
- The loss is set against the **first available** tax-adjusted profits from the **same trade**.
- The relief is automatic, i.e. no claim is required.
- The loss can be carried forward indefinitely.
- There is no need to make a current year or a prior year claim first.

Expandable text - Carry forward loss relief s393(1) ICTA 1988

- Where a company incurs a trading loss, it may carry the loss forward and set it off against profits from the **same trade**, in future accounting periods.
- The loss can be carried forward indefinitely, there is no time limit for obtaining relief, but it must be set-off against the **first available** trading profits.
- The only exception to carrying these losses forward indefinitely, is if the company changes their trading activity. Any remaining losses are then forfeited.
- Losses can be carried forward:
  - After a current year claim only.
  - After a current year and prior year claim.
  - Neither of the above.
- A claim to establish the amount of the loss available to carry forward, should be made within six years of the end of the loss-making accounting period.
- The carry forward relief automatically allows trading losses (s393(1)) to be set against future trading profits of the same trade, as soon as they arise. They cannot be relieved against any other profits.
- Such losses have to be used against the first available trading profits.

Example 2 - Trading losses

Poppy Ltd has a current year tax adjusted trading loss of £25,000, for the year ended 31 March 2009.

The company's projected trading profits are as follows:

	£
Year ended 31 March 2010	14,000
Year ended 31 March 2011	6,500
Year ended 31 March 2012	15,600

Poppy Ltd also receives property business income of £5,000 each year.

Calculate Poppy Ltd's PCTCT for the four years ended 31 March 2012 assuming that the loss for the year ended 31 March 2009, is carried forward and offset under s393(1) ICTA 1988.

Answer to example 2

Year ended:	**31.3.09**	**31.3.10**	**31.3.11**	**31.3.12**
	£	£	£	£
Trading income	Nil	14,000	6,500	15,600
s393(1) relief	–	(14,000)	(6,500)	(4,500)
	Nil	Nil	Nil	11,100
Property income	5,000	5,000	5,000	5,000
PCTCT	5,000	5,000	5,000	16,100

Current year relief – s393A ICTA 1988

Under current year loss relief trading losses are set off against:

- total profits before deduction of Gift Aid
- of the same accounting period.

A current year claim under s393A ICTA 1988, must be for the whole loss. It is not possible to restrict the amount of the loss offset.

A claim for the relief must be made within two years of the end of the loss-making accounting period.

Example 3 - Trading losses

Sage Ltd had the following results for the year ended 31 March 2009.

	£
Tax-adjusted trading loss	(40,000)
Property business income	10,000
Chargeable gain	50,000
Gift Aid payment	10,000

(a) **Show how the trading loss could be relieved in the current period under s393A ICTA 1988.**

(b) **Show how your answer would be different if the tax-adjusted trading loss was £60,000.**

Answer to example 3

(a) **PCTCT computation for the year ended 31 March 2009**

	£
Trading income	Nil
Property income	10,000
Chargeable gain	50,000
Total profits	60,000
s393A current year relief	(40,000)
	20,000
Less: Gift Aid	(10,000)
PCTCT	10,000

Loss memorandum

Year ended 31 March 2009	(40,000)
Relieved in current period	40,000
	Nil

Note: Setting off the loss before the deduction of Gift Aid, may result in the Gift Aid payments becoming unrelieved. Any unrelieved amounts, **cannot** be carried forward and relieved against future trading profits.

(b) **PCTCT computation for the year ended 31 March 2009**

	£
Total profits (as before)	60,000
s393A current year relief	(60,000)
PCTCT	Nil
Gift Aid (see Note)	(10,000)

Note: Gift Aid

The Gift Aid payments have become excess (i.e. not used), as there are insufficient profits. It is an important principle that, where there is an available loss, no restriction in set off is permitted.

This means that it would **not** have been possible here, to restrict the loss relief to (£50,000), so as to then relieve the Gift Aid payments of (£10,000), and find an alternative use for the remaining (£10,000) loss.

Excess Gift Aid donations cannot be carried forward or back and are therefore wasted.

Carry back relief – s393A ICTA 1988

Under carry back loss relief, trading losses are set off against:

- total profits (before deduction of Gift Aid) of the previous 12 months (LIFO basis).

A carryback claim can only be made, if a claim for current year loss relief has been made first.

The claim must be made within two years of end of the loss-making accounting period.

Example 4 - Trading losses

Marjoram Ltd has the following results for the three accounting periods to 31 March 2009.

Year ended 31 March:	**2007**	**2008**	**2009**
	£	£	£
Trading profits/(loss)	11,000	9,000	(45,000)
Building society interest	500	500	500
Chargeable gains	–	–	4,000
Gift Aid payment	250	250	250

Calculate the PCTCT for all periods affected, assuming that loss relief is taken as soon as possible.

Answer to example 4

Marjoram Ltd – Corporation tax computations

Year ended 31 March:	2008	2009
	£	£
Trading income	9,000	Nil
Interest income	500	500
Chargeable gain		4,000
Total profits	9,500	4,500
s393A current loss relief (W)		(4,500)
	9,500	Nil
s393A carry back relief (W)	(9,500)	
	Nil	Nil
Less: Gift Aid payment	Wasted	Wasted
PCTCT	Nil	Nil

Working – loss memorandum

	£
Loss for the year ended 31 March 2009	45,000
s393A current relief – y/e 31.3.09	(4,500)
	40,500
s393A carry back 12 months – y/e 31.3.08	(9,500)
Loss still available at 1 April 2009	31,000

Note: The year ended 31 March 2007 is not affected, as the loss cannot be carried back that far.

Test your understanding 1

The following are the profits of Alfred Ball Ltd, which commenced trading on 1 January 1991.

Year ended:	**31.12.06**	**31.12.07**	**31.12.08**
	£	£	£
Adjusted trading profit/(loss)	42,000	19,000	(67,000)
Bank interest received	3,000	2,000	1,000
Chargeable gains	4,000	4,000	4,000
Gift Aid paid	10,000	10,000	–

Calculate the PCTCT, for all of the accounting periods shown above, clearly indicating how you would deal with the trading loss, to obtain relief as soon as possible.

Test your understanding 2

Mint Ltd has the following results:

Year ended:	**31.3.07**	**31.3.08**	**31.3.09**
	£	£	£
Adjusted trading profit/(loss)	15,000	(100,000)	40,000
Interest income	5,000	10,000	10,000
Chargeable gain	–	40,000	–

Calculate the PCTCT, for all of the accounting periods shown above, clearly indicating how you would deal with the trading loss, to obtain relief as soon as possible.

Short accounting periods prior to year of loss

Under s393(A) ICTA 1988 the trading loss can be carried back 12 months.

If the company has a short accounting period preceding the period of loss, more than one accounting period may fall into the 12 months carry back period.

In this case:

- Where an accounting period falls partly into the 12 months carry back period, the profits of that accounting period must be time apportioned. The loss can only be offset against those profits which fall within the 12 month carry back period.

- The loss is offset on a LIFO basis (i.e. against the later accounting period first).

Example 5 - Trading losses

Lily Ltd has the following results for the periods to 31 March 2009:

	Year to 30.9.07	6 months to 31.3.08	Year to 31.3.09
	£	£	£
Tax-adjusted trading profit/(loss)	19,000	14,000	(50,000)
Gift Aid donations	500	1,000	1,000

Calculate the PCTCT for all three periods, assuming that relief is claimed for the loss in the year ended 31 March 2009, as soon as possible under s393A ICTA 1998. Show any losses available to carry forward at 1 April 2009.

Answer to example 5

The loss may be carried back against profits falling within the 12 months prior to the year to 31 March 2009, therefore:

- against 6 months, ended 31 March 2008
- against 6 months of the year, ended 30 September 2007 (the loss may be set against 6/12 × profits for this period).

Lily Ltd – PCTCT computations

	Year to 30.9.07	6 months to 31.3.08	Year to 31.3.09
	£	£	£
Trading income = Total profits	19,000	14,000	Nil
Less: s393A relief	(9,500)	(14,000)	–
Gift Aid	(500)	wasted	wasted
PCTCT	9,000	Nil	Nil
Unrelieved Gift Aid		1,000	1,000

Loss memorandum

	£
Loss for y/e 31.3.09	50,000
Less: s393A ICTA 1988 relief:	
6 months to 31.3.08	(14,000)
Y/e 30.9.07 (£19,000 × 6/12)	(9,500)
Loss to carry forward	26,500

Test your understanding 3

Catalyst Ltd has been trading for many years and the following results are available:

	Year ended 31.3.06	Period to 31.12.06	Year ended 31.12.07	Year ended 31.12.08
	£	£	£	£
Adjusted trading profit/ (loss) before capital allowances	33,000	16,500	(75,000)	25,000
Capital allowances	5,400	4,050	6,550	5,000
Non-trade interest receivable	1,200	1,300	1,400	1,600
Chargeable gain/ (loss)	Nil	(6,000)	Nil	12,000
Gift Aid donations	Nil	3,000	3,000	8,000

Assuming that Catalyst Ltd claims relief for its tax-adjusted trading loss as early as possible, calculate the company's PCTCT for the accounting periods ended 31 December 2008.

Your answer should show the amount of unrelieved losses as at 31 December 2008.

Loss-making period of less than 12 months

- Where the loss-making period itself is less than 12 months, no apportionment is necessary.
- The loss can be carried back in full, against profits falling within the preceding 12-month period.

Example 6 - Trading losses

Clover Ltd has the following results for the accounting periods ended 31 August 2008 and 31 March 2009

	Year to 31.8.08	7 months to 31.3.09
	£	£
Tax adjusted trading profit/(loss)	59,000	(49,000)
Property business profit	2,000	1,500
Gift Aid donations	500	500

Calculate the PCTCT for both periods, assuming that relief under s393A ICTA 1988 is claimed for the loss in the period ended 31 March 2009 as soon as possible. Show any losses available to carry forward at 1 April 2009.

Answer to example 6

Clover Ltd – PCTCT computations

	Year to 31.8.08	7 months to 31.3.09
	£	£
Trading income	59,000	Nil
Property income	2,000	1,500
Total profits	61,000	1,500
Less: CY and PY relief s393A	(47,500)	(1,500)
	13,500	Nil
Less: Gift Aid	(500)	Wasted
PCTCT	13,000	Nil

	£
Unrelieved Gift Aid	500

Loss memorandum

	£
Loss for 7 months ended 31.3.09	49,000
Less: s393A ICTA 1988 relief	
Current period – 7 months to 31.3.09	(1,500)
Carry back – Y/e 31.8.08	(47,500)
	Nil

3 Terminal loss relief – s393A ICTA 1988

When a company incurs a trading loss during the final 12 months of trading, then it is possible to make a carry back claim under s393A ICTA 1988.

However, such a loss can be carried back and set against **total profits** of the **three years** preceding the loss-making period, rather than the usual preceding 12 months.

Relief available

Terminal loss relief applies to trading losses incurred during the final 12 months of trading. The losses can be relieved as follows:

- The company must first claim to set the trading loss against total profits (before Gift Aid) of the accounting period of the loss.
- The terminal loss can then be carried back and set against total profits (before Gift Aid) of the three years preceding the loss-making period.
- The set-off is against later periods before earlier periods (LIFO basis).
- Unrelieved Gift Aid payments are wasted.
- Where the company has prepared accounts for a period other than 12 months during the three years preceding the loss-making period, apportionment will be necessary in the same way as for a normal s393A ICTA 1988 loss claim, so that losses are only carried back against the proportion of profits, falling within the three-year period.

Test your understanding 4

Brown Ltd has been trading for many years. The company prepared its annual accounts to 31 March, each year, but changed its accounting date to 31 December in 2007. The company ceased trading on 31 December 2008.

The following details are available:

Period ended:	**31.3.05**	**31.3.06**	**31.3.07**	**31.12.07**	**31.12.08**
	£	£	£	£	£
Tax adjusted trading profit	450,000	87,000	240,000	45,000	Nil
Bank interest received	9,000	3,000	6,000	1,500	1,500
Chargeable gain	7,500	–	–	–	–
Gift Aid donation	30,000	30,000	30,000	30,000	30,000

In the year ended 31 December 2008, Brown Ltd made a tax-adjusted trading loss of £525,000.

Calculate Brown Ltd's PCTCT, for all of the above accounting periods, assuming terminal loss relief is claimed for the trading loss for the accounting period ended 31 December 2008.

4 Choice of loss relief

There may be several alternative loss reliefs available for a loss. The following factors will influence the loss relief chosen.

Factors that influence choice of loss relief

- Tax saving.
- Cash flow.
- Loss of relief for Gift Aid payments.

In examination questions, it is usually the option that gives the most beneficial tax saving that is recommended.

Tax saving

- The aim is to save tax at the highest possible rate. The marginal rate of tax is used to work out this tax saving.
- The marginal rate of tax describes the rate of tax saved for each £1 of loss utilised.
- The following shows the preferred order to claim relief:
  (1) against profits subject to tax at the full rate, but obtaining marginal relief. The marginal rate of tax for FY2008 is 29.75% (FY2007 32.5%).
  (2) against profits subject to tax at the full rate. The marginal rate of tax for FY2008 is 28% (FY2007 30%).
  (3) against profits subject to the small companies rate. The marginal rate of tax for FY2008 is 21% (FY2007 20%).

Note: The rate of 29.75% (explained below) is not an **actual** rate of tax, it is a marginal rate of tax that is useful for planning purposes.

The marginal rates are not provided in the exam. You need to learn both the marginal rate for FY2008 (29.75%) and FY2007 (32.5%).

Marginal rate of tax

The illustration below demonstrates how a company in the 'marginal' band between the small company rate and the large company rate, pays tax of 29.75% in FY2008 on each extra £1 it earns above the lower limit.

Example 7 - Marginal rate of tax

A Ltd has PCTCT of £300,000, for the year ended 31 March 2009. B Ltd has PCTCT of £310,000, for the year ended 31 March 2009. Neither company received any dividends in the year.

Calculate the corporation tax liability payable by each company and the marginal rate of tax on the additional profits of £10,000 earned by B Ltd.

Answer to example 7

Year ended 31 March 2009	**A Ltd**	**B Ltd**
	£	£
PCTCT = Profits	300,000	310,000
Corporation tax:		
£300,000 @ 21%	63,000	
£310,000 @ 28%		86,800
Less: Marginal relief		
7/400 × (£1,500,000 – £310,000)		(20,825)
		65,975

Additional tax paid by B Ltd (£65,975 – £63,000) = £2,975

Additional PCTCT earned by B Ltd = £10,000

Effective extra rate of tax on extra profits over £300,000 (the small company lower limit):

£2,975/£10,000 × 100 = **29.75%**

Expandable text - Choice of loss relief

Cash flow

A company's cash flow position, will affect its choice of loss relief. A company may be prepared to accept loss relief at a lower marginal rate, if it results in an earlier receipt of cash.

- A carryback claim under s393A ICTA 1988, will probably result in a repayment of corporation tax, whereas carrying losses forward under s393(1) ICTA 1988, will only result in a reduction of a future tax liability.

Loss of relief for Gift Aid donations

Unrelieved Gift Aid donations cannot be carried forward and relieved against future trading profits. Therefore, certain claims for loss relief may lead to relief for Gift Aid being lost.

Approach to questions

Loss questions will often give you PCTCT information for a company for a number of years. This may initially appear daunting. The following pro forma and step by step approach will provide you with a logical way to attempt the question and ensure that you offset the losses correctly.

Trading loss pro forma

Loss arises in 2007	2006	2007	2008
	£	£	£
Trading income	X	Nil	X
s393(1) – Losses carried forward			(X)
Other income	X	X	X
Chargeable gains	X	X	X
Total profits	X	X	X
s393A – Current year offset		(X)	
s393A – Losses carried back	(X)		
	Nil	Nil	X
Gift Aid	Wasted	Wasted	(X)
PCTCT	Nil	Nil	X

Approach:

(1) Write out the skeleton PCTCT pro forma, remembering to leave space for loss relief claims.

(2) Fill in the pro forma with the PCTCT information provided, ignoring loss relief.

(3) In the year of the loss, the trading profit figure in the PCTCT computation is nil. Keep a separate memorandum of the loss and update it, as the loss is relieved.

(4) Consider the loss relief options available:

- Where there is more than one loss to offset:
  - Deal with the earliest loss first.
  - Losses brought forward are offset in priority to current year and carryback claims.

- If a question states 'relief is to be obtained as early as possible', the order of set-off is:
  - Current year claim followed by a carryback claim to the previous 12 months.
  - Carry forward any remaining loss and offset against future trading profits.
- If a question asks you to identify the option that will save the most tax, consider in turn the three options:
  - Carry forward only.
  - Current year claim and then carry forward any excess.
  - Current year claim, followed by a carry back claim and then carry forward any excess.
- Identify the amount of tax saving and loss of relief for Gift Aid under each option and conclude as to which option saves the most tax.

Example 8 - Choice of loss relief

Loser Ltd which prepared its accounts to 31 March 2007, has since changed to a 30 September accounting date. The company forecasts a substantial tax-adjusted trading loss for the current year to 30 September 2008. A small trading profit is forecast for the following year to 30 September 2009, with steadily increasing profits thereafter.

Loser Ltd's tax-adjusted trading profits for recent years, have been as follows:

	£
Year ended 31 March 2007	550,000
Period ended 30 September 2007	70,000

Advise Loser Ltd as to which loss relief claims would save the most tax.

Answer to example 8

Loser Ltd has the following options regarding the trading loss arising in the year to 30 September 2008:

(1) **Carry the loss forward to off-set against the first available future trading profits.**

As the trading profits in the year to 30 September 2009, are expected to be small, relief for the loss is likely to be at 21% (assuming the small companies rate is unchanged in the future).

(2) **Current year off-set against the total profits of the year ended 30 September 2008 and balance carried forward.**

Assuming that the non-trading income of the company in the current year is small, relief for the loss will be small companies rate of 20.5% (i.e. 21% in FY 2008 for 6 months and 20% in FY 2007 for 6 months).

(3) **Current year off-set followed by a carryback to the previous 12 months**

The carryback will be to the period ended 30 September 2007 and six months of the year ended 31 March 2007.

Relief in the current year and the period ended 30 September 2007, will be at the small companies rate. The significant level of profits in the year ended 31 March 2007, will mean that relief for the loss in this year will be at the marginal rate.

Conclusion

Option 3 will therefore save the most tax.

Test your understanding 5

Confused Ltd's results are as follows:

Period ended:	30.6.06	31.3.07	31.3.08	31.3.09
	£	£	£	£
Tax adjusted trading profit/(loss)	108,240	(116,140)	41,520	(93,960)
Property income	–	5,400	9,720	6,720
Gift Aid donation	(1,680)	(960)	(1,440)	(1,320)

Assuming that Confused Ltd claims relief for its losses as early as possible, calculate the company's PCTCT, for the four accounting periods ended 31 March 2009. Your answer should show the amount of unrelieved losses as at 31 March 2009.

5 Property business losses

- Property business losses are firstly off-set against total profits (before Gift Aid) for the current period.
- Any excess is carried forward and off-set against future total profits of the company.
- Relief is automatic – no claim is required.
- There is no carry back facility for property business losses.
- If there are both property business losses and trading losses available for relief in the same current period and total profits are not sufficient to utilise all available reliefs, then losses must be used in the following order:
  - Property business loss.
  - Trading loss.

Example 9 - Property business losses

Reas Ltd has the following results for the two years ending 31 March 2009.

	2008	**2009**
	£	£
Adjusted trading profit/(loss)	12,000	7,000
Property business profit/(loss)	(22,600)	800
Interest income	500	1,400
Gift Aid payments	(500)	(500)

Calculate PCTCT for both years assuming all reliefs are claimed at the earliest opportunity.

Answer to example 9

Year ended 31 March:	**2008**	**2009**
	£	£
Trading income	12,000	7,000
Property business income	Nil	800
Interest income	500	1,400
Total profits	12,500	9,200
Less: Property business loss (**W**)	(12,500)	(9,200)
	Nil	Nil
Less: Gift Aid	Wasted	Wasted
PCTCT	Nil	Nil

Working: Property business loss

	£
The loss in year ended 31 March 2008 will be relieved against total profits in that period	(22,600)
Year ended 31 March 2008	12,500
Then carried forward against total profits	
Year ended 31 March 2009	9,200
Unrelieved loss carried forward	(900)

Test your understanding 6

Comfy Ltd has the following results for the three years ending 31 December 2008.

	2006	2007	2008
	£	£	£
Adjusted trading profit/(loss)	12,450	(34,500)	4,000
Property business profit/(loss)	2,000	1,800	(500)
Interest income	1,000	600	1,000
Gift Aid payments	(400)	(400)	(400)

Calculate PCTCT for all three years assuming all reliefs are claimed at the earliest opportunity.

6 Capital losses

Relief for capital losses is given as follows:

- A capital loss incurred in an accounting period is automatically relieved against any gains arising in the same accounting period.
- Any excess losses are then carried forward for relief against gains arising in future accounting periods.
- A capital loss may never be carried back and relieved against chargeable gains for earlier periods.
- Capital losses may not be set against the company's income.

Example 10 - Capital losses

Rose Ltd has the following results:

Year ended 31 March	2008	2009
	£	£
Trading profit/(loss)	(20,000)	18,000
Interest income	6,000	9,000
Capital loss	(2,000)	
Chargeable gains		7,000

Calculate the PCTCT for the two accounting periods, assuming that the trading loss is carried forward under s393(1) ICTA 1988. Show any losses carried forward at 1 April 2009.

Answer to example 10

Under s393(1) ICTA 1988 trading losses are relieved against the first available trading profits.

Capital losses can only be set against current or future chargeable gains.

Rose Ltd – PCTCT computations

Year ended 31 March	**2008**	**2009**
	£	£
Trading income	Nil	18,000
Less: s393(1) relief		(18,000)
		Nil
Interest income	6,000	9,000
Chargeable gains (£7,000 – £2,000)	Nil	5,000
PCTCT	6,000	14,000
Trading loss carried forward at 31 March 2009 (£20,000 – £18,000)		£2,000

Test your understanding 7

Coriander Ltd has the following results:

Year ended:	**Trading profit/ (loss)**	**Interest Income**	**Gift Aid paid**	**Capital gains or (losses)**
	£	£	£	£
31.12.06	37,450	1,300	3,000	(6,000)
31.12.07	(81,550)	1,400	3,000	
31.12.08	20,000	1,600	3,000	12,000

Calculate PCTCT for all relevant periods assuming loss relief is given as early as possible.

7 Comprehensive example

Test your understanding 8

Eagle Ltd is a UK resident company that manufactures train components. The company's results for the year ended 31 March 2009 are summarised as follows:

	£
Trading loss (as adjusted for taxation but before taking account of capital allowances) (**Note 1**)	(254,400)
Income from property (**Note 4**)	56,950
Profit on disposal of shares (**Note 5**)	56,900
Donation to charity (**Note 6**)	(3,000)

Notes

(1) **Trading loss**

The trading loss includes £20,000 in respect of patent royalties which are paid for a trading purpose as follows:

	£
Payments made	20,600
Accrued at 31 March 2009	1,600
	22,200
Accrued at 1 April 2008	(2,200)
	20,000

(2) **Industrial building**

Eagle Ltd had a new factory constructed at a cost of £350,000 that was brought into use on 1 July 2008. The cost is made up as follows:

	£
Land	87,500
Site preparation	12,000
Architect's fees	5,000
Canteen for employees	32,000
General offices	72,500
Factory	141,000
	350,000

(3) **Plant and machinery**

On 1 April 2008 the tax written down values of plant and machinery were as follows:

	£
General pool	64,700
Expensive motor car	14,700

The expensive motor car was sold on 15 February 2009 for £12,400. The following assets were purchased during the year ended 31 March 2009:

		£
20 October 2008	Lorry	22,400
18 March 2009	Motor car (not a low emission car)	11,300

(4) **Income from property**

Eagle Ltd lets out two warehouses that are surplus to requirements.

The first warehouse was empty from 1 April to 30 June 2008, but was let from 1 July 2008. On that date the company received a premium of £50,000 for the grant of an eight-year lease, and the annual rent of £12,600 which is payable in advance.

The second warehouse was let until 31 December 2008 at an annual rent of £8,400. On that date the tenant left owing three months rent which the company is not able to recover. The roof of the warehouse was repaired at a cost of £6,700 during February 2009.

(5) **Profit on disposal of shares**

The profit on disposal of shares is in respect of a 1% shareholding in a UK company that was sold on 22 December 2008 for £257,250.

The shareholding was purchased on 5 June 1997 for £112,800. Assume that the indexation allowance from June 1997 to December 2008 it is £125,975.

(6) **Donation to charity**

The donation to charity was made under the Gift Aid scheme.

(7) **Other information**

Eagle Ltd has no associated companies. Its results for the year ended 30 September 2007 and for the six-month period ended 31 March 2008 were as follows:

	Year ended 30 September 2007	Period ended 31 March 2008
	£	£
Trading profit	137,900	52,000
Property business profit/(loss)	(4,600)	18,700
Chargeable gain/(allowable loss)	(8,900)	18,200
Donation to charity (gross)	(2,300)	(2,600)

(a) **Calculate Eagle Ltd's tax-adjusted trading loss for the year ended 31 March 2009.**

You should assume that the company claims the maximum available capital allowances.

(b) **Assuming that Eagle Ltd claims relief for its trading loss under s393A ICTA 1988 against total profits, calculate the company's PCTCT for the three accounting periods ended 31 March 2009.**

Your answer should show the amount of unrelieved trading losses as at 31 March 2009.

(c) **Describe the alternative ways in which Eagle Ltd could have relieved the trading loss for the year ended 31 March 2009.**

8 Chapter summary

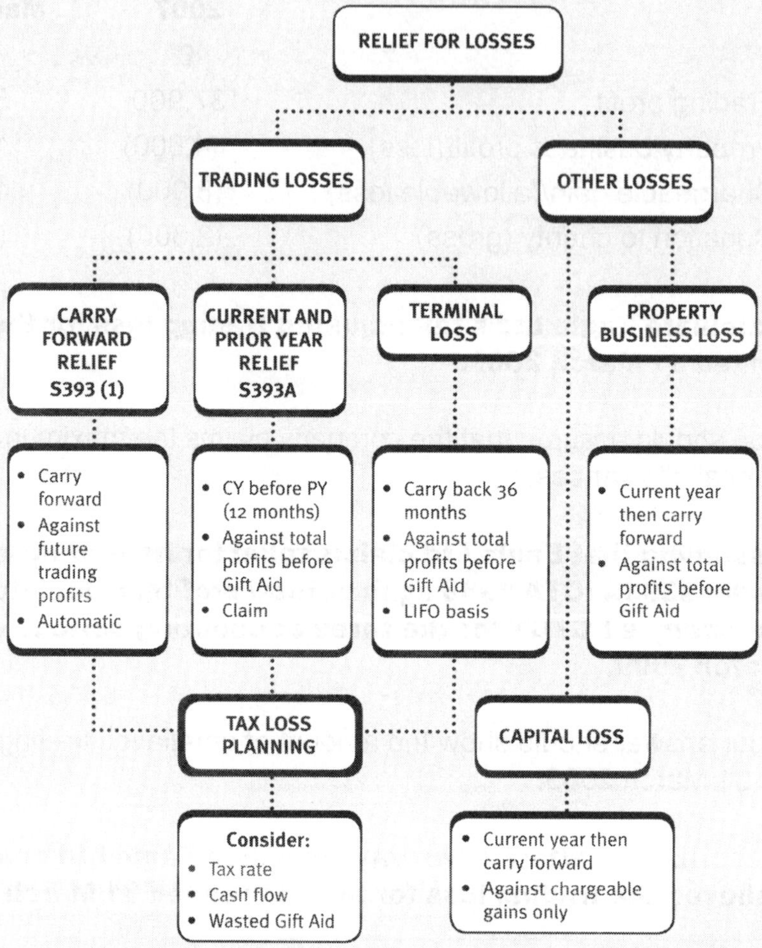

Test your understanding answers

Test your understanding 1

Alfred Ball Ltd – PCTCT computations

Year ended:	**31.12.06**	**31.12.07**	**31.12.08**
	£	£	£
Trading income	42,000	19,000	Nil
Interest income	3,000	2,000	1,000
Chargeable gains	4,000	4,000	4,000
Total profits	49,000	25,000	5,000
s393A current year relief			(5,000)
s393A carry back relief		(25,000)	
	49,000	–	–
Gift Aid (Note 1)	(10,000)	Wasted	Wasted
PCTCT	39,000	Nil	Nil

Loss memorandum

	£
Year ended 31 December 2008	(67,000)
Current year off-set – y/e 31.12.08	5,000
Carry back – 12 months to y/e 31.12.07	25,000
Loss unrelieved at 31 December 2008	(37,000)

Notes

(1) The Gift Aid of £10,000 paid in the year ended 31 December 2007 is wasted. Note that the amount of the loss off-set cannot be restricted to leave sufficient profits to be covered by the Gift Aid.

(2) The unrelieved loss of £37,000 as at 31 December 2008 is automatically carried forward for off-set against the first available future trading profits of the same trade.

Test your understanding 2

Mint Ltd – PCTCT computations

Year ended:	**31.3.07**	**31.3.08**	**31.3.09**
	£	£	£
Trading income	15,000	Nil	40,000
s393(1) carry forward relief			(30,000)
			10,000
Interest income	5,000	10,000	10,000
Chargeable gain	–	40,000	–
Total profits	20,000	50,000	20,000
s393A – current year		(50,000)	
s393A – carry back	(20,000)		
PCTCT	Nil	Nil	20,000

Loss memorandum

	£
Year ended 31 March 2008	(100,000)
Current year – y/e 31.3.08	50,000
	(50,000)
Carry back 12 months – y/e 31.3.07	20,000
Carried forward	(30,000)
Used – y/e 31.3.09	30,000
	Nil

Test your understanding 3

Catalyst Ltd - PCTCT computations

	12 m/e 31.3.06	9 m/e 31.12.06	12 m/e 31.12.07	12 m/e 31.12.08
	£	£	£	£
Trading income	33,000	16,500	Nil	25,000
Less: CA's	(5,400)	(4,050)	Nil	(5,000)
Trading profit	27,600	12,450	Nil	20,000
s393(1) relief				(20,000)
				Nil
Interest income	1,200	1,300	1,400	1,600
Chargeable gain (**W1**)		Nil		6,000
Total profits	28,800	13,750	1,400	7,600
s393A CY claim			(1,400)	
s393A PY claim	(7,200)	(13,750)		
	21,600	Nil	Nil	7,600
Less Gift Aid	Nil	(3,000) lost	(3,000) lost	(8,000) partly lost
PCTCT	21,600	Nil	Nil	Nil

Note: Unrelieved trading loss available to carry forward at 31 December 2008 is £39,200 (W2).

Workings

(W1) Chargeable gain/capital loss

	£
AP to 31.12.06 (Loss)	(6,000)
AP to 31.12.08 Gain	12,000
Net gain – CAP to 31.12.08	6,000

Note that the capital loss can only be off-set against future chargeable gains.

(W2) Tax-adjusted trading loss available and its utilisation

	£
Adjusted trading loss (given)	75,000
Add: capital allowances (given)	6,550
Tax adjusted trading loss available	81,550
Utilisation: Same period – y/e 31.12.07	(1,400)
	80,150
Carried back 9 months (AP to 31.12.06)	(13,750)
	66,400
Three months only (in AP to 31.3.06) Maximum: 3/12 × £28,800	(7,200)
Available to carry forward	59,200
First available future tax-adjusted trading profit (AP to 31.12.08)	(20,000)
Loss carried forward at 31.12.08	39,200

Test your understanding 4

Brown Ltd – PCTCT computations

	12 m/e 31.3.05	12 m/e 31.3.06	12 m/e 31.3.07	9 m/e 31.12.07	12 m/e 31.12.08
	£	£	£	£	£
Trading income	450,000	87,000	240,000	45,000	Nil
Interest income	9,000	3,000	6,000	1,500	1,500
Chargeable gain	7,500	–	–	–	–
Total profits	466,500	90,000	246,000	46,500	1,500
s393A-CY claim					(1,500)
s393A-Terminal loss relief	(116,625)	(90,000)	(246,000)	(46,500)	
	349,875	Nil	Nil	Nil	Nil
Less Gift Aid	(30,000)	(30,000) lost	(30,000) lost	(30,000) lost	(30,000) lost
PCTCT	319,875	Nil	Nil	Nil	Nil

Loss memorandum

	£
Tax-adjusted trading loss of final 12 months of trading	525,000
Utilisation: Same period – y/e 31.12.08	(1,500)
	523,500
Carried back:	
9 months to 31.12.07	(46,500)
12 months to 31.3.07	(246,000)
12 months to 31.3.06	(90,000)
3 months only for y/e 31.3.05 (3/12 × £466,500)	(116,625)
Balance of loss – unrelieved = lost	24,375

Test your understanding 5

Confused Ltd – PCTCT computations

Note: Remember, where there are two losses, deal with the earliest loss first.

	12 m/e 30.6.06	**9 m/e 31.3.07**	**12 m/e 31.3.08**	**12 m/e 31.3.09**
	£	£	£	£
Trading income	108,240	Nil	41,520	Nil
s393(1) – c/f			(2,500)	
Property income	Nil	5,400	9,720	6,720
Total profits	108,240	5,400	48,740	6,720
s393A relief				
– current period (**W**)		(5,400)		(6,720)
– carry back (**W**)	(108,240)		(48,740)	
	Nil	Nil	Nil	Nil
Less Gift Aid	(1,680) lost	(960) lost	(1,440) lost	(1,320) lost
PCTCT	Nil	Nil	Nil	Nil

Unrelieved trading loss as at 31.3.09 is £38,500 (**W**).

Working: Trading losses available and their utilisation

	£
Loss of AP to 31.3.07	116,140
Utilisation: Current year	(5,400)
	110,740
Carried back: 12 months (AP to 30.6.06)	(108,240)
Balance available to c/f	2,500
Trading income – AP to 31.3.08	(2,500)
	Nil

Loss of AP to 31.3.09	93,960
Utilisation: Current year	(6,720)
	87,240
Carried back: 12 months (AP to 31.3.08)	(48,740)
Balance available to c/f	38,500

Test your understanding 6

Comfy Ltd – PCTCT computations

Year ended 31 December:	**2006**	**2007**	**2008**
	£	£	£
Trading income	12,450	Nil	4,000
s393(1) relief			(4,000)
			Nil
Property income	2,000	1,800	–
Interest income	1,000	600	1,000
Total profits	15,450	2,400	1,000
Current year reliefs			
– Property business loss (**W2**)			(500)
– Trading loss (**W1**)		(2,400)	
Carry back relief – s393A	(15,450)		
	Nil	Nil	500
Gift Aid	Wasted	Wasted	(400)
PCTCT	Nil	Nil	100

Workings

(W1) Trading loss

	£
Trading loss – y/e 31.12.07	(34,500)
Current year relief – y/e 31.12.07	2,400
Carry back relief – 31.12.06	15,450
	(16,650)
Carry forward relief – y/e 31.12.08	4,000
Carry forward at 31 December 2008	(12,650)

(W2) Property business loss

	£
The loss in year ended 31 December 2008 will be relieved against total profits in that period	(500)
Year ended 31 December 2008	500
	Nil

Test your understanding 7

Coriander Ltd – PCTCT computations

Year ended:	**31.12.06**	**31.12.07**	**31.12.08**
	£	£	£
Trading income	37,450	Nil	20,000
s393(1) relief			(20,000)
			Nil
Interest income	1,300	1,400	1,600
Chargeable gains			
(£12,000 – £6,000 b/f)	Nil	Nil	6,000
Total profits	38,750	1,400	7,600
Current year relief		(1,400)	
Carry back relief	(38,750)	Nil	Nil
	Nil	Nil	7,600
Gift Aid	Wasted	Wasted	(3,000)
PCTCT	Nil	Nil	4,600
Gift Aid = unrelieved	3,000	3,000	

Loss memorandum

Year ended 31 December 2007	£
Trading loss	(81,550)
1. Used – current period	1,400
2. Carry back – year ended 31 December 2006	38,750
	(41,400)
3. Carry forward against trading profit – year ended 31 December 2008	20,000
At 31 December 2008 to carry forward	(21,400)

Test your understanding 8

Eagle Ltd

(a) **Tax-adjusted trading loss for the year ended 31 March 2009**

	£
Trading loss before capital allowances	(254,400)
Capital allowances	
– IBA (**W1**)	(5,700)
– P & M (**W2**)	(39,900)
Trading loss	(300,000)

The patent royalties are an allowable deduction against trading profits on an accruals basis, as they are paid for trade purposes. No adjustment is required to the trading loss figure as the amount has already been reflected in the trading loss given in the question.

Workings

(W1) Industrial buildings allowance

	£
Site preparation	12,000
Architect's fees	5,000
Canteen	32,000
Factory	141,000
Eligible expenditure	190,000
Industrial buildings allowance at (3%)	5,700

Notes:

(1) The cost of the land does not qualify.

(2) The general offices do not qualify as they cost more than 25% of the total qualifying cost (£350,000 – £87,500 = £262,500 × 25% = £65,625).

In practice some of the other costs may be treated as relating to the general offices and would therefore not qualify. This approach would be awarded equivalent marks.

(W2) Plant and machinery capital allowances computation

		General pool	Expensive car	Total CAs
	£	£	£	£
Year ended 31 March 2009				
TWDV b/f		64,700	14,700	
Additions:				
No AIA:				
Cars		11,300		
Qualifying for AIA:				
Lorry	22,400			
Less: AIA	(22,400)			22,400
		Nil		
		76,000	14,700	
Disposal proceeds			(12,400)	
		76,000	2,300	
Balancing allowance			(2,300)	2,300
WDA (20% x £76,000)		(15,200)		15,200
TWDV c/f		60,800		
Total allowances				39,900

(b) **Corporation tax computations**

Period ended:	**30.9.07**	**31.3.08**	**31.3.09**
	£	£	£
Trading income	137,900	52,000	Nil
Property income (W1)	–	18,700	49,950
Chargeable gains (W2)	–	9,300	18,475
Total profits	137,900	80,000	68,425
Property loss (W2)	(4,600)	–	–
	133,300	80,000	68,425
s393A relief (W4)	(66,650)	(80,000)	(68,425)
	66,650	Nil	Nil
Gift Aid (Note)	(2,300)	Wasted	Wasted
PCTCT	64,350	Nil	Nil

Tutorial note

A property business loss is set off automatically against total profits of the same period and takes priority over s393A relief (for trading losses).

Workings:

(W1) The property business profit for the year ended 31 March 2009 is calculated as follows:

	£
Premium received	50,000
Less: £50,000 × 2% × (8 – 1)	(7,000)
	43,000
Rent receivable	9,450
– Warehouse (£8,400 × 9/12)	6,300
– Irrecoverable debt (£8,400 × 3/12)	(2,100)
	56,650
Repairs to roof	(6,700)
Property income	49,950

(W2) **Property loss**

The property business loss in the year to 30 September 2007 is set off against non-property business income of that period in priority to utilising the trading loss.

(W3) **Chargeable gains**

The capital loss of the year ended 30 September 2007 is carried forward and set against the chargeable gain in the following period as follows:

Chargeable gain in period ended 31 March 2008
(£18,200 – £8,900) = £9,300

The chargeable gain in year ended 31 March 2009 is calculated as follows:

	£
Sale proceeds	257,250
Less: Cost	(112,800)
Unindexed gain	144,450
Less: Indexation allowance	(125,975)
Chargeable gain	18,475

(W4) **Loss relief**

	£
Loss in y/e/ 31.3.09	(300,000)
Used in current year claim	68,425
Carry back = p/e 31.3.08	80,000
	151,575
Carry back - y/e/ 30.9.07 (restricted)	
Max (£133,300 x 6/12)	(66,650)
Loss available to c/f	84,925

Note: The Gift Aid paid in the period ended 31 March 2008 and the year ended 31 March 2009 are unrelieved.

(c) **Alternative ways to relieve loss**

The claim against total profits under s393A ICTA 1988 need not be made. The total loss can then be carried forward under s393(1) ICTA 1988 against future trading profits of the same trade.

The claim against total profits under s393A ICTA 1988 could be restricted to just the year ended 31 March 2009. The balance of the loss can be carried forward under s393(1) ICTA 1988.

hapter

22

Groups of companies

Chapter learning objectives

Upon completion of this chapter you will be able to:

- define an associated company
- identify associated companies from information provided
- determine the effect of associated companies for corporation tax
- define a 75% group for group loss relief
- identify the members of a 75% group relief group from information provided
- explain and apply the rules for allowing surrender of losses between 75% group relief companies
- identify the key factors in using group losses to minimise corporation tax liabilities for the group
- define a 75% group for capital gains purposes
- identify a capital gains group from information provided
- explain and apply the reliefs available on capital transactions in a 75% capital gains group to minimise corporation tax liabilities.

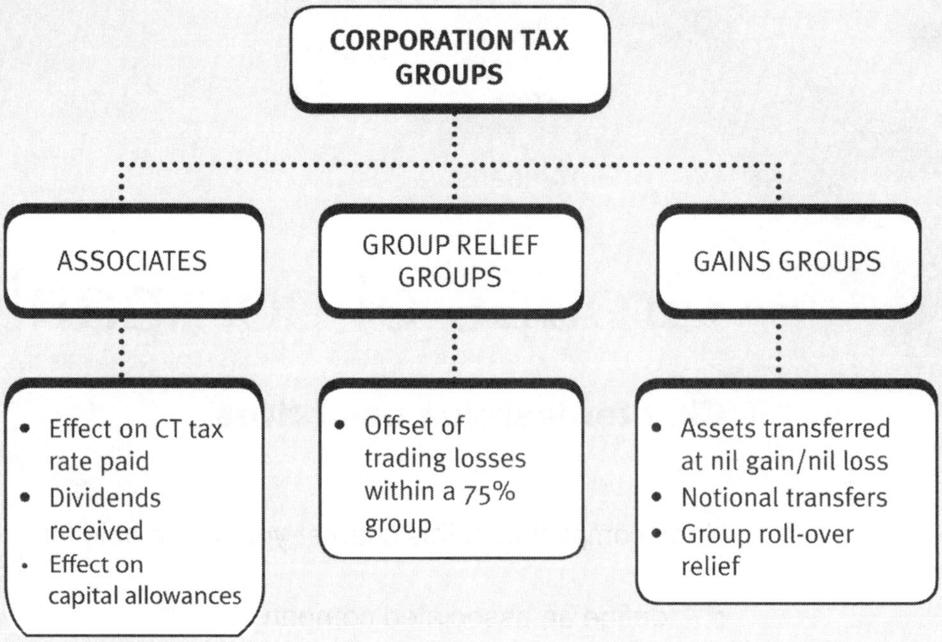

1 Introduction

This chapter deals with the tax position of groups of companies, i.e. where a company owns shares in another company.

For corporation tax purposes, each company within the group is treated as a separate entity and is required to submit its own tax return, based on its individual results.

Being a member of a group however, has other corporation tax implications and these vary, depending on the actual relationship of the group members.

This chapter sets out the corporation tax implications of:

- associated companies
- groups for group relief purposes
- capital gains groups.

2 Associated companies

Definition

For corporation tax purposes, two companies are 'associated' with each other if either:

- one of the companies is under the 'control' of the other; or
- they are both under the 'control' of the same person or persons (which can be a company, an individual or a partnership).

'Control' broadly means ownership of more than 50% of the company's issued ordinary share capital.

Expandable text - Control

For tax purposes 'control' means:

- ownership of over 50% of issued share capital, or
- holding over 50% of the voting rights, or
- entitlement to over 50% of the company's income, if all the income were to be distributed, or
- entitlement to over 50% of the company's assets, if the company were to wind up.

Points to note:

- Companies which are associated for only part of an accounting period are deemed to be associated for the whole of the accounting period.
- Both UK resident and overseas resident companies are included.
- Dormant companies are excluded.

Example 1 - Associated companies

A Ltd is the holding company for a group of four companies. The relationships between the companies in the group, are shown in the diagram below:

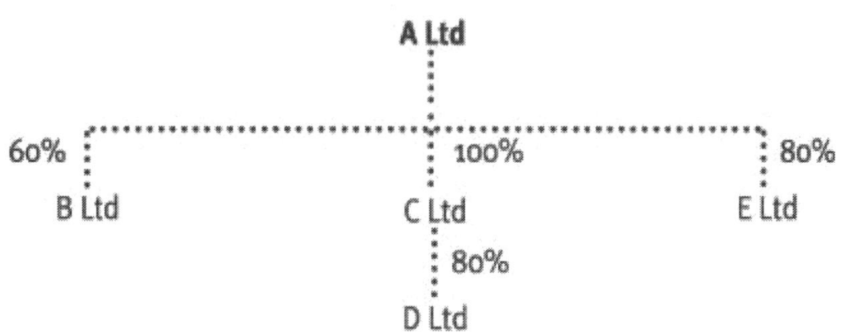

All of the companies are UK resident except for E Ltd, which is resident outside the UK and all its trading activities are conducted outside the UK.

B Ltd is a dormant company.

D Ltd was bought by C Ltd on 1 July 2008.

All of the companies have 31 December year ends.

State how many companies are associated for tax purposes in the year to 31 December 2008?

Answer to example 1

A Ltd is associated with:

- C Ltd (owns more than 50%).
- D Ltd (bought by C Ltd during the year, but associated for the whole year).
- E Ltd (even though it is resident overseas).

A Ltd is not associated with B Ltd, as it is dormant.

Therefore, there are four associated companies in the year to 31 December 2008.

Test your understanding 1

The relationship between the members of the W Ltd group are as follows:

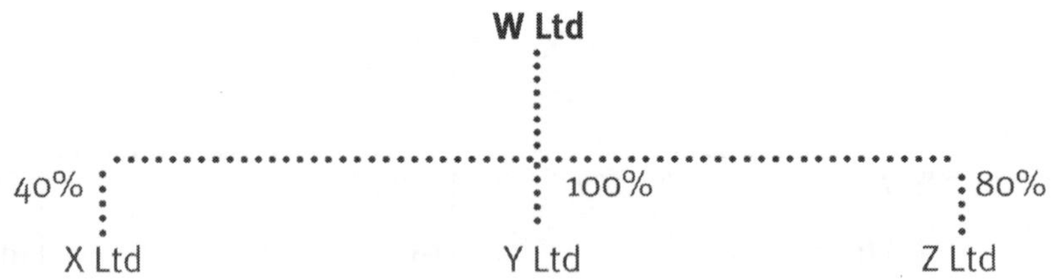

All of the companies are UK resident except for Y Ltd, which is resident outside the UK and all its trading activities are conducted outside the UK.

Z Ltd is a dormant company.

X Ltd was bought on 1 December 2008.

All of the companies have 31 December year ends.

State how many companies are associated for tax purposes, in the year 31 December 2008?

Implications of being associated

The tax implications of being associated are:

- The upper and lower limits, used to determine the rate of corporation tax, are divided by the number of associated companies.
- Intra-group dividends are not treated as franked investment income, for the purposes of calculating the company's 'profits'.
- only one annual investment allowance (maximum £50,000 p.a.) is available for the group.

Tax rate

The identification of the number of associated companies, is the starting point for every 'group question', as this establishes:

- the applicable lower and upper limit for each company, and therefore
- the rate of corporation tax applicable to each company.

Example 2 - Associated companies

A Ltd, shown in Illustration 1, has tax-adjusted trading profits for the year ended 31 December 2008 of £750,000. A Ltd had no dividend income during the year.

Calculate the corporation tax payable by A Ltd, for the year ended 31 December 2008.

Answer to example 2

A Ltd controls more than 50% of C Ltd, D Ltd and E Ltd – therefore (including A Ltd), we have four associated companies under common control.

Therefore, the corporation tax rate limits are as follows:

Upper limit: £1,500,000/4 = £375,000.
Lower Limit: £300,000/4 = £75,000.

A Ltd's profits exceed the revised upper limit and therefore, it will pay corporation tax at the full rate of 30% in FY 2007 (3 months) and 28% in FY 2008 (9 months).

Corporation tax payable

	£
FY 2007 £750,000 x 30% x 3/12	56,250
FY 2008 £750,000 x 28% x 9/12	157,500
	213,750

Test your understanding 2

Cob Ltd prepares accounts for the year ended 31 March 2009. On 1 April 2008, the company acquired 60% of the shares of a company, that is resident overseas. On 1 July 2008, it acquired 75% of the shares of a company, that is resident in the UK.

Cob Ltd has profits chargeable to corporation tax of £140,000, for the year ended 31 March 2009, and also received franked investment income of £10,000, during the year.

Calculate Cob Ltd's corporation tax liability, for the year ended 31 March 2009.

Dividends

- Dividends received by UK companies from other UK companies are not taxable.
- Normally they are grossed up by 100/90 and included as franked investment income (FII), when calculating the company's 'profits'. The company's 'profits' then determine the rate of corporation tax payable.
- Dividends received from associated companies however, do not form part of FII.

Example 3 - Associated companies

Holly Ltd is the parent company of two wholly owned subsidiaries, Berry Ltd and Sprig Ltd.

Holly Ltd recorded the following income for the year ended 31 December 2008:

	£
Trading profit	300,000
Interest income	50,000
Dividends received from Berry Ltd	60,000
Dividends received from Sprig Ltd	34,000
Dividends received from other UK companies	45,000

Calculate the corporation tax payable by Holly Ltd, for the year ended 31 December 2008.

Answer to example 3

Corporation tax computation – y/e 31 December 2008

	£	£
Trading income		300,000
Interest income		50,000
PCTCT		350,000
FY 2007		
(£350,000 x 30% x 3/12)	26,250	
Less: Marginal relief		
1/40 x (£500,000 – £400,000) x £350,000/£400,000 x 3/12	(547)	
		25,703
FY 2008		
(£350,000 x 28% x 9/12)	73,500	
Less: Marginal relief		
7/400 x (£500,000 – £400,000) x £350,000/£400,000 x 9/12	(1,148)	
		72,352
Corporation tax liability		98,055

Note

- Only dividends received from non-associated companies, are included as FII.
- Dividends received from UK companies are not taxable on Holly Ltd.

Workings: Rate of tax

Holly Ltd has 2 associates and therefore, the limits for determining the corporation tax rate must be divided by 3, as follows:

Upper limit: £1,500,000/3 = £500,000
Lower limit: £300,000/3 = £100,000

	£
PCTCT	350,000
FII (£45,000 × 100/90) (Note)	50,000
'Profits'	400,000

Therefore, Holly Ltd is a marginal relief company.

Note that the year ended 31 December 2008 falls into FY 2008 (9 months) and into FY 2007 (3 months).

Therefore a separte calculation for each financial year is required.

Test your understanding 3

Bill Ltd is the parent company of one wholly owned subsidiary, Ben Ltd.

Bill Ltd recorded the following income for the year ended 31 August 2008:

	£
Trading profit	380,000
Interest income	25,000
Dividends from Ben Ltd	60,000
Dividends from other UK companies	76,500

Calculate the corporation tax payable by Bill Ltd, for the year ended 31 August 2008.

Expandable Text - The annual investment allowance

For capital allowance purposes, only one AIA is available to a group of companies.

Note that:

- A 'group' for this purpose is defined by the Companies Act 2006 and essentially applies where a parent company holds a simple majority shareholding (> 50%) in another company or companies at the end of the accounting period.
- Therefore if there are associated companies, the allocation of the AIA between the group members will need to be considered.

When allocating the AIA:

- the group members can allocate the maximum £50,000 AIA in any way across the group
- the AIA does not have to be divided equally between them
- all of the allowance can be given to one company, or any amount can be given to any number of companies within the group.

3 Group relief group

Group loss relief is available to members of a 75% group relief group.

Losses of one member of the group can be surrendered to other group companies, which may then relieve the losses against their own profits chargeable to corporation tax.

Definition of a 75% group relief group

- Two companies are members of a 75% group relief group where:
  - one company is the 75% subsidiary of the other, or
  - both companies are 75% subsidiaries of a third company.
- One company is a 75% subsidiary of another if:
  - at least 75% of its ordinary share capital is owned directly or indirectly by the other company, and
  - it has the right to 75% or more of distributable profits, and
  - it has the right to 75% or more of net assets on a winding up.
- For sub-subsidiaries to be in a group, the holding company must have an effective interest in the sub-subsidiary of at least 75%.
- Groups can be created through companies resident anywhere in the world.
- For the purposes of the examination the companies claiming/ surrendering group relief must, however, be resident in the UK.

Example 4 - 75% group relief group

The following information relates to the Holding Ltd group:

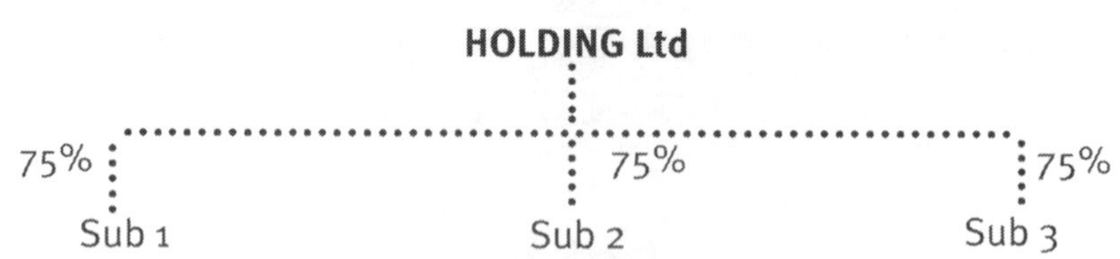

State which companies form a group for group relief purposes.

Answer to example 4

Holding Ltd has a 75% direct holding in Sub 1, Sub 2 and Sub 3 and therefore, all four companies are part of a 75% group for group relief purposes.

Example 5 - 75% group relief group

Beef Ltd owns 75% of Lamb Ltd. Lamb Ltd owns 75% of Bacon Ltd.

State which companies form a group for group relief purposes.

Answer to example 5

Beef Ltd and all its direct and indirect 75% holdings:

- Lamb Ltd (directly owns 75%)

Bacon Ltd does not belong to the same group relief group as Beef Ltd, as Beef Ltd only indirectly owns (75% × 75%) = 56.25%.

As Lamb Ltd directly owns 75% of Bacon Ltd, they will form a separate group relief group.

Therefore, there will be two group relief groups:

- Beef Ltd and Lamb Ltd.
- Lamb Ltd and Bacon Ltd.

Test your understanding 4

Toast Ltd owns:

- 75% of Honey Ltd.
- 100% of Marmalade Ltd.
- 65% of Jam Ltd.

Honey Ltd owns 75% of Butter Ltd.
Marmalade Ltd owns 75% of Bread Ltd.

State which companies form a group for group relief purposes.

Implications of being in a group relief group

Where a group of companies form a group relief group, losses may be surrendered to other companies in the group, which can then relieve the losses against their own profits chargeable to corporation tax.

A loss may be surrendered by any member company to any other member of the same group, provided they are UK resident.

Example 6 - 75% group relief group

HOLLAND Ltd
(RESIDENT OUTSIDE UK)

75% BIRMINGHAM Ltd

75% SHEFFIELD Ltd

Birmingham Ltd and Sheffield Ltd are both UK resident companies.

State which companies form a group for group relief purposes and between which companies losses can be transferred.

Birmingham Ltd and Sheffield Ltd are within a 75% group, as both companies are 75% subsidiaries of Holland Ltd. Remember, that non-UK resident companies can be used to establish a group relief group.

Birmingham Ltd and Sheffield Ltd can therefore transfer losses between each other, (i.e. Birmingham Ltd to Sheffield Ltd or vice versa).

Losses cannot be transferred to or from Holland Ltd, as the company is resident outside of the UK.

Test your understanding 5

GROUP 1

HOLDING Ltd
90%
Sub 1 Ltd
90%
Sub 2 Ltd

GROUP 2

HOLDING Ltd
80%
Sub 1 Ltd
80%
Sub 2 Ltd

From the above structures, identify which companies form a group for group relief purposes and between which companies can losses be transferred?

Mechanics of group relief

- Companies which form part of the same group relief group can transfer losses between each other.
- The surrendering company is the company that surrenders its loss.
- The claimant company is the company to which the loss is surrendered.

- The losses which may be surrendered are:
  - trading losses
  - unrelieved Gift Aid
  - unrelieved property business losses.
- Only current period losses are available for group relief.
- Capital losses cannot be surrendered to group companies.

The surrendering company

- The surrendering company may surrender any amount of its current period losses.
- There is no requirement for the surrendering company to relieve the loss against its own profits first.

The claimant company

- Offsets the loss against PCTCT of its corresponding accounting period.
- The surrendering company may surrender any amount of its eligible loss. However, the maximum loss which can be claimed by the claimant company, is the company's profits (after Gift Aid), assuming that current year losses and losses brought forward of the claimant company, are offset first.
- The maximum loss which can be claimed is:

	£
Total profits	X
Less: Gift Aid	(X)
PCTCT	X
Less: Current year losses	(X)
Less: Brought forward losses	(X)
Maximum loss relief	X

Test your understanding 6

Red Ltd has trading losses for the year to 31 December 2008, of £65,000. It has brought forward trading losses of £12,000.

Red Ltd owns 85% of Pink Ltd.

Pink Ltd has tax-adjusted trading profits of £85,000, for the year to 31 December 2008. It has brought forward trading losses of £35,000 and brought forward capital losses of £5,000.

Show the maximum amount of group relief available in the year to 31 December 2008 and state the amount of any unrelieved losses.

Corresponding accounting periods

Losses surrendered by group relief, must be set against the claimant company's profits of a 'corresponding' accounting period as follows:

- A corresponding accounting period is any accounting period falling wholly or partly within the surrendering company's accounting period.
- Where the companies do not have coterminous (same) year ends, the available profits and losses must be time apportioned, to find the relevant amounts falling within the corresponding accounting period.
- In this situation, the maximum 'loss' that can be surrendered is the lower of:

	£
(a) 'loss' in the surrendering (loss making) company for the corresponding accounting period, and	X
(b) 'PCTCT' in the claimant company for the corresponding accounting period	X

Example 7 - 75% group relief group

Sugar Ltd incurs a trading loss of £27,000, in its nine months accounting period to 31 March 2009.

The total 'profits' of Cup Ltd are £24,000 and £38,000 for the 12 months accounting periods to 30 September 2008 and 2009 respectively.

State the maximum amount of group relief which Cup Ltd can claim from Sugar Ltd, for the two accounting periods to 30 September 2009.

Answer to example 7

As the companies have non-coterminous year ends, firstly identify the corresponding accounting periods:

- 9 m/e 31.3.09 and y/e 30.9.08:

  The corresponding accounting period is 1 July 2008 to 30 September 2008 (i.e. three months).

- 9 m/e 31.3.09 and y/e 30.9.09:

  The corresponding accounting period is 1 October 2008 to 31 March 2009 (i.e. six months).

Cup Ltd can therefore claim the following group relief:

AP to 30.9.08

			£
Sugar Ltd	can surrender	3/9 × £27,000 loss	9,000
Cup Ltd	can claim	3/12 × £24,000	6,000

Therefore maximum loss claim is £6,000

AP to 30.9.09

Sugar Ltd	can surrender	6/9 × £27,000 loss	18,000
Cup Ltd	can claim	6/12 × £38,000	19,000

Therefore maximum loss claim is £18,000.

Test your understanding 7

White Ltd and Black Ltd are in a group relief group had the following recent results:

	£
White Ltd – trading loss for the year to 30 June 2009	(24,000)
Black Ltd – taxable profits:	
For the year ended 30 September 2008	36,000
For the year ended 30 September 2009	20,000

Explain the amount of group relief Black Ltd can claim from White Ltd, in respect of the two accounting periods, ended September 2009.

Tax loss planning

The following points should be considered, when deciding how to offset a trading loss which arises within a 75% group relief group company:

- Whether the loss should be surrendered.
- Order of surrender.

Choosing whether to surrender

A group member suffering a loss, has the choice to make a claim against its own profits, or to surrender the loss to another group member.

Consideration should be given to:

- the rate of tax saved
- the cash flow position (a claim to carryback the loss under s393A ICTA 1988, could lead to a repayment of tax).

Order of surrender

Losses should be surrendered in the following order, in order to save the maximum amount of tax:

(1) To companies that are subject to a marginal tax rate of 29.75% in FY 2008 or 32.5% in FY 2007 (see Chapter 21), to bring their profits down to the 'small company rate limit'

(2) To companies that are subject to the full tax rate of 28% in FY 2008 or 30% in FY 2007, to bring their profits down to the small company rate limit.

(3) To companies that are subject to tax at the small companies rate of 21% in FY 2008 or 20% in FY 2007.

Remember, that the upper and lower limits that determine the rate of tax, will be adjusted for the number of associated companies.

Example 8 - 75% group relief group

A Ltd has four wholly owned subsidaries, B Ltd, C Ltd, D Ltd and E Ltd.

The group companies had the following results for the year ended 31 March 2009.

	Profit/ (loss)
	£
A Ltd	(100,000)
B Ltd	20,000
C Ltd	83,000
D Ltd	96,000
E Ltd	375,000

None of the companies received any dividends in the year.

Calculate the corporation tax payable by each of the companies:

(a) **if no election for group relief is made**

(b) **if an election for group relief is made, on the assumption that the loss is allocated in such a manner as to save the maximum amount of tax.**

Answer to example 8

(a) **If no group relief**

Calculate the upper and lower limits for corporation tax rate purposes and calculate the tax payable by each company, assuming no election for group relief is made.

Upper limit	£1,500,000/5 = £300,000
Lower limit	£300,000/5 = £60,000

Corporation tax liability without group relief:

	A Ltd	B Ltd	C Ltd	D Ltd	E Ltd
	£	£	£	£	£
PCTCT	Nil	20,000	83,000	96,000	375,000
Corporation tax					
@21%		4,200			
@28%			23,240	26,880	105,000
Less: Marginal relief					
7/400 × (300,000 – 83,000)			(3,798)		
7/400 × (300,000 – 96,000)				(3,570)	
Corporation tax liability	Nil	4,200	19,442	23,310	105,000

(b) **With group relief**

Allocate the loss to other group companies. In order to save the maximum amount of tax, the loss of A Ltd, should be allocated as follows:

- The loss should be surrendered first to companies paying tax at the marginal rate of 29.75%, so as to bring their profits down to the lower limit, (i.e. to those companies with profits in the marginal rate relief band).
- The loss should then be surrendered to companies paying tax at 28%.
- Any remaining loss should be surrendered to companies paying tax at the small companies rate of 21%.

- Remember the upper and lower limit have been revised for the number of associated companies.

  Accordingly, the loss is first surrendered to C Ltd and D Ltd to bring their profits down to £60,000 (revised lower limit), the balance of the loss is surrendered to E Ltd.

	A Ltd	B Ltd	C Ltd	D Ltd	E Ltd
	£	£	£	£	£
PCTCT	Nil	20,000	83,000	96,000	375,000
Less: Group relief			(23,000)	(36,000)	(41,000)
PCTCT after group relief	Nil	20,000	60,000	60,000	334,000
Corporation tax					
@21%		4,200	12,600	12,600	
@28%					93,520
Corporation tax liability	Nil	4,200	12,600	12,600	93,520

Test your understanding 8

A Ltd is the holding company for a group of four companies. The relationships between the companies in the group, are shown in the diagram below:

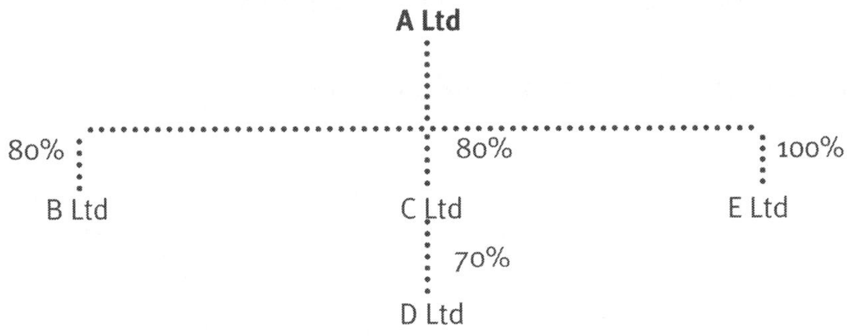

All of the companies are UK resident except for E Ltd, which is resident outside the UK and all its trading activities are conducted outside the UK.

All of the companies have an accounting year ended 31 March 2009 and their income/(losses) for this year, were as follows:

	Tax adjusted trading profit/(loss)	Bank interest (non-trade)
	£	£
A Ltd	100,000	–
B Ltd	110,000	15,000
C Ltd	(110,000)	12,000
D Ltd	(25,000)	–
E Ltd	15,000	–

On the assumption that the most efficient use is made by the group of any trading losses, compute the corporation tax payable by each UK resident company.

4 75% capital gains group

Special capital gains advantages are available to members of a capital gains group. They enable:

- assets to be transferred tax efficiently around the group
- the efficient use of capital losses within the group
- the advantages of roll-over relief to be maximised.

Definition of a 75% capital gains group

- A capital gains group comprises of the parent company and its 75% (direct or indirect) subsidiaries and also, the 75% subsidiaries of the first subsidiaries and so on.
- The parent company must have an effective interest of over 50%, in ALL companies.
- A company which is a 75% subsidiary, cannot itself be a 'parent company' and form a separate gains group.
- While applying the 75% test, the shares held by overseas companies, i.e. non-UK resident, can be taken into account. Non-UK resident companies, however, cannot take advantage of the special reliefs due to UK resident members.
- The 75% requirement only applies to the ordinary share capital.

It is important to note that the definition of a gains group, is different from that for a group relief group. It is essential to learn the different definitions.

Test your understanding 9

The A Ltd group consists of the following companies:

A Ltd
(PARENT COMPANY)

75%

B Ltd

75%

C Ltd

75%

D Ltd

(a) **State which companies form a capital gains group.**

(b) **State which companies form a group relief group,**

Implications of being in a 75% capital gains group

The reliefs that are available to members of a 75% capital gains group, are as follows:

(1) Assets are transferred at nil gain/nil loss.

(2) Assets can be 'notionally' transferred around the group, to take advantage of capital losses and lower tax rates.

(3) Roll-over relief is available on a group basis.

Transfer of assets within a group

- Assets transferred within a gains group, are automatically transferred at neither a gain nor a loss, i.e. without a chargeable gain or allowable loss arising.
- The transfer takes place, at a price that does not give rise to a gain or a loss to the transferor company, i.e. at original cost plus indexation allowance to the date of the transfer.
- The transferor's deemed proceeds figure, is also the deemed cost of the acquiring company.

- No claim is made – the treatment is automatic and mandatory.
- When the acquiring company sells the asset outside of the gains group, a chargeable gain/loss arises on the disposal in the normal way.

Example 9 - inter group transfer then sale outside group

Green Ltd acquired an asset on 1 April 1983, for £100,000. The asset was transferred to Jade Ltd, a wholly owned subsidiary, on1 October 1993, for £120,000, when the asset was worth £180,000.

On 1 December 2008, Jade Ltd sold the asset outside of the group for £350,000.

Calculate the chargeable gain, if any, arising on the transfer of the asset in October 1993 and the sale of the asset in December 2008.

Assume the RPIs as follows:

April 1983	84.28
October 1993	141.8
December 2008	215.7

Answer to example 9

Transfer of asset – October 1993

The transfer from Green Ltd to Jade Ltd, takes place at such a price that gives Green Ltd, no gain and no loss, i.e.

	£
Cost	100,000
Indexation allowance: April 1983 to October 1993:	
(141.8 – 84.28)/84.28 = 0.682 × £100,000	68,200
Deemed proceeds	168,200

Sale of asset – December 2008

When Jade Ltd sells the asset outside the group, its cost is deemed to be £168,200:

	£
Proceeds	350,000
Less: Deemed cost	(168,200)
Unindexed gain	181,800
Less: IA (Oct 1993 to Dec 2008):	
(215.7 – 141.8)/141.8 = 0.521 × £168,200	(87,632)
Chargeable gain	94,168

The gain is chargeable on Jade Ltd, the company which is selling the asset.

Example 10 – Inter group transfer and sale outside group

Orange Ltd acquired an asset on 1 June 1985, for £80,000. The asset was transferred to Amber Ltd, a wholly owned subsidiary, on 1 September 1991, for £115,000, when the asset was worth £160,000.

On 1 December 2008, Amber Ltd sold the asset outside the group for £385,000.

Calculate the chargeable gain, if any, arising on the transfer of the asset on 1 September 1991 and on its sale on 1 December 2008.

Assume the following RPIs:

June 1985	95.41
September 1991	134.6
December 2008	215.7

Answer to example 10

Transfer of asset – September 1991

The transfer from Orange Ltd to Amber Ltd, takes place at such a price as gives Orange Ltd no gain and no loss, i.e.

	£
Cost	80,000
Indexation allowance: June 1985 to September 1991:	
(134.6 – 95.41)/95.41 = 0.411 x £80,000	32,880
Deemed proceeds	112,880

Sale of asset – December 2008

When Amber Ltd sells the asset outside the group, its cost is deemed to be £112,880:

	£
Proceeds	385,000
Less: Deemed cost	(112,880)
Less: Indexation allowance	
September 1991 to December 2008	
(215.7 – 134.6)/134.6 = 0.603 x £112,880	(68,067)
Indexed gain	204,053

Notional transfer of assets

As we have seen, assets can be transferred around a capital gains group with no tax cost, i.e. assets are transferred at nil loss/nil gain.

A group may wish to transfer assets around the group, so that a capital gain/loss on the disposal of an asset outside of the group, is realised in a particular company.

This is useful for the following reasons:

- Capital losses realised by one company, cannot be transferred to another company. Transferring an asset before it is sold outside of the group at a gain, to a company with capital losses, will enable the capital losses to be utilised.
- Assets which are about to be sold outside of the group at a gain, can be transferred to the group member, which will pay the lowest rate of tax on the gain.

Notional transfer election

Members of capital gains groups can, rather than **actually** transferring assets about the group, elect that assets are **treated as if** they had been transferred between different group members, i.e. that there has been a notional transfer of assets.

The election must:

- be made within 2 years of the end of the accounting period, in which the asset is disposed of outside of the group
- specify which company in the group is to be treated for tax purposes, as having disposed of the asset.

Benefits of the notional transfer election

- As no actual transfer of assets is taking place within the gains group, there will be savings in legal and administrative costs.
- The two-year time limit for making the election, means that tax planning can be undertaken retrospectively.
- An election can apply to a specified portion of a disposal, i.e. effectively, only part of a gain or loss needs to be transferred. This gives increased flexibility with tax planning.

Test your understanding 10

In the accounting period to 31 March 2009, Alpha Ltd disposed of a chargeable asset which will result in a chargeable gain of £90,000.

Alpha Ltd also has a 80% subsidiary, Beta Ltd.

In the accounting period to 31 March 2009, Beta Ltd disposed of a chargeable asset, which resulted in a capital loss of £65,000.

Alpha Ltd and Beta Ltd are both UK resident companies.

Show how the tax liabilities of the Alpha Ltd group may be minimised.

Example 11 - 75% capital gains group

Red Ltd has brought forward capital losses of £60,000.

Its 100% subsidiary Blue Ltd, disposed of an asset on 15 June 2008, that resulted in a chargeable gain of £55,000.

Both companies prepare accounts to 31 March.

Explain how Red Ltd and Blue Ltd can make an election, so that Red Ltd is treated as making the disposal.

Answer to example 11

Although Blue Ltd has actually made the disposal outside of the group, the two companies can make an election so that Red Ltd, is treated for tax purposes, as making the disposal.

The election must be made by 31 March 2011 (i.e. two years after the year ended 31 March 2009). There is no need for the asset to actually be transferred from Blue Ltd to Red Ltd.

Red Ltd can then set-off its capital losses brought forward against the chargeable gain arising on the disposal outside of the group.

Note that capital losses brought forward can not be transferred around the group.

Group roll-over relief

Roll-over relief was covered in detail in Chapters 17 and 20.

- Companies within a 75% gains group, are treated as if they form a single trade, for the purposes of roll-over relief.
- Roll-over relief can therefore be claimed, where one company within a gains group, disposes of an eligible asset and makes a gain and another company within the same gains group, acquires a replacement eligible asset.

Example 12 - 75% capital gains group

Cheese Ltd sold a factory for £600,000, in the year ended 31 December 2008. The original cost of the factory was £200,000 and indexation to the date of sale was £65,000.

Cheese owns 75% of Ham Ltd.

Ham Ltd bought a warehouse costing £750,000, in the year ended 31 December 2009.

Calculate the chargeable gain arising on the sale of the factory, if all available reliefs are taken and state the base cost of the warehouse, in a future disposal.

Answer to example 12

Gain on sale of factory for Cheese Ltd

	£
Proceeds	600,000
Less: Cost	(200,000)
Unindexed gain	400,000
Less: Indexation allowance	(65,000)
Indexed gain	335,000
Less: Roll-over relief	(335,000)
Chargeable gain	Nil

Note: Full roll-over relief is available, as all proceeds were reinvested by a member of the gains group, within the required time limit.

Base cost of the warehouse for Ham Ltd

	£
Original cost	750,000
Less: Roll-over relief	(335,000)
Base cost	415,000

5 Chapter summary

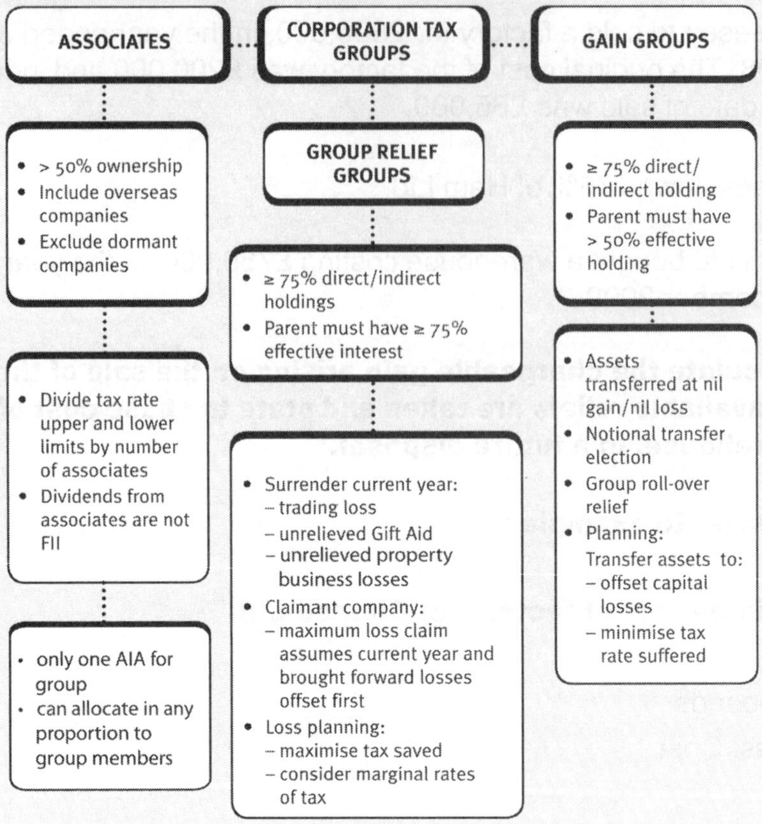

Test your understanding answers

Test your understanding 1

W Ltd

W Ltd is associated with Y Ltd only.

W Ltd is not associated with Z Ltd, as it is a dormant company, nor X Ltd, as it only owns 40% of the company's share capital.

Therefore, there are two associated companies.

Test your understanding 2

Cob Ltd

Cob Ltd is treated as having two associated companies, as it acquired more than 50% of the share capital of two companies, during the year.

The lower and upper corporation tax rate limits, must therefore, be divided by three (Cob Ltd plus two associates).

The lower limit is therefore £100,000 (£300,000/3) and the upper limit is £500,000 (£1,500,000/3).

Cob Ltd – year ended 31 March 2009	£
PCTCT	140,000
FII	10,000
Profits	150,000

The profits of £150,000 lie between £100,000 and £500,000, so marginal relief applies.

	£
Corporation tax liability (£140,000 × 28%)	39,200
Less: Marginal relief	
7/400 × (£500,000 – £150,000) × £140,000/£150,000	(5,717)
Corporation tax liability	33,483

Note: The revised upper limit is used in the marginal relief calculation.

Test your understanding 3

Bill Ltd

Corporation tax computation – y/e 31 August 2008

		£
Trading income		380,000
Interest income		25,000
PCTCT		405,000
	£	£
FY 2007		
(£405,000 x 30% x 7/12)	70,875	
Less: Marginal relief		
1/40 x (£750,000 – £490,000) x £405,000/ £490,000 x 7/12	(3,134)	
		67,741
FY 2008		
(£405,000 x 28% x 5/12)	47,250	
Less: Marginal relief		
7/400 x (£750,000 – £490,000) x £405,000/ £490,000 x 5/12	(1,567)	
		45,683
Corporation tax liability		113,424

Working: Rate of tax

Bill Ltd has one associated company and therefore the limits for determining the corporation tax rate, must be divided by 2:

Upper limit: £1,500,000/2 = £750,000
Lower limit: £300,000/2 = £150,000

	£
PCTCT	405,000
FII (£76,500 × 100/90)	85,000
'Profits'	490,000

Therefore, Bill Ltd is a marginal relief company.

Note that the year ended 31 August 2008 falls into FY2008 (5 months) and into FY2007 (7 months). Therefore separate calculations for each financial year is required.

Test your understanding 4

Toast Ltd

Toast Ltd and all its direct 75% holdings:

- Honey Ltd.
- Marmalade Ltd.

Toast Ltd only own 65% of Jam Ltd, therefore, it does not form part of the group.

Also include any 75% indirect holdings of Toast Ltd:

- Bread Ltd (Toast Ltd indirectly holds (100% × 75%) = 75% of Bread Ltd).

Note

Butter Ltd is not included, as Toast Ltd only indirectly holds (75% × 75%) = 56.25%.

Honey Ltd owns 75% of Butter Ltd, so they will form a second group relief group.

Therefore, there are two groups:

- Toast Ltd, Honey Ltd, Marmalade Ltd and Bread Ltd.
- Honey Ltd and Butter Ltd.

Test your understanding 5

Group 1	**Group 2**
Holding Ltd (H), Sub 1 (S1)and Sub 2 (S2) are within a 75 % group.	Holding Ltd (H) and Sub 1 are within a 75% group; Sub 1 and Sub 2 are within another 75% group.
The direct shareholding links between the group are all 75% and over.	Holding Ltd and Sub 2 are **not** within a 75% group **because** H's effective holding in Sub 2, is only 64% (80% × 80%).
In addition, Holding Ltd has an indirect shareholding in Sub 2 Ltd, of over 75% (90% × 90% = 81%).	
Losses can be transferred from:	**Losses can be transferred between:**
H to S1 and S2	H to S1 or S1 to H,
S2 to S1 and H	S1 to S2 or S2 to S1
S1 to H and S2.	**but** not from H to S2 **or** S2 to H.

Test your understanding 6

Red Ltd

Maximum group relief

	£
Profits	85,000
Less: b/f trading losses	(35,000)
Maximum claim	50,000

Maximum group relief, the lower of:

- Loss of Red Ltd £65,000
- Maximum claim by Pink Ltd £50,000

Therefore, Red Ltd can group relieve £50,000 of its current year trading losses, to Pink Ltd.

Unrelieved losses

Red Ltd:

Assuming maximum group relief is claimed:

Red Ltd will have £15,000 of current year trading losses unrelieved. A current year or prior year claim, can be made to relieve these losses against total profits.

Alternatively, they will be carried forward against the first available future trading profits.

Red Ltd's brought forward trading losses of £12,000, will continue to be carried forward and set against the first available trading profits.

Pink Ltd:

Pink Ltd's brought forward trading losses of £35,000, will be utilised in the year to 31 December 2008.

The company's capital losses b/f, will be carried forward and used against the first chargeable gains of the company.

Test your understanding 7

White Ltd and Black Ltd

Firstly, identify the corresponding accounting:

- Y/e 30.9.08 and y/e 30.6.09:

  The corresponding accounting period is 1 July 2008 to 30 September 2008, (i.e. three months).

- Y/e 30.9.09 and y/e 30.6.09

  The corresponding accounting period is 1 October 2008 to 30 June 2009, (i.e. nine months).

Black Ltd can therefore claim the following group relief:

y/e 30 September 2008

		£
Black Ltd can claim	(£36,000 × 3/12)	9,000
White Ltd can surrender	(£24,000 × 3/12)	(6,000)

Black Ltd can claim group relief of £6,000 against its profits, for the year ended 30 September 2008.

y/e 30 September 2009

		£
Black Ltd can claim	(£20,000 × 9/12)	15,000
White Ltd can surrender	(£24,000 × 9/12)	(18,000)

Black Ltd can claim group relief of £15,000, against its profits for the year ended 30 September 2009.

Test your understanding 8

A Ltd

Associated companies

A Ltd controls more than 50% of B Ltd, C Ltd, D Ltd as well as E Ltd – therefore (including A Ltd), there are five associated companies in the A Ltd group.

Group relief group

A Ltd, B Ltd and C Ltd form a group of companies for group relief purposes.

D Ltd is not a group member, as it is not a 75% subsidiary.

E Ltd is non-UK resident and therefore, cannot participate in a group relief claim.

Note: Non-UK resident companies are treated as associated companies.

Corporation tax computations – y/e 31 March 2009

	A Ltd	B Ltd	C Ltd	D Ltd
	£	£	£	£
Trading income	100,000	110,000	Nil	Nil
Interest income	Nil	15,000	12,000	
Total profits	100,000	125,000	12,000	
CY claim – s393A **(W2)**			(5,000)	
Group relief **(W2)**	(40,000)	(65,000)		
PCTCT	60,000	60,000	7,000	Nil
CT @ 21%	12,600	12,600	1,470	Nil

Note: The trading loss of D Ltd (£25,000), can only be carried forward in D Ltd for set-off against its first available future trading profits as it is not a member of the group relief group.

Workings

(W1) Associated companies

There are five associated companies; therefore, the upper and lower limits applicable to each company are:

£1,500,000/5 = £300,000 and £300,000/5 = £60,000

This is not required in the exam, but is done here for you to understand the implications of the relevant limits we have worked out, that are applicable to each company.

When 'profits' are:	PCTCT charged
≤ £60,000	Small company's rate (21%)
> £60,000 and ≤ £300,000	Full rate and MR (29.75%)
> £300,000	Full rate (28%)

The loss of C Ltd, is utilised most efficiently by surrendering sufficient of the loss to A Ltd and B Ltd to reduce their profits to the lower limit of £60,000.

Relief for the loss will be obtained at 29.75%. Any remaining loss can be relieved against C Ltd's other profits, where relief is obtained at 21%.

Note: Further loss relief to A Ltd or B Ltd would also save tax at 21%.

(W2) Utilisation of loss

Trading loss available in C Ltd and its efficient utilisation:

	£
Available loss in C Ltd	110,000
Utilisation: to A Ltd (Note)	(40,000)
to B Ltd (Note)	(65,000)
	5,000
in C Ltd	(5,000)
	Nil

Note: Loss given to bring the profits down to £60,000.

You could have started with B Ltd and then A Ltd, but in total you want to surrender £105,000 of the loss, from C Ltd to A Ltd and B Ltd.

The following would not be required in the examination but is provided to aid your understanding

If C Ltd had used its own loss and not transferred any loss under group relief to A Ltd and B Ltd, then it would not have any PCTCT and the loss available to carry forward would have been £98,000 (£110,000 – £12,000).

	A Ltd	**B Ltd**	**C Ltd**	**D Ltd**
	£	£	£	£
Trading income	100,000	110,000	Nil	Nil
Interest income	Nil	15,000	12,000	
Total profits	100,000	125,000	12,000	
Less: s393A – CY claim			(12,000)	
PCTCT = Profits	100,000	125,000	Nil	Nil

	A Ltd	B Ltd	C Ltd	D Ltd
	£	£	£	£
Corporation tax				
£100,000/£125,000 @ 28%	28,000	35,000		
Less: MR				
7/400 × (£300,000 – £100,000)	(3,500)			
7/400 × (£300,000 – £125,000)		(3,063)		
Corporation tax payable	24,500	31,937	Nil	Nil

From the 'group' viewpoint, the total corporation tax (CT) payable, **WITHOUT** making any claim for group loss relief, is **£56,437** (£24,500 + £31,937).

In our answer with group relief, the total CT payable was **£26,670** (£12,600 + £12,600 + £1,470).

We have allocated group relief as follows:

To A Ltd: £40,000 (to bring the PCTCT down to £60,000)

	£
CT of A Ltd (without group relief)	24,500
CT of A Ltd (with group relief)	(12,600)
Difference	11,900

This means that we have relieved the loss of £40,000 at an effective rate of 29.75%. ((£11,900/£40,000) x 100)

To B Ltd: £65,000 (to bring the PCTCT down to £60,000)

	£
CT of B Ltd (without group relief)	31,937
CT of B Ltd (with group relief)	(12,600)
Difference	19,337

This means that we have relieved the loss of £65,000 at an effective rate of 29.75% ((£19,337/£65,000) x 100).

Test your understanding 9

A Ltd group

Gains group

- A Ltd, B Ltd and C Ltd are in a gains group, as there is 75% ownership at each level and A Ltd (the parent) owns more than 50% (75% × 75% = 56.25%) in C Ltd.
- A Ltd does not own more than 50% of D Ltd (75% × 75% × 75% = 42.19%) and therefore D Ltd does not form part of the gains group.
- C Ltd and D Ltd, cannot form a separate gains group, as C Ltd is part of the A Ltd gains group and cannot therefore, be itself a 'parent' company and form a separate gains group.

Group relief group

- A Ltd and B Ltd form a group relief group.
- B Ltd and C Ltd form a group relief group.
- C Ltd and D Ltd form a group relief group.

Remember, that for a group relief group the parent company (A Ltd), must have an effective interest in all companies of at least 75%.

Test your understanding 10

Alpha Ltd

As the two companies satisfy the criteria of a gains group, they can make an election to either:

- treat Alpha Ltd as having made the disposal which results in a capital loss of £65,000 or
- treat Beta Ltd as having made the disposal which results in a capital gain of £90,000.

In both instances, the capital loss will be set-off against the chargeable gain, resulting in a net chargeable gain of £25,000, chargeable to corporation tax. It is therefore possible, to have the gain of £25,000, taxed in the company that is subject to the lower rate of corporation tax.

The time limit for making the election is 31 March 2011 (i.e. within two years from 31 March 2009).

hapter

23

Overseas issues for companies

Chapter learning objectives

Upon completion of this chapter you will be able to:

- explain the basis for charging overseas profits to UK corporation tax
- determine the amount of overseas chargeable profits
- explain how relief is given for overseas tax suffered
- calculate double tax relief when withholding tax is suffered
- identify when relief for underlying tax is allowed and calculate it for a single source
- calculate double tax relief where both withholding tax and underlying tax is suffered
- explain the purpose of the transfer pricing rules as they apply to transactions between a UK and overseas company.

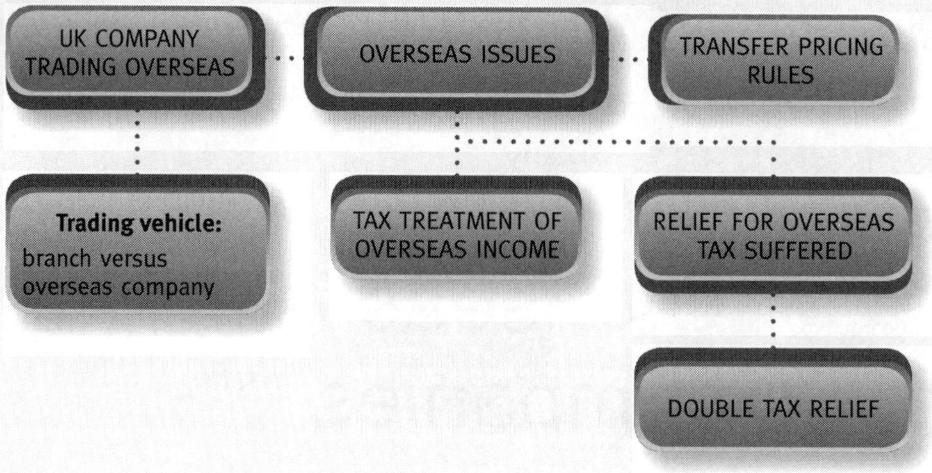

1 Overseas operations

Companies **resident** in the UK are chargeable to corporation tax on all profits and chargeable gains wherever they arise.

Definition – residency

The residency rules were covered in detail in Chapter 18. In summary, a company is resident in the UK if:

- it is incorporated in the UK, or
- it is 'centrally managed and controlled in the UK'.

A company which is incorporated in the UK or an overseas company which is centrally managed and controlled in the UK, will be chargeable to UK corporation tax on all of their profits, wherever earned.

Overseas operations of a UK company

A basic question to be considered by any UK resident company deciding to set up overseas, is whether to operate through an overseas resident company or a branch, as they have different tax implications.

Overseas branch of a UK resident company

An overseas branch of a UK company is effectively an extension of the UK trade. Accordingly, the tax implications of operating through an overseas branch, are as follows:

- 100% of the branch profits will be assessed to UK corporation tax. Whether profits are remitted to the UK or not is irrelevant.
- The branch profits will normally be taxed as UK trading profits.
- UK capital allowances are available on the branch's assets.

- Branch trading losses are eligible for UK loss relief, including group relief.
- UK trading losses can be offset against overseas branch profits.

Overseas resident company

A UK company may decide to establish its overseas operations through an overseas company.

An overseas resident company is a separate legal entity from the UK company. Accordingly, the tax implications of operating through an overseas resident company, are as follows:

- Only dividends paid to the UK parent company are liable to UK corporation tax.
- If the company is controlled (> 50% ownership) by the UK company, it will be classed as an associate, for the purposes of determining the rate of UK corporation tax payable by the UK company.

Note that the following benefits are not available:

- No UK capital allowances on the overseas company's assets.
- No relief in the UK for losses incurred by the overseas company.

Overseas chargeable profits

- Profits from an overseas branch are normally taxed as UK trading profits.
- Dividends received from an overseas company, are included in the UK parent company's corporation tax computation, as overseas dividend income. The 'gross' dividend is taxed and therefore, the dividend received must be grossed up for any overseas tax suffered.

Example 1 - Overseas operations

Probe plc, a UK resident company, has a tax-adjusted trading profit of £1,400,000, for the year ended 31 March 2009.

The company has a 5% shareholding in Deep Inc, an overseas resident company. During the year ended 31 March 2009, Deep Inc paid a total dividend of £388,000. This is after the deduction of overseas tax at the rate of 3%.

Calculate the profits chargeable to UK corporation tax of Probe plc for the year ended 31 March 2009.

Answer to example 1

Corporation tax computation – year ended 31 March 2009

	£
Trading profit	1,400,000
Dividend from non-UK company	
(£388,000 × 100/97 = £400,000 × 5%)	20,000
PCTCT	1,420,000

Test your understanding 1

Happy Ltd, a UK resident company, has tax-adjusted trading profits of £1,650,000, for the year ended 31 December 2008.

The company has an 8% shareholding in Jolly Inc, an overseas resident company. During the year Jolly Ltd paid a dividend to Happy Ltd of £27,300 (after the deduction of 22% overseas tax).

Calculate the profits chargeable to UK corporation tax of Happy Ltd, for the year ended 31 December 2008.

2 Double tax relief (DTR)

- UK resident companies are subject to UK corporation tax on all profits and chargeable gains wherever they arise.
- Overseas income (either branch profits or dividends) may be subject to both overseas tax and UK corporation tax.
- Relief for this double taxation is given by means of a 'tax credit' to the UK resident company.

Relief for overseas tax suffered

Relief for overseas tax suffered is given as follows:

- The overseas income is included gross of overseas tax in the corporation tax computation.
- Double tax relief (DTR) is given for the overseas tax suffered by way of credit against the corporation tax liability.

- The amount of DTR is limited to the lower of:
  - the amount of overseas tax on the overseas income
  - the UK corporation tax payable on that overseas income.

Operation of DTR

DTR must be calculated on a 'source by source' basis, not a global basis. Therefore, each source of overseas income and its related overseas and UK tax liability, must be dealt with separately.

Approach a question with different sources of overseas income as follows:

- Include overseas income inclusive of overseas taxes as part of the profits chargeable to corporation tax. Use a columnar layout to recognise each different overseas source of income.
- The overseas income is included as PCTCT and therefore, taxed at the appropriate UK rate.
- Deduct from the UK corporation tax liability, the lower of:
  - attributable UK corporation tax on overseas profits; and
  - overseas tax suffered.

Example 2 - Double tax relief

A Ltd, a UK resident company, has taxable trading profits of £500,000, during the year ended 31 March 2009. Due to the number of associates in the A Ltd group, the company pays tax at the rate of 28%.

The company also had the following overseas income during the year:

- a dividend of £10,000 (gross) from ABC Inc. This has been taxed overseas at the rate of 20%
- overseas branch profits of £10,000 (gross). These profits have been taxed overseas at the rate of 66%.

Calculate A Ltd's UK corporation tax liability, after double tax relief for the year ended 31 March 2009.

Answer to example 2

A Ltd

Corporation tax computation – year ended 31 March 2009

	Total	UK income	ABC Inc	Branch
	£	£	£	£
PCTCT	520,000	500,000	10,000	10,000
UK CT at 28%	145,600	140,000	2,800	2,800
Less: DTR – lower of				
(i) ABC Inc:				
UK CT: £2,800 (above)				
Overseas tax				
(20% × £10,000) = £2,000	(2,000)		(2,000)	
(ii) Branch profits				
UK CT: £2,800 (above)				
Overseas tax:				
(66% × £10,000) = £6,600	(2,800)			(2,800)
UK CT liability	140,800	140,000	800	Nil

Gift Aid

When calculating PCTCT for a company with overseas income, Gift Aid may be allocated in the most beneficial manner, (i.e. first against UK profits and then against overseas income).

If we do not do this, then we are reducing the foreign income and as a result, reducing the UK tax due on foreign income and as a direct consequence reducing the DTR available.

Expandable text - Double tax relief system

The system of DTR ensures that the overall charge to tax is not excessive, with one country giving credit for the tax paid in another.

As a general rule, the country of 'source' gets the first right to the tax, with the credit for the overseas tax paid being given by the country of residence.

There is, however, an overriding rule that credit will never be given, for more than the attributable UK tax on the overseas income, by the UK authorities.

UK resident companies can mitigate double taxation either:

- Bilaterally under a double taxation agreement between the UK and a specific overseas country; or
- Unilaterally by the UK tax authorities, irrespective of any double taxation agreement.

As far as the examination is concerned, there is no difference whether double taxation relief is given by an agreement or unilaterally.

Overseas tax suffered

There are two different types of overseas tax which may have been suffered on an overseas source of income. These are:

Withholding tax (WHT)

Any direct tax imposed at source by the overseas country:

- Can apply to any overseas income, (e.g. dividends, interest, rent).
- DTR for WHT is always available.

Underlying tax (ULT)

The overseas tax paid on the profits of the overseas resident company out of which the dividend is paid.

- Relief for ULT is only available where the UK resident company receiving the dividend, controls ≥10% of the voting power of the overseas company paying the dividend.
- Only applies to overseas dividends.

Relief for withholding tax (WHT)

Remember the following key points:

- WHT is any direct tax imposed at source by the overseas country.
- Relief for WHT is always available.

Example 3 - Double tax relief

Maxwell Ltd, a UK resident trading company, owns 6% of the share capital of Zulu Inc, and 8% of the share capital of Max Gmbh. Neither of these companies are resident in the UK for tax purposes. Maxwell Ltd also has a controlling interest in two other UK resident companies.

The following information relates to Maxwell Ltd's 12-month accounting year ended 31 March 2009

	£
Tax adjusted trading profits	500,000
Overseas Income:	
Dividend from Zulu Inc – after deduction of withholding tax of 30%	35,000
Dividend from Max Gmbh – after deduction of withholding tax of 5%	38,000
Gift Aid donation	10,000

Calculate the UK corporation tax payable for the above period by Maxwell Ltd, showing clearly your treatment of double taxation.

Answer to example 3

Corporation tax computation – year ended 31 March 2009

	Total	**UK income**	**Zulu Inc**	**Max Gmbh**
	£	£	£	£
Trading income	500,000	500,000		
Overseas dividends **(W1)**	90,000		50,000	40,000
Total profits	590,000	500,000	50,000	40,000
Less: Gift Aid	(10,000)	(10,000)		
PCTCT	580,000	490,000	50,000	40,000
Corporation tax				
(£580,000 @ 28%) **(W2)**	162,400	137,200	14,000	11,200
Less: DTR **(W3)**	(16,000)		(14,000)	(2,000)
CT payable	146,400	137,200	Nil	9,200

Workings

(W1) Grossing up the 'overseas dividends':

	Zulu Inc	**Max Gmbh**
	£	£
Dividend received	35,000	38,000
Add: WHT (30/70)/(5/95)	15,000	2,000
	50,000	40,000

(W2) Associated companies

There are three companies under common control, as Maxwell Ltd has a controlling interest in two other UK resident companies (Zulu Inc and Max Gmbh are not 'associated' companies).

Limits for determining the tax rate:

£1,500,000/3 = £500,000
£300,000/3 = £100,000

Therefore with profits of £580,000, the full rate of 28% applies.

(W3) DTR relief

	Zulu Inc	**Max Gmbh**
Lower of:	£	£
UK CT liability on overseas profits	14,000	11,200
Overseas taxes suffered	15,000	2,000

The following calculations would not be required in the exam – they are provided to aid your understanding.

If Gift Aid is not deducted from UK income first, then:

	Total	**UK income**	**Zulu Inc**	**Max Gmbh**
	£	£	£	£
Trading income	500,000	500,000		
Overseas dividend	90,000		50,000	40,000
Total profits	590,000	500,000	50,000	40,000
Less: Gift Aid	(10,000)		(10,000)	
PCTCT	580,000	500,000	40,000	40,000
Corporation tax @ 28%	162,400	140,000	11,200	11,200
Less: DTR **(Note 1)**	(13,200)		(11,200)	(2,000)
CT payable	149,200	140,000	Nil	9,200

Notes

(1) The DTR has been reduced by £2,800 to the amount of UK tax due on the income.

(2) Note that the CT payable has now become £149,200, (i.e. more than the original answer) because having allocated the Gift Aid against overseas income, we have restricted the DTR.

Therefore:

- Gift Aid should be initially allocated against UK income and then against overseas income, with the lower effective rate of overseas tax.
- This should, therefore, give the maximum amount of DTR for overseas income, with the higher effective rate of overseas tax.

Test your understanding 2

London Ltd, a UK resident trading company, owns 7% of the share capital of Paris Inc, and 4% of the share capital of Berlin Gmbh. Neither of these companies are resident in the UK for tax purposes. London Ltd also has a controlling interest in three other UK resident companies.

The following information relates to London's Ltd's year ended 31 March 2009:

	£
Tax-adjusted trading profits	400,000
Overseas income:	
Dividend from Paris Inc – after deduction of withholding tax of 40%	54,000
Dividend from Berlin Gmbh – after deduction of withholding tax of 15%	39,100
Gift Aid donation	20,000

Compute the UK corporation tax payable for the above period by London Ltd, showing clearly your treatment of double taxation.

Relief for underlying tax (ULT)

Remember the following key points:

- ULT only applies to overseas dividends.
- ULT is the overseas tax paid on the profits of the overseas resident company, out of which the dividend is paid.
- Underlying tax relief is only available where the UK resident company controls at least 10% of the voting power of the overseas company paying the dividend.
- Where relief for the underlying tax is available, the underlying tax is added to the gross amount of the overseas dividend. UK corporation tax is then charged on this total.

Example 4 - Double tax relief

Posh plc, a UK resident company, has the following income for the year ended 31 March 2009.

	£	£
Tax-adjusted trading profit		1,400,000
Income from shares held in an overseas company:		
Amount of dividend received		127,500
Foreign tax suffered:		
WHT (15%)	22,500	
ULT (25%)	50,000	72,500
Gross overseas dividend income		200,000

Posh plc owns 15% of the voting shares in the overseas company.

Calculate Posh plc's UK corporation tax liability for the year ended 31 March 2009.

Answer to example 4

Corporation tax computation: year ended 31 March 2009

		£
Trading profit		1,400,000
Dividends from non-UK companies		200,000
PCTCT		1,600,000
Corporation tax (1,600,000 at 28%)		448,000
Double taxation relief = lower of:		
(a) Overseas tax on overseas income	72,500	
(b) UK CT on overseas income		
(£200,000 at 28%)	56,000	(56,000)
UK corporation tax liability		392,000

Note: The dividend is shown gross of both WHT and ULT, as Posh plc owns more than 10% of voting rights in the overseas company.

Calculating underlying tax

If the amount of underlying tax is not given in the question it must be calculated by:

- taking the gross dividend received (that is after adding back any withholding tax that has been deducted)
- multiplying by the amount of overseas tax actually paid
- dividing by the after-tax accounting profits (the distributable profits) of the overseas company.
- The formula is therefore:

$$\frac{\text{Gross dividend}}{\text{After-tax accounting profit}} \times \text{Overseas tax actually paid}$$

Note that the calculation is based on the overseas company's after-tax profits per the financial accounts and not on the tax-adjusted profits.

Where credit is available for ULT as well as WHT (i.e. hold ≥ 10% of the voting rights), the gross taxable dividend is calculated by grossing up the dividend in two stages:

(1) For withholding tax to get 'gross dividend'.

(2) For underlying tax using the above formula.

Example 5 - Double tax relief

MN plc, a UK company, has a 100% owned overseas subsidiary, AB Inc.

For the year ended 31 March 2009, MN plc made a tax-adjusted UK trading profit of £2,000,000.

It also received foreign rental income of £302,250 (net). Overseas tax of £97,750, had been paid in respect of this income.

The results of the overseas subsidiary for the year ended 31 March 2009, are as follows:

	£	£
Trading profit		700,000
Corporation tax		(150,000)
Profit after tax		550,000
Dividends paid:		
Net	247,500	
Withholding tax	27,500	(275,000)
Retained profits		275,000

The dividends were all paid during the year ended 31 March 2009. AB Inc's actual tax liability was £15,000 higher than the figure provided for in its accounts.

Compute MN plc's corporation tax payable for the year ended 31 March 2009.

Answer to example 5

MN plc owns at least 10% of the share capital of AB Inc and so relief for the underlying tax paid overseas, will be available in respect of the dividends received.

Corporation tax computation: year ended 31 March 2009

	Total	UK	AB Inc	Overseas rent
	£	£	£	£
Trading profit	2,000,000	2,000,000		
Overseas dividend **(W1)**	357,500		357,500	
Property business profit (£302,250 + £97,750)	400,000			400,000
PCTCT	2,757,500	2,000,000	357,500	400,000
Corporation tax at 28%	772,100	560,000	100,100	112,000
Less: DTR **(W2)**	(197,850)		(100,100)	(97,750)
UK CT liability	574,250	560,000	Nil	14,250

Workings

(W1) Dividend from AB Inc

	£
Dividend received	247,500
Withholding tax	27,500
	275,000
Underlying tax: (£165,000* × 275,000/550,000)	82,500
Taxable dividend income	357,500

*(£150,000 + £15,000) = overseas tax actually paid

(W2) DTR

DTR on the dividend from AB Inc, is the lower of:

- the total overseas tax paid = £110,000 (£27,500 + £82,500)
- the UK corporation tax on the dividend received of £100,100.

DTR on the overseas rents is the lower of:

- the overseas tax paid = £97,750
- the UK corporation tax on the overseas rent = £112,000.

Note that the use of a columnar layout makes the DTR calculations easier to follow.

Test your understanding 3

Sammy Ltd is a UK resident company with two subsidiaries, one of which is situated abroad.

In the year to 31 March 2009, Sammy Ltd had the following results:

	£
Tax-adjusted UK trading profits	720,000
Dividends received from UK subsidiary	40,000
Chargeable gains	120,000
Dividend from overseas subsidiary (net of 30% withholding tax)	8,400
Gift Aid donation	80,000

Sammy Ltd owns 60% of the ordinary share capital of the overseas subsidiary.

The summarised profit and loss account of this subsidiary for the year ended 31 March 2009, is as follows:

	£
Profit before tax	75,000
Less: Provision for tax liability	(25,000)
Profit after tax	50,000
Dividends	(20,000)
Retained profit	30,000

The overseas company's actual tax liability for the year to 31 March 2009, was £20,000.

Calculate the corporation tax liability of Sammy Ltd for the year ended 31 March 2009, after claiming all possible reliefs.

Summary

- Overseas income is included gross of overseas tax in the corporation tax computation.
- The amount of DTR is limited to the lower of:
  - the amount of overseas tax on the overseas income
  - the UK corporation tax payable on that overseas income.
- DTR is calculated on a 'source by source' basis.
- Relief for withholding tax is always available.
- Relief for underlying tax is only available where the UK resident company controls at least 10% of the voting power of the overseas company paying the dividend.

3 Transfer pricing

If a UK resident company has a 'controlling' interest in an overseas resident subsidiary, then it might try to sell goods to the subsidiary at an undervalue or buy goods from it at an overvalue in order to manipulate where the profits should arise.

The aim of these arrangements would be to move the profits to a country with a lower corporation tax rate than the UK.

Transfer pricing – rules

- The transfer pricing rules prevent UK companies from charging artificial prices for goods and services in order to gain a tax advantage.
- The basic rule for transfer pricing is that transactions between group members should be charged on an arms-length basis.
- An 'arms-length' price is what it could have been sold for to an independent third party dealing on commercial terms, e.g. market prices.
- For example, where sales are made to an overseas resident 'group' company at an undervalue, then its true market price should be substituted for the transfer price.
- Under self-assessment rules, if transactions are not made on an arms-length basis, an adjustment to substitute arms-length prices should be made by the UK resident company in its corporation tax return.
- There are detailed rules for establishing which companies are within the scope of the transfer pricing rules, but the basic test is one of control.
- Advance pricing arrangements are available to enable a company to agree in advance with HMRC, that its 'transfer pricing policy' is acceptable.
- The transfer pricing rules can also apply between two UK resident companies. However, the examiner has stated that any question on transfer pricing will involve an overseas company.

Example 6 - Transfer pricing

Focus plc, a UK resident company, is to export cameras that it manufactures, to its 100% overseas subsidiary, at a discount of 30% to their normal trade selling price.

The company wishes to maximise the subsidiary's profits, as these are only subject to corporation tax overseas at the rate of 15%.

Discuss the tax implications of the above arrangement.

Answer to example 6

- The invoicing of cameras by Focus plc at a discount of 30% to the normal trade selling price, will have the effect of reducing its taxable trading profits, and hence UK corporation tax.
- The sales are at an under-valuation to an overseas company which it controls. Therefore a market price must be substituted for the transfer price when calculating Focus plc's profits chargeable to UK corporation tax.
- The market price will be an 'arm's length' one that would be charged if the parties to the transaction were independent of each other.
- Under self-assessment, transfer pricing adjustments are not made by HMRC, but should be made by the company concerned, in this case, Focus plc.

4 Comprehensive example

Test your understanding 4

Wash plc is a large UK resident company that manufactures kitchen equipment. The company's tax-adjusted trading profit for the year ended 31 March 2009 is £1,600,000. Wash plc has a 100% owned subsidiary, Dry Inc, that is resident overseas. Dry Inc sells kitchen equipment that has been manufactured by Wash plc.

The results of Dry Inc for the year ended 31 March 2009 are as follows:

		£	£
Trading profit			580,000
Corporation tax			(160,000)
Profit after tax			420,000
Dividend paid	– Net	270,000	
	– Withholding tax	30,000	
			(300,000)
Retained profits			120,000

Dry Inc's dividend was paid during the year ended 31 March 2009. The company's corporation tax liability for the year ended 31 March 2009 was £8,000 more than that provided for in the accounts.

All of the above figures are in pounds Sterling.

(a) Explain the difference between withholding tax and underlying tax in respect of an overseas dividend, and state the conditions that must be met for double taxation relief to be available in each case.

(b) Calculate Wash plc's corporation tax liability for the year ended 31 March 2009.

(c) Explain the tax implications if Wash plc were to invoice Dry Inc for the exported kitchen equipment at a price that was less than the market price.

5 Chapter summary

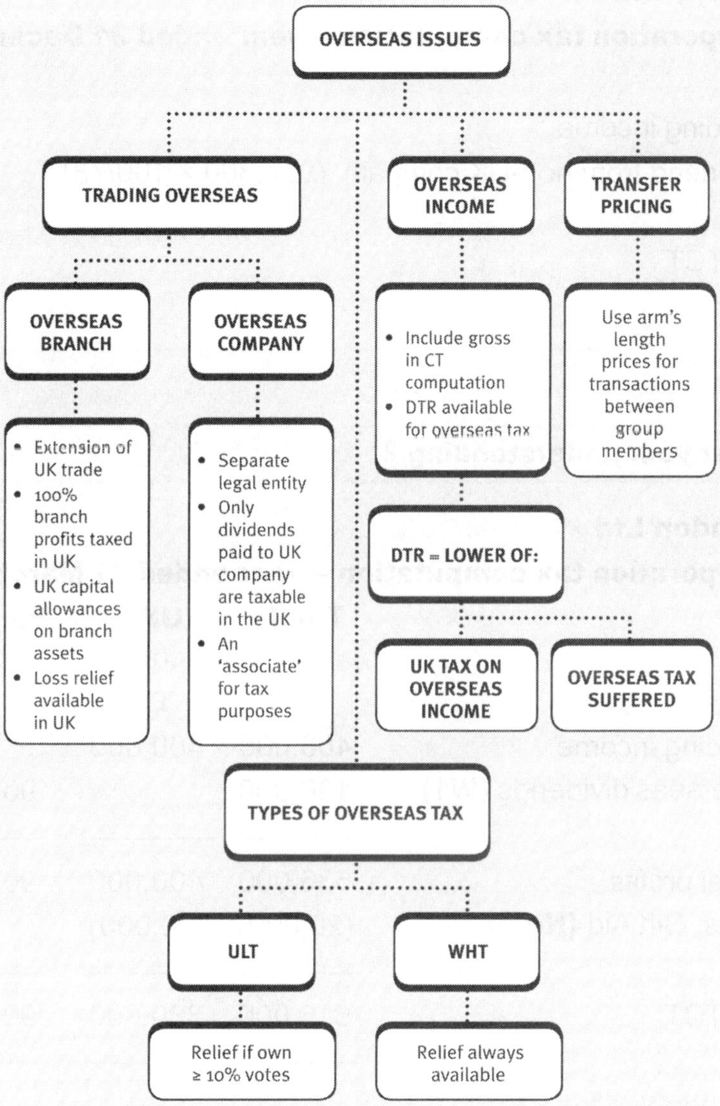

Test your understanding answers

Test your understanding 1

Happy Ltd

Corporation tax computation – year ended 31 December 2008

	£
Trading income	1,650,000
Dividend from non-UK company (£27,300 × 100/78)	35,000
PCTCT	1,685,000

Test your understanding 2

London Ltd

Corporation tax computation – year ended 31 March 2009

	Total	**UK** income	**Paris** Inc	**Berlin** Gmbh
	£	£	£	£
Trading income	400,000	400,000		
Overseas dividends **(W1)**	136,000		90,000	46,000
Total profits	536,000	400,000	90,000	46,000
Less: Gift Aid **(Note)**	(20,000)	(20,000)		
PCTCT	516,000	380,000	90,000	46,000
Corporation tax				
£516,000 @ 28% **(W2)**	144,480	106,400	25,200	12,880
Less: DTR **(W3)**	(32,100)		(25,200)	(6,900)
CT payable	112,380	106,400	Nil	5,980

Note: The Gift Aid is offset firstly against UK income in order to maximise the DTR available.

Workings

(W1) Grossing up the 'overseas dividends'

	Paris Inc	Berlin Gmbh
	£	£
Dividend received from Paris Inc	54,000	39,100
Add: WHT (40/60)/(15/85)	36,000	6,900
	90,000	46,000

(W2) Associated companies

There are three companies under common control, as London Ltd has a controlling interest in three other UK resident companies (Paris Inc and Berlin Gmbh are not 'associated' companies).

Therefore, the applicable limits for determining the tax rate for each company are:

£1,500,000/4 = £375,000
£300,000/4 = £75,000

Therefore, with PCTCT of £516,000, the full rate applies.

(W3) DTR relief

	Paris Inc	Berlin Gmbh
	£	£
UK CT on overseas profits	25,200	12,880
Overseas taxes suffered	36,000	6,900

Test your understanding 3

Sammy Ltd

Corporation tax computation – year ended 31 March 2009

	Total	UK	Overseas
	£	£	£
Trading income	720,000	720,000	
Chargeable gains	120,000	120,000	
Overseas dividend **(W1)**	16,800		16,800
Total profits	856,800	840,000	16,800
Less: Gift Aid	(80,000)	(80,000)	
PCTCT	776,800	760,000	16,800
Corporation tax			
£776,000 @ 28% **(W2)**	217,504	212,800	4,704
Less: DTR **(W3)**	(4,704)		(4,704)
Corporation tax payable	212,800	212,800	Nil

Workings

(W1) Dividend from overseas subsidiary

The gross overseas dividend received is:

	£
Net dividend	8,400
Add: Withholding tax credit (30/70)	3,600
Gross dividend	12,000

Sammy Ltd owns more than 10% of the overseas subsidiary, therefore we need to calculate the underlying tax as well.

(£12,000/£50,000 × £20,000) = £4,800

Note that it is the **actual** tax paid figure which is used in the calculation.

Therefore, the GROSS overseas dividend income inclusive of 'potentially recoverable overseas taxes' is £16,800 (£12,000 + £4,800).

The total foreign tax suffered is £8,400 (£3,600 + £4,800).

(W2) Associated companies

Sammy Ltd + 2 subsidiaries = 3 companies under common control.

The relevant main lower and upper limits applicable to each company are:

£300,000/3 = £100,000
£1,500,000/3 = £500,000

Sammy Ltd therefore, pays tax at the full rate (28%).

(W3) DTR

Maximum DTR = lower of:

(i) UK corporation tax on overseas income = £4,704

(ii) Overseas tax suffered = £8,400.

Test your understanding 4

Wash plc

(a) **Withholding tax and underlying tax**

(1) Withholding tax is the term used for any overseas tax deducted at source from a dividend payment.

(2) Relief for overseas withholding tax is always available.

(3) Underlying tax is the term used for the overseas tax paid on the profits of an overseas subsidiary, out of which a dividend is paid.

(4) Relief for underlying tax is only given where the UK holding company owns at least 10% of the overseas subsidiary's voting power.

(b) **Wash plc**

Corporation tax computation – year ended 31 March 2009

	£
Trading income	1,600,000
Overseas dividend **(Note 1)**	420,000
PCTCT	2,020,000
Corporation tax at 28%	565,600
Double taxation relief **(Note 3)**	(117,600)
Corporation tax liability	448,000

Notes:

(1) The dividend from Dry Inc must be adjusted for the underlying tax suffered overseas.

	£
Gross dividend (£270,000 + £30,000)	300,000
Underlying tax	
£300,000 × £168,000*/£420,000	120,000
Overseas dividend income	420,000

*Actual overseas tax paid £168,000 (£160,000 + £8,000)

(2) The total overseas tax suffered is £150,000 (£30,000 + £120,000).

(3) Double taxation relief is restricted to the amount of UK corporation tax on the dividend from Dry Inc (£420,000 at 28% = £117,600).

(c) **Tax implications of invoicing below market price**

(1) Invoicing for the exported kitchen equipment at less than the market price will reduce UK trading profits and hence UK corporation tax.

(2) As Wash plc controls Dry Inc and the terms of the transaction would have differed if the parties had been at arm's length then the transfer pricing rules apply to the transaction.

(3) A true market price will therefore have to be substituted for the transfer price.

(4) The market price will be an 'arm's length' one that would be charged if the parties to the transaction were independent of each other.

(5) Wash plc will be required to make the adjustment in its self-assessment tax return

hapter

24

Tax administration for a company

Chapter learning objectives

Upon completion of this chapter you will be able to:

- explain and apply the features of the self-assessment system as it applies to companies
- state the time limits for filing a tax return
- state the penalties for late submission of tax returns/notification of liability
- state when corporation tax is due for companies which are not large
- state the time limits for key claims
- define a large company and explain how they are required to pay corporation tax on a quarterly basis
- calculate interest on overdue tax
- state the penalties that can be charged on a late payment of tax
- explain the circumstances in which HM Revenue and Customs can enquire into a tax return
- list the information and records that the company needs to retain for tax purposes together with the retention period.

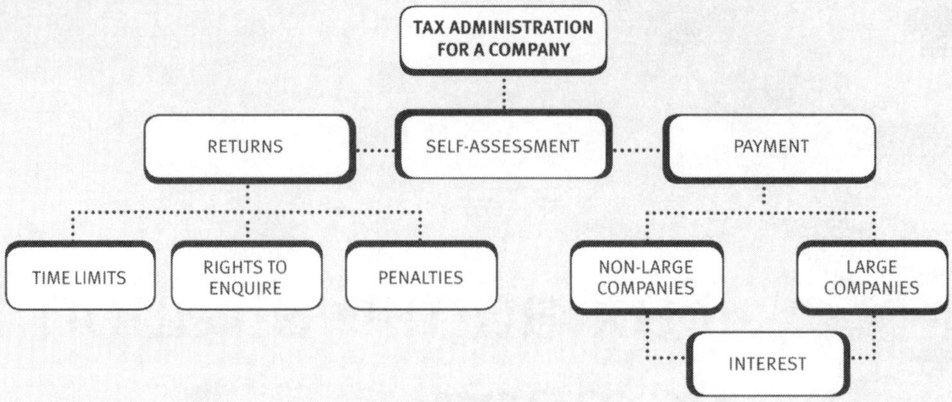

1 The self-assessment system for companies

Introduction

As with individuals, self-assessment exists for corporate taxpayers. Responsibility rests with the company to:

- calculate their own corporation tax liability for each accounting period
- submit a self-assessment corporation tax return **within 12 months** after the end of the accounting period
- pay any corporation tax due **within nine months** after the end of the accounting period.

Given the timing of the due date for payment of tax, in practice, many companies will aim to complete the self-assessment tax return prior to the nine-month deadline for paying the corporation tax.

The following session considers all aspects concerning the self-assessment system for companies and the related procedures.

The self-assessment tax return

The self-assessment tax return must be submitted either:

- **within 12 months** after the end of the accounting period; or
- **three months** after the issue of the return (if this is later than the normal submission date).

The return should contain all information required to calculate the company's profits chargeable to corporation tax.

A company has to submit a copy of its financial accounts together with the self-assessment tax return.

The return must include a self-assessment of the amount of corporation tax payable for that accounting period.

Making claims

Any claims must be included in the self-assessment tax return.

A claim for a relief, allowance or repayment must be quantified at the time that the claim is made. For example, if loss relief is claimed, then the amount of the loss must be stated.

Notification of chargeability

A company coming within the scope of corporation tax for the first time must notify HMRC when its first accounting period begins, **within three months** of the start of its first accounting period.

Companies that do not receive a tax return are required to notify HMRC if they have income or chargeable gains on which tax is due.

The time limit for notifying HMRC of chargeability is **12 months** from the end of the accounting period in which the liability arises.

Penalties for failure to submit a return

If the company fails to submit a tax return within the specified time, then, unless it can show reasonable excuse, an automatic fixed penalty arises.

The penalty structure is as follows:

- Penalty of £100 if the return is **up to three months** late.
- Penalty of £200 if the return is **more than three months** late.

These penalties are increased to £500 and £1,000 respectively if the return is the third (or more) consecutive return to be late.

Additional tax-geared penalties are also imposed:

- if a return is **more than six months** but less than 12 months late, this penalty is 10% of the corporation tax unpaid six months after the filing date.
- if a return is **more than 12 months** late, the penalty is 20% of the corporation tax unpaid six months after the filing date.

Example 1 - Self-assessment for companies

Late Ltd submits its self-assessment return for the year ended 31 March 2009, on 30 November 2010. The corporation tax due of £50,000 was paid on the same day. Late Ltd has submitted its previous tax returns on time.

State the penalties that are due as a result of the late submission of the tax return?

Answer to example 1

The tax return should have been submitted by 31 March 2010, and so it is eight months late. The fixed penalty is therefore £200, and the tax geared penalty is £5,000 (£50,000 at 10%).

Test your understanding 1

Everlate Ltd submits its corporation tax return for the year ended 28 February 2009, on 30 September 2010. This is the fifth consecutive occasion the company has submitted its return late. The liability eventually agreed for the year was £100,000; this was paid when the return was submitted.

State the penalties that are due as a result of the late submission of the tax return.

Expandable text - Determination assessments

To prevent companies deliberately delaying the submission of the return, HMRC have the following actions available:

- HMRC may determine the amount of corporation tax due by issuing a determination assessment.
- The determination assessment is treated as a self-assessment by the company, and will be replaced by the actual self-assessment when it is submitted by the company.
- There is no appeal against a determination assessment. Instead, the company must displace it with the actual self-assessment return.
- A determination assessment can be raised at any time **within five years** of the filing date.

2 Tax returns – amendments and errors

- HMRC may correct any obvious errors or mistakes **within nine months** of the date that the return is filed with them. For example, they will correct arithmetical errors or errors of principle. This process of repair does not mean that HMRC has necessarily accepted the return as accurate.
- A company can amend the return **within 12 months** of the filing date. For an accounting period ending on 31 March 2009, the filing date is 31 March 2010, and so the company has until 31 March 2011, to make any amendments.
- If an error is discovered at a later date, then the company can make an error or mistake claim to recover any corporation tax overpaid.

Error or mistake claims

Where an assessment is excessive due to an error or mistake in a return, the company can claim relief.

The claim must be made **within six years** of the accounting period to which it relates.

A claim can be made in respect of errors made, and mistakes arising from not understanding the law.

3 Due dates for payment

The payment date for corporation tax depends on the size of the company:

- For companies which are not 'large' – the due date is **nine months and one day** after the year end.
- For 'large' companies – the liability is settled under the **quarterly instalment scheme.**

4 Quarterly instalment payments for large companies

Introduction

HMRC does not provide large companies with the same delayed payment date for their corporation tax liability. Instead, a specific scheme is in place requiring such companies to settle their liability on an ongoing basis.

Definition of a large company

The key points here are:

- A large company is one paying the full rate of corporation tax (i.e. 28%).
- By definition, all other companies are not large (i.e. those paying the small company and marginal relief rates of corporation tax) are not required to pay corporation tax by instalments.

A company without any associated companies, will therefore pay tax by instalments, if profits are at least £1.5 million. This limit is reduced where a company has associates. But instalments are never due if a company's corporation tax liability is below £10,000.

Companies that become large during an accounting period do not have to make instalment payments provided:

- their profits for the accounting period do not exceed £10 million (reduced accordingly if there are associated companies), and
- they were not a large company for the previous accounting period.

Instalment dates

Four quarterly instalments are made in months 7, 10, 13 and 16 following the start of the accounting period.

Special rules apply where the accounting period is less than 12 months.

The instalments are due on the 14th of the relevant month.

Basis of payment

Instalments are based on the expected corporation tax liability for the current accounting period. It is, therefore, necessary for companies to produce an accurate forecast of their tax liability.

Companies will normally be able to obtain a refund, if they subsequently find that instalments have been overpaid.

Example 2 - Quarterly instalment payments for large companies

ABC plc estimates that its corporation tax liability for the year ended 31 December 2008, will be £800,000.

ABC plc is a large company for the purposes of quarterly instalment payments.

Show when ABC plc's corporation tax liability will be due.

Answer to example 2

ABC plc's corporation tax liability is due by instalments.

£200,000 on 14 July 2008

£200,000 on 14 October 2008

£200,000 on 14 January 2009

£200,000 on 14 April 2009

Test your understanding 2

XYZ Ltd has an expected corporation tax liability of £2,000,000 for the year to 31 March 2009. XYZ Ltd has been a large company for corporation tax purposes for a number of years.

State when XYZ Ltd's corporation tax liability for the year ended 31 March 2009 will be due.

5 Interest

The relevant interest rates will be provided in the Tax Rates and Allowances section of the exam.

Interest on corporation tax paid late

Interest is automatically charged if corporation tax is paid late. For the June 2009 and December 2009 exams, the rate to use is 7.5%.

Interest can also arise following an amendment to a self-assessment, or on corporation tax payable following a discovery assessment (see below).

Interest runs from the normal due date up to the date of payment. This is the case even if the tax was not actually due until a later date (for example, following the amendment of the self-assessment).

Interest paid to HMRC on corporation tax paid late is a deductible expense from interest income.

Test your understanding 3

Able Ltd prepares accounts to 31 March.

The company has a corporation tax liability of £75,000, for the year ended 31 March 2009. Able Ltd paid £25,000 of its corporation tax liability on 1 January 2010, but did not pay the balance of £50,000 until 15 March 2010.

Explain how interest is calculated on the late payment of corporation tax.

Interest paid on overpayments of corporation tax

Interest is paid by HMRC on any overpayment of corporation tax. For the June 2009 and December 2009 exams the rate to use is 3%.

Interest runs from the later of:

- the due date
- the date of actual payment

to the date of repayment.

Interest paid by HMRC on overpayments of corporation tax is taxable interest income.

6 Penalties

For returns commencing on / after 1 April 2008 where the return is due to be filed on / after 1 April 2009, the penalty is determined in the same way as penalties on incorrect income tax returns i.e. according to:

- The amount of tax understated
- The reason for the understatement
- The extent of disclosure by the taxpayer.

The level of the penalty is a percentage of the revenue lost as a result of the inaccuracy or under assessment and depends on the behaviour of the taxpayer as follows:

Taxpayer behaviour	**Maximum penalty (% of revenue lost)**
Genuine mistake	No penalty
Failure to take reasonable care	30%
Serious or deliberate understatement	70%
Serious or deliberate understatement with concealment	100%

The penalties may be reduced depending on the type of penalty and whether the taxpayer makes an unprompted disclosure.

Where the return is incorrect through deliberate intention of a third party, the penalty can be charged on the third party.

7 Enquiries into returns

HMRC have the right to enquire into the completeness and accuracy of any self-assessment tax return and issue discovery assessments. The procedures and rules are similar to those for individuals.

A reminder of the key points is given in expandable text.

Expandable text - Enquiries into returns

The enquiry may be initiated as a result of:

- suspicion that income is undeclared or a deduction incorrectly claimed
- information in HMRC's possession
- the choice of return as part of a random selection process.

Additionally:

- HMRC do not have to state a reason for the enquiry and are unlikely to do so.
- HMRC must give written notice before commencing an enquiry.

- The written notice must be issued **within 12 months** of the actual delivery of the tax return to HMRC.
- Once this deadline is passed, the company can normally consider the self-assessment for that accounting period as final.

Enquiry procedures

HMRC can demand that the company produce:

- documents
- accounts
- other written particulars
- full answers to specific questions.

The information requested should be limited to that connected with the return.

- The company has 30 days to comply with the request. An appeal can be made against the request.
- The enquiry ends when HMRC give written notice that it has been completed.
- The notice will state the outcome of the enquiry.
- If a company believes that HMRC have no grounds for continuing an enquiry, it is entitled to ask the General or Special Commissioners that a date be set for its completion. You should refer to Chapter 13 for details about appeal procedures and the Commissioners.
- A company has 30 days from the completion of the enquiry to amend its self-assessment.
- If the company declines to do so or makes an amendment that is not to the satisfaction of HMRC, HMRC have a further 30 days to impose their amendment. The company then has a further 30 days to appeal against HMRC's amendment. The appeal must be in writing.

Discovery assessments

HMRC has the capacity to raise additional assessments, referred to as discovery assessments. The key points are:

- The use of a discovery assessment is restricted where a self-assessment return has already been made. However, although enquiries must normally begin **within 12 months** of the actual submission date, a discovery assessment can be raised at a later date to prevent the loss of corporation tax.

- Unless the loss of corporation tax is due to fraud or negligence, a discovery assessment cannot be raised where full disclosure was made in the return, even if this is found to be incorrect.
- HMRC will only accept that full disclosure has been made if any contentious items have been clearly brought to their attention – perhaps in a covering letter.
- Only a company that makes full disclosure in the self-assessment tax return, therefore, has absolute finality 12 months after the actual submission date.
- The time limit for making a discovery assessment is **five years** from the filing date (six years from the end of the accounting period). This is extended to **20 years** from the filing date, in the case of fraud or negligence.
- A discovery assessment may be appealed against.

8 Records

Companies are required to keep and preserve records necessary to make a correct and complete return. The records that must be kept include records of:

- all receipts and expenses
- all goods purchased and sold
- all supporting documents relating to the transactions of the business, such as accounts, books, contracts, vouchers and receipts.

The records must be retained for **six years** after the end of the accounting period to which they relate.

A penalty of up to £3,000, may be charged for failure to keep or retain adequate records. The maximum penalty is only likely to be imposed in the most serious cases, such as, where a company deliberately destroys its records in order to obstruct a HMRC enquiry.

9 Chapter summary

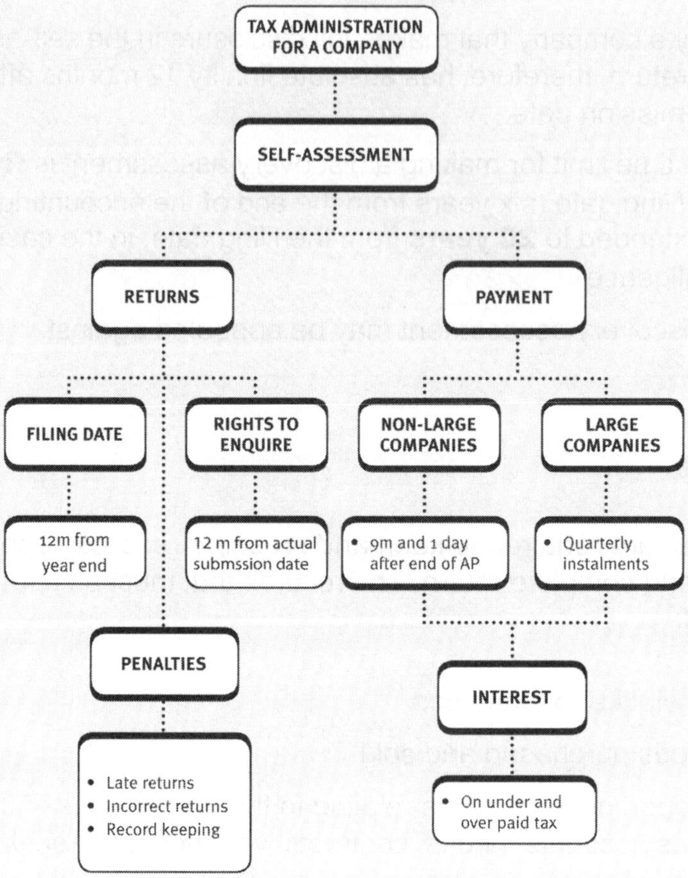

Test your understanding answers

Test your understanding 1

Everlate Ltd

The tax return should have been submitted by 28 February 2010, and so it is seven months late.

The fixed penalty is therefore £1,000 (as the return is more than three months late and Everlate is a persistent offender).

The tax geared penalty is £10,000 (£100,000 at 10%).

Test your understanding 2

XYZ Ltd

XYZ Ltd's corporation tax liability is due by instalments as follows:

£500,000 on 14 October 2008

£500,000 on 14 January 2009

£500,000 on 14 April 2009

£500,000 on 14 July 2009

Test your understanding 3

Able Ltd

Interest at the rate of 7.5% per annum will be charged from the due date of 1 January 2010 to 14 March 2010, on the underpayment of corporation tax of £50,000.

ıapter

25

VAT: outline

Chapter learning objectives

Upon completion of this chapter you will be able to:

- state the scope and nature of VAT
- explain the significance of the different types of supply for VAT
- list the principal zero-rated and exempt supplies
- identify the two key situations which require compulsory VAT registration
- discuss the advantages and disadvantages of voluntary registration
- identify when pre-registration input VAT can be recovered
- explain when a person must compulsorily/may voluntarily deregister for VAT
- outline the alternative VAT treatments on the sale of a business
- determine the date when goods and services are supplied
- identify the value of a supply and calculate the relevant VAT
- identify recoverable input VAT on key purchases and expenses
- compute the relief that is available for impairment losses on trade debts.

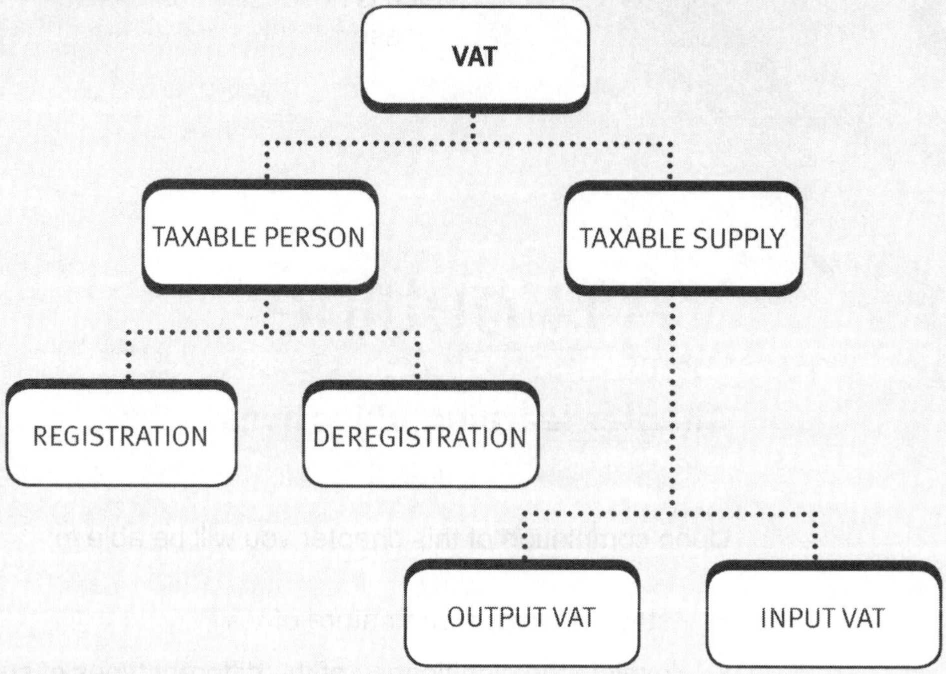

1 Introduction

VAT stands for value added tax.

VAT is:

- an indirect tax
- charged on most goods and services, supplied within the UK, and
- is borne by the final consumer.

VAT is an important tax for the examination. There will always be a minimum of 10 marks on VAT. VAT will normally be included within question one or question two, although there might be a separate question on VAT.

2 The scope and nature of VAT

There are three essentials needed before VAT can be charged

- A taxable person is one who is or should be registered for VAT, because they make taxable supplies (see registration section 4).

  A person can be an individual or a legal person, such as a company.

- A taxable supply is everything which is not exempt or outside the scope of VAT. It includes sales and purchases of most goods or services.
- For VAT to apply the taxable supply must be made in the course or furtherance of a business carried on by a taxable person.

Input and output VAT

It is important to distinguish between input and output VAT:

- Businesses pay input VAT on their purchases of goods and services.
- Input VAT is reclaimable from HMRC.
- Registered businesses charge output VAT on their sales of taxable goods and services.
- Output VAT is payable to HMRC.
- Every month or quarter the input and output VAT is netted off and paid to or recovered from HMRC.

Test your understanding 1

Which of the following statements are correct?

(1) VAT is an indirect tax.

(2) Lucy is an accountancy student. She sells some of her spare CDs to a friend. She should charge the friend VAT on the sale.

(3) Businesses may keep all the output VAT they charge to customers.

3 Types of supply

Supplies can be taxable, exempt or outside the scope of VAT.

Taxable supplies

- VAT is charged on taxable supplies but not on exempt supplies or supplies which are outside the scope of VAT. It is therefore important to be able to correctly classify supplies in order to determine whether VAT should be charged.
- It is also important to correctly classify supplies for the following reasons:
  - only taxable supplies are taken into account in determining whether a trader needs to register for VAT
  - input VAT related to exempt supplies is not recoverable.

- Taxable supplies are charged to VAT at one of three rates:
  - **zero rate:** This is a tax rate of nil. No VAT is charged but it is classed as a taxable supply. It is therefore taken into account in determining whether a trader should register for VAT and whether input VAT is recoverable
  - **standard rate:** This is currently a rate of 17.5%. Any taxable supply which is not charged at the zero or reduced rates is charged at the standard rate.
  - **reduced rate:** Some supplies, mainly for domestic or charitable use are charged at the reduced rate. Note that the reduced rate is not important for the examinations.

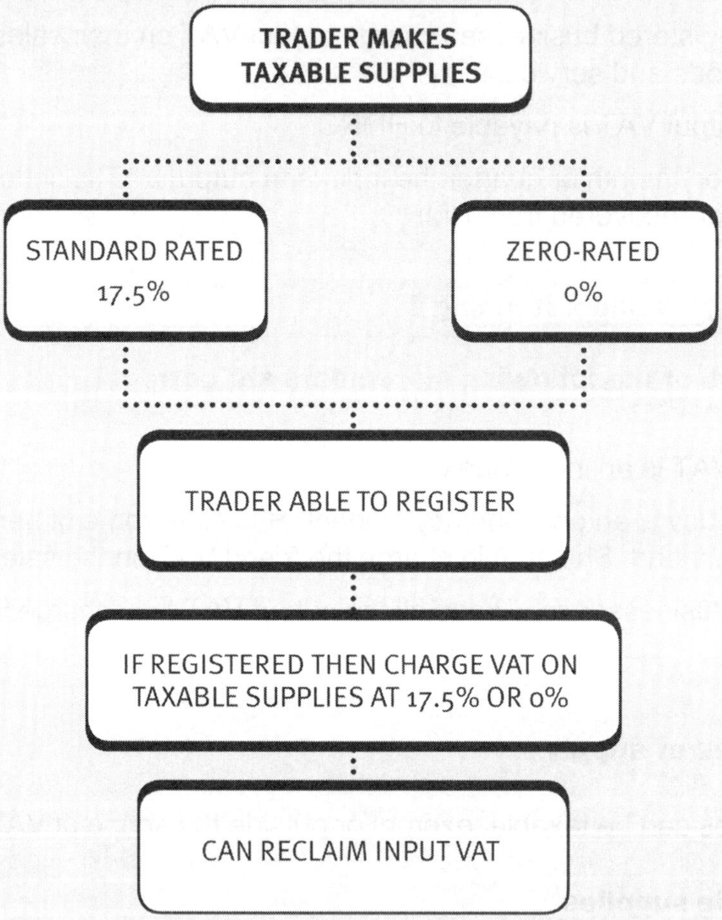

You must be careful to distinguish between zero-rated and exempt supplies.

Traders making exempt supplies cannot charge VAT to their customers. Traders making zero-rated supplies charge VAT but at 0%.

The key difference is that traders making zero-rated supplies **can** reclaim the input tax they suffer, those making exempt supplies **cannot**.

> **Test your understanding 2**
>
> **Fill in the blanks in the following statements:**
>
> (1) Traders making wholly exempt supplies .... register for VAT.
>
> (2) The standard rate of VAT is ....
>
> (3) Traders who are registered for VAT must charge VAT on all their taxable ....
>
> (4) The difference between zero-rated and exempt traders is that zero-rated traders .... recover input VAT, whilst exempt traders ....

Zero-rated and exempt supplies

You do not need a detailed knowledge of the rates of VAT which apply to different goods and services. However, it is useful to know the treatment of some of the more common types of supply. For example, items such as wages and dividends are outside the scope of VAT.

Remember that taxable supplies, which are not zero-rated or chargeable at the reduced rate, are standard rated.

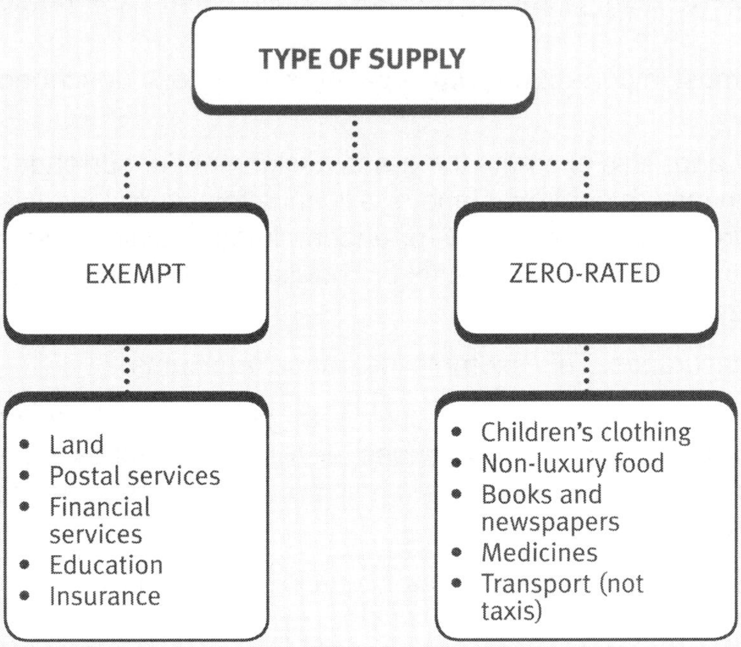

Expandable text - Zero-rated and exempt supplies

The most important **zero-rated items** are briefly described below.

- Food: Food of a kind used for human consumption is zero-rated unless it is either a supply in the course of catering (e.g. in a restaurant) or is classed as a luxury item, such as alcohol or confectionery.
- Books and other printed matter: This includes a wide range of reading material (e.g. newspapers, books, maps and sheet music).
- Construction of dwellings, etc: This includes new buildings for residential or charitable use. However, zero-rating does not cover the situation where an existing building is reconstructed, altered or enlarged.
- Transport: Transporting passengers by road, rail, sea or air is generally zero-rated, provided the vehicle or ship is designed to carry more than 11 passengers (e.g. not taxis).
- Drugs, medicines and appliances: Drugs supplied on prescription by a chemist are zero-rated, as are certain appliances and equipment supplied to the disabled.
- Charities: Gifts to charities are zero-rated.
- Clothing and footwear: Young children's clothing and footwear are zero-rated, provided they are unsuitable for older persons.

The most important **exempt supplies** are briefly described below.

- Land: This exempts the grant, assignment or surrender of an interest in land, a right over land or a licence to occupy land. However, the freehold sale of a new (or uncompleted) building is standard rated, unless it is for residential or charitable use (in which case it will be zero-rated).
- Insurance: This exempts insurance premiums.
- Finance: This exempts a wide range of financial services, such as: making loans, hire purchase, dealing in securities, such as shares, and banking services, such as providing current, deposit and savings accounts.
- Education: This exempts education provided by schools and universities.

- Health: This exempts the services of registered doctors, dentists, opticians, chemists, hospitals and other institutions (but not health farms).
- Sports: This exempts entry fees to sports competitions used to provide prizes or charged by non-profit making sporting bodies.

It is important to differentiate between zero-rated and exempt supplies. A trader making only exempt supplies will be unable to register for VAT and is not therefore able to recover input VAT on purchases.

Test your understanding 3

Fill in the following table by ticking the relevant column to indicate whether the item is zero-rated or exempt.

Item	Zero-rated	Exempt
Bread sold in a supermarket		
Children's shoes		
Sale of motor insurance policy		
Newspapers		
Sale of shares		
Railway ticket		

4 VAT registration – compulsory

Registration limits

If a person's taxable supplies (sales excluding sales of capital assets) exceed the registration limits, then registration is compulsory.

There are two separate tests for compulsory registration:

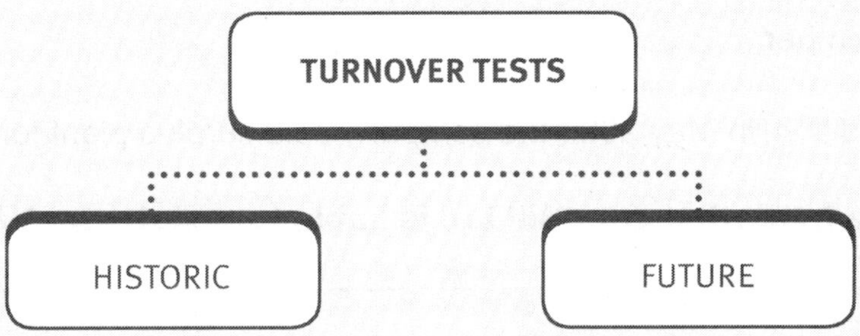

Historic turnover test

At the end of each month, the trader must look at the cumulative total of taxable supplies for the last 12 months, or since commencing trade, whichever is the shorter.

If the total exceeds the registration limit, currently £67,000, then the trader must register as follows:

- Notify HMRC **within 30 days** of the end of the month in which the turnover limit is exceeded.
- Registration is effective from the **end of the month** following the month in which turnover exceeded the limit, or an earlier agreed date.
- A trader need not register if his taxable supplies for the next 12 months are expected to be less than the deregistration limit (see below) currently £65,000.

Example 1 - VAT registration – compulsory

Hill Ltd commenced trading on 1 January 2008. Its monthly taxable supplies are as follows:

	2008	**2009**
	£	£
January	2,700	4,290
February	2,800	4,360
March	2,900	4,830
April	3,000	4,900
May	3,040	4,970
June	3,110	5,440
July	3,180	5,760
August	3,250	6,230
September	3,320	7,100
October	3,690	8,000
November	3,750	8,750
December	3,830	9,250

In addition, in May 2008 the company sold surplus plant for £3,100.

State from what date Hill Ltd is liable to register for VAT.

Answer to example 1

At the end of November 2009, Hill Ltd's taxable turnover for the previous 12 months is:

Value of supplies for registration purposes:	£
Supplies to customers	68,460
Supply of plant (disregarded)	Nil
	68,460

Hill Ltd is thus liable to register, and must notify HMRC by 30 December 2009.

The company will be registered from 1 January 2010, or such earlier date as may jointly be agreed.

Test your understanding 4

Jay owns a shop selling newspapers (zero-rated) and stationery (standard-rated). In his first year of trading to 30 September 2007, his sales of newspapers were £2,600 per month and of stationery £1,900 per month. In his second year of trading, these figures increased to £3,600 and £2,400, respectively.

State from what date Jay is liable to register for VAT.

Future prospects test

This test is considered at any time, when taxable supplies in the next 30 days in isolation are expected to exceed £67,000.

- HMRC must be notified before the end of the 30 days.
- Registration will be effective from the beginning of the 30-day period.

Example 2 - VAT registration – compulsory

Cat Ltd signs a lease for new business premises on 1 January 2009 and opens for business on 20 March 2009. The company estimates, from the outset, that taxable supplies will be in the region of £68,500 per month.

State when, if at all, Cat Ltd is liable to register.

Answer to example 2

Cat Ltd is liable to registration because supplies for the 30 days to 18 April 2009, are expected to exceed £67,000.

The company must notify HMRC of its liability to registration by 18 April 2009 and is registered with effect from 20 March 2009.

Note: Cat Ltd does not make any taxable supplies during the period 1 January 2009 to 19 March 2009, so the liability to register under the future limit test cannot arise during that period.

Test your understanding 5

State which of the following unregistered traders are liable to register for VAT and the effective date of registration.

Name	Supplies	Details
Majid	Accountancy services	Started in business 1 November 2008. Estimated fees £15,000 per month.
Jane	Baby wear	Established the business 1 March 2009 when Jane signed a contract to supply a local nursery. Sales for March 2009 are expected to be £75,000.
Sayso Ltd	Insurance	Commenced trading 2 January 2009. Sales are £100,000 per month.

Consequences of registration

Once registered, a taxable person must start accounting for VAT:

- Output tax must be charged on taxable supplies.
- Each registered trader is allocated a VAT registration number, which must be quoted on all invoices.
- Each registered trader is allocated a tax period for filing returns, which is normally every three months.
- Input tax (subject to some restriction) is recoverable on business purchases and expenses.
- Appropriate VAT records must be maintained.

There are penalties for late registration. In addition, the trader can be asked to pay over the VAT they should have collected in the period that they should have been registered.

Number of registrations

A person can be registered only once, and this registration includes all the businesses that that person carries on. Where a partnership is concerned, separate businesses carried on by the same partners, will have a single registration.

5 Voluntary registration

Actual or intending traders

Even if not required to register, a person may register voluntarily provided he is making, or intending to make, taxable supplies.

HMRC will register the trader from the date of the request for voluntary registration, or a mutually agreed earlier date.

Advantages and disadvantages of voluntary registration

Advantages	Disadvantages
• Avoids penalties for late registration. • Can recover input VAT on purchases. • Can disguise the small size of the business.	• Business will suffer the burden of compliance with all VAT administration rules. • Business must charge VAT. This makes their goods comparatively more expensive than an unregistered business, for customers who cannot recover the VAT, i.e. final consumers.

Example 3 - Voluntary registration

Alfred sells goods, which would be standard-rated if he were registered for VAT. All of his sales are to members of the public. His current annual turnover is £40,000. He incurs input VAT on purchases of £5,000 each year.

Assuming that, due to the competitive nature of his business, Alfred is unable to increase his prices to the public advise him whether it would be beneficial to register voluntarily for VAT.

Answer to example 3

If Alfred registered for VAT he would be required to charge his customers output VAT. As he is unable to increase his prices his VAT inclusive turnover would be £40,000 and he would have to account for output VAT to HM Revenue & Customs of £5,957 (£40,000 × 17.5/117.5). His profits would therefore decrease by £5,957.

He would however be able to reclaim input VAT of £5,000 pa. The net cost to Alfred of registering for VAT would be £957 (£5,957 – £5,000) and it is therefore not beneficial for him to register voluntarily.

If Alfred's sales were to other VAT registered businesses, he would be able to charge VAT in addition to his normal selling price, as his customers would be able to recover the VAT charged.

In this situation it would be beneficial for Alfred to register for VAT voluntarily. He would be able to recover the input tax, on his purchases and, as a result his profits would increase by £5,000.

6 Recovery of pre-registration input VAT

Normally, VAT incurred before registration cannot be accounted for as input VAT. If the conditions below are satisfied, however, then it can be treated as input tax and reclaimed accordingly.

Goods	**Services**
• The goods must be acquired for business purposes and should not be sold or consumed prior to registration, i.e. should still be in stock. • The goods have not been acquired more than **three years** prior to registration.	• The services must be supplied for business purposes. • The services should not have been supplied more than **six months** prior to registration.

Test your understanding 6

X Ltd registered for VAT with effect from 1 March 2009. The company incurred the following expenditure prior to registration:

(1) 14.8.08 Paid their accountants £500 plus VAT at 17.5%, for preparing cash flow forecasts.

(2) 15.10.08 Paid rent of £1,500, to a landlord who is an exempt trader hence no VAT paid.

(3) 1.11.08 Bought headed stationery, paying £1,175 including VAT at 17.5%.

(4) 14.12.08 Bought stock intended for resale, costing £5,000 plus VAT at 17.5%.

(5) 12.2.09 Bought machinery, costing £6,500 plus VAT at 17.5%.

At the date of registration, 60% of the stock intended for resale had already been sold. The stationery was unused and the company still owned the machine.

State the amounts of pre-registration input VAT that can be claimed.

7 Deregistration

Compulsory deregistration

A person must deregister when he ceases to make taxable supplies.

- HMRC should be notified **within 30 days** of ceasing to make taxable supplies.
- VAT registration is cancelled from the date of cessation or a mutually agreed later date.

Voluntary deregistration

A person may voluntarily deregister, even if the business continues, if there is evidence that taxable supplies in the next 12 months, will not exceed £65,000.

- The 12-month period is measured starting at any time.
- The onus is on the trader to satisfy HMRC that they qualify.
- VAT registration is cancelled from the date of request or an agreed later date.

Effect of deregistration

On deregistration, VAT output tax must be accounted for on the value of fixed assets and stocks held at the date of deregistration, on which a deduction for input tax has been claimed.

However, this final tax liability is waived if it is ≤ £1,000.

Test your understanding 7

(1) Jig Ltd closes down its business on 10 January 2009.

(2) At 1 January 2009, Elk Ltd thinks that taxable turnover for the year to 31 December 2009, will be £40,000. He immediately decides to apply for deregistration.

State when Jig Ltd should notify HMRC of his business cessation and from when he will be deregistered.

State when Elk Ltd will be deregistered.

8 VAT on sale of a business

Alternative treatments

Compulsory deregistration applies where a business is sold or otherwise transferred as a going concern to new owners.

The sale may be treated in one of two ways, depending on the circumstances:

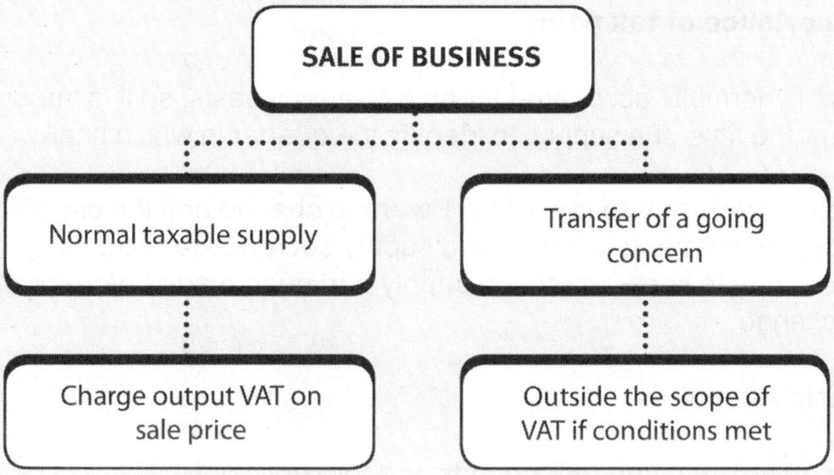

Conditions for transfer of business as a going concern

If the following conditions are satisfied, then the sale/transfer:

- will not be treated as a taxable supply
- no output tax will therefore be charged on the assets transferred by the seller, and
- no input tax is recoverable by the purchaser.

Conditions:

- The business is transferred as a going concern.
- There is no significant break in the trading.
- The same type of trade is carried on after the transfer.
- The new owner is or will be registered for VAT, immediately after the transfer.

Note that **all** these conditions **must** be met.

Transfer of registration

On the sale of a business it is normally compulsory to deregister. However, instead of doing so, both the transferor and the transferee may make a joint election, for the transferor's registration to be transferred to the transferee.

Where this is done, the transferee assumes all rights and obligations in respect of the registration, including the liability to pay any outstanding VAT.

9 The time of supply (the tax point)

Importance of tax point

VAT is normally accounted for on a quarterly basis, so it is important to know the time of a supply, to identify the quarter in which it falls.

Also, if the standard rate of VAT were to change or if the classification of a supply altered (e.g. a zero-rated supply became standard-rated), it would be necessary to know whether a supply had been made before or after the date of change.

Basic tax point

The rules are different for goods and for services:

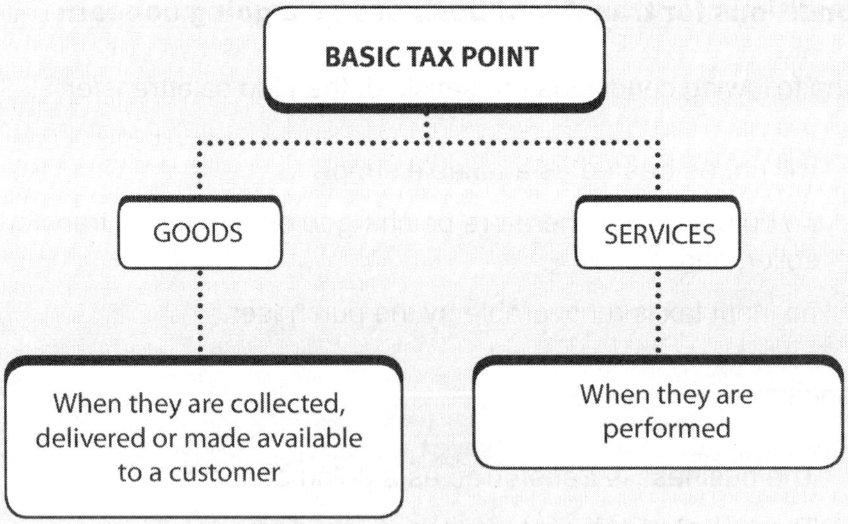

Example 4 - The time of supply (the tax point)

Queue Ltd received an order for goods from a customer on 14 August 2008. The goods were despatched on 18 August 2008 and the customer paid on 15 September 2008 when they received their invoice, which was dated 13 September 2008.

State what is the basic tax point date.

Answer to example 4

The tax point date is 18 August 2008 (i.e. the date of despatch).

Actual tax point

The basic tax point is amended in two situations:

ACTUAL TAX POINT

EARLIER

- A tax invoice is issued or a payment is received before the basic tax point.
- In these circumstances the date of invoice or date of payment is the time when the supply is treated as taking place.

LATER

- A tax invoice is issued within 14 days after the basic tax point.
- In these circumstances the date of issue of the invoice is the time when the supply is treated as taking place.

Note that traders can agree a different tax point with HMRC, to fit in with their invoicing routines.

Example 5 - The time of supply (the tax point)

Explain the effect if Queue Ltd, in example 4 above, were to issue an invoice for the goods dated 30 August 2008.

Answer to example 5

The tax point would become 30 August 2008 as an invoice is issued within 14 days after the basic tax point date.

Expandable text - Tax point - special rules

There are special rules for certain supplies of goods that do not fit naturally into the above scheme.

- **Goods on sale or return**: The time of supply is the earlier of the date when the sale is adopted by the customer, or 12 months after the dispatch of the goods
- **Continuous supplies**: Supplies such as electricity (goods) and tax advice (services) do not have a basic tax point. The time of supply is the earlier of a tax invoice being issued and a payment received.

  If the supplier wishes he may issue a tax invoice once a year in advance, showing the periodical payments and their due dates. In this case, there is a separate tax point for every amount due, being the earlier of the due date and the date on which payment is received.

- **Sales under hire purchase**. The goods are taxed as normal at the standard or zero-rate. The interest charge is an exempt supply, provided it is disclosed as a separate amount. The time of supply for the full value of the goods follows the normal rules, i.e. the time that the goods are collected, delivered or made available.

Test your understanding 8

On 30 November 2008, Oak Ltd ordered a new felling machine, and on 16 December 2008, paid a deposit of £25,000. The machine was despatched to Oak Ltd, on 31 December 2008. On 12 January 2009, an invoice was issued to Oak Ltd for the balance due of £75,000. This was paid on 20 January 2009.

State the tax point for:

(a) the £25,000 deposit?

(b) the balance of £75,000?

10 The value of a supply

Basic rule

The value of a taxable supply is the amount on which the VAT charge is based and this is normally equal to the price (before VAT) charged by the supplier.

VAT fraction for standard-rated goods

The price of goods before VAT is the **VAT exclusive amount**. If the price includes VAT, then this is the **VAT inclusive amount**.

- VAT is 17.5% of the VAT exclusive amount.

  If a standard-rated supply is made at a price of (£2,000 + VAT at 17.5%), then the value of the supply is £2,000 and the total consideration given for the supply is £2,350.

- If the VAT inclusive amount is given, then the VAT element is (17.5/117.5) of the gross amount. The fraction (7/47) gives the same result and is more commonly used.

Discounts

If a cash discount is offered, then VAT must be calculated as if the maximum discount available was taken.

Example 6 - The value of a supply

Gurminder sells standard-rated goods for £4,000, excluding VAT. A cash discount of 5% is allowed if the customer pays within seven days. Gurminder does not receive payment from the customer until a month after issuing the invoice.

Calculate the amount of VAT that should be charged on the sale.

Answer to example 6

VAT must be charged on the discounted amount even though the customer is not eligible for the discount.

VAT = (17.5% × 95% × £4,000) = £665

Goods for own use

Where the trader withdraws goods for his or her own use from the business, output VAT must be accounted for on the **replacement** value of the supplies.

Gifts

Gifts of stock or fixed assets are treated as taxable supplies at replacement value, except gifts of:

- goods to the same person which cost the trader £50 or less in a 12-month period
- samples, unless the recipient is given more than one sample of the same item.

Gifts of services are not taxable supplies.

Test your understanding 9

State the amount of VAT due in each of the following cases:

Description	Output VAT
Sale of standard-rated goods for £500, excluding VAT. A cash discount of 3% is offered.	
Sales of standard-rated goods for £5,500, including VAT.	
Gifts of 10 calendars costing £5 each, including VAT.	
Drawings of standard-rated goods by the owner. The goods cost £20 each and would cost £22 to replace, both figures exclude VAT.	

11 Recovery of input VAT

Conditions for obtaining input VAT relief

Input VAT is recoverable by taxable persons on goods and services which are supplied to them for business purposes. A VAT invoice (see below) is needed to support the claim.

Irrecoverable input VAT

Input VAT on the following goods and services cannot be recovered:

- Business entertaining, although VAT incurred on staff entertaining is recoverable.
- Cars, unless they are 100% used for business purposes (e.g. driving school cars).

Example 7 - Recovery of input VAT

Riker Plc sells standard-rated supplies and is registered for VAT. It incurs the following costs during 2008.

(1) £5,400 on business entertaining and £2,400 on staff entertaining.

(2) £30,000 on a new car for the managing director and £72,000 on new delivery lorries.

The managing director's car is used partly for private purposes.

All figures are VAT exclusive.

State the amount of input tax relief the business can claim and the figures that should be included in the financial statements in respect of these items.

Answer to example 7

(1) **Entertaining**

No VAT recoverable on business entertaining and the VAT inclusive figure of (£5,400 + 17.5%) = £6,345, should be charged against profits. Note that £6,345, will be a disallowed expense for the purpose of the tax-adjusted profit computation.

VAT of £420 (17.5% × £2,400), will be recoverable on staff entertaining and the VAT exclusive amount of £2,400 will be charged against profits.

(2) **Car and lorries**

No VAT recoverable on cars, so the VAT inclusive figure of (£30,000 + 17.5%) = £35,250, should be capitalised and will be eligible for capital allowances.

VAT of £12,600 (17.5% × £72,000) is recoverable on the lorries. £72,000 will be capitalised and be eligible for capital allowances.

Motor expenses

A business can recover input VAT incurred on the running costs of a car, such as fuel and repairs, even when there is some private use.

Note that VAT is not charged on the costs of insurance and road fund licence.

When a business pays for fuel costs for an employee, sole trader or partner and there is some private use of the vehicle, a VAT charge will be payable as follows:

- output VAT is payable on the cost of fuel reimbursed by the employee
- if the employee does not reimburse the employer, output VAT is due based on a prescribed scale charge.

The scale charge depending on the with CO_2 emissions of the car. The scale charges will be provided in the examination if necessary.

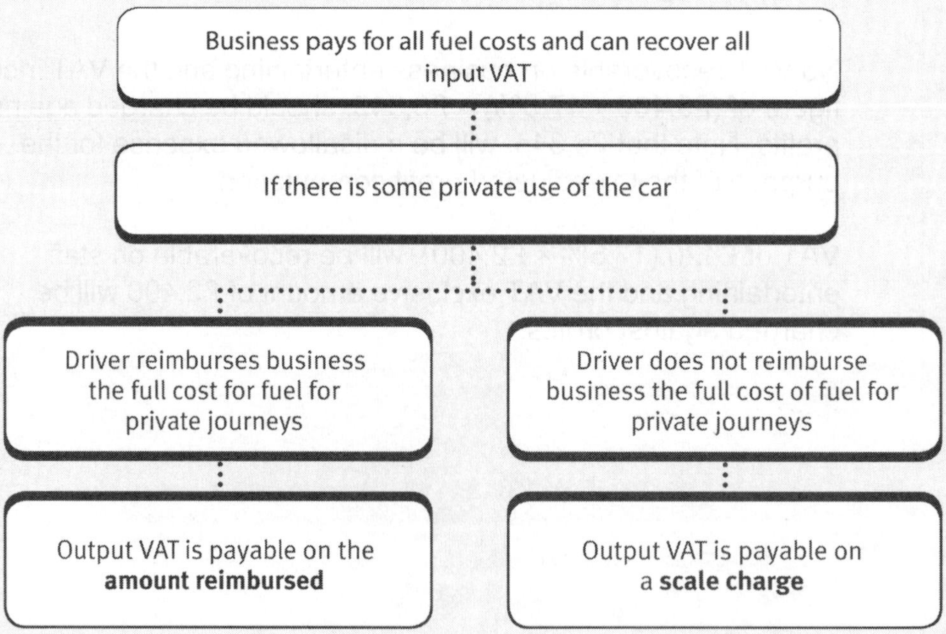

Example 8 - Recovery of input VAT

Forge Ltd provides a company car with CO_2 emissions of 205 g/km for the managing director for business and private use. The company pays for all running costs including petrol, with no reimbursement by the employee.

State the value of the output and output tax in respect of the running costs for this car for the quarter ended 31 March 2009.

Answer to example 8

The scale charge for a petrol car with CO_2 emissions of 205 g/km is £400. This means that £400 is the value of the VAT inclusive output.

The output VAT charge is £59.57 (£400 × 7/47).

Note the scale charge will be given in the question in the examination.

Test your understanding 10

State which of the following statements are true or false. Assume all the businesses in the question are VAT registered traders.

(1) VAT incurred by a business on staff entertaining is recoverable.

(2) Firmin plc can recover £2,625 on the purchase of an item of plant and machinery costing £15,000, including VAT.

(3) A business can never recover the VAT incurred on buying a car.

(4) A business supplies a company car with CO_2 emissions of 200 g/km to Albert. The company pays all the running costs of the car, incurring £2,100 of input tax for the VAT quarter and Albert reimburses the company 50% of the cost of his fuel for private use. The quarterly scale charge for a car with CO_2 emissions of 200g/km is £386 (VAT inclusive). The net input tax recoverable in respect of motor expenses is £2,043.

12 Relief for impaired debts

Normally, VAT output tax is accounted for when an invoice is issued. If the sale becomes irrecoverable, the seller has paid VAT to HMRC and never recovers this from the customer. This position is addressed by the seller being able to claim VAT bad debt relief.

The following conditions apply:

- At least **six months** must have elapsed since payment from the debtor was due.
- The debt must have been written off in the seller's VAT account.
- Relief is obtained by adding the VAT element of the bad debt to the input tax claimed.
- Claims for bad debt relief are subject to a three-year time limit.

Example 9 - Relief for impaired debts

Fox Ltd made sales to X Ltd as follows: £3,500 due for payment on 1 August 2008 and £2,260 due for payment on 1 September 2008. Fox Ltd wrote off the debts in January 2009.

State the amount of bad debt relief available to Fox Ltd, in the quarter to 31 March 2009.

Answer to example 9

At 31 March, both invoices are unpaid more than 6 months from the due date of payment.

The total debt to be written off is £5,760, including VAT. A claim for relief can be made for the VAT element of £858 (£5,760 × 7/47).

This claim can be made by adding £858 to the input tax claimed for the quarter.

Test your understanding 11

On 1 December, Berry Ltd wrote off two debts. The first was a debt of £2,456, due for payment on 1 May 2008 and the second a debt of £3,100, due for payment on 31 August 2008.

State the amount of bad debt relief available to the company in the return for the quarter ended 31 December 2008.

13 Comprehensive example

Test your understanding 12

Dynamo Ltd commenced trading as a wholesaler on 1 November 2008. Its sales have been as follows:

		£			£
2008	November	3,450	2009	June	4,750
	December	4,050		July	4,550
2009	January	3,550		August	5,350
	February	4,350		September	5,850
	March	3,750		October	7,750
	April	3,950		November	9,050
	May	4,150		December	10,050

The company's sales are all standard-rated, and the above figures are exclusive of VAT.

Dynamo Ltd only sells goods, and at present issues sales invoices that show:

(1) the invoice date and invoice number

(2) the type of supply,

(3) the quantity and a description of the goods supplied,

(4) Dynamo Ltd's name and address, and

(5) the name and address of the customer. The company does not offer any discount for prompt payment.

(a) Explain from what date Dynamo Ltd will be required to compulsorily register for VAT, and what action the company must then take.

(b) Explain the circumstances in which Dynamo Ltd will be allowed to recover input VAT incurred on goods purchased and services incurred prior to the date of VAT registration.

(c) Advise Dynamo Ltd of the VAT rules that determine the tax point in respect of a supply of goods.

14 Chapter summary

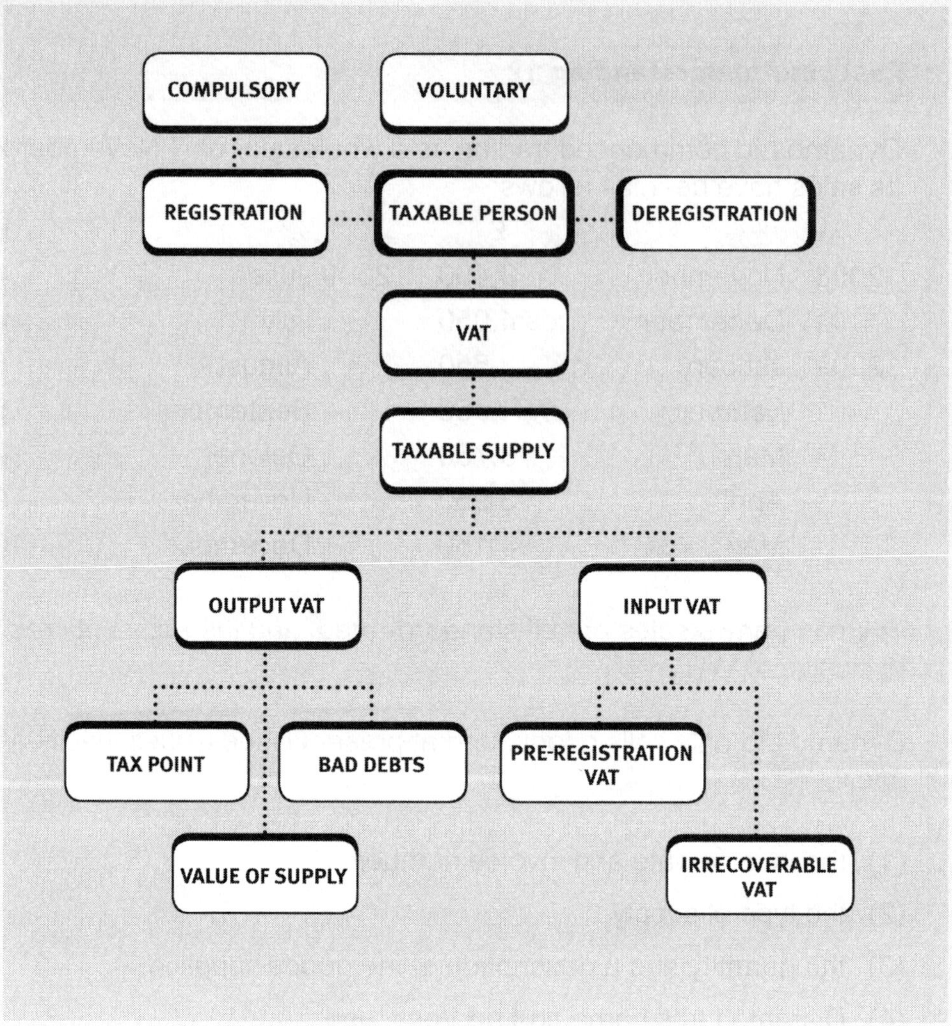

Test your understanding answers

Test your understanding 1

Correct or incorrect

(1) Correct.

(2) Incorrect. Lucy is not a taxable person and is not making a supply in the course of a business.

(3) Incorrect. Businesses must pay output VAT over to HMRC after deducting any input VAT they have suffered for the period.

Test your understanding 2

Missing words

(1) cannot

(2) 17.5%

(3) supplies

(4) can, cannot

Test your understanding 3

Zero-rated or exempt

Item	**Zero rated**	**Exempt**
Bread sold in a supermarket	√	
Children's shoes	√	
Sale of motor insurance policy		√
Newspapers	√	
Sale of shares		√
Railway ticket	√	

Test your understanding 4

Jay

Both newspapers and stationery are taxable supplies, so Jay must register when his sales for the previous 12 months exceed the registration limit of £67,000.

In his first year, sales are £4,500 per month, so his turnover for the year ended 30 September 2007, is £54,000. Thereafter, his sales are £6,000 per month, so each month he sells £1,500 more than one year ago.

Month end	Cumulative turnover for the last 12 months
	£
31 October 2007	55,500
30 November 2007	57,000
31 December 2007	58,500
31 January 2008	60,000
28 February 2008	61,500
31 March 2008	63,000
30 April 2008	64,500
31 May 2008	66,000
30 June 2008	67,500

He must notify HMRC by 30 July 2008 and will be registered with effect from 1 August 2008, or an earlier date agreed with HMRC.

Test your understanding 5

Name	Supplies	Details
Majid	Accountancy services	Taxable turnover will exceed £67,000 at the end of March 2009. Notify HMRC by 30 April 2009 and register with effect from 1 May 2009.
Jane	Baby wear	Sales for the next 30 days will exceed £67,000, so Jane must notify HMRC by the end of the 30 days on 30 March 2009 and will be registered with effect from 1 March 2009. Note that Jane could choose not to register as she is making wholly zero-rated supplies, but she would then be unable to reclaim any input tax.
Sayso Ltd	Insurance	Making wholly exempt supplies so cannot register.

Test your understanding 6

X Ltd

(1) Accountancy is a service. It is supplied more than six months prior to registration, hence, no input VAT can be reclaimed.

(2) Rent is exempt so no VAT paid and no VAT reclaimable.

(3) VAT of £175 (£1,175 × 17.5/117.5) is included in the cost of stationery. This can be recovered as the stationery had not been used prior to registration

(4) 40% of the stock is unsold at registration, so 40% of the VAT on the goods can be recovered. This is 40% of 17.5% of £5,000 = £350.

(5) The machinery is still owned by the company, so the VAT of £1137.50 (£6,500 × 17.5%) can be recovered.

Test your understanding 7

Jig Ltd and Elk Ltd

If Jig Ltd closes down its business on 10 January 2009, the company must notify HMRC on or before 9 February 2009 and is then deregistered from 10 January 2009, or an agreed later date.

If Elk Ltd thinks that taxable turnover for the year to 31 December 2009 will be £40,000, and applies for deregistration on 1 January 2009, the company can be deregistered with effect from 1 January 2009 or an agreed later date.

Test your understanding 8

(a) **£25,000 deposit**

The basic tax point is the date of despatch, 31 December 2008. As the deposit was paid before the date of despatch, this is the actual tax point (i.e. 16 December 2008).

(b) **The balance of £75,000**

As an invoice was issued within 14 days of the basic tax point; the date of the invoice is the actual tax point (i.e. 12 January 2009).

Test your understanding 9

Description	**Output VAT**
Sale of standard-rated goods for £500, excluding VAT. A cash discount of 3% is offered.	(17.5% × £500 × 97%) = £85
Sales of standard-rated goods for £5,500, including VAT.	(7/47 × £5,500) = £819
Gifts of 10 calendars costing £5 each, including VAT.	As less than £50 each, no output VAT
Drawings of standard-rated goods by the owner. The goods cost £20 each and would cost £22 to replace, both figures excluding VAT.	(17.5% × £22) = £4

Note that calculations in the examination are to the nearest £.

Test your understanding 10

True or false

(1) True

(2) False. (7/47 of £15,000) = £2,234.

(3) False. Input VAT can be recovered for cars with 100% business use.

(4) True. The business can recover £2,100 input tax but must account for £57 (£386 × 7/47) of output tax on the fuel scale charge. The net input tax recoverable is £2,043 (200 – £57).

Test your understanding 11

Berry Ltd

The second debt is less than six months old, so no relief is available yet.

On the first debt the VAT included of (7/47 × £2,465) = £366, can be recovered.

Test your understanding 12

Dynamo Ltd

(a) **Compulsory registration**

(1) Dynamo Ltd will become liable to compulsory VAT registration when its taxable supplies during any 12-month period exceed £67,000.

(2) This will happen on 31 December 2009 when taxable supplies will amount to £67,100 (£3,550 + £4,350 + £3,750 + £3,950 + £4,750 + £4,550 + £5,350 + £5,850 + £7,750 + £9,050 + £10,050).

(3) Dynamo Ltd will have to notify HM Revenue and Customs by 30 January 2010, being 30 days after the end of the period.

(4) The company will be registered from 1 February 2010 or from an agreed earlier date.

(b) **Recovery of input VAT on goods and services purchased prior to registration**

(1) The goods must be acquired for business purposes, and not be sold or consumed prior to registration.

(2) The goods were not acquired more than three years prior to registration.

(3) The services must be supplied for business purposes.

(4) The services were not supplied more than six months prior to registration.

(c) **The supply of goods**

(1) The basic tax point is the date goods are made available to the customer.

(2) If an invoice is issued or payment received before the basic tax point, then this becomes the actual tax point.

(3) If an invoice is issued within 14 days of the basic tax point, the invoice date will replace that in (1).

hapter

26

VAT: administration

Chapter learning objectives

Upon completion of this chapter you will be able to:

- prepare the computation of VAT payable/repayable for a return period
- explain the VAT return and payment procedures for different types of traders
- list the business records which must be retained for VAT purposes
- list the information required on a normal VAT invoice
- explain when a less detailed VAT invoice can be issued and list the content
- identify how a default surcharge penalty arises and calculate it
- explain the procedure and effect when errors on earlier VAT returns are identified
- define the circumstances when the serious misdeclaration penalty applies and state the amount of the penalty
- describe when a default interest charge will arise and calculate it
- understand the primary purpose of the cash accounting scheme and when it would be advantageous to use the scheme
- list the conditions to be met to operate a cash accounting scheme
- understand the primary purpose of the annual accounting scheme and when it would be advantageous to use the scheme
- explain how the annual accounting scheme operates and list the conditions
- demonstrate how a flat rate scheme operates compared to a normal scheme and state when this will be advantageous
- list the conditions for a flat rate scheme.

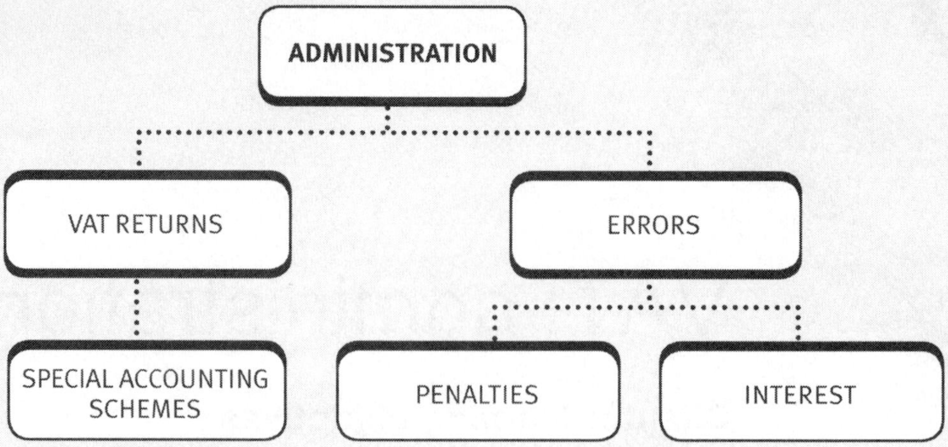

1 VAT computation

All registered traders have to complete a VAT return every return period (see below) and pay over any net VAT due to HMRC or reclaim net VAT repayable from HMRC.

Details of output and input VAT must be included, together with claims for bad debt relief and any errors made on earlier returns below a de minimus limit (see section 7).

Example 1 - VAT computation

Cart Ltd is registered for VAT, and its sales are all standard rated. The following information relates to the company's VAT return for the quarter ended 31 December 2008:

(1) Standard-rated sales amounted to £240,000. Cart Ltd offers its customers a 5% discount for prompt payment, and this discount is taken by half of the customers.

(2) Standard-rated purchases and expenses amounted to £71,280. This figure includes £960 for entertaining customers.

(3) On 15 December 2008, the company wrote off irrecoverable debts of £4,000 and £1,680, in respect of invoices due for payment on 10 May and 5 August 2008, respectively.

(4) On 30 December 2008, the company purchased a motor car at a cost of £32,900, for the use of a director, and machinery at a cost of £42,300. Both these figures are inclusive of VAT. The motor car is used for both business and private mileage.

Unless stated otherwise, all of the above figures are exclusive of VAT.

Calculate the amount of VAT payable by Cart Ltd for the quarter ended 31 December 2008.

Answer to example 1

VAT return – Quarter ended 31 December 2008

Output VAT	£	£
Sales (£240,000 × 95% × 17.5%)		39,900
Input VAT		
Purchases and expenses		
(£71,280 – £960 = £70,320 × 17.5%)	12,306	
Bad debt relief (£4,000 × 17.5%)	700	
Machinery (£42,300 × 7/47)	6,300	
		(19,306)
VAT payable		20,594

Notes:

(1) The calculation of output VAT must take into account the discount for prompt payment, even if customers do not take it.

(2) Input VAT on business entertaining cannot be reclaimed.

(3) Relief for an irrecoverable debt is not given until six months from the time that payment is due.

(4) Input VAT on motor cars not used wholly for business purposes cannot be reclaimed.

Test your understanding 1

Complete the following VAT return pro forma for the information given.

(1) Sales consisted of £45,000 of standard-rated sales and £15,000 of zero-rated sales.

(2) Purchases for resale were all standard rated and totalled £31,000.

(3) Standard-rated expenses were £7,600, including £350 for entertaining customers.

(4) One gift to a customer out of stock costing £250 was made. The replacement cost of the goods was £300.

(5) A photocopier costing £6,400 was purchased.

All figures exclude VAT. Work to the nearest £.

VAT return

	£	£
Output VAT		
Input VAT		
	———	
VAT payable/(repayable)		———
		———

2 VAT return and payment procedures

Normal VAT accounting

VAT return periods are normally three months long, but traders who regularly receive repayments, can opt to have monthly return periods to receive their repayments earlier.

- VAT returns show total output VAT and total input VAT for the period.
- VAT payable is due one month after the end of the quarter.
- VAT refunds are normally made within 28 days.

Expandable text - Substantial traders

These are traders with a VAT liability exceeding £2 million pa.

- Monthly payments on account are required.
- Payments at the end of months 2 and 3 in every quarter are 1/24th of the annual liability for the previous year.
- Any additional amounts are paid with the normal VAT return.

Other methods can be agreed with HMRC for calculating the payments on account.

3 VAT records

Records must be kept of all goods and services received and supplied in the course of a business. No particular form is specified, but they must be sufficient to allow the VAT return to be completed and to allow HMRC to check the return.

Records must be kept up-to-date and must be preserved for **six years**. In practice, the main records that must be kept are as follows:

- Copies of all VAT invoices issued.
- A record of all outputs, e.g. a sales day book.
- Evidence supporting claims for the recovery of input VAT, e.g. invoices.
- A record of all inputs, e.g. purchase day book.
- VAT account.

4 Normal VAT invoices

A VAT invoice must be issued when a standard-rated supply is made to a VAT registered business. No invoice is required if the supply is zero-rated.

A VAT invoice should be issued within 30 days of the date that the taxable supply is treated as being made.

The original VAT invoice is sent to the customer and forms their evidence for reclaiming input VAT, and a copy must be kept by the supplier to support the calculation of output VAT.

A VAT invoice must contain the following particulars:

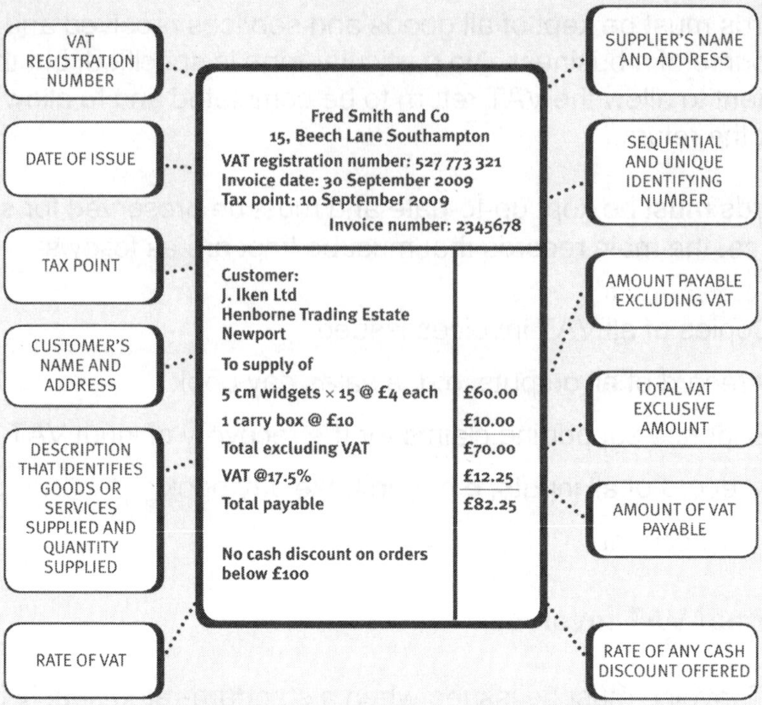

5 Less detailed VAT invoices issued by retailers

In broad terms, a retailer is someone who supplies goods and services to the general public, rather than to other traders. They are not necessarily retail shops, so a hairdresser is just as much a retailer as a newsagent or garage proprietor.

Retailers only have to provide a VAT invoice if a customer requests it. Such an invoice can be less detailed than normal, if the consideration for the supply is £250 or less.

This less detailed invoice must show the following information:

- The retailer's name, address and VAT registration number.
- The date of supply.
- A description of the goods or services supplied.
- The consideration for the supply.
- The rate of VAT in force at the time of supply.

Test your understanding 2

State which of the following statements are true or false:

(1) All VAT invoices must show the rate of VAT on the supply.

(2) A VAT invoice should show the customer's VAT registration number.

(3) Retailers must always supply a full VAT invoice to their customers when requested.

(4) Where the value of a supply is more than £250, a retailer should always issue a detailed VAT invoice.

6 The default surcharge

Introduction

A default occurs if a VAT return is not submitted on time or a payment of VAT is made late. The sequence is as follows:

- On the first default, HMRC will serve a surcharge liability notice on the trader.
- The notice specifies a surcharge period, starting on the date of the notice and ending on the 12-month anniversary of the end of the VAT period to which the default relates.
- If the trader has a further default during the surcharge period, there are two consequences:
  - The surcharge period is extended to the 12-month anniversary of the VAT period to which the new default relates.
  - If the default involves the late payment of VAT, then the trader will be subject to a surcharge penalty.
- There is no surcharge penalty where a late VAT return involves the repayment of VAT.

Calculating the surcharge penalty

The rate of surcharge penalty depends on the number of defaults in the surcharge period:

Default in the surcharge period	Surcharge as a percentageof the unpaid VAT due
First	2%
Second	5%
Third	10%
Fourth	15%

- Surcharge penalties at the rates of 2% and 5% are not made for amounts less than £400.
- Where the rate of surcharge is 10% or 15%, a surcharge penalty is the higher of:

  (i) £30, or

  (ii) the actual amount of the calculated surcharge.
- The surcharge liability period will only end when a trader submits four consecutive quarterly VAT returns on time, and also pays any VAT due on time.

Example 2 - The default surcharge

Mole Ltd's VAT return for the quarter ended 30 June 2008, was submitted late, and the VAT due of £14,500 was not paid until 16 August 2008.

The company's VAT return for the following quarter to 30 September 2008, was also submitted late and the VAT due of £26,200, was not paid until 9 November 2008.

State the consequences for Mole Ltd.

Answer to example 2

VAT return period for the quarter ended 30 June 2008	VAT return period for the quarter ended 30 September 2008
• First default	• First default within the surcharge period
• Surcharge liability notice issued	• Surcharge penalty 2% of £26,200 = £524
• Surcharge period ends 30 June 2009	• Surcharge period extended to 30 September 2009

Test your understanding 3

Fill in the missing blanks in the following statements:

(1) If a business submits its VAT return late then HMRC will issue a . . . . (3 words).

(2) The . . . . default within a surcharge period will attract a penalty of 5%.

(3) In order to avoid further surcharges, a business must submit all VAT returns and pay all VAT due, on time for a period of . . . . months.

(4) If a trader's first default produces a penalty of £300, then HMRC . . . . collect it.

7 Errors on VAT returns

Self-assessment

VAT is a self-assessed tax. The trader calculates their own liability or repayment.

- HMRC make occasional control visits to check that returns are correct.
- HMRC have the power to enter business premises, inspect documents, including profit and loss accounts and balance sheets, take samples, and inspect computers records.

Errors found on earlier VAT returns

If a trader realises that there is an error or misdeclaration on an earlier return, they will not suffer a penalty if they disclose it voluntarily.

Errors discovered by HMRC, may lead to penalties if the errors are large. In some cases interest may be due.

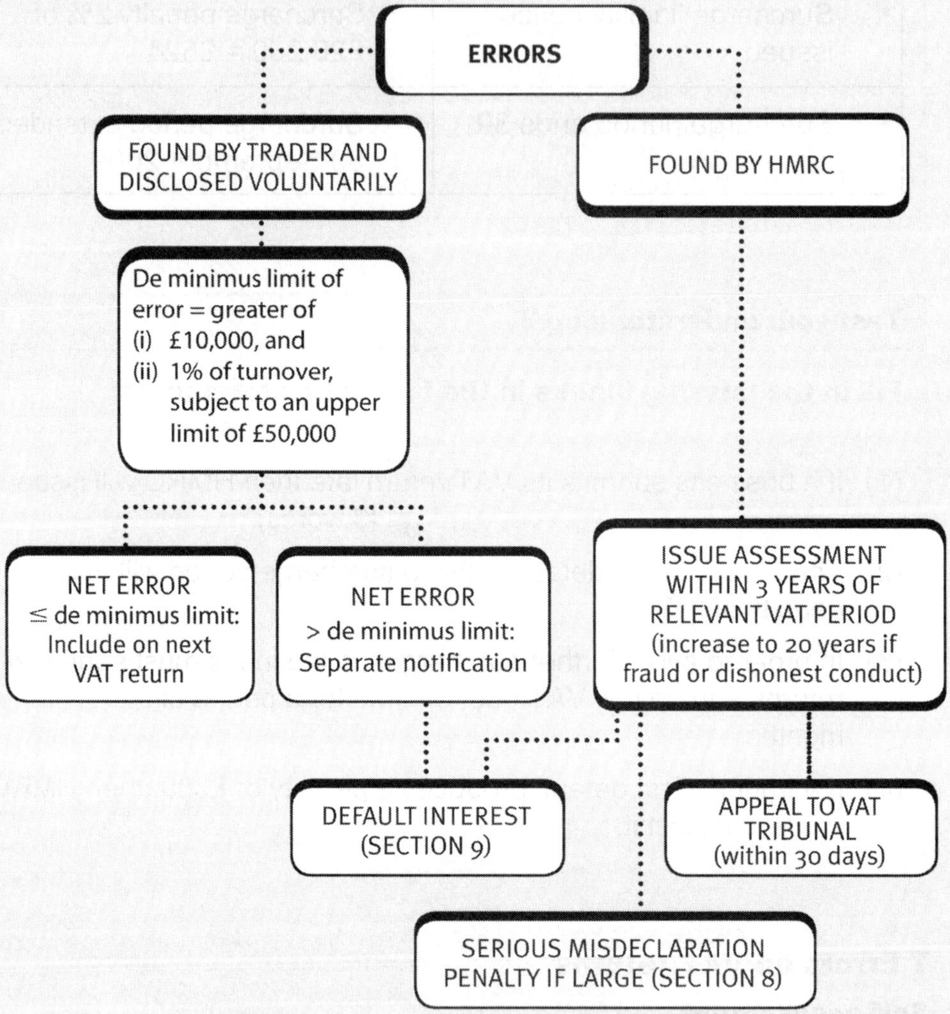

Example 3 - Errors on VAT returns

Bishop is a registered trader who prepares VAT returns quarterly. In his quarter to 30 June 2009, he has a turnover of £103,450 and he discovers the following errors in earlier returns:

(1) Bishop misread the total of output VAT for the previous quarter as £45,590, when it actually read £54,590. He entered £45,590 on his return.

(2) Input VAT on business entertaining of £180, was wrongly reclaimed as input tax in the same quarter.

(3) No input tax was reclaimed on the purchase of a computer in September 2008, costing £1,680 plus VAT.

State the action Bishop should take to correct these errors.

Answer to example 3

		£
(1) Output VAT	(£54,590 – £45,590)	9,000
(2) Entertaining		180
(3) Computer input VAT	(£1,680 x 17.5%)	(294)
		8,886

De minimus limit = greater of:

(i) £10,000

(ii) (1% x £103,450) = £1,034

As the net error of £8,886 < the de minimus limit of £10,000:

Bishop should include the amounts on his return to 30 June 2009.

This increases his VAT payable for the quarter ended 30 June 2009 by £8,886.

Expandable text - HMRC assessments

- HMRC may find that a VAT return is incomplete or incorrect. If so, they can issue an assessment to collect the VAT that has been underpaid, if applicable, by the trader.
- An assessment must be made within three years of the relevant VAT period. The three-year time limit is increased to 20 years where VAT has been lost, due to fraud or dishonest conduct.
- Appeals in connection with VAT, are made to an independent tribunal – the VAT tribunal. The normal time limit for appealing is 30 days.
- An unsuccessful party to an appeal, may appeal to the High Court on a matter or law, and thereafter, the Court of Appeal and House of Lords.

8 Serious misdeclaration penalty

Introduction

A serious misdeclaration penalty is imposed in two situations:

(1) A large misdeclaration is discovered by HMRC in respect of a trader's VAT return. Large means the lower of:

- 30% of gross amount of VAT (total of output VAT **plus** input VAT that should have been declared), or
- £1 million.

(2) HMRC issue an assessment for VAT underpaid, and the trader fails to inform them within 30 days that the assessment is too low.

The penalty

For returns commencing on/after 1 April 2008 where the return is due to be filed on/after 1 April 2009, the penalty is determined in the same way as penalties on incorrect income tax and corporation tax returns i.e. according to:

- The amount of tax understated
- The reason for the understatement
- The extent of disclosure by the taxpayer.

The level of the penalty is a percentage of the revenue lost as a result of the inaccuracy or under assessment and depends on the behaviour of the taxpayer as follows:

Taxpayer behaviour	**Maximum penalty (% of revenue lost)**
Genuine mistake	No penalty
Failure to take reasonable care	30%
Serious or deliberate understatement	70%
Serious or deliberate understatement with concealment	100%

The penalties may be reduced depending on the type of penalty and whether the taxpayer makes an unprompted disclosure.

Where the return is incorrect through deliberate intention of a third party, the penalty can be charged on the third party.

Test your understanding 4

For each of the following situations state whether a serious misdeclaration penalty is applicable.

Name	**Original net VAT declared**	**Correct output VAT**	**Correct input VAT**
	£	£	£
Avril	35,000	110,000	30,000
Blaise Ltd	120,000	350,000	100,000
Claim plc	900,000	4,000,000	1,150,000

9 Default interest

Interest is charged, if HMRC raise an assessment, or an error is voluntarily disclosed by the trader, and the net value of errors exceeds the de minimus limit.

Interest is charged from the date that the outstanding VAT should have been paid, to the actual date of payment.

Any interest charged by HMRC is limited to a maximum of three years, prior to the date of the assessment or voluntary disclosure.

Example 4 - Default interest

Hem Ltd discovers that in the quarter ended 31 May 2008, it made an error on its VAT return and output VAT of £12,800 was under declared. The company corrected this on its next VAT return, paying the VAT due on 30 September 2008.

Assuming the rate of default interest is 8.5%, calculate the charge made on Hem Ltd.

Answer to example 4

The under declared VAT should have been paid on 30 June 2008. Default interest will be charged from 30 June to 30 September 2008. This will be (£12,800 × 8.5% × 3/12) = £272.

Test your understanding 5

HMRC issue an assessment showing £4,100 VAT payable on 31 January 2009, for the quarter ended 31 March 2008. Grab Ltd pays the outstanding sum on 28 February 2009. Assume the rate of interest is 8.5%.

Calculate the default interest charged on Grab Ltd.

10 The cash accounting scheme

Purpose of the scheme

Normally VAT is accounted for on the basis of invoices issued and received in a return period. Accordingly, output VAT is paid to HMRC by reference to the period in which the invoice is issued regardless of whether payment has been received from the customer.

Similarly, input VAT is reclaimed from HMRC by reference to the invoices received in the return period, even if payment has not been made to the supplier.

- This can give cash flow and bad debt problems, particularly in the case of smaller businesses.
- 'Smaller' businesses may optionally use the cash accounting scheme if the conditions, set out below, are met.
- Under the cash accounting scheme VAT is accounted for on the basis of cash receipts and payments, rather than on the basis of invoice dates, issued and received.

- The tax point becomes the time of receipt or payment.

Advantages	**Disadvantages**
• Businesses selling on credit do not have to pay output VAT to HMRC until they receive it from customers.	• Input tax cannot be claimed until the invoice is paid. This delays recovery of input VAT.
• This gives automatic bad debt relief.	• Not suitable for businesses with a lot of cash sales or zero-rated supplies which would simply suffer a delay in the recovery of input VAT.

Conditions

The scheme is aimed at smaller businesses, hence, there are a number of conditions:

- Trader's VAT returns must be up-to-date and they must have no convictions for VAT offences or penalties for dishonest conduct.
- Taxable turnover, including zero-rated sales, but excluding sales of capital assets, must not exceed £1,350,000 pa.
- A trader must leave the scheme once their taxable turnover exceeds £1,600,000 pa.
- The cash accounting scheme cannot be used for goods that are invoiced more than six months in advance of the payment date, or where an invoice is issued prior to the supply actually taking place.

Test your understanding 6

State which of the following businesses would benefit from joining the cash accounting scheme:

(1) JB Ltd, which operates a retail shop selling directly to the public. All sales are for cash.

(2) Amber and Co, which manufactures and sells computer printers to other businesses.

(3) John Smith, who manufactures children's shoes and sells them to retailers.

11 Annual accounting

Purpose of the scheme

Smaller businesses may find it costly or inconvenient to prepare (the normal) four quarterly VAT returns.

An 'annual' accounting scheme is available, whereby, a single VAT return is filed for a 12-month period (normally, the accounting period of the business). This helps relieve the burden of administration.

How the scheme works

Only one VAT return is submitted each year, but VAT payments must still be made regularly. The scheme works as follows:

- The annual return must be filed **within two months** of the end of the annual return period.
- Normally, nine payments on account of the VAT liability for the year, are made at the end of months 4 to 12 of the year. Each payment represents 10% of the VAT liability for the previous year.
- A new business will base its payments on an estimate of the VAT liability for the year.
- A balancing payment (or repayment) is made when the return is filed.
- Businesses may apply to HMRC to agree quarterly payments on account instead of the normal nine monthly payments.

Conditions for the annual accounting scheme

As with cash accounting the scheme is aimed at smaller businesses:

- Businesses can join the scheme provided their taxable turnover (excluding the sale of capital assets) does not exceed £1,350,000.
- The business must be up-to-date with its VAT returns.

Test your understanding 7

Jump Ltd applies to use the annual accounting scheme from 1 January 2008. The company's net VAT liability for the year ended 31 December 2007, was £3,600. The actual net VAT liability for the year ended 31 December 2008, is £3,821.

Explain the returns and payments Jump Ltd must make for the year ended 31 December 2008.

12 The flat rate scheme

Operation of the scheme

The optional flat rate scheme is aimed at simplifying the way in which very small businesses calculate their VAT liability.

Under the flat rate scheme, a business **calculates its VAT liability** by simply applying a flat rate percentage to total turnover. This removes the need to calculate and record output VAT and input VAT and can save the business money.

- The flat rate percentage is applied to the gross (VAT inclusive) total turnover figure (inclusive of zero-rated and exempt supplies); with no input VAT being recovered.
- The percentage varies according to the type of trade that the business is involved in, and will be given to you in the examination.
- VAT at the rate of 17.5% is still charged on standard-rated supplies and a VAT invoice must still be issued. The flat rate scheme percentage is only used to calculate the VAT due to HMRC.

Conditions for the scheme

There are two conditions:

(1) The expected taxable turnover (excluding VAT) for the next twelve months does not exceed £150,000.

(2) The expected total income (excluding VAT but including exempt supplies and other income) for the next twelve months does not exceed £187,500.

Test your understanding 8

Apple Ltd has annual sales of £70,000, all of which are standard rated and to the general public. The company incurs standard-rated expenses of £4,500 pa. These figures are inclusive of VAT.

Calculate Apple Ltd's VAT liability using:

(1) **The normal method.**

(2) **The flat rate scheme.**

Assume that the relevant flat rate percentage for Apple Ltd's trade is 12%.

13 Chapter summary

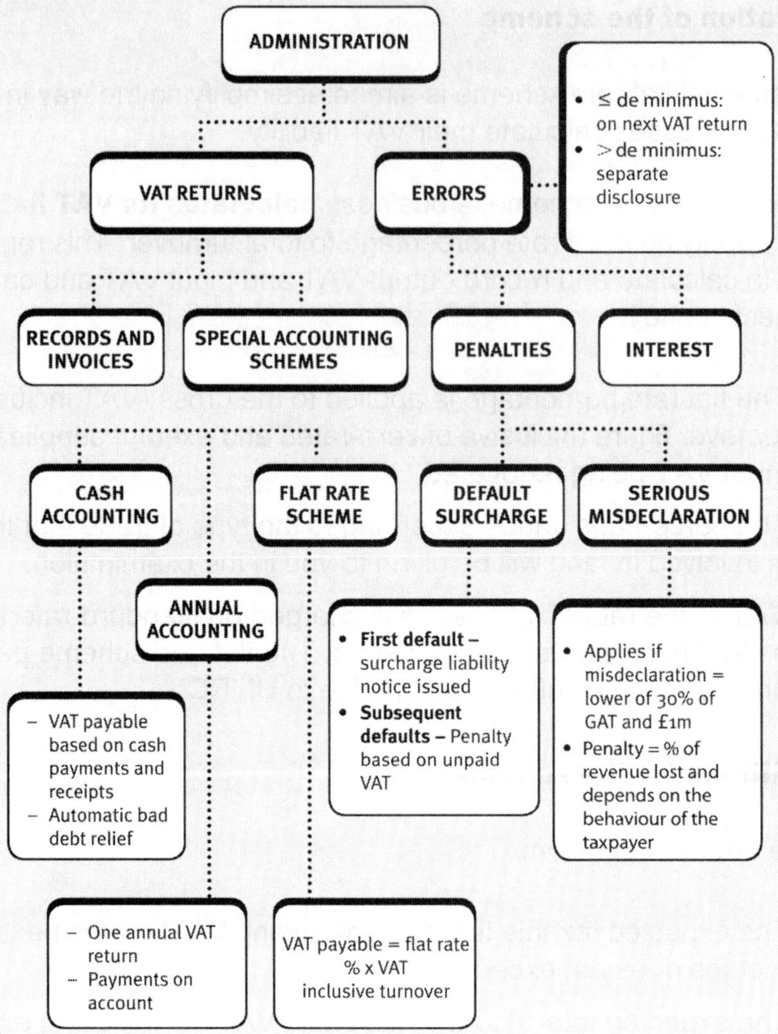

Test your understanding answers

Test your understanding 1

VAT return

	£	£
Output VAT		
Sales (£45,000 × 17.5%)		7,875
Gift to customer (£300 × 17.5%)		53
Input VAT		
Purchases (£31,000 × 17.5%)	5,425	
Expenses (£7,600 – £350 = £7,250 × 17.5%)	1,269	
Photocopier (6,400 × 17.5%)	1,120	
		(7,814)
VAT payable/repayable		114

Notes

(1) Output VAT due on gifts over £50 is always based on the replacement cost.

(2) VAT on business entertaining is not reclaimable. Only staff entertaining is allowed.

Test your understanding 2

True or false

(1) True.

(2) False – it should show the **supplier's** VAT registration number.

(3) False – for supplies below £250 they need only issue a less detailed invoice.

(4) False – only if the customer requests.

Test your understanding 3

Missing words

(1) Surcharge liability notice

(2) Second

(3) Twelve

(4) Will not

Test your understanding 4

Serious misdeclaration penalty

Penalty levied if error is greater than the lower of 30% of GAT or £1 milllion.

Name	**Original VAT declared**	**Correct VAT**	**Error**	**Lower of 30% of GAT or £1m (W)**	**Penalty due?**
	£	£	£	£	(Note)
Avril	35,000	80,000	45,000	42,000	Yes
Blaise Ltd	120,000	250,000	130,000	135,000	No
Claim plc	900,000	2,850,000	1,950,000	1,000,000	Yes

Working

(1) GAT is the total of output VAT **and** input VAT

Avril (£110,000 + £30,000) x 30% = £42,000

Blaise Ltd (£350,000 + £100,000) x 30% = £135,000

Claim plc (£4,000,000 + £1,150,000) x 30% = £1,545,000

Note: If the error is a genuine mistake, no penalty will arise. The amount of any penalty due will depend on the reason for the error and the extent of disclosure by the taxpayer.

Test your understanding 5

Grab Ltd

Interest runs from 30 April 2008 to 28 February 2009.

Default interest at 8.5% for 10 months will be charged:

(£4,100 × 8.5% × 10/12) = £290

Test your understanding 6

Cash accounting scheme

Amber and Co would benefit from joining the cash accounting scheme.

JB Ltd makes cash sales, and John Smith zero-rated sales, so neither of them have a problem with VAT on bad debts. Joining the scheme may also delay the recovery of input VAT on supplies. They are therefore unlikely to benefit from joining the cash accounting scheme.

Test your understanding 7

Jump Ltd

Jump Ltd's annual VAT return must be submitted by 28 February 2009.

Payments of VAT will be made as follows:

Monthly payments: April 2008 to December 2008	£
9 at £360 (£3,600 × 10%)	3,240
Final payment due on 28 February 2009	
(£3,821 – £3,240)	581
	3,821

Test your understanding 8

Apple Ltd

(1) Using the normal method, Apple has a VAT liability as follows:

		£
Output VAT	(£70,000 × 7/47)	10,426
Input VAT	(£4,500 × 7/47)	(670)
VAT payable		9,756

(2) Using the flat rate method Apple, has the following VAT liability:

(£70,000 × 12%) = £8,400

By using the flat rate scheme:

- there is a VAT saving of £1,356 (£9,756 – £8,400).
- Administration is also simplified; Apple Ltd will not have to issue VAT invoices, as none of its customers are VAT-registered.

hapter

27

Questions & Answers

1 The UK tax system

There are no questions for this chapter.

2 Basic income tax computation

There are no questions for this chapter.

3 Property and investment income

Amos Groves

Question 1

Amos Groves owns four houses that he lets out to tenants. Details of the income and expenditure incurred in respect of the houses in the year to 5 April 2009 is as follows:

House 1

Amos purchased this house on 1 June 2008. He immediately undertook repair work to the leaking roof that cost £5,000 and redecorated the house at a cost of £800. The house was rented out, unfurnished, from 1 September 2008 on a six-year lease at an annual rental of £4,500, payable quarterly in advance. The incoming tenant was charged a premium of £2,500.

House 2

This house was let furnished throughout the year at a monthly rent of £650, payable monthly in advance. Amos incurred the following expenditure during the year; water rates £300, council tax £850, property insurance £500, purchase of new cooker £400. He also incurred loan interest of £2,500 on a loan taken out to purchase the property.

Amos claims the wear and tear allowance for this property.

House 3

The tenants of this property left this unfurnished house on 30 November 2008, owing two month's rent totalling £1,000, which Amos was unable to recover. Decoration work was carried out in January 2009 at a cost of £2,500 and advertising costs of £450 were incurred in looking for new tenants. Other allowable costs for the year amounted to £550.The property was re-let on 1 April 2009, again unfurnished, at a monthly rent of £600, payable in advance.

House 4

This house was let out unfurnished to tenants throughout the year at a monthly rent of £450, payable in advance. Amos replaced a broken window at a cost of £100 during the year. The property was insured at a cost of £300 and £400 for the two years ended 30 June 2008 and 2009 respectively. Other allowable costs amounted to £200 for the year.

Other income

Amos received income from a part-time employment of £8,000 during the year to 5 April 2009 from which PAYE of £390 was deducted. In addition he received interest of £500 on a bank deposit account and dividends of £450 from UK quoted companies during the year.

Required:

(a) Calculate the amount assessable on Amos as property business income for the year to 5 April 2009 in respect of the above properties.

(11 marks)

(b) Calculate the income tax payable by Amos for the year ended 5 April 2009.

(4 marks)

(Total: 15 marks)

4 Section - Employment income

There are no questions for this chapter.

5 Income from self-employment

Peter

Question 1

For the past five years Peter has run a business importing electrical goods from the Far East, which he then sells to wholesalers in the UK.

His trading and profit and loss account for the year ended 31 December 2008 is as follows:

	£	£
Sales		325,000
Cost of goods sold		(172,500)
Gross profit		152,500
Rent received (**Note 1**)		9,500
		162,000
Wages and salaries	50,200	
Rent and rates (**Note 1**)	12,900	
Light and heat **(Note 1)**	5,250	
Depreciation of fixtures and fittings	1,500	
Insurance	3,550	
Travelling and entertaining (**Note 2**)	10,750	
Impaired debts (**Note 3**)	6,750	
Depreciation of vehicles	7,500	
Motor car expenses (**Note 4**)	4,500	
Sundry expenses (**Note 5**)	750	
Legal and professional charges (**Note 6**)	4,750	
Interest on bank overdraft	1,500	
Van expenses	9,300	
Telephone	3,350	
Repairs and renewals (**Note 7**)	3,500	
		(126,050)
Net profit		35,950

Notes:

(1) Rent received is in respect of a flat above Peter's business premises that is rented out. Peter estimates that a tenth of the rent and rates, and a seventh of the light and heat are in respect of this flat.

(2) **Travelling and entertaining expenses:**

	£
Peter's business travelling expenses	5,175
Christmas presents for staff	250
Entertaining overseas suppliers	2,750
Entertaining UK customers	2,300
Gifts to customers that carry the business name	
Boxes of chocolates costing £5.00 each	125
Calendars costing £1.50 each	150
	10,750

(3) **Impaired debts**

	£
Trading debts written off	3,750
Increase in allowance for debtors	1,750
Supplier loan written off	1,700
A trade debt recovered which had been written off the previous year	(450)
	6,750

(4) **Motor car expenses**

	£
Peter's motor car expenses	3,300
Salesman's motor car expenses	1,200
	4,500

Peter's total mileage for the year was 12,000 miles. During the year he drove 2,000 miles on a touring holiday and estimates that the balance of his mileage is 20% private and 80% business.

(5) **Sundry expenses**

	£
Donation to national charity	50
Donation to local political party	100
Subscription to chamber of commerce	25
A gift to a member of staff upon marriage	45
Peter's squash club subscription	250
Advertising in trade press	280
	750

Peter often uses his squash club as a place to take customers since several of them are keen squash players.

(6) **Legal and professional charges**

	£
The cost of renewing a 21-year lease in respect of the business premises	250
Accountancy	3,050
Debt collection	300
Legal fees in connection with an action by an employee for unfair dismissal	1,150
	4,750

Included in Peter's accountancy fee is £950 for taxation services. Of this, £200 is for the normal taxation work involved in submitting accounts to HM Revenue and Customs. The balance is in respect of calculating Peter's capital gains tax liability following the disposal of some shares that he had owned.

(7) **Repairs and renewals**

	£
Repairs to the office photocopier	175
A new printer for the office computer	650
The installation of new central heating for the office	2,200
Decorating the office	475
	3,500

(8) During the year ended 31 December 2008 Peter took various electrical goods out of stock for his own and his family's use without paying for them. These goods cost £450 and would have normally been sold at a mark up of 30%.

(9) Peter has a room in his private house that he uses as an office as he often works at home. The allowable amount for the use of the office is £250 and appears to be a fair estimate. Also, Peter makes business calls from his private telephone and he estimates the business use as two fifths. The total of his private telephone bill for the year was £450.

Required:

Calculate Peter's adjusted trading profit (before capital allowances) for the year ended 31 December 2008.

(Total: 15 marks)

6 Capital allowances – plant and machinery

Austin Scuba

Question 1

Austin Scuba commenced business as a self-employed decorator on 1 June 2008. His tax-adjusted trading profits before capital allowances, have been:

	£
Period ended 31 March 2009	51,000
Year ended 31 March 2010	45,600

The following capital transactions took place:

		£
15 May 2008	Purchased equipment	32,260
1 June 2008	Purchased a short-life asset	2,400
1 June 2008	Purchased a van	16,500
15 June 2008	Purchased a motor car	15,600
1 April 2009	Sold equipment (original cost £600)	500
12 April 2009	Purchased equipment	11,200
20 August 2009	Purchased furniture	22,020
18 January 2009	Sold the short-life asset	550

The motor car purchased on 15 June 2008 is used by Austin, and 15% of the mileage is for business purposes. The car is not a low emission car.

Required:

Compute the adjusted trading profits (after capital allowances) for the two periods of account ended 31 March 2010.

(Total: 12 marks)

7 Capital allowances – industrial buildings allowances

Herbert

Question 1

Herbert has been in business for a number of years manufacturing dining tables. He prepares his accounts to 31 March each year.

Herbert purchased a new factory from a builder on 15 March 2005 for £400,000. The factory was brought into industrial use on 1 April 2005. The cost of the factory was apportioned as follows:

	£
Freehold land	70,000
Site preparation for foundations	5,000
Construction of building comprising	
Employees' canteen	10,000
Drawing office	5,000
General offices	25,000
Factory	285,000
	400,000

On 1 February 2010 the factory was sold to Badger Ltd for £550,000 (including £50,000 for the land).

Required:

Calculate the IBAs available to Herbert for each of the years concerned.

(Total: 7 marks)

8 Sole traders: Basis of assessment

Rachel

Question 1

Rachel commenced in business as a fashion designer on 1 July 2007, and prepared her first accounts to 30 April 2009. Her profit for the period, adjusted for taxation, was £33,000.

Required:

(a) Calculate the trading profits assessable on Rachel for the first three years of assessment.

(6 marks)

(b) Calculate the 'overlap profits'.

(1 mark)

(c) State one disadvantage of having 'overlap profits'.

(1 mark)

(d) State how Rachel could have avoided the creation of 'overlap profits', supporting your statement with a relevant example.

(3 marks)

(Total: 11 marks)

Maggie Smith

Question 2

Maggie Smith commenced in business on 1 November 2005 manufacturing ladies clothing. Her tax-adjusted trading profits were as follows:

	£
Period to 31 December 2006	32,000
Year ended 31 December 2007	38,000
Year ended 31 December 2008	45,000

Capital allowances were as follows:

	Plant and machinery allowances	Industrial buildings allowances
	£	£
Period to 31 December 2006	18,000	Nil
Year ended 31 December 2007	11,675	4,000
Year ended 31 December 2008	13,550	4,000

Required:

Calculate the trading profits assessable on Maggie for the years 2005/06 to 2008/09 inclusive and the amount of any overlap profits.

(Total: 14 marks)

9 Partnerships

Roger, Brigitte and Xavier

Question 1 – Chapter 9

Roger and Brigitte commenced in business on 1 October 2005 as hotel proprietors, sharing profits equally.

On 1 October 2007 their son Xavier joined the partnership and from that date each of the partners, was entitled to one-third, of the profits.

The profits of the partnership adjusted for income tax are:

		£
Period ended	30 June 2006	30,000
Year ended	30 June 2007	45,000
Year ended	30 June 2008	50,000
Year ended	30 June 2009	60,000

Required:

(a) Calculate the assessable profits on each of the partners for all relevant years from 2005/06 to 2009/10

(7 marks)

(b) State the amount of the overlap profits for each of the partners.

(4 marks)

(Total: 11 marks)

10 Trading losses for individuals

Lucifer

Question 1

Lucifer commenced trading as a second-hand car dealer on 6 April 2006. He had had no taxable income prior to 2006/07.

His trading results, adjusted for income tax and capital allowances, were:

		£
Period ended	30 September 2006	(20,000) loss
Year ended	30 September 2007	(10,000) loss
Year ended	30 September 2008	10,000 profit

He received dividend income as follows:

	£
2006/07	3,375 net
2007/08	2,500 net
2008/09	1,800 net

In 2006/07 he had also realised a capital gain, before the annual exemption, of £15,000 on the sale of quoted shares.

Required:

(a) State the ways in which the trading losses may be relieved.

(3 marks)

(b) Show how the trading losses can be utilised most effectively by Lucifer, giving your reasoning.

(8 marks)
(Total: 11 marks)

11 Pensions

There are no questions for this chapter.

12 National Insurance

There are no questions for this chapter.

13 Tax administration for individuals

Tom Ching

Question 1

Tom has been a self-employed interior designer for a number of years, preparing his accounts to 30 April each year. His income for 2008/09 was as follows:

	£
Tax-adjusted trading profit	56,250
Property business income	5,200
Building society interest (net)	2,100
Dividends received from UK companies	3,200

During 2008/09 Tom paid £12,000 into his registered personal pension scheme.

Tom's payments on account for 2008/09 totalled £10,255.

Tom has a capital gains tax liability for 2008/09 of £3,000.

Required:

(a) Calculate the income tax and Class 4 NIC payable by Tom for 2008/09.

(8 marks)

(b) Calculate Tom's balancing payment for 2008/09 and his payments on account for 2009/10 and state the relevant payment dates.

(2 marks)

(c) State:

(i) the consequences of Tom not paying the balancing payment for 2008/09 by the due date.

(2 marks)

(ii) the due date by which Tom should file his tax return for 2008/09 assuming he wishes to file a paper return.

(1 mark)

(iii) how long Tom should retain his accounting records for the year to 30 April 2008.

(2 marks)
(Total: 15 marks)

14 Computation of gains and tax payable

Lorraine Campbell

Question 1

Lorraine Campbell disposed of the following individual assets during 2008/09:

(1) On 30 June 2008, Lorraine sold a freehold warehouse for £140,000. The warehouse was purchased on 1 September 2005 for £95,000 and had never been used for business purposes.

(2) On 30 November 2008, Lorraine sold a motor car for £25,000. The motor car was purchased in November 2006 for £23,500 and had always been used by Lorraine for business purposes.

(3) On 15 February 2009, Lorraine sold a factory for £320,000. The factory had been purchased on 14 October 1996 for £194,000, and was extended at a cost of £58,000 during March 1999. During May 2000, the roof of the factory was replaced at a cost of £44,000 following a fire. The building was not insured.

Lorraine had incurred legal fees of £3,600 in connection with the purchase of the factory, and £6,200 in connection with the disposal.

Lorraine had always used the factory for business purposes in her trade since it was bought in 1996. The factory is a small insignificant part of her business which she continues to operate.

Lorraine incurred a capital loss of £17,100 during 2006/07and made a capital gain of £10,500 during 2007/08.

Required:

Calculate Lorraine's capital gains tax liability for 2008/09 and advise her by when this should be paid.

Note: You should assume that the rate of annual exemption for 2008/09 applies throughout.

(Total: 15 marks)

15 Computation of gains: special rules

Mr and Mrs Steel

Question 1

Mr and Mrs Steel had the following transactions in assets in the year ended 5 April 2009.

Mr Steel

(1) A house, which had been bought for £4,000 on 3 April 1983 and let to tenants thereafter, was sold on 1 July 2008. On 2 April 1984 an extension costing £2,000 was built, and on 12 June 1986 the loft was converted into a bedroom at a cost of £3,000. The net proceeds of sale were £62,750.

(2) Sold a piece of sculpture for £6,500 on 30 August 2008, which he had bought for £5,500 on 31 May 2005.

(3) Sold a one-tenth share in a racehorse on 31 August 2008 for £6,200. The interest had cost £1,340 in November 2002.

(4) Sold a vintage Alfa Romeo motor car for £76,500 on 19 December 2008. The car had cost £17,400 on 31 March 2004. During his period of ownership Steel had never actually used the car on the road.

Mrs Steel

(1) Sold a rare Russian icon on 24 May 2008 for £5,600 which had cost £6,300 on 20 June 2005.

(2) Sold three acres out of a 12 acre plot of land on 14 December 2008 for £15,000. The whole plot had been purchased for £4,500 on 15 June 2005. On 14 December 2008 the unsold acres had an agreed market value of £25,000.

(3) Sold a piece of Chinese jade for £11,000 on 1 September 2008. This was purchased at auction in March 1982 for £6,500.

(4) Sold a plot of land for £12,000 on 1 October 2008. Mr Steel acquired the land for £2,000 in April 1995 and gave it to his wife in June 1997. The base cost of the land in June 1997 was £2,114.

Required:

Calculate the capital gains tax liability of both Mr Steel and Mrs Steel for 2008/09.

(Total: 20 marks)

16 CGT: Shares and securities for individuals

Jasper

Question 1

Jasper had the following transactions in securities during the year 2008/09:

(1) Sold 2,145 ordinary shares in Carrot plc on 19 November 2008 for net sale proceeds of £8,580.

His previous dealings in these shares were as follows:

July 2005	purchased 1,750 shares for £2,625
May 2006	purchased 200 shares for £640
June 2007	took up 1 for 10 rights issue at £3.40 per share

(2) Sold 400 £1 ordinary shares in Grasp plc for £3,600 on 31 March 2009. Jasper had acquired these Grasp plc shares as a result of a successful takeover bid by Grasp plc of Cawte plc on 5 December 2008.

Prior to the takeover Jasper had owned 12,000 £1 ordinary shares in Cawte plc, which he had acquired for £15,700 on 3 May 2006.

The terms of the takeover bid were:

- one £1 ordinary share in Grasp plc, plus
- two 10% preference shares in Grasp plc, plus
- 40p in cash

for every £1 ordinary share in Cawte plc.

The following are the quoted prices for the shares of Grasp plc at 5 December 2008:

£1 ordinary shares	350p
10% preference shares	110p

Jasper has never worked for Carrot plc, Grasp plc or Cawte plc.

Required:

Calculate the total capital gains arising in respect of the disposals in 2008/09.

(Total: 10 marks)

17 CGT: Reliefs for individuals

Jack Chan

Question 1

Jack Chan, aged 45, has been in business as a sole trader since 1 May 1997. On 28 February 2009 he transferred the business to his daughter Jill, at which time the following assets were sold to her:

(1) Goodwill with a market value of £60,000. The goodwill has been built up since 1 May 1997, and has a nil cost. Jill paid Jack £50,000 for the goodwill.

(2) A freehold office building with a market value of £130,000. The office building was purchased on 1 July 2007 for £110,000, and has always been used by Jack for business purposes. Jill paid Jack £105,000 for the office building.

(3) A freehold warehouse with a market value of £140,000. The warehouse was purchased on 1 September 2005 for £95,000 and has never been used by Jack for business purposes. Jill paid Jack £135,000 for the warehouse.

(4) A motor car with a market value of £25,000. The car was purchased on 1 November 2007 for £23,500, and has always been used by Jack for business purposes. Jill paid Jack £20,000 for the car.

Where possible, Jack and Jill have elected to hold over any gains arising.

Jack has unused capital losses of £6,400 brought forward from 2007/08.

Required:

Calculate Jack's capital gains tax liability for 2009/10, and advise him by when this should be paid.

(Total: 15 marks)

Sophie

Question 2

During 2008/09 Sophie made the following disposal of assets:

(1) On 1 May 2008 Sophie incorporated a business that she had run as a sole trader since 2001. All of the assets of the business were transferred, as a going concern, to the new company, Sophie Ltd:

	M.V. at 1 May 2008	**Cost**
	£	£
Goodwill	50,000	Nil
Freehold premises	200,000	80,000
Car	12,000	18,000
Stock and debtors	60,000	65,000
	322,000	

The goodwill had been built up since 2001. The freehold premises were purchased on 1 February 2001 and have always been used for business purposes. The car was purchased on 15 March 2005.

The consideration paid by Sophie Ltd for the assets transferred consisted of 200,000 £1 ordinary shares valued at £200,000 and £122,000 in cash.

(2) On 1 June 2008 Sophie sold a house for £450,000. Sophie had bought the house on 1 June 1999 for £120,000. She occupied the house as her main residence until 1 January 2002 when she went to live with her mother. The house was left unoccupied until she returned on 31 May 2003. She then lived in the house until 31 May 2004 when she purchased and moved into a new house. The house was left empty until its sale on 1 June 2008.

Sophie has made no other capital disposals during 2008/09.

Required:

(a) Assuming that Sophie elects not to claim incorporation relief, on the transfer of the business to Sophie Ltd, calculate her capital gains tax liability for 2008/09 on the above disposals.

(12 marks)

(b) State the conditions that must be met in order for incorporation relief to be available to Sophie on the transfer of her business to Sophie Ltd.

(3 marks)

(c) Calculate by how much Sophie's capital gains tax liability for 2008/09 would have changed if she had taken advantage of incorporation relief.

(5 marks)

(Total: 20 marks)

18 Introduction: to corporation tax

There are no questions for this chapter.

19 Profits chargeable to corporation tax

There are no questions for this chapter.

20 Chargeable gains for companies

Earth Ltd

Question 1

Earth Ltd sold the following shareholdings during the year ended 31 March 2009:

(1) On 20 November 2008 Earth Ltd sold 25,000 £1 ordinary shares in Venus plc for £115,000. Earth Ltd had originally purchased 40,000 shares in Venus plc on 19 June 1986 for £34,000. On 11 October 2002 Venus plc made a 1 for 4 bonus issue.

Assume the retail price indices (RPIs) are as follows:

June 1986	97.8
October 2002	174.3
November 2008	215.3

(2) On 22 January 2009 Earth Ltd sold 30,000 £1 ordinary shares in Saturn plc for £52,500. Earth Ltd purchased 30,000 shares in Saturn plc on 9 February 2001 for £97,500. The indexed value of the share pool on 3 January 2009 was £115,950.

On 3 January 2009 Saturn plc made a 1 for 2 rights issue. Earth Ltd took up its allocation under the rights issue in full, paying £1.50 for each new share issued.

(3) On 28 March 2009 Earth Ltd sold its entire holding of £1 ordinary shares in Jupiter plc for £55,000. Earth Ltd had originally purchased 10,000 shares in Mercury plc on 5 May 1994 for £14,000. The indexed value of the share pool on 7 March 2008 was £17,200.

On 7 March 2009 Mercury plc was taken over by Jupiter plc. Earth Ltd received two £1 ordinary shares and one £1 preference share in Jupiter plc for each £1 ordinary share held in Mercury plc. Immediately after the takeover each £1 ordinary share in Jupiter plc was quoted at £2.50 and each £1 preference share was quoted at £1.25.

Earth Ltd has never held more than a 1% shareholding in any of the above companies.

Required:

Calculate the chargeable gain or capital loss arising from each of Earth Ltd's disposals during the year ended 31 March 2009.

Each of the three sections of this question carries equal marks (i.e. 5 marks each).

(Total: 15 marks)

21 Losses for companies

There are no questions for this chapter.

22 Groups of companies

Gold Ltd

Question 1

Gold Ltd owns 100% of the ordinary share capital of Silver Ltd. Gold Ltd has an accounting date of 31 December, whilst Silver Ltd has an accounting date of 30 June. The results of Gold Ltd are as follows:

Year ended	**31.12.07**	**31.12.08**
	£	£
Trading profit	177,000	90,000
Property income	5,000	–
Chargeable gain	–	12,000
Gift Aid donation	(2,000)	(2,000)

For the year ended 30 June 2007 Silver Ltd had profits chargeable to corporation tax of £260,000. The company made a trading loss of £140,000 for the year ended 30 June 2008. No information is available regarding the year ended 30 June 2009.

Gold Ltd has no other associated companies.

Required:

(a) Assuming that the maximum possible claim for group relief is made in respect of Silver Ltd's trading loss of £140,000, calculate Gold Ltd's corporation tax liabilities for the year ended 31 December 2007 and the year ended 31 December 2008.

(8 marks)

(b) Explain how loss relief should be allocated within a group of companies in order to maximise the potential benefit of the relief for the group as a whole.

(4 marks)

(c) Based on the information available, advise Silver Ltd of the most beneficial way of relieving its trading loss of £140,000.

(3 marks)

(Total: 15 marks)

Apple Group

Question 2

Apple Ltd owns 100% of the ordinary share capital of Banana Ltd and Cherry Ltd. The results of each company for the year ended 31 March 2009 are as follows:

	Apple Ltd	Banana Ltd	Cherry Ltd
	£	£	£
Tax-adjusted trading profit/(loss)	(125,000)	650,000	130,000
Chargeable gain/(loss)	180,000	(8,000)	–

Apple Ltd's chargeable gain arose from the sale of a freehold warehouse on 15 April 2008 for £418,000. Cherry Ltd purchased a freehold office building for £290,000 on 10 January 2009.

Required:

(a) Explain the group relationship that must exist in order that group relief can be claimed.

(3 marks)

(b) Explain how group relief should be allocated between the respective claimant companies in order to maximise the potential benefit obtained from the relief.

(3 marks)

(c) Assuming that reliefs are claimed in the most favourable manner, calculate the corporation tax liabilities of Apple Ltd, Banana Ltd and Cherry Ltd for the year ended 31 March 2009.

(9 marks)

(Total: 15 marks)

23 Overseas issues for companies

There are no questions for this chapter.

24 Tax administration for a company

Ramble Ltd

Question 1

Ramble Ltd's profits chargeable to corporation tax for the two years to 31 March 2008 and 2009 were £2,150,000 and £2,456,000 respectively.

The company filed its tax return for the year ended 31 March 2008 on 15 October 2009 and on the same date made a payment of the tax outstanding.

Ramble Ltd made the following payments on account of its corporation tax liability for the year ended 31 March 2009:

	£
– 1 May 2009	470,900
– 1 January 2010	216,780

Required:

(a) State the date that the company's self assessment corporation tax return for the year ended 31 March 2008 was due and advise the company of the consequences of filing the return on 15 October 2009.

(3 marks)

(b) State the due date(s) for the payment of the company's corporation tax liability for the year ended 31 March 2009 and advise the company of any interest on overdue tax that will be payable in respect of this year (interest calculations are not required).

Assume that the rates of tax FY2008 continue in the future.

(7 marks)
(Total: 10 marks)

25 VAT: outline

There are no questions for this chapter.

26 VAT: administration

Mary

Question 1

You are provided with the following information for the quarter ended 31 March 2009 relating to your client Mary who is registered for value added tax.

	£
Supplies (all VAT-exclusive):	
Standard-rated supplies	
Sales invoices issued by Mary who also offers a 2½% discount	230,000
Zero-rated supplies	50,000
Purchases and expenses	
Standard-rated purchases (excluding VAT)	102,440
Standard-rated expenses (excluding VAT). The total of £18,000 includes £5,000 for entertaining customers	18,000
Exempt purchases	14,350
Cars (excluding VAT and bought on 1 February 2009)	16,200

Irrecoverable debts of £3,000 (exclusive of VAT) were written off in March 2009 in respect of three separate invoices, each of £1,000 for goods supplied on 1 May 2008, 1 August 2008 and 1 November 2008, payment for which was due on 1 June 2008, 1 September 2008 and 1 December 2008 respectively.

The car bought on 1 February 2009 was used 60% for business and has CO_2 emissions of 210 g/km. Petrol for both private and business mileage was paid for by the business. The quarterly scale charge figure is £414 (inclusive of VAT).

Required:

Calculate the VAT payable for the quarter ended 31 March 2009 and state when this will be payable to HM Revenue and Customs.

(Total: 11 marks)

Test your understanding answers

Amos Groves

Answer 1 – Chapter 3

(a) **Property business income – y/e 5 April 2009**

	House 1	House 2	House 3	House 4
	£	£	£	£
Rent accruing	2,625	7,800	4,000	5,400
Premium assessable	2,250	–	–	–
Repairs	(800)	–	(2,500)	(100)
Expenses	–	(1,650)	(1,000)	(575)
Irrecoverable debt	–		(1,000)	–
Loan interest	–	(2,500)	–	–
Wear and tear allowance	–	(665)	–	–
	4,075	2,985	(500)	4,725

The amount assessable as property business income for the year to 5 April 2009 is: (£4,075 + £2,985 - £500 + £4,725) = £11,285.

Profits and losses are automatically pooled together.

Workings

(W1) House 1

(i) Rent from 1 September 2008: (£4,500 × 7/12) = £2,625

(ii) Lease premium

	£
Premium	2,500
(6 - 1) × 2% × £2,500	(250)
Assessable premium	2,250

(iii) Roof repairs are not allowable as they were making good a deficiency on purchase, and are therefore capital expenditure.

(W2) House 2

(i) Rent: (£650 × 12) = £7,800.

(ii) The cooker is capital expenditure and is therefore disallowable.

(iii) Wear and tear allowance = (£7,800 – £300 – £850) × 10% = £665.

(W3) House 3

(i) Rent from expired lease: (£500 × 8) = £4,000.

(ii) Rent from new lease: £nil. Taxable on an accruals basis (ignore 5 days in April 2009).

(W4) House 4

(i) Rent: (£450 × 12) = £5,400.

(ii) Insurance for the year to 5 April 2009:
(£300 × 3/12 + £400 × 9/12) = £375.

(b) **Amos Groves – Income tax computation – 2008/09**

	Total	**Other income**	**Savings income**	**Dividend income**
	£	£	£	£
Employment income	8,000	8,000		
Property income	11,285	11,285		
Interest income (£500 × 100/80)	625		625	
Dividend income (£450 × 100/90)	500			500
Total income	20,410	19,285	625	500
Personal allowance	(6,035)	(6,035)		
Taxable income	14,375	13,250	625	500

	£	£
Income tax		
On other income	13,250 x 20%	2,650
On savings income	625 x 20%	125
On dividend income	500 x 10%	50
	14,375	
Income tax liability		2,825
Less: Tax credits		
Dividend		(50)
PAYE		(390)
Interest		(125)
Income tax payable		2,260

Peter

Answer 1 – Chapter 5

Adjusted trading profit before capital allowances – y/e 31 December 2008

	£	£
Profit per accounts		35,950
Less: Rent received	9,500	
Use of office	250	
Private telephone	180	
		(9,930)
		26,020
Add: Rent and rates (£12,900 × 1/10)	1,290	
Light and heat (£5,250 × 1/7)	750	
Depreciation of fixtures and fittings	1,500	
Entertaining suppliers	2,750	
Entertaining customers	2,300	
Gifts of food	125	
Supplier loan written off	1,700	
Depreciation of vehicles	7,500	
Private motor expenses (£3,300 × 4,000/12,000)	1,100	
Donation to national charity	50	
Political donation	100	
Squash club subscription	250	
Taxation services re capital gains tax	750	
New printer – capital	650	
Central heating – capital	2,200	
Own consumption (£450 × 130/100)	585	
		23,600
Adjusted trading profit (before capital allowances)		49,620

Austin Scuba

Answer 1 – Chapter 6

Capital allowances are computed for the two periods of account. The writing down allowance (WDA) for the period to 31 March 2009 is adjusted to reflect the 10 month period of account.

The expenditure incurred prior to the commencement of trade is deemed to have been incurred on the first day of trading.

Austin Scuba

Capital allowances computation

		General pool	Short life asset	Exp Car (B.U. 15%)		Total CAs
	£	£	£	£	B.U.%	£
10 m/e 31 March 2009						
Additions:						
No AIA or FYA:						
Car				15,600		
Qualifying for AIA:						
Equipment	32,260					
Van	16,500					
	48,760					
Less AIA (Note)	(41,667)					41,667
		7,093				
Equipment	2,400					
Less AIA (Note)	(Nil)					
			2,400			
		7,093	2,400	15,600		
WDA (20% x £7,093 x 10/12)		(1,182)				1,182
WDA (20% x £2,400 x 10/12)			(400)			400
WDA (max £3,000 x 10/12)				(2,500)	x 15%	375
TWDV c/f		5,911	2,000	13,100		
Total allowances						43,624

		General pool	Short life asset	Exp Car (B.U. 15%)		Total CAs
	£	£	£	£	B.U.%	£
y/e 31 March 2010						
Additions:						
Qualifying for AIA:						
Equipment	11,200					
Van	22,020					
	33,220					
Less AIA	(33,220)					33,220
		Nil				
Disposal proceeds		(500)	(550)			
		5,411	1,450	13,100		
Balancing allowance			(1,450)			1,450
WDA (20% x £5,411)		(1,082)				1,082
WDA (20% x £13,100)				(2,620)	x 15%	393
TWDV c/f		4,329		10,480		
Total allowances						36,145

Note: The AIA is pro-rated for the ten month period. The maximum allowance is therefore £41,667 (£50,000 x 10/12). The AIA is allocated to the general plant and machinery in priority to the short life asset.

Taxable trading profits

	Adjusted trading profit before CAs	Capital allowances	Tax-adjusted trading profits
	£	£	£
10 m/e 31.3.2009	51,000	(43,624)	7,376
y/e/ 31.3.2010	45,600	(36,145)	9,455

Herbert

Answer 1 – Chapter 7

Herbert – Allowances available

The expenditure qualifying for IBAs is as follows:

	£
Total cost	400,000
Less: Land	(70,000)
Cost of construction of whole building	330,000

The cost of the non-qualifying part of the building (i.e. the offices) of £25,000 does not exceed 25% of the cost of the whole building of £330,000. Therefore IBAs are available on the cost of the whole building.

The building was brought into industrial use on 1 April 2005 and therefore the first period of account for which IBAs are due is the year ended 31 March 2006.

	£
Year ended 31 March 2006	
WDA (4% x £330,000) (in use 31.3.06)	13,200
Years ended 31 March 2007 to 2008	
WDA @ £13,200 pa for two years	26,400
Year ended 31 March 2009	
WDA (3% x £530,000)	9,900
Year ended 31 March 2010	
No allowances – building sold 1 February 2010	Nil
Total allowances claimed	49,500

Rachel

Answer 1 – Chapter 8

(a) **Assessable trading profits**

Tax year	Basis period			Assessable profits
				£
2007/08	(1 July 2007 to 5 April 2008)			
	Actual basis	9/22 ×	£33,000	13,500
2008/09	(6 April 2008 to 5 April 2009)			
	Actual basis	12/22 ×	£33,000	18,000
2009/10	(1 May 2008 to 30 April 2009)			
		12/22 ×	£33,000	18,000

(b) **Overlap profits**

The profits assessed twice are those for the period 1 May 2008 to 5 April 2009 = (11/22 × £33,000) = £16,500

Key answer tips

Double check the number of months used in the profit apportionments and reconcile the overlap profits. Do they equal the profits assessed in excess of £33,000?

(c) **Disadvantage of overlap profits**

The disadvantage of overlap profits is that they can only be utilised in the future and will therefore lose value as no allowance is made for the effect of inflation.

(d) **Avoidance of overlap profits**

By choosing an accounting date co-terminous with the tax year it is possible to avoid the creation of 'overlap profits'.

If Rachel had chosen 5 April as her accounting date instead of 30 April the assessments for the first three years would have been based on the following basis periods with a consequent absence of 'overlap profits'.

Tax year	Basis period
2007/08	1.7.07 – 5.4.08
2008/09	6.4.08 – 5.4.09
2009/10	6.4.09 – 5.4.10

Tutorial note

Using a 5 April and not a 30 April year end may make a significant difference to assessable amounts in the year of cessation.

If Rachel ceases on 31 December 2014, for example, her 2014/15 basis period is nine months from 6 April 2014 in the first instance, but is 20 months from 1 May 2013 in the second instance, albeit with 11 months of overlap relief brought forward. In 2014 values the overlap relief created ten years earlier may not be sufficient to give a 'fair' nine months of assessable profits.

Maggie Smith

Answer 2 – Chapter 8

Trading profit assessments

Tax year	Basis period		Assessable profit
			£
2005/06	Actual		
	(01.11.05 – 05.04.06)	£14,000 **(W)** × 5/14	5,000
2006/07	Year ended 31.12.06	£14,000 **(W)** × 12/14	12,000
2007/08	Year ended 31.12.07	**(W)**	22,325
2008/09	Year ended 31.12.08	**(W)**	27,450

Overlap profits (01.01.06 – 05.04.06): (£14,000 × 3/14) = £3,000.

Working: Adjusted profit after capital allowances

	Adjusted profit	CAs	IBAs	Trading profit
	£	£	£	£
14 m/e 31.12.06	32,000	(18,000)	Nil	14,000
Y/e 31.12.07	38,000	(11,675)	(4,000)	22,325
Y/e 31.12.08	45,000	(13,550)	(4,000)	27,450

Roger, Brigitte and Xavier

Answer 1 – Chapter 9

(a) **Assessable profits for each partner**

The basis periods will be:

	Roger & Brigitte	Xavier
2005/06	01.10.05 – 05.04.06	–
2006/07	01.10.05 – 30.09.06	–
2007/08	01.07.06 – 30.06.07	01.10.07 – 05.04.08
2008/09	01.07.07 – 30.06.08	01.10.07 – 30.09.08
2009/10	01.07.08 – 30.06.09	01.07.08 – 30.06.09

The profits assessable will be:

	Roger	Brigitte	Xavier
	£	£	£
2005/06	10,000 **(W1)**	10,000 **(W1)**	–
2006/07	20,625 **(W2)**	20,625 **(W2)**	–
2007/08	22,500	22,500	8,333 **(W3)**
2008/09	18,750 **(W4)**	18,750 **(W4)**	17,500 **(W5)**
2009/10	20,000	20,000	20,000

Workings

(W1) (6/9 × £30,000) ÷ 2 = £10,000

(W2) [£30,000 + (3/12 × £45,000)] ÷ 2 = £20,625

(W3) (6/12 × £50,000) ÷ 3 = £8,333

(W4) (3/12 × £50,000 ÷ 2) + (9/12 × £50,000 ÷ 3) = £18,750

(W5) (9/12 × £50,000 ÷ 3) + (3/12 × £60,000 ÷ 3) = £17,500

(b) **Overlap relief**

	Roger	Brigitte
	£	£
2006/07 (01.10.05 – 05.04.06)	10,000	10,000
2007/08 (01.07.06 – 30.09.06)	5,625 **(W1)**	5,625 **(W1)**
	15,625	15,625

	Xavier
	£
2008/09 (01.10.07 – 05.04.08)	8,333
2009/10 (01.07.08 – 30.09.08)	5,000 **(W2)**
	13,333

Workings

(W1) (3/12 × £45,000 ÷ 2) = £5,625

(W2) (3/12 × £60,000 ÷ 3) = £5,000

Key answer tips

Note how the suggested answer manages to present the figures in a clearly intelligible form without needing detailed labels or explanations.

Lucifer

Answer 1 – Chapter 10

(a) **Utilisation of trading losses**

The loss may be relieved in three ways:

(i) The relief may be set off against total income of the year of the loss and/or against total income of the preceding year (s64 ITA 2007).

(ii) The relief may be carried forward against the first available trading profits of the same trade (s83 ITA 2007).

(iii) Where the loss exceeds the total income for the year, after a s64 ITA 2007 claim, relief may be set off against capital gains of the year (s261B TCGA 1992).

(b) **Most effective utilisation of the trading loss**

(i) **Calculation of loss**

	£
2006/07	
Period ended 30.09.06	20,000
Year ended 30.09.07 (01.10.06 – 05.04.07)	
(6/12 × £10,000)	5,000
	25,000
2007/08	
Year ended 30.09.07	10,000
Less period 01.10.06 – 05.04.07	(5,000)
	5,000

(ii) **Income tax computations after loss relief**

	2006/07	**2007/08**	**2008/09**
	£	£	£
Trading income	Nil	Nil	10,000
s83 relief			(1) (6,250)
			(2) (3,750)
			Nil
Dividends (× 100/90)	3,750	2,778	2,000
s64 relief	(3,750)		
Net income	Nil	2,778	2,000

(iii) **Capital gain computation**

	2006/07
	£
Capital gain	15,000
s261B TCGA 1992 relief	(15,000)
	Nil

(iv) **Explanation of optimum use of loss**

Although the method of loss utilisation chosen entails a loss of personal allowances for 2006/07 it is considered the best of the several options available, as relief can be given against capital gains in that year.

There is rarely a guarantee of future profits and in view of the poor trading results it is thought the maximisation of cash flow and claiming relief as early as possible is the critical factor.

The dividend income in 2007/08 is covered by the personal allowance. A s64 ITA 2007 claim is not therefore made in this year.

(v) **Loss memoranda**

2006/07	£
Loss (part (b) (i))	25,000
Used in 2006/07 (s64)	(3,750)
	21,250
Used in 2006/07 (s216B)	(15,000)
Loss left to carry forward	6,250
Used in 2008/09 (s83)	(6,250)
	Nil

2007/08	£
Loss (part (b) (i))	5,000
Used in 2008/09 (s83)	(3,750)
Loss left to carry forward to 2009/10	1,250

Key answer tips

Loss questions can be answered successfully by following a few simple rules.

Firstly, identify the loss of the tax year, and secondly, deal with each loss separately. The choice is usually to relieve total income in the tax year of loss and/or the previous year.

Where there is a capital gain, it can be worthwhile making a s261B TCGA 1992 claim.

Any loss remaining must be carried forward under s83.

Tom Ching

Answer 1 – Chapter 13

(a) **Tom Ching – Income tax and NIC payable – 2008/09**

	£
Trading profit	56,250
Property business income	5,200
Building society interest (£2,100 × 100/80)	2,625
Dividend income (£3,200 × 100/90)	3,556
	–––––
Total income	67,631
Personal allowance	(6,035)
	–––––
Taxable income	61,596
	–––––

Income tax	£		£
On other income			
Basic rate	49,800	x 20%	9,960
Higher rate	5,615	x 40%	2,246
	–––––		
	55,415		
On savings income	2,625	x 40%	1,050
On dividends	3,556	x 32.5%	1,156
	–––––		
	61,596		
	–––––		–––––
Income tax liability			14,412
Tax suffered at source			
– Dividends (£3,556 @ 10%)			(356)
– BSI (£2,625 @ 20%)			(525)
			–––––
Income tax payable			13,531
		£	
Class 4 NIC			
(£40,040 – £5,435) = £34,605 @ 8%		2,768	
(£56,250 – £40,040) = £16,210 @ 1%		162	2,930
		–––––	–––––
Total income tax and NIC payable			16,461
			–––––

Note: The basic rate band is extended by the gross amount of the personal pension contributions of £15,000 (£12,000 × 100/80). The extended basic rate band is therefore £49,800 (£34,800 + £15,000).

(b) **Tax payments**

(i) **Balancing payment – 2008/09**

	£
Total income tax and NIC payable	16,461
Capital gains tax liability	3,000
Total tax payable	19,461
Less payments on account	(10,255)
Balancing payment due 31 January 2010	9,206

(ii) **Payments on account – 2009/10**

	£
Payments on account for 2009/10 are based on the total income tax and Class 4 NIC liability of the previous tax year as follows	
Total income tax and NIC payable in 2008/09	16,461
Payments on account 2009/10:	
– 31 January 2010 (50% × £16,461)	8,231
– 31 July 2010 (50% × £16.461)	8,230
	16,461

Note that payments on account are not required for capital gains tax.

(c) (i) **Paying tax late**

If Tom does not pay the balancing payment for 2008/09 by the due date, interest will be charged from 31 January 2010 until the date of payment.

In addition, a 5% surcharge of £500 (£9,206 at 5%) will be imposed if the balancing payment is not made within 28 days of the due date. A further 5% surcharge will be imposed if the payment has still not been made six months after the due date.

(ii) **Filing date**

If Tom wishes to submit a paper return he should file his 2008/09 tax return by 31 October 2009.

(iii) **Retention of records**

The accounting records for the year to 30 April 2008 form the basis of the tax return for 2008/09.

Business records should be retained for five years after the 31 January filing date for 2008/09. The accounting records for the year to 30 April 2008 should therefore be retained for 5 years after 31 January 2010, i.e. 31 January 2015.

Lorraine Campbell

Answer 1 – Chapter 14

Capital gains computation – 2008/09

30 June 2008 – Warehouse

	£
Disposal proceeds	140,000
Less: acquisition cost	(95,000)
Capital gain	45,000

30 November 2008 – Motor Car

A motor car is an exempt asset

15 February 2009 – Factory

	£
Disposal proceeds	320,000
Less: Incidental costs of disposal	(6,200)
Net proceeds	313,800
Less: Acquisition cost	(194,000)
Incidental costs of acquisition	(3,600)
Enhancement expenditure	(58,000)
Capital gain (Note)	58,200
Net capital gains for the year	103,200
Less: Capital loss b/f (working)	(16,200)
Net capital gains	87,000
Less: Annual exemption	(9,600)
Taxable gain	77,400
Capital gain tax (£77,400 x 18%)	13,932
Due date 31.1.2010	

Note: The expenditure incurred in May 2000 for replacing the roof does not enhance the cost of the factory and is not an allowable deduction – as it is replacing a roof that was already there!

The factory is an insignificant part of Lorraine's business and the disposal is not associated with the disposal of the entire business. Therefore entrepreneurs relief is not applicable (see chapter 17).

Working: Capital losses

In 2007/08, £900 (£10,500 – £9,600) of the capital loss brought forward is used to reduce that years gains to the level of the annual exemption.

The remaining capital loss of £16,200 (£17,100 – £900) is available to carry forward to 2008/09.

Mr and Mrs Steel

Answer 1 – Chapter 15

Mr Steel – Capital gains tax computation – 2008/09

House	£	£
Net sale proceeds (1.7.08)	62,750	
Less: Cost (3.4.83)	(4,000)	
Extension (2.4.84)	(2,000)	
Loft (12.6.86)	(3,000)	
Capital gain		53,750
Sculpture		
Sale proceeds	6,500	
Less: Cost	(5,500)	
Capital gain	1,000	
Gain cannot exceed (£6,500 – £6,000) × 5/3	833	833
One-tenth interest in racehorse		
Exempt as a chattel which is also a wasting asset		Nil
Alfa-Romeo vintage car		
Cars are exempt assets		Nil
Total capital gains		54,583
Less: Annual exemption		(9,600)
Taxable gain		44,983
Capital gains tax (£44,983 x 18%)		8,097

Mrs Steel – Capital gains tax computation – 2008/09

	£	£
Icon		
Deemed sale proceeds	6,000	
Cost	(6,300)	
Allowable loss		(300)
Plot of land		
Sale proceeds (3 acres)	15,000	
Less: Cost (3 acres)		
£4,500 × £15,000/(£15,000 + £25,000)	(1,688)	
Capital gain		13,312
Jade		
Sale proceeds	11,000	
Less: Cost	(6,500)	
Capital gain		4,500
Land		
Disposal proceeds	12,000	
Less: Deemed acquisition cost (base cost)	(2,114)	
Capital gain		9,886
Net capital gains		27,398
Less: Annual exemption		(9,600)
Taxable gain		17,798
Capital gains tax (£17,798 x 18%)		3,204

Jasper

Answer 1 – Chapter 16

Jasper – Capital gains tax computation – 2008/09

	£	£
Shares in Carrot plc		
Net sale proceeds	8,580	
Less: Cost (W1)	(3,928)	
Capital gain		4,652
Takeover		
Cash received (W2)	4,800	
Less: Cost (W2)	(1,030)	
		3,770
Shares in Grasp plc		
Sale proceeds	3,600	
Less: Cost (W2) £9,008 x 400/12,000	300	
		3,300
Total capital gains		11,722

Workings

(W1) Carrot plc

		Number	Cost
			£
July 2005	Purchase	1,750	2,625
May 2006	Purchase	200	640
		1,950	3,265
June 2007	Rights issue (1:10) @ £3.40	195	663
		2,145	3,928
November 2008	Sale	(2,145)	(3,928)

(W2) Grasp plc

Apportionment of cost of Cawte plc securities to new securities and cash.

	5.12.08 Purchase consideration	Cost allocation
	£	£
For 12,000 Cawte plc ordinary shares:		
12,000 Grasp £1 ordinary shares at 350p	42,000	9,008
24,000 Grasp 10% preference shares at 110p	26,400	5,662
Cash (12,000 × 40p)	4,800	1,030
	73,200	15,700

Jack Chan

Answer 1 – Chapter 17

CGT liability for 2008/09

Net gains qualifying for entrepreneurs' relief	£	£
Goodwill		
Market value **(Note 1)**	60,000	
Less: Cost	(Nil)	
Capital gain before reliefs	60,000	
Gift relief (£60,000 – £50,000) **(Note 2)**	(10,000)	
		50,000
Freehold office building		
Market value	130,000	
Less: Cost	(110,000)	
Gain before relief	20,000	
Gift relief **(Note 3)**	(20,000)	Nil
		50,000
Less: Entrepreneurs' relief (£50,000 x 4/9)		(22,222)
		27,778
Net gains not qualifying for entrepreneurs' relief		
Freehold warehouse (Note 4)		
Market value	140,000	
Less: Cost	(95,000)	
		45,000
Motor cars (Note 5)		Nil
Net chargeable gains for the tax year		72,778
Less: Capital loss brought forward		(6,400)
Net chargeable gains		66,378
Less: Annual exemption		(9,600)
Taxable gains		56,778

	£
Capital gains tax (£56,778 x 18%)	10,220
Due date for CGT liability	31 January 2010

Notes:

(1) Jack and Jill are connected persons, and therefore the market values of the assets sold are used.

(2) The consideration paid for the goodwill exceeds the original cost by £50,000 (£50,000 – Nil). This amount is immediately chargeable to CGT.

(3) The consideration paid for the office building does not exceed the original cost, so full gift relief is available. Holdover relief is not restricted.

(4) The warehouse does not qualify for gift relief.

(5) Motor cars are exempt from CGT.

Sophie

Answer 2 – Chapter 17

(a) **Sophie – Capital gains computation – 2008/09**

Net gains qualifying for entrepreneurs' relief

Incorporation of the business

	£	£	£
Freehold premises			
Market value (May 2008)	200,000		
Less: Acquisition cost (Feb 2001)	(80,000)		
		120,000	
Goodwill			
Market value (May 2008)	50,000		
Less: Acquisition cost	(Nil)		
		50,000	
Total capital gains on incorporation		170,000	
Less: Entrepreneurs' relief (£170,000 x 4/9)		(75,555)	
Chargeable gain			94,445

Net gains not qualifying for entrepreneurs' relief

Gain arising on sale of house

	£	£
Sale proceeds (June 2008)	450,000	
Less: Acquisition cost (June 1999)	(120,000)	
Capital gain before reliefs	330,000	
Less: PPR exemption £330,000 x (96/108) **(W1)**	(293,333)	
Chargeable gain		36,667
Total chargeable gains		131,112
Less: Annual exemption		(9,600)
Taxable gains		121,512
Capital gains tax (£121,512 x 18%)		21,872

Workings

(W1) PPR relief

	Actual occupation (months)	Deemed occupation (months)	Absence (months)	Total (months)
1.6.99 – 31.12.01	31			31
1.1.02 – 31.5.03		17		17
1.6.03 – 31.5.04	12			12
1.6.04 – 1.6.08		36	12	48
Total	43	53	12	108

PPR relief = (43 + 53) = 96 months out of 108 months.

Notes:

(1) The period spent living with her mother is deemed occupation, being up to three years absence for any reason, as Sophie lived in the property both before and after the period of absence.

(2) The last three years of ownership represents a deemed period of occupation, even if the owner has elected for another property to be treated as his PPR in the same period.

(3) The remaining 12 month period of absence does not qualify as deemed occupation as the property was not reoccupied after the period of absence.

(b) **Incorporation relief**

Incorporation relief is available where the following conditions apply:

– The unincorporated business is transferred as a going concern.

– All of the assets of the business (other than cash) are transferred.

– The consideration for the transfer of the business must be wholly or mainly shares in the company.

(c) **Effect of incorporation relief**

Incorporation relief operates such that the gains arising on the deemed disposal of the individual assets are rolled over against the acquisition cost of the shares in the new company.

However where part of the consideration for the transfer of the business is not shares (e.g. cash), the gain eligible for relief is:

$$\text{Capital gain x} \frac{\text{Value of shares issued}}{\text{Total consideration}}$$

Therefore if Sophie had taken advantage of incorporation relief part of the gain would have been rolled over against the base cost of the shares in Sophie Ltd and would not have been chargeable in 2008/09.

The chargeable gains on incorporation would be:

	£
Total capital gains on incorporation	170,000
Less: Incorporation relief	
$\text{£170,000 x} \frac{\text{£200,000}}{\text{£322,000}}$	(105,590)
Chargeable gain after incorporation relief	64,410
Less: Entrepreneurs' relief (£64,410 x 4/9)	(28,627)
Chargeable gain on incorporation	35,783

Therefore if she had taken advantage of incorporation relief, Sophie's capital gains tax liability for 2008/09 would have been reduced by £10,559 ((£94,445 – £35,783) x 18%).

Earth Ltd

Answer 1 – Chapter 20

1 **Venus plc – sale of 25,000 shares**

	£
Disposal proceeds	115,000
Cost (W)	(17,000)
Unindexed gain	98,000
Indexation (£37,425 – £17,000) (W)	(20,425)
Chargeable gain	77,575

Share pool	**Number**	**Cost**	**Indexed cost**
		£	£
Purchase – June 1986	40,000	34,000	34,000
Bonus issue – October 2002 (£40,000 × ¼)	10,000	Nil	Nil
	50,000	34,000	34,000
Indexation to November 2008 £34,000 × (215.3 – 97.8)/97.8			40,849
	50,000	34,000	74,849
Disposal – November 2008 Cost × (£25,000/50,000)	(25,000)	(17,000)	(37,425)
Balance carried forward	25,000	17,000	37,424

(2) **Saturn plc**

	£
Sale proceeds	52,500
Cost	(80,000)
Allowable capital loss	(27,500)

Notes:

(a) Earth Ltd was issued with 15,000 (30,000 × 0.5) new shares under the rights issue at a cost of £22,500 (15,000 × £1.50).

(b) The cost of the shares sold is therefore £80,000 (£97,500 + £22,500 = 120,000 × 30,000/(30,000 + 15,000)).

(c) Indexation cannot be used to increase a capital loss.

(3) **Jupiter plc**

	£
Sale proceeds	55,000
Cost	(11,200)
Unindexed gain	43,800
Indexation allowance	(2,560)
Chargeable gain	41,240

Notes:

(a) On the takeover Earth Ltd received ordinary shares valued at £50,000 (10,000 × 2 × £2.50) and preference shares valued at £12,500 (10,000 × £1.25). The total value of consideration received is £62,500.

(b) The cost attributable to the ordinary shares is £11,200 (14,000 × 50,000/62,500).

(c) The indexation attributable to the ordinary shares is £2,560 (£17,200 – £14,000) = £3,200 × (50,000/62,500)).

Gold Ltd

Answer 1 – Chapter 22

(a) **Gold Ltd – Corporation tax liabilities**

Year ended	**31.12.07**	**31.12.08**
	£	£
Trading income	177,000	90,000
Property income	5,000	–
Chargeable gain	–	12,000
Total profits	182,000	102,000
Gift Aid donation	(2,000)	(2,000)
	180,000	100,000
Group relief	(70,000)	(50,000)
PCTCT	110,000	50,000
Corporation tax liability		
FY2006 (£110,000 x 19% x 3/12)	5,225	
FY2007 (£110,000 x 20% x 9/12)	16,500	
FY2007 (£50,000 x 20% x 3/12)		2,500
FY2008 (£50,000 x 21% x 9/12)		7,875
	21,725	10,375

Notes:

(1) The accounting periods are not coterminous, so both Gold Ltd's PCTCT and Silver Ltd's trading loss must be apportioned on a time basis.

(2) For the year ended 31 December 2007 group relief is restricted to the lower of Gold Ltd's available profits of £90,000 (£180,000 × 6/12) and Silver Ltd's available loss of £70,000 (£140,000 × 6/12).

(3) For the year ended 31 December 2008 group relief is restricted to the lower of Gold Ltd's available profits of £50,000 (£100,000 × 6/12) and Silver Ltd's available loss of £70,000 (£140,000 × 6/12).

(4) Gold Ltd has one associated company so the small companies rate lower limit is £150,000 (£300,000/2).

(5) The year ended 31 December 2008 straddles 31 March. As the small companies rate changed on 31 March 2007 and 2008 the corporation tax liability must be calculated for each financial year.

(b) **Maximising benefit of group relief**

(1) Relief should initially be claimed against profits subject to corporation tax at the marginal rate of 29.75% (FY2008) or 32.5% (FY2007) and then profits subject to the full rate of 28% or 30%.

(2) Where group relief is concerned, the amount surrendered should be sufficient to bring the claimant company's profits down to the small companies rate lower limit.

(3) Any remaining loss should be claimed against profits subject to corporation tax at the small companies rate of 21% (FY2008) or 20% (FY2007).

(4) Consideration should also be given to the timing of the relief obtained (an earlier loss relief claim is generally preferable), and the extent to which relief for Gift Aid donations will be lost if loss relief is carried back.

(c) **Most beneficial way to relieve Silver Ltd's trading loss**

(1) The group relief claim for the year ended 31 December 2007 should be restricted to £30,000 so that Gold Ltd's profits are reduced to exactly £150,000 (£180,000 – £30,000) and relief is obtained for the loss at the small companies marginal relief rate.

(2) No group relief claim should be made for the year ended 31 December 2008 since Gold Ltd's profits are already below the small companies rate lower limit and the losses are therefore only being relieved at 20.75% (W).

(3) The remaining £110,000 (£140,000 – £30,000) of the loss should be carried back to the year ended 30 June 2007 in order to reduce Silver Ltd's profits to £150,000 (£260,000 – £110,000), hence obtaining relief at the marginal rate.

Working: Small companies rate for year end 31 December 2008 – Gold Ltd

	%
FY2007 (20% x 3/12)	5.000
FY2008 (21% x 9/12)	15.750
	20.750

Apple Group

Answer 2 – Chapter 22

(a) **Group relationship – Group relief**

One company must be a 75% subsidiary of the other, or both companies must be 75% subsidiaries of the holding company.

The holding company must have an effective interest of at least 75% of the subsidiary's ordinary share capital.

The holding company must have the right to receive at least 75% of the subsidiary's distributable profits and net assets (were it to be wound up).

(b) **Allocation of group relief**

Surrender should be made initially to companies subject to corporation tax at the small companies marginal rate of 29.75%.

Surrender should then be to those companies subject to the full rate of corporation tax of 28%.

The amount surrendered should be sufficient to bring the claimant company's PCTCT down to the small company rate limit.

(c) **Corporation tax liabilities – year ended 31 March 2009**

	Apple Ltd	Banana Ltd	Cherry Ltd
	£	£	£
Trading income	–	650,000	130,000
Chargeable gain	120,000	–	–
Total profits	120,000	650,000	130,000
s393A relief	(20,000)		
Group relief		(75,000)	(30,000)
PCTCT	100,000	575,000	100,000
CT @ 21%/28%/21%	21,000	161,000	21,000

Apple Ltd has two associated companies, so the relevant lower and upper limits for corporation tax purposes are £100,000 (£300,000/3) and £500,000 (£1,500,000/3) respectively.

Apple Ltd's chargeable gain can be rolled over against the reinvestment by Cherry Ltd. The proceeds not reinvested of £128,000 (£418,000 – £290,000) remain chargeable in the year ended 31 March 2009.

Banana Ltd and Apple Ltd should elect that the disposal by Banana Ltd should be treated as made by Apple Ltd so that the capital loss may be set against Apple Ltd's gain.

Net chargeable gain = £128,000 – £8,000 = £120,000.

Apple Ltd's trading loss is relieved so as to reduce both its own and Cherry Ltd's profits down to the small company rate limit.

The order of the claims to use the losses would be as follows:

(1) Group relief to Cherry Ltd of £30,000.

(2) Group relief to Banana Ltd of £75,000.

(3) Current year relief against total profits of Apple Ltd of £20,000.

Ramble Ltd

Answer 1 – Chapter 24

(a) Self-assessment tax return

Ramble Ltd's self assessment corporation tax return for the year ended 31 March 2008 was due by 31 March 2009.

As the company did not submit the return until 15 October 2009 there will be a late filing penalty of £200 as the return was submitted more than three months late.

As a payment of tax was also made on 15 October 2009 there will also be a tax-geared penalty of 10% of the tax unpaid more than six months after the filing date.

(b) Corporation tax payments

Ramble Ltd's profits chargeable to corporation tax for the year ended 31 March 2009 exceed £1,500,000. It will therefore pay corporation tax at the full rate and be classed as a large company for the purposes of paying its corporation tax liability.

The company is therefore required to pay its corporation tax liability by quarterly instalments as follows:

– 14 October 2008 (month 7) (£2,456,000 × 28% × 1/4)	£171,920
– 14 January 2009	£171,920
– 14 April 2009	£171,920
– 14 July 2009	£171,920

Interest will be due on the late payment of corporation tax as follows:

– £171,920	– from 14 October 2008 to 30 April 2009
– £171,920	– from 14 January 2009 to 30 April 2009
– £127,060	– from 14 April 2009 to 30 April 2009
– £44,860 **(W)**	– from 14 April 2009 to 31 December 2009
– £171,920	– from 14 July 2009 to 31 December 2009

Working: underpayment	£
Outstanding payments (3 × £171,920)	515,760
Payment on 1 May 2009	(470,900)
Underpayment	44,860

Mary

Answer 1 – Chapter 26

VAT return for the quarter ended 31 March 2009

Output tax	£
Standard-rated supplies (£230,000 x 97½%) = £224,250	
(17½ % × £224,250) (net of discount sales)	39,244
Zero-rated sales (0% × £50,000)	Nil
Car fuel charge (2/3 × £414 × 17.5/117.5)	41
	39,285
Input tax	
Standard-rated purchases (£102,440 @ 17.5%)	(17,927)
Standard-rated expenses (£18,000 - £5,000) @ 17.5%	(2,275)
Bad debt relief (£1,000 + £1,000) @ 17.5%	(350)
VAT payable	18,733

Due and payable date is 30 April 2009.

Tutorial notes

The car was bought on 1 February 2009 – therefore, in this quarter there are only two months of private use.

Relief for bad debts was available for the sales invoice issued on 1 May 2008 and 1 August 2008 as the payment for these invoices was due on 1 June 2008 and 1 September 2008 – debt written off and more than six months overdue.

Relief for invoice issued on 1 November 2008, the payment for which was due on 1 December 2008 is not possible as the debt is not over six months old.

Index

Index

D

E

Index

Index

Index

U

V

W

APLAN

PUBLISHING

EN-gage Online Access Information

t EN-gage Online

EN-gage online gives access to the contents of this Complete Text anytime, anywhere, as well as providing students with extra online testing.

The online version of the book offers both the Complete and Essential text, allowing you to click in and out of the expandable content, or view the answers to a 'Test Your Understanding' when needed.

You will also find access to online testing which allows you to test your knowledge and instantly view and track your results, comparing your achievement to that of your peers and viewing your scores by topic.

to access your online resources

are a Kaplan Financial student

You will already have an EN-gage account and the contents of this book is already available to you online. You therefore do not need to register again, as this process would have been completed when you enrolled. If you have problems accessing the online materials, please ask your course administrator.

purchased through Kaplan Flexible Learning the Kaplan Publishing website

You will automatically receive an e-mail invitation to EN-gage online. Please register your details using this e-mail to gain access to your content. If you do not receive the e-mail or book content, please contact Kaplan Flexible Learning.

are already a registered EN-gage user

Go straight to www.EN-gage.co.uk and log in. Select the 'add a book' feature and enter the ISBN number of this book and the unique pass key at the bottom of this card. Then click 'finished' or 'add another book'. You may add as many books as you have purchased from this screen.

are a new EN-gage user

Please register your details at www.EN-gage.co.uk and click on the link contained in the e-mail we sent you to activate your account. Then all you need to do is select the 'add a book' feature and enter the ISBN number of this book and the unique pass key at the bottom of this card. Then click 'finished' or 'add another book'.

Code and Information

This code can only be used once for the registration of one book online. This registration will expire when the final sittings for the examinations covered by this book have taken place.

Please allow one hour from the time you submitted your book details for us to process your request.

N-gage

3eBa-99sg-0WPD-Rrxp

nnical support, please visit www.EN-gage.co.uk